THE MODERN LAW
OF TORT

AUSTRALIA
The Law Book Company
Brisbane • Sydney • Melbourne • Perth

CANADA
Carswell
Ottawa • Toronto • Calgary • Montreal • Vancouver

AGENTS:
Steimatzky's Agency Ltd., Tel Aviv;
N.M. Tripathi (Private) Ltd., Bombay;
Eastern Law House (Private) Ltd., Calcutta;
M.P.P. House, Bangalore;
Universal Book Traders, Delhi;
Aditya Books, Delhi;
MacMillan Shuppan KK, Tokyo;
Pakistan Law House, Karachi, Lahore

THE MODERN LAW OF TORT

By

K.M. STANTON, B.A., B.C.L.
Reader in Law,
University of Bristol

LONDON • SWEET & MAXWELL • 1994

Published in 1994 by
Sweet & Maxwell Limited
of South Quay Plaza
183 Marsh Wall, London E14 9FT
Computerset by York House Typographic Ltd.,
London W13 8NT
Printed in England by Clays Ltd.,
St Ives plc

1000174124

A CIP catalogue record for this book
is available from The British Library

ISBN 0421 377003

No natural forests were destroyed
to make this product only farmed
timber was used and re-planted.

The index was prepared by Patricia Baker

"To Isobel"

Preface

My aim in writing this book has been to provide undergraduate students with a different, and I hope more accessible, view of the law of tort than that provided by the existing texts. I have already developed much of my thinking on the teaching of tort in my contribution to the S.P.T.L.'s publication *Examining the Law Syllabus: The Core* which was published in 1992 and the reader will see that this book follows the "interest based" model which was outlined there. I hope that the structure adopted will help students to understand more easily the role and the working of modern tortious liability.

The limits of the space available have obviously called for decisions as to what material to include and omit. Ultimately the criterion has been a purely personal one. I have covered those areas of tort which I feel an undergraduate student needs to be introduced to in the 1990s. I have no doubt that many will disagree with my decisions. The most significant omission, and one over which I have some misgivings, is that of wrongful interference with goods.

Tort remains a fast moving subject in spite of the more conservative approach to negligence liability which is now being shown by the House of Lords. I have been forced by the pace of developments to make considerable amendments to the text which was originally submitted to the publishers. Even at the time of writing this preface I am faced by the decision of the House of Lords in *Cambridge Water Co. Ltd.* v. *Eastern Counties Leather plc* [1994] 1 All E.R. 53 which makes important changes to *Rylands* v. *Fletcher* liability and the reversal by the Court of Appeal (1993) 143 N.L.J. 1367 of the interesting first instance decision in *MacFarlane* v. *E.E. Caledonia Ltd.* which had appeared to give a new lease of life to *Dulieu* v. *White* [1901] 2 K.B. 669 in the post *Alcock* world.

This book has taken a long time to bring to publication and I owe considerable thanks to the publishers for the patience which they have shown to me. I would also like to thank all of my colleagues, and former colleagues, at Bristol who have shared in the development of the LL.B. Tort course and particularly Tony Dugdale and Robyn Martin with whom I have jointly taught the LL.M. Accident Compensation course. A number of other colleagues Stephen Cretney, David Feldman, Jonathan Hill and Richard Townshend-Smith all gave me useful assistance on particular parts of the text. Last, but by no means least, I would like to thank my wife Della for tolerating the absences from home which were entailed by my efforts to complete the manuscript, and for reading, commenting on and undoubtedly improving the whole work.

Keith Stanton
January, 1994

Contents

PART I: GENERAL PRINCIPLES

Part III: Economic Interests

Table of Cases

European Court of Justice Cases

National Cases

Table of Statutes

Table of Statutory Instruments

EEC Treaties and Conventions

E.C. Directives

National Legislation

International Treaties and Conventions

PART I

GENERAL PRINCIPLES

Chapter One

Introduction

THE SCOPE OF THE LAW OF TORT

The law of tort is one of the major divisions of the English law of obligations. The word tort is derived from the French word for wrong, but in English usage covers only part of what might be loosely referred to as the law of wrongs. The subject covers a variety of forms of action in which individuals use civil proceedings either to seek compensation for harm done to them by others or to prevent such harm occurring. Tort claims are based on duties which are imposed by the general law and which are owed to particular (although possibly unidentified) individuals rather than to society at large. Tort duties exist independently of any contractual relationship, that is, of any agreement between the parties and of any relationship founded on trust. They are also independent of any criminal offences which may have been committed on the same facts and for which a prosecution may be brought.

A problem which immediately confronts any student of the law of tort is the fragmented nature of the subject. The law of tort serves a variety of purposes and uses a number of different techniques to achieve its ends. A wide range of interests receive protection from the law of tort. A few illustrations will serve to emphasise the width of the subject. A familiar example of a tort is that of a damages claim made by a person who has suffered personal injury in a road, industrial or other kind of accident. A person who seeks compensation for damage to reputation caused by a libel or a wrongful arrest is invoking other areas of tort. So too, is the occupier of land who seeks an injunction either in nuisance on the grounds that a neighbour's conduct has interfered unreasonably with the use of land or in trespass to prevent another from encroaching onto it. A business is also invoking tort when it claims that its trading relationships have been improperly interfered with by trade rivals or trade union action. Only historical accident has brought these very different actions under the single heading of tort: different types of interest are being protected and the principles of law which provide the protection have developed, for the most part, independently of each other.

Writers who have attempted to provide a single definition of tort have been forced to settle for an unhelpful formula. In the words of one writer: "(t)he problem is that most definitions are either at too high a level of abstraction or are too cumbersome to be of any practical value."[1] For example, Winfield defined tort, not altogether accurately, in the following words: "Tortious

---

[1] M.A. Jones, *Textbook on Torts* (4th ed.), p.2.

liability arises from the breach of a duty primarily fixed by the law, such duty is towards persons generally and its breach is redressible by an action for unliquidated damages."[2] The major role played by injunctions in particular areas of tort is obscured by this definition as is the voluntary nature of some of the forms of negligence liability.[3]

TORT OR TORTS

A major academic debate has discussed whether tort is governed by a single underlying principle.[4] The debate can be conveniently summarised as turning on whether there is a unified law of "tort" of which different areas of liability are examples or whether there are merely a group of dissimilar civil liabilities, "torts," which have come to be grouped together. The truth is that the tort of negligence, based on the "neighbour test,"[5] has provided a conceptual unity for a significant part of the subject but has failed to embrace it all. Outside of negligence most of the subject consists of individual torts with their own specialised rules. "Torts" rather than "Tort" remains the more accurate title for the subject. On the other hand, the word "tort" has come, in modern usage, to describe the whole subject. This book is titled in accordance with this usage, although it is structured on the basis that there are different species of liability which operate differently according to the interests being protected.

RELATIONSHIP WITH OTHER FORMS OF LIABILITY

An attempt will be made in this book to place the modern law of tort in the context in which it operates. It is felt that by doing this it is possible to obtain a better impression of the role of this body of law and of the pressures which it is facing. In order to do this, it is necessary to attempt to distinguish tort from other forms of wrong recognised by the law.

Contract

Contract and tort are the two main areas of the English law of obligations. Contractual duties are based on an agreement whereby one person is to provide benefits for another in return for some form of benefit, whether in money or otherwise. Tort duties are imposed by operation of law and may be owed to a wide range of persons who may be affected by actions. The two areas of law complement each other and at times overlap. Some torts, such as intentional interference with trade,[6] play the role of supporting contractual relations by providing an additional remedy for their breach.

A question which is commonly asked in this context is whether a plaintiff who is in a contractual relationship with the defendant can invoke tort in

---

[2] P. Winfield, *Province of the Law of Tort*, p. 32. See also Salmond & Heuston, *Law of Torts* (20th ed.), pp. 14–15.
[3] See *post*, p. 341.
[4] The debate is summarised in Salmond & Heuston *op. cit.* pp. 17–20 and Winfield & Jolowicz on *Tort* (13th ed.), pp. 13–15.
[5] See *post*, p. 29.
[6] See *post*, Chap. 15.

order to benefit his case when there has been a breach of contract. There are a number of reasons relating to damages and limitation of actions which may make it advantageous to switch a claim out of contract and into tort.[7] The precise borderline between the two areas, particularly in respect of negligently inflicted economic losses, has changed over the years as fashions have changed. In the early 1980s it was widely believed that the tort of negligence was expanding into the territory of contract and had the capacity to take over a substantial part of contract's role. However, there has been a retreat from this idea in recent years.[8]

A substantial difference which exists between contract and tort rests on the distinction between non-feasance (failing to act in a way which would provide benefits) and misfeasance (acting, but doing the task badly). Tort duties essentially deal with misfeasance: one must not inflict harm on one's neighbour by one's negligent acts. In contrast, contract fulfils the role of imposing positive duties to provide benefits and can be used to specify the level of performance which is required. If a person wishes to ensure that 1000 tons of a commodity of a particular quality are supplied on a certain date, a contract with a supplier provides the mechanism for achieving this. The fact that tort obligations are owed generally rather than by particular individuals explains why tort cannot perform this role. Obligations to provide positive benefits imposed on the population at large would raise the question why any particular individual should be held liable rather than others. Contract marks out the area of liability for failures to act by use of the doctrine of consideration; only those who have paid for the act can sue if it is not performed to the agreed standard. This does not mean that obligations to take reasonable care, that is, not to be negligent, are unknown to the law of contract. Such obligations to avoid misfeasance can arise both in contract as an implied or express term of a contract and as the result of the imposition of a duty of care in tort. Contracts of employment, under which an employer will owe a duty to take reasonable care of the safety of an employee and contracts to provide professional services, such as those under which private medical services are supplied,[9] are the most obvious examples.

When personal injuries are at issue the existence of a contract between the parties does not act as a bar to an injured party basing a claim for damage on a tortious cause of action. The best example of this is a claim for damages for an industrial injury.[10] There is little, if any, significance in whether such claims are brought on the basis of an implied term in the contract of employment that the employer should take reasonable care of the employee's safety or under the tort of negligence.

The leading case of *Donoghue* v. *Stevenson*[11] shows tort to be capable of providing a remedy free from constraints of contract doctrine to third parties affected by the performance of a contract. In that case the plaintiff claimed she had been made ill by consuming ginger beer which had been contaminated by the decomposing remains of a snail. The beer had been purchased

---

[7] On the topic of damages see *post*, p. 000. Limitation of actions is not discussed in this book, see Dugdale & Stanton, *Professional Negligence*, Chap. 24 for a discussion of the differences.

[8] See *post*, p. 334.

[9] See s. 13 of the Supply of Goods and Services Act 1982 which incorporates the result which had previously been obtained in common law decisions.

[10] Contracts for the carriage of passengers have the same features.

[11] [1932] A.C. 562.

from a café by a friend of the plaintiff. As a result the plaintiff was not in a contractual relationship with either the café or the defendant manufacturer whose negligence was alleged to have caused the introduction of the snail into the bottle. The doctrine of privity of contract, which confines contractual actions to the parties to the contract, prevented her from bringing a claim in contract against either of these persons. The decision of the House of Lords, however, allowed the plaintiff to sue the manufacturer of the beer using the tort of negligence. This decision established that negligence is an independent tort, the operation of which is not limited by the constraints of privity of contract.[12]

Financial loss claims cause much more difficulty because the forms of financial loss which may be recovered in contract and tort differ. Tort obligations founded on negligence deal with damage to persons or to items of property other than that which has been purchased. Repair and replacement costs caused by the defective quality of property which has formed the subject of a contract are the exclusive preserve of contract. Such examples of loss are excluded from recovery in the tort of negligence as a form of pure economic loss because the only damage suffered by the purchaser is in the value of the property which has been acquired.[13]

In the case of financial losses a number of objections to a tort right operating have been identified. The fact that the conduct complained of occurred in a relationship where the allocation of risks has been the subject of detailed contractual regulation will point against the recognition of a tort duty. Such rejection has occurred in relation to contracts for the carriage of goods by sea[14] and in construction industry contracts.[15] On a similar basis, the courts have not been prepared to recognise tort duties owed by professional persons to third parties who were dealing with the professional's client if there is a risk that such a duty will face the professional with conflicting duties.[16] The contractual duty, having been freely entered into, takes precedence.

However, in spite of these objections, the existence of concurrent liability in tort and contract for financial losses is one of the assumptions upon which modern law concerning the liability of professional persons has been built. This assumption derives from the decision of Oliver J. in *Midland Bank Trust Co. Ltd.* v. *Hett, Stubbs & Kemp*.[17] A plaintiff is said to be able to opt to sue the professional adviser with whom he is in a contractual relationship, in the tort of negligence. The existence of a contractual relationship between the parties, and the fact that all relevant professional duties were created by that contract, do not preclude the bringing of an action in tort. The overwhelming reason for plaintiffs choosing to sue in tort has been to obtain the advantage of a longer limitation period.[18] In the early 1980s it was often difficult to tell whether a professional negligence case was being argued in tort or in contract.

---

[12] The rule that only the parties to a contract can sue and be sued on it.
[13] This issue is discussed in depth in Chap. 16.
[14] *Leigh & Sillivan Ltd.* v. *Aliakmon Shipping Co. Ltd.* [1986] A.C. 785.
[15] *Norwich City Council* v. *Harvey* [1989] 1 W.L.R. 828; *Pacific Associates Inc.* v. *Baxter* [1990] 1 Q.B. 993.
[16] *Clarke* v. *Bruce Lance & Co.* [1988] 1 W.L.R. 881.
[17] [1979] Ch. 384.
[18] The Latent Damage Act 1986 was clearly drafted on the assumption that concurrent liability is recognised by English law in the context of professional negligence law.

The right to choose to sue in tort rather than contract was threatened by dicta of Lord Scarman in *Tai Hing Cotton Mill Ltd.* v. *Liu Chong Hing Bank.*[19] He said:

"Their Lordships do not believe that there is anything to the advantage of the law's development in searching for a liability in tort where the parties are in a contractual relationship. This is particularly so in a commercial relationship. Though it is possible as a matter of legal semantics to conduct an analysis of the rights and duties inherent in some contractual relationships . . . either as a matter of contract law . . . or as a matter of tort law . . . their Lordships believe it to be correct in principle and necessary for the avoidance of confusion in the law to adhere to the contractual analysis: on principle because it is the relationship in which the parties have, subject to a few exceptions, the right to determine their obligations to each other and for the avoidance of confusion because different consequences do follow according to whether liability arises from contract or from tort, eg in the limitation of action."

Until recently these dicta have not appeared significantly to affect concurrent liability. *Tai Hing* was not, in the final analysis, a case of concurrent liability: it was a case in which the court refused to imply a term into a contract between a bank and its customer whereby the customer would be obliged to take reasonable care of the bank's interests. Having reached this decision, the court went on to refuse to recognise an equivalent obligation based on tort. It did not deal with the situation common in professional negligence cases of an attempt to use tort to supplement a well recognised contractual obligation in order to obtain a procedural advantage, such as a longer limitation period. There is a difference between a refusal to allow tort to provide rights which the law has refused to recognise in contract and allowing tort to intervene to give the advantage of better procedural rules, particularly if limitation defences which are invoked by tortfeasors are regarded as unattractive.

Different views of the acceptability of concurrent liability are now being expressed. In *Lee* v. *Thompson*[20] Lloyd L.J. seemed to support the view that concurrent liability had been fatally undermined when he suggested that a review of the relationship of *Midland Bank* to the old authority of *Groom* v. *Crocker*[21] is merited in the light of *Tai Hing*. He said:

"Parliament has provided that, in the case of a contractual action against a solicitor the period of limitation is six years. It may seem odd . . . that a client can . . . circumvent that contractual limitation period by suing in tort. If the client's action against his solicitor were confined to claims for breach of contract, then these difficult and, in some ways, artificial questions as to when actual damage is suffered would not arise."

There are some attractions in this approach which would return professional negligence liability to the position that the duty deriving from a contract is not actionable in tort. It is difficult to see why a plaintiff, rather than a defendant, should have the advantage of the rules of limitation which favour him. However, such an approach would mean that a third party damaged by work performed by a person who was not in privity with him might have the

---

[19] [1986] A.C. 80.
[20] [1989] 40 E.G. 89.
[21] [1939] 1 K.B. 194 in which it was held that a solicitor's contractual relationship with his client precluded the existence of a claim in tort by the client.

possibility of taking advantage of a longer limitation period than that which would be available to the professional's client. This may not matter greatly if the range of tort duties in relation to professional negligence continues to contract. In the light of his recent judgments[22] it is difficult to envisage Lord Oliver finding much to attract him in the views which he expressed in 1978 in *Midland Bank*.

A number of dicta in recent House of Lords cases appear, on the other hand, to accept concurrent liability. Lord Jauncey, in *Smith* v. *Eric S. Bush*, regarded a valuer's duty to a building society as founded in both contract and tort[23] and Lord Keith in *Murphy* v. *Brentwood District Council* was of the opinion[24] that *Pirelli General Cable Works Ltd.* v. *Oscar Faber & Partners*[25] remains good law. In *Pirelli* the House of Lords seemed to have accepted, albeit *sub silentio*, that concurrent liability represents the law. Lord Keith seemed to regard *Pirelli*, which was a tort claim concerning negligent design work performed by a civil engineer under a contract, as an example of concurrent liability for a negligent misstatement causing economic loss.

Criminal law

The purpose of the law of tort is to give an individual injured by another's act a remedy. The criminal law exists to express the State's condemnation of particular forms of misconduct by means of punishment. When tort provides compensation in the form of damages it directs it to be paid to the individual who has been injured by the misconduct; if the criminal law exacts a financial penalty in the form of a fine the money is paid to the state.

In spite of the different aims there is a substantial degree of overlap between the criminal law and tort. Many acts which are punished by the criminal law also give rise to compensation in tort. Poor driving and failures by an employer to take proper safety precautions, if they cause injury, are everyday examples. So too are assaults, misappropriation of goods and some nuisances and libels. In many, but not all of these examples there is a distinction in the fact that a criminal offence will have been committed once an act has been performed with the required state of mind irrespective of whether any damage was caused; in much of the law of tort no action will be possible without proof that the victim has suffered damage. A further example of overlap can be seen in the fact that damages designed to inflict punishment on the tortfeasor are permitted in a limited category of tort cases.[26]

Provisions exist which enable an individual's claim in tort to be assisted by proceedings brought in a criminal court. The fact of a conviction may be used as evidence in subsequent civil proceedings and a number of mechanisms exist whereby an individual can use the criminal process to obtain compensation for damage which has been suffered.[27] In effect, the criminal process can

---

[22] In particular his speeches in *D. & F. Estates Ltd.* v. *The Church Commissioners* [1989] A.C. 177 and *Murphy* v. *Brentwood D.C.* [1991] 1 A.C. 398.

[23] [1989] 2 All E.R. 514 at 540.

[24] *Murphy* v. *Brentwood District Council* [1991] 1 A.C. 398 at 466.

[25] [1983] 2 A.C. 1.

[26] See pp. 148–154.

[27] The Criminal Injuries Compensation Board provides compensation by means of an administrative process. Power also exists for the courts which try criminal offences to make a compensation order in favour of the victim of a crime. These mechanisms are described in Chap. 13.

assist an individual in bringing a tort claim or can remove the need to resort to one.

Breach of trust and other equitable obligations

Remedies for breach of trust or other equitable obligations, even though they may result in purely financial awards, are excluded from the law of tort. The reason for this is basically historical: tort derives from the work of common law courts whereas the Court of Chancery, developed completely separate equitable principles.

Restitution[28]

Restitution provides a number of remedies which are designed to enable a person to recoup money from another who has been unjustly enriched by its receipt or by the value of work or services which have been conferred outside of a contractual relationship. The recovery of money paid under a mistake of fact is an example of such a remedy. In such cases the liability is not based on any pre-existing duty or on the damage which has been done to the plaintiff's position, but on the unjust enrichment which will be conferred on the defendant if there is no obligation to repay the benefit. This area overlaps with tort at some points as it may be possible to forego a tortious remedy in favour of a restitutionary one under the rules of "waiver of tort."[29]

Bailment[30]

The law of bailment regulates the duties of a person to whom another's goods are entrusted subject to an obligation to return them. Traditionally, the duties of the bailee with respect to damage caused to the goods or misuse of them during the period of bailment have been regarded as based on a distinctive area of law which falls outside the law of tort. This is the case even when the bailment does not arise from a contractual relationship.

Non-tortious methods of protection

Compensation in the form of benefits may be provided by mechanisms other than the traditional judicial process. Many of the criticisms of the operation of tort as a compensation system centre on the requirement that the victim must surmount the hurdles created by the adversarial civil litigation system.[31] Other systems, such as the payment of social security benefits to accident victims, avoid such problems by making the benefits payable as of right to an applicant who meets the conditions of entitlement. Application for payment is made to the Government department concerned and no element of adversarial process is involved unless the initial decision on entitlement is disputed. Systems of this kind tend to be cheaper to operate and make payments to victims much more rapidly than litigation based systems.[32]

[28] See generally Goff & Jones, *The Law of Restitution* (3rd ed., 1986).
[29] See *post*, p. 157.
[30] See generally Palmer, *Bailment* (2nd ed., 1991).
[31] These difficulties will be discussed in detail in Chap. 8.
[32] See Chap. 8 for a discussion of these issues in the context of injury litigation.

Care needs to be taken when considering the issue of alternative methods of compensation because the terms "strict" and "no-fault" liability are often used loosely by commentators to cover two very different techniques. For the purposes of this book strict liability will be defined as a method of compensation which continues to use judicial proceedings to provide compensation, but making the standard of liability stricter by removing the need to prove negligence.[33] No-fault liability will be confined to the more radical suggestion of abandoning the courts completely in favour of an administrative process of paying compensation according to need.[34]

A LAW OF OBLIGATIONS?

This book accepts the traditional law of tort as its subject matter and does not attempt to present a picture of the English law of obligations as a single entity. There are a number of reasons for adopting this approach. First, as a matter of practicality, a book which sought to describe the whole of the English law of obligations would be unmanageably large, particularly if an attempt were made to treat the subject matter contextually. Secondly, many rules of law and procedure require a lawyer to recognise and to distinguish torts from breaches of contract: an attempt to describe the law of obligations in its entirety would depend greatly on the distinction. Thirdly, some areas of the law of obligations, such as the formation of contracts and relationships of trust are so far removed from the traditional subject matter of tort as to be irrelevant to it. Finally, the retreat of the duty of care in negligence in relation to pure economic loss[35] which has occurred in recent years has amounted to a strong judicial reassertion of the survival of important distinctions between the areas of contract and tort. As a result of these factors it is felt that although there may be some advantages in treating the law of obligations as a single subject they are not compelling.

Ultimately the decision on how to classify particular bodies of legal doctrine is largely a matter of personal preference, particularly in the case of a subject such as tort which is highly fragmented in its structure. There can be no doubt that tort overlaps with parts of contract, criminal law and property law. Indeed, traditionally structured contract textbooks are compelled to deal with tortious remedies in relation to topics such as misrepresentation. This book will attempt to place the traditional body of doctrine known as tort in its context by outlining non-tortious mechanisms, including those drawn from other parts of the law of obligations, which work alongside and have the capacity to replace tort. This provides a useful perspective on the role and adequacy of tort in a period in which tort is facing challenges as to its methods and existence. However, although the argument may be criticised as self-serving, it is felt that the continuing practice of lawyers to regard tort as a discrete area means that there is still a need for an approach which treats the subject in this way.

---

[33] Strict liability standards are discussed in Chap. 3.
[34] See Chap. 8 for discussion of no-fault alternatives to litigation in relation to personal injury.
[35] See Chap. 16.

THE AIMS OF THE TORT SYSTEM

Considerable effort has been expended in attempts to identify the aims of the law of tort. A justification ought to exist for the existence of a system which consumes resources in transferring money from one person (the injurer) to another (the victim). However, the range of interests protected by the law of tort makes any search for a single aim underlying the law a difficult one. Actions for wrongful interference with goods or trespasses to land serve fundamentally different ends from an action seeking compensation for a personal injury. In practice much of the discussion concerning the aims of the law of tort has concentrated on accidents and compensation for personal injuries.

The different aims which have been suggested seem to be capable of classification under a number of heads. Those who have studied tort from the perspective of economic theory have tended to favour the "deterrent" aim of tort.[36] This sees tort as a system which is designed to reduce the frequency and the severity of accidents. Fear of legal liability and the resulting awards of damages provides an incentive to persons, both injurers and potential victims, to indulge in safer conduct, both by avoiding hazardous activities and by increasing the level of safety precautions they provide. In practice, the "deterrent" approach will choose to sacrifice the interests of the victim in favour of those of the defendant by leaving injured plaintiffs to bear their own losses if the damage could not have been avoided by the use of cost-justified precautions.

In contrast, the "compensation" aim, which became very dominant among academic lawyers in the 1970s, sees the primary aim of tort as being to reduce the disruption which accidents cause to the lifestyles of victims and those dependent upon them. Victims may lose their income and may require expensive nursing care. An award of compensation alleviates this disruption and any attendant social problems. The whole thrust of the compensation aim is the protection of victims: the defendant is merely an agent by which this is achieved.

Additionally, the tort system can be seen as a mechanism for retribution and the appeasement of the injured person's feelings, as providing a mechanism for the protection of rights and as a technique whereby society is able to express judgment on the injurer's conduct. Recent practice, particularly in the context of "disaster" litigation seems to have brought this judgmental role of tort back to prominence, even if it has failed to attract academic support.

A subsidiary aim to those already mentioned is that any compensation system should be efficient in the sense of providing an effective mechanism for distributing the money paid into it to the victims of accidents. A large percentage of this money should not be consumed by the operating costs of the system.

The difficulty presented by the law of tort is that it has developed with only limited reference to these aims and that it may fail to achieve any of them

---

[36] See Department of Trade and Industry, White Paper, *Opening Markets: New Policy on Restrictive Trade Practices* Cm. 727 (1989), paras. 5.15–5.16 for an example of strong support from a government department for the deterrent effect of a privately instigated action in tort.

properly. In addition, the deterrence and compensation aims are almost certainly incompatible with each other.[37]

The assertion of rights

Some tort actions, for example trespass to land[38] and wrongful interference with goods,[39] are specifically intended to enable a person to assert rights which he possesses in property against interferences with them. These torts operate as an adjunct to the law of property and injunctive relief is commonly a more important remedy in such cases than a claim for compensation for any damage which has been inflicted. Other torts, such as false imprisonment and battery, play a similar role in relation to interferences with a person's freedom or physical integrity.

Deterrence and accident prevention

The deterrent approach to tort is based on the proposition that society seeks, in order to meet the demands of economic efficiency, to achieve a cost-justified level of care and accidents, rather than to eliminate all accidents at any cost. If the cost-justified level is not achieved, risk-creating activities will not be subject to an appropriate level of costs and an inefficient level of over or under production will occur. An underlying assumption of this approach is that the cost of accidents and of taking precautions to avoid them can be attributed either to the victim or the injurer and that, according to what is known as the "Coase Theorem,"[40] in a situation in which victim and injurer are able to bargain freely, with perfect knowledge and with no transaction costs being created by the bargaining, a cost-justified level of care will be achieved irrespective of the allocation of liability made by the law. The parties will simply contract to replace an inefficient result produced by the law with one which achieves the cost-justified result. The theory does not assume that a perfect world exists in which people freely negotiate accident bargains. It assumes that lack of knowledge, inability to assess the risks inherent in the situation,[41] inequality of bargaining power and the fact that injurer and victim will commonly have had no pre-existing relationship prevents a market solution being achieved to the problem of accidents. Rules of legal liability are regarded as a substitute mechanism for the creation of incentives in circumstances in which a market solution is unlikely to be achieved. On the basis of this approach, tort seeks to impose the cost of accidents on the person, victim or accident creator, who is able to take effective precautions against the risk at the least cost.[42] It is tort liability which provides the incentive to achieve the most efficient allocation of resources. In this way, society does not seek to avoid all accidents but rather seeks to achieve an economically efficient level of accidents. Victims should not be subjected to losses which others might easily have avoided, but, on the other hand, an uneconomic level of expenditure on safety is not to be required.

---

[37] See *post*, p. 16.
[38] See *post*, Chap. 19.
[39] See Clerk & Lindsell on *Torts* (16th ed., 1989), Chap. 23.
[40] Coase, "The Problem of Social Cost" (1960) 3 J.L. & Econ. 1.
[41] See Bowles & Jones, *Professional Liability: An Economic Analysis* for a strong development of this argument.
[42] See particularly Calabresi, *The Cost of Accidents*.

There are substantial difficulties with this approach. The basic assumption of the deterrent theory, that the level of accidents and man-made disease which is acceptable to a society should be determined solely by reference to economic considerations of efficiency, can be challenged as ignoring equally important considerations of justice and the distribution of wealth.[43] It can be contended that one of the major successes of the tortious remedy for personal injuries has been its recognition of pain and suffering and other forms of non-financial loss as meriting some degree of protection.

The approach is also open to the criticism that it assumes that all parties involved in accidents have, or can be given, by means of "signals" received from the courts or insurance companies, accurate knowledge of the costs created by accidents and of the precautions required to avoid them. The assumption is that the cost of economically unjustified accidents is trans-ferred to accident creating sources and that the incentive effect of this is not reduced or overwhelmed by distortions in the market created by the manage-ment of the economy[44] or price insensitivity.[45] It may prove impossible in practice to isolate from the factors which produce damage, a particular activity to which the cost of precautions should be attached. For example, in the case of a defective product, difficulties may be caused by the fact that production and design processes are complex and accidents may be caused by products which contain components designed and supplied by different manufacturers. The empirical evidence which exists on the operation of the tort system is in stark contrast to the theory. There is little evidence to suggest that accurate information of the potential liability costs of particular activ-ities is known by potential defendants or is "signalled" by insurance compa-nies or by judgments of the courts. It is difficult to believe that manufacturers "internalise" the particular risks created by specific products to that product; instead the risk is likely to be externalised to the pricing of the manufac-turer's other products or by means of insurance to other manufacturers.

The deterrent approach also assumes that the costs imposed on victims by accidents can be accurately quantified in advance of decisions being made as to the amount of precautions to be provided. But, in practice, the actual costs incurred as a result of an accident may bear little relationship to the degree of care or precautions taken. The assumption made by the theory, that there is an automatic relationship between the level and severity of accidents and the amount of precautions taken, is challengeable because minor examples of tortious conduct may have catastrophic consequences and because the amount of compensation payable will be calculated in accordance with the losses rather than the degree of misconduct which produced them. In addition, much of the subject matter of tort, pain and suffering, damage to the amenity of land and to reputation are interests which have no direct financial value. In one sense, the fact that tort attempts to attribute a value to such interests, albeit often on a conventional basis, means that it more accurately reflects the costs created by accidents than a system which confines itself to compensating direct pecuniary losses. However, it is impossible to deny that the conventional nature of the figures used must

---

[43] C. Veljanovski in Burrows & Veljanovski, *The Economic Approach to Law*, Chap. 5.

[44] Government decisions as to the appropriate levels of public expenditure may have a significant effect on the numbers of road accidents, on the levels of pollution controls and of medical care provided by the Health Service.

[45] A manufacturer who has a dominant share of a market may be able to adopt a pricing policy which pays little regard to the incentives created by tort liability.

mean that any decision as to whether a particular safety measure is cost-justified is made on the basis of conventional, rather than the, unobtainable, true costings.

Insurance creates major problems for the deterrent theory. If the theory is to work properly, insurance, the whole point of which is the "pooling" of risks, should be banned unless insurers are able or willing to fix premiums according to the accident costs created by a particular activity. In practice, it is unrealistic to regard insurers as seeing their main role as that of controlling the quality of the activities of their clients. An insurance company is likely to achieve far greater financial returns from concentrating its resources on resisting claims and settling them at a low figure than from expending the considerable sums of money which will be needed to achieve accurate premium rating.[46] It will be practically impossible for an insurer to achieve accurate premium rating in areas such as drug litigation where the true nature of the costs imposed by a particular product may only be revealed years after the manufacturer's insurance premium was fixed and possibly when the product had been withdrawn from the market. A general difficulty stems from the fact that if, as seems to be the case, a high proportion of accidents are the result of random conjunction of victim and another's negligence it is unlikely that insurers are able to glean useful information as to risk-creation from an individual's past claims record. Insurance, therefore, fails to impose the true costs of accidents on the activity which creates the risk and, since this is not done, the effect in economic theory of the tort liability of D1 is to increase the cost of insurance to D2, D3 and D4. The deterrent effect is therefore likely to be felt by different persons whose activities create different levels of risk. Stapleton when discussing the deterrent role of tort in relation to health hazards summarised the result in the following terms:

" . . . man-made disease illustrates most persuasively the minor role, if any, which tort can play (a) in specifically motivating those individuals in a position to reduce risks to do so, and (b) in achieving price deterrence through the market. Even in cases where liability can be successfully fixed and costs internalised to the appropriate person, the cheapest cost avoider, the deterrent impact on that tortfeasor is lost through a system of liability insurance which is incapable of re-establishing the deterrent effect via effective experience or classified rating. The tortfeasor's incentive to avoid future losses is undermined while price deterrence is severely limited by the difficulties in targeting losses to the correct product especially in areas of high product turnover and long latent diseases. Added to these rate-making difficulties in the real world are the general market imperfections . . . including the difficulty and vagueness of the process of seeking a single 'cheapest cost avoider'. Of course, the greatest imperfection is that the majority of losses will never be internalised in the first place because causal proof is impossible. As Pierce[47] notes this has 'led to an almost complete breakdown in the tort system as a mechanism of internalising [man-made]

---

[46] The deterrence theory can serve as an apology for the role of insurance companies in operating the tort system. Instead of being seen as the agents who sacrifice the interests of accident victims on the altar of third party liability; they become the watchdogs of quality control. Cf. post, pp. 169.

[47] R. Pierce, "Encouraging Safety: The Limits of Tort Law and Government Regulation" (1980) 33 Vand. L.R. 1281, 1298.

disease costs' and it is presumably for the same reason that even supporters of using liability rules to effect economic efficiency note – albeit in passing – that this may not be possible in the area of certain health risks such as pollution disease"[48]

The available evidence suggests that the incentive effect of criminal prosecution greatly exceeds that of tort liability. There are a lot of reasons for this. To be held liable in a negligence action a person need not only have misconducted himself but must also have caused damage. Even if damage is suffered and a tort claim is successful the amount payable as compensation will not be calculated on the basis of the fault of the actor. A very low percentage of accident victims initiate tort actions and it can take years for such proceedings to be brought to a conclusion and, if liability is established, the true cost is likely to be met by insurance. Criminal liability is more generally understood and correctly perceived as a far more immediate risk. However, although criminal liability may play a far more effective deterrent role than tort in areas such as road and industrial accidents, it is not a real alternative to it in other areas, such as medical accidents, press misconduct, the protection of persons against infringement of their civil liberties by the police and professional negligence which causes economic loss. In all of these areas the best alternative to commencing proceedings in tort offered to an aggrieved person may well be to invoke non-litigious remedies such as professional disciplinary or other complaints procedures. However, as all of these tend to operate on the basis of self regulation and have been widely criticised as lacking independence and being ineffective, tort is regarded as an important technique for deterring unacceptable conduct in these areas.

Tort liability may well have some deterrent effect even in the areas in which criminal liability operates. People probably fail to appreciate the low percentage of victims which obtains compensation from the tort system. At times tort may achieve an effective degree of deterrence. In some situations a successful tort claim may generate sufficient publicity to achieve an educative effect: it is unlikely that many car ferries leave harbour with their bow doors open after the Zeebrugge disaster. Publicity relating to claims may also generate further claims as it may encourage potential claimants to seek legal advice on the possibility of bringing a case.[49] This educative role may be of particular importance given the fact that the large scale failure of accident victims to obtain compensation from tort is commonly attributed to a failure to initiate proceedings. It can also be of particular importance in relation to processes which inflict illness on those exposed to them over a period of time, especially if the link between exposure and illness has been disputed.

There is no doubt that insurance practice plays some role in discouraging dangerous conduct. Young persons wishing to drive high powered cars may find the insurance costs of doing so exorbitant and examples are recorded of manufacturers faced by the prospect of crippling levels of tort liability and escalating insurance premiums withdrawing from a particular market.[50]

---

[48] J. Stapleton, *Disease and the Compensation Debate* (1986), p. 134.

[49] The best recorded example of this is the increase in claims against surveyors with respect to residential valuations and surveys which followed *Yianni v. Edwin Evans & Sons* [1982] Q.B. 438. In 1980, R.I.C.S. Insurance Services Ltd. received 35 claims in respect of residential valuations and paid £114,982 to claimants. In 1982 the equivalent figures were 403 claims and £996,607 paid. See D.T.I., *Professional Liability: Report of the Study Teams*, Surveyors' Study Team, para. 3.6.

[50] Such as the manufacture of asbestos.

What is argued is that as the vast majority of tort cases are either abandoned or settled out of court for relatively small sums, the deterrent effect achieved by tort varies and is often small. It is possibly best seen in areas such as professional work and product development in which a finding of negligence may put a professional or trading reputation in issue. But even here the deterrence appears to operate in a very general way. It appears as a general perception that negligence litigation is a problem. For example, it is commonly asserted that the expansion of medical negligence litigation has given rise to the practice of defensive medicine.[51] Potential tortfeasors almost certainly do not make a precise calculation of the likely costs of accidents and of the costs of an increased level of care. In the areas of road and industrial accidents, in which cases are likely to be abandoned or settled with little publicity, the immediacy of criminal liability is likely to be a far greater encouragement to safe conduct than tort.

Distributive justice

In theory a finding of liability in tort shifts the costs of an accident from the victim to the tortfeasor. In practice it goes further and distributes the cost widely into society because the potential tortfeasor allows for his having to bear such costs in the price which is charged for his products and services and "pools" the risk with others through the insurance market. This process of risk distribution, which replaces losses suffered unexpectedly by an individual with small budgeted expenditure spread throughout society, is a legitimate aim for tort. Unexpected losses may cause substantial dislocation to the victim's finances and have significant "knock on" consequences for others. On the other hand, the aim of redistributing losses widely is irreconcilable with the deterrence aim of directing the cost of the accident to the person who could most easily control the risk. The distributive justice aim sees tort as part of a collective social response directed to protecting accident victims by the provision of compensation. Many of the familiar rules of the law of tort concerning the calculation of damages and joint and vicarious liability, as well as the secondary rules which make insurance compulsory for many potential tortfeasors, are easily explained on the basis that the dominant aim of the law is the achievement of distributive justice by means of the "compensation" approach.

The problem with this approach is that the protection of victims is imperfectly achieved in practice because many accident victims do not, whether consciously or through lack of knowledge of their rights, pursue tort claims and because those who do commonly fail to achieve full, or any, compensation because of the difficulties of proving fault, the effect of contributory negligence and their weakness in the bargaining process. Even if compensation is achieved it will generally be paid so long after the damage was suffered that it will not avoid disruption to the plaintiff's life.

Although social security benefits offer a lower level of protection than tort, they are a markedly superior technique for loss distribution. They provide instant protection irrespective of the cause of the injury to a far greater number of people and are funded by the whole of society. These arguments

---

[51] See Jones, *Medical Negligence*, paras. 1.06–1.09 for a discussion of the problems created by the concept of defensive medicine.

will be developed in more detail in relation to accident compensation in subsequent chapters.[52]

Those who favour distributive justice as the main aim of tort, but who accept that tort performs poorly in this respect, often favour a move to a no-fault system of accident compensation: one which concentrates on the victim's needs rather than the cause of the injury. The problem with doing this is that any deterrent effect which tort has is sacrificed and the spectre of an increased level of injuries is created. It is for this reason that, as happened in New Zealand, moves towards no-fault liability may well be coupled with measures designed to promote accident prevention.[53]

A different argument which has been made criticises tort on the political ground that it supports the existing distribution of wealth in society and that it is actually regressive because its commitment to full compensation compels the poorer members of society to obtain insurance to cover damage to the property and income of the richer.[54] The third party insurance which the driver of the 10 year old Lada is compelled to buy protects the income of the driver of the new Rolls Royce and his car. At the most general level there is some truth in this but only in so far as tort, in common with many areas of common law, has the aim of protecting property and wealth. Tort is overtly designed to protect the status quo, although the extent of the protection is limited in an area such as nuisance[55] and, nowadays, very poor when negligently caused economic losses are involved.[56] Even if the existing distribution of wealth in our society is unacceptable, it is difficult to believe that the elimination or restriction of tort claims for accidental damage would have a substantial redistributive effect. The reallocation of wealth caused by tort claims is probably small and other techniques, such as first party insurance, can be used successfully to defend the status quo. The regressive effect of tort is unproven and the system works both ways: drivers of Rolls Royces carry insurance to protect other Rolls Royces and 10 year old Ladas. Furthermore, the argument breaks down completely in areas such as industrial injury and product liability litigation in which there is no system of mutual insurance between persons who might be both victims and tortfeasors.

Vindication

Tort has at times been regarded as a means whereby an individual may seek redress for injured feelings. In some areas of tort this would seem to be the predominant purpose underlying the plaintiff's pursuit of his rights. Claims for defamation,[57] malicious prosecution[58] and false imprisonment[59] will commonly be brought not for the purpose of obtaining compensation but to prove that the defendant acted wrongfully and thus to vindicate the plaintiff.

[52] Chaps. 8 and 13.
[53] See *post*, pp. 172–173.
[54] Abel "Should tort law protect property against accidental loss?" in *The Law of Tort* (Furmston ed. 1986), p. 155.
[55] See *post*, Chap. 20.
[56] It is an interesting scale of values which protects such losses when they are consequential on physical damage to the plaintiff's property.
[57] See *post*, Chap. 24.
[58] See *post*, Chap. 23.
[59] See *post*, Chap. 23.

Although this basis for tortious liability does not feature greatly in the theoretical literature concerning accidents, it is difficult to deny that there is a deeply held belief within society that those who have caused damage should be seen to make recompense for it. The view has been expressed that the dramatic increase which has been recorded in New Zealand in complaints against doctors made to the Medical Council and the Medical Practitioners' Disciplinary Committee is attributable to patients who have been denied access to judicial proceedings by the advent of a no-fault compensation system seeking an alternative forum in which to "express their anger."[60] Organisations representing the interests of the victims of medical accidents have argued that proposals for the introduction of no-fault compensation into this country should be opposed unless they contain measures designed to ensure that doctors are "accountable" for their acts.[61]

The vindication approach has been very widely expressed in recent years in relation to cases of major disasters and has been the basis of the argument that the level of damages awarded for pain and suffering and, in particular, for bereavement, are inadequate compensation for the interests of those injured by tortious conduct. The idea that a bereavement award should be set at a modest level because it is impossible to reflect the loss suffered in financial terms is lost from sight when the figure awarded is condemned on emotional grounds as an "insulting" response to the loss suffered.

Again the failure of tort to deliver a remedy to the great majority of victims makes this aim a questionable basis for tort. Even when claims are started the majority are settled for small sums after considerable time with little attendant publicity. It is difficult to believe that victims obtain a great deal of satisfaction from such results.

A more major objection to this approach is that it confuses the functions of criminal and civil law: a claim instigated by an individual should not be used to express society's disapproval of a tortfeasor's actions. This is unacceptable because it relies on the vagaries of individual willingness to fund proceedings and because any compensation awarded will reflect the damage done rather than the need to punish the defendant's conduct by the infliction of a suitable penalty.

Efficiency

It is clear that the tort system is very expensive to operate. The costs incurred by insurance companies, their experts and the lawyers who administer it consume a large proportion of the money which enters it as insurance premiums. The Pearson Commission,[62] when it conducted its survey into the workings of the accident compensation system, estimated that only 55 per

---

[60] I.G. Simpson, "No-Fault Compensation" (1991) *July Independent Solicitor* 18.

[61] "Accountability" may well be a concept which entails elements of both vindication and deterrence. The National Health Service (Compensation) Bill 1991 contained a provision which would have empowered a compensation board, when administering the no-fault compensation scheme proposed, to refer the conduct of the doctor in question to the General Medical Council. The British Medical Association, which supports the introduction of no-fault compensation, refused to support this particular bill because of this provision. One may surmise that some members of the medical profession support the introduction of no-fault compensation because it would lessen the identification of the injury with a particular doctor's conduct.

[62] Royal Commission on Civil Liability and Compensation for Personal Injury, Cmnd. 7054 (1978).

cent. of the money paid into the accident compensation system in the form of insurance premiums was ultimately paid to victims as tort damages.[63] Other areas are possibly even more inefficient. In relation to professional liability in the construction industry it has been suggested that only about a third of premium income reaches claimants as compensation.[64] The social security system, by abandoning the adversarial approach, operates much more efficiently.[65]

A particular inefficiency of litigation procedure, which is encouraged by the tort system, and at times compelled by law, is double insurance. If my car or house is damaged I am likely to have purchased insurance cover to enable me to repair or replace it, whether or not that damage is the result of another's tort. Such first party insurance is efficient: it can be tailored to meet my particular requirements and I am likely to be the person who best appreciates the value of the property. It is also likely to be relatively effective at the task of arranging for repairs to be undertaken and at minimising the disruption caused by the damage. The tort system effectively requires potential tortfeasors to duplicate this protection with an inferior product. Third party insurance has to be priced in accordance with the whole range of losses likely to be inflicted on possible victims of the conduct. The adversarial system of liability inevitably slows down payments. It is also possible that administrative costs are increased by the necessity of writing two insurance policies rather than one to cover the same risk, although this point should not be overstated as first and third party cover is commonly marketed as a single combined package.[66] It is not particularly surprising that motor insurers have attempted to avoid some of these inefficiencies by operating "knock for knock" agreements under which first party insurers agree to bear the costs of repairing damaged vehicles and third party liability claims for such losses are not pursued.[67]

The fault principle

If tort has failed to achieve the aims which might be set for it we may legitimately ask why it has survived. The answer would seem to be that lawyers have concentrated their attention on legal principle rather than on the aims underlying the law. In addition, tort has come to be dominated by the principle of fault liability which has a powerful internal logic of its own. No one who has read *Donoghue* v. *Stevenson*[68] could doubt that the

---

[63] para. 83.

[64] D.T.I., *Professional Liability* (1989), p. 86. The Construction Industry Study Team reported that insurers were reluctant to provide information as to the efficacy of professional indemnity insurance and the proportion of premiums paid out in damages. It calculated that in this area 30–40 per cent. of premium income is consumed in legal and expert witnesses costs and inferred that roughly 33 per cent. represented administration costs and profit for the insurer and broker.

[65] Pearson (para. 121) estimated that the cost of administering social security benefits to accident victims was approximately 11 per cent. of the amount paid out as benefit. The equivalent figure for accident compensation claims in tort was 85 per cent.

[66] For example a motor car insurance policy will commonly provide first party cover against theft and accidental damage (whether inflicted by the policy holder or others) and will cover the policy holder's liabilities to third parties for injuries and damage to their cars which his torts inflict on them.

[67] For more information on the working of such agreements see Atiyah, *Accidents, Compensation and the Law* (5th ed.), p. 196.

[68] [1932] A.C. 562.

principle of fault liability is a form of ethical response to the problem created by accidents and their attendant damage. Lord Atkin's "neighbour" principle is a limited legal response to the commandment to love one's neighbour. Arguments for the retention of tort are commonly based on the moral attraction of the fault principle, supported, at times, by the pragmatic attractions of deterrence. The Royal Commission on Civil Liability and Compensation for Personal Injury[69] (commonly known as the Pearson Commission), which reported in 1978, was not averse to using such arguments. When outlining its strategy[70] the Commission said "there is elementary justice in the principle of the tort action that he who has by his fault injured his neighbour should make reparation. The concept of individual responsibility still has value. In addition, a tort action may draw attention to dangerous practices, especially in the industrial sphere." The Commission was of the same mind when it summarised its conclusions[71]:

" . . . there is another factor which goes deeply into the structure of society. A sense of responsibility for the effect of one's actions on others, and a sense that one does have a duty of care towards one's fellow citizens, is an essential element in a civilised community, and a lapse in the discharge of that responsibility is a matter of blame, in other words fault or culpa."

The attraction of the fault principle to lawyers schooled in a system which sets individual against individual in litigation is easy to see. Notions of the collective social interest and of collective social responsibility for the victims of society's activities are difficult to express in a common law system. The modern tort system has its roots in nineteenth century laisser-faire thinking under which the fault principle provided a degree of protection for the industrial activities and mass transportation which were changing the face of the economy of the time. The main challenges to the dominance of fault have been based on later twentieth century Welfare State thinking. The moral justification for tort has come to look somewhat threadbare in an era in which the demands of the compensation approach have resulted in widespread liability insurance; in liability being imposed for conduct which no moralist would condemn and in levels of damages which do not reflect the blameworthiness of the conduct.

Tort and a mixed economy

The historical analysis of tort liability which is generally accepted is that strict liability dominated the period before the industrial revolution. At this time tort was seen as a means of satisfying the need for retribution felt by victims and of avoiding the increase in social costs which self-help remedies would have caused. The increase in accidents resulting from industrialisation and mass transportation caused the law to move towards the less stringent negligence standard of liability. The cost of accidents thus came to be shared between victims and injurers; the emerging forces of capital were subsidised and encouraged to operate in areas of risk by the protection of the negligence

[69] Cmnd. 7054.
[70] Vol. 1, para. 262.
[71] Vol. 1, para. 1717.

standard of liability, the "privity" fallacy[72] and the total defences of contributory negligence and common employment. Against this background, the decision of the House of Lords in *Rylands* v. *Fletcher*[73] to impose strict liability for the escape of dangerous things from land, was an attempt to cling to a disappearing world which inevitably failed to stand the test of time.

There were signs of a reaction against the dominance of negligence before the end of the nineteenth century. 1897 saw the appearance of the first Workmen's Compensation Act and the arrival of strict liability for injuries caused by breach of industrial safety legislation.[74] However, the negligence based accident compensation remedy only faced a sustained challenge, based on Welfare State thinking, in the 1970s. Although New Zealand pioneered the path into a brave new world by replacing the tort action for personal injuries and death with a state administered no-fault accident compensation scheme, tort survived in the United Kingdom as a result of a combination of factors. The Pearson Commission proved unable to produce recommendations which people could rally to and, as occurred in Australia, the arrival of a government committed to cutting public expenditure sounded the death knell for any proposal for large scale public funding of accident compensation schemes. Indeed, it can be argued that there has been a strong political move since 1979 to reduce the ambit of the Welfare State and to encourage individual self-reliance and responsibility and that the challenge facing tort's role as an accident compensation remedy has declined correspondingly. Indeed, some of the most recent challenges to the fault principle, such as the proposals for no-fault compensation for medical accidents seem to have been motivated as much by professional self-interest as by a desire to provide additional protection for injured patients.[75]

Parallel, but different arguments as to the role of tort in a mixed economy can be made in relation to tort's role as a remedy for the protection of financial losses. Particular problems have been created for industrial relations by the need to protect the collective interest summarised as "the right to strike" against the torts derived from the nineteenth century authority of *Lumley* v. *Gye*[76] which provide strong legal support for the industrial status quo as expressed in the individual contract of employment. The political consensus in the twentieth century has been to recognise the legitimacy of the right to strike in the form of defences to the torts and the arguments have centred on the appropriate limits to the defences in a mixed economy. The collective interest received the greatest protection as a result of the Labour Government's Trade Union and Labour Relations Act of 1974 which attempted to provide a comprehensive defence against tort liability to those engaged in industrial action. The Conservative Government's policy since entering office in 1979 has been to limit, but not remove, this protection. The role of tort has been revived as society's concerns have moved away from protecting the collective interests of employees to encouraging free enterprise.

The last 10 years have seen a dramatic expansion of the role of negligence in relation to financial losses followed by an even more remarkable retreat to

---

[72] The idea that a party who was not in a contractual relationship with the person who injured him could not sue for the loss.
[73] (1868) L.R. 3 H.L. 330 discussed at p. 407.
[74] *Groves* v. *Lord Wimborne* [1898] 2 Q.B. 402.
[75] See *ante* note 61.
[76] (1853) 2 E & B 216. The modern versions of this tort are described in Chap. 14.

a conventional position.[77] In this context tort is commonly regarded, in contrast to the law of contract, as having a protective purpose. One writer has expressed the point as follows:

"Contract law was at its zenith in the nineteenth century with its prevailing free enterprise and laisser-faire predilections. Tort law was suited to a different society. The pinnacle of its influence was reached in the twentieth century with its concept of the mixed economy and society. Tort law represents a compromise between the extremes of collectivism and libertarianism."[78]

Writing in 1984, the same writer correctly anticipated the retreat which was to come;

"The speculative question is thus posed: if the tide of the welfare state is now beginning to run out may (we) expect a retreat from negligence and a reassertion of contractually based liability."[79]

If the current political consensus is that the frontiers of the State are to be drawn back this will entail the encouragement of individual self-reliance. In such an era it ought not to be surprising that the courts should conclude that the law should be that people cannot necessarily shift their financial disasters onto the shoulders of others, such as professional persons, from whom they have not bought contractual protection. The wide ranging protective purposes of the tort of negligence no longer reflect the values of the society in which we live. The function of professional persons is to protect the interests of their clients; it is not to be the guardians of society as a whole.

---

[77] See Chap. 15.
[78] D. Partlett, *Professional Negligence* (1984), p. 27.
[79] See p. 29.

Chapter Two

Types of Tortious Liability

INTRODUCTION

It is proposed for the purposes of this chapter to classify torts into four types. They are: (1) Torts in which proof of intention is necessary; (2) Torts based on proof of negligence; (3) Strict liability torts (those in which liability is established on proof of an act and, possibly, damage caused thereby, without negligence or intention having to be shown); (4) Torts based on statutory duties.

The reason for adopting this division is that it illuminates the techniques which are used in the central areas of tort, such as accident compensation and economic losses, and allows a more coherent picture of the law to be presented than that provided by the older "nominate" tort approach; that is, the approach which describes the rules governing each tort individually.

Certain problems raised by this division of material should be noted at the outset. The first is that statutory torts raise problems as to their existence and are therefore treated separately in this chapter. However, those statutory torts which exist have characteristics which place them in one of the other three categories. In later sections of the book they will simply appear as examples of negligence based or strict tortious liability. Secondly, as we will see, the concept of an intentional tort carries different meanings and the classification of torts such as trespass may depend on this. This particular problem is accentuated by the fact that the role of trespass has evolved over the years, particularly in relation to personal injuries, as tort has abandoned the distinction between direct and indirect damage which formerly governed the choice of the appropriate writ[1] to be used and negligence has become a general basis of liability. Trespass, in particular trespass to the person, now has something of a split personality. It is commonly regarded, in distinction to negligence, as the remedy for intentionally inflicted personal injuries. However, it has other roles as a strict basis of liability for which no damage need be proved. It is used to protect an individual's freedom from physical constraint or interference.

A notable feature of the modern law of tort is that negligence has become a general basis of liability and so, to a much smaller extent, has breach of statutory duty. However, torts based on intention and strict liability have not been generalised. Torts of these kinds exist in nominate form. This means that named torts with their own particular rules cover these areas.

---

[1] Form of action.

INTENTIONAL TORTS

Any survey of the principles governing torts which require intention to be proved must recognise that the word intention has more than one meaning. An act may be intentional in the sense that it is a voluntary act of an individual's will. Alternatively, it may be the consequences of an act which must be shown to have been intended. The tort of trespass to land illustrates the first category. A person who is involuntarily pushed onto another's land will not commit the tort, whereas one who consciously places himself on it will be liable irrespective of his knowledge of another's rights over it and of whether any damage was intended or actually caused. On the other hand, the tort of conspiracy will only be held to have been committed if the defendant's acts were consciously directed to the objective of inflicting a particular kind of harm on the plaintiff.

Several attempts have been made to identify a generalised basis of tortious liability founded on intentional acts. The best example of this in the personal injury sphere is found in the judgment of Wright J. *Wilkinson* v. *Downton*[2] "The defendant has wilfully done an act calculated to cause physical harm to the plaintiff, that is to say, to infringe his right to personal safety. That proposition without more appears to me to state a good cause of action, there being no justification alleged for the tort." In *Beaudesert Shire Council* v. *Smith*[3] the High Court of Australia seemed to have applied a similar general principle to other forms of loss when it held that "a person who suffers harm as the inevitable consequence of the unlawful, intentional and positive acts of another is entitled to recover damages from that other." However, *Wilkinson* has had scarcely any affect on the law and the *Beaudesert* dicta has been expressly rejected.[4] The consequence has been that the law concerning intentionally inflicted injury has remained based on nominate torts such as battery and interference with trade which are distinguishable according to the nature of the interest receiving protection.

For most purposes the general assumption is made that recklessness (knowing that a consequence is likely to result from one's acts yet proceeding to do the act regardless of those consequences, without actively intending them) is equivalent in the law of tort to intending a consequence. A person is said to have intended the natural consequences of his act.

A number of well established House of Lords authorities[5] make the point that malice, in the sense of a motive to inflict damage on an individual, does not, of itself, render an act tortious. There is no tort of abuse of rights. A person has an unfettered right to do acts which are lawful albeit that the act is done with the intention of damaging another person. These propositions need to be treated with caution. The motive of causing damage to the plaintiff is clearly an essential component of the cause of action in torts such as conspiracy and malicious abuse of process. Furthermore, proof of malice will defeat a number of defences in defamation cases. Even in the context of the tort of nuisance, a defendant's intention to inflict damage on his neighbour seems to have been deemed relevant to deciding whether the

---

[2] [1897] 2 Q.B. 57.
[3] (1966) 120 C.L.R. 145.
[4] *Lonrho Ltd.* v. *Shell Petroleum Ltd.* [1982] A.C. 173.
[5] *Mayor of Bradford* v. *Pickles* [1895] A.C. 587; *Allen* v. *Flood* [1898] A.C. 1.

neighbour's property has been subject to an unreasonable interference.[6] It may well be that a better statement of the law would be that malice does not invariably render a lawful act tortious.

THE PROBLEM OF TRESPASS

The historical antecedents of much of the present law of tort lie in the forms of action[7] of *trespass vi et armis* (commonly called trespass) and trespass on the case (case). The basic distinction between these remedies was that trespass was the appropriate form when an injury was directly inflicted whereas case was used for indirect injuries. Although the forms of action were abolished by the Common Law Procedure Act 1852, it is still contended by some writers[8] that they have some effects on English law. It is clear that the modern torts of assault, battery and false imprisonment are derived directly from the writ of trespass and that negligence has its roots in case (although the evolution of this tort has been so marked in the twentieth century that history of this age is scarcely relevant). The surviving problem stems from the fact that the writ of trespass was used to remedy directly inflicted injuries irrespective of whether the conduct producing the damage was intended or not. Does this mean that negligently inflicted trespass survives as an alternative to negligence?[9] A range of advantages has been suggested as available to a plaintiff who chooses to frame a claim as negligent trespass rather than negligence on such matters as the burden of proof; limitation periods; defences and damages. Most of these advantages have not stood the test of time.[10]

As long ago as 1933 Winfield and Goodhart were prepared to concede that negligent trespass had fallen into disuse as plaintiffs were content to rely on the tort of negligence.[11] Further, although there is a good historical basis for the argument (and accepting that one should not criticise legal advisers who seek to utilise historical survivals for the advantage of their clients) it is still impossible to accept that there can be reasons of logic or policy in recognising two sets of rules giving different results covering the same situation when the distinction depends on history rather than the substance of the issue at hand. If, for example, the present rules on the burden of proof are defective, we should alter them for all cases rather than allow haphazard avoidance of them according to whether the plaintiff could have invoked the writ of trespass before 1852. Viewed in this way, we should welcome the fact that English courts when faced by claims based on negligent trespass have denied any advantages to the tort and have come close to denying its existence.

The issue was first faced in *Fowler* v. *Lanning*[12] in which it was argued that the plaintiff's statement of claim which simply alleged that "the defendant shot the plaintiff" was sufficient to disclose a cause of action and to shift the burden of proof to the defendant to show that the injuries had been caused

---

[6] *Post*, p. 394.
[7] For a discussion of the nature of forms of action see Street on *Torts* (9th ed.), pp. 8–9.
[8] Winfield & Goodhart, (1933) 49 L.Q.R. 359; Trinidade, (1971) 20 I.C.L.Q. 706. *Cf.* Millner, (1965) 18 C.L.P. 20
[9] Winfield & Goodhart and Trinidade *op. cit.*
[10] Winfield & Jolowicz on *Tort* (13th ed.), pp. 70–71.
[11] (1933) 49 L.Q.R. 359.
[12] [1959] 1 Q.B. 426.

unintentionally or without negligence. Diplock J., having reviewed the development of the writ of trespass, held that whether the claim was phrased as one of negligence or of unintentional trespass, the burden of proving negligence rested on the plaintiff and that, as a result, the statement was insufficient. In the subsequent decision of *Letang* v. *Cooper*[13] the Court of Appeal took the discussion a stage further. In that case the plaintiff, who had been run over by the defendant's car, attempted to rely on unintentional trespass to the person in order to avoid provisions of the Limitation Acts which would have barred a claim in negligence. The court was unanimous that this was not possible. Diplock L.J. took the view that negligent trespass to the person and negligence are nowadays simply different names for the same tort and that no differences of substance can flow from the choice of description. Lord Denning M.R. (with whom Danckwerts L.J. agreed) took the more radical approach of arguing that the law had abandoned the distinction between direct and indirect injuries in favour of one between torts based on intention and those based on negligence.[14] If trespass to the person was still to be used as a term of art, it was to be confined to the intentional torts of assault, battery and false imprisonment. The choice between these views is not of any great importance in relation to unintentionally inflicted injuries as their whole tenor is to deny any continuing advantages to negligent trespass. It is, however, suggested that Lord Denning's views on the matter should be adopted for the simple reason that they accord with modern approaches to the subject. Distinctions between torts of intention and those based on negligence remain of great importance, whereas the refinements of the old learning on trespass and case founded on the nebulous distinction between direct and indirect injuries disappeared long ago.

It remains the case, however, that the role of the tort of trespass in modern law is left uncertain by these cases. Trespass would now seem to be a remedy for intentionally inflicted injuries and also, because it exists to protect rights and is actionable *per se* (without proof of damage), is capable of providing a strict liability remedy for damage caused by certain forms of conduct such as medical treatment which has not been consented to. If Lord Denning's views in *Letang* are not accepted trespass is not capable of providing a remedy in the small number of cases of intentional acts which inflict damage indirectly. The split personality of the modern tort of trespass to the person is illustrated further in Chapter 9.

Negligence

If a person fails to take reasonable care to avoid foreseeable harm to another, but did not intend to cause the harm, he will be described as having acted negligently. Such a description passes a judgment on his state of mind. However, to lawyers the word negligence not only describes a factor which may render conduct tortious it is also a distinct and independent tort in its own right. It is a tort of dynamic characteristics which has come, in the twentieth century, to protect a wide range of interests. Its dominant influence

---

[13] [1965] 1 Q.B. 232.
[14] Lord Denning would appear to have been echoing American law on this. See Prosser on *Torts* (4th ed.), pp. 29–30.

has also been felt in the development of other nominate torts, particularly nuisance.

For a plaintiff to succeed in a negligence action three things need to be proved. The defendant must have been under a duty to take care; that duty of care must have been owed to the plaintiff and must have been broken and, finally, that breach of duty must have been the cause of the damage which was suffered by the plaintiff. All three elements must be proved and they can be difficult to distinguish. The requirement that the loss should have been reasonably foreseeable is relevant at all three stages of the enquiry and lawyers have been known to disagree as to the correct classification of a particular problem, although this has rarely involved disagreement as to the result of the case. For the purposes of this book the following classification will be adopted.

The duty of care question will be confined to the purely legal issue of whether certain conduct or kinds of damage are actionable or attract an immunity. It is discussed in the following section of this chapter. Breach raises the factual question of whether the required standard of conduct has been reached. It is only of relevance if a duty of care has been held to exist in law.[15] Damage, which encompasses a number of different issues, is similarly a question of fact.[16] In practice, the majority of negligence cases centre on disputes as to the facts (*i.e.* whether the defendant's conduct reached accepted standards and whether that conduct, if found to be negligent, was sufficiently connected to the damage to count as a cause of it). The cases, therefore, usually raise questions of breach and damage. However, great attention has been paid by lawyers to duty of care issues. This is not altogether surprising as the boundaries of the subject are an obvious matter of interest to lawyers in a period in which the tort of negligence has advanced into new fields of activity and then retreated.

Immunities and the duty of care

The concept of the duty of care fixes the boundaries of the tort of negligence. If conduct is condemned as being negligent it is because it fails to comply with generally accepted standards of behaviour. In this sense, the term negligence merely signifies a critical judgment on a piece of conduct. There is nothing distinctively legal about the statement that an activity was conducted negligently. Negligence is a powerful tool with which to evaluate conduct because of its flexibility; it is capable of applying to all human activities from the mundane (such as driving) to the highly sophisticated (such as brain surgery). For the lawyer this width of application raises the question whether all forms of conduct which a moralist or the man in the street would condemn as negligence are torts. It is not the case that all conduct which fails to meet generally recognised standards of conduct is capable of forming the basis of an action for damages in court. As was once said, "In most situations it is better to be careful than careless. But, it is quite another thing to elevate all carelessness into a tort. Liability has to be based on a legal duty not to be careless."[17] The concept of the duty of care marks

---

[15] Issues of breach are discussed in Chap. 3.
[16] These issues are discussed in Chap. 4.
[17] *Moorgate Mercantile Co. Ltd.* v. *Twitchings* [1977] A.C. 890.

out those areas of negligence which the courts, as a matter of law, recognise as giving rise to a claim for damages.

To say that a duty of care exists in relation to a category of conduct is a proposition of the same kind as "murder is a crime." It is a legal proposition that a particular form of conduct has particular legal consequences. In the context of tort the question is whether the conduct is, or is not, immune from an action in tort. For example, the leading case of *Rondel* v. *Worsley*[18] established that a barrister owes no duty of care to a client in relation to work which is done in court. However negligently a barrister acts and however much damage is caused as a result of this negligence, the lack of a duty of care creates a complete immunity. Conversely, the recognition of a duty of care, for example, that motorists owe a duty of care to other road users, merely asserts the fact that the area of conduct is not protected by an immunity. To establish liability it is necessary to go further and to prove that the defendant was actually negligent (the breach question) and that the negligence caused the plaintiff's damage. These latter issues turn on the facts of the particular case whereas the duty of care issue is purely a question of law.

Duty of care issues arise in a number of forms. The issue may be raised by the nature of the damage (examples of this are cases of pure economic loss and nervous shock) or by the way in which the damage is inflicted (as in the case of misstatements) or by the task being performed (the immunity of advocates illustrates this). The role of the law of tort may dictate the result. The distinction between misfeasance (doing the task badly) and non-feasance (failing to act) is based on perceptions of the appropriate role of tort: tort applies to activities which inflict harm on others not to failures to provide others with benefits. An immunity from the duty of care may be complete or partial. In the latter case liability will be possible, exceptionally, if certain unusually restrictive conditions, sometimes termed "control factors" are satisfied.[19]

Case law has resolved many duty of care issues. It is well established that motorists and employers owe a duty of care to other road users and to their employees respectively. Duty of care questions do not arise in the courts every day of the week. They are posed when existing immunities are challenged or when a novel kind of negligence claim is brought. For example, the limits of the immunity which protects a person whose negligence has caused pure economic loss[20] to another has been debated continually since 1963 and, in 1970, the House of Lords was faced by a wholly novel claim when persons whose property had been damaged by escaping borstal trainees brought negligence proceedings against the prison authorities.[21]

Generalised principles

How does a court determine whether certain conduct or damage is within the ambit of a duty of care if the issue has not been settled previously by case law or statute? Do the areas of negligence for which a duty of care is recognised exhibit a common factor which distinguishes them from those

---

[18] [1969] 1 A.C. 191.
[19] The area of nervous shock (discussed at pp. 203–210, *post*) is possibly the best example of "control" factors in operation.
[20] See *post*, Chap. 16.
[21] *Home Office* v. *Dorset Yacht Co. Ltd.* [1970] A.C. 1004.

other areas in which what a moralist would treat as negligence attracts an immunity? It is not surprising to find that attempts have been made to identify this common factor because, if it exists, it is a principle which underlies and unifies the large part of the law of tort based on fault liability.

The best known attempt to provide a general theory of negligence as a tort is found in Lord Atkin's speech in *Donoghue* v. *Stevenson*.[22] This is undoubtedly the most important tort case decided in the twentieth century. The plaintiff and a friend went to a café where the friend ordered a bottle of ginger beer for the plaintiff. The beer, which had been manufactured by the defendant, was supplied in an opaque glass bottle and, as a result, it was impossible to see the contents. The plaintiff consumed some of the beer and claimed that when she poured the rest into her glass she was confronted by the decomposed remains of a snail. She sued the defendant manufacturer in tort alleging that this sight and the beer which she had already consumed rendered her ill. The claim raised important issues of principle concerning a manufacturer's liability in tort to persons who were not in a contractual relationship with him, but its relevance for present purposes lies in the principle which is set out in Lord Atkin's speech:

> "(I)n English law there must be, and is, some general conception of relations giving rise to a duty of care, of which the particular cases found in the books are but instances. The liability for negligence . . . is no doubt based upon a general public sentiment of moral wrongdoing for which the offender must pay. But acts or omissions which any moral code would censure cannot in a practical world be treated so as to give a right to every person injured by them to demand relief. In this way rules of law arise which limit the range of complainants and the extent of their remedy. The rule that you are to love your neighbour becomes, in law, you must not injure your neighbour; and the lawyer's question who is my neighbour? receives a restricted reply. You must take reasonable care to avoid acts or omissions which you can reasonably foresee would be likely to injure your neighbour. Who then, in law, is my neighbour? The answer seems to be – persons who are so closely and directly affected by my act that I ought to have them in contemplation as being so affected when I am directing my mind to the acts or omissions which are called in question."

A careful reading of these words reveals a difficulty. Lord Atkin distinguishes the moralist's conception of negligence from the legal notion and sets himself the task of providing a criterion with which to test this distinction. But, although he poses the correct question, if the aim is to provide a general criterion for tortious liability in negligence, the answer which he gives is too wide. The "neighbour" test could equally provide a moralist with a definition of negligence as the test offers no distinctive element which justifies the intervention of the law. The truth of this criticism can be shown by the fact that the law in 1932 recognised, and it still recognises some, immunities from the duty of care which fall within the ambit of Lord Atkin's formula and which should, therefore, on his reasoning, be actionable. Pure economic loss inflicted by negligence is the most important in modern law. The immunity of an advocate is another. A barrister who does his job negligently in court should undoubtedly have the client in contemplation as "a person closely and directly affected" by the work. Injury to the client can be reasonably

[22] [1932] A.C. 562.

foreseen. But, although an application of Lord Atkin's test would lead to a duty of care being imposed, the decision in *Rondel* v. *Worsley*[23] establishes that an advocate is immune from suit. The fact that some of the immunities which existed in 1932, when *Donoghue* was decided, have been subsequently removed or restricted suggests that the search for a factor common to all areas of liability, but absent from areas of immunity, is likely to be fruitless.

If Lord Atkin's test fails to achieve its purpose why does it continue to hold such an important place in common law thinking? The answer is that although it was too wide as a statement of the law in 1932, and although it failed to draw a firm line between the lawyer's conception of negligence and that of the moralist, these very features made it the perfect instrument with which to extend the scope of the tort of negligence. The significance of the test is historical and lies in the development of the law: a development which was made easier by the moral foundation on which Lord Atkin based his statement of the law. In 1932 negligence was a factor which needed to be proved in order to establish liability in a number of specific areas of tort liability. By 1980 the "neighbour principle" had been recognised as a general principle of tort liability and the different areas of negligence based liability had been unified by it and new ones introduced. Negligence had become a tort in its own right. The courts took to heart Lord MacMillan's words in *Donoghue* that "the categories of negligence are never closed." The width and authority of Lord Atkin's words provided his successors with authority to invoke when developing new areas of negligence liability and when overturning established immunities. As a result the law moved closer to the moralist's idea of negligence. The expansion of the duty of care, on the authority of Lord Atkin's general principle, ultimately led to the position being reached that a duty of care is almost always owed in relation to negligently caused personal injuries, death and property damage. However, the expansion did not stop at this point. In the late 1970s negligence liability expanded rapidly into the area of economic losses and challenged the traditional preserve of the law of contract.

In the 1970s the generalised principle of negligence liability resulted in the judiciary adopting a presumption that a duty of care would be imposed in situations within the neighbour test, unless good policy reasons could be discerned for rejecting it. This approach is usually associated with a dictum of Lord Wilberforce in *Anns* v. *Merton L.B.C.*[24] The case concerned the question of whether a local authority, which had the statutory function of approving building work, owed a duty of care to a subsequent owner of the building if its negligent performance of its functions resulted in the building being defective.[25] Lord Wilberforce recognised that the result of the neighbour principle was that the tort of negligence could impose a duty of care on an activity previously untouched by the law. He said:

"(T)he position has now been reached that in order to establish that a duty of care arises in a particular situation, it is not necessary to bring the facts of that situation within those of previous situations in which a duty of care has been held to exist. Rather the question has to be approached in two

[23] [1969] 1 A.C. 191.
[24] [1978] A.C. 728. The approach had surfaced earlier in the speeches of Lords Reid and Pearson in *Home Office* v. *Dorset Yacht Co. Ltd.* [1970] A.C. 1004.
[25] The issue is discussed in detail in Chap. 16.

stages. First one has to ask whether, as between the alleged wrongdoer and the person who has suffered damage there is a sufficient relationship of proximity or neighbourhood such that, in the reasonable contemplation of the former, carelessness on his part may be likely to cause damage to the latter, in which case a prima facie duty of care arises. Secondly, if the first question is answered affirmatively, it is necessary to consider whether there are any considerations which ought to negative, or reduce or limit the scope of the duty or the class of person to whom it is owed or the damages to which a breach of it may give rise . . . Examples of this are *Hedley Byrne* v. *Heller* where the class of potential plaintiffs was reduced to those shown to have relied on the correctness of statements made, . . . and . . . cases about 'economic loss' where, a duty having been held to exist, the nature of the recoverable damages was limited."

The practical result of combining the neighbour test with a consideration of the demands of public policy obviously depended on how prepared courts were to use policy factors to limit the expansionary characteristics of the neighbour test. In practice, the two-stage test served as the basis of the rapid expansion of the duty of care which occurred between 1977 & 1982. Since 1984, however, courts have rejected this approach and, particularly in the context of the recovery of damages for economic losses, have adopted a more stringent ad hoc approach to imposing a duty of care.

Before turning to look at the current position, it is worth considering the nature of the task which courts are undertaking in relation to duty of care questions. Formally the role of courts is to apply existing law derived from statute and precedent; it is not to create new law. However, no student of tort could accept this as an accurate description of the role of the judiciary. The great bulk of tort was created by judicial development. A court faced by a novel duty of care question has to give an answer. As "don't know" is neither a permissible nor a helpful judicial response, the task in relation to a novel point is inevitably a legislative one unless the law is to remain static and is not to be adapted to changing social needs. The result of *Anns* v. *Merton L.B.C.*[26] was that the House of Lords imposed on all local authorities administering building regulations a tort duty owed to subsequent purchasers to take care in relation to the quality of buildings. Subsequently, in *Murphy* v. *Brentwood District Council*[27] the House reversed this policy and restored protection to local authorities by overruling *Anns*. But, although the process is essentially a legislative one, the "neighbour test" allows it to be justified in terms of precedent. *Donoghue* provides a precedent pitched at a high level of generality which provides authority for extending the scope of the tort of negligence. The fact that the neighbour principle is derived from case law satisfies the demands of formal theory.

In the 1970s the courts emphasised their legislative function on duty of care issues by openly referring to public policy considerations.[28] This method of deciding duty of care issues opened up an unlimited field of inquiry. Rather than shrouding the legislative function involved in the task behind a mechanical application of the neighbour principle, the courts

[26] [1978] A.C. 728.
[27] [1991] 1 A.C. 398.
[28] Symmons, (1971) 34 M.L.R. 394, 528.

looked beyond statute, precedent and legal principle at a variety of extra-legal factors. For example, they considered whether the nature of the conduct at issue made it suitable for control by the law[29]; which of the parties was best placed, through being able to take out insurance or use other forms of protection, to bear the loss; whether the imposition of the duty would encourage the taking of care or, alternatively, discourage individuals from undertaking socially desirable activities; whether inconsistencies with other areas of the law would be created and whether the imposition of a duty would impede the administration of justice, either by overwhelming the judicial system in a mass of claims (the "floodgates" argument) or by raising the possibility of issues being relitigated.[30] In doing this the courts were accepting the legislative character of their role and considering the social consequences that possible decisions might have. There was nothing intrinsically new in this in so far as good courts have always considered the consequences that their decisions might have. What was important in the context of the duty of care, was that courts in the 1970s, emphasised public policy considerations as having the central role as the main limitation on the neighbour test which was accepted as having an all-embracing and expansionary character. Some judges, seized by an enthusiasm for modernism, treated public policy as the answer to all duty and causation issues.[31]

This open reference to considerations of public policy was clearly preferable to allowing such issues to be lost from sight behind the smokescreen of the neighbour test. But, it raised its own difficulties in opening up a potentially unlimited field of inquiry and it was open to the charge that it made the results of cases unpredictable. Even more fundamentally, it raised questions as to the judicial role in achieving law reform. A court's task is to resolve a dispute between two parties; it is not ideally suited to the evaluation of conflicting policy considerations. The effect of a decision on the interests of third parties who are not represented in the proceedings may be particularly difficult for a court to assess. It is revealing to contrast the techniques adopted by the judiciary in *Dutton* v. *Bognor Regis U.D.C.*[32] and *Anns* v. *Merton L.B.C.*,[33] in imposing liability on persons whose negligence has caused defects in buildings, with the process of consultation and debate through the Law Commission and Parliament which produced the Defective Premises Act 1972. The Parliamentary technique of law reform provides for more consideration of the appropriate limits of consumer protection. However, the judiciary actually provided a far more powerful consumer protection remedy. Nonetheless, the councils and professional persons who were to meet the bill for the common law remedy had scarcely any say in its creation and ultimately the courts concluded that the statutory remedy was the more satisfactory one in terms of legal principle and that the limits of important measures of consumer protection were for Parliament, rather than the courts, to define.[34]

---

[29] *Ashton* v. *Turner* [1981] Q.B. 137.
[30] *Rondel* v. *Worsley* [1969] 1 A.C. 191.
[31] Lord Denning M.R. was the leading proponent of this approach. See particularly his judgments in *Spartan Steel & Alloys Ltd.* v. *Martin & Co. (Contractors) Ltd.* [1973] Q.B. 27 and *Lamb* v. *Camden L.B.C.* [1981] Q.B. 625.
[32] [1972] 1 Q.B. 373.
[33] [1978] A.C. 728.
[34] *Murphy* v. *Brentwood District Council* [1991] 1 A.C. 398.

Although the introduction of policy based limitations on the neighbour test might have been intended to place a brake on the expansion of the duty of care, in practice this did not happen. Courts applied the neighbour test, treated the requirement of proximity as identical to foreseeability and, having raised the prima facie inference of actionability, failed to discover policy reasons for denying the existence of a duty of care. The moralist's and lawyer's concepts of negligence were increasingly assimilated. This process reached its peak in the early 1980s in two decisions of the House of Lords. In *McLoughlin* v. *O'Brian*[35] a minority of the members of the House seemed to wish to set the neighbour test free from the constraint imposed by policy factors. Lord Scarman, who was ahead of his time in regarding policy issues as unsuitable for resolution by the judicial process, said that the courts' task was to apply principle (presumably the neighbour test) and that it was for Parliament to impose limitations if the results proved unacceptable. In *Junior Books Ltd.* v. *Veitchi Co. Ltd.*[36] the House threw doubts on the ability of the "floodgates" criterion to limit the duty of care: if principle justified recovery the court should not disallow it merely because many people would benefit. This supported the House of Lords' reversal of the Court of Appeal's decision in *McLoughlin*, which had been firmly based on a "floodgates" argument. Yet the "floodgates" argument had, in practice, been one of the few policy criteria capable of placing an effective limitation on the expansion of the neighbour test in this period.

The retreat from generality

The retreat to a more guarded position has involved a rejection of the *Anns* test for the existence of a duty of care. Senior appellate courts clearly decided that the expansion of the duty of care was going too far, particularly in the area of financial losses. Different approaches appear in the recent duty of care cases.

1. Proximity

The first approach involves replacing Lord Wilberforce's two stage test with a three stage one. A duty of care will be imposed if damage is foreseeable; a sufficient relationship of proximity exists between the parties and it is held to be "just and reasonable" to recognise a duty. Under this approach the process of equating foreseeability with proximity is rejected. Foreseeability is said to be an essential, but not a sufficient, requirement of liability and attention is focused on whether the relationship under consideration reveals adequate proximity to justify the imposition of a duty of care. The difficulty with this is that "proximity" is an ambiguous term and is being used as a smokescreen behind which policy decisions are taken. In Lord Oliver's words[37] "it has to be accepted that the concept of 'proximity' is an artificial one which depends more on the court's perception of what is the reasonable area for the imposition of liability than upon any logical process of analogical deduction." Because the notion of a foreseeable risk can, and has been, widely defined as the equivalent of any conceivable risk and thus, if

[35] [1983] 1 A.C. 410.
[36] [1983] 1 A.C. 520.
[37] *Alcock* v. *Chief Constable of the South Yorkshire Police* [1992] 1 A.C. 310 at 411.

unlimited, may offer no real scope for judicial discretion to limit the scope of negligence a new test is introduced which re-establishes discretion. In practice, although the traditional *Donoghue* v. *Stevenson* foreseeability test has continued to be applied in cases of personal injuries,[38] the courts have imposed a stringent proximity requirement in the problem areas of negligence: nervous shock[39]; duties to protect against the malicious acts of third parties[40] and duties to avoid the infliction of financial losses.[41] Something close to direct dealings between the parties has been required. The "just and reasonable" test, which seems to be little more than a reformulation of the "public policy" approach, has the capacity to block the existence of a duty of care in spite of the presence of a sufficient relationship of proximity.[42] However, in practice, it has had a subsidiary role to play as few of the difficult cases have satisfied the proximity test. The three stage test is the latest attempt to provide a general working formula for determining duty of care issues. It continues the *Donoghue* v. *Stevenson*[43] tradition which is receiving criticism in modern cases on the basis that general tests may produce results which are inappropriate on the facts of particular cases.

2. The incremental approach

The second approach, which now seems to be favoured by the House of Lords in economic loss cases,[44] is more radical. It contends that the law would be better served by an approach of determining duty of care issues on a pragmatic basis in relation to the different areas which raise problems. The central text is now that of Brennan J. in *Sutherland Shire Council* v. *Heyman*[45]

> "It is preferable . . . that the law should develop novel categories of negligence incrementally and by analogy with existing categories, rather than by massive extension of a prima facie duty of care restrained only by indefinable 'considerations which ought to negative, or to reduce or limit the scope of the duty or the class of person to whom it is owed.'"[46]

This openly accepts the legislative function of senior appellate courts on these issues at the cost of rejecting the existence of general principles of negligence liability derived from *Donoghue* v. *Stevenson*. Proximity and fairness are seen as lacking the capacity to operate as precise tests for the resolution of particular issues; at best they are used to cloak results achieved on an ad hoc basis. The advantage of this approach is that it signals a return to openness; the disadvantage, that it seems capable of freezing the tort of negligence in its present form unless Parliament can be induced to intervene.

It will be interesting to see whether common lawyers are capable of coping with the abandonment of a general approach to negligence liability in favour of an ad hoc one. The courts in recent cases have engaged in the development

---

[38] *B.* v. *Islington H.A.* [1992] 1 A.C. 310.
[39] *Alcock* v. *Chief Constable of the South Yorkshire Police* [1992] 1 A.C. 310.
[40] *Smith* v. *Littlewoods Organisation Ltd.* [1987] A.C. 241.
[41] See *post*, Chap. 16.
[42] As in *Rondel* v. *Worsley* [1969] 1 A.C. 191.
[43] [1932] A.C. 562.
[44] *Murphy* v. *Brentwood District Council* [1991] 1 A.C. 398.
[45] (1985) 60 A.L.R. 1.
[46] *Op. cit.* p. 48.

of discrete rules concerning the liabilities of professional persons working in a number of areas.[47] However, whilst a general approach carries the risk of giving a result which is inappropriate in particular circumstances, the incremental one can be criticised as unpredictable and capable of producing apparently inconsistent results when different areas are compared.[48] Problems are to be expected given the dominance that the variants of the neighbour principle have exercised in the past. Ingrained habits die hard and the common lawyer's desire to discern and use general principles is one of the most deeply entrenched habits. The real test will come when the courts are faced by a novel problem. The practical difficulty of moving to an incremental approach is already showing as there is a growing body of decisions of the lower courts which have continued to use the three stage test.[49] Examples are recorded of it being argued[50] that an auditor owed a duty of care because his relationship with the plaintiff was similar to that which existed in a decision on a surveyor's liability[51] rather than to that in the leading case on auditors.[52] Even speeches in cases which support the incremental approach make use of arguments based on general theories of liability such as reliance.[53] Those who doubt the capacity of incremental development to provide a working test for duty of care issues can derive some support from *Alcock* v. *Chief Constable of the South Yorkshire Police*,[54] the claim for damages for nervous shock brought by relatives of victims of the Hillsborough football disaster. Although the speeches in the case deal only with shock and therefore provide support for the view that the tort of negligence must now be divided into discrete areas, the result is heavily dependent on notions of foreseeability and proximity which would normally be regarded as derived from general principles of negligence liability. In view of the emphasis placed on incremental development by the House of Lords in cases such as *Murphy* v. *Brentwood D.C.*[55] it is surprising to find a similarly constituted House of Lords making no reference to it when deciding an important duty of care case less than two years later.

---

[47] On the liability of auditors see *Al Saudi Banque* v. *Clark Pixley* [1990] Ch. 313; *Caparo Industries plc* v. *Dickman* [1990] 2 A.C. 605; *James McNaughton Paper Group Ltd* v. *Hicks Anderson & Co* [1991] 2 Q.B. 113; *Morgan Crucible Co. plc* v. *Hill Samuel & Co. Ltd.* [1991] Ch. 259. *Smith* v. *Eric S. Bush* [1990] 1 A.C. 831 is the starting point for the modern law concerning surveyors. The construction industry is developing principles of professional liability of its own based on *D. & F. Estates Ltd.* v. *The Church Commissioners* [1989] A.C. 177 and *Murphy* v. *Brentwood D.C.* [1991] 1 A.C. 398. On lawyers see *Gran Gelato Ltd.* v. *Richcliffe (Group) Ltd.* [1992] 1 All E.R. and *White* v. *Jones* [1993] 3 All E.R. 481.

[48] The classic problem is why the law still recognises the recovery of economic losses caused by a negligent misstatement but not by most other forms of negligence.

[49] *Lonrho plc* v. *Tebbit* [1991] 4 All E.R. 973; *Gran Gelato Ltd.* v. *Richcliff (Group) Ltd.* [1992] 1 All E.R. 865; *Spring* v. *Guardian Assurance plc* [1993] 2 All E.R. 273; *White* v. *Jones* [1993] 3 All E.R. 481.

[50] *Al Saudi Banque* v. *Clark Pixley* [1990] Ch. 313.

[51] *Smith* v. *Eric S. Bush. Harris* v. *Wyre Forest D.C.* [1990] 1 A.C. 831.

[52] *Caparo Industries plc* v. *Dickman* [1990] 2 A.C. 605. The decision in *Al Saudi Banque* predates that of the House of Lords in *Caparo*.

[53] *Murphy* v. *Brentwood D.C.* [1991] 1 A.C. 398. General statements as to the scope of liability for negligent misstatements are still appearing in cases, see *Caparo Industries plc* v. *Dickman* [1990] 2 A.C. 605; *James McNaughton Paper Group Ltd.* v. *Hicks Anderson & Co.* [1991] 2 Q.B. 113; *Morgan Crucible Co. plc* v. *Hill Samuel & Co. Ltd.* [1991] Ch. 295.

[54] [1992] 1 A.C. 310.

[55] [1991] 1 A.C. 398.

3. The purpose approach

A "purpose" doctrine has been used by the courts in relation to negligence duties in recent years in order to limit the imposition of duties of care. By this approach, the courts can specify and hence limit the nature of the interest which is to be protected by a legal duty. It confers on appellate courts a wide discretion to bar recovery on the ground that a particular duty does not exist to protect particular classes of person against particular forms of loss. The doctrine, which has its roots in the tort of breach of statutory duty,[56] can effectively restrict the obligations of a public authority because the duties imposed on such bodies may be held to exist to protect the public interest rather than to confer individually enforceable rights on a defined class of persons. This approach first had a significant impact on the modern law of negligence in *Governors of the Peabody Donation Fund* v. *Sir Lindsay Parkinson & Co. Ltd.*[57] in which the *Anns* result was limited by a finding that the role envisaged for the building inspector by the governing legislation on building control was to protect users of a building against risks to their health and safety, rather than to protect the financial interests of the developer. The approach has subsequently been to the fore in cases concerning governmental bodies[58]; in defining the role of the statutory audit[59] and, outside the area of financial losses, in blocking claims brought by individuals against the police.[60]

Summary

The truth of the matter is that the particular formula chosen for the purpose of determining duty of care issues is of less significance than whether the court is keen to extend, contain or reduce the scope of the duty of care. All of the approaches used since 1932 have left the courts with considerable scope for creativity and changes in the test used generally signify that an attempt is being made by a court to break free from the approach accepted in the immediate past. Whichever of the approaches outlined above is preferred, the picture has changed fundamentally in recent years. The confident advance of the tort of negligence into new areas in the 1970s and early 1980s has been stopped and reversed. The boundaries of the duty of care have retreated, particularly in relation to financial losses in respect of which the fear that novel tort duties will undermine established contract rules and produce unduly extensive liability has been widely expressed. Tort has not been allowed to overturn well known results which possess the advantage of certainty.

The decision of the House of Lords in *Hill* v. *Chief Constable of West Yorkshire*[61] is a good example of the modern approach at work. The defendant was sued on the basis of an allegation that his officers had been

---

[56] *Atkinson* v. *The Newcastle & Gateshead Waterworks Company* (1877) 2 Ex. D. 441.
[57] [1985] A.C. 210.
[58] *Yuen Kun-yeu* v. *A. G. for Hong Kong* [1988] A.C. 175; *Minories Finance Ltd.* v. *Arthur Young* [1989] 2 All E.R. 105; *Davis* v. *Radcliffe* [1990] 1 W.L.R. 821.
[59] *Al Saudi Banque* v. *Clark Pixley* [1990] Ch. 313; *Caparo Industries plc* v. *Dickman* [1990] 2 A.C. 605; *James McNaughton Paper Group Ltd.* v. *Hicks Anderson & Co.* [1991] 2 Q.B. 113; *Morgan Crucible Co. plc* v. *Hill Samuel & Co. Ltd.* [1991] Ch. 295.
[60] *Hill* v. *Chief Constable of West Yorkshire* [1988] 2 W.L.R. 1049; *Clough* v. *Bussan* [1990] 1 All E.R. 431; *Ancell* v. *MacDermott* [1993] 4 All E.R. 355.
[61] [1989] A.C. 53.

negligent in failing to detect the identity of Peter Sutcliffe, the so-called "Yorkshire Ripper," who had committed a series of murders and attacks in the area. The plaintiff was the mother of the last of Sutcliffe's victims. The court held the claim to be unsustainable. The police force had a duty to detect criminals but this was a general one owed to the public at large and not enforceable by particular individuals in private law proceedings for damages. At the root of this finding was the belief that the police force's discretion as to the allocation of their available resources should not be questioned in common law proceedings. An additional reason for denying the existence of a duty of care was that no "special relationship" existed between the police and Sutcliffe, who had not been taken into custody at the relevant time. The facts were contrasted with those of *Dorset Yacht Co. Ltd* v. *Home Office*,[62] a case in which a duty of care was held to be owed by prison authorities in respect of damage which had been caused to property in the vicinity of the place of detention by prisoners who were negligently allowed to escape from custody.

The use of policy factors to decide cases has virtually disappeared and the role of negligence in the sphere of consumer protection has declined. Courts are now taking the view that their task is to apply existing legal principles, whereas the creation of new areas of protective liability is the task of Parliament.[63] In the context of defective buildings the existence of consumer protection legislation such as the Defective Premises Act 1972 is now given as a reason for denying the existence of a common law duty of care and as defining the limits of the necessary protection. Judicial legislation, particularly that based on the broad brush of the neighbour principle, is now regarded as incapable of determining with sufficient precision the appropriate limits for any such remedies which are to be introduced. It is a notable feature of recent decisions of the House of Lords that the only sustained discussion of the policies underlying the competing interests of persons in the positions of the plaintiff and defendant occurs in *Smith* v. *Eric S. Bush*[64] in relation to the issue of whether the disclaimer used by the valuer was reasonable under the Unfair Contract Terms Act 1977.[65] In effect, the courts are considering the policies when Parliament has directed them to do so, but not otherwise.

History seems to have a habit of repeating itself in this area. When the neighbour test appeared to be dominating the subject the courts rejected its mechanical application, and gave themselves the real power by using policy as an additional test. When this failed to stop the advance of the duty of care, the courts turned first to more overtly discretionary criteria and then adopted an incremental approach which has the capacity to stifle any further development in the tort of negligence. The House of Lords has now opted for a very conservative approach which seems to owe more to the demands of formal doctrine than to the need for a considered development of the law.[66] The days are long past when Lord Denning could decide duty of care issues according to a personal consideration of the demands of public policy. The very role of *Donoghue* v. *Stevenson* as a instrument to achieve a generalised

---

[62] [1970] A.C. 1004.

[63] Lord Bridge, *Murphy* v. *Brentwood D.C.* [1991] 1 A.C. 398 at 480–481.

[64] [1990] 1 A.C. 831.

[65] See p. 119.

[66] Stanton, (1991) 44 C.L.P. 83.

theory of negligence liability must now be questioned, particularly in the context of financial losses.

STRICT AND ABSOLUTE LIABILITY

It is important to draw the distinction between absolute and strict tortious liability. If liability is truly absolute a person who is proved to have caused damage is liable to compensate for it. No scope is allowed for defences or for the courts to adjust the liability according to considerations such as the cost and feasibility of taking precautions against the risk. Liability of this kind is exceptionally rare: it places the defendant in the position of insuring the victim against a particular category of risk. Strict liability, in contrast, may be much more lenient to defendants. A wide variety of duties fall under the head of strict liability and the only factor which is common to all of them is that proof that the defendant took reasonable care to avoid damage is no defence. The duties are strict in being more powerful than negligence even though the stringency of the duty imposed may be qualified significantly by defences and by the fact that any duty imposed may depend on such matters as the "practicability" of taking precautions against the loss. The imposition of absolute or strict liability by tort infringes the principle that no liability should be imposed in the absence of fault. From one perspective it therefore conflicts with the idea that tort liability is a morally based response to a person's conduct and it may be thought to need particular justification.

A common justification offered is that strict liability is an appropriate standard to exact in the case of ultra-hazardous activities. Society may permit a person to indulge in activities of this nature, but only on the condition that compensation is automatically provided to anyone who is damaged by the activity irrespective of the degree of care with which it is conducted.[67] Some writers who adopt this approach view strict liability as an appropriate response to the risks inherent in life in a developed society in the late twentieth century. Modern technology has greatly increased the possibility of an individual's activities causing extensive damage to others and strict liability for such damage should be the response.

There are several difficulties in the way of accepting this "ultra-hazardous risks" approach. The most basic is that it is predicated on a very narrow perception of the boundaries of tort: it is based on the fallacy that tort is no more than the law concerning accidents and as a result it oversimplifies and misrepresents the values which are at issue in a significant area of tort. The true position is that strict liability is a very common feature of "rights" based torts such as the different species of trespass, conversion and defamation. There is a simple explanation for the imposition of strict liability by these torts. If rights to property and reputation are to be protected by tort mechanisms they would not be protected adequately if the remedy which supports them was qualified by the criteria of reasonable care or "practicability." The protection of rights over property and equivalent interests rates high in the hierarchy of values recognised by tort[68] and it should not be surprising that strict duties are imposed to support this protection.

---

[67] Fleming, *Introduction to the Law of Tort* (2nd ed.), Chap. 8.
[68] Cane, *Tort Law and Economic Interests*, Chap. 2.

Even if attention is confined to accident law the "ultra-hazardous activities" approach is difficult to accept. It seems to be firmly based on the mistaken assumption that the central principle of strict liability in tort is to be derived from the case of *Rylands* v. *Fletcher*[69] and is to be found, in a more modern guise, in statutory provisions such as the Nuclear Installations Act 1965. However, the truth is that *Rylands* v. *Fletcher* is effectively moribund and that it is impossible to distinguish, by reference to the level of danger created, those activities which are subject to regimes of strict liability (such as the manufacture of defective products; the keeping of dangerous animals and injuries suffered in the course of commercial air transport) from those such as motoring, medical practice and other public transport which are subject to negligence.

The controls placed by tort on those industrial hazards which threaten the safety of employees at work pose a number of difficulties for the "ultra-hazardous activities" approach. First, they are controlled by an amalgam of negligence and strict liability duties which seems to be based on no discernible assessment of the exceptional nature of the risk created by the activity. Why, for example, should a factory operator be under a strict liability duty in respect of a failure to maintain a safe means of access to a place of work?[70] Secondly, a study of the role of tort in relation to industrial hazards emphasises the gulf which can exist between strict and absolute liability. The ultra-hazardous activities approach seems to be founded on the idea that a person who undertakes such an activity becomes the insurer of those injured by it. But this is absolute liability, a form of liability which is unqualified by defences or the phrasing of the particular obligation. This form of liability rarely, if ever, exists. The torts used in relation to industrial injuries show that many strict liability duties approximate more closely to negligence than to absolute liability and allow considerable scope to the actor to consider and weigh the risks of the activity.[71]

The economic analysis of accident law has produced a variety of approaches to strict liability. At the most simple level it is possible to argue that the imposition of strict liability and the associated inability to avoid liability by pleading that it was not reasonable to adopt a particular precaution may produce inefficiencies in so far as it may create an incentive for persons to adopt accident prevention measures which are not cost-justified or to withdraw from an activity which would, given a correct allocation of incentives, have been economically beneficial. In short, strict (or absolute) liability, by making legal liability for damage unavoidable, may mean that the actor no longer has the incentive produced by negligence to weigh the advantages and costs of a precaution so as to discover the cost justified level of care.[72]

This approach is probably too unsophisticated. In practice, strict liability may well be capable of achieving a more efficient internalising of the costs of accidents to the person who is likely to be the least cost avoider.[73] It may well

---

[69] (1868) L.R 3 H.L. 330. See *Cambridge Water Co. Ltd.* v. *Eastern Counties Leather plc* [1994] 1 All E.R. 53.

[70] Factories Act 1961, s. 29.

[71] See *post*, p. 59–61.

[72] For an early criticism of strict liability on the lines that a justification needs to be found for the transfer of resources between an injured person and the injurer see Holmes, *The Common Law*, Lecture 3.

[73] A term used by the writers on law and economics to describe the person who is capable of eliminating the risk most efficiently.

also be capable of helping to correct many of the operational inefficiencies of the tort system and thus of achieving a more accurate allocation of incentives. In the case of defective products,[74] the Consumer Protection Act 1987 adopted the approach that the manufacturer of products was the person best placed to assess the risks created by the design and marketing of a product and the costs involved in eliminating those risks whereas the consumer, as a result of information failure, was unable to assess those risks and was therefore likely to be hindered in any attempts to establish negligence on the part of the manufacturer. These inefficiencies in the operation of the system could be addressed, if only in part, by imposing strict liability on the manufacturer who was almost certain to be the least cost avoider of accidents.

Other forms of economic analysis contend that the choice between a strict and a negligence based standard of liability is likely to have only a marginal effect in terms of efficiency. First, there is a widely accepted view[75] which holds that in a situation of perfect market competition, the parties to legal proceedings will negotiate to substitute an efficient result for an inefficient one imposed by the law. If this is correct, the choice between negligence and strict liability may be of little importance so long as (which is unlikely) the parties have full information about the costs of all of the potential results and so long as the costs of transacting an efficient result are not exorbitant. A second, and more convincing, argument which produces the same result is to the effect that an individual who faces the prospect of being held strictly liable if damage results from an activity will still indulge in a calculation to determine the efficiency of additional precautions to avert the risk of liability. The change from negligence to strict liability merely alters one of the elements in the equation and, in practice, given that strict liability may not differ very significantly from negligence, the equation may not be changed greatly. The liability element in the equation requires quantification, but so does the likelihood of liability being established; the quantum of compensation likely to be paid and the benefits to be obtained by the risk creator from running the risk. There is no obvious evidence of those risk creators who are subject to strict liability abandoning their activities.

Strict liability has had a somewhat chequered history in the English law of tort. It is a common feature of torts based on the old writs of trespass. Indeed, the existence of some examples of strict liability torts, such as the liability for dangerous animals and trespassing livestock, may be best explained as survivals from a period before negligence made its mark on English civil liability. In the nineteenth century there was a possibility that strict liability would emerge as the dominant general principle unifying the English law of tort. In *Rylands* v. *Fletcher*[76] Lord Cranworth was of the view that "when one person in managing his own affairs causes, however innocently, damage to another, it is obviously only just that he should be the party to suffer." If this, rather than the *Donoghue* v. *Stevenson* "neighbour" principle, had become the dominant principle of English tortious liability the law might now offer a road accident victim an automatic right to claim compensation against the insurance of a motorist whose car was involved in an accident which injured him. French law has successfully developed a strict liability

---

[74] See *post*, p. 220.
[75] The "Coase Theorem." See Coase, "The Problem of Social Cost" (1960) 3 J.L. & Econ. 1.
[76] (1868) L.R. 3 H.L. 330.

remedy governing motoring accidents.[77] As late as the 1930s it is possible to find courts developing Lord Cranworth's approach to the extent of imposing strict liability for dangerous (or ultra-hazardous) activities,[78] apparently on the assumption that *Rylands* was authority for such a general principle of liability. However, the actual scope of the decision in *Rylands* v. *Fletcher*[79] has increasingly been subject to restrictive conditions and, by 1970, the Law Commission could comment that the application of strict liability under English law was "complex, uncertain and inconsistent in principle."[80] English law had chosen to build its general theory of tort liability on the basis of fault and, as a result, the nominate torts which impose a strict liability standard had come to be regarded as somewhat anomalous.

The Pearson Commission[81] made an attempt to revive strict liability. The Commission felt that a narrower principle than that favoured by Lord Cranworth, that strict liability should be imposed in the case of personal injury caused by exceptionally hazardous things or activities, would be beneficial if more widely and consistently applied. The Commission would have applied this form of liability both to things which are unusually hazardous, such as explosives and flammable liquids, and those, such as dams, bridges and stadiums, which, although usually safe, are likely, if they do go wrong, to cause serious and extensive casualties. The difficulty of deciding which things and activities were to be subject to the strict liability regime was to be answered by a system under which only activities stipulated by statutory instrument would be covered. No attempt has been made to implement this proposal.

Strict liability continues to exert an attraction for commentators who are dissatisfied with the working of the fault based system of liability and who want to ensure a more efficient channelling of the costs of damage to the responsible parties. In a consumer orientated society there is considerable attraction in the simplicity of the strict liability principle, whether or not the activity can be classified as ultra-hazardous. It is such concern for the interests of consumers which is almost certainly the best explanation of the fact that injuries caused by defective products have become subject to a strict liability regime as a consequence of legislation[82] instigated by a European Community directive. Other similar developments based on European Community initiatives relating to the provision of services and to waste disposal are under discussion at the time of writing.[83]

STATUTORY TORTS

Tortious liability derived from statute cuts across the types of liability already described because liability based on a statute may have the character-istics of either negligence or strict liability. However, the subject requires

---

[77] Civil Code Art. 1384 and Road Traffic Law (No. 85–677 of July 5, 1985).
[78] *Honeywill & Stein Ltd.* v. *Larkin Bros.* [1934] 1 K.B. 191.
[79] (1868) L.R. 3 H.L. 330.
[80] Law Commission Report No. 32.
[81] Chap. 31.
[82] Consumer Protection Act 1987.
[83] A draft directive on liability for harm done by waste disposal has been issued. The draft directive on the provision of services which would reverse the burden of proof in relation to negligence which resulted in personal injuries would arguably impose a form of strict liability.

separate treatment as the forms of liability are derived from a different basis. The different forms of statutory tort are the basis of a sizeable and expanding part of the modern law of tort.

Express statutory schemes of liability

Statutory torts take a number of different forms. A number of modern statutes expressly create a detailed scheme of tortious liability. The Occupiers' Liability Acts of 1957 and 1984; the Animals Act 1971 and the Consumer Protection Act 1987 exemplify this approach. The conditions for the existence of a duty; the standard of conduct required and the available defences are all defined. The law created is part of the mainstream of tort liability. Indeed, rules enacted in this way are often modelled closely on common law principles. Claims brought on these statutes may be described as being for breach of statutory duty but no consequences follow from this loose use of the term.

Inferred breach of statutory duty

In its second, more sophisticated, meaning, breach of statutory duty denotes a common law tortious liability created by courts to allow an individual to claim compensation for damages suffered as a result of another breaking the provisions of a statute which does not on its face provide a remedy in tort. A tortious remedy is obviously available if a statute says that it is, but the converse is not the case. If the statute is silent on the issue a remedy may or may not be implied; if it is implied, it is said that the defendant is liable under the tort of breach of statutory duty. The most familiar example of this arises in relation to those areas of industrial safety legislation which have traditionally imposed criminal penalties upon an employer for breach of safety provisions, but have given no express tortious remedy to an employee injured by such a breach. The decision of the Court of Appeal in *Groves* v. *Lord Wimborne*[84] is the leading authority supporting the inference of a tortious remedy in relation to such legislation. English law has firmly committed itself to the view that breach of statutory duty is a distinct tort.[85] In doing this it has rejected the theory which has become fashionable in North America that the tort is simply a species of negligence. The "statutory negligence"[86] approach is to say that as the reasonable person does not break the law the existence of statutory provisions serves to establish a duty of care and to "crystallise" the standard of conduct required to meet it. However, the difficulty with forcing breach of statutory duty into the framework of negligence is that problems, such as the recovery of pure economic loss, are imported artificially into the tort and the possibility of actionability for every breach of a minor statutory provision is raised.

This tort is important for several reasons. The first is that it governs a substantial part of the important area of litigation concerning industrial injuries. At a more general level it can be said that the quantity of legislation produced by the modern Parliament means that the question whether the tort of breach of statutory duty should be inferred is asked frequently, not only in

---

[84] [1898] 2 Q.B. 402.
[85] *L.P.T.B.* v. *Upson* [1949] A.C. 155.
[86] For a more detailed discussion see Stanton, *Breach of Statutory Duty in Tort*, p. 25 *et seq.*

relation to statutes which impose duties enforced by the criminal law, but also in the case of those which place duties on public bodies. Finally, the tort has supplied the theoretical basis for the recognition in English courts of damages remedies for breach of certain European Community legislation.

In practice, the question of attempting to determine when this tort will operate is exceptionally difficult to answer. The techniques adopted to answer this question, which are generally viewed as inadequate and liable to lead to arbitrary results, are discussed below.

Express breach of statutory duty

The difficulties involved in deciding whether a tort right is to be inferred has led to calls for Parliament to remove the difficulty by express wording. In *Cutler* v. *Wandsworth Stadium Ltd.*[87] Lord du Parcq said:

"To a person unversed in the science or art of legislation it may well seem strange that Parliament has not by now made it a rule to state explicitly what its intention is in a matter which is often of no little importance, instead of leaving it to the courts to discover, by a careful examination and analysis of what is expressly said, what that intention may be supposed probably to be. There are no doubt reasons which inhibit the legislature from revealing its intention in plain words. I do not know, and must not speculate, what those reasons may be. I trust, however, that it will not be thought impertinent in any sense of that word, to suggest respectfully that those who are responsible for framing legislation might consider whether the traditional practice, which obscures, if it does not conceal, the intention which Parliament has, or must be presumed to have, might not safely be abandoned."

The Law Commission subsequently adopted a different and more radical approach and suggested that a statutory presumption in favour of actionability should be introduced.[88]

Neither of these suggestions has been adopted in full, although an increasing number of modern statutes do make explicit provision on the issue. For the most part such statutes adopt one of a number of standard phrases to achieve the desired result. Statutes which deny a civil law claim generally adopt a formula along the lines of "nothing in this Act shall be construed as conferring a right of action in any civil proceedings."[89] One notable example of a different form is section 170(1) of the Consumer Credit Act 1974 which reads: "A breach of any requirement made (otherwise than by any court) by or under this Act shall incur no civil or criminal sanction as being such a breach, except to the extent (if any) expressly provided by or under this Act."

There has been a marked growth in recent years in the number of statutes which establish such remedies. Parliament when passing regulatory legislation seems increasingly prepared to support it by the creation of a private law remedy under which compensation can be claimed. Statutes of this kind,

[87] [1949] A.C. 398.
[88] *The Interpretation of Statutes*, 21st Report (1969).
[89] Radioactive Substances Act 1960, s. 19(5)(a). See also Water Resources Act 1963, s. 135(8)(a); Fair Trading Act 1973, s. 26(a); Guard Dogs Act 1975, s. 5(2)(a); Health and Safety at Work Act 1974, s. 47(1)(a); Safety of Sports Grounds Act 1975, s. 13; Medicines Act 1968, s. 133(2)(a) and the Consumer Protection Act 1987, s. 41(2). The Representation of the People Act 1949, s. 50(2) and 51(2) are in a slightly different form.

which create a tortious right but do not enact a full statutory scheme governing such liability, create significant problems. In the industrial safety sphere the normal technique adopted in the legislation is simply to adopt the formula to the effect that breach of a duty "shall be actionable."[90] In view of the detailed learning which has grown up in relation to employer's liability this approach is likely to be adequate. However, in other areas a variety of formulae is used. Although the Telecommunications Act 1984 follows the industrial safety model and provides that "any breach of the duty . . . shall be actionable,"[91] a more common formula is that "any breach of that duty is actionable accordingly (subject to the defences and other incidents applying to actions for breach of statutory duty)."[92] In 1988 Parliament used two other formulae. Section 4 of the Landlord and Tenant Act 1988 makes a claim possible "in like manner as any other claim in tort for breach of statutory duty"[93] whereas the Copyright, Designs and Patents Act 1988 says that "an infringement . . . is actionable (. . .) as a breach of statutory duty."[94]

The general problem posed by these forms of wording[95] is the assumption that a unified tort of breach of statutory duty exists, with clearly identified characteristics and to which the application of defences is well known. It might be thought that the industrial safety cases provide sufficient material from which to draw these principles and that Parliament in enacting remedies of this kind was intending to model the new remedy on that area. On the other hand, it is not at all clear that the policies which apply in the industrial safety cases, particularly in relation to the imposition of a strict standard of liability, should be transferred by analogy to different areas. It is also arguable, that what are commonly treated as the normal features of an industrial safety case founded on breach of statutory duty are in fact not invariable features but derive from a construction of the particular provision at issue. If this is correct, the reliance on analogies drawn from this area may be misconceived. At best this technique is unhelpful and liable to cause difficulty; Parliament has created a tort but has left the courts with the task of filling out the details of the remedy. Often the class of persons who may invoke such remedies is stipulated, even though this is done in general, and unhelpful, terms such as "any person who may be affected."[96] What is commonly omitted is any consideration of the kinds of damage which are

---

[90] Health and Safety at Work Act 1974, s. 47(2); Building Act 1984, s. 38 and Mineral Workings (Offshore Installations) Act 1971, s. 11. See also Health & Safety, The Classification, Packaging, and Labelling of Dangerous Substances Regulations 1984 (S.I. 1984 No. 1244), reg. 15(1).

[91] s.18(6)(a).

[92] Resale Prices Act 1976, s. 25. See also Restrictive Trade Practices Act 1976, s. 35(2); Employment Act 1982, s. 12(7) and 13(4); Financial Services Act 1986, s. 62 and Consumer Protection Act 1987, s. 41(1).

[93] See also Sex Discrimination Act 1975, s. 66(1) and Race Relations Act 1976, s. 57(1).

[94] ss. 103(1), 194.

[95] The Telecommunications Act 1984 avoids this. However, there are still doubts as to who owes the duty. See Carty, (1984) 13 I.L.J. 165.

[96] Resale Prices Act 1976, s. 25; Restrictive Trade Practices Act 1976, s. 35(2); Trade Union and Labour Relations (Consolidation) Act 1992, ss. 145(5) and 187(5); Telecommunications Act 1984, s. 18(5) and Consumer Protection Act 1987, s. 41. The Trade Union and Labour Relations (Consolidation) Act 1992 uses this form of words as a fall back after giving more explicit guidance. S. 62 of the Financial Services Act 1986 speaks of "a person who suffers loss."

actionable; the standard of liability and the available defences.[97] These are fundamental questions. The result is that explicit Parliamentary guidance on the availability of the tort has lessened the problems inherent in breach of statutory duty but has not removed them. The adoption of the Law Commission's presumption of actionability would have produced a similar result on a wider scale.

Inferring the tort of breach of statutory duty: presumptions and principles of construction

Having described the different species of statutory tortious liability which exist it remains to consider the process of statutory interpretation which operates when courts have to decide whether the tort of breach of statutory duty should be inferred. The problem facing the courts is that of discerning the intention of Parliament on a question which it has, by definition, failed to answer. The question is whether the existence of a statutory duty imposed on one person implies that another person who is injured by its breach has a right to seek damages in tort. In the words of Lord Jauncey " . . . it must always be a matter for consideration whether the legislature intended that private law rights of action should be conferred in respect of breaches of the relevant statutory provision."[98]

The cases reveal two distinct approaches. The first (the "presumption" approach) seeks assistance in resolving the issue by using presumptions to assist courts to determine whether the tort should be inferred. The alternative approach denies that there is any possibility of bringing order to the subject. Lord Denning M.R. took this view in *Ex parte Island Records Ltd.*[99]:

> "The truth is that in many cases the legislature has left the point open. It has ignored the plea of Lord du Parcq in *Cutler's* case (for the legislature to provide express guidance). So it has left the courts with a guesswork puzzle. The dividing line between the pro-cases and the contra-cases is so blurred and ill-defined that you might as well toss a coin to decide it."

Proponents of this approach tend to adopt as their starting point the words of Lord Simonds in *Cutler* v. *Wandsworth Stadium Ltd.*[1] that "(t)he only rule which in all circumstances is valid is that the answer must depend on a consideration of the whole Act and the circumstances, including the pre-existing law, in which it was enacted." In effect, the court is left free to make its own ad hoc assessment of each statutory provision. The supporters of this view criticize the presumption approach for the fact that it is often difficult to predict how a statute will be classified in terms of the presumptions and because some of the results in the cases are undoubtedly contradictory.

In spite of the force of these criticisms the presumption approach must be considered for a number of reasons. First, breach of statutory duty is of considerable practical importance in view of the volume of legislation issuing from Parliament and there are obvious advantages to be gained from any technique which assists in the prediction of results. Secondly, the criticism of the presumptions must be set against the fact that they are of considerable

---

[97] *Cf.* Telecommunications Act 1984, s.18(7).
[98] *Hague* v. *Deputy Governor of Parkhurst Prison* [1992] 1 A.C. 58.
[99] [1978] Ch. 122.
[1] [1949] A.C. 398.

antiquity and were approved in Lord Diplock's seminal speech in *Lonrho Ltd.* v. *Shell Petroleum Co. Ltd.*[2] Lord Diplock's words seem to have been accepted as correctly stating the law: the cases decided subsequently[3] show the judiciary to be treating his words with the reverence which was once granted to Lord Wilberforce's two stage test in *Anns*. Thirdly, the critics do, on occasion, misunderstand the limited role of presumptions. For instance, Ormrod L.J. in *McCall* v. *Abelesz*[4] attacked those who seek to formulate rules to apply to this subject. But presumptions are not binding rules, they will yield to competing evidence for the contrary result which is found in the statute. Finally, the Law Commission has favoured the use of presumptions in this area. In its 21st Report the Commission criticised the traditional approach to breach of statutory duty on the grounds that it was difficult to determine the weight that the various presumptions used by the courts should bear, but recommended the enactment of an Interpretation Act which would contain a new presumption that all statutory duties introduced subsequently would be actionable in a civil court unless the statute expressly denied this. The proposal attracted severe criticism on the only occasion that it was placed before Parliament[5] and has not been enacted. This is not surprising as experience has marked out generally accepted categories of "public" and "individually enforceable" rights which the Commission's inflexible irrebuttable presumption would not have respected. Nonetheless the fact that the Commission regarded the use of presumptions as the way forward in this area must be of some comfort to those who believe that the common law has already developed techniques of this kind.

None of this means that the existing presumptions are wholly satisfactory. The law on the subject has been severely, and justifiably, criticised on account of the diverse and arbitrary results produced. However, in view of the continuing, and authoritative, judicial support for the use of presumptions they must be considered. It is possible that this consideration may lead to the conclusion that the presumptions are worthless. Alternatively, it may be possible to use them as the basis of a revised, and more successful, approach.

The use of presumptions in relation to issues of breach of statutory duty should not be surprising. The problem is not the normal one faced by those who have to construe statutes of attributing a particular meaning to a form of words. It is the more difficult one of discerning the intention of the legislature on a matter which has not been dealt with expressly. The use of presumptions is ideal in such a case. A presumption is, in effect, a judicial pronouncement that a particular result is to be assumed unless the contrary is stated with precision. As Lord du Parcq emphasised in *Cutler* the legislature is assumed to know the relevant presumptions and if they leave the matter undecided, to have done so knowing what the judicial response will be. In effect, the judicial intent is attributed to the legislature.

The fact that presumptions are not decisive creates most of the difficulties which give rise to the charge that the law on breach of statutory duty is uncertain. If the court holds that the statutory intention is clearly opposed to

---

[2] [1982] A.C. 173.
[3] *Rickless* v. *United Artists Corp.* [1987] 1 All E.R. 679.
[4] [1976] Q.B. 585.
[5] Interpretation of Legislation Bill 1979/80. H.L. Deb., Vol. 405, Cols. 276–306, February 13, 1980.

the result derived from the presumption it must uphold that intention. The words of the statute are construed carefully for any available assistance with which to test the result derived from the presumption. The leading cases on breach of statutory duty provide a good illustration of the wide range of judicial approaches used nowadays to interpret statutes. At times a precise reading of the provision at issue is used; at other times the court evaluates the provision against other associated provisions, against the whole structure of the statute and against the purposes discerned as lying behind the passing of the statute. Commentators on the English approach to statutory interpretation have argued that the "literal" approach, that is, concentration on the natural and ordinary meaning of the words and nothing else, as the primary approach, has been abandoned in favour of a "unified" approach. This treats as equal, factors such as the rest of the statute and the purposes for which it was passed. There can be no doubt that the cases on breach of statutory duty are a good illustration of this approach to interpretation.

There is support in early cases for the wide presumption that if Parliament has created a duty by statute, the common law should provide a remedy to a person injured by breach of it.[6] Had this presumption been accepted, breach of statutory duty would be central to the English rules of civil liability. The most notable modern example of such thinking are the words of Greer L.J. in *Monk* v. *Warbey*[7] that "prima facie a person who has been injured by the breach of a statute has a right to recover damages from the person committing it unless it can be established by considering the whole of the Act that no such right was intended to be given." However, by the time of *Monk* the tide of judicial reasoning was flowing strongly in a different direction. The presumption which had come to the fore was that actionability would only be inferred in the case of a statute which created an obligation but provided no express mode of enforcing its performance.

The modern version of the presumption approach is based on the application of two presumptions which were first stated by Lord Tenterden in *Doe dem. Murray, Lord Bishop of Rochester* v. *Bridges*[8]:

" . . . (W)here an Act creates an obligation and enforces the performance in a specified manner, we take it to be a general rule that performance cannot be enforced in any other manner. If an obligation is created, but no mode of enforcing its performance is ordained, the common law may, in general, find a mode suited to the particular nature of the case."

Two exceptions exist to the presumption of non-actionability derived from the first presumption. First, it will be presumed that a tort right should be inferred in the case of a statute passed with the intention of protecting the interests of a defined group of individuals as opposed to one passed to protect the public interest. Secondly, an exception exists in the case of a statute which creates "public rights" breach of which has caused an individual "special damage". Little is known about this second exception. Lord Diplock's speech in *Lonrho* provides authoritative modern support for this approach.

---

[6] Lord Campbell C.J. in *Couch* v. *Steel* (1854) 3 El. & Bl. 402 stated that "in every case, where a statute enacts or prohibits a thing for the benefit of a person, he shall have a remedy upon the same statute for the thing enacted for his advantage, or for a recompense of a wrong done contrary to the said law."

[7] [1935] 1 K.B. 75.

[8] (1831) B. & Ad. 847.

" . . . (O)ne starts with the presumption . . . that 'where an Act creates an obligation, and enforces the performance in a specified manner . . . that performance cannot be enforced in any other manner' . . . (T)here are two classes of exception to this general rule. The first is where on the true construction of the Act it is apparent that the obligation or prohibition was imposed for the benefit or protection of a particular class of individuals, as in the case of the Factories Acts and similar legislation . . . The second exception is where the statute creates a public right . . . and a particular member of the public suffers... 'particular, direct and substantial' damage 'other and different from that which was common to all the rest of the public.' "

Some variations in the phrasing of the presumptions appear in the cases. Lord Tenterden's "general rule" is based upon the statute "enforcing the performance" of its obligations in a specified manner, whereas the Earl of Halsbury L.C. in *Pasmore* v. *Oswaldtwistle U.D.C.*[9] spoke of the statute providing a "specific remedy." The latter wording has been adopted on many occasions, notably by the members of the Court of Appeal which decided *Phillips* v. *Britannia Hygienic Laundry Co. Ltd.*[10] What is clear is that the word "remedy" does not require financial recompense to be available to the injured person before the presumption against a tort right will arise. In this respect Lord Tenterden's formulation is preferable in leaving open the possibility that powers vested in Ministers to compel the performance of public duties and purely criminal penalties which cannot benefit the victim of a breach of duty can be presumed to bar the inference of a private law remedy.[11]

1. When no mode of enforcement is contained in the statute

At first sight it is an attractive proposition that if Parliament has not provided a remedy to enforce the duty the courts should provide one. Closer consideration reveals a number of problems. First, to what extent does the existence of administrative law remedies[12] operate to exclude the operation of this presumption. Secondly, this presumption may lead to the tort being inferred in circumstances which might be thought to be the least likely to justify it. Statutory duties which lack enforcement machinery are commonly found in the general enabling legislation governing public bodies. For example, subsection 1(2) of the Employment Protection Act 1975 places the Advisory Conciliation and Arbitration Service (ACAS) under "the general duty of promoting the improvement of industrial relations, and in particular of encouraging the extension of collective bargaining and the development and, where necessary, reform of collective bargaining machinery." It is difficult to conceive of a breach of a duty of this generality being held to be actionable at the suit of an individual, even though the legislation contains no explicit enforcement machinery. The duty exists at the policy or planning

---

[9] [1878] A.C. 387.
[10] [1923] 2 K.B. 832.
[11] *Pasmore* and *Phillips* support this.
[12] Such as mandamus, derived from general principles of law and special statutory remedies of complaint conferred by particular statutes. Some modern authorities, such as *Reffell* v. *Surrey C.C.* [1964] 1 W.L.R. 358, *Thornton* v. *Kirklees M.B.C.* [1979] Q.B. 626 and *Meade* v. *Haringey L.B.C.* [1979] 2 All E.R. 1016, suggest that such remedies, even if created by the statute, may not invoke the presumption of non-actionability. The reason for this is not clear.

level.[13] The responsibility is essentially a political one. The normal approach is to bar tort remedies from the political sphere as it is regarded as inappropriate for courts to become involved in questioning such decisions. This reluctance to use tort remedies is directly opposed to the result stated by the presumption.

The leading modern authorities in this area are not of great assistance as the issue has only been raised in the course of the trial of preliminary issues. *Booth & Co. (International) Ltd.* v. *National Enterprise Board*[14] concerned the duties of the Board under subparagraph 2(2)(b) of the Industry Act 1975 which included "promoting or assisting the reorganisation or development of an industry or any undertaking in an industry." By the terms of section 7 the Secretary of State might "give the Board directions of a general or specific character as to the exercise of their functions and it shall be the duty of the Board to give effect to any such directions." Directions had been issued to the Board by the Secretary of State to the effect that (a) the Board should only make acquisitions and investments where there was a prospect of an adequate rate of return within a reasonable period; (b) the Board should avoid showing undue preference in its trading relationships, and (c) the Board, in taking investment decisions, should always have regard to the profitability of the investments. The plaintiffs, who had been trading profitably in the United Kingdom tanning industry in spite of a recession, sought damages from the Board on the basis that it had broken these duties when it intervened to provide financial assistance for loss making firms in the industry. The defendant's application to have the action struck out was unsuccessful. Forbes J. expressed the view that it was difficult to believe that Parliament had intended that a private person was to have the right to enforce these duties by civil action through the courts, but held that the plaintiff's case, which was based on the presumption of actionability, was not so obviously wrong that it should be struck out. The final outcome of the case is not reported. When a similar issue was raised in *Re HIV Haemophiliac Litigation*,[15] Ralph Gibson L.J. took a more robust view to the suggestion that the Department of Health had broken the general statutory duties imposed by the National Health Service Act 1977 by importing HIV infected blood from the United States. He stated that it was unlikely that Parliament, when legislating, wished to confer a civil remedy on all persons entitled to receive NHS benefits. However, he did not have to reach a final decision on whether the point was arguable as he held the plaintiffs to have an arguable case in negligence.

2. When there is an alternative mode of enforcement

Possibly the best example of the second presumption in action is *Thornton* v. *Kirklees M.B.C.*[16] The plaintiff claimed that he was a homeless person with a priority need for accommodation and that as a result the defendant local authority was under a statutory duty imposed by the Housing (Homeless Persons) Act 1977 to provide him with accommodation while inquiries were made into his situation. The defendants were prepared to concede that

---

[13] Terms borrowed from Lord Wilberforce's judgment in the negligence case of *Anns* v. *Merton L.B.C.* [1978] A.C. 728. For further discussion of this point see *post*, Chap. 25 and Buckley, "Liability in Tort for Breach of Statutory Duty" (1984) 100 L.Q.R. 204.

[14] [1978] 3 All E.R. 624.

[15] (1990) 140 N.L.J. 1349.

[16] [1979] Q.B. 625

such a duty was owed to the plaintiff, but argued that it was a duty which, if broken, was actionable only by means of an application for judicial review with the result that a private law claim for breach of statutory duty was not available. This contention, which might be thought to follow from the presumption drawn from *Doe* was well supported by analogous modern authority on similar legislation.[17] *Thornton*, however, fell to be decided on the effects of the 1977 Act which had replaced earlier legislation governing the issue of homelessness and which, unlike its predecessors, contained no power of ministerial intervention. This change of legislative wording was the decisive factor in leading the Court of Appeal to allow an action for breach of statutory duty in the teeth of the older authority. *Thornton* illustrates the application of the *Doe* presumption. When the statutory enforcement procedure was removed the private law remedy appeared.

The case is also relevant for its refusal to regard the plaintiff's right to challenge the authority's decision by an application for judicial review as an alternative remedy sufficient to invoke the *Doe* presumption of non-actionability. The defendants argued that the duty at issue involved the exercise of a substantial degree of discretion and judgment, and that as there was a large element of political content in the decision, any legal remedy should be drawn from the area of administrative law. This approach might seem to have a lot to recommend it, but it was condemned by Megaw L.J. as unsatisfactory and as creating a distinction which was vague and impossible to apply. There is support in the leading cases for this approach in so far as the presumptions are stated to apply according to the existence of remedies conferred by the governing statute rather than the general law. However, there is contrary authority in *McCall* v. *Abelesz*[18] in which the Court of Appeal regarded the existence of rights under a tenancy agreement as excluding an inference of the tort based upon the criminal offence of harassing a tenant. The *Thornton* approach is supported by the industrial safety area in which the common law remedy of negligence does not bar the inference of breach of statutory duty. However, this latter result is traditionally explained as turning on other presumptions.[19] It is suggested that the authority of *Thornton* should not be followed on this point. It seems unreal for a court to decide whether or not to infer the existence of a tort without reference to remedies conferred by the general law. It can scarcely be supposed that the legislation was drafted in ignorance of the legal background.

3. Obligations imposed to protect a particular class of persons

If a statutory obligation or prohibition was imposed for the benefit or protection of a particular class of persons a presumption will arise that the tort of breach of statutory duty is to be inferred. This presumption is an exception to the presumption of non-actionability derived from *Doe*. It therefore only applies to a statute which provides its own enforcement machinery.

This presumption requires the statute to be interpreted to see whether it was intended to benefit the interests of the public as a whole or a defined

---

[17] *Southwark London Borough Council* v. *Williams* [1971] Ch. 734; *Wyatt* v. *Hillingdon L.B.C.* (1978) 76 L.G.R. 727.
[18] [1976] Q.B. 585.
[19] That concerning the protection of a particular class of persons.

group of members of the public. The decisions in *Cutler* v. *Wandsworth Stadium Ltd.*[20] and *Atkinson* v. *The Newcastle and Gateshead Waterworks Company Ltd.*[21] are the leading examples of courts deciding that statutes were designed to protect the public as a whole. The question in *Cutler* was whether section 11(2)(b) of the Betting and Lotteries Act 1934, which obliged the occupier of a dog racing track upon which a totalisator was operated to provide space for the use of bookmakers, could be used by a bookmaker to compel an occupier to admit him to a track. The House of Lords concluded that it could not because the statutory intention was to protect the public interest by regulating the operation of dog tracks. Any benefit accruing to bookmakers was incidental to this purpose. *Atkinson* followed the same lines. The obligation to fix and maintain fire plugs and to keep the pipes to them charged with water at a certain pressure was held to be owed to the public in general; not to any member of the public whose property was damaged as a result of breach of this obligation.

The opposite result was reached in *Groves* v. *Lord Wimborne*[22] which established the proposition that industrial safety legislation enforced by criminal penalties is intended to protect the interests of "employees" as a defined class and that a tortious remedy is therefore to be inferred. This result shows the problem of defining in advance the degree of common interest sufficient to constitute a defined class of society. The fact that "employees" are capable of being so classified shows that this is not a stringent requirement. The critics of the presumption approach would go further and argue that this degree of uncertainty shows the approach to be unworkable. The inference of the tort does not turn on whether a defined class exists or on whether Parliament intended that the class should receive protection from the statutory provision, but on whether it is possible to infer an intention of providing a remedy in tort to the members of the class.[23] A statute which provides incidental advantages to the members of a class must be distinguished from one which is intended to confer rights upon them. Although the bookmakers in *Cutler* possessed sufficient common identity and interests to constitute a defined class their claim failed because the relevant provisions of the Betting and Lotteries Act 1934 were regarded as not intended to confer tort rights upon them.

The defined class approach has been criticised on the basis that a statutory duty passed in the interests of the public should be regarded as more important than one passed merely to protect a restricted category of persons and because it has produced inconsistent results.[24] However, Lord Diplock's speech in *Lonrho* shows that it is still regarded as the correct approach.

4. Principles of construction

Presumptions are not decisive. When it has been decided which presumption applies to the case it will still be necessary for the court to review the statute in question in order to determine whether the prima facie result is to be upheld. In the words of Lord Simonds in *Cutler* v. *Wandsworth Stadium*

[20] [1949] A.C. 398.
[21] (1877) 2 Ex. D. 44.
[22] [1898] 2 Q.B. 402.
[23] *Hague* v. *Deputy Governor of Parkhurst Prison* [1992] 1 A.C. 58.
[24] *Cf. Read* v. *Croydon Corporation* [1938] 4 All E.R. 631 and *Atkinson* v. *The Newcastle and Gateshead Waterworks Company Ltd.* (1877) 2 Ex. D. 441 which concerned different sections of the same statute. See also *Knapp* v. *Railway Executive* [1949] 2 All E.R. 508.

Ltd.[25] "the answer must depend upon a consideration of the whole Act and the circumstances including the pre-existing law in which it was enacted."[26]

5. Public rights and special damage

Lord Diplock's speech in *Lonrho Ltd.* v. *Shell Petroleum Co. Ltd.*[27] recognises a second exception to the presumption of non-actionability derived from *Doe*. "The second exception is where the statute creates a public right (*i.e.* a right to be enjoyed by all those of Her Majesty's subjects who wish to avail themselves of it) and a particular member of the public suffers what Brett J. in *Benjamin* v. *Stoor*[28] described as 'particular, direct and substantial damage' other and different from that which was common to all the rest of the public." It is not clear whether this exception is a presumption or a binding rule.

The true ambit of the exception is a matter of conjecture. A wide interpretation might suggest that it would be capable of subverting the restrictions imposed by the narrow categories of the first exception. All criminal and administrative law duties might be treated as creating public rights on the basis of which individuals might be able to claim. There can be no doubt that Lord Diplock would reject this interpretation, but the difficulty remains of explaining what limitations are to be imposed on the second exception.

One thing which is made clear by the reference to *Benjamin* v. *Storr* is that this exception is related to the well recognised rules relating to public nuisance, which is actionable by an individual as a tort upon proof of his having suffered special damage.[29] The exception may thus transcend the boundaries of statute law in as much as a public nuisance constitutes a crime at common law. Lord Diplock recognises this and cites Buckley J.'s judgment at first instance in *Boyce* v. *Paddington Borough Council*[30] as one of the few examples of a public right conferred by statute. All of this shows Lord Diplock to regard the second exception as founded on well established principle. The difficulty is that this exception was not applied in either *Lonrho* or *Boyce*. It remains to be seen to what extent and under what conditions it can operate to create torts beyond the sphere of public nuisance.

The principles enunciated by Buckley J. in *Boyce* dealt not with public nuisance but with the situations in which an individual could seek an injunction in a civil court on the basis that another had interfered with rights vested in the public, without the assistance of the Attorney-General. Two such cases are recognised. First, where the infringement of the public rights at the same time constitutes an infringement of private rights vested in the plaintiff and secondly, where, although no private right has been interfered with, the plaintiff has suffered special damage peculiar to himself from the interference with a public right. Lord Diplock in *Lonrho* cited these principles with approval but discounted the relevance of the first example in as much as the actionability might have been founded equally upon the private

---

[25] [1949] A.C. 398.
[26] For a review of the techniques used see Stanton, *Breach of Statutory Duty in Tort*, pp. 44–49.
[27] [1982] A.C. 173.
[28] (1874) L.R. 9 C.P. 400.
[29] See *post*, p. 402.
[30] [1903] 1 Ch. 109.

right (an inference of the tort of breach of statutory duty under the more familiar principles would create such a private right).

It is Buckley J.'s second example on which Lord Diplock bases what is, in effect, a new category of breach of statutory duty. Several factors seem to point towards the second exception having limited use. First, Lord Diplock asserts that it will not be invoked by a mere prohibition upon members of the public generally doing an act. Something more substantial is required which amounts to creating a legal right to be enjoyed by all of Her Majesty's subjects. In *Ward* v. *Hobbs*[31] it was held that a provision of the Contagious Diseases (Animals) Act 1869 which prohibited persons from sending animals suffering from contagious diseases to market, created a public right that such animals should not be sent into a public place. The relevant Act in *Boyce* designated certain land as "open space, for the perpetual use thereof by the public." The great majority of statutory duties, particularly those which simply create criminal offences, would not meet this criterion. Secondly, in view of the reluctance shown by the courts to recognise a damages remedy available to persons injured by the unlawful actions of an administrative authority it is very unlikely that many statutes imposing such duties would be characterised as intended to create a public right. Thirdly,the whole tenor of Lord Diplock's speech in *Lonrho* is opposed to the creation of vaguely defined tortious obligations which might prove disruptive of established principle. In particular, he denies that the decision of the High Court of Australia in *Beaudesert Shire Council* v. *Smith*[32] is good authority for the existence of an innominate tort which would benefit a person who suffers damage as the inevitable consequence of the unlawful, intentional and positive act of another. In arguing this he points to the fact that subsequent Australian decisions, in distinguishing the case, had rejected the view that every form of breach of statutory duty can be classified as unlawful for this purpose. If the decision in *Beaudesert* was intended to extend the operation of the tort of breach of statutory duty beyond the principles recognised by English law, Lord Diplock would not be prepared to recognise it as stating the law accurately.

These factors suggest that the special damage exception to the presumption of non-actionability may in practice add little to the learning relating to the first exception.[33] Such a result would correspond with the normal judicial reluctance to permit individual enforcement of obligations owed to the public. Nonetheless the exception should not be discounted completely. If, in an appropriate case, an injunction could have been obtained to prevent the breach of a duty owed to the public, it would seem logical to allow a claim for damages if the breach has occurred and produced special damage.

[31] (1878) 4 App. Cas. 13.
[32] (1966) 120 C.L.R. 145.
[33] Nonetheless, an attempt was made to invoke it in *Mercury Communications Ltd.* v. *Scott-Garner* [1984] 1 All E.R. 204. The plaintiff company argued that the defendant union members, who had refused to connect the plaintiff's telecommunications system to that of British Telecom had committed offences under s. 45 of the Telegraphs Act 1863 by committing a wilful act which prevented or delayed the transmission or delivery of any message. It was contended that this offence created a public right, the breach of which had caused the plaintiff to suffer special damage and that as a result the plaintiff could base a cause of action on it. Sir John Donaldson M.R. was clearly alive to the fact that a claim of this kind, if successful, would render most industrial action taken by British Telecom employees unlawful, as it would be unprotected by the Trade Union and Labour Relations (Consolidation) Act 1992. The point did not need to be decided.

6. Conclusion

It is impossible to disagree with critics who argue that the processes used by the courts in this area make the outcome of cases extremely difficult to forecast. If results can be predicted it is because of factors other than the presumptions which are stated by the courts to govern. The most significant problems stem from the difficulty of deciding whether a sufficient alternative remedy exists to invoke the presumption of non-actionability and in determining whether a defined class which is intended to have enforceable rights vested in it can be identified. These unsatisfactory techniques seem to have been sanctified by Lord Diplock's speech in *Lonrho*. There is no hint in that speech of any moves to modernise the law. Judges will continue to make ad hoc and discretionary decisions on statutes. Courts and prospective litigants will be given no substantial guidance as to the likely outcome of a case which raises the issue of whether a breach of statutory duty remedy exists. It is possible to hope that the problem will be lessened if Parliament can be persuaded to provide explicit guidance in the interpretation sections of new legislation; but, even if a consistent policy is adopted, the difficulty will take years to disappear because older legislation will continue to raise it. There are a number of other approaches which might improve the law.

The least radical alternative is to suggest that the existing presumptions allow sufficient freedom of manoeuvre for courts to ensure that sensible decisions are reached. If the courts were to regard statutes containing no enforcement machinery and all other duties over which they had any doubt as being passed in the public interest rather than as intended to vest rights in a defined class of private individuals; were to regard the existence of standard common law and administrative law remedies as raising the presumption of non-actionability and were to keep Lord Diplock's concept of rights vested in the public for highly exceptional cases, the results would not be very different from those reached by the existing cases. However, the chance of a new area of breach of statutory duty appearing would be effectively eliminated. There are, of course, great practical problems in ensuring that the judiciary adopt a common approach of this kind. It could probably only be achieved as a result of an authoritative statement given by the House of Lords.

More fundamental change would involve replacing the existing presumptions. Buckley has propounded the view that "the correct approach is the adoption of a presumption to the effect that, subject to other factors, an action for breach of statutory duty is more likely to lie the more specific is the nature of the statutory obligation. Conversely, the less specific the obligation the less likely it is that the obligation will arise."[34] This approach assumes that a lack of precision in the formulation of the duty indicates an intention on the part of Parliament to confer a degree of discretion and hence a freedom from intervention by the courts. The result would tend to free most statutory duties placed on public authorities from the tort. However, it is not really acceptable; the question whether a duty is sufficiently specific to raise the presumption of the tort's existence is likely to raise so many difficulties that only a limited improvement over the present law would result. The examples given in support of the approach are not convincing. For example, *Phillips* v. *Britannia Hygienic Laundry Co. Ltd.*[35] is cited as an instance of a non-specific obligation. However, motor vehicle construction regulations of

---

[34] Buckley, "Liability in Tort for Breach of Statutory Duty" (1984) 100 L.Q.R. 204.
[35] [1923] 2 K.B. 832.

the kind which were under consideration in that case may, on occasions, be highly specific in the requirements stipulated, yet there can be little logic in holding breach of specific regulations in this area to be actionable while less specific obligations on the same topic are not. In any case, if strict tortious liability for damage caused by the use of a motor vehicle in breach of construction regulations is deemed to be a desirable legal development it should be imposed consciously by an Act of Parliament after full debate; it should not appear as a consequence of the adoption of a particular theory which has nothing to say directly about the topic of road accidents.

Buckley also makes no attempt to explain the fact that certain non-specific industrial safety obligations, such as that to provide a safe means of access to a place of work "so far as is reasonably practicable" are well established as actionable.

A more acceptable approach would be to return to Williams' "oversimplification" to the effect that the inference of the tort should be made in the case of industrial safety legislation, but not elsewhere.[36] However, as the Health Safety at Work Act 1974 makes express provision as to actionability in the industrial context, this would amount to denying any new role to the inferred species of the tort. Views would probably differ as to whether this would be a matter of concern. An alternative, less drastic, variant of this approach would be for the courts to place greater emphasis on the kind of interest which is sought to be protected by the tort. Is it safety from personal injury; personal welfare benefits or financial losses? To do this would almost certainly result in the courts paying greater attention to the underlying policies at issue, rather than shrouding them behind a discussion of the mysteries of the presumptions. The courts qualified the *Donoghue* v. *Stevenson*[37] "neighbour" test in this way.[38] It should not be beyond their capacity to do the same to breach of statutory duty.

If complete predictability is the overriding criterion there is no real substitute for the enactment of a presumption in a Interpretation Act, as recommended by the Law Commission. The Commission's preferred presumption in favour of actionability is probably not the best approach. It would revolutionise English civil liability by imposing individually enforceable rights where none have previously existed. A rational system only enacts rights and duties when they are shown to be required; it does not do so on the basis of a briefly argued recommendation which paid little attention to the areas in which the presumption might operate. It is not surprising that the Commission's proposal found little support in Parliament. A possible answer to this criticism is that the operation of such a presumption might be severely limited in practice by a standard form exclusion contained in the interpretation section of every new Act of Parliament which was passed. If this was to be done, it would go a long way to answering the criticism that the presumption would create civil liability by default and Parliamentary draftsmen and legislators would need to pay constant attention to the question whether they intend to create civil liability.

A less dramatic statutory presumption would be one which stipulated nonactionability unless the statute in question expressly stipulated the contrary. This would produce a result which would resemble the present law whilst

---

[36] Williams, "The Effect of Penal Legislation in Tort" (1960) 23 M.L.R. 233.
[37] [1932] A.C. 562.
[38] See p. 30.

being free from the difficulties which dog it. On the debit side, it would remove the possibility of the courts utilising the tort to play new roles or to plug gaps in the overall picture of legal protection. This would not be a great loss in view of the uncertainty which must exist at present as to whether rights are going to be inferred. Such a presumption would be unlikely to apply retrospectively to existing legislation, but it would tend to promote a policy of discouraging new forms of the tort, based on older legislation, in the absence of express authority. It is suggested that this is the best way of removing the existing difficulties and allowing the tort to evolve on a principled basis.

Chapter Three

Standards of Liability

General

The subject of standards of liability defines the conduct which needs to be proved for tortious liability to be established. At this point the discussion shifts from the legal issue of duty, the existence of which is now assumed, to a factual issue. The English law of tort uses a number of standards but the dominance of the tort of negligence means that it is the standard of reasonable care and skill which receives the greatest attention. However, other standards govern significant parts of the subject and the practical problems involved in proving that a person has failed to take reasonable care mean that alternatives should be considered. The introduction, in the Consumer Protection Act 1987, of strict liability for injuries caused by defective products was an example of the dissatisfaction with negligence producing a move to a more stringent standard of liability.

Four different standards of liability operate in tort. The most important is the negligence standard which requires the taking of reasonable care and skill. This imposes liability for damage caused as a result of a person's conduct falling below generally accepted levels of behaviour. Low standards, which are less stringent, exist in several forms. These range from those under which liability will not be established unless the defendant is shown to have consciously intended to cause the damage, or to have been reckless as to whether it would result, to cases in which the conduct required is judged according to the defendant's personal, subjective, abilities. Absolute standards are rare. The torts based on trespass, which protect peoples' basic rights, and the breach of a statutory duty based on an unqualified obligation are the examples most likely to be encountered. If an absolute standard applies the defendant's liability is based on proof that his conduct was the cause of the damage irrespective of whether any means were available to avoid it. Strict liability is more common. It operates in the area between reasonable care and absolute liability and denotes a range of standards which impose liability more readily than negligence but which fall short of being absolute because they are qualified in some way. The most familiar examples of breach of statutory duty, industrial safety duties, are usually qualified in some way and therefore fall into this category.

Although this division of standards provides a working distinction it is important to realise that the different categories actually cover a wide range of standards. For example, strict standards come in a number of forms with the only common feature being that a lack of reasonable care on the part of the defendant need not be proved to establish liability. Negligence based standards rest on a unified theory, but there is a clear distinction in practice between the degree of discretion and margin for error given to medical practitioners and the virtually strict standard exacted from motorists.

Absolute Standards

An absolute standard imposes liability on proof that an act caused damage, irrespective of whether the defendant could have foreseen the damage in the circumstances and of whether any precautions could have been taken to avoid it. In view of the rarity of examples of absolute standards some of the cases which best illustrate the features of this standard are drawn from the field of strict liability.[1]

In the leading case on animals liability, *Behrens* v. *Bertram Mills Circus Ltd.*,[2] the defendant company was held liable for injuries caused by an elephant. Strict liability for damage caused by animals is imposed according to the species[3] and elephants are a species subject to this strict liability. On the facts of the case the defendants were held liable in spite of their argument that the elephant in question was trained and could not have been foreseen to be any more dangerous than a domesticated animal such as a cow. The fact that damage might not have been foreseeable was no defence when an activity subject to a strict liability duty resulted in damage.

In *John Summers & Son Ltd.* v. *Frost*[4] an employee was injured when his hand came into contact with the moving wheel of a grindstone. He sought damages on the basis that the machine was being operated in breach of the fencing requirements contained in section 14(1) of the Factories Act 1937. In spite of the employer's argument that a secure fence would have made it impossible to operate the machine in question, the House of Lords upheld the employee's claim. The decision was the result of a close analysis of the structure of the Factories Act which showed the particular provision to be subject to none of the qualifying techniques found elsewhere in that legislation. In particular, power had been given to the Minister to relax the statutory requirements by regulation if he thought fit, but, at the relevant time, he had not done so in the case of grindstones.[5] The result was the recognition of an absolute and unqualified obligation which owed nothing to reasonableness. If the statute required the wheel to be fenced it was a breach not to fence it, even though that led to the extraordinary result that an everyday item of machinery was rendered inoperative.

Torts derived from trespass commonly have absolute characteristics. In *Allan* v. *New Mount Sinai Hospital*[6] a doctor was held to have committed a battery against a patient when he overrode her objection to his injecting

---

[1] The absolute nature of the basic duty may be the same under both absolute and strict liability. The duty will be strict if qualifications or defences are available to reduce the level of obligation imposed.

[2] [1957] 2 Q.B. 1.

[3] See *post*, Chap. 11.

[4] [1955] A.C. 740.

[5] Regulations concerning grindstones were finally enacted in the Abrasive Wheels Regulations of 1970.

[6] (1980) 109 D.L.R. (3d) 634. The decision was subsequently reversed (1981) 125 D.L.R. (3d) 276 on the grounds that battery had not been pleaded in the original proceedings.

anaesthetic into her left arm. He followed the normal and perfectly accept-able procedure in administering the anaesthetic to the left arm and was unfortunate to find that the patient suffered a serious and unusual reaction to a minor mishap in the course of the procedure. Nonetheless, his actions were tortious; once he overstepped the boundaries of the consent he was abso-lutely liable for all damage caused by his acts.

STRICT STANDARDS

There is no single form of strict liability; rather there are a variety of duties which are more stringent than reasonable care but which fall short of being absolute because they are subject to some qualification.

The strictness of an obligation will commonly derive from the particular phrasing of the statutory duty which created it. For example, section 1 of the Defective Premises Act 1972 requires those who owe duties under it in relation to the building of dwellings to see that the work "is done in a workmanlike or, as the case may be, professional manner, with proper materials and so that as regards that work the dwelling will be fit for habitation when completed." Under a duty of this kind the defendant will be held liable if his acts failed to produce the required result. The reasons for any failure and, in particular, the fact that the person under the duty had taken all reasonable care to avoid the failure are not relevant. The plaintiff's burden of proving his case is therefore much easier to discharge.

In many cases the strict nature of a duty derives from its having the characteristics of the absolute standards described above but being qualified by the availability of defences. The burden of proving such defences will commonly be placed on the defendant. The provisions of Part I of the Consumer Protection Act 1987[7] illustrate this approach. If damage is caused by a defective product, the producer[8] will be liable unless he can prove, the burden being on him, that the case falls within one of the defences allowed by section 4 of the Act. The liability is strict because none of these defences allows the producer to escape liability by proving that he took reasonable care in the design and manufacture of the product.

The stringency of an obligation will often have been determined by judicial authority. In some cases, particularly in relation to strict industrial safety duties, the courts have placed an interpretation on the wording of strict standards which has had the effect of reducing the stringency of the obliga-tion and it has therefore become relevant to ask whether such obligations differ significantly from negligence based ones. There are a number of techniques which are commonly used by Parliament which have opened the way to the appearance of such qualifications.[9] The result is that the standard should be regarded as being strict, but as far from being absolute.

A statutory standard of liability may be qualified by a defence based on the impracticability of meeting the obligation. The best example of this is section 157 of the Mines and Quarries Act 1954 which creates a defence which is

---

[7] See p. 22 for full details.
[8] Consumer Protection Act 1987, s. 1(2).
[9] For further examples of judicial interpretations of statutory provisions which have reduced the standard of liability see Stanton, *Breach of Statutory Duty in Tort*, pp. 105–113.

generally available in civil or criminal proceedings founded on a breach of the duties created by that Act.

"157. It shall be a defence in any legal proceedings to recover damages and in any prosecution, in so far as the proceedings or prosecution are or is based on any allegation of a contravention in relation to a mine or quarry of—

   (a) a provision of this Act, or of an order made thereunder or of regulations . . .
   (c) . . . to prove that it was impracticable to avoid or prevent the contravention."

A qualification based on impracticability gives very limited protection to the person who bears the duty. It is generally taken to allow a defendant to escape liability only if he can meet the burden of proving that it was physically impossible to take the relevant precaution. For example, if machinery has broken in such a way as to place the employer in breach of the duty there may have been insufficient time to remove the danger before the injury occurred.[10] The cost of taking a precaution[11] and the fact that such a precaution, if taken, might have created more risks than it would have removed[12] are not regarded as capable of being used to prove that it was impracticable to fulfil the duty.

Some statutes use the slightly different criterion of "reasonable practicability" as the standard of liability. A good example of this is section 29(1) of the Factories Act 1961 which stipulates that:

"There shall, so far as is reasonably practicable, be provided and maintained safe means of access to every place at which any person has at any time to work, and every such place shall, so far as is reasonably practicable, be made and kept safe for any person working there."

The introduction of reasonableness as the governing factor allows the court to consider issues relating to the costs of and the benefits to be derived from taking the precaution. A strict standard of this kind is much closer to negligence than the unqualified impracticability standard. In *Coltness Iron Co. Ltd.* v. *Sharp*[13] the criterion of reasonable practicability was held to protect an employer against liability for injuries suffered by an employee which had resulted from an engineer, who was repairing a machine, running a test on it with the guard removed; it was impossible for the engineer to observe the workings of the machine when the guard was fitted properly. Lord Atkin took the view that on these facts "the time of non-protection is so short, and the time, trouble and expense of any other form of protection is so disproportionate that I think that the defence is proved." However, although such a standard of liability is closer to negligence than that of impracticability the important difference remains that the burden of proving the defence is on the defendant.

If a strict liability duty depends on the meaning of words such as "dangerous" or "defective" the courts are commonly able to introduce

---

[10] *Sanderson* v. *National Coal Board* [1961] 2 Q.B. 244 (the defence was not established on the facts).
[11] *Sanders* v. *F. H. Lloyd & Co. Ltd* [1955] 3 All E.R. 205.
[12] *Boyton* v. *Willment Brothers Ltd.* [1971] 1 W.L.R. 1625.
[13] [1938] A.C. 90.

concepts, drawn from the law of negligence, such as foreseeability of harm into consideration. The treatment accorded to the strict tortious liability for public nuisances created by dangers on the highway is a classic example of this.[14] A highway has only been held to be dangerous if in the ordinary course of affairs danger may reasonably be anticipated.[15] As a result it is difficult to distinguish the standard of liability applied to such an issue from that which arises in the tort of negligence other than on the basis that the burden of proof remains on the defendant.

Non-delegability tends to be a feature of absolute and strict standards of liability. This does not mean that the actual performance of a duty cannot be delegated, but that the legal responsibility for that performance cannot be. A person who owes such a duty will remain liable for damage caused by the acts of an independent contractor who has been reasonably appointed to perform the duty. The leading strict liability case of *Rylands* v. *Fletcher*[16] illustrates this. The defendant landowner was held liable for work performed by his independent contractors which had resulted in water brought onto the land escaping onto neighbouring property.[17]

THE STANDARD OF REASONABLE CARE

The negligence standard of liability is that which requires the taking of reasonable care and skill to avoid foreseeable harm. It uses socially accepted standards of behaviour as the test of legal responsibility, the defendant's conduct being tested against the criterion of what ought to have been done in the circumstances. It is a depersonalised criterion of liability; what the defendant actually knew or could predict is not relevant as he is judged by what ordinary reasonable people in the position he was in would have done. The test is used widely by the common law of tort and has been adopted by legislation such as the Occupiers' Liability Act 1957.[18] The standard itself is fixed by law, but, as most cases in this area concern the subsidiary question of fact; (whether conduct has satisfied the standard) decisions are strictly not authority for future cases. Nonetheless, as the whole purpose of the reasonable care test is to evaluate conduct on the basis of generally accepted standards, a fair degree of predictability is possible. Indeed, the test would be unworkable if this were not the case.

A foreseeable risk

An obligation to take reasonable care only arises with regard to harm which is foreseeable. At times this is expressed as harm which is "reasonably foreseeable." If this qualification is intended to place a substantial limitation on the operation of foreseeability it is unjustifiable. It is important to attribute a wide meaning to foreseeability in this context in order to ensure that obligations exist to provide protection against risks which may be

---

[14] See also the industrial safety cases discussed in Stanton, *Breach of Statutory Duty in Tort*, pp. 103–105.
[15] *Littler* v. *Liverpool Corporation* [1968] 2 All E.R. 343n.
[16] (1868) L.R. 3 H.L. 330, discussed at pp. 407–414.
[17] The issue of delegability of duties is discussed in more depth in Chap. 6.
[18] It also has a role as an implied contractual term, particularly in relation to contracts to provide services.

unlikely or improbable. To say that a risk is foreseeable is the equivalent of saying that people may conceive of it as a being a risk. Whereas a probable risk is more likely to happen than not, a risk may be foreseeable even though it is only likely to happen in one case in a thousand or less. The law takes the view that a risk which is unlikely, but conceivable, may ground liability if it was easy to guard against and there was no justification for running it.[19] It is not acceptable for a chemist who is researching the characteristics of a new drug to confine his attention to probable risks: the remote ones may have catastrophic effects on persons who take the drug.

Nonetheless, exceptional cases may occur in which it can be shown that the risk which occurred was beyond the contemplation of a person in the position of the defendant at the time that he acted or that it was only a "fantastic possibility."[20] If this is the case the inquiry will go no further. There is no obligation to take reasonable care to guard against the unforeseeable. The leading example of this is *Roe* v. *Minister of Health*[21] in which two plaintiffs who had developed paralysis after undergoing surgery sought to hold a hospital liable in negligence for their disabilities. An inquiry into the accident revealed that the problem had been caused by the anaesthetic administered to the patients. This had been supplied to the hospital in sealed glass ampoules and had been stored, in order to minimise the risk of infection, in a solution of a disinfectant called phenol. It was known that phenol was dangerous and the accepted procedure when anaesthetic was required was to wash the ampoules and to inspect them to ensure that they were free from cracks or breakages. This procedure had been used in this case. The inquiry revealed that this precaution was not adequate. It was found to be possible for the phenol to penetrate the glass and contaminate the anaesthetic through microscopic flaws which were not visible to the human eye. It was the fate of the plaintiffs which alerted the medical profession to this risk. At the time of the acts in question the risk was not within accepted medical knowledge. It was therefore unforeseeable and there was no obligation to guard against it. The doctors could not be criticised for failing to provide protection against a risk which they could not appreciate even though the consequence was that individuals who had been permanently paralysed by a medical accident went without tort compensation.

A second general feature of the reasonable care test is also emphasised in the judgments in *Roe*. A defendant is entitled to be judged according to standards accepted at the time that he acted. The lessons of hindsight, which could operate to condemn all defendants as negligent, are excluded from consideration by the courts. On the other hand, once a risk has been publicised, accepted procedures may change in response to it and the law will reflect this change. But, as Denning L.J. said in *Roe* "we must not look at a 1947 accident through 1954 spectacles."

The obligation of reasonable care

If harm is foreseeable the obligation to take reasonable care to avoid it applies. A court will consider the facts and test them against the hypothetical actions of a reasonable person faced by them.

---

[19] *Overseas Tankship (U.K.) Ltd.* v. *Miller Steamship Co. Pty. Ltd. The Wagon Mound (No. 2)* [1967] 1 A.C. 617.
[20] *Fardon* v. *Harcourt-Rivington* (1932) 48 T.L.R. 215.
[21] [1954] 2 Q.B. 66.

A number of factors are traditionally considered by courts to be relevant to the question of whether the defendant has taken reasonable care. First, the likelihood of the damage. The more likely the damage is to occur the more likely it is that the courts will require precautions to be taken to guard against it. Secondly, the seriousness of the damage. A risk may be remote, but if it creates the possibility that serious consequences may ensue it is likely to require a high level of precaution to be taken.[22] Thirdly, the ease with which protection against the risk can be provided; considering in particular the practical difficulties and the expense involved in eliminating or reducing it.[23] Finally, the benefits to be gained. An activity which creates a risk may provide benefits which society is not prepared to forego.

The leading cases in this area show the courts to be balancing these considerations in order to make what is, in essence, a value judgment on the acceptability of the defendant's conduct. In *Bolton* v. *Stone*[24] a cricket club which had provided 17 foot high fencing around its ground was held not to have been negligent in failing to eliminate the recognised, but small, risk that persons might be injured by cricket balls hit from the centre of the pitch over the fence into the neighbouring road. The expense involved in taking additional precautions was disproportionate to the risk which existed. The result might well have been different had the risk been greater; for example, if balls had been knocked into the road with greater frequency.[25] In *Daborn* v. *Bath Tramways*[26] it was held to be acceptable for the ambulance services to use, during the Second World War, American built left hand drive ambulances which were not fitted with mechanical indicators. It was reasonable to use the only equipment available in order to keep the ambulance service operating, even if the use of such vehicles on British roads increased the likelihood of accidents occurring. These cases show the distinction between absolute liability and the standard of reasonable care. The latter standard does not make a defendant an insurer of all risks created by his conduct. Many activities of a modern developed society, such as high speed motoring, create risks, but it is only those risks which society, as personified by the courts, deems unacceptable which attract legal liability. For example, there are few, if any, forms of medical treatment which do not carry the risk of side-effects being suffered by the patient. However, if an acceptable balancing of the potential benefits of the treatment against the risks has been carried out, the decision to proceed will be unimpeachable. In practice it may require significant expenditure to eliminate remote risks and it may be excessive to demand that such precautions are taken. For example, in *Latimer* v. *A.E.C. Ltd.*[27] a factory owner was held not to have been negligent for choosing not to close the factory after its floor had become slippery as a result of flooding when it was discovered that insufficient sawdust was

---

[22] *Paris* v. *Stepney Borough Council* [1951] A.C. 367. The general practice was not to provide eye protection for employees doing a particular job. The plaintiff employee was known by the employer to be blind in one eye. This disability did not increase the chance of an accident occurring but loss of the sight of the only good eye was held to be a more serious consequence than loss of one eye and the employer was held negligent for this failure to provide protection for the one-eyed employee.

[23] *Overseas Tankship (U.K.) Ltd.* v. *Miller Steamship Co. Pty. Ltd. The Wagon Mound (No. 2)* [1967] 1 A.C. 617.

[24] [1951] A.C. 850.

[25] *Hilder* v. *Associated Portland Cement Manufacturers Ltd.* [1961] 1 W.L.R. 1434.

[26] [1946] 2 All E.R. 333.

[27] [1953] A.C. 643.

available to make all of the floor safe. In economic terms the court was holding that the marginal additional deterrence to be derived from imposing liability could not be justified. From a different perspective, extreme circumstances such as the need to save life, may make it reasonable for doctors to incur the risk of their patients suffering severe, and even unavoidable, side-effects.

An alternative way of looking at this process is provided by writers on the economics of law. They have argued that the technique adopted by the courts is an imprecise method of achieving a cost-justified level of care. The American, Judge Learned Hand,[28] proposed that a defendant should be held liable if the cost of his taking adequate precautions against a risk (B) was less than the cost caused if the risk did occur (L) multiplied by the probability that the risk would occur (P). If the cost of avoiding the accident (B) exceeds the true costs of the accident (P x L), a decision to take the precaution is not cost justified. Conversely, if B is less than P x L it is economically desirable that the precaution should be taken and the defendant should be held liable for failure to do so as he was the "cheapest cost avoider." There can be no doubt that current practice represents an imprecise and ad hoc way of achieving the results which the "Learned Hand formula" seeks. In Veljanovski's words[29]: "the basis on which the judge decides and the process by which he arrives at the decision are very similar to the way in which an economist would approach the problem." However, it is not argued that the traditional technique could be replaced by that of the economists as it seems highly unlikely that the courts would be prepared to become embroiled in the time and cost consuming analysis of statistical evidence that use of the approach would require.

Each case will be tested in the light of its particular circumstances. For example, although English courts have emphasised that persons who take part in fast moving sports owe an objective duty of reasonable care towards other competitors and spectators and have rejected the idea of a special relationship under which only limited obligations are owed,[30] they have accepted that the aim of winning a contest may justify forms of risk creating conduct which would undoubtedly be deemed negligent in other contexts.[31] An analogy has been drawn in these cases with the cases dealing with mistakes made "in the agony of the moment."[32] This approach is possibly not confined to sports. The need to apprehend a suspected criminal[33] or to rush a seriously ill person to hospital may justify driving in a way which would not be acceptable under normal circumstances. On a similar basis, a person's reaction to being placed in a situation of imminent danger may be judged to have been reasonable even though it can be shown with hindsight to have caused damage.[34]

---

[28] *United States* v. *Carroll Towing Co.* 159 F.2d. 169. See C. Veljanovski, *The Economics of Law: An Introductory Text*, pp. 67–72 for the application of this reasoning to some of the leading English cases and for a refinement of the test to take account of the factor of marginal cost.

[29] C. Veljanovski *op. cit.* p. 72.

[30] *Condon* v. *Basi* [1985] 1 W.L.R. 866.

[31] *Wooldridge* v. *Sumner* [1962] 2 All E.R. 978; *Wilks* v. *The Cheltenham Home Guard Motor Cycle & Light Car Club* [1971] 2 All E.R. 369.

[32] See *post*, p. 92.

[33] *Marshall* v. *Osmond* [1983] Q.B. 1034.

[34] *Ng Chun Pui* v. *Lee Chuen Tat* [1988] R.T.R. 298.

Delegation of task

In certain circumstances it may be a perfectly reasonable for a person who is under a duty of care to employ another person to discharge it on his behalf. In effect, the person under the duty takes reasonable care by choosing an apparently competent contractor to perform the task. Indeed, if the duty requires highly specialised work it would probably be negligent for a person who lacked such skills not to seek expert assistance; an occupier's duty to keep his lift properly serviced[35] is the classic example of such a duty. If the duty at issue is of a delegable nature[36] the result will be that any negligence in the course of the work will be the responsibility of the contractor rather than of the employer.

Section 2(4)(b) of the Occupiers' Liability Act 1957 is an example of the law on this issue and its limitations:

"In determining whether the occupier of premises has discharged the common duty of care to a visitor, regard is to be had to all the circumstances, so that (for example) –

(b) where damage is caused to a visitor by a danger due to the faulty execution of any work of construction, maintenance or repair by an independent contractor employed by the occupier, the occupier is not to be treated without more as answerable for the danger if in all the circumstances he had acted reasonably in entrusting the work to an independent contractor and had taken such steps (if any) as he reasonably ought in order to satisfy himself that the contractor was competent and that the work had been properly done."

Once an apparently competent contractor has been chosen, the obligations of the employer are probably not very extensive. In *Ferguson* v. *Welsh*,[37] Lord Goff said that he did not "subscribe to the opinion that the mere fact that an occupier may know or have reason to suspect that the contractor carrying out work on his building may be using an unsafe system of work can of itself be enough to impose on him a liability under the 1957 Act, or indeed, negligence at common law." However, he accepted that exceptional circumstances might occur in which the occupier's involvement was such as to render him a joint tortfeasor with the contractor. Although it is not completely clear how the line should be drawn between the two categories, Lord Goff did seem anxious to ensure that an ordinary householder[38] should not be held liable for injuries caused by the negligence of an apparently competent specialist, such as an electrician, who has been engaged to perform work. On principle, this approach should be limited in so far as if the work, when completed, should reasonably have been appreciated by the occupier to be defective, that person may well be held to have broken his personal duty of care if he fails to take reasonable steps to have it remedied.

---

[35] *Haseldine* v. *C.A. Daw & Son Ltd.* [1941] 3 All E.R. 156.
[36] For the distinction between delegable and non-delegable duties see *post*, p. 128.
[37] [1987] 3 All E.R. 777.
[38] *Cf.* the attitude taken to a professional building owner's duty to supervise the work of the independent building contractor by Mocatta J. in *A.M.F. International Ltd.* v. *Magnet Bowling Ltd.* [1968] 1 W.L.R. 1028.

The characteristics of the plaintiff

The characteristics of foreseeable victims are included in the circumstances which are taken into account when the degree of care required is determined. Duties are not owed in the abstract, but to particular individuals who are known, or ought to be foreseen as likely, to be affected by the defendant's conduct. This rule may increase or decrease the level of required precautions. The leading example of a case in which the plaintiff's characteristics increased the level of required precautions is *Paris* v. *Stepney Borough Council*.[39] In that case an employer was held to have been negligent in failing to supply a particular employee with goggles to protect his eyes from the risk of injury. The accepted practice in the trade did not require such equipment to be supplied. However, the plaintiff was known to be already blind in one eye and although this fact did not increase the likelihood of an accident occurring it did mean that any accident which did occur would have far more serious consequences for him than for a fully sighted employee. The employer's knowledge of the employee's characteristics therefore raised the level of precautions which were required to meet the standard of reasonable care.[40]

An obvious example of a factor which is likely to increase the precautions which are necessary is that the presence of children may create special risks. In his speech in *Hughes* v. *Lord Advocate*[41] Lord Morris explained the law in the following words:

> "it is within common experience and knowledge that children may be allured by and tempted to play and meddle with objects which for others would have no special attraction. In such playing or meddling children may be heedless of danger and may bring neither method nor reason nor caution to bear."

Section 2(3)(a) of the Occupiers' Liability Act 1957 summarises the position succinctly: "an occupier must be prepared for children to be less careful than adults."

Conversely, a defendant is entitled to take account of the foreseeable victim's capacity to deal with risks.[42] In the leading occupiers' liability case of *Wheat* v. *E. Lacon & Co. Ltd.*[43] several members of the House of Lords were of the opinion that an unlit staircase on which the handrail finished above the foot of the stairs did not represent a danger to a person who was taking proper care of his own safety. It has been held that in certain areas there may be a foreseeable risk that blind persons will be walking alone,[44] but a person who digs a hole in a pavement will be entitled to assume that any blind person will take the normal precautions of making use of a guide dog or

---

[39] [1951] A.C. 367.
[40] See also *Haley* v. *London Electricity Board* [1965] A.C. 778 which deals with the risk of a blind person using a footpath protected only by his use of a white stick. On the facts it was held that the persons conducting work on the path should have foreseen the presence of such a person and taken adequate precautions to ensure that he could pass safely.
[41] [1963] A.C. 837.
[42] This is also the case in some areas of strict liability. For example, in the area of public nuisance concerning an authority's responsibility for maintenance of the highway (see *post*, p. 247) the courts have been exceptionally reluctant to allow persons injured as a result of minor imperfections in pavements to obtain damages, presumably on the basis that such a person should be able to look after themselves.
[43] [1966] A.C. 552.
[44] *Haley* v. *London Electricity Board* [1965] A.C. 778.

white stick. In *Phipps* v. *Rochester Corporation*[45] Devlin J. was of the view that an occupier of land is entitled to assume that a very young child permitted to enter his property will be accompanied by a responsible adult. The occupier will therefore satisfy the duty of care which he owes to the child by providing such precautions as would enable the accompanying adult to ensure that the child is safe.

Warnings

A duty to provide protection may be satisfied by giving the potential victim an adequate warning of the risk to enable him to take his own satisfactory precautions for dealing with it. The duty of reasonable care owed by a manufacturer may therefore require adequate warnings to be supplied with the product as to its nature and ways in which it should be used. Similarly, a skilled individual, such as an electrician, may be well able to appreciate the true nature of the risks created by a particular task and be able to protect himself against them. Both of these approaches are codified for the purposes of occupiers' liability by provisions of the Occupiers' Liability Act 1957. Section 2(4)(a) of this Act states that:

> "where damage is caused to a visitor by a danger of which he had been warned by an occupier, the warning is not to be treated without more as absolving the occupier from liability, unless in all the circumstances it was enough to enable the visitor to be reasonably safe."

and section 2(3)(b) is in the following terms:

> "(relevant circumstances) include the degree of care, and of want of care, which would ordinarily be looked for in such a visitor, so that (for example) in proper cases- (b) an occupier may expect that a person in the exercise of his calling, will appreciate and guard against any special risks ordinarily incident to it, so far as the occupier leaves him free to do so."

Both of these provisions were relevant to the decision of the Court of Appeal in *Roles* v. *Nathan*.[46] The occupier of premises had a boiler which was proving troublesome and which was discovered to be producing dangerous quantities of carbon monoxide. Two chimney sweeps were engaged to do work on the chimney flue attached to the boiler. They were warned about the danger and on one occasion were physically removed from the area of danger. They were told not to work on the chimney when the boiler was alight. Nonetheless, they ignored these warnings and were overcome by carbon monoxide and died. Their widows succeeded in establishing that the occupier had broken a duty in permitting the boiler to be alight before vents in the flue had been sealed. However, the claims failed because the warnings given were held to have been sufficient to enable the sweeps to have been safe and because the risks created by carbon monoxide were held to be special risks ordinarily incident to the calling of a chimney sweep. The second finding is somewhat dubious on the facts; it is not altogether clear that the unusual dangers created by the defects in the defendant's boiler should have

---

[45] [1955] 1 Q.B. 450.
[46] [1963] 1 W.L.R. 1117.

counted as a "special risk ordinarily incident" to the calling of a relatively unskilled person such as a chimney sweep.[47]

The giving of a warning will not automatically discharge a duty of care, but must be considered in relation to the nature of the risk. The decision in *Baker* v. *T.E.Hopkins & Sons Ltd.*[48] provides a useful contrast to *Roles*. In *Baker* the defendant contractors, who were engaged in the task of draining a well, had adopted a method which involved mounting a petrol driven pump inside the well. This was exceptionally dangerous because the pump was almost certain to produce a lethal concentration of carbon monoxide within the confines of the well. The defendant's director, who had been alerted to this risk by a chance remark made by one of his workers, warned his men not go down the well the next day until the fumes had cleared. On the next day he gave further instructions that no one was to go down the well until he had arrived at the site. One of the workmen ignored these instructions and was killed as were another workman and a doctor who made vain attempts to perform rescues. The Court of Appeal refused to accept the defence's argument that the warnings given had been sufficient to satisfy any duty of care and to place the risk of the accident on the workmen. The warnings given did not emphasise that the work was likely to have to be suspended; neither did they spell out the lethal and hidden nature of the risk in such a way as would bring home its true nature to those who were facing it. The nature of the risk in *Baker* was very similar to that in *Roles*. The contrast in the result of the cases is almost certainly attributable to the far more emphatic nature of the warning given in *Roles*.

The objective standard

Although the foreseeable plaintiff's characteristics and abilities are relevant to determining the level of precautions required of the defendant, the characteristics and personal abilities of the individual defendant are the elements in the factual equation which are not considered.[49] This is what is meant by saying that the standard of care in negligence is objective. Any individual who is in a particular situation will have to meet the required standard of care and, if this is impossible to achieve, will conduct the activity at his risk. The classic example is provided by *Nettleship* v. *Weston*.[50] A learner driver had injured her instructor in the course of her third lesson in a crash caused by her failure to straighten the car after turning a corner. Before turning to the question of whether any defences could be founded on the relationship of instructor to driver, the majority of the Court of Appeal held that a learner driver cannot plead incompetence to lower the applicable standard of care. In the classic words of Lord Denning M.R.:

> "It is no answer for him to say: 'I was a learner driver under instruction. I was doing my best and could not help it.' The civil law permits no such excuse. It requires of him the same standard of care as of any other driver. 'It eliminates the personal equation and is independent of the idiosyncrasies of the particular person whose conduct is in question' . . . The learner driver may be doing his best, but his incompetent best is not good enough.

---

[47] See the dissenting judgment of Pearson L.J.
[48] [1959] 3 All E.R. 225.
[49] *Glasgow Corporation* v. *Muir* [1943] A.C. 449. 457, *per* Lord Macmillan.
[50] [1971] 2 Q.B. 691.

He must drive in as good a manner as a driver of skill, experience and care, who is sound in wind and limb, who makes no errors of judgment, has good eyesight and hearing, and is free from infirmity."

Subsequently the Court of Appeal applied the same objective approach to the acts of a trainee doctor[51] in spite of the objection that doctors need to be trained on the job and that the Health Authority in question did not have the financial means to staff all of its wards with qualified staff. Patients were said to be entitled to the same standard of treatment irrespective of the chance factors of recruitment and rostering. It may seem harsh that the law should adopt this stance. Even harsher than *Nettleship* was the decision in *Roberts* v. *Ramsbottom*[52] to hold as negligent the acts of a driver who caused an accident when he drove with impaired consciousness at the time that he was suffering a stroke. It is difficult to accept that the defendants in these cases were "at fault" in the commonly accepted meaning of the term; and it is unlikely that the decisions will exert a deterrent effect on the future conduct of learner drivers and stroke victims. Nonetheless, those who have sympathy for such drivers should ask themselves how they would react if they were injured in a road accident and then confronted by a driver who said "I'm sorry about that, but I don't know how to drive." The objective standard of care ensures that the compensatory purpose of tort is not undermined by arguments founded on moral responsibility and the need to achieve effective deterrence. The result in motoring cases is that what is formally an obligation to take reasonable care acquires the appearance of strict liability. Lord Denning justified the decision in *Nettleship* by saying that the damages would, in any case, be paid by an insurance company and not by the driver held to be at fault. A stringent standard of care ensures that the victim obtains access to the insurance funds.

The alternatives to the objective rule adopted in *Nettleship* are not attractive. In the words of Megaw L.J. "the certainty of a general standard is preferable to the vagaries of a fluctuating one."[53] A subjective standard provides scarcely any basis for evaluating a person's conduct. A defendant would be likely to escape liability on the ground that he performed as well as could be expected in the light of his own abilities. Even if it is alleged that he fell below those abilities there will be great difficulty in determining what those abilities are and a court might be reluctant to enter into an examination of the defendant's finances in order to determine whether it was reasonable to expect additional precautions to have been taken.[54] The position is no more attractive if a modified objective standard is adopted. The standard of a reasonable learner driver is meaningless as it is obvious that different learners have different abilities; if it were to be used, the absolute beginner might well be treated as harshly as was Mrs Nettleship if the reasonable learner was expected to have some abilities. A suggestion, which was rejected by the majority in *Nettleship*, that the level of duty owed may vary according to the

---

[51] *Wilsher* v. *Essex Area Health Authority* [1986] 3 All E.R. 801, the appeal to the House of Lords (discussed at p. 88) did not consider the standard of care.

[52] [1980] 1 All E.R. 7. Neill J. held that "The driver will be able to escape liability if his actions at the relevant time were wholly beyond his control. The most obvious case is sudden unconsciousness. But if he retained some control, albeit imperfect control, and his driving, judged objectively, was below the required standard, he remains liable."

[53] [1971] 2 Q.B. 691 at 707.

[54] This reluctance appears to have been present in *Leakey* v. *National Trust* [1980] 1 All E.R. 17, a case in which a subjective duty was used in relation to a naturally occurring nuisance.

plaintiff's knowledge of the defendant's idiosyncrasies is equally unacceptable. It would introduce virtually unanswerable issues of fact and might lead
to serious anomalies in that, for instance, different passengers in a car might
be held to have different levels of knowledge and hence to be owed different
levels of protection.

The motoring cases impose a particularly exacting standard. Other areas
have possibly shown a greater degree of leniency towards the position of
defendants. For example, although a child may be held liable in negligence on
the basis of an objective test in so far as its conduct will not be judged
according to its personal perception of the risks created by its conduct, it will
be judged by the standards of a reasonable child of its age,[55] rather than by
the standards of an adult. Childhood is not regarded as an individual
idiosyncrasy. Furthermore, whereas a uniform standard of care is required of
all persons who practice a particular skill, whatever their level of expertise,
persons exercising different functions will be subject to the standard required
of the particular function even though their work is closely related to that of
other skills. It was on this basis that Pill J. held in *Knight* v. *Home Office*[56]
that the standard of precautions required of a prison hospital which is
treating a mentally ill patient is not to be set by reference to the standards
required of a specialist psychiatric hospital. Another case has been recorded
in which a court has applied the reasonable care test to the work of volunteer
first aiders[57] by reference to the standard of treatment required of reasonable
first aiders; it did not apply a uniform standard to all persons who provide
different forms of medical treatment.

The compensatory purpose of negligence is also emphasised by the fact
that liability can be based on any conduct which falls below the standard of
reasonable care and skill and which causes damage, however trivial the
degree of fault proved. People make many mistakes in the course of everyday
activities such as driving. It is virtually a matter of chance whether damage
results from their mistakes. A tort action commonly requires a minute
analysis of the defendant's conduct at a particular time and may be determined
by chance factors such as the quality of evidence available. A classic example
of this was *Whitehouse* v. *Jordan*[58] in which a claim was brought on behalf of
a child who suffered irreversible brain damage at birth. It was alleged that the
doctor who had delivered the child had caused the damage by pulling "too
hard and too long" on its head whilst attempting delivery by forceps. The
judge at first instance held the doctor negligent and awarded £100,000
damages, but, both the Court of Appeal and the House of Lords held that the
evidence did not establish that the doctor had departed from accepted
practice. As a result the child obtained no tort compensation.

Accepted practice

The fact that the standard of reasonable care is designed to reflect the
standards of conduct generally accepted by the community means that
persons against whom negligence is alleged may seek to defend themselves on

---

[55] *McHale* v. *Watson* (1965) 115 C.L.R. 199.
[56] [1990] 3 All E.R. 237.
[57] *Cattley* v. *St. John's Ambulance Brigade* (1989) unreported. See Griffiths, (1990) 6 P.N. 48
and (1990) 53 M.L.R. 255.
[58] [1981] 1 W.L.R. 246.

the basis that their conduct complied with a practice generally accepted by reasonable persons. Proof of compliance with such a practice will usually mean that a negligence claim based on such facts fails, although there are examples recorded of courts rejecting the argument that an accepted practice was reasonable. At times such refusals seem to have been based on a judicial decision that the alleged general practice was not proved or was not appropriate for the particular circumstances of the case.[59] However, occasionally courts have effectively assumed a legislative role and condemned a recognised practice as failing to take account of obvious risks.[60]

Particular difficulties are created by evidence of general practice when it is clear that the standards acceptable in a particular context are evolving. *Thompson* v. *Smiths Shiprepairers (North Shields) Ltd.*[61] raised such an issue in relation to the protection of employees in the shipbuilding industry against damage to their hearing from exposure to high noise levels. The evidence was that the risk of such damage had been recognised for many years but that no effective means of countering it had been available until the late 1950s and that general apathy to the problem fostered by lack of any official guidance had reigned. Mustill J. founded his judgment on the principle that:

> " . . . where there is a recognised and general practice which has been followed for a substantial period in similar circumstances without mishap, he is entitled to follow it, unless in the light of common sense or newer knowledge, it is clearly bad; but, where there is developing knowledge, he must keep reasonably abreast of it and not be too slow to apply it . . . "[62]

The judge accepted that the court must not condemn an employer for failing to be ahead of the rest of the industry but held, on the facts, that the reasonable employer in the industry would have provided protection for the hearing of his employees from 1963.

Accepted practice has proved particularly important as the technique used to define the standard of skill required in relation to skilled professional work. The courts will be highly dependent in such cases on expert evidence as to what constitutes accepted practice and difficulties may be caused by the fact that these experts may themselves favour different approaches to a particular problem. The courts are prepared to receive expert evidence as to what constitutes acceptable conduct, although they retain the right to reject it, as is inevitable if the evidence differs, or if they feel that a recognised practice fails to provide proper safeguards against obvious risks.[63] A professional person's obligation to act with reasonable skill and care will be satisfied by showing the skill of an ordinary practitioner of the profession. There is no obligation to show the skill of the greatest expert or even to come up to the standards of an "average" practitioner.[64] If more than one school of thought exists within a profession as to the appropriate course of action to

---

[59] *Morris* v. *West Hartlepool Steam Navigation Co. Ltd.* [1956] A.C. 552.
[60] *Lloyds Bank Ltd.* v. *E. B. Savory & Co.* [1933] A.C. 201; *Edward Wong Finance Ltd.* v. *Johnson, Stokes and Master* [1984] 2 W.L.R. 1.
[61] [1984] Q.B. 405.
[62] Swanwick J. in *Stokes* v. *G.K.N. (Bolts and Nuts) Ltd.* [1968] 1 W.L.R. 1776.
[63] For examples of such rejections see Dugdale & Stanton, *Professional Negligence* (2nd ed.), paras. 15.22–23.
[64] The notion of an average implies that a considerable number of the practitioners of the particular skill would be below average.

deal with a particular issue it will be sufficient to adopt any accepted approach. The classic statement of this approach was given by McNair J. in *Bolam* v. *Friern H.M.C.*[65]:

"where you get a situation which involves the use of some special skill or competence, then the test whether there has been negligence or not is not the test of the man on top of the Clapham omnibus, because he has not got this special skill. The test is the standard of the ordinary skilled man exercising and professing to have that special skill. A man need not possess the highest expert skill at the risk of being found negligent. It is well established law that it is sufficient if he exercises the ordinary skill of an ordinary competent man exercising that particular art . . . there may be one or more perfectly proper standards; and if a medical man conforms with one of those proper standards then he is not negligent . . . a mere personal belief that a particular technique is best is no defence unless that belief is based on reasonable grounds . . . a doctor is not negligent if he is acting in accordance with . . . a practice (accepted as proper by a responsible body of medical men skilled in that particular art), merely because there is a body of opinion that takes a contrary view. At the same time, that does not mean that a medical man can obstinately and pig-headedly carry on with some old technique if it has been proved to be contrary to what is really substantially the whole of informed medical opinion."

This rule is applied generally to all professions and may give a professional person considerable discretion as to the course of action to pursue. This is particularly the case in relation to professional functions such as valuation which involve predicting the sum which third parties might be prepared to pay for property. The scope for genuine differences of opinion between different members of a profession in relation to such matters is so great that it is very difficult, if not entirely impossible,[66] to establish negligence. In *Luxmoore-May* v. *Messenger May Baverstock*[67] it was alleged that the defendant firm of auctioneers had been negligent in failing to appreciate that two paintings might be the work of the artist Stubbs. The paintings were auctioned by the defendants at a reserve price of £40 and fetched £840. Five months later they were resold at a London auction house for £88,000. The judge at first instance held the defendants negligent. However, the Court of Appeal reversed this saying that there was no evidence that no competent auctioneer could have failed to spot the potential of the paintings.

It may not be entirely realistic to contrast the *Bolam* test with the equivalent result in motoring cases, because the latter area may show a particularly stringent interpretation of the demands of reasonable care. However, it is impossible to believe that a motorist who drives into the back of a stationary vehicle could defend a negligence action on the basis that a body of reasonable motorists exists which would have done the same thing. The *Bolam* test has the advantage of being relatively easy to work: the result depends on expert evidence rather than a judicial imposition of standards the court considers appropriate to skills it knows little or nothing about. However, the test is open to the charge that it exacts a wholly insufficient

---

[65] [1957] 1 W.L.R. 582.
[66] For a discussion of the cases on valuation see Dugdale & Stanton, *Professional Negligence* (2nd ed.), paras. 17.41–46.
[67] [1990] 1 W.L.R. 1009.

standard of care from professional defendants and that by allowing professionals to determine their own standard of care, as opposed to fixing it by reference to external factors, the search for the cost-justified "efficient" level of precautions is defeated: professionals receive insufficient incentives to avoid damage and hence are liable to cause an excessive amount of damage.

The fact that the *Bolam* test means that, for the most part, professions are allowed to set their own standards of practice has caused particular difficulties in relation to the medical profession given the widely held view that that profession is unduly defensive in relation to negligence claims. These difficulties came to a head over the question of the appropriate level of warnings to be given by a doctor to a patient prior to treatment. Whilst there is no doubt that the *Bolam* test governs the giving of treatment, it was argued in *Sidaway* v. *Bethlem Royal Hospital Governors*[68] that the fundamental nature of a patient's right to determine for himself whether to undergo treatment would be undermined if the duty on a doctor to disclose information, on the basis of which the patient could make an informed decision, was to be determined according to what an accepted body of reasonable doctors would choose to disclose. If, as some people argue, doctors as a profession tend to be unwilling to disclose information, a test which adopts recognised practice as the standard of liability does nothing to improve the position. Lord Scarman's dissenting judgment in *Sidaway* purported to recognise a doctrine of "informed consent" as a part of English law. The patient was said to have a right to know of real or material risks inherent in the proposed procedure and, to take account of this, the standard of care was to be fixed by the courts rather than doctors. The majority of the House, however, rejected this approach and held that the decision in *Bolam* established a comprehensive duty which covered all aspects of medical practice.[69] A subsequent rearguard action in which it was argued that there could be no acceptable medical reason for non-disclosure of risks created by non-therapeutic treatment, such as sterilisations, suffered the same fate.[70] As a result the *Bolam* test now applies the standard of care adopted by reasonable doctors to all forms of medical treatment.

Specialists

It is technically incorrect to speak of the work which is done by highly specialised professional persons as being subject to a higher standard of care than that done by other members of their professions. The legal test of reasonable care and skill does not vary according to the nature of the work which is at issue. The correct approach is to say that the conduct which satisfies that standard will vary according to all the circumstances and that exceptionally difficult work will call for a high level of precautions to be used. All doctors, whether general practitioners or surgeons performing intricate procedures on the frontiers of medical practice, are therefore subject to an identical legal standard of care. However, a doctor who undertakes a high technology procedure in the absence of proper training, facilities and research support will not satisfy the standard of reasonable care and skill.

---

[68] [1985] A.C. 871.
[69] See also *Blythe* v. *Bloomsbury Health Authority* (1987) 5 P.N. 167.
[70] *Gold* v. *Haringey Health Authority* [1988] Q.B. 481.

Errors of judgment

On occasions courts have held defendants not to be negligent saying that they merely made an "error of judgment." The most famous example of this was in Lord Denning M.R.'s reversal of the judge's finding in *Whitehouse* v. *Jordan*[71] that a doctor had been negligent when he "pulled too hard and too long" on a child's head when trying to deliver it. This is an imprecise use of language. Many activities which may be tested by the standard of reasonable care involve the exercise of judgment and that judgment may be erroneous either because it is shown, with the benefit of hindsight, to have caused damage or because it did not comply with any accepted body of opinion as to the appropriate conduct. The first case may not constitute negligence; the second certainly does. To say that conduct amounted to an error of judgment is not to ask the critical question and to say, as Lord Denning did, that a doctor should not be liable in negligence for errors of judgment appears to open the door to their escaping from liability even though they have failed to meet professionally accepted standards. The House of Lords in *Whitehouse*[72] rejected this use of "error of judgment" for these reasons.

LOW STANDARDS

Occasional examples of standards below that of reasonable care can be found in the English law of tort. They fall into two classes: duties to avoid damage by intentional acts and subjective standards of care.

The tort of deceit,[73] which provides a damages remedy for deliberate fraud, is the best example of a standard to avoid causing damage intentionally. As long as it cannot be proved that the defendant deliberately or recklessly misled the plaintiff, no tort will have been committed.

Subjectively-based duties of care are very rare, but have been used in relation to an occupier's duties towards trespassers entering his land and towards his neighbours when naturally arising nuisances are at issue. The first situation is now governed by the Occupiers' Liability Act 1984, which, for the most part, has adopted an objective standard of liability, but the subjective standard still governs the second situation. An occupier's duty to abate a nuisance which is created on his property by the forces of nature is assessed according to his subjective ability and resources to deal with it. This rule has been applied to duties to extinguish fires started by lightning[74] and to duties to stop falls of soil caused by the natural weathering of a bank.[75]

These examples of subjective standards are highly exceptional and probably add little to the law. They have appeared in situations in which there has been some doubt as to whether any duty at all is to be imposed and it may not be overcynical to suggest that the courts have adopted subjective standards as a compromise solution. In both of the examples the duties at issue come close to infringing the traditional common law refusal to impose liability in tort for a failure to assist others. The duty which is being imposed creates an obligation to react to dangers created by outside forces, the arrival of the

[71] [1980] 1 All E.R. 650.
[72] [1981] 1 W.L.R. 246.
[73] See *post*, p. 330.
[74] *Goldman* v. *Hargrave* [1967] 1 A.C. 645.
[75] *Leakey* v. *National Trust* [1980] Q.B. 485.

trespasser or the whims of nature, rather than because of the defendant's decision to undertake an activity. It makes far more sense to apply subjectivity when duties to provide benefits for others are at issue than when an individual has chosen to undertake an activity himself. If, for example, English law was to impose liability for a failure to swim out to sea and save a drowning man it would surely have to assess the duty subjectively in order to account for differing abilities as lifesavers and swimmers.

The fact that the Occupiers' Liability Act 1984 replaced the subjective duty of an occupier towards a trespasser with an objective one may suggest that the objective test is both more suitable and preferable. It seems likely that the occasional use of subjectivity has had little effect on the results in the cases. In practice, a subjective standard may be unworkable because it may prove exceptionally difficult to obtain evidence as to a particular individual's abilities and resources.

SATISFYING THE STANDARD

The burden which is generally placed upon a plaintiff of proving breach of a particular standard of liability may be assisted by two legal devices. These devices can, in practice, render a negligence standard of liability much stricter.

Res ipsa loquitur

This maxim (in English, "the thing speaks for itself") is based on the assumption that certain kinds of accidents do not happen unless caused by negligence. It follows that if a person is injured by such an accident its very occurrence provides evidence of negligence. The maxim is commonly traced to the judgment of Erle C.J. in *Scott* v. *The London & St. Katherine's Dock Company*.[76] The plaintiff had been injured whilst walking past the defendant's premises when a bag of sugar had fallen onto him. The judge summarised the position in the following words:

> "There must be reasonable evidence of negligence. But where the thing is shown to be under the management of the defendant or his servants, and the accident is such as in the ordinary course of things does not happen if those who have the management use proper care, it affords reasonable evidence, in the absence of explanation by the defendants, that the accident arose from want of care."

This maxim can provide very useful assistance to a plaintiff who has been damaged by an activity which falls within the particular expertise of the defendant, as it can place pressure on a defendant who has access to information as to the cause of the accident to make it available rather than simply relying on the plaintiff's inability to meet the burden of proof on him. Medical negligence cases provide a good illustration of this. If, as in *Cassidy* v. *Ministry of Health*,[77] a patient is discovered to be suffering from an unexpected side effect at the end of a course of treatment, this may provide evidence that negligence must have occurred in the course of the treatment.

[76] (1865) 3 H. & C. 596.
[77] [1951] 2 K.B. 347.

Denning L.J. explained the working of the maxim in the following words: "I went into hospital to be cured of two stiff fingers. I have come out with four stiff fingers and my hand is useless. Explain it, if you can."

Control

In order for the maxim to operate the defendant must have had control of the activity in question. If the facts raise an inference of negligence, but that negligence could have been caused by the conduct of one of a number of people the maxim will not operate. Neither will it operate if other people had the opportunity to interfere with an activity for which the defendant was responsible. In *Easson* v. *London & North Eastern Railway Company*[78] the defendants were held not to have exclusive control of the offside doors of the carriages of their trains throughout a journey. As a result, when a child fell from a door in the course of a journey, it was inferred that the cause must have been interference with the door by another passenger. The one exception to this rule is that if all of the persons who might have been at fault were employees of the defendant the maxim can be used as evidence of his vicarious liability for the damage. Therefore, if a patient can raise res ipsa against the medical staff who provided the treatment involved in an operation, he will be able to use it against the health authority so long as all of the relevant staff were employees of the authority.

In *Lloyde* v. *West Midlands Gas Board*[79] it was pointed out that an inflexible application of the control requirement would exclude the maxim's application in any case in which work had been completed on the plaintiff's premises and handed over to him. The defendant's control of the item would have ceased before the damage occurred. In that case a gas meter and pipe on the plaintiff's premises had exploded injuring him. The court was prepared to allow the maxim to operate so long as it could be shown that it was improbable that another person had interfered with the work.

The inference of negligence

Res ipsa loquitur only operates to provide evidence of negligence in the absence of an explanation of the cause of the accident. If the facts are known, the inference is impermissible and it is the task of the court to review the facts and to decide whether they amount to the plaintiff having satisfied the burden of proof which is upon him.[80]

Not every item of damage is evidence of negligence. For the inference of negligence to be made the simple fact of the damage having occurred must point to it. Although the result in *Cassidy* may be correct on its facts, it is not authority for the proposition that all untoward consequences following medical treatment are evidence of negligence. Medical treatment carried on with all reasonable care entails the running of many risks. This approach was strongly supported by the result in *Stafford* v. *Conti Commodity Services Ltd.*,[81] in which the plaintiff's allegation that his broker had damaged him by negligence could not be established by the simple fact that the plaintiff's dealings in the commodity futures market had resulted in loss. This market

---

[78] [1944] 1 K.B. 421.
[79] [1971] 1 W.L.R. 749.
[80] *Barkway* v. *South Wales Transport Co. Ltd.* [1950] 1 All E.R. 392.
[81] [1981] 1 All E.R. 691.

was of a "wayward and rapidly changing" kind: losses occurred on it in the ordinary course of things even though the advisers of investors had taken all reasonable care.

Effect of the maxim

If res ipsa loquitur operates it does not shift the burden of proof onto the defendant. It remains for the plaintiff to prove that negligence was the cause of the damage. The maxim merely provides the plaintiff with a piece of evidence in support of his case. If the defendant adduces no evidence the plaintiff will have satisfied the burden of proving his case by invoking the maxim. However, if the defendant does adduce evidence, it will be for the judge to evaluate all of the evidence provided by both sides in order to decide whether the plaintiff's case is proved.[82] On this basis the Privy Council held that the plaintiff's case failed in the leading modern case of Ng Chun Pui v. Lee Chuen Tat.[83] A coach had crossed the central reservation of a dual carriageway road and collided with oncoming traffic. The court accepted that the plaintiffs were entitled to invoke res ipsa on these facts because properly maintained and driven coaches should not crash in this fashion. However, the defendant's evidence that the coach had gone out of control because of the driver's attempts to avoid a vehicle which had cut across its path was accepted and deemed to be sufficient to negative the effect of the maxim.

The actual burden facing a defendant who seeks to rebut an inference of negligence created by res ipsa loquitur has been the subject of a great deal of debate. As a result of the Ng case it can now be confidently asserted that a defendant cannot be faced by the legal burden of disproving negligence. All that a defendant needs to do is produce an answer which is adequate to displace the prima facie inference. However, some of the earlier cases decided by the House of Lords show that res ipsa can be a powerful weapon which can give a negligence action strict liability characteristics. In Colvilles Ltd. v. Devine[84] it was held that a defendant could not rebut the prima facie presumption merely by offering a plausible explanation of the accident. It needed to be shown that reasonable precautions had been taken in relation to these matters. Henderson v. Henry E. Jenkins & Sons[85] set an even stricter standard. The defendants' lorry had crashed as a result of brake failure caused by corrosion of a brake pipe. The defendants showed that the vehicle had been serviced in accordance with the standard practice laid down in the manufacturer's and Ministry of Transport's recommendations and that the defect could not have been discerned in the course of such servicing. Nonetheless, they were held not to have rebutted the inference created by the maxim. Reasonable care demanded that they service the vehicle according to the risks created by its particular history and usage. The defendants lost because they failed to show that the lorry had not been subject to unusual factors which would have required a higher level of precautions to be taken. This is a standard which is likely to be exceptionally difficult to meet in practice.

---

[82] The result is confusingly said to be that the evidential burden of proof is shifted by the maxim whereas the legal burden remains with the plaintiff.

[83] [1988] R.T.R. 298.

[84] [1969] 1 W.L.R. 475.

[85] [1970] A.C. 282.

Civil Evidence Act 1968

Section 11 of the Civil Evidence Act 1968 provides a further aid to proving liability in tort. It is in the following terms:

11(1) In any civil proceedings the fact that a person has been convicted of an offence by or before any court in the United Kingdom . . . shall . . . be admissible in evidence for the purpose of proving, where to do so is relevant to any issue in those proceedings, that he committed that offence . . .

(2) In any civil proceedings in which by virtue of this section a person is proved to have been convicted of an offence by or before any court . . .–

(a) he shall be taken to have committed that offence unless the contrary is proved; and

(b) without prejudice to the reception of any other admissible evidence for the purpose of identifying the facts on which the conviction was based, the contents of any document which is admissible as evidence of the conviction, and the contents of the information, complaint, indictment or charge-sheet on which the person in question was convicted, shall be admissible in evidence for that purpose.

This provision may be of use in many personal injury cases. Intentional batteries, road and industrial accidents may all lead to a criminal prosecution and conviction. It is likely that the criminal law proceedings will be resolved more rapidly than any tort claim based on the same facts. The plaintiff in the tort case may therefore decide to allow the prosecuting authorities to collect the evidence and to convince the court of its veracity before seeking to resolve the claim for damages. A defendant who has been convicted by a criminal court on the higher standard of proof which that court will apply will commonly see little prospect of success in subsequent civil proceedings and will choose to settle the plaintiff's claim.

However, section 11 is not conclusive of the issue posed in the civil proceedings and it does not prevent a convicted person from introducing into the civil proceedings evidence designed to prove that the conviction was mistaken. The issues raised by criminal proceedings are not necessarily identical to those posed by subsequent civil proceedings. The criminal offence may have different requirements to the tort and defences may be available to a tortfeasor which would not defeat a criminal charge. A good example of this is provided by *Nettleship* v. *Weston*.[86] The learner driver had been convicted of careless driving prior to the tort claim reaching court. This conviction was obviously not decisive in the civil proceedings as it was open to the defence to argue that the standard of care imposed by tort on the learner driver was a limited one and defences such as contributory negligence and *volenti*, which were wholly irrelevant to the criminal proceedings, were raised.[87]

---

[86] [1971] 2 Q.B. 691.
[87] The first argument was disallowed as a matter of law and the defence of *volenti*, which failed on the facts of the case, is now disallowed as a result of Road Traffic Act 1988, s. 149. It is also possible to plead illegality against a person who has been convicted of an offence. See *Pitts* v. *Hunt* [1991] 1 Q.B. 24.

Chapter Four

Causation and Remoteness of Damage

INTRODUCTION

A number of related issues are discussed under the heading of causation and remoteness of damage. The central question is whether a connection can be made between the tortious conduct of the defendant and the damage suffered by the plaintiff. Causation and remoteness of damage offer a number of devices which limit the scope and extent of liability for admittedly tortious conduct.

The principles discussed in this chapter are common to all torts, although the rules relating to remoteness of damage vary to a degree according to the tort committed. In the case of many torts, such as negligence, proof that damage was caused by the breach of duty is a necessary element in the cause of action: the tort is not complete until damage has been caused. In other cases a tort may be actionable *per se*, (*i.e.* without proof of damage). This means that nominal damages can be recovered on the basis of the defendant's conduct even if the plaintiff has not suffered damage. However, even in the case of these torts, causation will have to be proved before substantial damages can be recovered.

Duty and remoteness of damage

Difficulties exist as to the relationship between negligence, duty of care and remoteness of damage. Some of the best known problem areas of negligence, for example, nervous shock and economic loss, have been regarded by some judges and commentators as raising issues of duty of care and by others as a matter of remoteness of damage. Lord Denning on several occasions stated that the two areas were different ways of achieving the same result and that they ultimately raised the same issues of policy.[1] The example of *Doughty* v. *Turner Manufacturing Co. Ltd.*[2] may be used as an example. In that case the plaintiff was injured at work when an asbestos cement cover was negligently knocked into a cauldron of hot liquid. The lid and liquid produced an unforeseeable chemical reaction which caused the liquid to erupt and scald the plaintiff. His claim for damages failed because the risk of such an eruption was found to be unforeseeable. If the damage which occurred was unforeseeable the plaintiff's claim can be rejected at any of the

---

[1] See particularly his judgments in *Spartan Steel & Alloys Ltd.* v. *Martin & Co. Contractors Ltd.* [1973] 1 Q.B. 27 and *Lamb* v. *Camden L.B.C.* [1981] Q.B. 625.
[2] [1964] 1 Q.B. 518.

stages of the negligence test. The fact that a risk is unforeseeable can block the creation of a duty of care, mean that there is no harm against which reasonable care should be taken at the level of breach of duty or mean that any damage which is suffered will be too remote a consequence of a breach of a duty to take reasonable care. To an extent the classification of the problem is a matter of taste. However, the degree of generality with which the questions are posed will affect the classification. In *Doughty* Diplock L.J. described the duty of care in the case as one to "take reasonable care to avoid knocking the cover into the liquid or allowing it to slip in in such a way as to cause a splash which would injure the plaintiff." If these words express the whole picture no duty of care exists to guard the employees against the different risk of the liquid erupting. On the other hand, the approach which commonly appears in modern cases is to phrase issues of duty of care in much more general terms than this. The duty of care deals with abstract issues of immunity created by wide categories of conduct and damage. On this basis the employer in *Doughty* clearly owes a duty of care; it is one to take reasonable care of the safety of his employees. The issue raised by the case falls to be decided by the rules of breach (on the facts the employer negligently endangered the employee's safety) and remoteness of damage (the actual consequence which ensued from the breach was unforeseeable and therefore too remote). In practice most of the modern cases approach issues such as nervous shock and economic loss on the basis that they raise questions of the duty of care. This approach has already been adopted in the previous two chapters. Issues of causation and remoteness of damage will therefore be restricted to factual issues as to whether a particular item of damage is recoverable on the facts of the case. Arguments as to whether such damage can ever be recovered as a matter of law are the concern of the duty of care.

CAUSE IN FACT (THE "BUT FOR" TEST)

The issue of cause in fact excludes from consideration items of tortious conduct which are irrelevant to the damage suffered. If no link between cause and effect can be proved by use of the "but for" test there will be no tortious liability. On the other hand, even if a duty of care exists and has been broken, proof of factual causation is not sufficient to establish liability. Questions of legal causation and remoteness of damage may remain to be considered. They will decide which of the factual causes which form the situation in which damage is suffered is the legally relevant one. The test excludes irrelevant causes, but cannot define the cause. The "but for" test requires a court to construct a hypothetical version of the facts of the case from which the defendant's tortious conduct is removed. Would the damage have occurred "but for" the tort? If the damage would still have occurred on this alternative scenario the tortious conduct was irrelevant to its causation and is to be ignored.

The classic example of this approach is provided by *Barnett* v. *Chelsea & Kensington H.M.C.*[3] in which a hospital's casualty officer was held to have been negligent in failing to examine, admit for tests and treat a man who had

---

[3] [1969] 1 Q.B. 428.

come to the hospital complaining of vomiting fits. The doctor had given instructions by telephone to the nurse who had seen the man that he should return home and call his own doctor in the morning if the symptoms persisted. The man was suffering from arsenic poisoning and died five hours after leaving the hospital. An action brought by his widow failed on the grounds that the evidence showed that the man would have died even if he had been given all proper treatment. A reasonably run hospital could not have diagnosed the cause of the symptoms in time to save his life. It followed that the negligence of the defendants was not a factual cause of the death. A similar decision was reached in *Robinson* v. *The Post Office*[4] in which a doctor's negligent failure to follow correct procedure by administering a small test dose of a drug to guard against the possibility of an allergic reaction was held not to be a factual cause of a severe allergic reaction suffered by the patient on the administration of the full dose. As the reaction to the full dose had taken three days to manifest itself, it was inherently unlikely that a properly conducted test dose of a much smaller quantity would have revealed the patient's susceptibility in the half hour allowed by the test for a reaction. Again the negligence was irrelevant. The damage would have occurred in any event.

Cases such as *Barnett* and *Robinson* are relatively simple to decide given that convincing evidence may be available as to what would have happened in the absence of negligence. The position may be much more difficult when an alternative scenario dependent on human actions must be considered. A well known case in which the court was confident as to the result is *McWilliams* v. *Sir William Arrol & Co. Ltd.*[5] This case concerned an employer who had broken an industrial safety duty by failing to provide safety belts for employees working at height. The plaintiff's husband had been killed in a fall and it was claimed that the removal of the safety equipment from the site several days before the accident was the cause of his death. The House of Lords rejected this claim on the grounds that the evidence was unequivocal, that the deceased had never used a belt when it was available. The widow's argument that this faced her with the impossible burden of proving what her husband would have done in the absence of his evidence was discounted on the basis that his likely action could be inferred from the overwhelming evidence which existed.

However, the evidence will not always establish a consistent pattern of behaviour. An example of the kind of problem which may occur is provided by the doctor who negligently fails to warn a patient of the risks inherent in a medical treatment which is being proposed. In the absence of the warning, the treatment is given and the patient is damaged by the risk. Is it open to the doctor to argue that if he had given a proper warning the patient would still have suffered damage because he would have chosen to go ahead with the treatment? A second issue arises in the event that the doctor is permitted to use this causation based argument. By what standard is the patient's response to the hypothetical proper warning to be judged? Is it by the hypothetical reaction of a reasonable, sensible patient (the objective test) or is it that of the particular patient with his own peculiar sensitivities and fears (the subjective test)? The objective standard is capable of sacrificing an individual's

---

[4] [1974] 1 W.L.R. 1174.
[5] [1962] 1 W.L.R. 295.

undoubted right to decline medical treatment to the argument that reasonable people follow their doctor's advice; whereas the subjective may be
thought to give too great a scope to patients to support their grievances with
impermissible hindsight. The contention "I would not have agreed had I
known the truth," may be exceptionally easy to make if the risk has
eventuated, wholly untrue, and impossible to disprove in the face of the
patient's evidence as to his fears concerning the treatment. English courts[6]
have not, as yet, had to face this issue directly although Lord Diplock in the
Sidaway case seemed to prefer the subjective standard, at least in relation to
battery. It is suggested that English law should adopt the subjective
approach. A patient's right to decline treatment is a fundamental right which
should not be compromised by the assertion that a reasonable patient would
have accepted it. Courts are surely capable of evaluating critically a patient's
assertion that he would have declined treatment.

Simultaneous causes

Although there seems to be little, if any, authority directly in point, it is
generally accepted that the "but for" test must give way to the demands of
policy in a situation in which two parties independently commit torts which
would have inflicted the same damage on the plaintiff. Were this not the case
both parties whose independent acts of negligence started fires which spread,
merged and jointly damaged the plaintiff's property would escape liability on
the argument that the damage would have been inflicted by the other even if
he had not acted.

Evidence that the courts will adopt a common sense attitude to factual
situations of this kind can be found in cases in which a nuisance is
attributable to the combined acts of a number of defendants acting independently. In *Lambton* v. *Mellish*[7] two defendants who operated organs independently of each other on their properties as accompaniment to merry-go-
rounds argued that "two rights cannot make a wrong": as neither organ
constituted a nuisance on its own the combined noise could not be actionable. The court rejected this and held both defendants liable for the combined
noise.[8] In *Pride of Derby Derbyshire Angling Association Ltd.* v. *British
Celanese Ltd.*[9] Harman J. was prepared to extend this approach to a
situation in which one of the defendants had committed an act which would
have been actionable on its own.

Successive independent causes

The problem of successive causes is closely related to that of simultaneous
causes. What is the position when two successive events independently inflict
the same damage upon the plaintiff? Is it open to a tortfeasor to deny that
causation has been established on the basis that the same damage had

---

[6] For a discussion of the Canadian authority see Dugdale & Stanton, *Professional Negligence*
(2nd ed.), para. 18.09.
[7] [1894] 3 Ch. 163.
[8] Chitty J.'s suggestion that for liability to be established each defendant must be aware of the
acts of the other is almost certainly wrong.
[9] [1952] 1 All E.R. 1326.

happened or was going to happen in spite of his conduct? It is helpful to distinguish a number of situations.

The most straightforward case is that of the tortfeasor who damages a person or object which is already damaged. The principle that a tortfeasor must take his victim as he finds him may benefit a tortfeasor. For example, a person who inflicts injuries on another who was already disabled and unable to earn cannot be held liable for loss of earnings. If the plaintiff previously had a reduced earning capacity, it is only the damage to that reduced capacity which will enter the calculation. In the leading case of *Performance Cars Ltd.* v. *Abraham*[10] the defendant's negligence caused damage to the plaintiff's Rolls Royce car. The damage called for respraying at a cost of £75. However, a previous accident, in relation to which the plaintiff had obtained an unsatisfied judgment, had made this work necessary in any case. The Court of Appeal held that the defendant's negligence had inflicted no additional loss on the plaintiff and that he bore no liability.

Greater difficulties occur when the defendant has undoubtedly inflicted damage on the plaintiff but the consequences of that damage are over-whelmed by the consequences of a subsequent event. There are a number of leading cases on this issue which are not entirely consistent. In *Carslogie Steamship Co. Ltd.* v. *Royal Norwegian Government*[11] the plaintiff's ship was damaged in a collision due to the fault of the defendants. Temporary repairs were effected and the vessel proceeded on a normal voyage to a port at which permanent repairs were to be carried out. In the course of the voyage the vessel encountered heavy weather and suffered further damage which rendered immediate repair essential. Both sets of repairs were carried out simultaneously when the ship reached port. The repairs detained her in port for 30 days. The question posed for the House of Lords was whether the defendants were liable for loss of earnings resulting from 10 days of delay, this being the period which the collision damage would have taken to repair. The House held that they were not liable. The claim was for the loss of a profit-earning vessel for a period; but, at the time that the ship suffered the weather damage, she was a seaworthy profit earning vessel in spite of the collision damage. It was the damage caused by the weather which rendered her unseaworthy and this would have detained her in port for 30 days whether or not she had suffered damage previously. The collision damage was therefore not a cause of the delay. The position would have been different if the owner had put the vessel into dock to repair the collision damage and taken the opportunity of doing other advisable, but not essen-tial, repairs at the same time or if two successive events both rendered the vessel unseaworthy.[12] In both of these situations the first event would constitute a cause of the delay.

A similar result was reached in *Jobling* v. *Associated Diaries Ltd.*[13] In 1973 the plaintiff suffered an accident at work, caused by his employer's breach of statutory duty, which left him with a partial disability and fit only for sedentary work. In 1976 he was discovered to be suffering from a degenerative disease which would, in any case, have inflicted a greater disablement upon him. By the middle or end of 1976 he would have been

---

[10] [1962] 1 Q.B. 33.
[11] [1952] A.C. 292.
[12] The *Performance Cars* result.
[13] [1982] A.C. 794.

totally unfit for work. The question which arose was whether the superven-
ing naturally arising event was to be taken into consideration when assessing
the consequences of the tort on the grounds that the disablement would have
occurred by 1976 even if no tort had taken place. The House of Lords held
that the illness had the effect of terminating the tortfeasor's liability from the
date on which it overwhelmed the effects of the tort. A plaintiff's award of
damages for future losses is discounted because of the "vicissitudes" of life,
the range of factors which might have damaged the plaintiff even if the tort
had not occurred. However, if such an occurrence had eventuated before trial
it will be taken fully into account because the court will not "guess when it
knows." Illness is one of the vicissitudes taken into account and it therefore
operated on the facts of *Jobling* to determine the liability, whether or not the
disablement was the result of a condition which predated the tort.

The reason that the House of Lords had difficulty in deciding *Jobling* was
that it was faced by its previous decision in *Baker* v. *Willoughby*.[14] If the
reasoning in *Baker* remains correct it is possible that the *Jobling* result will
not apply when the successive events which afflict the plaintiff are both torts.
Alternatively, the decision in *Baker* may have been so damaged by *Jobling*
that the case would not survive a direct challenge. The facts of *Baker* were
simple. The plaintiff had been injured in 1964 in a road accident for which
the defendant bore responsibility and as a result of the injury his left leg was
disabled. The case in which he sought compensation for this loss came to trial
in 1968. However, a few months before the trial took place the plaintiff had
suffered a second tortiously inflicted injury, at the hands of an armed robber,
which had caused his disabled leg to have to be amputated. The question was
whether the defendant's responsibility for the disablement ceased at the date
of the amputation. Could he continue to be liable for the pain, suffering and
loss of amenity caused by a disabled leg when that leg no longer existed?

The House unanimously held that the defendant's liability continued
beyond the date of the amputation. The majority view, expressed by Lord
Reid, was that liability would continue, as a matter of principle, in a case in
which later injuries become a concurrent cause of damage but do not reduce
it. Lord Pearson, on the other hand, based his approach on the pragmatic
need to avoid injustice. The second tortfeasor was bound to take the plaintiff
as he found him. In a case in which injuries are inflicted on a person who is
already disabled, this principle favours the defendant who is only liable for
the additional disablement which results from his acts. If, for example, the
first tort causes a 30 per cent. disablement and the second total disablement,
the second tortfeasor will only be liable for the 70 per cent. difference. If the
liability of the first tortfeasor ceases at the time of the second tort the
unacceptable result would occur that the plaintiff, having received damages
appropriate to a 30 per cent. disablement for the period from the first to the
second tort, would only be awarded compensation for a 70 per cent
disablement from the moment that 100 per cent. disablement afflicts him.
The only way to avoid this is to do what the House of Lords did in *Baker* and
create an exception to the "but for" test which prevents the first defendant
from arguing that the plaintiff would have been totally disabled from the
date of the second tort irrespective of the first tort.

The House in *Jobling* took the view that the authority relied upon in *Baker*
did not support the result reached and that the House should have considered

---

[14] [1970] A.C. 467.

the vicissitudes argument and the existence of the Criminal Injuries Compensation Board as providing a remedy for the second tort.[15] The wider approach of Lord Reid, which expresses a general approach to cases of concurrent causes, is now expressly rejected. However, it is not clear whether the actual decision will survive either on the basis that the prospect of further tortiously inflicted injuries is not one of the vicissitudes of life or as a necessary response to the inadequate compensation in the post second tort period which the thin skull rule would produce. The House in *Jobling* left the authority of *Baker* open. On balance it is suggested that the decision should be upheld if directly challenged.

Causation and calculation

The issues of causation and of calculation of damage may be easily confused. The issue of causation is whether there exists a legally recognised link between tortious conduct and damage. If there is such a link a defendant is responsible for the damage; if not, there is no tort, even though the defendant has breached a duty which the law imposed on him. How the law calculates compensation for a loss which has been proved to have been suffered is a question for the law of damages. These issues may prove exceptionally difficult to disentangle because factual uncertainties may be relevant at every stage. The example of a man exposed, at his place of work as a result of negligence, to a carcinogenic chemical, may help. If the man develops lung cancer and dies and his widow brings an action against his employer under the Fatal Accidents Act, the issues are as follows. (a) Was the cancer caused by the tort? (the causation issue). (b) If, and only if, causation is established, what losses are attributable to the damage caused by the tort? (the quantification of damage). There are substantial difficulties to be overcome at this point if, as may well be the case in our example, it is argued that the cancer was attributable to causes other than the exposure. It may have arisen naturally or resulted from other carcinogens such as tobacco. In practice, absolute certainty will be impossible in this situation. The law has developed a number of rules to deal with this issue, but there is no consistency as to whether they favour or disfavour a plaintiff who is faced by these uncertainties.

First, the plaintiff bears the burden of proving causation on the normal civil standard of proof. The plaintiff merely has to show, on the balance of probabilities, that his damage was attributable to the defendant's conduct. On our example, the widow must show that it was more likely than not (*i.e.* that there was a 51 per cent. probability) that the exposure at work was the cause of the cancer. An "all or nothing" approach is adopted. If a 51 per cent. probability is established, the defendant is held wholly responsible for the cancer and the other possibilities are disregarded. If the widow fails to satisfy this standard of proof, which is quite possible in a situation of factual uncertainty, the employer will bear no responsibility for the cancer at all (an apportionment is not possible). The effect of these rules is variable. A defendant may be held wholly responsible for damage although there is a substantial possibility that the damage is attributable to other causes and, conversely, people who create real risks of damage may find that the

---

[15] Lord Wilberforce's argument relating to the possibility of overcompensation in the event of a C.I.C.B. award ignore the fact that such awards are recouped from damages.

combination of rules of proof and factual uncertainties confers immunity on them. These results are not consistent with deterrent theories of tort which require the true cost of tortious conduct to be placed on the person best placed to control the risks and may create substantial injustices.

Secondly, in a situation of concurrent causes, the picture is complicated by the operation of the test established by the case of *Bonnington Castings Ltd.* v. *Wardlaw.*[16] Under this test the plaintiff will succeed by proving, on the balance of probabilities, that the tort made a material contribution to his damage, along with the other factors. It is unclear how substantial a contribution the tortious conduct has to make. However, if the test is satisfied, the tortfeasor is liable for all of the damage, not just for a proportion of it.

Finally, uncertainties are undoubtedly relevant to the calculation of damages. If it is clearly established that the tort caused the plaintiff's death, there may still be uncertainties as to what would have happened had the tort not occurred and thus as to what losses are attributable to the established tortious damage. The plaintiff's prospective earnings will obviously form an important part of any calculation, but they are likely to be dependent on evidence as to promotion prospects and possible illnesses. The difficulty of keeping the issues of causation and calculation apart are shown by the fact that even if our plaintiff establishes that her husband's cancer was attributable to his employer's fault, as opposed to other possible causes of cancer, the multiplier used to calculate the compensation should be discounted because of the possibility that non-tortious factors would have reduced the husband's earning capacity in any event. A naturally occurring cancer would be one such factor.[17]

If these rules cause difficulty in relation to negligently inflicted harm, they create almost insuperable problems in cases of negligent failure to provide protection against harm. The leading case on this is *Hotson* v. *East Berkshire Area Health Authority*[18] in which the plaintiff child had suffered an injury in an accident at school which created a 75 per cent. risk of permanent disability. The defendant hospital's negligence delayed proper treatment of the injury and the probability of disability became a certainty. The hospital argued that the plaintiff's case should fail because he could not prove, on the balance of probabilities, that he would have been better off had there been no negligence. The judge and Court of Appeal rejected this and held that the plaintiff's loss was not the disability but the loss of the chance of a successful outcome. They valued this loss as 25 per cent. of the value of the permanent disability and calculated the damages awarded to the plaintiff accordingly. The House of Lords reversed this decision and held that the judge's finding was actually a determination on the balance of probabilities,[19] that the original accident was the cause of the disability and that the hospital's negligence was causally unconnected with it. By doing this the House defined the problem in such a way as to render discussion of the possibility of recovering damages in tort for loss of a chance irrelevant. There are

---

[16] [1956] A.C. 613, discussed *post*, p. 87.

[17] *Smith* v. *Leech Brain & Co. Ltd.* [1962] 2 Q.B. 405 was such a case. The defendant employer was held to have caused the cancer, but the damages took into account the strong possibility that cancer would have developed in the near future.

[18] [1987] A.C. 750.

[19] There being less than a 50 per cent. chance that the hospital's conduct had made any difference.

considerable difficulties with the approach of the House of Lords. The most obvious is that it effectively gives a plaintiff who complains about a doctor's failure to provide proper treatment the burden of proving that he had more than an even chance of recovery given proper treatment. A doctor faced by a patient who has less than a 50 per cent. chance of recovery is immune from liability if he does nothing.

Only time will tell whether it will prove unacceptable for *Hotson* to be authority for such results. One possible escape route might be for its authority to be confined to situations in which the problem is to determine what had happened in the past; but that it should not apply when the question is what would have happened in a hypothetical situation or what might have happened in the future. As has been correctly pointed out[20] the difficulty with this approach is that a court must consider a hypothetical alternative fact situation whenever a factual causation issue is raised. But, the fact that the situations may prove impossible to separate may open the door to a narrow interpretation of *Hotson* which will avoid unacceptable results.

Proof of factual causation

Proof of factual causation raises some of the most difficult issues confronting the modern law of tort. The burden of proving causation, on the balance of probabilities, rests with the plaintiff, even if the defendant is in clear breach of a strict industrial safety duty. Causation may be very difficult to prove in many situations in which a person has been exposed to a continuing process or to a number of different factors which are possible explanations for the damage. The example of an employee who develops lung cancer after being exposed to a carcinogenic chemical at work is, again, of use. What needs to be done to establish that it was this exposure rather than the fact of regular smoking which produced the illness? Similarly, how is it to be proved that disabilities with which a child was born were caused by tortious events before its birth rather than occurred naturally.[21] The rules which have been developed have not favoured a plaintiff's chances of recovering tort compensation.

In simple terms the issue is what a plaintiff has to prove. The test can be set at a number of levels. Is it that the defendant caused the damage; that the defendant made a material contribution to the damage; that the defendant increased the risk of the damage occurring, or merely that the defendant added an additional risk factor?

There can be no doubt that proof that the defendant caused the damage will suffice to establish liability and that the law is prepared to go beyond this and thus to assist plaintiffs to win their cases. The decision of *Bonnington Castings Ltd.* v. *Wardlaw*[22] establishes that proof that the tortious conduct has made a material contribution to the damage does suffice. In that case the plaintiff developed a disease after having been exposed to silica dust produced by two machines in the defendant's factory. Only one of these machines had been operated in breach of statutory duty. Nonetheless, it was held that the defendant could be held liable for all of the plaintiff's damage

---

[20] Jones, *Textbook on Torts* (4th ed.), p. 146–47.
[21] See Chap. 26 of the Report of the Pearson Commission and the criticisms there made of the Congenital Disabilities (Civil Liability) Act 1976.
[22] [1956] A.C. 613.

on the basis that the machine which had been operated in breach of statutory duty had made a material contribution to the damage. This result is of great importance in circumstances of joint liability as it means that it is not open to a person who has contributed to damage to escape liability on the basis that another defendant bore the primary responsibility.

In *McGhee* v. *National Coal Board*[23] the House of Lords seemed to go further than this in a case in which it was impossible to determine exactly how the damage occurred. *McGhee* was an industrial safety case in which an employer had broken a duty of care by negligently failing to provide showers for the use of employees who worked in a dusty atmosphere in a brick kiln. The plaintiff employee developed dermatitis. The evidence showed that the failure to provide the showers and the resultant longer exposure of the plaintiff's skin to the dust had increased the risk of the disease developing, but that there was no way of being certain whether it would have been produced by the shorter exposure that the plaintiff would have been subject to if the showers had been provided. The court held that, in these circumstances proof of a material increase in the risk was equivalent to proving that the defendant had made a material contribution to the damage; otherwise the impossibility of medical evidence determining the cause of the damage would leave the defendant in a position of immunity.

In *Wilsher* v. *Essex A.H.A.*[24] a slightly different issue was raised. A hospital which had treated the plaintiff child had been negligent with the result that he had received excessive amounts of oxygen. The child developed an eye disorder and it was shown that great uncertainty existed within the medical profession as to the causes of such a disorder, but that excessive oxygen was one explanation. It was impossible to tell whether it was the oxygen or one of the other factors which accounted for the child's condition. In the Court of Appeal *McGhee* was said to cover this case and the hospital was held liable. The result was criticised on the basis that it ignored the important distinction between increasing the risk of damage resulting from an identified danger and adding a different and wholly independent risk factor. The significance of the Court of Appeal's approach in *Wilsher* was shown by *Fitzgerald* v. *Lane*,[25] a road accident case in which a court was faced by the inability of witnesses to say which of two impacts was more likely to have caused the plaintiff's injuries. On an application of *Wilsher* the Court of Appeal held that both motorists had added an additional risk factor and both were liable.

However, the Court of Appeal's approach, which tilts the scales in the plaintiff's favour, must now be regarded as incorrect. When *Wilsher* came before the House of Lords, the Court of Appeal's interpretation of *McGhee* was emphatically rejected. The decision in *McGhee* was said to be no more than a robust and pragmatic finding that the defendants conduct had made a material contribution to the plaintiff's injury.[26] It was emphasised that the burden of proving causation rests with the plaintiff and is not satisfied by proof that the defendant had failed to take precautions against one of a number of possible causes of the damage. It is clear that, as a result of this case, causation can now only be established by the plaintiff meeting the

---

[23] [1973] 1 W.L.R. 1.
[24] [1987] Q.B. 730, C.A; [1988] A.C. 1074, H.L.
[25] [1987] 2 All E.R. 455.
[26] And, as such, fell within the authority of *Bonnington*.

burden of proving that the tort caused or made a material contribution to his damage.

The final result in *Wilsher* is of particular relevance to cases in which it is claimed that an illness has been caused by exposure to a particular substance. The example of a group of employees who are negligently exposed to a carcinogenic chemical creates an insoluble dilemma if the illness suffered is indistinguishable from naturally occurring cancers as it will be impossible to tell which employees would have developed cancer from natural, or non-tortious, causes irrespective of the employer's acts and which only developed it because of the exposure at work. The Court of Appeal's result in *Wilsher* would hold the employer liable to all of the employees who become ill: they have all suffered damage and can prove that the employer was responsible for increasing the risk that they would develop the disease. This is harsh on the employer and, to the economist's eyes, is liable to lead to an inefficient level of underproduction as it holds the employer liable to compensate for some cancers which would have occurred naturally. The House of Lords' approach is equally bad from the plaintiff's view and imposes inadequate incentives on the employer to take precautions. Under this approach none of the employees will recover compensation. Even though it can be shown statistically[27] that the increase in the rate of cancer was caused by the employer, none of the sufferers will be able to show that his particular illness was attributable to him. This is just one example of the point that the burden of proving causation can create insuperable obstacles to success in disease cases.

One can envisage courts being faced by substantial disputes in the post-*Wilsher* world as to whether they may legitimately make the inference that the defendant's conduct made a material contribution to the plaintiff's damage or must deny the claim on the basis that all that was suffered was a material increase in the risks faced. The actual decision in *Fitzgerald* v. *Lane*[28] might be capable of being upheld on the basis of a finding that both motorists had made a material contribution to the plaintiff's damage. However, *Wilsher* gives defendants scope for resisting such claims and, at a more general level, establishes a classic example of a meaningless distinction behind which courts are likely to be able to shelter their value judgments.

CAUSE IN LAW AND REMOTENESS OF DAMAGE

Factual causation is an essential, but not a sufficient, condition of tortious liability. There are several reasons for this: a single act may have a long sequence of consequences; conduct which is unarguably a factual cause of damage may produce a form of damage which is radically different from that which might have been envisaged at the time that the responsible person acted and an item of damage may be factually attributable to a number of acts and the law may need to exclude some of these causes from responsibility.

An example which is commonly given is that of a person (P) negligently injured by another's (D1's) driving. P is then rushed to hospital in an

---

[27] Hill, (1991) 54 M.L.R. 511, argues that there is a distinction between "personal" and "statistical" chances and that compensation should not be payable in respect of loss of the latter. See also Scott, (1992) 55 M.L.R. 521.

[28] [1989] A.C. 328.

ambulance driven by D2. D2's negligent driving causes the ambulance to crash and P is killed. Which defendant is the cause of P's death? In terms of factual causation both D1 and D2 are. The death would not have occurred had D1's negligence not required P to be taken to hospital; neither would it have occurred had D2 not driven negligently. The law has to decide to which of these causes the legal responsibility for the death should be attributed.

The process involved in attributing legal responsibility for damage to factual causes is essentially one of judicial discretion. No simple rule is possible because the facts of every case are likely to be different. All that the courts can do is to use their "instinctive, common sense," in the light of experience, to decide such issues. Many of the problems which beset this area derive from the fact that the courts have shrouded their decisions behind what appear to be substantial legal doctrines when they are in fact using different, and interchangeable, verbal formulae to shield the discretionary nature of the process. If, on the facts of the example given previously, the court decides that the responsibility for the death is to be attributed to the ambulance driver (D2), it may discharge D1 from responsibility by saying either that the chain of causation from D1's negligent act was broken by D2's intervening negligence (the latin novus actus interveniens is commonly used); that D1's negligence was an essential condition of the death, but that D2's acts were its "real" or "effective" cause, or, finally, that the death was too remote a consequence of D1's negligence for him to be liable for it. These different ways of expressing the conclusion are drawn from the categories of law traditionally called legal causation and remoteness of damage. At times these are treated as distinctly different areas of law. However, there is a substantial overlap because many of the problems which arise can be formulated so as to fall under either heading. Nonetheless, two issues are being discussed. The first is that of "multiple cause." The ambulance crash is an example of this. In such a case there is one item of loss (the death) and a number of causes to which legal responsibility for it may be attributed. The second situation is one in which only one tortious act is at issue. Difficulties arise because it has resulted in damage of an unusual kind or extent and the question is whether there should be responsibility for such untoward consequences. As a working rule it is possible to say that multiple cause problems are commonly treated under the heading of cause in law, whereas differences in the kind or extent of damage are classified as raising issues of remoteness of damage. But, although attractive, this cannot be a watertight distinction, because the effect of a second factual cause may be that a form of damage results which is very different from that which the person responsible for the first cause could have envisaged. In addition, there can be no doubt that the remoteness of damage approach has become increasingly fashionable in modern law[29] and has come to be used in relation to problems of multiple cause. A good example of this occurred in Lamb v. Camden L.B.C.[30] when Oliver L.J. stated that the Wagon Mound Cases,[31] which are the leading

---

[29] There are however, examples of the causation approach being used by the House of Lords in the post-Wagon Mound era. The most important is McKew v. Holland, Hannen & Cubitts (Scotland) Ltd. [1969] 3 All E.R. 1621.

[30] [1981] Q.B. 625.

[31] Overseas Tankship (U.K.) Ltd. v. Morts Dock and Engineering Co., The Wagon Mound [1961] A.C. 388; Overseas Tankship (U.K.) Ltd. v. Miller Steamship Co. Pty. Ltd., The Wagon Mound (No. 2) [1967] 1 A.C. 617.

modern authorities on remoteness of damage "established that the test of causation is reasonable foreseeability."

Multiple causes – Legal causation

The previous discussion of legal causation has assumed the accuracy of an argument that has been made forcefully by some commentators. The process of determining legal causation is not a value-free one of producing an explanation for an item of damage; neither, unless the deterrent aim of tort is accepted as relevant to this issue, is it designed to prevent such accidents from happening in the future. It is rather a process of attribution of responsibility and blame; one which is heavily influenced by the policies[32] and philosophies underlying the tort system. An ordinary road accident situation may illustrate this point. In terms of factual causation the damage produced by such an accident may derive from a host of factors including the layout and lighting of the particular road; the weather conditions; the design of the vehicles involved and the behaviour of the drivers. It may well be the case that the configuration of the road at the point at which the accident occurred is such as to increase the chance of accidents occurring. However, the process of attribution conducted under the banner of legal causation concentrates heavily, if not exclusively, on the human conduct involved in the scenario. An injured person cannot sue an inanimate object, such as a piece of ice, for causing an accident. Such items are not available as defendants and are not insured. But, one can sue a driver for failing to take proper precautions to anticipate the dangers created by freezing conditions and one may be able to sue public authorities for failing to keep roads clear of ice. Many otherwise perfectly competent drivers may encounter difficulties in controlling their vehicles on ice, but to allow the ice, rather than the human reaction to it, to constitute the legal cause of any resulting damage would be to declare that the damage was attributable to a pure accident and remove any chance of compensation being payable. Causal principles, by concentrating on the human variables in the factual equation, reflect the compensatory and deterrent aims of tort. The emphasis which is placed by these principles on personal responsibility is a good example of the dominance of thinking derived from negligence in general tort theory and goes a long way to explain why the distinctions between issues of duty of care and legal causation have become so blurred in practice.

The position becomes more difficult when the task of attribution of damage relates to several independent items of tortious human conduct. In such a case the options are to attribute the damage wholly to one or other cause or to regard them as joint causes of the damage. As the final decision will depend on the facts of the particular case it would be misleading to suggest that there are any firm rules governing this subject. Nonetheless, the cases do reveal fairly consistent patterns of results in commonly occurring scenarios. These were possibly best summarised in Stephenson L.J.'s judgment in *Knightley* v. *Johns*[33]:

" . . . it is helpful but not decisive to consider which of these events were deliberate choices to do positive acts and which were mere omissions (or)

[32] Atiyah, *Accidents, Compensation and the Law*, Chap. 4.
[33] [1982] 1 W.L.R. 349.

failures to act; which acts and omissions were innocent mistakes or miscalculations and which were negligent having regard to the pressures and the gravity of the emergency and the need to act quickly. Negligent conduct is more likely to break the chain of causation than conduct which is not; positive acts will more easily constitute new causes than inaction. Mistakes and mischances are to be expected when human beings, however well trained, have to cope with a crisis; what exactly they will be cannot be predicted, but if those which occur are natural the wrongdoer cannot, I think, escape responsibility for their consequences simply by calling them improbable or unforeseeable."

The different possible approaches to determining which of a number of factual causes is the legal cause of a particular item of damage are well illustrated by the speeches given in the House of Lords in the case of *Singleton Abbey* v. *Paludina*.[34] In that case negligence in the operation of a ship (the *Paludina*) had caused two other ships (the *Singleton Abbey* and the *Sara*) to break their moorings. Both of these vessels were forced to manoeuvre in the confined space of a harbour to avoid further collision. Twenty minutes after the original incident a second collision occurred between the *Singleton Abbey* (which suffered further damage) and the *Sara* (which was holed and sunk). The question for decision was whether the damage suffered in the second collision was attributable to the initial negligence of those operating the *Paludina*. The majority of the House of Lords held that it was not: by the time of the second collision the master of the *Singleton Abbey* had manoeuvred his vessel into a position of relative safety and the second collision was held to have been caused by his then failing to switch his engines off quickly enough when the collision with the *Sara* appeared likely. The negligence of the *Paludina* provided the occasion for the second item of damage to occur but was not the cause of it. In contrast, two judges dissented on the grounds that the master of the *Singleton Abbey* should not be criticised for making what turned out to be a damaging decision in "the agony of the moment." On this reasoning the *Paludina* had placed the other two vessels in a position of extreme difficulty from which they were attempting to extricate themselves and the master of the *Singleton Abbey* could not be criticised for taking what, in retrospect, proved to be a damaging decision in the heat of the moment. The *Paludina's* acts remained an operative cause of the later items of damage. The truth of the matter is that either of these approaches may be the correct analysis on the facts of a particular case and that, in view of the facts of the case, the difference of opinion was not surprising. The actual decision in *Knightley* v. *Johns*[35] followed that of the majority in the *Singelton Abbey* when a police inspector's negligence in failing to close a road tunnel to traffic after an accident had occurred close to the exit and his subsequent attempt to remedy the situation by ordering two of his officers to ride through the tunnel on motorcycles against the flow of the traffic in order to close the entrance, was held to be the legal cause of injuries suffered by one of those officers in a collision with an oncoming car. The inspector's acts were such as to make the officer's injuries too remote a consequence of the negligence which had caused the original accident to be attributable to it.

---

[34] [1927] A.C. 16.
[35] [1982] 1 W.L.R. 349.

It is clearly established that intervening human action does not act automatically to break the chain of causation. In the classic words of Lord Wright in *The Oropesa*,[36] "To break the chain of causation it must be shown that there is something which I will call ultroneous, something unwarrantable, a new cause which disturbs the sequence of events, something which can be described as either unreasonable or extraneous or extrinsic." On the facts of that case the decision of the master of a ship which had been seriously damaged in a collision to go, by lifeboat, to the other vessel to discuss measures to salve his vessel was held to have been reasonable and not to have broken the chain of causation leading from the negligence which had caused the collision. It followed that the original collision was the cause of a death which occurred in the course of the trip between the vessels. From one perspective, the facts of this case are a good illustration of a case in which acts taken to deal with an emergency were treated as a natural response to it.

The results in the *Singleton Abbey* and *Knightley* illustrate the fact that a second example of negligent conduct which increases the consequences which flow from a tort will generally be held either to be unforeseeable or to have broken the chain of causation from the original tort with the result that the first tortfeasor will bear no responsibility for the additional damage inflicted. Medical negligence which occurs in the course of treating a person for injuries suffered as a result of an earlier tort is probably the best example of this. In the leading English case of *Hogan* v. *Bentinck West Hartley Collieries (Owners) Ltd.*,[37] a case which concerned entitlement under the Workmen's Compensation Acts, Lord Normand said that it was:

"axiomatic, that if a surgeon, by lack of skill or failure in reasonable care, causes additional damage or aggravates an existing injury and so renders himself liable in damages, the reasonable conclusion must be that his intervention is a new cause and that the additional injury or the aggravation of the existing injury should be attributed to it and not to the original accident. On the other hand an operation prudently advised and skilfully and carefully carried out should not be treated as a new cause, whatever its consequences may be."

An application of this approach is found in the more modern employers' liability decision of *Robinson* v. *The Post Office*.[38] The discussion in that case assumed that if a doctor's failure to test a patient for a reaction to an anti-tetanus serum could be classified as causally relevant negligence, the chain of causation from the employer's tort which had inflicted the original injury would be broken and the employer would escape liability. The policy basis underpinning this area of law is emphasised by the fact that it seems certain that the results which tort reaches in such cases are very different from those achieved by the criminal law in which responsibility for causing injuries tends to survive negligent medical treatment which damages the victim's condition.

If the second causal factor is an act of negligence by the plaintiff there is a strong possibility that the chain of causation from the original act will be broken. In *McKew* v. *Holland, Hannen Cubitts (Scotland) Ltd.*[39] a man who

[36] [1943] P. 32.
[37] [1949] 1 All E.R. 588.
[38] [1974] 1 W.L.R. 1174.
[39] [1969] 3 All E.R. 1621.

had suffered injuries which occasionally resulted in his left leg giving way beneath him was held to have acted unreasonably when he attempted to descend, in the company of his young daughter and without assistance, a steep flight of stairs which lacked a hand rail. The defendants who were responsible for the injury to his leg escaped liability for additional injuries the plaintiff suffered as a result of this conduct because his acts had been totally unreasonable and, as such, had broken the chain of causation from the original tort. However, the availability of the defence of contributory negligence needs to be taken into account in such situations. It is open to a court in circumstances such as occurred in *McKew* to hold that the plaintiff's unreasonable acts contributed to the second item of damage but were not so bad that they broke the chain of causation leading from the defendant's acts. The difference between the two situations is one of degree. In the latter case the plaintiff's damages will be reduced on account of contributory negligence.[40] A finding that both plaintiff and defendant jointly caused the plaintiff's damage is essential if contributory negligence is to be pleaded successfully.

An important exception to the idea that a second item of negligence will become the effective cause of any subsequent damage is created by cases which hold that a person who creates a situation of danger on the road will not escape liability for the ultimate consequences merely because another road user negligently made matters worse. In *Rouse* v. *Squires*[41] a lorry driver whose negligent driving resulted in two lanes of a motorway being blocked was held partially liable for the death of a person who was killed while assisting at the scene of the accident by another vehicle the driver of which had negligently failed to appreciate the danger. The second negligent driver bore the brunt of the responsibility for the death but the first driver remained jointly responsible. As a matter of common sense a driver cannot assume that all other road users will exercise the appropriate standard of care and will be able to avoid dangers which they have created and may therefore be liable for the ultimate consequences if another's negligence exacerbates a dangerous situation which they have created. However, a dictum of Cairns L.J. in *Rouse* suggests that the result would be different if the second driver's acts could be classified as reckless. This approach was adopted in *Wright* v. *Lodge*.[42] In that case the driver of a car which broke down on an unlit dual carriageway road at night in conditions of fog was held to have been negligent in failing to move the car off the road onto the verge. She was therefore held to have broken the duty of care which she owed to a passenger in the car and to be liable to that passenger for injuries suffered when a lorry collided with the car. However, the lorry driver's act of driving at speeds in excess of the speed limit in conditions of poor visibility were castigated as reckless and injuries caused to other motorists when the crashing lorry crossed the central reservation and overturned were held not to be attributable to the negligence of the car driver. It was said that these injuries were wholly attributable to the excessive speed at which the lorry had been driven.

The chain of causation is unlikely to be broken by the negligent or even intentional act of a third party if the defendant owes a duty of care to guard the plaintiff against the risks created by such acts. Examples of such

[40] See Chap. 5.
[41] [1973] Q.B. 889.
[42] [1993] 4 All E.R. 299.

"supervisory" duties include the professional person's duty to protect the client and others affected by the work against risks created by the work of those being supervised[43] and the duty of prison officers to take reasonable care to ensure that prisoners on a work party do not escape and damage property in the neighbourhood.[44]

Unusual consequences – remoteness of damage
Directness and reasonable foreseeability

When the remoteness of damage approach is used the law makes a distinction according to whether the tortious conduct is based on intentional conduct, negligence or strict liability. The law in this area uses two tests of remoteness of damage. The first test, which is commonly identified with the decision of the Court of Appeal in Re Polemis and Furness, Withy & Co.[45] is that a defendant is liable for all the natural and direct consequences of his tort. Under this test a defendant who commits a breach of a tort duty is liable for all resulting consequences which are within the ambit of the tortious duty. It does not matter that the extent of the damage inflicted or the manner of its infliction could not have been foreseen by the defendant. Neither does it matter that the type of loss was unforeseeable on the facts, the type needs to be recognised only as a form of loss, damages for which are recoverable under that tort. This test is recognised as being favourable to plaintiffs. Once a breach of a tort duty has been recorded it will be difficult for the defendant who is subject to such a duty to avoid liability for the full consequences of his acts. The only real possibility is to resort to causation principles and argue that the loss was inflicted "indirectly"; however, there is little evidence of such an approach being used successfully in a great number of cases.

The natural and direct consequence test no longer applies to negligence as a result of the decision of the Privy Council in Overseas Tankship (U.K.) Ltd. v. Morts Dock & Engineering Co. Ltd., The Wagon Mound (No. 1).[46] The subsequent decision in Wagon Mound (No. 2)[47] went further and stopped it from applying to nuisance and possibly to other forms of strict liability. It is doubtful whether many results of substance followed from this change. The Wagon Mound Cases featured the defendant's ship which negligently allowed bunkering (fuel) oil to spill into the waters of Sydney harbour. The plaintiffs, in the first case, owned a wharf near to where the defendant's vessel was moored and at which they were carrying out welding operations. It was established, as a fact, in this case that it was unforeseeable that this type of oil could be ignited when spread in a thin film on the waters of a harbour because it would not ignite at less than a temperature of approximately 170 degrees centigrade. It was also established that the plaintiffs had suffered damage as the direct result of the spillage from the fact of oil having congealed on their slipway. In fact, the oil did catch fire, probably as a result of waste material floating in it being ignited by sparks from the plaintiff's welding operations, and the plaintiff's property was seriously damaged by

---

[43] The classic example is that of the architect or building inspector employed to supervise the work of a contractor.
[44] Home Office v. Dorset Yacht Co. [1970] A.C. 1004.
[45] [1921] 3 K.B. 560.
[46] [1961] A.C. 388.
[47] [1967] 1 A.C. 617.

fire. Faced by these facts, the Privy Council refused to accept that the fact that some of the damage suffered (the congealing of the oil) was a direct consequence of the defendant's negligence made them liable for the fire damage. The rule derived from *Re Polemis* was roundly rejected as a satisfactory test for remoteness of damage in negligence. It was said not to be consonant with current ideas of justice and morality that a person should be liable for all possibly unforeseeable consequences of negligence so long as those consequences could be said to be direct. Whereas directness, which imposes a harsh regime, leads, in Viscount Simonds' words to "the never ending and insoluble problems of causation" the preferred test of reasonable foreseeability "corresponds with the common conscience of mankind."

This result is one of the major triumphs of the principle of fault liability. On the facts of the *Wagon Mound* the new test narrowed the range of consequences for which the admittedly negligent defendant was held liable. It was possible to view the result as producing an internally consistent body of law: all three stages of the negligence test, duty, breach and damage had been made subject to tests based on the concept of foreseeability.

Although the *Wagon Mound* principle has clearly been accepted by English law the reasoning on which it is based is not unassailable. As a matter of policy it is not immediately apparent why the law should opt for a rule which limits the liability of a defendant who has broken a legally recognised duty at the expense of an innocent victim of this act. If it is an important part of the deterrent role of tort that the costs of accidents should fall on the least cost avoider it is presumably the case that it is the real rather than notional costs which should be placed in the equation. In addition, in efficiency terms the cost of obtaining additional insurance cover against unlikely marginal risks is likely to be cheaper for the person who bears the cost of insuring the standard risks.[48]

It is also arguable that the vagueness of the criterion of reasonable foreseeability coupled with the exceptions to the rule which have been recognised has meant that few, if any, cases have been decided differently as a result of the change. The concept of reasonable foreseeability is difficult to define and any search for internal consistency in the theory underlying negligence is almost certain to be fruitless. Foreseeability is not the sole determinant of liability at any stage of the negligence process. As a test of the existence of a duty of care it has been heavily qualified by notions of policy and proximity and can have little role to play in an era of incremental development of the law. Foreseeability is relevant, but not central, to issues of breach of a negligence duty; of more relevance are questions of the likelihood of the risk, its magnitude, the ease of protecting against it and the advantages of running it. In any event it is by no means certain that foreseeability bears the same meaning in all three contexts. The view has been expressed in Chapter 3 that foreseeability in the context of the standard of care in negligence is the equivalent of the word conceivable. This places a person who is under a duty of care in a position of having to take reasonable care to avoid remote risks. The word may not bear so wide a meaning when it is used to test the existence of a duty of care as notions such as proximity and a special relationship may be used to restrict its meaning.

---

[48] Although in the *Wagon Mound* situation of property damage the result may be different because the plaintiff is likely to have first party insurance against fire and the result may therefore discourage the wasteful practice of double insurance.

In the context of remoteness of damage, to use foreseeability as the equivalent of conceivable may produce results which are wider than would be achieved under *Re Polemis*. The problems that this can create were well illustrated by the difficulties which the Court of Appeal encountered in *Lamb* v. *Camden L.B.C.*[49] In that case the defendant council's negligence had damaged the plaintiff's house which as a consequence was left unoccupied. The house suffered further damage as the result of the acts of squatters who moved into it. The plaintiff attempted to include in her negligence action against the defendant authority, a claim for the damage done by the squatters. This raised a classic example of an issue which has been posed in a series of modern cases: is a person who has been negligent liable for additional losses caused by the fact that third parties acting independently have increased the loss? In *Dorset Yacht Co. Ltd* v. *Home Office*[50] Lord Reid had appeared to lay down the rule that a person would only be liable for the acts of an independent third party when those acts were the "very likely" consequence of the negligence. The dilemma facing the court in *Lamb* was that, whereas Lord Reid's test seemed to bear no relationship to the rules established by the *Wagon Mound*, an unlimited application of the foreseeability test to the acts of independent third parties imposes scarcely any constraint on liability. If foreseeable means conceivable in this context the whole range of malicious and careless conduct of such persons meets the test of remoteness of damage: it is in no way inconceivable that a house left unoccupied in North London will be taken over by squatters. A possible escape from this dilemma is offered by Oliver L.J.'s insistence in his judgment in *Lamb* that the *Wagon Mound* test is that of "reasonable foreseeability" rather than "foreseeability" and that the addition of the word reasonable requires a consequence to be much higher on the scale of probability than foreseeability does when used as a criterion of the standard of care. An alternative approach would be to say that the case would have presented no problem had it been treated as one concerning causation: the acts of the squatters were undoubtedly the real or effective cause of the loss and broke the chain of causation from the council's negligence. In fact, more recent cases on the issue of a person's liability for the malicious acts of an independent third party have chosen to analyse the problem as one of duty of care.[51]

Limitations on the Wagon Mound principle

The final problem with the *Wagon Mound* principle is that it has been made subject to a number of exceptions which mitigate its effect. In *Hughes* v. *Lord Advocate*[52] the House of Lords decided that, although the consequence suffered by the plaintiff must be of a kind which ought to have been foreseen by the defendant, there is no necessity for the precise sequence of events which produced the damage to have been foreseen. In that case Post Office employees had negligently failed to post a nightwatchman to guard an open manhole cover which was covered by a tent and surrounded by paraffin warning lamps. The eight year old plaintiff who entered the tent and knocked

[49] [1981] Q.B. 625.
[50] [1970] A.C. 1004.
[51] *Smith* v. *Littlewoods Organisation Ltd.* [1987] A.C. 241.
[52] [1963] A.C. 837.

one of the lamps into the hole was severely burned when paraffin vapour which escaped from the lamp ignited and exploded. The House took the view that the defendant's negligence had made it foreseeable that the child would be burned and that this had happened, albeit in a fashion and to an extent that was unforeseeable. To demand too high a degree of precision when operating the reasonable foreseeability test would create an unreasonable barrier to the plaintiff succeeding in his action.

The decision in *Hughes* spawned a further restriction on the *Wagon Mound* principle. All that needs to be foreseen if the remoteness of damage test is to be satisfied, is the particular kind of damage which was actually suffered. The fact that the extent of damage suffered was unforeseeable is irrelevant. In *Hughes* the House of Lords refused to accept that the injuries resulting from the explosion of the paraffin vapour were of a different kind from the burns which were a foreseeable consequence of a lamp being knocked over and broken. In subsequent cases this approach has led to an employer being held liable when he could foresee that he had exposed an employee to the risk of injury by cold and the exposure resulted in the employee suffering frostbite, which is exceptionally rare in this country[53] and to another defendant who could foresee that his actions created a risk that the plaintiff would suffer nervous shock being unable to argue success-fully that the plaintiff's exceptionally violent reaction was unforeseeable.[54]

The distinction between the kind and the extent of damage is obviously capable of placing a significant limit on the *Wagon Mound* principle. A tortfeasor is liable to an unlimited extent for all losses caused by his act which are of a foreseeable kind. However, this distinction can only operate satisfac-torily if there is agreement on the kinds of damage which exist. Unfortuna-tely, apart from some dicta to the effect that nervous shock is a different kind of damage to personal injury,[55] the courts have given little indications as to how such questions are to be answered. The case of *Doughty* v. *Turner Manufacturing Co. Ltd.*[56] is an illustration of these difficulties. The plaintiff had been injured at work as the consequence of an asbestos cement cover fitted to a cauldron of hot liquid being negligently knocked into the liquid. An unforeseeable and violent chemical reaction between the cover and the liquid caused the liquid to erupt and the plaintiff was struck and injured. In reliance on *Hughes* the plaintiff argued that it was a reasonably foreseeable consequence of knocking the cover into the liquid that those working close to the cauldron would be splashed by hot liquid and that what had happened amounted to an injury of this kind but of a much greater extent than could have been foreseen. The Court of Appeal preferred the view that the kind of risk, the chemical reaction and resulting eruption of the liquid, was wholly different in kind from the foreseeable risk of splashing and that as it was unforeseeable no damages were recoverable.

A further exception to the *Wagon Mound* is created by the eggshell or thin skull rule which states that a tortfeasor must take his victim as he finds him. If the victim suffers from a peculiar weakness which makes his injuries far worse than could have been envisaged the defendant is liable for the full loss.

[53] *Bradford* v. *Robinson Rentals Ltd.* [1967] 1 W.L.R. 337.
[54] *Brice* v. *Brown* [1984] 1 All E.R. 997.
[55] See Lord Ackner's speech in *Alcock* v. *Chief Constable of the South Yorkshire Police* [1992] 1 A.C. 310.
[56] [1964] 1 Q.B. 518.

It is not open to him to argue that the damage was unforeseeable. This is a fundamental rule of tort which reflects the compensatory aim of the law. It predates the *Wagon Mound* and fits more easily with the "natural and direct" consequences test of remoteness of damage. The rule was challenged in the light of the advent of the reasonable foreseeability test but, given the importance of the rule, it was not surprising that it survived. In *Smith* v. *Leech Brain & Co. Ltd.*[57] the plaintiff's husband suffered a burn at work caused by his employer's negligence. The husband was suffering from a pre-malignant condition which made it likely that he would develop cancer in the future. The burn promoted a cancer which caused his death. His wife succeeded in a Fatal Accidents Act claim in establishing that the employers were liable for the death. Lord Parker C.J. was satisfied that the Privy Council, when deciding the *Wagon Mound* did not intend to question the thin skull rule.

It is possible to argue that the thin skull rule is merely an application of the kind/extent of damage distinction. On this argument plaintiffs with peculiar vulnerabilities recover the whole of their loss because the kind of damage they suffer (personal injuries) is foreseeable; the only thing which is unforeseeable is the extent of their loss. If this is correct, the thin skull rule has no independent existence. This approach is clearly supported by Lord Parker's judgment in *Smith*:

> "The test is not whether these employers could reasonably have foreseen that a burn would cause cancer and that he would die. The question is whether these employers could reasonably foresee the type of injury he suffered, namely the burn. What in the particular case is the amount of the damage which he suffers as a result of that burn depends on the character-istics of the victim."

This approach may well be correct, but it must be realised that it is dependent on the vagaries of the kind/extent distinction. If all personal injuries are to be classified as belonging to the same kind, the approach can be adopted with confidence. However, if that is not the case, there are no advantages in jettisoning a well established and understood rule which offers significant protection to plaintiffs.

There are doubts as to whether the thin skull principle applies beyond the area of personal injuries. These doubts derive from the decision of the House of Lords in *Owners of Dredger Liesbosch* v. *Owners of Steamship Edison.*[58] In that case the plaintiffs, who were engaged on a contract which required the use of a dredger, suffered considerable financial losses when the defendant's negligence caused the dredger to sink. The plaintiffs were, at the time of the accident, in a weak position financially and this weakness delayed the completion of the contract as it meant that they were unable to purchase a suitable alternative immediately. The House of Lords held that any losses which resulted from the plaintiff's weak financial position were too remote a consequence of the original damage to be attributable to it. Financial weakness could not be assimilated to the kinds of physical weakness protected by the thin skull rules.[59]

---

[57] [1962] 2 Q.B. 405.
[58] [1933] A.C. 449.
[59] See Lord Wright, [1933] A.C. 449. 461.

The present authority of the *Liesbosch* decision is, however, a matter of some doubt as it has been distinguished in a number of important modern cases. The leading modern authority of *Dodd Properties (Kent) Ltd.* v. *Canterbury City Council*[60] concerned a claim by the owners of a building that the defendant's pile driving operations on land next to it had resulted in structural damage. The damage was suffered in 1968 but the defendants did not admit their liability until 1978. A dispute remained as to the date by reference to which the cost of the necessary repairs should be assessed. The plaintiff's claim was for £30,327 assessed on the basis of the cost of repairing the property as at the time of the trial, whereas the defendant argued that the reasonable owner would have conducted the repairs in 1970 and that £4,108 was the appropriate figure. The plaintiffs supported their case by arguing that they did not have the means to conduct the repairs in 1970 and that it did not make commercial sense for them to undertake the work during the period in which the defendants were resisting liability. The Court of Appeal accepted the plaintiff's case and awarded damages according to the cost of the work at the date of trial. The central plank of the reasoning was an application of mitigation of damage: in the light of the defendants' resistance of the claim the plaintiff had acted reasonably in delaying the work. The authority of the *Liesbosch* was distinguished on the basis that the financial stringency which led to the postponement of the repairs was not "the cause" of the postponement but merely one factor which helped to render it commercially prudent to postpone the work.[61]

The result of the restrictions which are placed on the *Wagon Mound* principle is that it will rarely place severe limitations on the extent of loss which is to be compensated by a tortfeasor. The aim of ensuring that compensation reaches the victims of accidents is therefore not as seriously prejudiced by the reasonable foreseeability test as appeared to be possible in 1961. This is particularly the case in the area of accident compensation and it is right that this should be so because it is the area in which victims are least likely to carry first party insurance against the risks. In the case of property damage, there is a strong argument in efficiency, if not deterrent, terms in leaving the victim and his insurers to bear the loss.

Torts outside Wagon Mound

Some vestiges of the "natural and direct" consequences test have survived to govern remoteness of damage issues in relation to torts other than negligence. However, the precise rules are difficult to state as much of the relevant authority dates from before 1961. Nonetheless, it seems possible that the remoteness of damage test applied to torts based on intentional conduct and to strict liability torts is that of the "natural and direct" consequences of the tort.

One clearly established example of such a survival is deceit. In *Doyle* v. *Olby (Ironmongers) Ltd.*[62] the Court of Appeal established that a person held liable for a deliberate fraud under the tort of deceit is liable "for all the actual damages directly flowing from the fraudulent inducement." Lord Denning M.R. commented that a person who had committed a deliberate

---

[60] [1980] 1 All E.R. 705.
[61] This approach was followed in *Perry* v. *Sidney Phillips* [1982] 3 All E.R. 705.
[62] [1969] 2 Q.B. 158.

fraud against another should not be allowed to avail himself of the argument that a particular form of loss could not reasonably have been foreseen.

There is some support for the contention that a similar rule applies to battery. A Canadian judge has said that one result of successfully framing a case in battery is that the defendant is liable for all the consequences of his act whether they were foreseeable or not.[63] A similar approach to the effect that a successful claim in battery overrides normal causation principles emerged in a dictum of Bristow J. in *Chatterton* v. *Gerson*.[64] It was said that if a doctor was proved to have committed a battery because a non-disclosure of risks vitiated an apparent consent it would not be relevant to consider the hypothetical reaction of the patient if proper information had been given.

The rules applicable to strict liability torts have been subject to even less investigation. In *The Wagon Mound (No. 1)* the Privy Council expressly denied that its decision was intended to apply to cases decided under the *Rylands* v. *Fletcher* principle. However, more recently, in *Cambridge Water Co. Ltd.* v. *Eastern Counties Leather plc*,[65] the House of Lords held, by analogy to the law of nuisance, that it is a prerequisite of liability under *Rylands* that the type of damage which occurred was reasonably foreseeable to the defendant.

It is not clear which test applies to matters of defamation. In *Slipper* v. *British Broadcasting Corporation*[66] the plaintiff alleged that he had been defamed by a television programme and that press reviews of the programme, which had repeated the allegation, were relevant to the assessment of the damages. The Court of Appeal held that such a case of republication of defamatory matter was no more than an example of the general issue of remoteness of damage and that the issue was to be decided according to whether the damage flowing from republication was to be regarded as a reasonably foreseeable or as a natural and probable consequence of the original publication. The case law on this issue is almost unanimous in using the "natural and probable consequence" test,[67] but all of it predates the decision in *The Wagon Mound (No. 1)*.[68] In the *Slipper* Case Slade L.J. admitted to the difficulty of drawing any distinction between the tests and opted to regard the tests as coterminous.

In practice, remoteness of damage issues do not tend to arise in cases of breach of statutory duty as the definition of the statutory purpose required before a duty is deemed actionable in tort tends to determine the range of losses which can be recovered. Thus, in *Gorris* v. *Scott*[69] a statutory duty imposed by the Contagious Diseases (Animals) Act 1869 to keep animals penned when on board ship was held to be directed to controlling the spread of disease amongst them. When unpenned animals were lost by being swept overboard in a storm the loss was deemed to fall beyond the scope of the duty, rather than being treated as too remote a consequence of the tort.

[63] *Allan* v. *New Mount Sinai Hospital* (1980) 109 D.L.R. (3d) 634.
[64] [1981] Q.B. 432.
[65] [1994] 1 All E.R. 53.
[66] [1991] 1 Q.B. 283.
[67] *Lynch* v. *Knight* (1861) 9 H.L. Cas. 577; *Weld-Blundell* v. *Stephens* [1920] A.C. 956.
[68] [1961] A.C. 388.
[69] (1874) L.R. 9 Ex. 125.

Chapter Five

Defences

A number of defences which are generally available to answer tort claims will be discussed in this chapter. They are contributory negligence; consent; lawful justification; necessity and illegality. Contributory negligence is a partial defence: it reduces the value of, but does not extinguish, the plaintiff's claim. The others provide a tortfeasor with a complete defence. Other specialised defences which are peculiar to particular torts will be discussed in the appropriate context. Two defences, inevitable accident and mistake, to which reference may occasionally be found in the cases will not be discussed in this book as they are effectively redundant.[1]

CONTRIBUTORY NEGLIGENCE

A plaintiff who is a partial cause of the damage which he suffers as a result of another person's tort will be held to be contributorily negligent. In such a case the damages recoverable by the plaintiff will be reduced under the provisions of the Law Reform (Contributory Negligence) Act 1945. Before the 1945 Act was enacted a finding of contributory negligence constituted a total defence to tortious liability. Section 1(1) removes this harsh rule and, in doing so, prevents a court from making a holding of 100 per cent. contributory negligence on the part of the plaintiff which would reduce the award of damage to nil.[2] Section 1(1) of this statute provides that:

> "Where any person suffers damage as the result partly of his own fault and partly of the fault of any other person or persons, a claim in respect of that damage shall not be defeated by reason of the fault of the person suffering the damage, but the damages recoverable in respect thereof shall be reduced to such an extent as the court thinks just and equitable having regard to the claimant's share in the responsibility for the damage."

---

[1] See Winfield & Jolowicz on *Tort* (13th ed.), pp. 701–703 for details.

[2] The concept of 100 per cent. contributory negligence, although creating logical difficulties, has attracted respectable support, see Lord Reid's speech in *Imperial Chemical Industries Ltd.* v. *Shatwell* [1964] 2 All E.R. 999. However, it is now rejected. It cannot stand with the wording of the 1945 Act as such a finding would amount to the claim being "defeated by reason of the fault of the person suffering the damage." *Pitts* v. *Hunt* [1991] 1 Q.B. 24. A finding that the plaintiff was the true cause of his damage remains possible, but may be difficult to achieve in circumstances such as occurred in *Pitts* in which the defendant driver, encouraged by the plaintiff, had been acting in a thoroughly reckless manner.

This is a general defence which applies to most forms of tortious liability because section 4 of the Act gives the word "fault" an exceptionally wide meaning in this context. It is defined as "any negligence, breach of statutory duty or other act or omission which gives rise to liability in tort or would, apart from this Act, give rise to the defence of contributory negligence." It is now established that the defence is available in relation to intentional torts such as assault[3] and to any cause of action based on negligence, including the statutory negligence remedy created by section 2(1) of the Misrepresentation Act 1967.[4] If the claim can be framed as one of negligence it is open to the defendant to plead the defence even though the plaintiff might wish to invoke concurrent liability and bring the claim in contract.[5] The only important areas of tortious liability to which the defence does not apply are the torts of deceit, conversion and intentional interference with goods.[6] In practice, it is likely to be the case that the defence will only operate in exceptional cases of negligent misstatement; it is well recognised that a defendant will face almost insurmountable difficulties if he wishes to allege that the plaintiff failed to take reasonable care of his interests by choosing to believe what the defendant told him.[7]

Contributory negligence requires the defendant to prove on the balance of probabilities that the plaintiff failed to take reasonable care of his own safety. In the great majority of cases this is a simple question of fact. Atiyah has commented that "there is little 'law' left in contributory negligence cases today."[8] However, occasionally it may be necessary to ask whether a neglected precaution was designed to protect the plaintiff against the particular form of damage which he suffered. The case of *Jones* v. *Livox Quarries Ltd.*[9] suggests that courts will not be too ready to allow the defence to be defeated by fine distinctions as to the likely form of damage. In that case the plaintiff employee had disobeyed instructions issued by his employer by riding on the towbar of a vehicle. It was argued on his behalf that the instructions were directed against the danger of injuries being caused to an employee by his falling from the vehicle, whereas he had actually suffered injury when a following vehicle, as a result of its driver's negligence, ran into the back of the one on which he was travelling. The Court of Appeal held that the plaintiff's conduct showed that he had contributed one of the causes of the injury by riding on the vehicle in a dangerous position. He had failed to show a proper regard for his own safety and his damages should be reduced. The damages would not have been reduced if the accident which had occurred had been wholly unconnected in terms of causation with the kind of risks against which the precaution was directed. Denning L.J. gave as an example injuries inflicted on the plaintiff by the negligent firing of guns by huntsmen while he was riding on the vehicle: in such a case the plaintiff's conduct would have amounted to an essential condition of the harm but would not have been a cause of it.

---

[3] *Murphy* v. *Culhane* [1976] 3 All E.R. 533.
[4] *Gran Gelato Ltd.* v. *Richcliff (Group) Ltd.* [1992] 1 All E.R. 865.
[5] *Forsikringsaktieselskapet Vesta* v. *Butcher* [1989] A.C. 852.
[6] Torts (Interference with Goods) Act 1977, s. 11(1). This provision is subject to an exception created by the Banking Act 1979, s. 47.
[7] *Gran Gelato Ltd.* v. *Richcliff (Group) Ltd.* [1992] 1 All E.R. 865.
[8] Atiyah, *Accidents, Compensation and the Law* (4th ed.), p. 119.
[9] [1952] 2 Q.B. 608.

The standard of care

The standard of care applied to contributory negligence is an objective one. An individual's personal view that a safety precaution is unnecessary or positively harmful will be discounted if the court finds that a reasonable person would use it. The Court of Appeal's decision in *Froom* v. *Butcher*[10] is regarded as establishing this result. The court in that case, which concerned an injured person's failure to wear a seat belt in a car, held that the reasonable driver makes use of the seat-belts fitted to his car, even though at the time of the decision there was no legal obligation to wear a belt and a wide variety of views were held as to the advisability of doing so. The failure was therefore held to amount to contributory negligence in spite of the plaintiff's argument that he had merely been following a school of thought accepted at that time and should not be criticised just because others thought differently. A possible explanation of the decision is that the court simply held, as a matter of fact, that no reasonable person could hold the view that failing to wear a seat-belt was a reasonable thing to do in 1975. However, the case is usually regarded as having the wider significance that the court held that the standard of care in contributory negligence is an objective one which pays no attention to the views or abilities of the plaintiff.

This objective approach to the defence should not be taken too far. The stringent interpretation placed on the concept of negligence in order to ensure that liability is established is not always appropriate in relation to defences. For example, the courts have not allowed contributory negligence to be used to reduce a defendant's liability as a result of a hypercritical evaluation of the injured person's conduct. It may be possible, with the benefit of hindsight, to show that the reactions of a plaintiff when confronted by a situation of danger (in the "agony of the moment") actually increased his loss, but a defendant who put the plaintiff in a position in which he made, what proved to be, the wrong decision cannot be allowed to criticise reasonable reactions to the danger. Courts have similarly been wary of arguments that a child should be held to be contributorily negligent and have applied a test which asks what dangers a child of the particular age[11] could be expected to appreciate.[12] In *Yachuk* v. *Oliver Blais & Co. Ltd.*[13] it was held that a person who had sold petrol to a child of nine could not plead that the child was contributorily negligent when he was injured while using the petrol to make a burning torch for the purposes of a game.

The result in *Yachuk* may turn on the nature of the duty imposed on the defendant rather than on whether the defence has subjective characteristics. Duties owed to children are an illustration of the principle that the standard of conduct owed by a defendant is often assessed according to the subjective characteristics of the person to whom it is owed. A further example is that an

10 [1976] Q.B. 286.
11 This test is therefore a variable form of objective test rather than a subjective one. The child is not tested according to its own ability to appreciate the danger.
12 The Pearson Commission (para. 1077) recommended that the defence should cease to be available in respect of injuries caused in road accidents to children under the age of 12. It is not at all clear why this particular category of injuries should be accorded special treatment. The recommendation has not been enacted. In *Armstrong* v. *Cottrell* [1993] P.I.Q.R. P109 the Court of Appeal held that a child of 12 should lose a third of her compensation for injuries which she suffered in a collision with a car whilst attempting to cross a busy main road on the grounds that someone of her age ought to be familiar with the basics of the Highway Code.
13 [1949] A.C. 386.

employer will be obliged to take additional precautions to safeguard an employee whose characteristics[14] or inexperience makes him an identified risk. In such cases, it cannot be correct to assess the degree of that employee's contribution to his damage by the standard of care to be expected of a hypothetical reasonable employee. On the other hand, if the defendant cannot foresee the peculiar risks presented by the plaintiff he may well be held not to have been negligent and not to require any defence.

Contributory negligence is available in cases of industrial injuries, but the balancing of responsibility between employer and employee has been influenced by the fact that it is the employer's responsibility to provide proper safety equipment; to instruct that it is used and to guard against employees becoming casual in the face of risks. This policy would be defeated if injuries caused by the employee's inattention justified a finding of contributory negligence. This is particularly the case when an employer is held to have been in breach of a strict statutory safety duty. In *Staveley Iron and Chemical Co. Ltd.* v. *Jones*[15] Lord Tucker summarised the position as being that in "Factory Act cases the purpose of imposing the absolute[16] obligation is to protect the workman against those very acts of inattention which are sometimes relied upon as constituting contributory negligence so that too strict a standard would defeat the object of the statute." In addition, there is support in the cases for the proposition that a person does not act unreasonably by assuming that others have fulfilled statutory duties imposed upon them.[17] This is in strong contrast to the accepted proposition that motorists should be prepared for other road users to be negligent. It does not follow from these propositions that the defence is unavailable in cases of industrial injuries, indeed the wording of section 4 of the 1945 Act insists that it is. What it does mean is that the results achieved in these cases can be very difficult to predict because the courts are faced with the task of comparing, as an issue of fact, items which are not truly capable of comparison against a background of the conflicting policies as to how the burden of accident prevention should be borne between the parties.

Accident and damage

A plaintiff's unreasonable conduct may either be a partial cause of an accident or, although it does not help to cause the accident, increase the consequences of an accident caused wholly by the negligence of another. This is particularly important with regard to failures to use safety equipment. A motorist who fails to use a seat-belt may drive with all reasonable care and only be involved in an accident because of the fault of another. However, if the failure to wear the belt increased the injuries suffered a reduction in the injured party's damages will be made on account of contributory negligence. This was established in *Froom* v. *Butcher*.[18] The reasonable road user is taken to know that there is a risk that other people will cause a road accident. Lord Denning in *Froom* summarised the position in the following terms:

---

[14] *Paris* v. *Stepney B.C.* [1951] A.C. 367.
[15] [1956] A.C. 627.
[16] This is a loose use of the word, "strict" would be more accurate.
[17] *Grant* v. *Sun Shipping Co. Ltd.* [1948] A.C. 549; *Westwood* v. *Post Office* [1974] A.C. 1.
[18] [1976] Q.B. 286.

"The question is not what was the cause of the accident. It is rather what was the cause of the damage . . . in seat belt cases the cause of the accident is one thing. The cause of the damage is another. The accident is caused by the bad driving. The damage is caused in part by the bad driving of the defendant, and in part by the failure of the plaintiff to wear a seat belt."

The apportionment

The reduction in damages made on account of contributory negligence is a question of fact which is left to the discretion of the courts. A full range of reductions from 1 per cent. to 99 per cent. is available.[19] Two issues are considered; the causal effect of the plaintiff's act and the blameworthiness which can be attributed to him. A child's conduct may be identical to that of an adult in contributing to the accident but its blameworthiness is likely to be much less, if not non-existent. Results will vary according to the court's assessment of the plaintiff's conduct in contrast to that of the defendant. In practice, the variables can create a great deal of unpredictability. If, for example, a driver and passenger have been jointly engaged in heavy drinking before setting out on a journey in which the driver's negligence causes injury to the passenger, is the joint nature of the risk taken such that damages should be apportioned on a 50/50 basis or should the driver bear the brunt of the responsibility on the basis that the act of driving under the influence of drink was far more reprehensible than the act of the passenger? Both results are recorded in the cases.[20]

In "seat-belt"[21] cases the Court of Appeal's decision in Froom v. Butcher[22] removed the possibility of many road accidents leading to a problematic, detailed consideration of the comparative conduct and blameworthiness of the parties by imposing a result which it regarded as likely to be "just and equitable" in the great majority of cases. Under this 25 per cent. of damages is deducted if wearing the belt would have protected the plaintiff from all harm and 15 per cent. if it would have provided partial protection. This must have simplified the proceedings in many cases, but is open to the objection that it may require a detailed inquiry as to the cause of the injury and that it can

---

[19] There is no rule that a reduction of less that 10 per cent. should be ignored, although very minor fault might be disregarded as de minimis. Capps v. Miller [1989] 1 W.L.R. 839. A finding of 100 per cent. contributory negligence is a logical impossibility and is banned by the wording of the 1945 Act. See note 2, above.

[20] In Pitts v. Hunt [1991] 1 Q.B. 24, Dillon L.J. would have reduced the plaintiff's damages by 50 per cent. on the basis that the parties were equally to blame. In Owens v. Brimmell [1977] Q.B. 859 a 20 per cent. reduction was applied. In Morris v. Murray [1991] 2 Q.B. 6 the Court of Appeal, obiter, criticised a 20 per cent. apportionment in the case of an injured passenger who had embarked on a pleasure trip in a light aircraft piloted by a person who had drunk 17 whiskies, the court favoured a 50 per cent. reduction in these circumstances. In Stinton v. Stinton [1993] P.I.Q.R. P135 Simon Brown J. regarded Pitts as a "very special case" on account of the passenger having actively encouraged the dangerous driving. In a case of the "greatest blameworthiness," short of actual participation, he made a reduction of one third in the plaintiff's damages. For another "very special case" see Donelan v. Donelan [1993] P.I.Q.R. P205. See also Stapley v. Gypsum Mines Ltd. [1953] 2 All E.R. 478 for an example of the same problem in the industrial safety context.

[21] The guidelines probably also apply to a failure to wear a crash helmet on a motor cycle. However, the Court of Appeal in Capps v. Miller [1989] 1 W.L.R. 839 was prepared to apply a lesser reduction (10 per cent. instead of 15 per cent.) to the case of a moped rider who was wearing an unfastened helmet contrary to the law.

[22] [1976] Q.B. 286.

produce anomalous results. Both features were evident in *Owens* v. *Brim-mell*[23] in which the plaintiff who had been seriously injured in a road accident lost 20 per cent. of his damages either because he knew that the defendant driver of the car in which he was travelling had been drinking heavily or because knowing that he was going to be driven he accompanied the driver in a bout of drinking which deprived him of the capacity to appreciate the danger. His damages would have been subject to the greater reduction of 25 per cent. if it could have been shown that his failure to wear a seat-belt was a cause of the damage. The guidelines required the court in *Owens* to undertake a detailed inquiry into the possible ways in which the plaintiff's head injuries might have been inflicted when the car struck a lamp post. No answer emerged from the evidence and, given this uncertainty, the defendant was held to have failed to establish his defence that wearing the belt would have made a difference to the injuries suffered by the plaintiff. A lesser 20 per cent. deduction applied, not because travelling in a car driven by someone who has been drinking heavily is less culpable than failing to wear a seat-belt, but as a result of a comparative assessment of the responsibilities of the drunken driver and his passenger. In this case the passenger and driver were not regarded as equally to blame as a result of joint participation in heavy drinking prior to making the journey. The driver of the car was held to bear the brunt of the responsibility for any accident caused. It is this process of assessing the comparative fault of plaintiff and defendant which is prevented from being used in seat-belt cases by the guidelines.

An assessment

There is a superficial logic in the idea that a person who has contributed to cause the damage for which compensation is being sought should be met by a defence. Defences based on such logic are a familiar feature of all legal systems and are used by social security legislation.[24] They do, however, create difficulties. A common justification for the defence is that of accident prevention. This reflects the assertion of the deterrent approach to tort that accidents should be regarded as caused by the conflicting activities of victim and tortfeasor and that their prevention is a joint responsibility. It is said that if people could obtain compensation from those who injure them irrespective of their own conduct there would be no incentive for them to make use of safety equipment and the number and severity of accidents would rise. The difficulty with this argument is that the available evidence suggests that, as most people are unaware of the role of the defence, it cannot be expected to influence their conduct. The majority of drivers and passengers in cars did not wear seat belts until a failure to do so was made a criminal offence. This happened more than six years after *Froom* v. *Butcher*[25] had held such a failure to amount to contributory negligence. If drivers did not use a safety precaution to guard against the clearly appreciated risk of their suffering

---

[23] [1977] Q.B. 851.

[24] Note, however, that the Lord Chancellor's Department's proposal for a no-fault compensation scheme for road accident victims (*Compensation for Road Accidents: A Consultation Paper* (1991)) would not permit a reduction of compensation on the basis of contributory negligence. See paras. 4.87–88. However, it has been suggested that injuries following from certain driving offences and intentionally self-inflicted injuries should be excluded from the scheme.

[25] [1976] Q.B. 286.

personal injuries they are hardly likely to be influenced by the remote and barely understood possibility that any damages which might be awarded to them in several years time on account of injuries inflicted on them by another person will be reduced.

A second problem is that the effect of contributory negligence differs from that of a finding of negligence. A finding of liability rarely imposes a direct loss on a defendant because his insurance company will meet the damages; such a finding therefore achieves one of the aims of tort, that of spreading the financial consequences of an accident widely into society. In contrast, contributory negligence denies a plaintiff[26] a percentage of the money which the rules on damages deem to be needed to cope with the injury which has been suffered. As this reduction is uninsurable, certain financial consequences of the accident are left to rest with the victim. Contributory negligence provides the only example of a situation in which the quantum of compensation received actually varies according to the degree of fault of the parties. It is wholly at variance with the compensatory aim of tort.

In addition, there can be no doubt that the existence of contributory negligence gives insurance companies a powerful weapon with which to pressure a plaintiff into settling a claim for a low sum. One survey of solicitors found that contributory negligence had been taken into account in almost half of the settlements covered.[27] This feature of the defence is exacerbated by the fact that the percentage reduction, depending, as it does, on the court's assessment of the conduct of the plaintiff and defendant compared, may be very difficult to predict.[28] Given the unequal bargaining position of the plaintiff in relation to the defendant's insurance company such uncertainty is very likely to reduce the figure at which the plaintiff is prepared to settle his claim.

A final difficulty stems from the doctrine of relative fault. The percentage deduction in the damages is made by comparing the plaintiff's conduct with that of the defendant. A plaintiff's negligent driving might merit a 50 per cent. deduction if he was injured by a momentary act of negligence on the part of another driver but only a 20 per cent. deduction if the other was a reckless drunk. An individual injured by the combined acts of himself and a number of others will be likely to bear a lesser proportion of the responsibility than if only one other defendant was involved. In *Fitzgerald* v. *Lane*[29] the House of Lords rejected a contention that the plaintiff's contribution should be tested against that of each defendant. The rules can be particularly bizarre when combined with vicarious liability. If two workmen's combined acts cause them injury there is a possibility that both can sue their employer as vicariously liable for the other's acts subject only to a deduction for their personal fault.

In spite of these criticisms the defence is deeply embedded in English law. The criticisms levelled at it centre on its role in personal injury litigation, as

---

[26] The defence extends to claims brought by the estate of a deceased person under the Law Reform (Miscellaneous Provisions) Act 1934 and to those brought by the dependants of a deceased under the Fatal Accidents Act 1976.

[27] Harris, *Compensation and Support for Illness and Injury* (1984), p. 91.

[28] Given the 20 per cent. reduction applied in *Owens* v. *Brimmell* it would have been difficult to predict that the judge in *Pitts* v. *Hunt* [1989] 3 W.L.R. 795 would have favoured a 100 per cent. reduction. The facts of the cases may not have been identical, but they were not that different. See *ante* note 20 for further examples.

[29] [1989] A.C. 328.

opposed to claims for property damage. It is an interesting comment on the competing interests in the personal injury sphere that Professor Atiyah, who is one of the most vocal critics of the defence, has ceased to argue for its abolition. He now takes the view that abolition would accentuate the anomaly that only a small percentage of accident victims recover any damages in tort in so far as it would provide those persons with increased benefits.[30] These are the arguments of someone who can see no purpose in the continued existence of the tort system. If, as seems likely, it is going to survive for the foreseeable future it is a matter of opinion whether it is preferable to accomplish reforms which would improve a system which is fundamentally defective or to allow the faults to survive in the hope that they will hasten the system's demise.

DEFENCES BASED ON CONSENT

Consent, or, as it is sometimes known, assumption of risk, provides a complete defence to a tort action rather than an apportionment of damages. A variety of different forms of the consent defence which have different characteristics are recognised by the law of tort. Indeed, it may be better to say that the law recognises a number of different defences all founded on the common basis of consent. A defence of consent may result from an express agreement to run a risk or be implied from the plaintiff's conduct.

Implied consent: *volenti non fit injuria*

The implied consent defence is commonly referred to by the Latin name of *volenti non fit injuria*. The reasoning underlying this species of the defence of consent is that the plaintiff's actions showed such a lack of care that an agreement must be inferred that the tortfeasor should be relieved from the consequences of his conduct. As contributory negligence is likely to be available, as an alternative, to provide the less drastic result of a reduction of the damages to be awarded to the plaintiff, it is not surprising that a heavy burden must be satisfied before the defence is proved. In order to establish this defence it must be shown that the plaintiff, who had freedom of choice in the matter and knowledge (*sciens*) of the risk, consented (was *volens*) to run the risk of the tort.

1. Knowledge

In order to establish the defence it must be proved that the plaintiff knew of the risk which was being run. A person cannot consent to risks which there was no reason to anticipate. This knowledge requirement can restrict the operation of the defence in cases of negligence because a plaintiff may have had no prior knowledge of the risks created by the defendant's negligent conduct before suffering damage. A classic example of this is provided by the facts of *Slater* v. *Clay Cross Co. Ltd.*[31] in which the plaintiff was injured by a train whilst using a railway tunnel in a quarry as a short cut. The court held that the plaintiff, by entering the tunnel, had accepted the risk of injury from the normal running of trains, but not from those which were driven

---

[30] Atiyah *op. cit.* p. 125.
[31] [1956] 2 Q.B. 264.

negligently. On the facts, the defence of consent was not established because it was held that the driver had acted negligently by failing to slow down and to signal a warning that he was entering the tunnel which he knew to be used by members of the public.

A point which was raised, but not decided, in *Morris* v. *Murray*[32] is whether a plaintiff can defeat a defence of *volenti* by showing that the fact that he was drunk at the time precluded his having the requisite knowledge of the risks which were created by the defendant's conduct. The most likely result is that the courts will not permit self-induced intoxication to defeat the defence. In *Morris*, Stocker L.J. commented that it would be paradoxical if a sober person who had gone on a pleasure flight in a light aircraft piloted by someone who had been drinking heavily would be held *volens* whereas someone who had become drunk as a result of accompanying the pilot in the drinking would not.[33]

2. Consent

Knowledge of the risk is therefore an essential condition for the defence to be established, but it is not a sufficient condition. For example, the leading case of *Smith* v. *Baker & Sons*[34] establishes that an employee's consent to a risk cannot be inferred from the simple fact of his continuing to work knowing that the employment creates a risk of his suffering injury. The additional requirement which must be shown is that the consent to assume the risk was freely given. Consent, here, does not mean that the plaintiff knowingly put himself in a position of danger. It must be established that the plaintiff willingly consented to exempt the prospective defendant from any legal liability. A person may have decided to run the risk involved in crossing a busy city road, but it does not follow that he has agreed to exempt from liability any motorist who negligently injures him whilst he is doing this. This is the distinction between running a physical risk and assuming the legal risk. A clear example of a refusal to waive rights is provided by *Nettleship* v. *Weston*.[35] The amateur driving instructor who knew of his pupil's inexperience could not be held *volenti* to injuries caused by this inexperience as his conduct of checking that the car's insurance extended to passengers proved that he clearly intended to retain his rights. Although the evidence will rarely be this explicit, the result will commonly be the same. A person who travels as a passenger in a car with knowledge that the driver is inexperienced or has been drinking alcohol is taking a risk, and, if injured, is liable to be met by the defence of contributory negligence, but the leading cases show that such a person will not necessarily be found to have consented to exempt the driver from all liability. In *Dann* v. *Hamilton*[36] a passenger was held not to be *volenti* merely because she chose to continue on a journey with a driver whom she knew to have been drinking alcohol. Her conduct may have been unwise and might allow contributory negligence to be pleaded against her, but it was insufficient to establish her agreement to waive all rights which she might have against the driver. However, extreme facts may produce the opposite result. *Volenti* barred a claim in *Morris* v. *Murray*[37] in which the

---

[32] [1991] 2 Q.B. 6.
[33] On the facts the passenger was held to have been able to appreciate the risks.
[34] [1891] A.C. 325.
[35] [1971] Q.B. 691.
[36] [1939] 1 K.B. 509.
[37] [1991] 2 Q.B. 6.

plaintiff and defendant, both of whom had been drinking heavily, embarked on a pleasure flight in a light aircraft piloted by the defendant. The pilot was killed and the passenger injured when the plane crashed. An autopsy showed that the pilot had consumed the equivalent of 17 measures of whisky. A claim brought by the passenger against the pilot's estate was blocked by *volenti*. *Dann* was distinguished, on its facts, as a case of an ordinary social outing in which the driver was sober at the outset. The facts of this case were said to be of a wild and irresponsible joint venture, fraught with danger, on which the passenger had willingly embarked.

3. Freedom of choice

A further rule which limits the application of the defence is that a valid consent can only be given if the plaintiff had complete freedom of choice in the matter. This effectively prevents the defence of consent from having any role in industrial injury cases. The pressures on an employee to obey the employer's orders in order to earn a living remove any freedom of choice as to whether to run risks created by the job.[38]

4. An assessment

It is not completely clear what role the defence has to play in modern law. Being based on the plaintiff's conduct, it has a similar rationale to contributory negligence. That defence, although not a total one, has the capacity to provide a far more accurate assessment of the responsibilities of the parties. The defences can operate in parallel, although *volenti* is far more difficult to prove. It is arguable that, in view of the overlap between the defences and doctrines of causation, and given the fact that *volenti* does not apply in motoring and industrial cases, the law would scarcely suffer from its disappearance. However, the contrary argument is that it expresses a fundamental principle that consent should remove liability and that, in practice, it can provide a useful technique for denying liability in cases of exceptional misconduct, particularly those in which the defendant's acts were so culpable that they demanded a relatively low reduction in the damages awarded to the plaintiff. This role of the defence is well illustrated by the decision of the House of Lords in *Imperial Chemical Industries Ltd.* v. *Shatwell*.[39] In that case the plaintiffs were two brothers who were employed by the defendant as shotfirers in a quarry. Part of their work involved the testing of the electrical circuits which connected the detonators and the charges. Because a risk of premature detonation existed, they had been instructed by their employers to take cover when conducting such tests. A statutory duty existed which made it an offence on the part of the shotfirers to test without taking cover and the plaintiffs knew that the employer had taken disciplinary action against a fellow employee who had conducted a test in the open. Nonetheless, the two plaintiffs conducted a test without taking cover and were both injured. They both brought negligence proceedings against their employer arguing that the company was vicariously liable for the other's negligence and that their joint blame for the accident merited no more than a reduction in the damages to be awarded on the grounds of contributory negligence. The court used *volenti* as the method of escaping from this unattractive result. This was a case of a deliberate joint decision to disobey an order of which the employees were

---

[38] *Smith* v. *Baker & Sons* [1891] A.C. 325.
[39] [1964] 2 All E.R. 999.

fully aware. They were *volens* in the fullest sense of the term; the imposition of the statutory duty on the employee, rather than the employer, served to distinguish the case from a normal case concerning industrial injuries in which *volenti* is allowed no role. In effect, *volenti* operated to override the 50 per cent. apportionment which contributory negligence might have produced when two people combine to injure themselves. If I blow myself up by my own negligence I get no compensation. The result is the same if I blow myself up in the course of my employment. If I combine with another person, in the course of our employment, to act negligently and I get blown up as a result, contributory negligence might allow me to recover from our employer, subject to a deduction. But, *volenti* operates to avoid this result.

Even Parliament seems to have been unable to decide whether the defence has a useful role to play. It encouraged its survival by making a number of statutory torts (for example, those arising under the Animals Act 1971 and the Occupiers' Liability Acts 1957 and 1984) subject to it but banned its use in the case of motoring accidents.[40]

In a number of contexts the term *volenti* has been used loosely to justify non-recovery of damages. For example, spectators at or competitors in sporting events are said to have consented to the risk of injury created by conduct within the rules of the game.[41] The better view is that this approach is misconceived[42]: no defence is needed in such cases as the conduct in issue is not tortious. The cricketer who hits the ball into the crowd of spectators causing injury is not negligent. He is merely indulging in conduct which is within the rules of the game and which creates an acceptable risk of injury to others. In many situations nothing will turn on whether such a claim is rejected on grounds of consent or no tort, but this is not always the case. If, for instance, the cricket ball was to cause injury to a young child brought to the match by its parents it is difficult to see how the child could be held to be *volenti* as it would lack the required knowledge of the risk and the capacity to consent to it. Yet it surely cannot be the case that the cricket player must pay compensation to children, but not adults, in the crowd injured by his best shots. The correct result is that he is liable to none of these people because no tort has been committed.

Consent to intentional torts

Consent has a role to play as a defence to intentional torts, in particular trespass to the person. What amounts to a valid consent is not altogether clear. It is, for example, a well recognised rule of criminal law that a person's consent provides no defence in criminal law to a charge of assault.[43] However, it is quite likely that the result would be otherwise in a tort claim, as fundamentally different policies are involved. A person who was injured by a criminal assault which was consented to should surely have any damages claim in relation to the injuries blocked by a defence of consent, if not by illegality, even though the person who committed the assault should not escape criminal conviction for the act.

[40] Road Traffic Act 1988, s.149. This interpretation of the provision was confirmed by the Court of Appeal in *Pitts* v. *Hunt* [1991] 1 Q.B. 24.

[41] See also *Marshall* v. *Osmond* [1983] Q.B. 1034. (police pursuit of a suspected criminal).

[42] *Wooldridge* v. *Sumner* [1962] 2 All E.R. 978; *Wilks* v. *The Cheltenham Home Guard Motor Cycle & Light Car Club* [1971] 2 All E.R. 369.

[43] *R.* v. *Donovan* [1934] 2 K.B. 498; *R.* v. *Brown* [1993] 2 W.L.R. 556.

Consent renders lawful, medical procedures and those contacts incurred in legitimate sports, such as boxing or rugby, in which intentional physical contact is within the rules of the game. In such cases the consent will be limited, in the medical case to the procedures agreed to, and in the sporting context, to injuries incurred within the rules of the game. The consent will not extend to damage caused by negligence which occurs during such activities and it is difficult to envisage a court supporting the view favoured by some commentators that sportsmen consent to a certain amount of intentional foul play.

A number of specialised rules have been developed in relation to medical treatment to deal with the problems which can be created by the need to obtain a valid consent. In the context of medical practice consent as a defence to the tort of battery differs from normal *volenti* in as much as full disclosure of all risks created by a medical procedure is not required. In order to avoid liability for trespass a doctor needs only to disclose to a patient in broad terms the general nature of the treatment which is being proposed.[44] Non-disclosure of the general nature of a proposed medical procedure will therefore be necessary in order to vitiate an apparent consent. A doctor cannot be liable in trespass if the patient has freely[45] and validly consented to treatment so long as no deviation from the procedure consented to occurs.[46] If the more stringent rule used in negligence were to be applied to this tort, doctors would be strictly liable for all adverse consequences of medical treatment unless they could show that they had disclosed all the risks created by the treatment, however remote they might be. The question of whether an appropriate degree of disclosure of the risks entailed by medical treatment has been made to a patient is tested according to accepted medical practice by the tort of negligence.[47]

Consents to major medical treatment are usually made by the patient signing a consent form, but it is clear that a consent may be implied from conduct and that such consents undoubtedly legitimate a great number of minor medical procedures.

Consent is generally regarded as being implied in an emergency situation in which it is impossible to obtain the patient's express consent before providing treatment; however, it may now be preferable to regard the legality of providing treatment in such circumstances as resting on necessity rather than a fictitious consent.[48] Special rules exist concerning the giving of consent on behalf of children and persons who are incapacitated. The general rule is that the right of consent is vested in the person who is to receive the treatment, a rule which was strictly applied in *Paton* v. *British Pregnancy Advisory Service Trustees*[49] to refuse a husband an injunction designed to prevent his wife from lawfully aborting their child.

Parents or guardians are regarded as having the right to give a valid consent on behalf of their children.[50] However, the decision of the House of

---

[44] *Chatterton* v. *Gerson* [1981] Q.B. 432.
[45] See Dugdale & Stanton, *Professional Negligence*, para. 11.69.
[46] *Allan* v. *New Mount Sinai Hospital* (1980) 109 D.L.R. (3d) 634; *Nash* v. *Sheen* [1953] C.L.Y. 3726.
[47] See p. 191.
[48] *F.* v. *West Berkshire Health Authority* [1990] 2 A.C. 1, see *post*, p. 122.
[49] [1979] Q.B. 276.
[50] Dicta of Lords Reid and Hodson in *S.* v. *McC.* [1972] A.C. 24 suggest that a parent has a right to insist that his young child submits to medical treatment.

Lords in *Gillick* v. *West Norfolk and Wisbech Area Health Authority*[51] establishes that an infant can give its own valid consent to medical treatment if it is of such an age and intelligence as to be fully capable of understanding the proposed procedure. Subsection 8(1) of the Family Law Reform Act 1969 avoids some of the evidential problems which might be raised by the *Gillick* decision by providing that a person of the age of 16 or more has a right to give a valid consent on his or her own initiative. The right of a child to give its own consent in such circumstances must inevitably entail the right to decline treatment which the parent wishes it to have.

The provision of medical treatment to the great majority of patients who suffer from mental illness is governed by the normal rules of consent. Part IV of the Mental Health Act 1983 makes specialised provision in relation to mental health treatment.[52] It does not, however, make provision for the giving of consent in relation to many forms of treatment on behalf of patients who lack the capacity to consent. It has fallen to the courts to find a justification for such treatment by use of the defence of necessity.[53]

Express consent

Express consent provides a defence to a number of torts, including nuisance, defamation and the tort based on the authority of *Rylands* v. *Fletcher*.[54] A plaintiff's agreement to be subject to the disciplinary rules of an association may provide that association with a defence to a charge of libel relating to the findings of its disciplinary tribunal.[55]

Exclusion clauses and notices

A second form of defence based on express consent is the exclusion clause or notice. It is somewhat fictitious to regard such a defence as based on the plaintiff's express consent to waive rights. In most situations in which an exclusion clause is used it is the defendant's idea to draft and use the clause in order to remove rights which the plaintiff might otherwise have. However, the best theoretical justification for the efficacy of exclusion clauses is that the plaintiff consented to become subject to the clause.

The great majority of exclusion clauses which purport to remove rights in tort derive their force from incorporation in a contract. It is perfectly normal for clauses which derive their efficacy from a contract to seek to remove or limit liability in tort. The judicial methods of interpreting such clauses and their statutory regulation are discussed in detail in the standard works on the law of contract.[56] The discussion in this chapter is confined to the small number of clauses which operate outside of contract. The great majority of these are notices erected on land and disclaimers of liability in respect of negligent misstatements. A point which must be appreciated is that notices may be drafted to perform a variety of different functions. Some will purport to exclude liability or to deny the existence of a duty of care. Others may

---

[51] [1986] A.C. 112.
[52] See generally Hoggett, *Mental Health Law*, Chap. 6.
[53] See *post*, p. 122.
[54] (1868) L.R 3 H.L. 330 See *post*, pp. 244–245 and Chap. 21.
[55] Chap. 24.
[56] Treitel, *Law of Contract* (8th ed.), pp. 197–244; Cheshire, Fifoot and Furmston's *Law of Contract* (12th ed.), pp. 155–198.

merely warn of risks, in which case they will not provide a complete defence but may mean that the defendant's duty has been discharged or, if less effective, give grounds for a plea of contributory negligence. Other possibilities are that the notice simply ensures that a person who enters the property is classified as a trespasser and is thus subject to a less favourable level of protection or that the authority of an employee to do particular kinds of work or to make representations is restricted and the employer's vicarious liability for such acts removed.

The efficacy of exclusion clauses which are not based on a contract has been the subject of considerable debate. The leading modern case is *Ashdown* v. *Samuel Williams & Sons*.[57] The plaintiff in that case had been injured when struck by a railway truck which was being shunted on the defendant's property. At the time the plaintiff was using a recognised short cut across the property to get to her place of work. A notice, which was visible to persons using the short cut, was to the effect that the property was private and that persons using it would have no claim against the defendant for injury or damage caused to them. The plaintiff admitted that she had read the first few lines of the notice in the past and had had the opportunity to read it all. The Court of Appeal held that the notice was effective to exclude the plaintiff's rights because the terms of the notice had become a condition of the plaintiff's permission to enter the property. The defendants had done sufficient to bring the terms of the notice home to the plaintiff. This result attracted severe criticism[58] on the grounds that it allowed a defendant, on his own initiative, to reduce the duties which he owes to a lawful visitor to less than those which are owed to trespassers.[59] The reasoning in *Ashdown* survived a severe attack from Lord Denning M.R. in his judgment in *White* v. *Blackmore*.[60] This case concerned the death of the plaintiff's husband while watching a motor race. The husband had not been charged for admission to the event as he was competing in other races. Notices displayed prominently at the entrance to the ground warned of the risks inherent in motor racing and stated it to be a condition of admission that the organisers were to be absolved from all liabilities for accidents to spectators 'howsoever caused." The warning was repeated inside the programme which was handed to persons who entered the ground. The organisers having been held to be negligent in the way in which they had erected the safety ropes between the track and the spectator areas, the effect of the notice on the plaintiff's claim became critical. Lord Denning M.R. sided with the critics of *Ashdown* and held that an exclusion of liability would only be effective if incorporated into a contract. The majority of the Court of Appeal disagreed arguing that Parliament had intended to approve the *Ashdown* result when it spoke in subsection 2(1) of the Occupiers' Liability Act 1957 of excluding the common duty of care owed to lawful visitors "by agreement or otherwise." The words "or otherwise" could only have meaning if they recognised forms of exclusion which were not contractually based.

The result of these cases would seem to be that non-contractual exclusion clauses used in relation to the occupation of land obtain their effectiveness by

---

[57] [1957] 1 Q.B. 409.
[58] Gower, (1956) 19 M.L.R. 532.
[59] Although it is arguable that the duty of common humanity recognised by the common law as owed to trespassers is the minimum below which it is impossible to reduce the duty.
[60] [1972] 2 Q.B. 651.

being a condition attached to a permission to enter. Although the situation is close to being contractual, the best explanation for the effectiveness of such notices is that it derives from the plaintiff's consent to the condition. This consent is inferred objectively.[61] All that a landowner has to do is give reasonable notice of the exclusion. If this is done all entrants are bound by the clause, whether or not they actually appreciated or understood its significance. The defence is very effective. A lawful visitor who enters property subject to such a clause may have fewer rights than a trespasser. In *White* v. *Blackmore* the notice proved to be more effective than the standard *volenti* defence. The fact that the husband had no knowledge of the negligence which caused his death, the fact that the defendants had negligently erected the safety ropes, meant that he could not be held *volenti* to the risk. However, the exclusion notice placed at the entrance to the ground removed his rights irrespective of his knowledge. The only common law rule which limits the operation of such clauses is that which requires the plaintiff to have had a free choice whether to become subject to the clause. Persons entering property in the course of their employment are apparently regarded as lacking such freedom and are not subject to the clause.[62]

At one level the distinction between the "conditional permission" and the "consent" explanation for the efficacy of non-contractually based exclusion notices used in relation to land would seem to be negligible. If I persist in entering property knowing that the price of being permitted to do so is that I waive any rights I might otherwise have against the occupier, I am, in effect, consenting with knowledge to run the risk.[63] However, the different explanations are possibly important if such clauses are to be pleaded against trespassers. The consent of a trespasser to a risk is recognised as a defence to the statutory duty owed to a trespasser by an occupier under the Occupiers' Liability Act 1984. On the other hand, if the true explanation of the efficacy of the notice lies, as *Ashdown* and *White* appear to hold, in the condition attached to the permission to enter, such a notice cannot, ex hypothesi, bind a person who entered without permission. The ability of occupiers to use exclusion notices against trespassers is therefore uncertain.[64] If such notices can be effective there are no statutory controls on their use.

The efficacy of disclaimers of liability for negligent misrepresentation giving rise to economic loss was accepted in the leading decision of *Hedley Byrne & Co. Ltd.* v. *Heller and Partners Ltd.*[65] The defendants had given a reference on one of their clients stating that they did not accept responsibility for the accuracy of the information. The explanation which is commonly given for this result is that the duty of care derives from the fact of the person giving the advice "voluntarily accepting" responsibility for the accuracy of that advice and that the disclaimer negatives that voluntary assumption and removes the duty of care. This explanation has become increasingly difficult to accept in the light of recognition of the fact that as the "voluntary assumption" can be implied from the facts of the case it is actually a legal

---

[61] *Bennett* v. *Tugwell* [1971] 2 Q.B. 267.

[62] *Burnett* v. *British Waterways Board* [1973] 1 W.L.R. 700.

[63] Alternatively, it would require a little judicial ingenuity to hold that there was in fact a contract, the consideration for the permission to enter being my waiving my rights. See *Gore* v. *Van der Lann* [1967] 2 Q.B. 31.

[64] Law Commission Report No. 75, *Liability for Damage to Trespassers and Related Questions of Occupiers' Liability*, paras. 60–66.

[65] [1964] A.C. 465.

fiction.[66] The duty is, in effect, imposed by the law and the representor is recognised as having the ability to disclaim responsibility for it. If consent explains the efficacy of the disclaimer it must be on the basis that the representee having notice of the disclaimer proceeds with the transaction accepting that he will take responsibility for any losses suffered.

The ability to use exclusion clauses and notices can obviously produce unfair results. Certain statutory controls therefore exist in order to redress the balance between the parties. However, the controls are not comprehensive and, as a result the common law rules may still operate occasionally.

Road traffic legislation

Two pieces of overlapping legislation effectively ban the use of exclusion clauses in relation to traffic accidents. The most important is section 149 of the Road Traffic Act 1988. This invalidates any attempt by the user of a motor vehicle to impose an exclusion clause on a passenger. Previously cases had been reported[67] of drivers who had not insured their liability to passengers attempting to exclude it by fixing exclusion notices to the dashboards of their cars. Such attempts were deprived of effect by the legislation[68] which made such insurance compulsory. An equivalent provision, derived from earlier legislation, prohibits the operators of public service vehicles from excluding or restricting their liability to passengers for personal injuries or death.[69]

The Unfair Contract Terms Act 1977

A fairly comprehensive set of controls was placed on exclusion clauses by the Unfair Contract Terms Act 1977 which, in spite of its title, is not confined to contractually based exclusions of tortious liability but extends its controls to notices which are not enforced as part of a contract. Section 2(1) of the Act renders inoperative any contract terms or notices used in relation to "business liability" which "exclude or restrict" negligence liability for personal injuries or death. Section 2(2) makes the validity of clauses which exclude or restrict liability for other forms of loss or damage resulting from negligence depend on whether they can be shown to be reasonable. Section 2(3) ensures that the statutory controls are not circumvented by a plea that a person's agreement or awareness of a clause or notice makes that person *volenti* to the risk. Each of the main requirements of the Act will be examined.

1. Business liability

The Act does not apply to all exclusion clauses and notices. Its operation is confined to situations of "business liability," that is, where the clause excludes liability for breach of obligations or duties arising from things done in the course of a business or from the occupation of premises used for business purposes. As a result the controls do not apply to exclusions used by

---

[66] See *post*, p. 341.
[67] *Buckpitt* v. *Oates* [1968] 1 All E.R. 1145; *Bennett* v. *Tugwell* [1971] 2 Q.B. 267.
[68] Originally the Motor Vehicles (Passenger Insurance) Act 1971 and subsequently the Road Traffic Act 1972.
[69] Public Passenger Vehicles Act 1981, s. 29.

private persons or in relation to non-business activities. In those areas the results established by *Ashdown* and *White* survive. The precise definition of business is a matter of some difficulty. The Act provides no definition, but the term is commonly thought to entail the carrying on of trade with a view to making a profit. It is by no means clear how substantial an element of money making is required. For example, would a charity count as a business in relation to a fund raising event, even though it is not able to make a profit without prejudicing its charitable status? The Act seems to confirm that some kind of profit making is required because it specifically extends the definition of business to include the activities of professional persons, of government departments and of local and public authorities[70] which might fall outside of a restrictive definition. An exception which was created by the Occupiers' Liability Act 1984,[71] allows businesses which grant access to their property for recreational or educational activities, to use exclusion clauses in relation to dangers created by the state[72] of the premises provided that the granting of such access is not part of the occupier's business purposes. The purpose behind the introduction of this amendment was to allow farmers and other landowners to exclude any potential liability which their premises might create to ramblers and potholers.

2. Contract terms or notices

Non-contractual notices such as signs erected on land purporting to exclude liability and "disclaimers" of liability for negligent misstatements are all within the scope of the Act. The statutory definition includes notices directed to particular individuals and those aimed at the world at large.[73] The notice need not even be in writing: an oral disclaimer of liability is within the statutory controls.[74]

3. Negligence

Section 2 of the Act controls contract terms or notices which exclude or restrict liability for negligence.[75] Negligence is given a particular definition for these purposes by section 1 of the Act. It covers obligations of reasonable care and skill created by an express or implied contractual term; common law duties of care and the common duty of care imposed by the Occupiers' Liability Act 1957. It does not extend to any stricter form of liability, such as that which arises under the Animals Act 1971, or to the statutory obligation of care owed to persons other than lawful visitors under section 1(5) of the Occupiers' Liability Act 1984.[76] The Act therefore has no application to exclusions of such kinds of liability.

---

[70] s. 14.
[71] s. 2.
[72] Not by activities conducted upon them.
[73] s. 2.
[74] s. 14.
[75] Other parts of the Act deal with specific forms of contractual liability.
[76] This may not be important. The "conditional permission" explanation for the efficacy of exclusion clauses may mean that it is impossible to make an exclusion notice efficacious against a trespasser who, ex hypothesi, has been given no permission onto which the exclusion notice can be attached. Note, however, that the Law Commission in its Report (No. 75) on Occupiers' Liability to Trespassers would have permitted all occupiers, other than those acting in the course of a business, to exclude their liability to all entrants, subject to a test of resonableness.

4. Exclude or restrict

In order to ensure that the statutory controls are comprehensive, the Act applies them to a wide range of techniques which a draftsman might adopt. For example, a clause which limits the defendant's liability to a nominal sum is technically not an exclusion clause, even though it operates to deprive the plaintiff of rights which he might legitimately have expected. The Act gives protection in such circumstances by applying controls to all clauses and notices which "exclude or restrict" liability. Section 13 of the Act extends the meaning of these words to cover making liability or its enforcement subject to restrictive or onerous conditions; excluding or restricting any right or remedy in respect of the liability, or subjecting a person to any prejudice in consequence of his pursuing any such right or remedy; and, excluding or restricting rules of evidence or procedure.

In addition, section 2 is applied by section 13 to clauses which prevent, exclude or restrict liability by excluding or restricting the relevant obligation or duty. This provision is of considerable importance. In *Smith* v. *Eric S. Bush*; *Harris* v. *Wyre Forest District Council*[77] the House of Lords rejected the widely held view that the Act does not apply to *Hedley Byrne* type disclaimers because they operate to prevent a duty of care from arising, as opposed to providing a defence to an established liability. Some support for the rejected approach can be derived from the drafting of the statute which, by speaking of liability, obligations and duties, suggests that it only operates in the case of existing duties. However, acceptance of this approach would grant draftsmen considerable scope for the development of techniques which would be likely to remove much of the statute's controls and the wording of section 13 was clearly designed to cover the point. It is not surprising that the court in *Harris* treated section 13 as unambiguous and rejected a technical reading of the Act which would have deprived courts of the power to subject the whole range of clauses to control. Lord Griffiths adopted an approach based on causation principles and asked whether liability would have existed "but for" the existence of the exclusion clause. If it would have the clause is subject to section 2.

5. Personal injuries and death

The Act places a complete ban on the use of clauses and notices which exclude or restrict liability for negligence which causes these kinds of damage. The actual results on the facts of *Ashdown* and, probably *White*,[78] would not be reached today as a result of this.

6. Reasonableness test

Clauses which do not exclude or restrict liability for personal injuries or death are subject to a reasonableness test. In the case of clauses which do not derive their effect from a contract the question whether it is fair and reasonable to place reliance on the clause is tested, according to section 11(3), in the light of the circumstances at the time when the liability arose. The burden of proving that a clause was fair and reasonable rests with the person who seeks to rely on the clause.

No exhaustive list of the relevant factors could, or should, be made. However, courts are likely to pay particular attention to the relative positions

---

[77] [1990] 1 A.C. 831.
[78] Depending on whether the holding of the jalopy race would count as a business.

of the parties; whether the plaintiff received an inducement to become subject to the clause and whether alternative sources of the service which did not involve such restrictions were available. The courts are also likely to consider the clarity with which the clause was brought to the plaintiff's attention.

The reasonableness test used by the Act has subjective characteristics. The question is whether it was reasonable to use this clause against the particular plaintiff. The same clause may be reasonable when used against one person but unreasonable against another. In *Smith* v. *Eric S. Bush*; *Harris* v. *Wyre Forest District Council*[79] it was held to be unreasonable for a surveyor undertaking a valuation for mortgage purposes, to exclude liability against a private individual who proposed to buy at the cheaper end of the residential market. The surveyor was a professional person who carried professional indemnity insurance and who knew that he was likely to be relied upon. The borrower had, indirectly, funded the valuer's work. In contrast, it was held to be reasonable to use a similar clause in *Stevenson* v. *Nationwide Building Society*[80] in which the borrower, who traded as an estate agent and insurance broker, was held to be perfectly familiar with the clauses commonly attached to mortgage valuations.

Other areas

Because the operation of the Unfair Contract Terms Act in relation to tort is confined to exclusions of negligence liability there are no general controls on the use of exclusion clauses in relation to strict forms of tortious liability. However, a number of modern consumer protection statutes have banned the use of such clauses in relation to the strict duties which they create. The most noteworthy examples of this are section 7 of the Consumer Protection Act 1987, which prohibits the exclusion or limitation of any liability in respect of defective products which arises under Part I of that Act[81] and section 6(3) of the Defective Premises Act 1972 which renders void any attempt to exclude the duties[82] which arise under that measure. In the field of employer's liability, the obligation placed on an employer by section 1 of the Employer's Liability (Defective Equipment) Act 1969 cannot be excluded.[83]

The use of exclusion clauses in relation to other areas of strict liability tort has not been investigated in depth. It is generally assumed that the non-availability of *volenti* as a defence to an employers' liability claim excludes the use of exclusion clauses in the case of breach of statutory duty claims.[84] In *Baddeley* v. *Earl Granville*[85] Wills J. said that "(t)here ought to be no encouragement given to the making of an agreement between A and B that B shall be at liberty to break the law which has been passed for the protection of A . . . such an agreement would be in violation of public policy and ought

---

[79] [1990] 1 A.C. 831.

[80] (1984) 272 E.G. 663.

[81] See also s. 41(4) which bars any exclusion of the breach of statutory duty remedy created by s. 41(1).

[82] Including the duties of care which arise under ss. 3 and 4.

[83] s. 2. The duty placed on the employer is actually a duty of reasonable care (see pp. 136 and 238 for a full discussion of the provision). However, the duty was created by statute before the 1977 Act was passed and is not brought within the 1977 Act as a result of the definition of negligence contained in s. 1.

[84] Stanton, *Breach of Statutory Duty in Tort*, pp. 121–124.

[85] (1887) 19 Q.B.D. 423, 426.

not to be listened to." In contrast to this the Animals Act 1971 bars the *volenti* defence in relation to an employee of the animal's keeper who incurs a risk incidental to his employment,[86] but recognises the availability of *volenti* as a general defence to the strict liability which it creates.[87] It would seem to follow from this that a properly worded and notified exclusion clause would be effective in removing such liability. There is no evidence of *Rylands* v. *Fletcher* or nuisance liability being controlled by an exclusion clause. However, as the consent of the plaintiff is a recognised defence to the first of these torts it would seem likely that an exclusion clause would be effective.

STATUTORY AND COMMON LAW JUSTIFICATION

If a person can show that his acts have been authorised by Act of Parliament they will not be tortious. In addition, certain rules of common law exist which permit conduct which would be tortious in other circumstances. Statutory and common law justification of acts which would constitute intentional torts to the person and interference with real and personal property forms a substantial subject which encompasses self defence and other forms of self help, lawful chastisement, powers of arrest, entry and search as well as the statutory authority for acts which constitute a nuisance. These defences will be discussed in detail in the context of the torts in relation to which they provide a defence.

There is no evidence of Parliament being prepared to sanction negligence by means of a statute. Indeed, when authority has been given to perform an act which would be tortious in other circumstances, the scope of the authorisation is generally construed as not extending to protecting negligent performance of that act. In the classic words of Lord Blackburn: " . . . it is now thoroughly well established that no action will lie for doing that which the legislature has authorised, if it be done without negligence, although it does occasion damage to anyone; but an action does lie for doing that which the legislature has authorised, if it be done negligently."[88]

NECESSITY

Necessity is recognised as a defence in relation to a number of torts, in particular nuisance and the various forms of trespass. Necessity has provided a defence against liability in nuisance when a ship discharged oil into an estuary[89]; against trespass to land in cases in which the police were attempting to apprehend an armed psychopath[90] and in which property was destroyed in order to create a fire break[91]; against battery in a case of forcible feeding of a prisoner who was on hunger strike[92] and against liability for

---

[86] s. 6(5).
[87] s. 5(2).
[88] *Geddis* v. *The Proprietors of the Bann Reservoir* (1878) 3 App. Cas. 430 at 455.
[89] *Esso Petroleum Co. Ltd.* v. *Southport Corporation* [1956] A.C. 218.
[90] *Rigby* v. *Chief Constable of Northamptonshire* [1985] 1 W.L.R. 1242.
[91] *Cope* v. *Sharpe (No. 2)* [1912] 1 K.B. 496.
[92] *Leigh* v. *Gladstone* (1909) 26 T.L.R. 139. The justification for medical treatment in an emergency situation may lie in either implied consent or necessity. Necessity now seems to be the explanation favoured.

interference with chattels which would have arisen on the killing of a dog which was worrying sheep[93] and the throwing goods from a vessel which was in danger of sinking.[94]

The conditions governing the availability of the defence are relatively clear. First, there must be a danger which creates an imminent threat to the safety of persons or property; secondly, the defendant's acts must be a reasonable response aimed at averting the danger. Several points are raised by these requirements. It is sufficient that the threat endangers property.[95] Human safety need not necessarily be in issue, although it is likely to be easier to satisfy the reasonableness test when it is. The existence of the danger must be objectively established as "imminent"; a defendant's subjective belief in it will not suffice.[96] However, the reasonableness of the defendant's reaction will be tested at the time of the act. Hindsight is excluded with the result that the defence cannot be defeated by proof that another's intervention made that of the defendant unnecessary.[97] The criterion of reasonableness will compare the value of the damage done by the trespass to that of the property which it was sought to save. A defendant will lose the defence if it is shown that the occasion which produced the necessity was caused by his own negligence.[98]

It is uncertain whether necessity can be based on factors other than the need to protect life or property from physical damage. The Court of Appeal has refused to accept that a person's homelessness can justify trespass onto another's land in order to find shelter on the basis that recognition of such an excuse would open the door to unacceptable encroachments on property rights.[99] Similarly, the common law refused to accept that entry, without permission, onto another's property for the purpose of effecting essential repairs to one's own property could be justified by necessity.[1] However, a limited right to enter in such circumstances has now been created by the Access to Neighbouring Land Act 1992.[2]

A more liberal, but specialised, version of the defence of necessity was recognised by the House of Lords in *F. v. West Berkshire Health Authority*,[3] a case which concerned the proposed sterilisation of a mentally handicapped woman aged 36. Because of her mental capacity the woman was incapable of giving her consent to the treatment and no power was vested in the court or other persons to give consent on her behalf. Nonetheless, the medical staff treating the patient formed the view that sterilisation would be in the woman's best interests because she had formed a relationship with a male patient in the hospital in which she was resident. The court was asked to declare that the performance of such an operation would be lawful in spite of the absence of consent. The House of Lords acceded to this request holding

---

[93] *Cresswell v. Sirl* [1948] 1 K.B. 241.
[94] *Mouse's Case* (1608) 12 Co. Rep. 63.
[95] *Cope v. Sharpe (No. 2)* [1912] 1 K.B. 496; *Cresswell v. Sirl* [1948] 1 K.B. 241.
[96] *Cope v. Sharpe (No. 2)* [1912] 1 K.B. 496
[97] *Cope v. Sharpe (No. 2)* [1912] 1 K.B. 496
[98] *Rigby v. Chief Constable of Northamptonshire* [1985] 1 W.L.R. 1242. Negligence in this context means the ordinary standard of care at the time of the defendant's supposedly negligent acts.
[99] *Southwark L.B.C. v. Williams* [1971] Ch. 734. Similarly a person's hunger would not excuse the theft of food.
[1] *John Trenberth Ltd. v. National Westminster Bank Ltd.* (1979) 39 P. & C.R. 104.
[2] See *post*, p. 383.
[3] [1990] 2 A.C. 1.

that treatment of such a patient may lawfully be given in the absence of consent if it is necessary[4] or is in the best interests of the patient[5]; that the responsibility for determining whether treatment satisfies these tests is to be judged according to the tenets of accepted professional practice as laid down in the *Bolam*[6] decision and, finally, that, although it is strictly unnecessary for an application to be made to a court for a declaration that such treatment is lawful, it is a matter of good practice to do so in respect of irreversible and contentious procedures such as the sterilisation of an adult.[7]

This decision has attracted severe criticism, not least because its use of the *Bolam* test means that contentious forms of medical treatment may be imposed on a patient on the basis that a body of responsible doctors regard it as in the patient's best interests or as necessary even though a body of equally responsible medical opinion would oppose it. Critics of the decision regard it as a leading modern example of the judiciary's determination to ensure that difficult questions of medical ethics are determined by doctors rather than judges. It is certain that the courts will confine the ratio of the decision to patients who are incapable of giving a valid consent and are likely to restrict it in a case of temporary incapacity only to justifying emergency treatment. As a form of the defence of necessity the decision breaks new ground in justifying treatment which is not life-saving. Lord Brandon speaks of treatment being in the patient's best interests "if, but only if, it is carried out either to save their lives or to ensure improvement or prevent deterioration in their physical or mental health." It is difficult to envisage forms of medical treatment (other than non-therapeutic experimentation) which do not fall within this test. Lord Brandon's words were carefully chosen to legitimate treatment ranging from major life-saving procedures to minor procedures of preventive medicine or dentistry. From one standpoint it can be argued that adults who cannot give a valid consent should not be deprived by the technicalities of the tort of trespass of advantageous treatment that capable persons would be willing to accept and that it is preferable to found the legitimacy of such treatment on necessity rather than a fictitious consent. But, on the other hand, the decision opens the door to doctors who seek to impose, possibly contentious, treatment on patients being subject to scarcely any legal controls.

ILLEGALITY

If damage is suffered which is tainted by criminal conduct, the defence of illegality (known in Latin as *ex turpi causa non oritur actio*) may provide a complete defence to any tort claim brought. This defence can block a claim even though nothing which the plaintiff did increased the risk of damage being suffered. The wide variety of ways in which illegality can affect different torts and the fact that the defence is based on inherently vague notions of public policy create considerable difficulties in predicting when it

---

[4] *Per* Lord Goff.

[5] *Per* Lords Bridge and Brandon.

[6] *i.e.* that a doctor's decision must conform to a view accepted as proper by a body of reasonable practitioners. See *ante*, p. 72.

[7] A practice note has been issued by the *Official Solicitor* concerning the procedure to be adopted in such cases [1989] 2 F.L.R. 447.

will operate to defeat a claim. Modern authority[8] dealing with this topic as a defence to negligence has tended to treat illegality as a policy reason for denying the existence of a duty of care rather than as a separate defence. However, as such reasoning is now suspect in view of the decline of the *Anns* principle and as illegality is a general tort defence which extends beyond negligence to trespass to the person,[9] interference with goods[10] and deceit[11] it is suggested that it should be regarded as a distinct defence, albeit one founded on the public policy consideration that the courts should not be seen to be assisting wrongdoers. If the public policy basis for the defence were to be accepted it is possible that it might apply to conduct which is against public policy but not illegal. However, there is no recorded example of the defence working on such facts.[12]

No single test has been accepted as governing the operation of the defence. The court faced by an issue of this kind considers a number of factors, in particular, the nature of the illegality and how closely related it was to the damage. The most common approach found in modern cases is the "conscience" test. In *Thackwell* v. *Barclays Bank plc*.[13] Hutchison J. explained that this ". . . involved the court looking at the quality of the illegality relied on by the defendant and all the surrounding circumstances, without fine distinctions, and seeking to answer two questions: first, whether there had been illegality of which the court should take notice and, second, whether in all the circumstances it would be an affront to public conscience if, by affording him the relief sought, the court was seen to be indirectly assisting or encouraging the plaintiff in his criminal act." The dilemma facing the courts was summarised by Bingham L.J. in *Saunders* v. *Edwards*,[14]

> "Where issues of illegality are raised, the courts have . . . to steer a middle course between two unacceptable positions. On the one hand it is unacceptable that any court of law should aid or lend its authority to a party seeking to pursue or enforce an object or agreement which the law prohibits. On the other hand it is unacceptable that the court should, on the first indication of unlawfulness affecting any aspect of a transaction, draw up its skirts and refuse all assistance to the plaintiff, no matter how serious his loss or how disproportionate his loss to the unlawfulness of his conduct."

The "conscience" test encountered severe criticism in the Court of Appeal in *Pitts* v. *Hunt*[15] in which it had been argued that public conscience would be affronted by a denial of compensation to a seriously injured accident victim. Dillon L.J. countered this by saying that the "conscience" test was difficult to apply as the public conscience might well be affected by matters of an emotional nature. Two different approaches were preferred by the members

---

[8] *Ashton* v. *Turner* [1981] Q.B. 137.
[9] *Murphy* v. *Culhane* [1977] Q.B. 94, C.A., a claim brought by the dependants of a person killed in the course of a fight which was alleged to have been provoked by his initial assault.
[10] *Thackwell* v. *Barclays Bank plc* [1986] 1 All E.R. 676.
[11] *Saunders* v. *Edwards* [1987] 1 W.L.R. 1116.
[12] The most likely example might have been a negligence claim for damage caused by a suicide attempt. However, claims of this kind have tended to succeed in spite of public policy arguments. See *post*, pp. 211–212.
[13] [1986] 1 All E.R. 676 at 687. This approach was followed by the Court of Appeal which decided *Saunders* v. *Edwards* [1987] 1 W.L.R. 1116.
[14] [1987] 2 All E.R. 651 at 665–666.
[15] [1991] 1 Q.B. 24.

of the court. Beldam L.J. was of the view that the defence should operate in motoring cases only if the offence committed was so serious as to preclude the driver on grounds of policy from claiming indemnity under the terms of his motor insurance. Balcombe and Dillon L.J., on the other hand, preferred the view that a plaintiff should fail where the conduct was such that the court was unable to determine a standard of care to be imposed on the tortfeasor. It is unlikely that these reformulations are an improvement on the "conscience" test. The first is merely a change in the phrasing of a public policy bar to recovery and the majority view adopts the incorrect view that it is impossible to fix a standard of care applicable to activities such as safe breaking or, as in *Pitts* itself, for the acts of an uninsured, unlicensed and drunken motor cycle rider.[16]

Not all criminal offences committed at the time of an injury bar a subsequent claim in tort. Employees injured in industrial accidents may well have committed offences under the Health and Safety at Work Act 1974.[17] The approach adopted in such cases, since the decision of the House of Lords in *National Coal Board* v. *England*,[18] is to treat the plaintiff's conduct as merely reducing damages on the grounds of contributory negligence. This is surely correct. To bar completely the claim on the grounds of a minor illegality would be exceptionally harsh in the light of the protective purpose of industrial safety legislation. The financial consequences suffered by even a moderately injured plaintiff might dramatically exceed the maximum penalty which the criminal law would impose. Similar considerations apply to some traffic accident cases. Many injured motorists may have been breaking speed limits or driving carelessly but this should not bar their tort claims. However there are undoubtedly limits to this approach. In *Pitts* v. *Hunt*[19] an illegality defence stopped a claim by a plaintiff who had been a passenger on a motor cycle and who was held to have been encouraging the rider to drive dangerously. In the leading case of *Ashton* v. *Turner*[20] illegality blocked the claim of a passenger injured in a road accident whilst escaping from the scene of a crime. As one writer[21] has commented, the result in *Ashton* was that the accident victim was effectively fined £70,000 for the theft of three radios.

The decision in *Ashton* raises the question of the link which must exist between the illegality and the tort before the defence will operate. In that case the defendant, at the time of the accident, was driving at high speed in an attempt to escape arrest. But the facts will not always be this clear. Would the fact that the occupants of a car were travelling in a normal fashion towards the scene of intended criminal activity when an accident occurred raise the defence? The non-technical approach of the courts to the defence means that the ability of a plaintiff to mount his claim without making reference to any illegal conduct does not automatically stop the defence from operating. The

---

[16] In the slightly earlier decision of *Kirkham* v. *Chief Constable of the Greater Manchester Police* [1990] 2 Q.B. 283 a differently constituted Court of Appeal had used the "conscience" test.

[17] s. 7 of the Health & Safety at Work Act 1974, which puts all employees at work under an obligation, enforceable by a criminal penalty, to take reasonable care for the safety of themselves and of others, is the provision most likely to have been broken. See also s. 8.

[18] [1954] A.C. 403.

[19] [1991] 1 Q.B. 24.

[20] [1981] Q.B. 137.

[21] Hervey, (1981) 97 L.Q.R. 537.

background which is known to the court may make it against conscience to grant recovery. In *Thackwell* v. *Barclays Bank plc*[22] the plaintiff claimed that the defendant bank had converted a cheque to which he was entitled. All of the relevant facts could be proved without the plaintiff being forced to admit that the cheque represented the proceeds of a scheme to defraud a finance company. However, the court held that the claim was barred. It was against public policy for the judicial process to be used to ensure that the proceeds of fraud reached the person who instigated it. Similarly in *Burns* v. *Edman*[23] a Fatal Accidents Act claim on behalf of the dependants of a deceased who had derived all his income from crime was held to be barred even though the claimants were personally innocent of criminal conduct. These cases do not mean that lack of a connection between the tort and the illegality is invariably irrelevant, but rather that certain forms of illegality may be deemed to be so reprehensible that they taint transactions which are only remotely connected to the illegality. *Saunders* v. *Edwards*[24] is a case on the other side of the line. The court in that case did not regard an attempt to evade stamp duty on the sale of a property as sufficiently important to bar the plaintiff from claiming damages for an unconnected fraudulent misrepresentation which had been made, concerning the extent of the property included in the sale.

Illegality as a tort defence attracts considerable criticism because of the uncertainty surrounding it and the harsh results which it can produce. The approach which it adopts of allowing the loss to lie where it falls can provide a defendant implicated in illegality with a defence against claims brought by others injured in the course of the criminal conduct. It seems very unlikely that the defence has any deterrent effect on criminal behaviour.

[22] [1986] 1 All E.R. 676.
[23] [1970] 2 Q.B. 541.
[24] [1987] 1 W.L.R. 1116.

Chapter Six

Vicarious Liability and Contribution

Vicarious liability is a general doctrine of law under which the legal responsibility for one person's act is imposed upon another person. In the context of the law of tort it is generally identified with the rule under which an employer is made liable for torts committed by his employee in the course of the employee's employment. The same result is obtained in relation to the responsibility of the members of a partnership for each other's acts and some vicarious liability may exist in the case of the delegation of a task to an agent. Special statutory rules govern the vicarious responsibility of trade unions for the tortious acts of their members.[1] However, some situations which might be thought suitable for vicarious liability are not covered by it; for example, a parent is not vicariously liable for the acts of its child.[2] As vicarious liability operates to imposes liability on a person who has not been negligent it is possible to regard it as a form of strict tortious liability.

It should not be thought that vicarious liability, by placing responsibility upon the employer, provides the employee with a defence. It creates a situation of joint liability[3] on the part of employer and employee. Although the survival of the right to sue the employee will rarely be important if the employer and his insurance are available to meet the claim, the joint liability may have a role to play if the employer is no longer available. A company may have been wound up and an individual employer may be bankrupt or dead.[4] In such a case the claim against the ex-employee may still have some value.

Distinctions: primary and vicarious liability and delegable and non-delegable duties

Vicarious liability is only one of the ways in which a person may be held responsible in law on account of damage resulting from the acts of another

---

[1] Trade Union and Labour Relations (Consolidation) Act 1992, ss. 20–22. These rules will not be discussed in this book as they are a basic part of the defences to the economic torts granted by trade union legislation.

[2] *McHale* v. *Watson* (1964) 111 C.L.R. 384. Note that primary liability may be imposed upon a parent or school for damage done by a child as a result of negligent failure to supervise the child, *Carmarthenshire County Council* v. *Lewis* [1955] A.C. 549; *Vicar of Writtle* v. *Essex County Council* (1979) 77 L.G.R. 656.

[3] See p. 140 for a discussion of the working of joint liability.

[4] This is particularly important in the case of professional indemnity insurance which is bought from year to year and covers "claims made" rather than work done within the currency of the policy.

person. Liability which is imposed on account of such acts may be either primary or vicarious. It is only vicarious if the employer has broken no duty which is owed personally on the facts of the case but has acquired responsibility for the other persons's acts by operation of law. If the liability is a primary one, it is imposed because of the breach by the employer of a duty which was imposed on him personally rather than because his relationship with another person transferred a duty to him. A primary responsibility will be created by a person's authorising, assisting, procuring or ratifying another's tortious act. Similarly, negligent failures in supervision are a classic situation of primary liability. Modern examples, drawn from leading cases, include prison officers who negligently supervise a prison working party with the result that prisoners escape and cause damage[5] and a building inspector who negligently fails to stop a builder constructing a house in such a way that subsequent owners are damaged.[6] Any tort liability imposed in these cases is a primary liability based on a personal failure to perform a duty with reasonable care.

A distinction must also be drawn between delegable and non-delegable duties. A duty is delegable if a person can satisfy it by employing an independent contractor[7] to perform the function on his behalf. Where a duty is delegable it must still be proved that it was reasonable to delegate the task in question and that a reasonable check was made on the competence of the person doing the work and on the quality of it when completed. If these conditions are satisfied the responsibility for defects in the work rests with the person who performed it and not with the employer, who has established that he has taken reasonable care in the performance of his duty. A good example of this is the duty of an occupier of premises to make property reasonably safe for lawful visitors. A lift will constitute a potential source of danger and the occupier will owe a duty to take reasonable care in respect of it. This duty may be satisfied by the employment of an apparently competent lift engineer to service the lift.[8] Indeed, the employer might be negligent to attempt such specialised work himself. Any negligence which occurs in the course of the servicing will create liability on the part of the engineer, but not the employer.

Some duties, however, are non-delegable.[9] In these circumstances, although the performance of the work may be delegated, the legal responsibility for defects remains with the employer. Unfortunately no clear criterion exists for distinguishing the two types of duty. Non-delegability tends to be a feature of strict liability duties; the *Rylands* v. *Fletcher* tort is a good example of this.[10] The defendant landowner in that case was held liable for damage caused by the acts of his independent contractors. In contrast, duties to take reasonable care may be either delegable or non-delegable. Section 2 of the Occupiers' Liability Act 1957 confirms the result in the case of the lift engineer by making the common duty of care owed to lawful visitors which it creates delegable. However, an employer's duty to take reasonable care to provide a safe system of work for his employees is undoubtedly non-

---

[5] *Home Office* v. *Dorset Yacht Co. Ltd.* [1970] A.C. 1004.
[6] *Anns* v. *Merton L.B.C.* [1978] A.C. 728. For the current law on this topic see pp. 350 and 472.
[7] See below for the distinction between an employee and an independent contractor.
[8] *Occupiers' Liability Act 1957*, s.2(4)(b) and see *Haseldine* v. *C. A. Daw & Son Ltd.* [1941] 2 K.B. 343.
[9] They are listed below at p. 134.
[10] See *post*, Chap. 21.

delegable,[11] as is a health authority's duty to take care in the provision of services to patients.[12]

Vicarious liability in the strict sense of the term is imposed in two situations. First, when the employer owes no primary duty; for example an employee's duty to drive carefully is not owed personally by his employer. Secondly, when a delegable duty is imposed on the employer and he chooses, reasonably, to fulfil it by delegating performance to an employee. Vicarious liability is commonly summarised as the rule that an employer is responsible for the torts of his employee but not for those of his independent contractor. Examples of what may appear to be vicarious liability for the torts of independent contractors are in fact cases of an employer's non-delegable duties imposing primary liability. Liability for such acts of an independent contractor has always rested with the employer.

The purpose of vicarious liability

Various justifications, which reflect the debate on the purposes of tort, may be made for the imposition of vicarious liability. The most important is the financial one. The rule, and the ways in which it has been developed, is an embodiment of the compensatory and loss distribution aims of tort. Liability rests with the person best placed in terms of resources and information to insure or to distribute the risk. It is to the plaintiff's advantage to be given an additional defendant to sue, particularly if that defendant is likely to be able to meet any award of damages which is made. The employer, rather than the employee, is likely to have the knowledge required to obtain the correct amount and kind of insurance. Through pricing policy he should be able to pass the cost of the risk back into society through his customers. There is logic in the idea that the employer, who obtains the benefits of the employee's work, should meet the responsibilities created by it. The employee is only performing the act in order to fulfil the business requirements of the employer and, in one sense, the damage can be attributed to the employer's choice of employee.

The role of vicarious liability in encouraging accident prevention is less clear. It might be thought to be likely to have a positive effect on accident rates in so far as an employer might be thought to be better placed to understand the risks created by an activity and to implement the training and other measures necessary to reduce those risks. However, the operation of vicarious liability may actually lessen any deterrent effect of tort by reducing the personal involvement of employees in proceedings.

At a practical level, vicarious liability may assist a plaintiff by providing a defendant to sue. It may be impossible to identify the particular employee within an enterprise whose fault caused the damage, but the employer will still be liable if it can be shown that the damage must have been caused by the negligence of one of his employees. The leading example of this is provided by *Hill* v. *James Crowe (Cases) Ltd.*[13] the facts of which were that the plaintiff had been injured when some negligently nailed boards on a packing

---

[11] *McDermid* v. *Nash Dredging & Reclamation Co. Ltd.* [1987] A.C. 906.
[12] National Health Service Act 1977, s. 3.
[13] [1978] 1 All E.R. 812. It has been argued (L. Lustgarten, *The Governance of Police*, p. 136) that this feature is of particular use in cases brought concerning tortious acts of the police, as it may have been difficult for an injured party to identify the particular police offier who caused his injuries in the course of events such as crowd disturbances or picket lines.

case gave way when he stood on the case when loading a lorry. The court held that the manufacturer of the case could not escape liability by proving that he had a proper system of work and supervision in his factory. Although the employee who had nailed the offending case could not be identified, he had done it negligently and the employer was responsible for all such employees.

Employee and Independent Contractor

If true vicarious liability is at issue it becomes necessary to decide whether the person whose acts caused the damage was an employee or a self employed independent contractor as true vicarious liability only exists for the acts of employees.[14] This distinction plays an important role in a number of other areas of English law. In particular, employed and self-employed persons are subject to different taxation and social security regimes and the self-employed are given fewer remedies than the employed under employment protection legislation. The distinction commonly proves difficult in practice because of the wide variety of arrangements under which people work and because people attempt to classify the relationships under which they work as falling within the category which they expect to be the most favourable to their interests. The courts' response to such manoeuvres has been to insist that it is for them to make the final decision, as a matter of law, on the facts of the case. The parties' own labelling of their relationship is not conclusive, although it is an important factor. The judicial willingness to police agreements made by the parties was emphasised by *Ferguson* v. *Dawson*[15] in which the Court of Appeal held that a building labourer was an employee and thus within the protection of certain industrial safety legislation in spite of an express agreement when he started work that he should be treated as self-employed. The decision was based on the nature of the work and the kind of directions given by the employer.

The courts' decision on the character of the relationship is ultimately one of impression to be made in the light of all the facts of the case. In the words of Somervell L.J.[16] it should be asked "was his contract a contract of service within the meaning which an ordinary person would give to the words." No single factor is decisive. Previously it was thought that the degree of control exercised by the employer over the methods employed to do the work was the critical factor. However, although the right to control the way in which the work is done, as opposed to the right to determine what task is to be done, is an important factor indicating the existence of a relationship of employment, it is not the sole determinant. There is no bar to highly skilled persons, whose actions cannot in reality be controlled by an employer, being classified as employees.[17] More recently courts have placed emphasis on a wider range of factors such as the degree to which the work is integrated into the employer's business[18] and which of the parties bears the financial risks; in

---

[14] The distinction is variously described as that between employee and independent contractor or between a "contract for services" and a "contract of service." The employer/employee usage has generally supplanted the older master/servant. However, the newer usage has the disadvantage that the word employer is used in relation to persons who engage employees and independent contractors.

[15] [1976] 3 All E.R. 817.

[16] *Cassidy* v. *Ministry of Health* [1951] 2 K.B. 343.

[17] *Gold* v. *Essex C.C.* [1942] 2 K.B. 293; *Cassidy* v. *Ministry of Health* [1951] 2 K.B. 343.

[18] *Stevenson, Jordan & Harrison Ltd.* v. *MacDonald & Evans* [1952] 1 T.L.R. 101.

effect, on whose account are the services being performed?[19] An obligation to perform work personally points towards the relationship being one of employment, whereas the fact that payment is wholly dependent on the satisfactory completion of the work is a pointer towards self-employment.

Borrowed employees

Employees may be borrowed by one employer from another. Common examples include operators who are hired out with machinery and employment agency employees who are allocated to another employer as temporary labour. In such cases the presumption is that the general (or original) employer remains vicariously liable for any tort committed whilst the employee is working for the temporary employer.[20] The leading case on this issue is *Mersey Docks & Harbour Board* v. *Coggins & Griffiths (Liverpool) Ltd.*[21] A mobile crane and a driver had been hired to a firm of stevedores under a contract, the terms of which stipulated that the driver was to become an employee of the hirers. In spite of this term, the Board continued to pay the driver's wages and retained the right to dismiss him. The hirer directed the tasks which were to be performed but not the method by which the work was done. In the course of the work the driver negligently injured the plaintiff who brought an action for damages against both employers. The House of Lords held that the terms of the hiring agreement could act as an indemnity agreement between the employers but could not be decisive on the issue as to which of the parties counted as employer as against a third party. An employer who sought to shift the prima facie responsibility for the torts of persons whom he engaged and paid faced a heavy burden. To be effective an agreement to change the identity of a person's employer requires the express or implied consent of the employee. The decisive factor was who bore the ultimate control[22] over the manner in which the work was performed, and, on the facts of the case, this control had remained with the Harbour Board.

Course of employment

In order for vicarious liability to operate the tort must have occurred within the course of the employee's employment. An employer bears no responsibility for torts committed by an employee which are unconnected with that person's job. Questions concerning the scope of an individual's employment are issues of fact. For example, a body of case law has discussed whether an employee who commits a tort whilst travelling to work[23] or whilst taking refreshments in the course of performing a job,[24] remains

---

[19] *Ready Mixed Concrete (South East) Ltd.* v. *Minister of Pensions* [1968] 2 Q.B. 497.

[20] Although this is the result in relation to tort claims brought by third persons the employers may well have entered into a valid indemnity agreement which shifts the financial consequences between them, *Thompson* v. *T. Lohan (Plant Hire) Ltd.* [1987] 1 W.L.R. 649.

[21] [1942] A.C. 1.

[22] In *Bhoomidas* v. *Port of Singapore Authority* [1978] 1 All E.R. 956 the Privy Council spoke of a transfer of entire and absolute control being necessary to transfer vicarious responsibility from the shoulders of the general employer.

[23] In general such an employee is outside the course of his employment. But, the result is different if the employer pays the employee travelling time to enable him to reach a site at a distance from his normal place of work, *Smith* v. *Stages* [1989] A.C. 928.

[24] *Crook* v. *Derbyshire Stone Ltd.* [1956] 1 W.L.R. 437; *Harvey* v. *O'Dell* [1958] 2 Q.B. 78; *Hilton* v. *Thos. Burton (Rhodes) Ltd.* [1961] 1 W.L.R. 705.

within the course of his employment. Blatant misconduct may allow an employer to argue successfully that the scope of employment was exceeded; in the well known phrase it may be held that the employee was on a "frolic of his own." However, the notion of the course of employment is interpreted liberally. If this were not the case it might be possible for an employer to subvert the purpose of vicarious liability by pleading that he did not employ the employee to misconduct himself. This kind of plea was raised in *Century Insurance* v. *Northern Ireland Road Transport*[25] which concerned an employer's liability for the acts of a petrol tanker driver who caused damage by lighting a cigarette whilst off-loading petrol. In one sense it is difficult to conceive of the employer employing the driver to do this act. However, the law does not accept this. It distinguishes the actions which an employee was employed to perform from the manner in which they were performed. Only the first issue matters. In the *Century Insurance* Case the driver was actually doing his job at the relevant time. He was delivering petrol, albeit in an exceptionally negligent manner, and his acts were therefore within the course of his employment. It is a question of fact whether an employee's acts have reached the point at which he is doing something which he is not employed to do and fairly extreme facts seem to be required. In one case a bus conductor's assault on a passenger was held to fall outside of the course of his employment.[26] The argument that he had merely chosen an extreme and unauthorised mode of performing his duty of keeping order on the bus was rejected! This was probably the correct result on the facts, but it did leave a seriously injured person to pursue his, possibly worthless, remedies against the employee.

It is possible that the courts will regard even an express prohibition on the doing of an act as merely directed to the methods by which a job is to be done. Prohibitions on drivers giving lifts fall into this category. Older cases[27] allowed the employer to restrict the course of a driver's employment in this way and even classified such passengers as trespassers on the vehicle. However, the Court of Appeal's approach in *Rose* v. *Plenty*[28] seems likely to be followed in the future. That case concerned a milkman who disobeyed instructions not to have children assist him in delivering the milk and not to carry passengers on his milk float. The plaintiff, a boy aged 13, was injured by the milkman's negligence whilst riding on the float in the course of helping on the round. The majority of the Court of Appeal clearly appreciated that the child's rights could only be secured by making the employer's insurance available to meet the claim. They held that the milkman was doing his job, he was delivering the milk, albeit that he was acting in a prohibited fashion.

It seems likely that the employer in *Rose* would only have escaped liability if it could have been shown that the purpose of the employee's activities at the relevant time was unconnected with the employer's business; for example, if he was delivering items on his own behalf. In *Kooragang Investments Pty. Ltd.* v. *Richardson & Wrench*,[29] a surveyor had been told by his employers, the defendants, that he was not to undertake work on behalf of a particular group of companies which had failed to pay for work performed

---

[25] [1942] A.C. 509.

[26] *Keppel Bus Co. Ltd.* v. *Ahmad* [1974] 1 W.L.R. 1082.

[27] *Twine* v. *Bean's Express Ltd.* (1945) 62 T.L.R. 458; *Conway* v. *George Wimpey Co. Ltd.* (No. 2) [1951] 2 K.B. 266.

[28] *Rose* v. *Plenty* [1976] 1 W.L.R. 141.

[29] [1982] A.C. 462.

previously by the practice. In breach of this instruction the surveyor undertook such work on his own behalf and issued valuation reports using the defendant's letterhead. The plaintiff moneylenders placed reliance on two of these valuations and, on discovering them to have been conducted negligently, attempted to hold the defendants vicariously liable for the negligence of their "moonlighting" employee.[30] The Privy Council found in favour of the defendant. The conduct of the surveyor amounted to an unauthorised act, not merely to an unauthorised method of performing an authorised act. The mere fact that he was doing acts of the same kind as those which he was employed to do did not render his employer responsible for acts of this kind which he performed on his own behalf. Similarly, an act of a kind which the employee is employed to perform, but which is done in a manner which shows the employee to have the specific aim of frustrating the employer's business purposes, is unlikely to be classified as merely an unauthorised mode of performing the job. In *General Engineering Services Ltd.* v. *Kingston & Saint Andrew Corporation*[31] a local authority was held not to be vicariously liable when firemen deliberately delayed their arrival at a fire until the building was destroyed as part of a "go slow" policy in support of a pay claim.

The desire of the courts to develop vicarious liability in ways which will ensure that the interests of plaintiffs are safeguarded is well illustrated by the fact that an employer may be vicariously liable even though his employee's tortious acts were for the purpose of benefitting himself rather than his employer. Employers have been held responsible for frauds committed by employees at work in circumstances in which they have given the employee authority as part of his job to handle the transaction or items in question. The decision in *Kooragang*, in contrast, turns on the fact that the employee had no actual or ostensible authority from the employer to conduct the particular transaction. The leading decision is *Lloyd* v. *Grace, Smith & Co.*[32] in which a firm of solicitors was held vicariously liable for the acts of a managing clerk who fraudulently persuaded a client to sign property over to him. Earl Loreburn L.C. summarised the law in the following terms:

> "If the agent commits the fraud purporting to act in the course of business such as he was authorised, or held out as authorised, to transact on account of his principal, then the latter may be held liable for it."

In *Armagas Ltd.* v. *Mundogas S.A.*[33] Lord Keith emphasised that the use of the agency terminology of actual and ostensible authority in this context is merely an alternative way of expressing the question of whether an act falls within the course of an employee's employment. It is likely that this authority will extend to thefts committed in the course of employment. In *Morris* v. *C.W. Martin & Sons Ltd.*[34] the defendant was the bailee of the plaintiff's mink stole, which had been sent to him for cleaning. He was held liable when the employee who had been given responsibility for cleaning the fur, stole it.

---

[30] No question of ostensible authority or "holding out" arose because the plaintiff was unaware of the name of the valuer who had conducted the survey which was not disclosed in the copy of the valuation which they received. The Privy Council accepted that the result would have been "wholly different" had this been the case.

[31] [1989] 1 W.L.R. 69.

[32] [1912] A.C. 716.

[33] [1986] A.C. 717.

[34] [1966] 1 Q.B. 716.

Although some of the reasons given in the case rest the decision on the particular responsibilities of a bailee towards the owner of goods, it seems certain that the result can also be based on standard vicarious liability principles derived from the decision in *Lloyd*.

Liability for the torts of independent contractors

As a general rule an employer bears no liability for the negligence of his independent contractor. Persons damaged by such work must seek redress directly from the contractor. Apparent cases of liability for such negligence are in truth cases of a primary non-delegable duty owed by the employer. This result was emphatically reaffirmed by the House of Lords when it held in *D. & F. Estates Ltd.* v. *The Church Commissioners for England*[35] that a building contractor owes no non-delegable duty in the tort of negligence in relation to the work of a subcontractor even though his contractual responsibility to his client for such work would be non-delegable. The contractor's primary tortious duty would be satisfied by showing that he had acted reasonably in choosing to delegate the work, in his choice of contractor and in supervising the work.

A variety of forms of non-delegable duty are recognised by the English law of tort. However, it should be noted that an employer's responsibility for the acts of independent contractors engaged in the task of fulfilling his personal non-delegable duties does not extend to what is termed incidental, casual or collateral negligence. These are forms of negligence which fall outside of the particular duty owed by the employer, for which the performance, but not the responsibility, is delegated to the contractor. The contractor bears the sole responsibility in relation to these matters. The result is that a person subject to a non-delegable duty, will be liable for a narrower range of conduct of his independent contractor than would be the case in relation to vicarious liability for the acts of an employee. In *Padbury* v. *Holliday & Greenwood Ltd.*[36] the defendants were engaged in the construction of a building and had subcontracted the task of putting metallic casements into the windows. One of the subcontractor's employees placed a tool on a window sill which fell into the road injuring the plaintiff. Placing the tool on the window-sill was not part of the normal method of fixing the casements. The Court of Appeal held that as the subcontractor's acts formed no part of the performance of the task which had been delegated, the negligence was collateral. Even though the case concerned a danger on the highway of a kind which is recognised as entailing a non-delegable duty, the negligence was collateral to the task delegated and the defendant was not liable for it. The problem with this exception is the practical one of distinguishing "collateral" negligence from that which forms part of the task delegated.[37]

The following non-delegable duties have been identified.

1. Torts based on strict liability

It should not be surprising that strict liability duties are of a non-delegable character. It is a logical consequence of the rule that the standard of care cannot be satisfied by the taking of reasonable care, that delegation of a task

---

[35] [1989] A.C. 177.
[36] (1912) 28 T.L.R. 494.
[37] See the doubts expressed by Harman L.J. in *Salsbury* v. *Woodland* [1970] 1 Q.B. 324.

to an apparently competent contractor will not satisfy the duty. The problems which exist in relation to this area derive from the difficulty of defining
the true ambit of strict liability for dangerous activities. The leading case of
Rylands v. *Fletcher*[38] is a classic example of non-delegability. A landowner
employed an engineer and a contractor to construct a reservoir on his land
and it was their negligence in performing the work which caused damage to
the plaintiff's property. Nevertheless, in spite of the fact that he had
employed apparently competent persons and had taken no part in the work
himself, the landowner was held responsible for the damage. A number of
cases have developed this result by saying that a person who undertakes
dangerous activities is under a non-delegable duty.[39] However, as no such
general duty is recognised by the law, it seems preferable to regard these cases
as an application of the *Rylands* principle and to question whether the result
remains correct in the light of the restrictions which modern courts have
placed on that tort.[40] Non-delegability is clearly a characteristic of the strict
liability for damage caused by fire.[41]

2. Highways

Certain acts which create a danger on the highway are also recognised as
giving rise to a non-delegable duty. The precise limits of this principle are
difficult to define. The leading authority is the nineteenth century case of
Tarry v. *Ashton*[42] in which an occupier of premises was held liable for
injuries caused when a lamp, which was attached to his premises, fell into the
road. The attachment by which the lamp was fixed to the building was in a
poor state of repair; however, a reputable contractor who had been
employed to put the lamp into a state of good repair had negligently failed to
take the necessary measures. The defendant's liability in *Tarry* was a species
of public nuisance. Some of the other cases dealing with injuries caused by
dangers on the highway are probably best explained as based on the *Rylands*
v. *Fletcher* category.[43] It is not the case that all nuisances or other torts
creating dangers on the highway give rise to a non-delegable duty. Indeed the
tendency in the twentieth century to bring negligence thinking into the tort of
nuisance has made *Tarry* appear to be a questionable authority. It was not
particularly surprising that in *Salsbury* v. *Woodland*[44] the Court of Appeal
refused to extend the principle of non-delegability to a danger created by a
contractor's acts near to, as opposed to on, the highway.

3. Industrial safety

All industrial safety duties, whether founded on breach of a strict statutory
duty[45] or the employers' common law duty to provide a safe system of

---

[38] (1868) L.R. 3 H.L. 330.
[39] *Honeywill & Stein Ltd.* v. *Larkin Bros.* [1934] 1 K.B. 191.
[40] See *post*, Chap. 21.
[41] *Balfour* v. *Barty-King* [1957] 1 Q.B. 496; *H. & N. Emanuel Ltd.* v. *Greater London Council*
[1971] 2 All E.R. 835.
[42] (1876) 1 Q.B.D. 314. See also *Penny* v. *Wimbledon U.D.C.* [1899] 2 Q.B. 72.
[43] *Holliday* v. *National Telephone Company* [1899] 2 Q.B. 392. This case may also be
explicable as an example of a statutory duty. The statements of principle in this case are
clearly too wide in view of the decision in *Salsbury*.
[44] [1970] 1 Q.B. 324.
[45] *Hosking* v. *De Havilland Aircraft Co. Ltd.* [1949] 1 All E.R. 540.

work,[46] are non-delegable. Thus where an employee is borrowed from his employer and works for another, the general employer bears the responsibility for any breach of a safety duty which injures the employee.[47] The Employers' Liability (Defective Equipment) Act 1969[48] adds an equivalent obligation. It places an employer under a statutory non-delegable duty for negligence on the part of a supplier of equipment.

"Where . . .
  (a) an employee suffers personal injury in the course of his employment
       in consequence of a defect in equipment provided by the employer
       for the purposes of the employer's business; and
  (b) the defect is attributable wholly or partly to the fault of a third party
       (whether identified or not), the injury shall be deemed to be also
       attributable to negligence on the part of the employer . . . "

The purpose of this measure is to ensure that an injured employee does not have to pursue a claim against the manufacturer of the item, who may have gone out of business, be unidentifiable or trading overseas. The definition of "equipment" in the section is a wide one, it extends to "any plant or machinery, vehicle, aircraft and clothing."[49] It is not confined to the individual parts that go to make up a larger item. In *Coltman* v. *Bibby Tankers Ltd.*,[50] a case in which it was alleged that the plaintiff's husband had been killed when an unseaworthy ship sank, the House of Lords held that a ship can count as equipment for the purposes of this statute. It was said that it would be absurd to hold that machinery attached to the vessel should be within the provision whilst the hull itself was not.

4. Statutory duties

Duties imposed by statute are usually non-delegable. The leading examples of this are found in the area of industrial safety. However, the principle is not confined to that area.[51] The duty to provide medical services imposed by the National Health Service legislation[52] has been held to be of a non-delegable character[53] with the result that a hospital authority is liable for the torts of any independent consultants which it engages to perform its functions. The result will obviously depend on the wording of the particular provision. If the governing statute specifically authorises the delegation of

---

[46] *Wilsons & Clyde Coal Co. Ltd.* v. *English* [1938] A.C. 57. For further discussion of this duty
      see *post*, p. 237.
[47] *McDermid* v. *Nash Dredging & Reclamation Co. Ltd.* [1987] A.C. 906.
[48] Discussed further at p. 238.
[49] s. 1(3).
[50] [1988] A.C. 276.
[51] *Darling* v. *A.G.* [1950] 2 All E.R. 793; *Hardaker* v. *Idle D.C.* [1896] 1 Q.B. 335; *Ministry of
      Housing and Local Government* v. *Sharp* [1970] 2 Q.B. 223. See generally Stanton, *Breach
      of Statutory Duty in Tort*, pp. 115–117.
[52] National Health Service Act 1977, s. 3.
[53] *Razzel* v. *Snowball* [1954] 1 W.L.R. 1382.

the task the person delegating will not be responsible for the negligence of an independent contractor to whom the task was delegated.[54]

Liability for the torts of agents

The use of concepts of agency in relation to vicarious liability for tortious conduct can create some difficulties. The fact that a person is the agent of another should not, in principle, affect the imposition of vicarious liability as it is undoubtedly the case that many persons who act as agents in the sense of having authority to conclude contracts on behalf of their principals, are independent contractors, who should personally bear the consequences of any tortious conduct which occurs in the course of the agency. However, cases such as *Lloyd* v. *Grace, Smith & Co.*[55] have resulted in thinking derived from agency cases, particularly that relating to actual or ostensible authority, entering the law of tort. Although this may be confusing, it is probably inevitable as the circumstances of these cases generally relate to frauds and misrepresentations and are closely related to the conclusion of contracts. It is important to appreciate that, for the most part, this usage relates to the acts of employees, not to independent agents[56] and to remember that Lord Keith in *Armagas Ltd.* v. *Mundogas S.A.*[57] asserted that this usage was nothing more than an alternative way of phrasing the question of whether an act fell within the course of an individual's employment.

There is no general principle that a person is vicariously liable for the torts of his non-employee agent.[58] However, an anomalous example of vicarious liability may make the owner of a car liable for torts committed by a person who is permitted to drive it. This result is said to depend on the driver acting as the agent of the owner, but, the rule is undoubtedly better viewed as a special one confined to motoring which has outlived its usefulness,[59] rather than as representing a general principle of vicarious liability for the acts of non-employee agents.

The root of this line of authority in English law is *Hewitt* v. *Bonvin*.[60] In that case a passenger in a car was injured by the negligence of the driver. The car was owned by the driver's father and the driver had received permission to use it for the purpose of giving a lift home to some friends. The plaintiff sought, unsuccessfully, to hold the father vicariously liable for the son's negligence. However, the Court of Appeal accepted that the result would have been different if the son had been driving the car for the father's

---

[54] In *Rivers* v. *Cutting* [1982] 1 W.L.R. 1146 the plaintiff had abandoned a car illegally on a motorway. The police called a garage and requested them to move it. The garage damaged the car whilst doing the job and it was argued that the police owed the owner a non-delegable duty created by statute in relation to the damage. The Court of Appeal rejected this on the basis that the particular statutory regulation obliged the police either to "remove" the vehicle or to "arrange" for its removal. On the facts, they had opted to "arrange" and could not be liable for negligence of the independent contractor in the course of the removal.

[55] [1912] A.C. 716.

[56] However, in *Gordon* v. *Selico Co. Ltd.* [1986] 1 E.G.L.R. 71 the lessor of a block of a flat was held responsible for fraudulent misrepresentation by his managing agent on the basis of the ostensible, if not actual, authority given to the agent.

[57] [1986] A.C. 717.

[58] Leaving aside cases of non-delegable duties and cases of specific authorisation of the act. This latter case may explain cases such as *Gordon* v. *Selico Co. Ltd.*, *supra*.

[59] See *post*, p. 139.

[60] [1940] 1 K.B. 188.

purposes. On the facts, the father, who had permitted use of the car, had no interest in the particular activity of the son. *Hewitt* opened the way to a new form of vicarious liability for the acts of non-employees based on the delegation of the performance of a task or duty to another person. In practice, this has been confined to motoring cases. Subsequent decisions held that it was not a bar to such liability arising that the driver was driving partly in his own interests and partly in the performance of a task delegated to him by the owner[61] and that a person who was driving on behalf of a group of persons who had contributed to the costs of the journey was their agent even though the other members of the group did not own the car.[62]

The definitive modern case on this topic is *Morgans* v. *Launchbury*.[63] Central to the dispute in that case was the concept of the "family car." A car is commonly used by the members of a family for a variety of individual and joint purposes. Which member of the family insures and registers the vehicle may be a matter of little significance. In order to ensure the availability of insurance cover some jurisdictions have developed the rule that the person who insures the family car should be vicariously responsible for all torts committed by other members of the family when using the vehicle. In spite of Lord Denning M.R. favouring such a development in his judgment in the Court of Appeal in *Morgans*, the House of Lords remained committed to the "delegation of task" approach derived from *Hewitt*. In *Morgans* a car was owned, registered and insured in the wife's name, although it was regarded by husband and wife as jointly owned. The husband used the car each day to travel to his place of work and had agreed with his wife previously that if he had ever had too much to drink he would ask her to pick him up or would ask someone who was sober to drive the car. The plaintiffs were injured when travelling away from a public house as passengers in the car when it was being driven by a friend who had been asked to drive by the husband. The plaintiffs sought unsuccessfully to hold the wife vicariously responsible for the friend's driving, on the basis of her understanding with her husband. The House reasserted the rule that permission to drive did not, on its own, constitute the driver an agent of the owner. The purposes for which the car was being driven at the time of the accident were purely those of the husband and the friend; indeed, the driver was not bringing the husband home but driving away from the couple's home towards a restaurant. The House confined the agency principle to situations involving the delegation of a task and asserted that it was for the legislature, not the courts, to determine whether it was appropriate to introduce a "family car" principle into English law and the terms on which this should be done.

Although the decision in *Morgans* conferred House of Lords authority on the limited version of the agency principle, it is submitted that it is now not needed and should be rejected. If it had any rationale, it was to plug gaps in the insurance cover when the owner of a car permitted it to be used by another who was not insured because of restrictions applicable to the policy. The decision in *Morgans* limits the situations in which this device will work and it was, in any case, inferior to the direct breach of statutory duty remedy

---

[61] *Ormrod* v. *Crosville Motor Services Ltd.* [1953] 1 W.L.R. 1120.

[62] *Scarsbrook* v. *Mason* [1961] 3 All E.R. 767. This decision was doubted by Oliver L.J. in *S.* v. *Walsall M.B.C.* [1985] 3 All E.R. 294; however, it would seem to be a perfectly logical application of the *Hewitt* principle. What is wrong is the principle of vicarious liability for agents, not merely its application to non-owners of vehicles.

[63] [1973] A.C. 127.

placed on an owner who permits an uninsured driver to drive it by the case of *Monk* v. *Warbey*.[64] The whole problem of uninsured drivers is, in practice, dealt with by the Motor Insurers' Bureau which provides insurance cover in favour of the victims of uninsured drivers and since that scheme now covers third party property damage as well as all third party injuries, there is really no role left for the agency principle to play. The law of vicarious liability would present a much more logical appearance if this line of authority were rejected.

Special statutory rules

A Chief Constable is, as a result of section 48 of the Police Act 1964, vicariously liable for the acts of his officers in purported execution of their duty. It has been argued that this is a significant assistance to those who wish to bring civil proceedings against the police because it can avoid the plaintiff having to prove the identity of the officers against whom the complaint is being made.[65] It may be difficult for an individual subjected to police misconduct at a public demonstration or similar occasion to identify the particular officer involved.

Special statutory rules govern the vicarious liability of trade unions for the acts of their officials and members in the course of an industrial dispute.[66]

The Employer's indemnity

A number of legal devices exist which may enable an employer who has been held vicariously liable for damage to recoup his losses from the negligent employee. This is a difficult area of law because it has the capacity to undermine a great deal of the reasoning on which vicarious liability is based. If the devices work, the losses caused by an accident are not distributed into society but channelled back to a single individual. Furthermore the incentive on the employer to insure against the risk of being held liable is reduced. If the claim for an indemnity is brought in the form of a subrogation on behalf of the employer's insurance company there is a very real risk of the insurer seeking to recoup its losses from one of the parties that it had insured.[67] In the light of these factors it is not surprising that measures have been taken to restrict the operation of the employer's indemnity. However, it has not been wholly excluded from the law.

It is likely to be an implied term of most contracts of employment that the employee will take reasonable care when performing his job to protect the employer against financial losses. It follows that the negligence of an employee in the course of the employment will justify a damages claim by an employer who suffers loss as a result. In *Lister* v. *Romford Ice and Cold Storage Co. Ltd.*[68] such a term was recognised by the majority of the House of Lords as justifying a successful claim for indemnity by an employer against

---

[64] [1935] 1 K.B. 75.
[65] L. Lustgarten, *The Governance of Police*, p. 136.
[66] Trade Union and Labour Relations (Consolidation) Act 1992, ss. 20–22.
[67] The employer's insurance is almost certain to have covered liabilities of both the employer and employee.
[68] [1957] A.C. 555.

its employee, a lorry driver, whose negligent driving had led to the employer paying damages to a person who had been injured. The employee's argument that there was a necessary implied term that this right would not be exercised in circumstances in which the insurance policy covered both the employer's and the employee's liability was rejected. However, the insurance implications of the decision were such that, faced by the prospect of legislation to reverse the decision, the insurance industry was induced to reach a "gentleman's agreement" with the government to the effect that it would not exercise these rights in future other than in cases of collusion or wilful misconduct by the employee.

Although the "gentleman's agreement" has solved most of the difficulties created by the employer's indemnity, cases still occasionally arise. Shortly after *Lister*, in *Harvey* v. *O'Dell*,[69] an employer who had been held vicariously liable attempted to recoup the sum which he had paid as damages from the negligent employee,[70] a storekeeper, whose riding of his motor cycle, in the course of his employment, had injured a fellow employee. McNair J. succeeded in avoiding the implied term basis of *Lister* by arguing that it was impossible to imply a term into the contract of employment of a storekeeper that the employee should drive carefully, merely because he occasionally used his motor cycle in the course of his employment to help out. However, the judge still held that the employer was entitled to recover a 100 per cent. contribution[71] from the employee under the terms of the contribution legislation.[72]

JOINT LIABILITY AND CONTRIBUTION

Joint liability[73] covers a variety of situations in which two or more people are liable to the same person for the same damage. Examples of this situation are familiar in tort. The joint acts of a number of motorists may combine to injure the plaintiff; an employer will be jointly responsible with his employee for torts committed by the employee in the course of his employment and the various persons who are responsible for the design and construction of a building may be jointly liable to subsequent occupiers for injuries caused by negligently created defects. The two related topics of joint liability and contribution in tort are governed by the Civil Liability (Contribution) Act 1978.

It is a general principle of English law that any person whose tortious conduct causes damage to another may be held liable for the full loss incurred by the injured party. This remains the case even though a particular defendant's contribution to the damage was manifestly smaller than that made by others. A plaintiff can pursue a number of cases against different

---

[69] [1958] 2 Q.B. 78.

[70] It is likely that the case was in reality a dispute between insurance companies, *i.e.* between the company which covered the employer's liability and that which insured the employee's third party liabilities in respect of his motor cycle.

[71] For a discussion of the principles governing contribution claims, see *post*, p. 141.

[72] For a further example of judicial manipulation of implied contractual terms to limit the use of the employer's indemnity see *Morris* v. *Ford Motor Co. Ltd.* [1973] Q.B. 792.

[73] For a discussion of the distinction between joint and several tortfeasors see Clerk & Lindsell on *Torts* (16th ed.), para. 2–53 *et seq.*

defendants in relation to the same damage, although the loss which has been suffered cannot be recovered more than once. This rule secures the interests of the victims of a tort by allowing them to pursue more than one defendant and to enforce liability against the one who has the means of meeting the judgment. As a result, a defendant who is insured or solvent may find that his minor share in responsibility for damage leaves him underwriting the liability of others. It is likely that this factor explained much of the expansion, in the late 1970s and early 1980s, in the negligence liability of local authorities and professional persons working in the construction industry: their assets and insurance policies were being used as a way of securing the interests of injured consumers who would otherwise have had to face the difficulty of suing, possibly insolvent, building contractors.

The Civil Liability (Contribution) Act 1978 allows tortfeasors who are jointly liable for tortiously caused damage to a particular victim to seek a contribution which will apportion the liability between themselves. The result of the two rules of joint liability and contribution is that the law does not compel a plaintiff to collect his damages from different defendants according to their share of responsibility for the damage, but it allows the liability of one defendant to be redistributed to others who are jointly responsible for the damage.

Contribution claims can arise in two ways. A plaintiff can bring proceedings against a group of defendants and the court can dispose of the plaintiff's claim against the tortfeasors and of the appropriate apportionment of responsibility between those tortfeasors in a single set of proceedings. Alternatively, a defendant may seek to recoup part of his liability to the plaintiff by instituting separate proceedings for a contribution against others once the initial proceedings brought against him have been concluded in the plaintiff's favour. The 1978 Act operates on the same basis in either situation.

In order to succeed in a contribution claim, it must be shown that the person claimed against (D2) is liable in law to the same plaintiff for the same damage as the person claiming contribution (D1). The basis of that liability need not be identical: one defendant may be liable under the tort of negligence whereas the other may be liable for breach of contract, breach of trust or otherwise.[74] Neither need the extent of the two defendant's liability be identical. If, for example, the plaintiff's initial injuries are caused by D1 and further damage is caused by negligent medical treatment provided by D2, in such a way as not to break the chain of causation from D1's tort, apportionment should be possible in respect of the additional injuries.

Under the 1978 Act a person may normally seek a contribution to his liability from another tortfeasor even though the case against him has not gone as far as to establish his liability. Section 1(4) allows a settlement or compromise to be the basis of contribution proceedings because it is felt that not to do this might unnecessarily prolong proceedings by discouraging defendants from settling claims. D2 is protected in such circumstances by the fact that the settlement must have been made in good faith and because it still needs to be proved that D2 was liable to the plaintiff for the damage which was the basis of the settlement. The one problem which affects the operation of this subsection is that it is dependent upon the person who is seeking a

---

[74] subs. 6(1).

contribution being liable in law if the factual case made against him were to be established.

The subsection therefore applies to cases which concern disputed facts which are settled, but not to those which raise an issue of law. In such a case it has been suggested that a defendant will need to submit to a judgment in order to maintain his right to claim contribution from other tortfeasors.[75]

Under section 2(1) of the Act the amount of contribution to be made by one tortfeasor to another is "such as may be found to be just and equitable." Although fairly consistent results can be discerned in the cases concerning familiar relationships between tortfeasors,[76] this provision effectively gives the court a wide discretion which is to be exercised on the facts of the particular case. The wording of the subsection mirrors that which governs the apportionment of damages between plaintiff and defendant on the basis of contributory negligence under the Law Reform (Contributory Negligence) Act 1945. It is generally thought that the factors of causation and blameworthiness which are considered in that context are equally relevant to the operation of the discretion under the 1978 Act. However, the 1978 Act does go further than the 1945 Act in so far as section 2(2) permits a nil or 100 per cent. contribution.

If a contribution is claimed from a tortfeasor who has limited his liability by means of a contract, or who is able to plead the defence of contributory negligence to reduce the damages payable to the plaintiff, the amount which can be claimed in contribution proceedings against him cannot be greater than the amount he would have had to pay the plaintiff if directly sued.

Nothing in the 1978 Act affects any rights of one party to enforce his rights to an indemnity, created by the express or implied terms of a contract, from another in respect of liability to a third party. In addition there is nothing in the Act to prevent parties from entering into private contractual arrangements which exclude the statutory results.

Joint liability is a fundamental rule of English law which is firmly based in the full compensation theory. The rule protects plaintiffs by increasing the chances of their collecting compensation at the price of possible injustice to defendants who may have to pick up the whole bill for damage for which they have only a minor responsibility. The rule has vocal critics. Bodies representing professional persons, particularly those in the construction industry, have argued that it is unfair that their indemnity policies should underwrite the liabilities of those with whom they are involved. It is argued that, in relation to non-personal injury cases in excess of a certain value, a successful plaintiff should only be able to collect from each defendant the proportion of the loss which it is just and equitable for that person to pay.[77] Adherents to the deterrent theory of tort may also argue that the rule has the potential of making those defendants who are likely to have the means of paying damages produce an inefficient level of care. As the rule can lead to the damages payable by that person exceeding the loss attributable to their work it may produce an incentive to increase the level of precautions used beyond those which would be justified by the criterion of efficiency. It may be

[75] Dugdale, (1979) 42 M.L.R. 182.
[76] Dugdale, (1985) 1 P.N. 11.
[77] D.T.I., *Professional Liability*, Report of the Study Teams (1989) Construction Industry Team, para. 10.2.2. The financial limit was designed to exclude claims brought on behalf of domestic clients.

doubted whether these criticisms are likely to achieve any changes in a rule as basic to the working of the tort system as joint liability. It is certainly highly unlikely that a particular area of activity, such as the construction industry, will be granted exceptional treatment.[78]

---

[78] It is slightly more likely that the standard conditions of engagement of professional persons working in the construction industry will be amended to exclude the statutory rules. The Construction Industry Study Team of the Likierman Committee saw this as a possible way forward.

Chapter Seven

Remedies

This chapter will consider certain principles which are generally applicable to tort remedies. The detailed rules concerning the operation of particular remedies in relation to particular forms of damage (for example the calculation of damages for personal injuries) will be discussed in the appropriate context.

DAMAGES

The most familiar remedy in a tort claim is an award of damages: a payment of money by the defendant to the successful plaintiff.

The purpose of the award

The traditional view of the purpose of an award of damages in tort is that the aim is compensation rather than deterrence or punishment. It is to remove the consequences of the tort by providing full compensation to the injured party. The classic statement of this principle is that of Lord Blackburn in *Livingstone* v. *Raywards Coal Co.*[1]: " . . . in settling the sum of money to be given for reparation of damages you should as nearly as possible get at that sum of money which will put the party who has been injured, or who has suffered, in the same position as he would have been in if he had not sustained the wrong for which he is now getting his compensation or reparation." The aim is to remove the harm attributable to the tort, rather than to ensure, as actions brought in contract do, that the plaintiff receives the benefits which he hoped to receive had the tort not occurred.

These principles have been illustrated by cases of deceit or negligent misrepresentation which are on the borderline between contract and tort. A defendant who, on selling a business to the plaintiff, promises that it will achieve a certain level of profit, will be bound to make good that promise. If, as is more likely, the vendor merely misrepresents the potential of the business (*i.e.* commits a tort), the damages will be calculated according to the money which the plaintiff lost as a result of investing in the project, including a sum which would have been earned had the money been invested elsewhere.[2]

---

[1] (1880) 5 App. Cas. 25.
[2] *Esso Petroleum Ltd.* v. *Mardon* [1976] Q.B. 801; *Swingcastle Ltd.* v. *Alistair Gibson* [1991] 2 A.C. 223; *East* v. *Maurer* [1991] 1 W.L.R. 461.

This distinction is at times summarised as being that contract takes the plaintiff forward whereas tort restores the status quo. This is potentially misleading. Tort seeks to remove the losses as they exist at the date of the assessment and it is perfectly capable of compensating for losses which can be predicted as likely to be incurred in the future and which are based on damage to interests founded on contractual promises. A personal injury case in which loss of earnings will continue into the future is an obvious example of this.

The traditional view that the essential function of damages is compensation has not gone unchallenged.[3] It should not be particularly surprising that a body of law which pursues a variety of aims should recognise a variety of remedies with different purposes. According to this approach the compensatory aim of damages should be seen as representing the major, but not the exclusive, aim of tort remedies. If this is accepted some of the remedies which are traditionally regarded as species of compensation, damages for the upset and annoyance caused by a defamatory statement or a wrongful arrest and damages for the non-financial losses resulting from a personal injury may be better viewed as designed to console rather than to compensate. Similarly, it may be preferable to regard some of the measures of damages available for trespass to land and wrongful interference with goods[4] as directed to obtaining restitution of an unfair advantage obtained by a tortfeasor rather than as an artificial form of compensation for the losses suffered by the plaintiff. Any assertion of the traditional view of the purpose of an award of damages needs to be qualified to take account of the availability of contemptuous, nominal and punitive awards. However, the more radical view is that the traditional view, that there exists a general rule subject to exceptions, should be abandoned and that the position should be accepted that awards of damages are designed to achieve different ends according to the circumstances in which the award is made.

General principles

Damages are generally awarded in the form of a lump sum on a "once and for all" basis.[5] Once an award has been made no change in the plaintiff's position is allowed to alter it. This principle is relatively simple to operate in relation to property damage but has the potential to cause substantial injustice in a personal injury case in which the loss suffered by the victim is expected to continue to be suffered into the future.[6]

A distinction which is commonly made is that between "general" and "special" damages. In the context of the liability rules relating to certain torts, such as public nuisance[7] or slander[8] "special" damage means that, before any cause of action will be vested in him, the plaintiff must prove that

---

[3] Birks, *Civil Wrongs: A New World.*
[4] *Strand Electric & Engineering Co. Ltd.* v. *Brisford Entertainments Ltd.* [1952] 2 Q.B. 246 and *B.B.M.B.Finance (Hong Kong) Ltd.* v. *Eda Holdings Ltd.* [1990] 1 W.L.R. 409.
[5] Certain apparent exceptions exist in the case of a single wrong which infringes two distinct rights of the victim and in the case of a continuing wrong which inflicts damage which constitutes a fresh cause of action each day for as long as the tort continues.
[6] These issues are discussed at p. 256.
[7] See *post*, p. 402.
[8] See *post*, p. 443.

he suffered losses over and above those suffered by the rest of the community. However, in the context of the calculation of damages, the distinction is between those items of loss which are capable of being calculated with reasonable precision, such as damage to property and expenses and earnings losses incurred by a personal injury victim before the date of trial and those items such as pain and suffering and future losses, the "general" damages, which are of their nature incapable of being reduced to precise figures. Special damages, unlike general damages, need to be specifically pleaded.

Damages in most tort cases are assessed by the judge who hears the case. In this way judicial knowledge of other cases tends to produce conformity in the levels of damages awarded to persons who suffer similar injuries. However, jury trial is still available in a limited number of areas; most notably, defamation, false imprisonment and malicious prosecution.[9] The level of damages awarded by juries in defamation cases in recent years has caused considerable disquiet, particularly because the highest awards[10] have been far in excess of the money which would be awarded to a person who suffered the most serious forms of personal disability as a result of a tort.

There has been a slow, but steady, move towards restricting the level of awards made by juries in this area. The problem has been to find a satisfactory mechanism which is not seen as usurping the function of juries. In *Sutcliffe* v. *Pressdram Ltd.*[11] the Court of Appeal took a faltering step in this direction when it was prepared to order a retrial on the grounds that a jury's award of £600,000 must have been made on an erroneous basis. It was said to be acceptable for the judge to direct the jury that it should have regard to the income which would be produced by the capital awarded. On the facts, an award of £600,000 would, if invested properly, have given the plaintiff an income of over £1,000 a week. However, the court reiterated the conventional rules that although judges can direct juries not to take into account any knowledge which they may have acquired of other awards for similar torts it is not open to the judge to suggest a bracket of figures as the acceptable range of damages for the particular tort as this would usurp the function of the jury and be likely to give grounds for appeal.

The powers of the Court of Appeal to intervene in relation to jury awards were increased by section 8 of the Courts and Legal Services Act 1990. This gives the court power to substitute, for an award made by the jury which it regards as either inadequate or excessive, its own assessment of what would have been a "proper" sum to be awarded. This provision expands the powers of the court (previously it could only remit the case for consideration by another jury) but it was debatable, until the decision of the Court of Appeal in *Rantzen* v. *Mirror Group Newspapers*,[12] whether it made a significant difference to the circumstances in which the powers could be exercised. However, in *Rantzen*, the court interpreted the word "excessive" as having been intended to lower the threshold at which it was appropriate for it to intervene. It took the test to be whether a reasonable jury could "have

<hr>

[9] Supreme Court Act 1981, s.69.
[10] Recent awards include: £450,000 to Barney Eastwood in March 1992; £250,000 (subsequently reduced to £110,000) to Esther Rantzen in January 1992; £1.5 million to Lord Aldington in December 1989 and £500,000 to Jeffrey Archer in July 1987. An out of court settlement made in December 1988 paid £1 million to Elton John and the jury's award to Sonia Sutcliffe (which was subsequently reduced) was for £600,000.
[11] [1991] 1 Q.B. 153.
[12] [1993] 4 All E.R. 975.

thought that this award was necessary to compensate the plaintiffs and to re-establish his reputation?" The court supported the practice whereby juries could not be referred to previous jury awards or to judge made personal injury awards. The first category was excluded because earlier awards could not be regarded as having been made on a principled basis and the second because no satisfactory link could be made between the different areas. However, the court did believe that it was appropriate for juries to be referred to awards substituted by the Court of Appeal under its section 8 powers as it felt that the intention behind that section was to build up a corpus of authority as to appropriate level of damages to be awarded by juries. In the light of this stance it is slightly disappointing that the Court of Appeal did not enunciate its reasons for using its section 8 powers to reduce the jury's award in that case from £250,000 to £110,000. The truth is, of course, that any attempt to produce a tariff for the kind of intangible losses caused by defamation will face severe problems.

Mitigation of damage

The duty which is placed on a plaintiff to mitigate his damage requires that he act reasonably to limit the losses caused by the tort. The doctrine is not truly a duty owed to another person. An accident victim can be as extravagant as he wishes; he is merely barred by the doctrine of mitigation from charging the cost of that extravagance to the tortfeasor.

Mitigation plays a central role in the process of calculating awards of damages. It is commonly the basis governing the question of whether the appropriate measure in the case of property damage is the cost of repairing or of replacing the item[13] or for determining whether a relative's loss of earnings or the cost of professional nursing services is the measure of the costs caused to a victim by an accident.[14] Furthermore, in a period of inflating costs, mitigation can determine the date by reference to which the cost of effecting repairs should be determined.[15] The doctrine can have a more drastic effect on an award than doctrines of causation because it can limit the extent of a defendant's responsibility for a type of damage which is foreseeable. In personal injury cases mitigation of damage issues may arise in relation to whether the victim has failed to return at a suitable time to his previous or alternative work and in relation to a failure to submit to recommended medical treatment aimed at assisting a recovery. The burden of proof shifts in these cases to the defendant to prove that in all the circumstances, the plaintiff acted unreasonably.[16] However, the courts do not allow mitigation to be used by tortfeasors as the basis for a hypercritical assessment of the plaintiff's conduct. The obligation to act reasonably is

---

[13] Cf. Darbishire v. Warran [1963] 1 W.L.R. 1067 and O'Grady v. Westminster Scaffolding [1962] 2 Lloyds Rep. 238.

[14] See p. 266.

[15] In Dodd Properties (Kent) v. Canterbury City Council [1980] 1 W.L.R. 433 the Court of Appeal held that the cost of repairs to a building may be assessed as at the date of trial if it was reasonable for the plaintiff to delay the repairs and that the defendant's denial of liability combined with the plaintiff's impecuniosity might make such a delay reasonable.

[16] In Selvanayagam v. University of the West Indies [1983] 1 W.L.R. 585 the Privy Council suggested that the burden of disproving a failure to mitigate was on the plaintiff. However, this is generally regarded as conflicting with established House of Lords authority to the effect that the burden of proving a failure to mitigate is on the defendant. McGregor, (1983) 46 M.L.R. 758.

interpreted with a degree of latitude for the difficulties in which the victim was placed by the defendant's act. It was on the basis of this approach that a defendant who had negligently performed a sterilisation was not successful in arguing that the plaintiff should have mitigated her loss by terminating her pregnancy.[17] Mitigation will also not bar the recovery of expenses reasonably incurred in fruitless attempts to limit the loss.

Non-compensatory damages

Although an award of damages in tort is generally designed to provide compensation to the victims of the conduct there exist a number of forms of damages which have other aims.

1. Nominal damages

Nominal damages are small awards of money which are awarded in cases in which the plaintiff has established that the defendant committed a tort against him but is unable to show that he suffered any loss. By definition such awards can only be made in the case of those torts which are actionable *per se*; that is, without damage being an essential part of the cause of action. Nominal awards are particularly appropriate in relation to torts such as trespass which have the role of vindicating the plaintiff's rights.

2. Contemptuous damages

Contemptuous damages are awarded when a court considers that the plaintiff's action, although successful, should not have been brought. Such an award, which is not unknown in defamation cases, will usually be for the smallest coin in the currency. It may well lead to the plaintiff, although successful, having to bear some, or all, of the costs of the action.

3. Punitive damages[18]

In these cases the damages awarded may exceed the losses which have been suffered by the injured plaintiff. The principles governing such awards of damages were thoroughly reviewed in Lord Devlin's speech in *Rookes* v. *Barnard*[19] and further amplified in the House of Lords decision in *Broome* v. *Cassell & Co. Ltd.*[20] The starting point for Lord Devlin's approach is that tort actions are generally designed to provide compensation and that these awards, by introducing punitive considerations into tort, confuse the functions of criminal and civil law. However, Lord Devlin accepted that the weight of authority favouring such awards of damages made it impossible to remove them from the law and that circumstances may occur in which an award of this kind may serve the useful purpose of "vindicating the strength of the law." His speech in the case was an attempt to regularise what he regarded as the anomaly of punitive damages.

As part of this regularisation Lord Devlin drew a firm distinction between "exemplary" and "aggravated" damages. Before *Rookes* these terms had

---

[17] *Emeh* v. *Kensington A.H.A.* [1985] Q.B. 1012.
[18] See generally; Ghandhi, (1990) 10 L.S. 182; Anderson, (1992) C.J.Q. 233 and Law Commission Consultation Paper No. 132.
[19] [1964] A.C. 1129.
[20] [1972] A.C. 1072.

been used interchangeably to describe any form of punitive award of damages and it is likely that most of the older authorities dealt with what would now be termed aggravated damages. After *Rookes* "aggravated" damages denotes an area of compensatory damages which may be awarded in cases in which the loss is "at large"; that is, where a range of figures is acceptable as compensation because no precise monetary figure can be fixed for the compensation. An award of damages for injured feelings and damage to reputation caused by a libel is an obvious example. Awards of this kind may be "aggravated" in two ways: first, they may be fixed at the higher end of the bracket of acceptable compensatory figures to take account of the injury to the plaintiff's feelings and reputation resulting from the nature of the defendant's conduct; secondly, conduct of the defendant subsequent to the time at which the tort occurred may be allowed to increase the level of the damage and hence the compensation merited. In *Sutcliffe* v. *Pressdram Ltd.*[21] Nourse L.J. described the latter class of aggravation as including:

"a failure to make any or any sufficient apology or withdrawal; a repetition of the libel; conduct calculated to deter the plaintiff from proceedings; persistence, by way of a prolonged or hostile cross-examination of the plaintiff or in turgid speeches to the jury, in a plea of justification which is bound to fail; the general conduct either of the preliminaries or of the trial itself in a manner calculated to attract further wide publicity; and persecution of the plaintiff by other means."

"Exemplary" damages go further and are truly punitive in nature. As a result of *Rookes* an award of exemplary damages is now only appropriate in three categories of case: oppressive, arbitrary or unconstitutional action by government servants; wrongful conduct which is calculated by the defendant to make a profit for himself and, cases where such an award is justified by statute.[22] Although these limits are now firmly established they have not escaped criticism on the grounds that they are unduly rigid and illogical.[23] The truth is that there is no logical reason for limiting the scope of such awards in this way but that Lord Devlin was not prepared to extend what he regarded as an anomalous form of damages beyond the limits strictly recognised by earlier authority and the categories represent those limits.

The category of oppressive arbitrary or unconstitutional behaviour by servants of the government is derived from a number of eighteenth century authorities[24] which sought to protect the liberties of the subject from the power of the State. This category of exemplary damages was regarded by Lord Devlin as too valuable to be lost. In *Broome* v. *Cassell & Co. Ltd.*[25]

---

[21] [1990] 1 All E.R. 269 at 288.

[22] See the Reserve & Auxiliary Forces (Protection of Civil Interests) Act 1951, s. 13(2) (Lord Kilbrandon in *Broome* regarded this as an example of the older usage of the term exemplary damages and as in fact dealing with what modern usage would term aggravated damages) and s.97(2) of the Copyright, Designs and Patents Act 1988 which gives a right to "additional damages" (the authorities differ as to whether an award made under this section is of aggravated or exemplary damages).

[23] The *Rookes* limitations have received a hostile reception in other common law jurisdictions. For a short survey see Law Commission Consultation Paper No. 132.

[24] *Wilkes* v. *Wood* (1763) Lofft. 1 (Trespass to land); *Huckle* v. *Money* (1763) 2 Wils. K.B. 205 (Trespass to the person); *Benson* v. *Frederick* (1766) 3 Burr. 1845 (Trespass to the person).

[25] [1972] A.C 1072.

Lord Hailsham was of the view that liability under this category should not be confined to government servants in the strict sense but might extend to the police and local government officials. Awards of exemplary damages have, as a result, become a familiar feature of claims brought against the police for false imprisonment and the various kinds of trespass.[26] In *Holden* v. *Chief Constable of Lancashire*[27] the Court of Appeal encouraged this development when it held that Lord Devlin's words should be read disjunctively: it was open to a court to make an award of exemplary damages if the behaviour of the police was unconstitutional even though it was neither oppressive nor arbitrary. There has been debate in the cases as to the forms of activity which may fall within the first category. In *AB.* v. *South West Water Services Ltd.*[28] the Court of Appeal held that the defendant, which was a nationalised body, was not performing a governmental function when conducting its main commercial activity of supplying a product to its customers. However, in the earlier case of *Arora* v. *Bradford City Council*[29] the Court of Appeal held that an activity which justified an award of exemplary damages under the first category need not be of a nature that it could only be committed by a public body. It could not be argued that a local authority when conducting an interview for a job was exercising a private rather than a governmental function.

The main criticism levelled at the first category is that it is irrational to exclude examples of oppressive or arbitrary conduct by big businesses from the ambit of exemplary damages as such bodies may be capable of causing as much, if not more, damage than a public body. Why, for example, should the police, but not private store detectives, be liable for abusing their powers? Secondly, it is argued that there are pragmatic objections to imposing punitive awards on public bodies as it is likely that they will be funded, ultimately, not by the public official whose conduct is at issue, but from general public expenditure.[30]

The profit-earning class of exemplary damages is most commonly found in two areas of tort: cases of defamation in which a defendant damages another's reputation in order to sell a publication and cases of trespass to land, the typical example being one in which a landlord wrongfully evicts a tenant in order to make the property available for a more profitable use. As is the case with the previous category, Lord Devlin's words, to the effect that the defendant must have "calculated" that his conduct would make a profit which might exceed the compensation payable for the tort, have been given a liberal interpretation. Lord Devlin himself was of the view that this category was not confined to money making in the strict sense but included the defendant making any gain at the plaintiff's expense. However, in *Broome* the members of the House of Lords emphasised that the mere fact that the conduct occurred in a business context, for example, the fact that defamatory matter was published in a newspaper, would not justify the making of an

---

[26] *White* v. *Metropolitan Police*, *The Times* April 24, 1982; *Holden* v. *Chief Constable of Lancashire* [1987] Q.B. 380.

[27] [1987] Q.B. 380.

[28] [1993] 1 All E.R. 609.

[29] [1991] I.R.L.R. 165. The result in this case cannot stand with that in *AB*.

[30] American practice has tended to protect public bodies from such awards rather than singling them out as peculiarly appropriate subjects. See Law Commission Consultation Paper No. 132, p. 180.

award of exemplary damages and in *AB. v. South West Water Services Ltd.*[31] the Court of Appeal refused to accept that an allegation that a defendant had covered up the fact that it had committed a tort brought the case within the category even though its acts might have led to pecuniary advantage in avoiding a liability to pay damages. Even though the courts do not require the defendant to have made a precise arithmetical calculation of the benefits to be obtained from the tortious conduct he must be shown to have knowingly or recklessly proceeded with the conduct knowing it to be wrong because the advantages of going ahead outweigh the risks involved. In practice, this requirement seems to have meant that exemplary damages are not sought in many cases of defamation by the press as it is difficult to produce evidence that the defendant calculated that the defamation would yield a profit by boosting the sales of the publication. Many of the largest awards made by juries in such cases have apparently been cases in which only aggravated damages were sought.[32]

Some commentators[33] have regarded this category of exemplary damages as a species of restitutionary remedy under which a benefit wrongfully obtained by the defendant at the plaintiff's expense is recouped. However, cases are recorded in which the exemplary damages awarded have exceeded the benefit obtained by the defendant[34] and it can therefore be assumed that the punitive purpose of teaching the defendant that tort does not pay, can require an award in excess of the sum required to make restitution of any benefits obtained from the tort. Criticism of the second category has tended to centre on the contention that conduct maliciously designed by the defendant to damage the victim rather than to make a profit is just as reprehensible and should also justify a punitive award of damages.

A further constraint on the making of an award of exemplary damages does not feature in Lord Devlin's speech in *Rookes*, but is now clearly established. Exemplary damages may only be awarded in relation to certain torts. In *AB. v. South West Water Services Ltd.*[35] the Court of Appeal held that, as the intention in *Rookes* had been to restrict the awards of exemplary damages to those areas which were covered by previous authority, such awards could not be made in the absence of pre-1964 authority establishing the availability of exemplary damages for the particular tort. Such awards are supported by authority in relation to defamation; unlawful interference with business[36]; private nuisance[37]; malicious prosecution[38]; and the different species of trespass.[39] However it is not certain whether such an award

---

[31] [1993] 1 All E.R. 609.
[32] The jury award of £600,000 which was overturned on appeal in *Sutcliffe* v. *Pressdram Ltd.* [1991] 1 Q.B. 153 was a case in which exemplary damages were not claimed.
[33] McGregor on *Damages* (15th ed.), para. 422. Lord Diplock in *Broome* adopted this approach.
[34] *Macmillan* v. *Singh* (1984) 17 H.L.R. 120.
[35] [1993] 1 All E.R. 609.
[36] *Messenger Newspapers Group Ltd.* v. *National Graphical Association* [1984] I.R.L.R. 397.
[37] *Guppys (Bridport) Ltd.* v. *Brookling* (1983) 269 E.G. 846, 942.
[38] *Bishop* v. *Commissioner of Police of the Metropolis, The Times,* December 5, 1989.
[39] *Merest* v. *Harvey* (1814) 5 Taunt. 761; *Wilkes* v. *Wood* (1763) Lofft. 1; *Drane* v. *Evangelou* [1978] 1 W.L.R. 455 (Trespass to land); *Huckle* v. *Money* (1763) 2 Wils. K.B. 205 (Trespass to the person); *Bennson* v. *Frederick* (1766) 3 Burr. 1845 (Trespass to the person) and the more modern case on police powers. See particularly *White* v. *Metropolitan Police, The Times* April 24, 1982 and *Holden* v. *Chief Constable of Lancashire* [1987] Q.B. 380.

can be made in the case of deceit[40] or wrongful interference with goods.[41] Exemplary damages may not be awarded in claims brought in public nuisance or in negligence.[42] As a result, such awards are not available in the great majority of personal injury claims, although they have become established as a remedy in cases based on trespass which feature oppressive, arbitrary or unconstitutional action by government servants such as police officers. This result reflects the generally accepted view that awards of damages made for a personal injury are designed to compensate rather than to punish.[43] As a result, exemplary damages cannot be awarded in English law in negligence proceedings following a major accident however reprehensible the conduct of the defendant may have been in flouting safety requirements. Punitive awards in such situations have become familiar in North America, particularly in product liability cases.[44]

A court is not obliged to make an award of exemplary damages in every case which falls within Lord Devlin's categories. A number of general considerations apply to all cases in which a court is considering making an award of exemplary damages. The most important is that it must be accepted that all awards of damages, particularly aggravated ones, have a punitive effect. It is only if the punitive effect achieved by the compensatory award is felt to be insufficient punishment that an award of exemplary damages is appropriate.[45] The second consideration is that, as the punishment inflicted should be appropriate to the defendant, the court when calculating exemplary damages should take into account the means of the defendant. A rule which follows from this is that if a number of persons are jointly liable for a

---

[40] The availability of the award in such a case was conceded in *Mafo* v. *Adams* [1970] 1 Q.B. 548; however, the members of the court disagreed whether the concession was correctly made. Lord Hailsham L.C. in *Broome* regarded the concession in *Mafo* as incorrect. The judge in *Archer* v. *Brown* [1985] Q.B. 401 favoured the availability of the award in deceit but did not have to decide the point. A possible explanation of the difficulty is the close relationship that such claims have to contract. Exemplary damages cannot be awarded for breach of contract. However, such awards have been made for trespasses and nuisances by landlords against their tenants in spite of the fact that such claims might have been founded in the alternative on the implied covenants in the lease.

[41] In *Mafo* v. *Adams* Sachs L.J. doubted whether either conversion or detinue could give rise to an award of exemplary damages.

[42] *AB.* v. *South West Water Services Ltd.* [1993] 1 All E.R. 609; *Barbara* v. *Home Office* (1984) 134 N.L.J. 888.

[43] In *Kralj* v. *McGrath* [1986] 1 All E.R. 54 an award of aggravated damages was sought in a case in which an obstetrician's conduct in the course of delivering a child had been condemned as "horrific and wholly unacceptable." Woolf J. held that it is not appropriate to make such an award in a medical negligence case because to do so would conflict with the general principle that damages for personal injuries should be compensatory. However, the judge accepted that an increased compensatory award would be appropriate if it could be shown that the defendant's condition as a result of the tort had been worsened by the nature of the defendant's conduct; for example, if the impact of the treatment given made it more difficult for the plaintiff to make a full recovery.

[44] Christie, (1991) Anglo-American L.R. 349.

[45] The authorities conflict as to whether a civil court which is contemplating making an award of exemplary damages should take into account any punishment which has already been inflicted by means of criminal process. *Cf. Archer* v. *Brown* [1985] Q.B. 401 and *Messenger Newspapers Group Ltd.* v. *National Graphical Association* [1984] I.R.L.R. 397. In *AB.* v. *South West Water Services Ltd.* [1993] 1 All E.R. 609 Stuart-Smith L.J. was of the opinion that the criminal process was relevant. He spoke of the risk of serious injustice occurring if a defendant, who had already been convicted and fined by the criminal process, was then subject to an exemplary award.

tort, any award of exemplary damages should be at the lowest level which is appropriate punishment for any one of the tortfeasors; thus an author who has knowingly sought to profit by publishing defamatory matter may be shielded from an exemplary award by the lesser responsibility of other parties involved in the publication of the work with the result that any restitutionary aim underlying the award may be defeated. If exemplary damages are sought by more than one plaintiff in proceedings brought against a single defendant the correct approach is for the court to determine a single sum which constitutes appropriate punishment for the conduct and to divide it equally among the successful plaintiffs.[46] Finally, a judge is entitled to direct the jury that it is entitled to take the conduct of the plaintiff into account when deciding what sum to award.[47] Provocative conduct which results in a wrongful arrest may therefore reduce the punitive damages awarded. This rule is slightly surprising in view of the nature of the conduct which must be proved before an award of exemplary damages is merited.

Rookes v. *Barnard*, by effectively codifying the grounds on which awards of exemplary damages might be made, gave the topic a new lease of life even though the purpose of Lord Devlin's speech was to condemn such awards as an anomaly. The objections to such awards are both theoretical and pragmatic. It is argued, first, that they confuse the functions of the civil and criminal law and give rise to a successful plaintiff receiving an unjustified windfall and, secondly, that they are objectionable because the usual protections provided by the criminal process are absent from this form of punishment: there is no firm definition of the offence; little realistic chance of appealing the extent of the penalty; the penalty may be assessed by a jury and is subject to no maximum and cases are decided according to civil law procedure and burden of proof. The Faulks Committee on Defamation recommended that legislation should abolish awards of exemplary damages in cases of defamation.[48] and the Court of Appeal in *AB*. v. *South West Water Services Ltd*.[49] limited the availability of such awards by a rule based on precedent rather than logic. However, in spite of the objections, it seems possible that awards of exemplary damages may expand into new areas of English law. The subject had shown some vitality in the years before *AB*. was decided and powerful arguments are now being made to the effect that such awards should be made in cases concerning major accidents.[50] The Law Commission has recently published a Consultative document on non-compensatory

---

[46] *Riches* v. *News Group Newspapers* [1986] Q.B. 256. There is support in the *AB*. Case for the view that the existence of multiple victims and the problems of apportioning an award between such persons (not all of whom may be before the court) is a reason for the court deciding not to make an award of exemplary damages.

[47] *Bishop* v. *Commissioner of Police of the Metropolis*, The Times December 5, 1989.

[48] paras. 351–360. The Committee took the view that it was irrational to punish the person who published defamatory matter to make a profit, but not the person who acted out of malice. The Neill Committee (The Supreme Court Procedure Committee's Working Group on Practice and Procedure in Defamation) repeated this recommendation in 1991 (para. IV 11).

[49] [1993] 1 All E.R. 609.

[50] Attempts to achieve judicial support for such awards have been made, but were blocked by the decision of the Court of Appeal in *AB*. v. *South West Water Services Ltd*. [1993] 1 All E.R. 609. The Association of Personal Injury Lawyers in a submission to the Law Commission has argued that punitive damages should not be widely available in personal injury cases, but that they could serve a useful purpose in "cases involving the most serious torts committed in the most reckless of circumstances."

damages[51] which has canvassed a whole range of possibilities ranging from a general recognition of the availability of such awards to their total abolition.

INJUNCTIONS

An injunction is a court order which requires a person to cease to commit tortious conduct. There are various kinds of such order. A prohibitory injunction will compel a person to cease to commit a tort, whereas a mandatory injunction will order a person to take positive action to remove the item, such as an obstruction, which constitutes the tort. A quia timet injunction is one issued to restrain conduct before any damage has been caused and an interlocutory one is a provisional and temporary order pending full trial of the issue between the parties.

The topic of injunctions is of importance in relation to torts such as nuisance, trespass and defamation in which a plaintiff may be concerned to ensure that the defendant's conduct does not continue to cause damage to him. The main problem which arises in relation to injunctions is that the remedy is a discretionary one. However, the discretion is exercised in accordance with well recognised principles. For example, an injunction will not be awarded if damages would be an adequate remedy for the loss suffered in the circumstances or if the harm can be classified as trivial. A long line of cases[52] has emphasised that these principles do not mean that it is an answer to a claim for an injunction against a trespass that it has done no damage to the plaintiff's real property. The plaintiff's right to enjoy property free of interference has been infringed and the fact that any award of damages would probably be nominal means that granting an injunction is necessary to protect the plaintiff's rights from expropriation. Other generally accepted principles are that an injunction will not be awarded if it is impossible for the defendant to comply with it, although, the fact that compliance would entail considerable effort or expense is no bar. The plaintiff's conduct in acquiescing in the defendant's conduct may well act as a bar to the award of an injunction.[53] However, it now seems certain that any public interest in the defendant's acts will not bar the award of an injunction if the plaintiff's rights have been substantially interfered with.[54]

In the case of an interlocutory injunction the general rule is that the court will exercise its discretion to consider whether to grant such as order "on the balance of convenience" if it finds that there is a "serious question to be

---

[51] Consultation Paper No. 132.
[52] *Kelsen* v. *Imperial Tobacco Co. Ltd.* [1957] 2 Q.B. 334; *Anchor Brewhouse Developments Ltd.* v. *Berkeley House (Docklands Developments) Ltd.* (1987) 38 B.L.R. 82; *John Trenberth Ltd.* v. *National Westminster Bank* (1979) 39 P. & C.R. 104. The decision of Stamp J. in *Woollerton & Wilson Ltd.* v. *Richard Costain Ltd.* [1970] 1 W.L.R. 411 to postpone the operation of an injunction for twelve months in order to give the defendants time to complete the work was regarded in *Anchor Brewhouse* and *Trenberth* as incorrect. An attempt to argue that damages calculated according to the rental value of the property trespassed on should provide adequate compensation proved unsuccesful in *Anchor Brewhouse*.
[53] In *Woollerton & Wilson Ltd.* v. *Richard Costain Ltd.* [1970] 1 W.L.R. 411 the plaintiff's decision to refuse the defendant's offer to pay for the right to have their crane enter the airspace above the plaintiff's property was a factor which induced the judge to postpone the operation of an injunction.
[54] *Kennaway* v. *Thompson* [1981] 1 Q.B. 88.

tried"; that is, that the claim is not frivolous and vexatious.[55] Imposition of the higher standard of requiring the plaintiff to establish a prima facie case or a probability of success at trial would compel a court to give a detailed consideration to the evidence at the interlocutory stage. The defendant's position will usually be safeguarded by the fact that the plaintiff who is granted an interlocutory injunction will generally be required to give an undertaking to the court to pay damages for any losses suffered by the defendant as a consequence of the injunction if he fails to establish his case at trial. Special rules govern the award of interlocutory injunctions in two areas of tort. In cases concerning industrial disputes the court is directed to consider the likelihood of the defendant establishing a defence under section 13 of the Trade Union and Labour Relations Act 1974[56] and such an injunction will not normally be granted in a case of an alleged defamation if the defendant intends to plead justification as a defence.[57]

Courts have the power[58] to give an award of damages in lieu of awarding an injunction. This is a difficult power both because it consists of a discretion which is to be exercised on top of a discretion and because it amounts, in effect, to giving damages for future interferences with the plaintiff's rights which the award of an injunction would have prevented. In essence, this jurisdiction allows a defendant who is committing a tort to buy the right to continue to commit it. It is therefore a power which is only exercised sparingly in circumstances in which the court is of the opinion that the grant of an injunction is not merited. In *Shelfer* v. *City of London Electric Lighting Co.*[59] A.L. Smith L.J. stated that "as a good working rule" an award of damages in lieu of an injunction would only be appropriate if the injury to the plaintiff's legal rights is small; if it is one which is capable of being estimated in money; if it is one which can be adequately compensated by a small money payment and if the case is one in which it would be oppressive to the defendant to grant an injunction. If these criteria are not satisfied the injured plaintiff will be protected by the award of an injunction. In *Kennaway* v. *Thompson*[60] the Court of Appeal held that the defendant's activities in using their property as a centre for power boat racing was causing a nuisance to the plaintiff which was of a magnitude which meant that it did not satisfy the *Shelfer* criteria and that it was therefore appropriate to grant an injunction.

---

[55] *American Cyanamid Co.* v. *Ethicon Ltd.* [1975] A.C. 396.

[56] Trade Union and Labour Relations (Consolidation) Act 1992, s. 221(2).

[57] *Bonnard* v. *Perryman* [1891] 2 Ch. 269. The same rule was held not to apply to an allegation of conspiracy to libel another in *Gulf Oil (G.B.) Ltd.* v. *Page* [1987] 3 Ch. 327. However, this decision probably turns on the facts of the case. It was distinguished in the later conspiracy case of *Femis Bank (Anguilla) Ltd.* v. *Lazar* [1991] Ch. 391 on the basis that the plaintiff in *Gulf Oil* had made out a strong prima facie case of conspiracy. In *Femis* the judge exercised his discretion not to grant an interlocutory injunction on the basis of the general public interest in preserving freedom of speech and of the specific interest of allowing allegation to be made which might alert investors and regulatory authorities of the possibility of malfeasance in the affairs of financial institutions.

[58] Supreme Court Act 1981, s. 50. For a full survey of this jurisdiction see Jolowicz, (1975) C.L.J. 224.

[59] [1895] 1 Ch. 287.

[60] [1981] 1 Q.B. 88.

SELF-HELP

In a limited range of circumstances the law may permit a person to redress a tort without the assistance of the judicial process. Self-help in the form of abatement of nuisances or trespasses on land is regarded by the law as a summary remedy which is only appropriate in simple cases or in an emergency; it is not acceptable for a person to attempt to utilise a self-help remedy a long time after the tort has occurred or when a court has heard and rejected a claim by the plaintiff for a mandatory injunction against the interference.[61] Such remedies possess the advantages of being cheap in not requiring an application to be made to a court and in some circumstances may allow a person to defend rights when there is no time to seek judicial assistance. However, they are subject to a variety of legal restrictions, such as the requirement that self-help should be a reasonable response to the tort, which may make it inadvisable for a person to attempt to exercise them without having first obtained legal advice.[62] Self-help remedies are generally discouraged by legal systems because their exercise always carries the risks of exacerbating the problems between the parties and of the stronger party using them to assert and enforce a claim of dubious merit. It is often more satisfactory to compel a person to establish his claim to the satisfaction of a court.[63]

Commonly, self-help remedies involve a degree of interference with the person or property of the wrongdoer, which might, in the absence of justification, be regarded as tortious in itself. It is therefore possible to regard such remedies either as redressing the initial wrong or as creating a defence to a tort claim brought by the wrongdoer.

The most important examples of self-help remedies which survive are the use of reasonable force in response to a threatened battery (whether in self-defence or in defence of a third party)[64] or wrongful arrest, to prevent the commission of a crime or to effect the arrest of offenders or persons unlawfully at large,[65] to resist an attempt to enter land or to take goods unlawfully or to recover goods which have been unlawfully seized. Reasonable force may also be used to eject a person who is trespassing on land. However, this rule is now subject to significant restrictions which are likely to mean that the law of tort will no longer regard many methods of retaking possession of land as reasonable. A landlord may not reclaim possession of a dwelling without a court order[66] and the use of force to re-enter land is now a criminal offence in most circumstances.[67] Self-help remedies are also recognised by the Animals Act 1971 in relation to trespassing livestock[68] and the protection of livestock against dogs[69] and by the law of nuisance, particularly in relation to encroaching roots and branches of trees.

---

[61] *Burton v. Winters* [1993] 3 All E.R. 847.
[62] Lawson, *Remedies of English Law* (2nd ed.), p. 25.
[63] s. 3 of the Protection from Eviction Act 1977 prevents a landlord from evicting a tenant from a dwelling house in the absence of a court order.
[64] The degree of force used must be proportional to the need of the case. See *Lane v. Holloway* [1968] 1 Q.B. 379.
[65] Criminal Law Act 1967, s. 3.
[66] Protection from Eviction Act 1977, s. 3.
[67] Criminal Law Act 1967, Pt. II.
[68] See *post*, p. 383.
[69] Animals Act 1971, s. 9.

RESTITUTIONARY REMEDIES[70]

Restitutionary remedies aim to compel a person who has been "unjustly enriched" to pay over the value of the benefits obtained to those at whose cost the enrichment was made. Restitutionary remedies have a small, but not insignificant, role in tort. In order to obtain a restitutionary remedy it is necessary for a plaintiff to prove that the defendant has been unjustly enriched by his commission of a tort or other wrong against the plaintiff such that a definite sum of money or a readily assessable benefit can be identified as attributable to the tort.

The traditional area of restitutionary remedies in tort is referred to as "waiver of tort." This description is something of a misnomer as the relevant process involves electing to pursue restitution, as opposed to damages, as the remedy for a tort rather than abandoning or waiving the claim in tort. Thus if a person converts the plaintiff's chattels and sells them for more than their market price it is open to the owner to opt to recoup the sum obtained by the defendant and to forgo the damages remedy which would be measured according to the market price. Waiver of tort has been held to be possible in cases of deceit,[71] trespass to land[72] and goods[73] and conversion.[74] There is, however, no conclusive authority as to whether it can apply to other torts such as assault and defamation. There are also examples of statutory rights to claim in tort for an account of the profits obtained by a tortfeasor in the areas of intellectual property[75] and housing law.[76]

The development of restitutionary remedies in tort has been hampered by three factors. First, its role is undertaken, to an extent, by the "profit-earning" category of exemplary damages. This is almost certainly the reason for the lack of authority dealing with restitutionary remedies for defamation. Exemplary damages, when they are available, offer an even more generous measure of recovery untrammelled by any need to produce evidence as to the precise gains made by the defendant from the tort. Secondly, certain remedies, for example the award of the rental value of goods which a person has used to save himself expense,[77] have been treated as a compensatory form of damages even though they might be susceptible to analysis as restitution.[78] Finally, however, the role of restitutionary remedies in tort was significantly limited by the refusal of the Court of Appeal in *Phillips* v. *Homfray*,[79] a case

---

[70] See generally Goff and Jones, *The Law of Restitution* (3rd ed.), Chap. 32.

[71] *Hill* v. *Perrott* (1810) 3 Taunt. 274; *Billing* v. *Ries* (1841) Car. & M. 26; *Kettlewell* v. *Refuge Assurance Co.* [1908] 1 K.B. 545; [1909] A.C. 243.

[72] *Powell* v. *Rees* (1837] 7 A. & E. 426. See also *Penarth Dock Engineering Co. Ltd.* v. *Pounds* [1963] 1 Lloyd's R. 359; *Bracewell* v. *Appleby* [1975] Ch. 408.

[73] *Oughton* v. *Seppings* (1830) 1B. & Ad. 241; *Strand Electric & Engineering Co. Ltd.* v. *Brisford Entertainments Ltd.* [1952] 2 Q.B. 246, 254–255 (*per* Denning L.J.; Somervell and Romer L.JJ. analysed the award as compensatory).

[74] *Lamine* v. *Dorrell* (1705) 2 Ld. Raym. 1216; *Re Simms* [1934] Ch. 1.

[75] Patents Act 1977, ss. 61–62; Copyright, Designs and Patents Act, 1988, ss. 96, 97, 229.

[76] Housing Act 1988, s. 28 (discussed *post*, p. 384).

[77] *Strand Electric & Engineering Co. Ltd.* v. *Brisford Entertainments Ltd.* [1952] 2 Q.B. 246.

[78] See the difference of opinion of the members of the Court of Appeal in *Strand Electric* noted in note 69, above.

[79] (1883) 24 Ch. D. 439.

of trespass by means of the wrongful use of land, to allow their operation in a situation in which the benefit obtained by the defendant was not matched by a loss suffered by the plaintiff. Critics of this rule have argued that it is mistaken in treating what is a personal remedy as a proprietary one.[80]

---

[80] Goff & Jones, *The Law of Restitution* (3rd ed.), p. 611.

PART II

PERSONAL INJURIES AND DEATH

Chapter Eight

Compensation for Injuries and Death

INTRODUCTION

This section deals with compensation for personal injuries and death. A great deal of empirical evidence on the operation of tort exists in relation to this subject and much of the debate on the aims and possible reforms of the tort system has centred on accidents and the physical injuries which they cause. In line with the modern approach to the subject[1] the terms "accident" and "compensation" will be given a wide meaning. "Accident" will be treated as including the intentional infliction of injuries by assaults and cases in which an illness develops as a result of exposure, possibly over a long term, to a particular industrial process or environmental factor. "Compensation" will be taken to encompass the whole range of benefits in money or kind which may be payable to an accident victim through tort, wages, taxation, insurance and the operation of the Welfare State.

It will rapidly become apparent that the role of tort in this area is a limited one. Tort is merely one of several accident compensation systems which overlap and offer different levels of benefit. Harris[2] summarises the overall position in the following words:

"The many systems which currently coexist in this country have evolved in a piecemeal fashion over the last century. New benefits have been introduced to meet the needs of particular categories of people and the law has been modified in an ad hoc manner without any apparent overall strategy. The result has been much criticised as absurdly complex, as embodying serious anomalies, as inefficient and as unnecessarily expensive to administer."

STATISTICS

A fair amount of statistical information is now available on the operation of the accident compensation systems in England and Wales.[3] The Report of the

---

[1] Pearson Commission, Vol. 1, para. 27; Atiyah, *Accidents, Compensation and the Law* (5th ed.), p.3.
[2] Harris and Others, *Compensation and Support for Illness and Injury*, p. 1.
[3] There are inevitably some differences in the results achieved by the different surveys. Those conducted on behalf of the Pearson Commission relate to the position in the early 1970s whereas the Civil Justice Review is based on the position between 1980 and 1986.

Royal Commission on Civil Liability and Compensation for Personal Injury[4] of 1978 (known as the "Pearson" Commission) contained detailed statistics and these have been supplemented by a research project conducted by the Oxford Centre for Socio-Legal Studies[5] and by the work of the Civil Justice Review.[6] For lawyers who believe that tort is the primary remedy for the victims of accidents, the statistics make surprising reading.

Every year there are approximately three million significant injuries[7] and 21,000 deaths caused by accidents in the United Kingdom.[8] The great majority of injuries have no long lasting consequences with only 1.6 per cent. of victims still suffering the effects of the accident after six months.[9] The role of tort in providing compensation for the victims is limited. Only 6 per cent. of victims successfully obtain any compensation from tort[10] and the great majority of these obtain comparatively small sums. The Pearson Commission found that in 1973 over 60 per cent. of successful claimants obtained awards of less than £500 and only 1 per cent. of such people (or 0.065 per cent. of all victims) obtained over £10,000.[11] These figures tell only part of the story. The cause of an accident victim's injury makes a great difference to the likelihood of success. Approximately 25 per cent. of road accident victims obtain money as opposed to 10 per cent. of those injured at work and 1 per cent. of other victims.[12] The tort system, once invoked, seems relatively successful at producing some, albeit small, compensation. If a claim is made, the chance that some money will be forthcoming jumps to between 85 per cent. and 90 per cent.[13] The low percentage of accidentally injured persons obtaining money from tort is due to the fact that many victims do not initiate a claim.[14] The seriousness of the injury suffered is also an important factor in the likelihood of obtaining money from tort. Victims incapacitated from work for more than six months have a 31 per cent. success rate[15] and 21 per cent. of the money paid as tort compensation goes to the 1 per cent. of successful claimants who obtain compensation of more than £1,000.[16]

At the time of the Pearson Commission's report it was calculated that the tort system was paying approximately £202 million each year to 215,000 accident victims.[17] Although only 6 per cent. of social security expenditure was directed to accident victims the amount expended on such persons was

---

[4] Cmnd. 7504.

[5] Published as Harris and others, op. cit. The financial information contained in these pieces of research is obviously out of date. However, as there have been no fundamental changes in the structure of the system since the research was done, it is likely that the general picture is unchanged.

[6] Report of the Review Body on Civil Justice, Cm. 394 (1988).

[7] Those causing four or more days absence from work, or the equivalent injury for the non-employed.

[8] Pearson op. cit. para. 35. The 1986 Consultative Paper (para. 12) issued as part of the Civil Justice Review gave the same figure for England and Wales.

[9] Pearson op. cit. para. 40.

[10] Pearson op. cit. para. 78.

[11] Pearson op. cit. para. 80.

[12] Pearson op. cit. para. 78.

[13] Ibid.

[14] Some, obviously, would not have had a valid claim in tort. For example, the injury may have been the result of the victim's own conduct.

[15] Pearson op. cit. para. 78.

[16] Pearson op. cit. para. 80. Other relevant factors include the sex and age of the victim. Harris refers to the typical successful claimant as being male, aged 21–65 and in full time employment (Harris and others op. cit. p. 51).

[17] Pearson op. cit. para. 44.

more than double that of tort at £421 million and there were 1.55 million new claimants each year.[18] Social security therefore compensated a much greater number of victims but the level of support provided to each was, on average, lower than that provided by tort.

THE OPERATION OF THE TORT SYSTEM

The operation of the tort system is dominated by the fact that it involves an adversary process in which there is little chance of the adversaries meeting on equal terms. The accident victim, who is likely to have no previous experience of tort claims, bears the burden of assembling the evidence needed to convince the defendant's insurance company to settle the claim. The tort system is also notable for the fact that there is no external control on the large number of claims which are concluded by negotiation[19]: the terms of any settlement are left to the parties who may well not meet on equal bargaining terms.

Access to the system

For an accident to give rise to compensation in tort the victim must take the initiative by visiting a solicitor or seeking the advice of a trade union official. Accident victims are likely to be unsure of their legal rights and to be more concerned, in the first instance, with achieving recovery and it is not surprising that the evidence suggests that the great majority of victims do not take the first step. Seventy-five per cent. of the accident victims covered by the Oxford survey claimed never to have considered the question of seeking compensation[20] and only 14 per cent. actually consulted a lawyer.[21] As the great majority of those who took that step obtained some compensation it is likely to be the case that many, but not all, of the 86 per cent. who did not consult a lawyer would have obtained some compensation had they done so.

Different explanations have been offered for the failure of tort to reach vast numbers of accident victims. A great deal of the general literature on access to legal services has centred on arguments to the effect that access to and use of lawyers is, in practice, confined to the richer members of society.[22] The difficulty with this proposition in the context of accident compensation, is that the Oxford research[23] showed that accident victims from the professional and managerial classes were less likely to obtain damages than their counterparts engaged in manual work. The researchers concluded that the most important factor governing the decision to make a claim was access to informal sources of advice. In the case of road accidents this tended to come from the police, medical services and insurance companies whereas in industrial accidents, trade union officials played a substantial role. These two

---

[18] Pearson *op. cit.* para. 44.

[19] Except in the case of cases brought on behalf of infant plaintiffs.

[20] The leading reasons usually advanced for this are ignorance as to rights, fear of costs and lack of evidence. See Civil Justice Review *Consultation Paper: Personal Injuries Litigation*, paras. 16–19 for a survey of the research in this area.

[21] Harris and others *op. cit.* p. 46.

[22] The different approaches found in the literature are summarised in Harris and others *op. cit.* pp. 47–48.

[23] Harris and others *op. cit.* pp. 49–76.

categories of accident are the ones in which the greatest success in obtaining damages is recorded, presumably because there is no equivalent source of informal advice generally available to victims of other categories of accident.

Bargaining inequality

Even if legal advice is sought, the inequalities in the bargaining position of the parties are obvious. This is particularly important because the great majority of personal injury cases are either settled or dropped. Only 2 per cent. of the cases notified to insurers[24] actually reach trial.[25] The personal injury victim is unlikely to have had any previous experience of the operation of the system and will not be able to enter into any negotiations with a firm idea of what the claim is likely to be worth. On the other hand, an insurance company, which, more often than not, will be handling the defence, will be an experienced operator in the field with access to specialist lawyers and witnesses. It is clear that insurance companies see their role as being to operate the system as they find it. Genn[26] expresses their philosophy in terms which scarcely reflect the compensatory purpose of tort:

> "(T)hey operate within a fault system and if, according to the rules of that system, they are liable in law to pay damages to the plaintiff they do so; but if, on the evidence, they are not so liable, then they will not pay damages, regardless of the situation of the plaintiff. The primary obligation of insurance company claims departments is seen as being toward the interests of policy holders, and this obligation is discharged by keeping costs to a minimum. This involves concluding claims at the lowest possible level, and taking what is seen as legitimate advantage of whatever opportunities are presented."

The fact that the balance of power favours the defence means that the processing of claims can be delayed, uncertainties as to the outcome increased and the plaintiff's willingness to continue the case, sapped. An insurance company which resists the payment of damages retains the use of its money and puts pressure on the plaintiff to agree to a settlement. The more pressures which afflict a plaintiff the less likely it is that a settlement will be struck at the level of damages that a court would award and, in view of the pressures, it is not surprising that the vast majority of victims accept the first offer which is made to them.[27]

It might be thought that the balance of power between plaintiff and insurance company could be redressed by the employment of a solicitor by the plaintiff, to handle his case. Unfortunately, the research which has been done reveals that there is likely to be a great difference in the performance of

---

[24] *i.e.* those in relation to which the earliest steps in the litigation process have been taken. Pearson *op. cit.* para. 180. *Cf.* the slightly higher rate recorded by the Civil Justice Review.

[25] The majority are settled, or disposed of in some other way (usually discontinued), by negotiation without any formal legal proceedings having been commenced. The Civil Justice Review statistics were that approximately 340,000 victims make a claim in tort each year but that 300,000 of these are settled without a writ being issued. Only 1 per cent. of the cases in this survey were disposed of by trial.

[26] Genn, *Hard Bargaining*, pp. 50–51.

[27] Harris recorded (*op. cit.* p. 93) that the first offer to settle was accepted in 63 per cent. of the cases covered by the Oxford survey. A second offer, if made, was on average between one-third and one-half higher than a first offer and any third offer that was made was on average one-third higher than the second one (pp. 101–104).

different solicitors in handling personal injury litigation. Solicitors who specialise in the area undoubtedly have the skill to value a claim, assemble the relevant evidence and use the rules of procedure in a way which will put pressure on the insurers to settle the claim on realistic terms. On the other hand, unless the plaintiff has access to information as to the specialisms of particular solicitors, as will be the case if the claim is supported by trade union funds, there is little guarantee that it will be handled by a specialist. Personal injury litigation is still regarded as a part of general legal practice and is commonly conducted by non-specialist solicitors.[28] A number of problems may beset personal injury work which is performed by general practitioner solicitors.[29] Most importantly, they may adopt too co-operative an approach towards insurers; they may delay the commencement of proceedings and hence reduce the pressure on the insurer to settle; they may fail to appreciate the need to assemble the relevant evidence quickly and may, as a result, give inadequate information to counsel and, finally, they may be too keen to settle the case because of the financial pressures on the plaintiff. The plaintiffs probably lack the knowledge which would enable them to instruct a suitable firm and to evaluate any advice which is given. It is likely to be a matter of chance whether they instruct a specialist firm which handles hundreds of such claims a year (such quantities of work will often result from that firm being instructed by a trade union to handle injury claims on behalf of its members) or one which conducts such work as a side line to its conveyancing and probate work. Once the instructions have been given, the client will almost certainly be unable to exert any meaningful control over the conduct of the case.

Costs and the funding of claims

A person who is contemplating commencing a claim for tort compensation has to consider the financial burden which litigation can entail. In the words of the Civil Justice Review "The risk of having to bear all the costs, which can be very substantial, at the end of the case is a major inducement to settlements short of a trial. This risk bears more heavily on the economically weaker party which, in personal injury cases, is usually the plaintiff."[30]

It has been estimated that the average cost to a claimant of taking a personal injury case through to trial in the High Court in 1984 was £6,830.[31] A comparison of the costs incurred by both sides with the average compensation recovered in tort proceedings tells a particularly remarkable story. The Civil Justice Review estimated that in High Court proceedings an average of £50 or £70 was spent for every £100 recovered; in County Court proceedings, where the damages recovered were lower, the equivalent figures for costs were £125 or £175.[32] As one writer has commented "the system is . . .

---

[28] Genn's survey of solicitors showed that 73 per cent. of respondents regarded personal injury work as one of their specialisms whereas only 44 per cent. spent more than 20 per cent. of their time on such work (Genn *op. cit.* p. 37).

[29] See generally Genn *op. cit.*

[30] Civil Justice Review, *Consultation Paper: Personal Injuries Litigation*, para. 46.

[31] Civil Justice Review, *Consultation Paper: Personal Injuries Litigation*, para. 69. The equivalent figure for County Court proceedings was £1,540.

[32] The different figures were produced by different bases of calculation. The first was based on information obtained from solicitors whereas the second was derived from a sample of taxed solicitors' bills.

operated in a fashion which accumulates substantial expenses not only in the unusual case, but also in the ordinary. Although most cases settle, they settle after the vast majority of the costs of litigation have already been incurred."[33]

A self-funding plaintiff who is confident that the claim will be successful can rely on the fact that the costs incurred are likely to be recovered on the basis that "the costs follow the event." This means that if the confidence is justified the losing defendant will be liable to meet the plaintiff's costs. Many settlements are made on the basis that the plaintiff's solicitor's costs are to be paid by the defence. However, a successful plaintiff may well find that the full costs that have been incurred will not be recovered. This is particularly the case if the costs payable by a losing defendant are "taxed" by the court,[34] as the costs allowed to be recovered by a court on taxation do not always represent the full amount which has been expended on the plaintiff's behalf. These difficulties are obviously increased when the outcome is uncertain and there is a real prospect of the plaintiff losing and having to bear the defence's costs.

It is only those plaintiffs who are supported financially by trade unions[35] or who are entitled to receive legal aid without obligation to make a contribution to the costs of the case who are in the enviable position of not having to find the money to fund the work of their own solicitor and who are not at risk of being held liable for the other side's costs if the claim fails.

The uncertainty created by the operation of the rules concerning costs is increased by rules which allow a defendant to pay money into court. This is a method by which a defendant may make an offer to the plaintiff of a sum of money in respect of his claim. A payment in usually places the plaintiff under pressure to settle because a plaintiff who declines to accept the payment in and who is subsequently awarded the same or a lesser sum by the court as damages, will be liable for the costs incurred by the losing side from the date of the payment in. In effect, he will be held to have been wrong to have continued to pursue the case beyond that date.[36]

A plaintiff who is entitled to legal aid is obviously in a more secure position than the self-funding plaintiff as the costs of pursuing the case will be either wholly or partially funded and a winning defendant will usually be unable to recover any costs. However, there has been a very significant reduction in recent years in the number of people entitled to receive civil legal aid. Research published in 1989 concluded that approximately 14 million people had ceased to be eligible for legal aid in the previous decade as a consequence of the failure to ensure that the financial limits applied, reflected the increase in earnings and the cost of living.[37] Additional heavy cuts in entitlement were made in 1993 as a cost saving measure. It was estimated that a further seven to 14 million people were excluded from receiving legal aid at that time.

---

[33] Swanson, (1990) 43 C.L.P. 185, 190.

[34] Taxation, in this context, refers to the process whereby the court has power to control the level of costs to be recovered from the losing party.

[35] Trade unions generally provide their members with access to free legal services in relation to accidents at work. In addition, the union will bear the financial risks involved in the case being unsuccessful. Protection of this kind is preferable to legal aid as it is not means tested and because trade unions direct claims to solicitors who specialise in personal injury work.

[36] Genn, (*op. cit.* p. 111) produced evidence from claims negotiators and counsel which suggested that payment in was used "less ruthlessly and less efficiently than might be imagined."

[37] (1989) 86/35 L.S.G. 7.

Even if legal aid is available it does not always constitute an outright grant to the assisted person. Some legally aided plaintiffs will be expected to make a contribution towards the costs of the litigation. The level of contribution which might be required was increased substantially by the 1993 changes. In particular, the rule that restricted the obligation to contribute to costs incurred during the first year of the case was removed. Many commentators see the contribution requirement as a major disincentive to a plaintiff pursuing litigation. In the decade before 1993 the proportion of legal aid cases in which contributions were made had fallen from 22 per cent. to 14 per cent. Any damages recovered by a legally aided person will be subject to a "statutory charge" in favour of the Legal Aid Board. The effect of the statutory charge is that in the event of the proceedings failing the costs paid by the Legal Aid Board will amount to a non-returnable grant to the plaintiff, whereas, if they are successful, such costs will be regarded as a loan to be repaid out of the damages and costs recovered. Sir John Donaldson M.R. summarised the position in *Davies* v. *Eli Lilly & Co.*,[38] one of the cases which dealt with the anti-arthritis drug Opren, when he said that legal aid makes grants to losers and loans to winners.

The result of the recent changes to eligibility for legal aid would seem to be that such aid is now only of real benefit to the poorest members of society. It was therefore not wholly surprising that the income limits which govern the eligibility for such aid were assimilated, in 1993, to those which entitle a person to receive income support. The result is that the large proportion of society which does not meet these criteria is likely to have very severe difficulty in funding civil litigation. The financial balance of power in personal injury litigation is therefore heavily in favour of the defence.

The operation of legal aid and the "statutory charge" can cause particular difficulties in a group action situation. This is one in which there are many plaintiffs and in which much of the work involved in preparing the claim is common to all of them. Large scale transport accidents or product litigation in relation to drugs are obvious examples in the area of personal injuries. English law has no special procedure for the bringing of "class actions" and the alternative of choosing a member of the group who is entitled to legal aid to fight a "lead action" is not always satisfactory. Several problems are created if this is done. Although the Legal Aid Board will bear the cost of such an action if the plaintiff loses, the statutory charge may eliminate any damages which a successful plaintiff obtains. For example, the individual claimants in the Opren litigation were unlikely to receive large sums as damages[39] and the recoupment of costs from the lead plaintiff, if successful, was almost certain to deprive that person of all compensation. The judge had attempted to overcome this problem by directing that all the members of the group of plaintiffs, whether legally aided or not, should share the costs of the lead case. Any recoupment of legal aid expenditure would therefore be spread over all of the successful claims. However, although the Court of Appeal held that this was a valid exercise of the judge's discretion,[40] it left the non-legally aided plaintiffs facing the risk of having to contribute to the defendant's costs if the lead action failed. It was only the intervention of a

---

[38] [1987] 3 All E.R. 94.
[39] This factor was held not to justify the refusal of legal aid.
[40] *Davies* v. *Eli Lilly & Co.* [1987] 3 All E.R. 94.

private benefactor who agreed to underwrite the costs of the non-legally aided plaintiffs which enabled them to continue the proceedings.

A number of proposals have been made for overcoming these difficulties. The Law Society favours the view that group litigation should be encouraged in major disaster cases. It has proposed that no means test should be applied to such cases so that the Legal Aid Board would bear all of the costs of the litigation and that no recoupment of legal aid should be made from any damages obtained from the litigation. The National Consumer Council has adopted the slightly less radical view that no claimant should be liable to contribute more than a fixed sum (£1,000 was suggested) to the costs of the proceedings.

Privately entered legal expenses insurance policies might be thought to offer another possible method of funding personal injury litigation. However, although such policies have made an appearance as an additional area of cover in some motor insurance policies their coverage is still limited and this form of insurance could not at present be viewed as having a great impact on the practice of injury litigation.

Delays

A central criticism of the tort system is the delay which it allows to occur before an accident victim receives compensation. Research[41] has shown that the average time between an injury being suffered and the conclusion of High Court proceedings in respect of it is over five years (the equivalent period in County Court proceedings is three years). An individual who has pressing financial needs as a result of a tort cannot therefore rely on tort for protection[42] and is bound to have to fall back on non-tortious forms of compensation such as social security benefits. The evidence also suggests that the great majority of cases which are settled without trial do not treat victims significantly better in terms of the time taken to pay compensation. The reason for this seems to be that the majority of settlements are reached at a late stage in proceedings, if not "at the door of the court." The reason for the delay in such cases would seem to be the failure of insurance companies to come up with acceptable, or indeed any, offers to settle at an earlier stage in the proceedings.[43]

It should not, however, be assumed that delay in processing a claim is necessarily always to the disadvantage of a claimant. A firm medical prognosis, which will be required in order for an accurate calculation of the damages to be awarded for future losses, may take months to emerge after an accident and it is well known that significant delays can occur in obtaining satisfactory reports on the medical condition of a victim. An experienced plaintiffs' solicitor may need considerable time in order to ensure that the client's case is presented in a form in which it is most likely to succeed.[44]

A plaintiff is also likely to favour delaying bringing the case to trial if there is any prospect of a negotiated settlement being reached because a trial is a "win or lose" situation which carries little prospect of a compromise result.

---

[41] Report of the Review Body on Civil Justice, Cm. 394 (1988), para. 421. This research relates to the period before the transfer of jurisdiction over many cases to the County Court following the Courts & Legal Services Act 1990.

[42] Although an interim award of damages (see *post*, p. 251) may be payable in some cases.

[43] Swanson, (1990) 43 C.L.P. 185.

[44] Dingwall, Durkin & Felstiner, (1990) 9 C.J.Q. 353 develop these arguments strongly.

Although research suggests that the majority of personal injury cases which come to trial are successful and, if successful, produce, on average, awards of damages significantly in excess of any offer made to settle before the trial, there remains the possibility that a trial will resolve the case in the defendant's favour with all the cost implications that an unfavourable verdict entails. Plaintiffs, but not insurance companies, are "one off" participants in personal injury litigation and are generally "risk averse" and as a result they are likely to view further negotiations which carry the prospect of an agreed compromise of the claim as far more attractive than a trial with its attendant risks.

Insurance

The traditional approach of the courts when assessing liability is to pay no attention to whether the parties have insurance. The reason given for this is that insurance premiums are calculated according to an estimation of the risk of the insurer being called on to make a payment according to existing legal liabilities.

However, it is impossible to explain the working of the system without reference to the role of insurance. At one level it works to the advantage of the plaintiff, in making funds available to meet any award of damages which is made, and of the defendant in providing the facilities to fund and manage the defence of a claim. The damages awarded in many cases would be crippling to defendants if insurance funds were not available to meet the bill.

In many situations the fact that potential defendants are insured can be assumed. The Road Traffic Act 1988 and The Employers' Liability (Compulsory Insurance) Act 1969 make it a criminal offence for the most important risk creators, vehicle users and employers, to fail to have a valid insurance policy in force. First party insurance policies, under which people insure their property, commonly provide public liability insurance, which covers them against occupiers' liability. In the case of motoring, the Motor Insurers' Bureau, a body funded by the insurance industry, provides funds to meet the liabilities of uninsured or unidentifiable "hit and run" drivers.

The role played by liability insurers in the tort system is, however, regarded as the cause of many of the problems which confront the accident victim. Insurers have the role of operating the system according to its rules[45] to the advantage of their clients. As regular participants in the tort system they acquire considerable expertise in its operation and have ready access to skilled advisers. This gives them a considerable advantage over accident victims who are not "repeat players." Insurance companies may have the luxury of being able to take tactical decisions as to whether a particular case should be fought or settled according to what they perceive as their long term interest rather than the strength of the plaintiff's case.[46] Delay both lengthens the time over which the insurer can keep the insurance premiums invested

---

[45] See the quotation from Genn reproduced at p. 164.
[46] Swanson, (1990) C.L.P. 185 argues that much of the delay in the system is caused by the failure of insurers to make any offer to settle. This is attributed to a "hard bargaining" strategy. Swanson argues that there is a tendency to refuse to make any offer in what are regarded as "test cases" and that the level of expenses incurred in defending cases can only be justified in economic terms if it reduces the general level at which settlements are made.

and tends to pressure the plaintiff into abandoning the case or accepting any settlement offer which is made.[47]

Conclusion

The tort system's operation in the area of personal injuries has been castigated as inefficient, dilatory and disproportionately expensive.[48] Ignorance of the law and of techniques of invoking it, difficulties in assembling evidence, costs, delays and defence tactics all contribute to reducing the number of tort claims brought and the amounts for which any which are brought, are settled. Victims may, not unnaturally, be unwilling to pursue a claim against their employer or a relative or friend who was driving the car in which they were injured. The result is that tort is an accident compensation system which rarely and haphazardly achieves its aims.

THE PLETHORA OF SYSTEMS[49]

As will be shown in Chapter 13 protection in money or benefits can be obtained for accident victims from sources other than tort.[50] Wages may continue after the accident in the form of sick pay and a drop in income is likely to produce a tax rebate. Insurance benefits may be obtained from pension funds or from privately contracted income protection or life assurance policies. The Welfare State may provide a variety of benefits or services through the National Health Service or local social services departments and reduced income or increased needs may make a victim eligible for housing and other social security benefits. At times well publicised disasters may lead to the setting-up of a special fund which will make payments to victims. In addition there are a number of schemes funded by central government which pay compensation to particular classes of victim; the best known of these are the Criminal Injuries Compensation Scheme and payments made under the Vaccine Damage Payments Act 1979.

The overall picture is of a variety of systems which award different kinds and levels of benefit according to the nature of the victim's loss and the way in which the accident occurred. To a degree the systems operate with no regard to each other. The result is that accident victims who suffer similar injuries may obtain widely differing levels of compensation and that a victim may obtain compensation for an injury from more than one source.

REFORM

Varieties of approach

The debate on the reform of the accident compensation system has ranged over a variety of possibilities. The least radical approach involves accepting

---

[47] See *ante*, p. 168.

[48] Civil Justice Review, *Consultation Paper: Personal Injuries Litigation*, para. 88.

[49] See Chap. 13 for a more detailed description of all of the methods of support listed in the first paragraph.

[50] The Report of the Review Body on Civil Justice Cm. 394 (1988) gave the following figures: every year 1,800,000 accident victims obtain social security payments; 1,000,000 obtain occupational sick pay; 250,000 benefit from private insurance and 340,000 make claims on the basis of tort proceedings.

that a fault based tort system will continue to operate and attempting to improve it by limited procedural and legal reforms. This approach accepts that radical reform is either undesirable or a practical impossibility and seeks to make the existing system more effective. It assumes that most of the problems with the present system stem from the failure of accident victims to enter it and from inefficiencies within it which can be eliminated.

A second approach is simply a more radical variant of the first. It would involve transferring certain areas, such as road and medical accidents, from the category of negligence based common law liability to a strict liability system under which liability would still be sought through judicial processes, but where the standard of liability or the burden of proof[51] would be changed to favour the claimant. Under this approach a claimant would still have to face many of the practical problems involved in seeking compensation by means of litigation. The problems created by issues such as causation and contributory negligence would be likely to remain.

The most radical approach would involve the total or partial abandonment of court based processes in favour of no-fault compensation.[52] This approach is based on the arguments that the tort system creates unacceptable barriers to an accident victim obtaining compensation and that the variety of systems which co-exist make unjustifiable distinctions in the protection provided to accident victims, according to the cause of their injury. A victim's needs do not vary according to whether the disability results from a criminal assault, a road accident or a naturally occurring illness. If the different compensation systems which exist are all to be regarded as techniques by which society responds collectively to individual need, the discrimination which exists in the levels of benefit and in the ease of access to those benefits, is unacceptable. A comprehensive system with simpler access than that provided by a civil claim for damages is seen as the only technique capable of meeting the needs of victims fairly and of being capable of eliminating some of the inefficiencies of the tort process. A no-fault system sees the payment of compensation through an efficient system as its goal and abandons what are regarded as the unattainable aims of deterring accidents, vindicating the feelings of victims and passing moral judgments on the activities of those who cause accidents. These aims are left to the criminal courts and other legal techniques.[53]

The problems faced by such proposals are immense. First, can such a scheme be said to be truly comprehensive and based on compensating on the basis of need if it does not include cover for illnesses which create identical needs? Secondly, if illnesses are not included within the protection, difficult problems as to the definition of an "accident"[54] and causation are likely to dog the system and, if this is the case, some litigation may still be produced. Thirdly, the more comprehensive such a scheme is made the more expensive

---

[51] The draft directive on services produces such a reversal of the burden of proof. However, medical accidents have been removed from the latest version. See p. 193.

[52] The most comprehensive example of such a scheme is the New Zealand Accident Compensation Scheme which covers all kinds of personal injuries. There are also a significant number of North American schemes which provide limited levels of benefit to the victims of traffic accidents. Sweden has a no-fault scheme in relation to medical accidents.

[53] s. 26 of the New Zealand Accident Compensation Act 1982 treats the provision of no-fault compensation as one of three purposes underlying the Act. The others are the promotion of safety and the rehabilitation of those injured.

[54] Under the New Zealand Accident Compensation Scheme benefits are only paid if it can be shown that the claimant has suffered a "Personal Injury by Accident."

it is likely to be. In spite of achieving savings by means of eliminating many of the inefficiencies inherent in the adversary tort litigation system, a no-fault scheme may well cost more overall to run than tort because of the greater number of accident victims who are entitled to claim benefits from it. This is likely to be the case even if the benefits which the scheme pays are capped. In practice, most of the no-fault schemes which exist in the United States of America are designed only to provide a level of basic and limited financial protection for the victims of motor accidents.[55] If the benefits provided by a no-fault scheme are capped in this way, it may be politically impossible to establish the scheme without allowing tort to survive to "top up" the benefits in cases of the most serious injuries. If this is done, comprehensive no-fault protection and the disappearance of the plethora of protective schemes is not achieved and there is the possibility of tort's role reviving in the future if the benefits of the no-fault scheme are limited as a result of funding pressures[56] or devalued by inflation.[57] Finally, such schemes tend to be opposed by those who believe that deterrence and vindication are legitimate and worthwhile aims for the tort system which should not be abandoned.[58]

The Pearson Commission

The Royal Commission on Civil Liability and Compensation for Personal Injury[59] chaired by Lord Pearson was set up in 1973. At that time many people confidently expected it to lead to a radical reform of the accident compensation systems. The inadequacies of tort had been emphasised by the difficulties which had faced the claims brought by children who had been born with physical disabilities caused by their mothers having taken the drug thalidomide during pregnancy. New Zealand was in the process of abolishing tort rights in relation to personal injuries and death, in favour of a no-fault accident compensation system and Australia was contemplating taking an even more radical approach which would have included illnesses within the protection provided.[60] Europe and North America offered examples of specialised no-fault and strict liability schemes which appeared to have advantages over the traditional negligence action.

The Commission's report, when it arrived in 1978, proved to be a major disappointment. It provided a compelling critique of the existing system, but the proposals made were technical and were flawed by inconsistencies of approach. The Commission's recommendations were, to an extent, circumscribed by its terms of reference. In particular these precluded it from

---

[55] The proposed motor vehicles scheme in the United Kingdom would limit the benefit payable to £2,500. See post, pp. 302–303.

[56] The New Zealand Compensation Scheme has recently been subject to limiting amendments designed to save money.

[57] Most of the no-fault traffic accident schemes in the United States do not offer inflation linked benefits. There is clear evidence that the proportion of compensation attributable to tort paid to accident victims in states which have no-fault cover has increased as inflation has eroded the capped value of the no-fault benefits. See the All-Industry Research Advisory Council study, Compensation for Automobile Accidents in the United States (1989).

[58] The evidence of the effect of no-fault schemes on accident rates in the United States is disputed. However, in 1985 the United States Department of Transportation Report, Compensating Auto Accident Victims concluded that the data did "not support the hypothesis that no-fault insurance influences fatal and injury accident rates."

[59] Cmnd. 7054.

[60] This proposal fell with a change of government.

considering compensation for accidents in the home (about one-third of the total) and from recommending the introduction of a comprehensive scheme covering all accidentally caused injuries, let alone one covering incapacity caused by illness. Faced by these constraints the Commission had little alternative but to base its recommendations on alterations to the existing systems. It accepted that compensation should continue to be derived from both social security and tort but argued that there should be a shift in the balance between the systems in favour of social security. It argued that the developed social security system which already existed in this country made the introduction of a no-fault compensation system unnecessary. Social security benefits should be upgraded by an extension of the industrial injuries scheme and by the introduction of new benefits for severely handicapped children and road accident victims (the latter benefit being modelled on the industrial injuries scheme). The value of tort damages would be reduced by two measures. Damages for non-pecuniary losses would be confined to the most serious cases and a full offset of the value of social security benefits from any subsequent award of damages would reflect the fact that tort damages and social security benefits both ultimately derive from society at large.

Both measures would result in social security benefits being the main method of compensating accident victims and would remove the incentive for many people to pursue a claim in tort by reducing the value of any such awards which were made, particularly in relation to more minor injuries. Somewhat inconsistently, other recommendations made by the Commission, such as the introduction of the periodic payment of tort damages awarded for long term pecuniary losses and new methods of calculating the value of long term financial losses,[61] would have increased the value of awards and thus the incentive for the more seriously injured to claim in tort. The inconsistencies in the proposals dealing with the grounds for liability were even greater. The chances of success in tort were to be improved by the introduction of strict liability for injuries caused by defective products, vaccinations and nominated categories of ultra-hazardous activities. On the other hand no change was recommended to the basis of liability for road and medical accidents and occupiers' liability. Tort liability for industrial accidents and injuries caused by animals was also to be left untouched.

The Commission admitted that its members were not agreed as to the long term aim. Some foresaw a comprehensive extension of the social security system to cover all accidentally produced damage and even disabilities resulting from illness. Tort compensation for personal injuries would either be abolished when adequate state protection existed or would wither away through disuse. Others envisaged tort continuing with a reduced role. It might act as a supplementary remedy providing compensation for forms of loss which were outside the social security system and as topping up the compensation received by high earners. Some were keen for tort to survive: it was seen as embodying the socially valuable principle of making a tortfeasor make amends for the consequences of his fault. A sense of responsibility for the effect of one's acts on others was seen as an essential element in a civilised society.

The Commission's report probably arrived five years too late. By 1978 financial stringency was in the air. Even if the Commission had produced a unanimous recommendation for reform along the lines of the New Zealand

[61] See *post*, p. 26.

model it was unlikely that the incoming Conservative government would have regarded such a plan as consistent with its aim of cutting public expenditure. As it was, the divergence of views expressed by the Commissioners could not provide a rallying point. In retrospect the Commission may be regarded as almost a total failure. Its existence froze discussions in the 1970s and its report produced little of value. The tort and social security systems were left intact to evolve on an ad hoc basis.

Post-Pearson

The period since the Pearson Commission reported has seen significant changes in the law of tort governing accident compensation; in many of the rules under which social security benefits are paid and in the procedural rules governing personal injury litigation. However, the majority of the Commission's most important recommendations have not become law.

Tort law reform

Parliament, by means of the Administration of Justice Act 1982 and section 22 of the Social Security Act 1989, has made significant reforms to the quantification of damages for personal injuries and death.[62] In Part I of the Consumer Protection Act 1987 it created a new tort right when it introduced a regime of strict liability for injuries caused by defective products[63] and by the Occupiers' Liability Act 1984 it attempted to resolve the difficulties which had surrounded an occupier's liability to those who enter property without permission.[64] In reality, none of these measures owed a great deal to the work of the Pearson Commission.[65] The judiciary has been left to operate an unreformed tort system based on negligence. Its main contribution since Pearson has been to increase significantly the level of damages awarded. The lump sums of damages awarded in the most severe cases now regularly top the £1 million barrier and the potential value of some structured settlements has been far in excess of this.[66] The courts have been less adventurous when principles of liability have been at issue. A number of attempts have been made to introduce stricter forms of liability into medical cases by use of the tort of trespass and by arguing for stricter tests of negligence, but the courts have rejected these attempts and reasserted the traditional rules.[67]

Social security

The social security system has changed dramatically since Pearson reported. In the early 1980s a government committed to cutting public

---

[62] See Chap. 12.

[63] Discussed in Chap. 11, *post.*

[64] See *post*, pp. 199–201.

[65] The reforms in the Administration of Justice Act 1982 were derived from Law Commission Report No. 56 and the Consumer Protection Act 1987 from an E.C. Directive. The recoupment provisions in s. 22 of the Social Security Act 1989 are in a very different form from the offsetting of benefits recommended by Pearson.

[66] See *post*, pp. 263–264. Press publicity of the value of such settlements has tended to concentrate on the highest payments which might be made on extremely unlikely facts.

[67] See pp. 113–114 and 191–192.

expenditure was faced by rising levels of unemployment which dramatically increased social security expenditure. Its response was to remodel parts of the system. A great deal of the industrial injuries scheme, including industrial injury benefit, have disappeared. The administration of short term sickness benefit was "privatised" by the introduction of statutory sick pay administered by employers and the earnings related supplements which enhanced the value of short term benefits were abolished. Supplementary benefit was replaced by a new form of means tested income support which was likely to lead to lower levels of benefit for many claimants. Expenditure on social security benefits directed to accident victims was reduced by the introduction of recoupment of the value of benefits paid from tortfeasors.[68] For the most part the Pearson Commission's aim of unifying the industrial and other forms of benefit has been achieved. But, instead of all accident victims being raised to the preferential level of benefit received by those who formerly obtained benefits from the industrial injuries scheme, the standardisation has been at the lower level.

The period since Pearson has seen an increased amount of coordination in the protection provided by the different schemes of accident compensation. The most obvious example of this is the full recoupment by the D.S.S. of the value of social security benefits from awards of damages of more than £2,500.[69] In addition, the replacement of sickness benefit by the employer administered Statutory Sick Pay gave employers the ability to deduct the value of this benefit from any wages which they continued to pay. As a result the possibility of an accident victim benefitting in financial terms from a tort has been reduced.

The Civil Justice Review

The Civil Justice Review[70] has led to a range of reforms in civil procedure which are designed to make the litigation process quicker and cheaper. At the centre of these proposals is the provision in the Courts and Legal Services Act 1990 which requires all claims for damages for personal injury and death valued at less than £50,000, to be started in a County Court. Whether the actual trial occurs in the County or High Court is now determined according to its financial substance and its importance and complexity, but the intention is that the general practice will be that claims of less than £25,000 will be tried in a County Court whereas those of more than £50,000 will go to the High Court. The aim of this reform is to ensure that a greater number of personal injury cases are tried by County Courts and that only cases which demand special attention are heard by the High Court. The County Court is preferred as the normal venue for trial because it is thought to be able to dispose of cases more effectively than the High Court in terms of costs and delays. It remains to be seen whether the problems of delay and cost encountered previously in the High Court were the result of the procedure that that court adopted or were in fact caused by the well recognised difficulties facing a plaintiff in acquiring the necessary medical evidence and inducing the defendant's insurers to settle the more serious claims. If the second interpretation is the correct one the transfer of more valuable cases to

---

[68] s. 22 of the Social Security Act 1989. See *post*, p. 274.
[69] See *post*, pp. 274–275.
[70] Report of the Review Body on Civil Justice Cm. 394 (1988).

the County Court is likely to achieve little in terms of speeding up or reducing the costs of such cases.

Other reforms which have resulted from the Review have sought to expedite the litigation process by favouring a "cards on the table" approach to litigation which compels the parties to reveal the evidence on which they will rely, to their opponents at an early stage in the proceedings and by allowing courts to order a split trial under which issues of liability may be resolved before those of quantum.[71]

In 1993 proposals were made by the Lord Chancellor's Department to bring small personal injury claims within the jurisdiction of the small claims court. This proposal was strongly criticised because it opened the way to plaintiffs having to conduct their cases without representation against an experienced insurance company.

Funding

One reform which has been proposed is that English law should allow solicitors to represent their clients in personal injury cases on a contingency fee basis, under which no remuneration would be received by the solicitor unless the case was successful.[72] Funding arrangements of this kind are a familiar feature of litigation in the United States of America but have been traditionally rejected by English lawyers on the grounds that a lawyer working under such an arrangement would have an unacceptable personal interest in the outcome of the litigation. Proponents of such arrangements[73] argue that they are advantageous in removing much of the financial risk created by the possibility of the claim being lost from a plaintiff and that the personal interest acquired by the plaintiff's solicitor in the outcome would help to even the scales in negotiations between the parties by giving the solicitor an incentive to monitor the progress of the claim efficiently and to seek the best possible outcome for the client. Section 48 of the Courts Legal Services Act 1990 makes provision for a limited move in this direction by permitting "conditional fees." Whereas the American system of contingency fees allows a lawyer to receive a percentage of the damages awarded to a winning client, this system will only permit a solicitor who is prepared to work on a "no win no fee" basis to receive the standard level of fee increased by a fixed percentage. A further difference from American practice is that costs would continue to "follow the event"[74] with the consequence that a losing plaintiff would remain at risk of having to meet the costs incurred by the other side.[75] In 1993 the Lord Chancellor's Department announced that conditional fees would be permitted from 1994 in personal injury and death cases with the plaintiff's solicitor permitted to charge a maximum uplift of 100 per cent. on the standard fee. Critics of the proposal have argued that this level of uplift could bear very heavily on plaintiffs who were awarded comparatively small sums as damages, and moves have been made to devise

[71] The principle behind this is that the evidence available on the liability issue may deteriorate in the period when the plaintiff's medical condition is stabilising.

[72] The issues are fully discussed in the Lord Chancellor's Department's paper *Contingency Fees* Cm. 571 (1989).

[73] Swanson, (1991) 11 Ox.J.L.S. 193.

[74] In American practice parties bear their own costs whatever the outcome of the litigation.

[75] This is seen as acting as a disincentive to the pursuit of claims which are unlikely to succeed. See Lord Chancellor's Department paper, *Contingency Fees* (1989), para. 4.14.

forms of insurance which would protect a losing plaintiff from the risk of bearing the costs incurred by the defence.

Specialisation

The Law Society has also reacted to the widely expressed concern as to the competence of many of the solicitors who handle personal injury work on behalf of plaintiffs, by proposing that panels of solicitors who have particular competence in general personal injury litigation and in medical negligence work be established.[76] A solicitor who wishes to join the appropriate panel will be required to demonstrate competence, in terms of both experience and knowledge, in the particular area of work.[77] Membership of the panel will enable the public to identify those members of the profession who are skilled in the area of practice. However, there will be no prohibition on members of the profession who are not members of the panel undertaking such work. In November 1993 it was reported that only 405 applications had been received from solicitors wishing to become members of the personal injury panel.

In any event, recent years have witnessed the emergence of solicitors' firms which are increasingly specialised in the conduct of personal injury litigation. Some have even gone as far as to present themselves as specialising in the claims which follow major disasters. The Association of Personal Injury Lawyers has become a powerful body which represents the interests of solicitors conducting this kind of work. In addition the Association for Victims of Medical Accidents now provides assistance to solicitors who are conducting medical negligence cases on such matters as the identity of possible expert witnesses.

Group actions

Recent years have seen increased attention being paid to the procedural and funding problems posed by group actions; for example, actions brought by a number of persons injured in a transport accident, by a defective drug or other product or by exposure to hazardous substances at work. English law has no special procedure dedicated to cases of this kind but considerable efforts have been devoted to ensuring that such claims are processed with a minimum of duplication of effort, with adequate and fair funding arrangements and with the professional work of the solicitors being co-ordinated by firms which have the expertise to handle highly specialised work.

The result of these efforts can be seen in a variety of developments. The Law Society now operates a disaster co-ordination service which seeks to alert victims of a major incident to their rights, to co-ordinate the work of solicitors who may be representing the victims and to direct potential claimants to firms of solicitors who have particular experience in the matters at hand.[78] The Legal Aid Board now has the right, in cases concerning 10 or more claimants, to select and enter into contracts with specific firms of solicitors who will conduct the generic work (*i.e.* that common to all of the plaintiffs in the litigation, particularly issues of liability as opposed to

---

[76] The Society's consultation document is reproduced at (1990) 87/16 L.S.G. 36.
[77] See (1991) 88/12 L.S.G. 7 for details of the latest consultative document on the subject.
[78] For additional details see Appendix 1 of the Supreme Court Procedure Committee's publication *Guide for use in Group Actions* (1991).

quantum) for all of the legally aided plaintiffs. Such firms of solicitors will often act as the co-ordinators of those firms which are representing the individual interests of the claimants. The courts have developed cost sharing orders[79]; the Supreme Court Procedure Committee has published a guidance paper on the conduct of group litigation[80] and practice notes have been issued by the Lord Chief Justice designed to ensure that all preliminary issues concerning a particular piece of group litigation are directed to a particular judge for a decision.

No-fault

Interest in considering no-fault based alternatives to tort compensation has revived in recent years. In particular, the medical profession, faced by steep increases in the cost of insurance, has moved in favour of the introduction of a no-fault accident compensation scheme for the victims of medical accidents and this proposal has gained the support of many politicians, although not the present Government.[81] However, the Lord Chancellor's Department has produced a consultative document which recommends the introduction of a limited no-fault scheme for the victims of road accidents.[82]

CONCLUSION

Well publicised disasters such as the Zeebrugge ferry capsize and the deaths at the Hillsborough football stadium as well as a number of tragic results of medical negligence have kept the issue of accident compensation on the political agenda. At times such cases have shown that the tort system can produce quick settlements which are advantageous to victims if defendants are anxious to be seen to be reacting responsibly to major disasters. Unfortunately the ordinary traffic or industrial accident does not generate the kind of publicity which creates pressure on the defendant to settle and which tends to mean that the litigation is conducted by one of the firms of solicitors which specialise in the area of personal injury litigation. The tort system is still far from guaranteeing financial protection for the victims of all accidents.

In the long term it remains to be seen whether a more comprehensive accident compensation system can be devised to replace the existing "plethora" of systems which provide widely different benefits to persons who suffer similar injuries in different ways. The problem of achieving major reform is certain to be immense. Our society remains to be convinced of the anomalies created by the existing systems and that a limited level of benefit payable to all may be preferable to tort's rarely fulfilled promise of full compensation. The fault principle and the belief that tort deters accident creating conduct still attract wide support. In political terms the dilemma remains that the problem of finding the resources to fund a comprehensive no-fault accident compensation system is likely to be insurmountable whereas a limited scheme will merely serve to add more complexity to the overall picture.

---

[79] *Davies* v. *Eli Lilly & Co.* [1987] 3 All E.R. 94.
[80] *Guide for use in Group Actions* (1991).
[81] This is discussed in more detail at p. 192.
[82] For discussion see p. 302.

Chapter Nine

Intentional Infliction of Personal Injuries

A GENERAL PRINCIPLE?

It is possible that English law recognises a general principle to the effect that intentional or reckless conduct which results in personal injury is actionable in tort. The authority for this proposition rests on the judgment of Wright J. in *Wilkinson* v. *Downton*.[1] The defendant in that case had visited the plaintiff and told her, as a practical joke, that her husband had been injured in an accident and had broken both of his legs. This story, which was false, resulted in the plaintiff suffering severe shock. Wright J. held the defendant's conduct to be actionable on the ground that:

> "the defendant has . . . wilfully done an act calculated to cause physical harm to the . . . plaintiff . . . That proposition, without more, appears to me to state a good cause of action, there being no justification alleged for the act."

Although the principle laid down by Wright J. was subsequently approved on similar facts by the Court of Appeal,[2] English law has subsequently based the recovery of damages for intentionally inflicted personal injuries on the torts of battery and assault which are species of trespass to the person. In addition, as we have seen,[3] English law has refused to recognise generally based grounds for tortious liability outside of the tort of negligence. The current status of the general principle is therefore not entirely clear.

However, the *Wilkinson* principle may still have a role to play. Trespass to the person may be confined to directly inflicted injuries, and, if this is the case, *Wilkinson* may survive as a remedy for intended, but indirectly inflicted, personal injuries. It has recently been held that the case provides authority for the grant of an injunction in cases of harassment or molestation by such means as threatening phone calls, at least where injury to the victim's health is likely to result.[4]

BATTERY

The torts of assault and battery are both species of trespass to the person. The tort of battery is defined as the intentional and impermissible touching of the

---

[1] [1897] 2 Q.B. 57.
[2] *Janvier* v. *Sweeney* [1919] 2 K.B. 316.
[3] *Ante*, p. 24.
[4] *Khorasandjian* v. *Bush* [1993] 3 All E.R. 669, discussed Stanton, (1993) 1 Tort L.R. 179.

person of another. There is considerable latitude in the terminology adopted in relation to assault and battery. In a strict sense battery concerns the intentional infliction of an unlawful touching of the person of another, whereas assault denotes acts which threaten an imminent battery. In practice an assault will often be followed by a battery, but this need not always be the case. A battery committed whilst the victim is unconscious or from behind his back will not be coupled with an assault and, conversely, if the assailant's blow misses his victim or if he is restrained before he can strike or desists in the attack, he may well have committed an assault without a battery. In common usage the term assault is the more familiar and is used indiscriminately, even by the courts, to include battery. Both torts are also commonly referred to as trespass to the person. No consequences would appear to turn on these usages. The torts will be described here according to the stricter terminology.

The role of battery

There are three main roles for the tort of battery which reflect the split personality that history has conferred on the modern tort of trespass to the person:

1. Intentionally inflicted harm

The most obvious role of battery is to give a damages remedy in cases of intentionally inflicted physical injuries, such as those inflicted in the course of murders or attempted murders; fights[5]; rapes[6] or other forms of assault whether or not weapons are used. It will also extend to injuries caused by deliberate fouls in the course of sports.

2. The protection of the right to physical integrity

The role of the tort may go beyond this into the sphere of the protection of a person's civil liberty to be free from unwanted and deliberate physical contacts which are objectionable, although not physically damaging.[7] Battery, being a species of trespass to the person, is actionable *per se* and, therefore, a battery which causes no physical damage, of which examples may include the unwanted kiss and some indecent assaults and wrongful arrests, will be actionable in battery. An action of this kind may be used by a plaintiff to assert basic rights of physical integrity and to recover damages for any fear, annoyance and insult caused by such acts. Exemplary damages may be awarded in claims of this kind made against police or prison officers.[8]

3. Medical consent[9]

The role of the tort in the context of medical treatment straddles both of the previous categories. It may be used in relation to medical treatment which has not been consented to,[10] whether that treatment proves to be harmful or not (in the latter case the action would effectively serve as an assertion of

---

[5] *Murphy* v. *Culhane* [1977] Q.B. 94.
[6] *W.* v. *Meah* [1986] 1 All E.R. 935.
[7] For further consideration of this role of the tort see Chap. 25.
[8] See p. 150.
[9] For a full survey see Jones, *Medical Negligence*, paras. 6.03–6.67.
[10] See particularly the decision of Linden J. at first instance in *Allan* v. *New Mount Sinai Hospital* (1980) 109 D.L.R. (3d) 634.

(Consent)

rights). If harm is caused by a "medical battery" the tort provides a strict liability remedy to the patient. A substantial amount of authority exists on the requirements of establishing a valid consent in the medical context. In particular, a debate[11] as to whether a failure to disclose risks inherent in a medical procedure may invalidate an apparent consent, has raised the possibility that such a failure will provide the basis for a strict liability claim in respect of any untoward consequences which result from the procedure, irrespective of whether it was conducted with all reasonable care. It now seems unlikely that there is any real scope for the development of this haphazard form of strict liability for medical misadventure.[12]

In practice battery claims based on intentionally inflicted harm are probably not very common. Many persons who commit battery may not have the resources to enable them to pay any damages and the role of the tort in providing compensation has been replaced, to an extent, by the creation of compensation schemes benefitting the victims of criminal injuries.[13] As has been said, an expansion of the role of battery in relation to medical practice is now very unlikely.[14] On occasion, the modern dominance of negligence has led to claims which have evidenced battery being pleaded in negligence,[15] presumably in order to simplify issues of proof and to avoid the claims falling within exclusions applicable to the defendant's insurance policy. This does not mean that the tort has no role to play. Criminal injuries compensation may not always be available, and, even if it is, the amount awarded may be subject to significant restrictions.[16] In the civil liberties field a successful allegation of battery may open the way to the award of exemplary damages payable by a police authority,[17] even if the plaintiff has suffered no substantial physical hurt. The picture is, therefore, one in which the advantages to be gained from bringing a case in battery need to be considered against the alternatives on the particular facts of every case.

The successful tort claims brought by surviving victims and dependents of victims against Peter Sutcliffe, "the Yorkshire Ripper," have resulted in battery claims in relation to criminal assaults becoming more fashionable, particularly if the tortfeasor has assets, such as a house, which suggest a capacity to meet an award of damages or if the plaintiff is seeking a legal mechanism with which to establish the facts of a case. The tort has been used by persons who have sought to challenge a failure to prosecute for murder[18] and as a means of pursuing allegations of rape[19] and sexual abuse.[20] In theory, tort claims of this kind might be thought to offer a lower burden of

---

[11] See *ante*, p. 113–114.
[12] See Dugdale & Stanton, *Professional Negligence*, para. 11.65.
[13] See p. 295.
[14] *Ante*, note 12.
[15] *Williams* v. *Humphrey The Times*, February 20, 1975.
[16] See *post*, p. 297 for the current limits applied to the scheme. In *W.* v. *Meah* [1986] 1 All E.R. 935 tort damages were awarded to the two victims in excess of the compensation which had been paid to them by the Criminal Injuries Compensation Board. See p. 297.
[17] See *ante*, p. 150.
[18] See particularly *Halford* v. *Brookes* [1992] P.I.Q.R. P42, in which the mother of a murder victim brought tort proceedings against two men alleging that one of them had murdered her daughter. One of the defendants to the civil proceedings had been previously acquitted of the charge in criminal proceedings having defended the case on the ground that the other man had killed the daughter, no prosecution had been brought against the other man after the acquittal of the first.
[19] *Miles* v. *Cain, The Independent*, December 15, 1989.
[20] *Stubbings* v. *Webb* [1993] A.C. 498.

proof and to avoid some of the safeguards which protect defendants in criminal proceedings, such as the need for certain kinds of evidence to be corroborated.[21] However, it is clear that the courts are alive to the dangers involved in permitting civil proceedings to circumvent such safeguards. In *Miles* v. *Cain*,[22] a case in which civil proceedings alleging rape and sexual assault were brought, the Court of Appeal argued that a high degree of certainty was required in the evidence by which it was sought to satisfy the court on the balance of probabilities that the battery had occurred.[23] In the later case of *Halford* v. *Brookes*[24] Rougier J. decided that a person should not be declared guilty of murder in civil proceedings unless the evidence achieved the criminal law standard of satisfying the court beyond reasonable doubt of the defendant's guilt.[25] In spite of this, the judge accepted that differences between civil and criminal proceedings exist on such matters as the inferences to be drawn from the defendant's failure to testify in civil proceedings and as to the rules governing the admissibility of certain items of evidence.

The definition of battery

The paucity of leading modern authorities on the tort of battery means that there are difficulties in defining some of its technical requirements. Much of the received learning on the subject is derived from old authorities on trespass, whilst some is borrowed from the criminal law of assault. The evolution in the law which followed the demise of the writ of trespass and the fact that different policies may be at issue when criminal liabilities are involved suggest that a modern appellate court might wish to approach some of the standard authorities in a critical fashion.

1. Intentional

In view of the dominance of negligence in relation to unintentional physical injuries, it is for all practical purposes possible to confine the law of battery to intentionally inflicted injuries. It is the act which is done rather than the harm which results which has to be intended.[26] In addition, it is relatively certain that some positive action on the part of the defendant is required to constitute a battery: the passive act of blocking a person's entrance to a building is insufficient.[27]

2. Direct

Historically, trespass to the person could only be committed if the touching had been inflicted "directly." In view of the Court of Appeal's

---

[21] See Major, (1990) 140 N.L.J. 1692 for a discussion of the advantages of using civil proceedings in cases concerning the sexual abuse of children.

[22] *The Independent*, December 15, 1989.

[23] Note also that civil proceedings which constitute a collateral attack on a finding made by a court in criminal law proceedings will be treated as an abuse of process and struck out. *Hunter* v. *Chief Constable of the West Midlands* [1982] A.C. 529. Failures to prosecute and prosecutions which lead to a conviction must therefore be distinguished from prosecutions which produce an acquittal which the plaintiff would wish to challenge. *Hunter* concerned a different scenario of a convicted person alleging assault by the police in the course of questioning.

[24] [1992] P.I.Q.R. P42.

[25] It is not clear whether this approach should be applied to offences other than murder.

[26] *Wilson* v. *Pringle* [1987] Q.B. 237.

[27] *Innes* v. *Wylie* (1844) 1 Car. & K. 257, although it might amount to an assault.

decision in *Letang* v. *Cooper*[28] there must be doubts whether this requirement survives in modern law. As the distinction between intentionally and
negligently inflicted injuries is far more comprehensible and in accordance
with modern thinking than that between directness and indirectness, it is
submitted that it should be discarded.[29] However, even if this is wrong, it
must be recognised that the notion of what constitutes a direct injury was
significantly extended in the old cases. Actual touching of one person by
another was not necessary. Not only was it sufficient if the defendant used an
instrument within his control,[30] such as a stick or a bullet from a gun, to
effect the touching, but it also sufficed if the contact was made with an object
in the plaintiff's control, so long as the force which initiated the incident was
still continuing when the plaintiff was injured.[31] On this basis, defendants
whose acts caused a collision involving the plaintiff's carriage were held
liable in trespass when the plaintiff was thrown from the carriage and
injured[32] or where the horses drawing it ran away and the plaintiff was
injured in jumping clear.[33] A good example of the extended meaning given to
directness in order to retain a case within the boundaries of trespass is
provided by the well known case of *Scott* v. *Shepherd*.[34] In that case the
defendant threw a lighted squib into a market, and two persons in succession
threw it away in order to protect their persons and property. The squib
finally exploded blinding the plaintiff who was held entitled to sue the
defendant in trespass for his injuries. It is clear from this decision that even if
the notion of directness continues to be applicable in modern law it may not
constitute a significant barrier to success in an action for battery.

3. Reckless

It seems probable that reckless conduct which causes personal injury falls
within the scope of battery.[35] If this is the case, battery will be the appropriate remedy in many cases in which vandalism results in injury; for example, it
would lie against youths who throw things from a block of flats or who leave
items obstructing railway lines. The recognition of reckless conduct as
sufficient grounds for an action in battery would also solve the problem of
"transferred malice"; that is, those cases in which the defendant intends to
injure a specific person, but by mistake injures another. The action of
trespass was held to be appropriate on such facts in the cases of *James* v.
Campbell[36] and *Ball* v. *Axten*[37] and although these decisions are probably
best regarded as merely showing that trespass was the appropriate form of
action for such cases at a time when the intention of the defendant was not of
primary legal significance, they do seem capable of supporting the proposition that a recklessly inflicted injury constitutes a battery in modern law.

---

[28] [1965] Q.B. 232. See *ante*, p. 29.
[29] See *ante*, p. 29.
[30] *Hopper* v. *Reeve* (1817) 7 Taunt. 698.
[31] *Scott* v. *Shepherd* (1773) 2 W. Bl. 892.
[32] *Hopper* v. *Reeve* (1817) 7 Taunt. 698.
[33] *Leame* v. *Bray* (1803) 3 East 593.
[34] (1773) 2 W. Bl. 892.
[35] *R.* v. *Venna* [1976] Q.B. 421, a case of a criminal prosecution for assault occasioning actual
bodily harm.
[36] (1832) 5 C. & P. 372.
[37] (1866) 4 F. & F. 1019.

4. Minor touchings

There is a natural disinclination to regard minor acts, such as a person tapping another on the shoulder to attract attention, as tortious. In *Cole* v. *Turner*[38] Holt C.J. was of the opinion that the "least touching of another in anger is a battery." In the more recent case of *Collins* v. *Wilcock*,[39] which concerned a police officer's act of taking hold of the arm of a woman to whom she wished to speak to prevent her from walking away, Goff L.J. regarded these words as reflecting the fundamental nature of the interest being protected, but held that the principle had to be subject to an exception to allow for the exigencies of everyday life. As a result he argued that nobody can complain of the jostling which is inevitable in a busy society, nor of the physical contacts which are used to attract a person's attention or to welcome them. Although these cases could be justified on the basis that a person impliedly consents to them, the judge preferred the view that there was a "broad exception to Holt C.J.'s principle which embraced all physical contact which is generally acceptable in the ordinary conduct of daily life. He argued that this approach is preferable to one which restricts battery to situations in which the contact is "angry, revengeful, rude or insolent." A subsequent decision[40] which reverted to the disapproved approach by making proof of "hostility" on the part of the defendant a requirement of battery, has not been followed.[41]

Although Goff L.J.'s approach has been accepted it is subject to certain limitations. For example, the notion of "physical contact which is generally acceptable in the ordinary conduct of daily life" does not justify a doctor providing treatment, however minor, to patients, without obtaining their consent. In *T.* v. *T.*[42] Wood J. refused to accept that operative treatment performed by a doctor could fall within "the exigencies of everyday life" and in *F.* v. *West Berkshire Health Authority*[43] Lord Goff took the same view. It is also clear that a police officer will only be justified by these words in touching another person in order to attract their attention. Any imposition of a restraint will have to constitute a lawful arrest in order for the constable to escape liability for battery.[44]

Defences

1. Consent[45]

The operation of consent as a defence to intentional torts has been described in Chapter 5.[46] In view of the strict nature of the tort of battery the defence of consent is of great significance, in particular in relation to medical procedures and to sports in which physical contact is of the essence of the

---

[38] (1704) 6 Mod. 149.

[39] [1984] 1 W.L.R. 1172.

[40] *Wilson* v. *Pringle* [1987] Q.B. 237.

[41] *T.* v. *T.* [1988] 1 All E.R. 613. Lord Goff in his speech in *F.* v. *West Berkshire Health Authority* [1990] 2 A.C. 1 doubted the "hostility" requirement and followed his approach in *Collins*.

[42] [1988] 1 All E.R. 613.

[43] [1990] 2 A.C. 1.

[44] On the facts of *Collins* v. *Wilcock* it was held that the officer had gone beyond the exception by attempting to restrain the woman by taking hold of her arm and had therefore committed a battery against her.

[45] See *ante*, p. 109.

[46] *Ante*, pp. 112–114.

game. Implied consent may also operate to render permissible a whole range of minor contacts which would otherwise be tortious.[47] The burden of proving consent rests with the defendant. The tort's role of protecting a person's physical integrity is supported by placing the burden of justifying any invasion on the defendant. The consent established must be real; by which is meant not only that it must not have been extracted by fraud or violence, but also, in the medical context, that the consent must not have been obtained at a time when the patient was under sedation.[48]

Outside of the medical and sporting spheres, the role of consent as a defence to an act of battery needs to be treated with some caution as it must not be supposed that the law will automatically permit a person to consent to all forms of battery. This is certainly the case in criminal law where it has been held to be no defence to a charge of assault that the accused was engaged in a prize fight,[49] or a street fight[50] with the consent of the other party or indeed that the assault was an act done with the victim's consent for the purpose of sexual gratification.[51] However, the public interest in preventing assaults of these kinds by imposing a criminal penalty raises totally different policy questions from those raised by a tort claim. In tort, the question is whether a person injured in such an occurrence should be able to claim compensation. There can be little doubt that the courts will have scant sympathy for a person who seeks compensation in such circumstances and, from this standpoint, it is surprising that the judges had some difficulty in accepting that the plaintiff who seeks compensation for a battery might, in appropriate circumstances, be met by the defences of illegality, *volenti* or contributory negligence.[52]

2. Justification

Lawful punishment and restraint of adults and children, arrest[53] and self-defence are all capable of providing a defence to an allegation of battery.[54]

A person is entitled to use reasonable force, such as would amount to a battery, against another in self-defence of himself or of his property, for example in repelling an attack on him by another or in ejecting a trespasser from his land. The amount of force used must be the minimum necessary in the circumstances and in proportion to the conduct of the other party. In practice it is likely that a greater degree of force will be deemed to be reasonable in the case of defence of a person's physical well being than in the defence of property. A statutory right to use reasonable force in the prevention of crime[55] overlaps with this common law right, but makes it clear that force may be used in order to protect the interests of third parties.

A parent is entitled to administer reasonable punishment to his or her children, and it is clear that this entitlement extends to the administration of corporal punishment.[56] What counts as reasonable punishment is a question

---

[47] See *ante*, p. 184.
[48] See Dugdale & Stanton *op. cit.* paras. 11.69–11.74 and the authorities there cited.
[49] *R. v. Coney* (1882) 8 Q.B.D. 534.
[50] *Attorney-General's Reference (No. 6 of 1980)* [1981] Q.B. 715.
[51] *R. v. Donovan* [1934] 2 K.B. 498; *R. v. Brown* [1993] 2 All E.R. 75.
[52] See *Murphy v. Culhane* [1977] Q.B. 94 discussed at pp. 000 and 000.
[53] See *post*, p. 425 for a description of these powers.
[54] See *ante*, p. 121.
[55] Criminal Law Act 1967, s. 3(1).
[56] See Barton, (1992) 142 N.L.J. 1262 for a more complete survey of the current law on this topic.

of fact. The relevant considerations are likely to include the age and sex of the child, its strength, the conduct for which it is being punished and the mode of punishment used. Changing views within society as to the acceptability of corporal punishment may well have reduced the range of acceptable forms of such punishment, but, it seems certain that the right of a parent to punish children in this way still survives.[57] School teachers were traditionally regarded as standing in *loco parentis* and as having equivalent powers to punish children, even in relation to out of school conduct. However, successful proceedings brought against the British Government alleging that the practice of corporal punishment in schools constituted a breach of the European Convention on Human Rights led to it being abolished in state schools by section 47 of the Education (No. 2) Act 1986.[58] More recently further proceedings have held to be admissible, claims that the Government has broken the Convention by permitting corporal punishment to be administered in private fee paying schools.[59]

3. Offences against the Person Act 1861

The effect of section 45 of this Act is that criminal proceedings for assault brought in a magistrates' court may bar further civil proceedings in respect of the same incident. The section may operate whether the proceedings resulted in an acquittal on the merits or in a conviction following which the convicted person has paid the fine or served the sentence of imprisonment imposed. It is difficult to see what justification can be made for this rule and it is not surprising that the Criminal Law Revision Committee[60] has recommended the repeal of the provision.

4. Other defences

The law concerning the availability of contributory negligence, illegality and *volenti non fit injuria* as defences to battery was settled by the Court of Appeal's decision in *Murphy* v. *Culhane*.[61] In that case the defendant, who had previously been convicted, following a plea of guilty, of the manslaughter of the plaintiff's husband, sought to defend himself against her damages claim brought under the Fatal Accidents Act by alleging that the deceased had initiated the criminal affray in which he was killed and that his provocative conduct, if proved, could give rise in tort to the defences of illegality, *volenti* or contributory negligence.

The Court of Appeal accepted this contention, and in so doing, departed from its earlier decision in *Lane* v. *Holloway*.[62] The finding that these

---

[57] The Scottish Law Commission (Report No. 135) has recommended that the parent's right to punish a child by hitting it should no longer allow the use of an implement or any act which caused, or risked causing, injury or pain or discomfort lasting for more than a very short time.

[58] The section operates by making a teacher who administers such punishment liable in tort for battery. The operation of the section was extended to grant maintained schools by the Education Reform Act 1988, Sched. 12 and to some independent schools by S.I 1989 No. 1233 & 1989 No. 1825. A schoolteacher retains the right to use reasonable force against a pupil in self-defence or to prevent injury to other persons or property. See also S.I. 1991 No. 1506 which prohibits the use of corporal punishment in children's homes.

[59] *Applications Nos. 13134/87 & 14229/88* noted (1991) 88/15 L.S.G. 39. See *Costello-Roberts* v. *U.K.*, The Times, March 26, 1993.

[60] 14th Report (1980), paras. 163–164.

[61] [1977] Q.B. 94.

[62] [1968] 1 Q.B. 379.

defences were not available to the defendant in *Lane* must now be regarded as turning on the facts of the case in which the defendant had delivered a savage blow out of all proportion to the minor verbal provocation given by the elderly and not entirely sober plaintiff.

ASSAULT

The tort of assault consists of conduct which raises in another a reasonable apprehension that a battery will be committed against him.[63] The role of the tort is to serve to vindicate the rights of an individual who has been threatened with violence[64] or against whom a battery has failed[65] or been restrained. It will commonly be the case that the torts of assault and battery will be committed in close proximity to each other, but as the plaintiff's knowledge of the imminent battery is essential before he can reasonably apprehend it, the two torts will not coexist where the plaintiff is unconscious at the time of the battery (as in a medical case) or where, for instance, he is attacked from behind. Assault also operates in circumstances in which the battery fails, as where the blow misses, and where the assailant is restrained or desists from the final act. Finally it can operate where the threat was incapable of accomplishment, as where an unloaded gun is pointed at a person.

It is a question of fact whether the defendant's conduct was sufficient to raise the necessary reasonable apprehension of an imminent battery in the plaintiff's mind. What is required is an indication of an immediate intention to commit a battery, coupled with the capacity to carry that intention into effect. It is no assault to make a threatening telephone call or to shake a fist or to make other threatening gestures from such a distance that there is no imminent possibility of a battery occurring. It was on this basis that Scott J. held in *Thomas* v. *National Union of Mineworkers (South Wales Area)*[66] that violent and abusive language and threats directed at strike breaking miners by 60 to 70 mineworkers who were picketing a colliery in the course of a strike did not constitute an assault. The requirement of imminence could not be satisfied as the pickets were being restrained by a police cordon and the strike breakers were being bussed into the colliery. However, the question is ultimately one of fact and it is not a defence for the defendant to prove that he never got sufficiently close to the plaintiff to strike a blow as it is the threat of the blow which must be imminent. In *Stephens* v. *Myers*,[67] the defendant advanced with threats upon the plaintiff who was chairing a meeting, but was restrained by others before he came within reach. It was held that his acts were sufficient to comprise the tort of assault on the plaintiff. This was undoubtedly correct as the apprehension would seem to have been reasonable and the prospective battery could scarcely have been more immediate.

It should be noted that although the plaintiff must have apprehended an imminent battery he need not actually have been put in fear by it. The tortious character of the defendant's conduct does not depend on the degree

---

[63] Assault is here being used in its strict sense as opposed to the wide and common usage which subsumes both assault and battery. See *ante* p. 180.

[64] *Martin* v. *Shoppee* (1828) 3 C. & P. 373; *Read* v. *Coker* (1853) 13 C.B. 850.

[65] *Stephens* v. *Myers* (1830) 4 C. & P. 349.

[66] [1986] Ch. 20.

[67] (1830) 4 C. & P. 349.

of fortitude with which it is faced by the plaintiff.[68] The plaintiff must, naturally, have had actual knowledge of the threats in order to reasonably apprehend them.

Threats made with a firearm which proves to have been a fake or to have been unloaded almost certainly constitute a tort. There are judicial statements to the contrary,[69] but it is submitted that they are misconceived. The basis of the tort is the raising of a reasonable apprehension in the plaintiff and it would negate this to deny a remedy on the basis that, whatever the appearance, the defendant did not have the means to carry his threat into effect.

Words or acts which accompany an act which would otherwise constitute an assault may operate to remove the apprehension and thus negative the tort. The best known example of this is to be found in the decision in *Tuberville* v. *Savage*[70] in which it was claimed that the defendant had put his hand upon his sword and said "If it were not assize time, I would not take such language from you." It was held that these words were sufficient to remove the tortious quality of the act since it was assize time. Similarly, it has been said to be no tort to point a gun at someone if it is made clear at the time that it is not loaded.[71] This may well be correct in theory, but there must remain scope for argument on the facts as to whether the plaintiff was reasonably to believe the oral assertion.

The question of whether words alone are sufficient to constitute an assault is a matter of some doubt.[72] In terms of policy it is difficult to see why these doubts should exist, if words are capable of negativing the implication that an act is an assault, they are equally capable of explaining conduct in a way which raises the necessary reasonable apprehension and it is not unreasonable to suggest that they can alone constitute an assault in appropriate circumstances. There can be little doubt that the rule in battery that some active conduct is needed to comprise the tort, is equally applicable in assault.[73]

The categories of loss available for an assault are relatively wide and if the victim did suffer physical injury (the obvious example being shock) as a result of the tort, he would seem certain to succeed in a damages claim. The authority of *Wilkinson* v. *Downton*[74] and *Janvier* v. *Sweeney*,[75] although not strictly dealing with an assault, would seem to point in this direction.

[68] *Brady* v. *Schatzel* [1911] St. R. Qd. 206.
[69] *Blake* v. *Barnard* (1840) 9 C. & P. 626; *cf. R.* v. *St. George* (1840) 9 C. & P. 483, (a criminal case); and *Brady* v. *Schatzel* [1911] St. R. Qd. 206.
[70] (1669) 1 Mod. Rep. 3.
[71] *R.* v. *St George* (1940) 9 C. & P. 483.
[72] *Mead & Belt's* Case (1823) 1 Lew. 184; *cf. Barton* v. *Armstrong* [1969] 2 N.S.W.L.R. 451.
[73] *Innes* v. *Wylie* (1844) 1 Car. & K. 257.
[74] [1897] 2 Q.B. 57.
[75] [1919] 2 K.B. 316.

Chapter Ten

Negligence and Personal Injuries

This and the next chapter describe the most important grounds of liability used in cases of unintentionally inflicted personal injury and death. This chapter concentrates on negligence based liabilities and the next on strict liabilities. It is impossible to draw an absolutely firm line between the two bodies of material. As will be seen, most of the interests which are protected by strict liability are protected, in the alternative, by negligence. The title of the next chapter might thus be more correct if it was mixed liability. The division adopted is a pragmatic one between those areas which are primarily governed by negligence and those where strict liability plays a significant or the leading role.

The examples of negligence liability for personal injuries given in these two chapters illustrate the most important areas in which the tort of negligence operates and those which have attracted the greatest attention from the courts. Negligence, being a tort in its own right, is not confined to these areas and is capable of giving a remedy in situations which fall beyond the common ones which are illustrated here. Two areas of negligence liability which are not discussed in this chapter are injuries incurred in the course of sports by competitors and spectators and injuries incurred in the course of carriage by public transport on road and rail.[1] Both areas are governed by the standard general principles of negligence liability. The subject of public road and rail transport is slightly different because the quantum of damages recoverable in cases of international carriage may be "capped" as a result of the incorporation of international conventions into English law.[2]

ROAD ACCIDENTS

In 1990 approximately 5,100 people were killed in road accidents in Great Britain and 340,000 injured.[3] Road accidents therefore form a significant part of the accident compensation system accounting for approximately a quarter of all accidentally caused deaths and a ninth of all accidental injuries. The majority of victims of these accidents are either drivers of or passengers

---

[1] Commercial carriage by air, which is subject to a regime of strict liability, is discussed at p. 241.

[2] For details see Chitty on *Contracts* (26th ed.), Vol. II, Chap. 5.

[3] Lord Chancellor's Department, *Compensation for Road Accidents: a Consultation Paper*, p. 7. These figures are provisional.

in cars. However, the fact that almost a third of persons killed are pedestrians shows that such persons tend to suffer the more serious consequences.

Road accidents are the leading example in English law of a negligence based duty owed in relation to personal injuries. The general principles of negligence liability and the defences described in the first section of this book apply to this area; the only substantial modifications to general principle being that the defence of *volenti non fit injuria* cannot operate in many motoring cases as a result of section 149 of the Road Traffic Act 1988[4] and that special rules of apportionment are used when contributory negligence is pleaded in a case in which a person travelling in a car has failed to use a seatbelt.[5] Isolated examples of strict liability based on breach of statutory duty[6] and public nuisance[7] may very occasionally offer a remedy to a road accident victim, but they are of no significance in the ordinary case. The Pearson Commission's proposal[8] for the introduction of a special social security benefit, modelled on the industrial injury scheme, to protect the road accident victim was never accepted. More recently the Lord Chancellor's Department, following recommendations made in the Civil Justice Review, has proposed the introduction of a scheme of no-fault accident compensation for minor injuries.[9]

Medical Negligence

Negligence is the basis of most litigation concerning medical practice,[10] although a doctor's failure to obtain the necessary consent to a proposed treatment will involve strict liability based on the tort of battery.[11] Medical negligence litigation is dominated by the "schools of thought" approach derived from *Bolam* v. *Friern H.M.C.*[12] which is to the effect that a doctor is not to be held negligent if he acted in accordance with a responsible body of opinion accepted within the profession. This result has been criticised as making it far too difficult for patients injured by poor quality treatment, to bring a successful claim because it is too easy for a doctor to defend a case by finding other practitioners who would approve of the action taken.[13] On the

---

[4] *Pitts* v. *Hunt* [1991] 1 Q.B. 24.
[5] See *ante*, p. 106.
[6] *Monk* v. *Warbey* [1935] K.B. 75 (breach of compulsory insurance requiremens); *London Passenger Transport Board* v. *Upson* [1949] A.C. 155 (pedestrian crossing regulations). *Cf. Phillips* v. *Britannia Hygienic Laundry Co. Ltd.* [1923] 2 K.B. 832 (vehicle construction regulations) and *Coote* v. *Stone* [1971] 1 W.L.R. 279 (breach of parking regulations).
[7] *Dymond* v. *Pearce* [1972] 1 Q.B. 496 and the rules relating to those who have responsibility for maintaining a highway. These areas are discussed at p. 245.
[8] Chap. 18.
[9] Lord Chancellor's Department, *Compensation for Road Accidents: a Consultation Paper.* See *post*, p. 302.
[10] No data exists on the number of medical accidents or claims for compensation made in this area. However, the rapid increase in the premiums charged by the medical defence societies in the early 1980s probably confirms the generally held belief that the number and value of such claims has increased significantly.
[11] See *ante*, p. 180.
[12] [1957] 1 W.L.R. 582.
[13] The Pearson Commission (para. 1326) found that the success rate of those who claimed compensation for medical negligence was between 30 per cent. and 40 per cent. This was much lower than the 86 per cent. rate recorded for all personal injury claims.

other hand, in spite of this, the medical profession seems to take the prospect of negligence claims very seriously. This is an area in which the deterrent effect of tort is at its most effective because doctors perceive their professional reputations to be at risk following an allegation of negligence.

Wrongful life and wrongful birth

"Wrongful life" actions, those brought by a child born with disabilities claiming negligence on the part of doctors in failing to prevent its birth by advising its parents of the desirability of an abortion, were excluded from English law as a matter of public policy by the decision in *McKay* v. *Essex Area Health Authority*.[14] This was on the grounds that such an action would open the way to children suing their parents for failure to procure an abortion and because it is impossible to compare the value of life with disabilities with never having been born at all. In any case, such claims were made impermissible for births occurring after 1976 by the wording of subparagraph 1(2)(b) of the Congenital Disabilities (Civil Liability) Act 1976.[15] However, "wrongful birth" claims by parents for the cost of maintaining a child who has been born after the failure of negligently conducted sterilisations or abortions, are now well recognised. In *Thake* v. *Maurice*[16] Peter Pain J. rejected the contention that public policy would bar the award of damages to parents following the birth of a healthy child after the father had undergone a vasectomy which was alleged to have been conducted negligently. The judge accepted that the birth of a child is not always a blessing and, in the light of the legality and widespread acceptance of family planning, refused to countenance policy objections to the awarding of damages in such circumstances.[17]

The standard of liability

The *Bolam* "schools of thought" test governs the standard of liability applied to all forms of medical treatment.[18] It was extended to the question of the counselling given to a patient and the warnings given of the risks entailed in the proposed treatment, by the decision of the House of Lords in *Sidaway* v. *Bethlem Royal Hospital Governors*.[19] That case involved a major challenge to the *Bolam* test on the grounds that to fix the standard of the amount of information to be given to a patient according to the level of information given by reasonable doctors, was tantamount to sacrificing the patient's "right to know" and the associated right of refusing to accept recommended treatment to the demands of medical paternalism: if a body of reasonable doctors feel that patients need not be informed of a particular risk

---

[14] [1982] Q.B. 1166.
[15] For an action to be possible under the Act the tort must have been the cause of disabilities "which would not otherwise have been present." In wrongful life cases this condition is not satisfied as the disability is naturally caused and the claimed negligence relates to a failure to advise on the desirability of an abortion.
[16] [1986] Q.B. 644.
[17] See also *Emeh* v. *Kensington & Chelsea & Westminster A.H.A.* [1985] Q.B. 1012.
[18] The most recent affirmation of the role of the test in this context occurred in *Maynard* v. *West Midlands Regional Health Authority* [1984] 1 W.L.R. 634.
[19] [1985] A.C. 871.

inherent in a recommended treatment, no doctor will be negligent in failing to disclose it. Lord Scarman, in a powerful dissenting speech, argued that a patient's right of self-determination could only be protected by introducing a judicially determined standard of medical disclosure into English law along the lines of American doctrines of "informed consent." However, the majority of the House asserted that the *Bolam* test applied the "medical standard" to the issue of disclosure. A decision on what risks should be disclosed to a patient was regarded as just as much an exercise of professional medical judgment as decisions taken on the appropriate form of treatment. Subsequently *Bolam* has had a number of further triumphs over attempts to set some limits to the width of the *Sidaway* decision and can, as a result, be said to apply a single comprehensive criterion of liability to all areas of medical negligence. In *Gold* v. *Haringey Health Authority*[20] the Court of Appeal refused to recognise an exception to *Sidaway* in the case of non-therapeutic or elective treatments such as sterilisations and cosmetic surgery. The argument that non-disclosure of risks could not be justified in such a case as there could be no medical grounds for encouraging the patient to undergo the treatment, failed to justify an exception being made to the *Bolam* principle asserted by *Sidaway*. In *Blythe* v. *Bloomsbury H.A.*[21] it was held that answers to specific questions asked of doctors by patients do not create an obligation to make a complete disclosure of available information: the answer given by the doctor need only correspond with the accepted schools of thought approach.

Reform

The Pearson Commission[22] was of the view that, at the time that it reported, negligence remained the appropriate basis for the compensation of medical injuries, although it did accept that the introduction of strict liability might be appropriate in relation to particular areas.[23] The Commission's approach seemed to be based on the belief that the negligence action served to maintain professional accountability and on the practical difficulties of introducing a no-fault system in this area.

In spite of the Pearson approach, a number of proposals for radical reform of medical litigation by the introduction of a no-fault compensation scheme have been made in Great Britain in the last couple of years and have gained the support of a diverse group of bodies including the British Medical Association, the Royal College of Physicians, the Law Society, and the Labour Party. Although the details of the various proposals have differed, they have generally involved the creation of compensation boards to administer a fund which would provide compensation for those who suffer adverse consequences as a result of medical treatment. Most of these proposals envisage that the tort system will continue to exist as an alternative to the benefits which would be available from the fund. The level of benefits which

---

[20] [1988] Q.B. 481.
[21] (1987) 5 P.N. 167.
[22] para. 1347.
[23] Vaccine damage and injuries suffered by volunteers undergoing medical research or clinical trials. Some drug related injuries might also have been covered by the Commission proposals for product liability; these predated the Consumer Protection Act 1987.

it is proposed should be derived from the fund has varied between the different proposals, although the scale of the expenditure required was emphasised when the British Medical Association calculated that the cost of its proposed scheme would be in the region of £100 million per annum.[24] The present Government has set itself against the introduction of such a scheme on the basis that it is a kind of insurance which it is not a function of the State to provide.[25] The different attitude of the Government to this scheme and to the proposal for a no-fault road accident scheme,[26] is explained by the role of health authorities as defendants in medical cases and by the fact that these authorities now adopt a policy of self-insurance for the risks of negligence liability. Although a no-fault road accident scheme funded by private insurance is feasible, it is practically impossible to introduce such a scheme for medical accidents without government funding.

The original draft of a proposed E.C. Directive[27] on the liability of the suppliers of services for damage to the health or physical integrity of persons, would have made the liability of medical practitioners stricter by placing them under the burden of disproving negligence. This would have been a limited reform as the basis of compensation for medical accidents would have remained within the mainstream of litigation and would still ultimately have turned on the criterion of fault. It was suggested that this might have proved to be an effective method of overcoming the perceived problem of the medical profession being unduly defensive when faced by allegations of negligence as it would have given the doctors, against whom such allegations were made, an incentive to investigate the circumstances of the accident in order that negligence could be disproved. However, the most recent versions of the draft directive have exempted the supply of medical services from its provisions, presumably on the basis that the question of medical accidents raised so many difficulties that it was certain to impede the passage of the legislation.[28]

OCCUPIERS' LIABILITY AND DEFECTIVE PREMISES

Liability for personal injuries caused by dangerous premises is traditionally treated under two categories of tort. Occupiers' liability deals with the duties owed to visitors by a person who has control of premises. Defective premises defines the duties of those who dispose of property by sale or lease to others who are affected by the state of the premises. Both of these topics are now governed by statute but are, in essence, species of negligence liability.

---

[24] *No Fault Compensation Working Party Report* (1991), paras. 7.1–7.2. See also Ham, Dingwall, Fenn and Harris, *Medical Negligence: Compensation and Accountability* (1988), p. 31 which estimated costs of between £177 million and £235 million.

[25] See the statement of the Lord Chancellor reported in (1991) 88/20 L.S.G. 3 and also the proposals for improving the present system made by the Secretary of State for Health at the time that the private members National Health Service (Compensation) Bill 1991, which would have introduced a no-fault scheme, failed to obtain a second reading in the House of Commons (1991) 88/5 L.S.G. 9.

[26] See *post*, p. 302.

[27] January 18, 1991: [1991] O.J. C12.

[28] The British Government had opposed the application of the directive to the supply of medical services.

Occupiers' liability to visitors

The law of occupiers' liability is now to be found in the Occupiers' Liability Acts (O.L.A.s) of 1957 and 1984. These statutes create a comprehensive code which is clearly intended to place the liability within the mainstream of the tort of negligence. The 1957 Act defines the duties owed to a "visitor." The 1984 Act deals with other categories of entrant, primarily trespassers.

Traditionally, occupiers' liability governed injuries caused by the state or condition of premises, rather than by activities conducted upon them. However, the fact that the statutes have assimilated the occupiers' liability rules to the mainstream negligence principles which govern "activity" duties, has made the distinction redundant for most purposes. The actual wording of the statutes is very unclear on the issue: both the 1957 and 1984 Acts appear to deny the validity of the distinction when they speak of "dangers due to the state of the premises *or to things done or omitted to be done on them*"[29] and the 1984 Act replaces the common law in relation to "any danger due to the state of the premises *or to things done or omitted to be done on them.*" On the other hand, the 1957 Act is stated to "regulate the nature of the duty imposed by law in consequence of a person's occupation or control of premises."

1. Who is the occupier?

The duties created by both the 1957 and 1984 Acts are owed by "occupiers." Occupation is not defined by either Act. The rules developed at common law are allowed to govern the question.[30] It is well established that occupation is not synonymous with the ownership of property, but is based on the factual question of who has control of it. An owner who lets property to a tenant will therefore cease to occupy it. An occupier need not be in exclusive possession of the property and the occupation may be through the agency of employees (this is inevitably the result in the case of companies). The leading decision on the question of occupation is that of the House of Lords in *Wheat* v. *E. Lacon Co. Ltd.*[31] which concerned a death which occurred on premises owned by a brewery. The brewery permitted its manager to reside on the premises, but had not given him a tenancy. The deceased had been staying at the premises as a paying guest and was killed when attempting at night to descend a back staircase in the residential part of the building which was unlit and on which the handrail ended above the foot of the stairs. The ratio of the decision is that the staircase was not a danger to a person who took proper care for his safety. However, the House of Lords also discussed whether the manager or the brewery was the occupier of the building. The House held that the brewery, by employing a manager rather than letting the premises to a tenant, had retained sufficient control over the property to count as the occupier. There was no need for it to be shown that the brewery had exclusive control. It was enough that it was in joint occupation of the property with the manager.

In the absence of any factual control, the assertion of a right to control premises may suffice to establish occupation. The Court of Appeal applied

---

[29] O.L.A. 1957, s. 1(1); O.L.A. 1984, s. 1(1)(a).
[30] s. 1(2).
[31] [1966] A.C. 552.

such an approach in *Harris* v. *Birkenhead Corporation*[32] when it held that the assertion of an immediate right to enter and control property, even if not supported by any actual, symbolic or "deemed" taking of possession, was sufficient to constitute occupation from the time that the previous occupier vacated the premises. A local authority was, on the facts of the case, held to be the occupier of a vandalised and dangerous house over which it had asserted its right to compulsory purchase even though the authority took no actual measures to assert its control from the time when the previous occupier moved out.

A contractor undertaking work on property may be held to be in joint control of it with the person on whose behalf the work is being undertaken. In *A.M.F. International Ltd.* v. *Magnet Bowling Ltd.*[33] a contractor was held to be in joint occupation with the owner of a construction site and therefore to owe duties under the O.L.A. 1957 to the plaintiff who was supplying and installing equipment on the site. This rule is of limited significance, because a contractor who is not an occupier, because he has insufficient control over the premises, will still owe a duty of care to those whom he can foresee as being affected by the work under standard negligence principles.[34] As the duties owed by an occupier to a trespasser remain more limited than the standard negligence duty to take reasonable care to avoid foreseeable harm to those who can be foreseen as being affected by one's acts, it is possible that a non-occupier might owe a greater duty of care to a trespasser than an occupier, although any anomaly created by this result has been reduced as the level of duty owed to trespassers by occupiers has been increased by the O.L.A. 1984.

2. Premises

The law of occupiers' liability is not limited to land or immoveable structures. Section 1(3) of the O.L.A. 1957 extends the duties created by the Act to:

"a person occupying or having control over any fixed or moveable structure, including any vessel, vehicle or aircraft."

The result is that the Act may apply to dangers created by the state of a wide variety of items which a person has been permitted to use. The best known case is *Bunker* v. *Charles Brand & Sons Ltd.*[35] in which section 1(3) was held to justify the Act applying to a case in which the plaintiff was injured when climbing over tunnelling equipment at his place of work.[36]

3. Visitor

The 1957 Act removed the distinction which the common law made previously between different categories of lawful entrant. An occupier now owes the same duty to all "visitors" who enter his premises with his permission. "Visitor" is defined to mean those persons who would have been held at common law to be invitees or licensees.[37] Actual permission need not

---

[32] [1976] 1 W.L.R. 279.
[33] [1968] 1 W.L.R. 1028.
[34] *A.C. Billings & Sons Ltd.* v. *Riden* [1958] A.C. 240.
[35] [1969] 2 Q.B. 480.
[36] See also *Wheeler* v. *Copas* [1981] 3 All E.R. 405 in which dangers created by the defective state of a ladder were said to be within the Act.
[37] s. 1(2).

have been given by the occupier. People who enter property on the basis of statutory or other powers to do so, for example, police with warrants, employees of statutory bodies and factory inspectors, are also classified as lawful visitors.[38] However, three classes of lawful entrant do not count as "visitors." They are those who are using a private[39] or a public[40] right of way and persons who enter property in the exercise of rights conferred by an access agreement or order under the National Parks and Access to the Countryside Act 1949.[41]

In *Ferguson* v. *Welsh*[42] Lord Goff considered that as it is possible for two persons, such as the owner of property and his contractor, to be in occupation of the same piece of land at the same time, it is inevitable that a person may be classified as a trespasser against one of them but a lawful visitor as against the other. However, the actual result in *Ferguson* shows that entrants who rely on a permission to enter given to them by a contractor, will usually count as lawful visitors against the owner as they will be able to plead that the contractor had the owner's ostensible authority to permit others to enter his property.[43]

A permission need not have been given expressly. It may be implied from the conduct of the occupier. In the leading case of *Lowery* v. *Walker*[44] an occupier's conduct of tolerating the use of his property as a short cut was held to have amounted to impliedly permitting entry to his property. The precise point at which an occupier's knowledge of entries onto his property can be regarded as implying permission to enter may be difficult to pinpoint. The fact that a trespass has been repeated does not, of itself, raise the implication that the occupier must have agreed to permit the entry[45] and it would seem that at least acquiescence with knowledge is required. At the time that *Lowery* was decided a finding of implied permission was important because of the great contrast between the treatment which the law accorded to trespassers and those who entered property with permission. It is generally thought that courts will be less willing to imply permissions fictitiously now that trespassers receive a significant degree of protection from the law.[46]

This does not mean that genuine implied permissions have no role left to play. An implied permission would seem to be the best explanation for the fact that many normal everyday entries onto property do not constitute a trespass. In practice, most people tolerate entries onto their property by persons such as door to door salesmen. In *Robson* v. *Hallett*[47] Lord Parker C.J. said that "It seems to me that the occupier of any dwelling house gives implied (permission) to any member of the public coming on his lawful business to come through the gate, up the steps, and knock on the door of his house." It is, of course, possible for a person expressly to deny such permission to enter by erecting a notice reading "no salesmen" or to revoke a

[38] s. 2(6).
[39] *Holden* v. *White* [1982] Q.B. 679.
[40] *Greenhalgh* v. *British Railways Board* [1969] 2 Q.B. 286.
[41] s. 1(4).
[42] [1987] 1 W.L.R. 1553
[43] See *Robson* v. *Hallett* [1967] 2 Q.B. 939 for an application of principles of ostensible authority in everyday circumstances.
[44] [1911] A.C. 10.
[45] *Edwards* v. *Railway Executive* [1952] A.C. 737.
[46] O.L.A. 1984, discussed *post*, pp. 199–201. The use of fictitious implied permissions was criticised by the House of Lords in *Herrington* v. *British Railways Board* [1972] A.C. 877.
[47] [1967] 2 Q.B. 939.

permission impliedly given with the consequence that the visitor will become a trespasser if he fails to leave within a reasonable time. The courts have, however, refused to allow implied permission to justify entry into dwellings, particularly when the consequence of doing so would be to expand the rights of the police to enter premises without a warrant. In *Great Central Railway v. Bates*[48] a police officer who was injured on premises which he had entered at night after seeing an open door was held unable to plead implied permission and was held to be a trespasser.

A person who exceeds the scope of an invitation becomes a trespasser. This applies even though the person was innocent of any intention to trespass. In *Mersey Docks and Harbour Board v. Proctor*[49] this rule was applied to a person who exceeded the geographical bounds of his permission when he became lost in fog. An invitation may be limited in either of two ways. The invitation of a person permitted to enter an extensive piece of property may be confined, as occurred in the *Mersey Docks* case, to a particular part of that property. Similarly a permission to enter property may be limited to the use of the property for specific purposes. In either case going beyond the limits of the permission will have the effect of turning a lawful visitor into a trespasser. The precise bounds of an invitation may create difficult issues of facts in practice because of the informal ways in which permission to enter property is granted.

An exception to these rules exists in relation to children who are injured by "allurements." An occupier who permits children to be present on land should foresee that children are inquisitive, may meddle with and be endangered by items which an adult would ignore. If a child is injured by such an "allurement" it will be held that the occupier ought to have foreseen the possibility of such behaviour. As a result the occupier will not be able to claim that the child has exceeded the limits of its permission and become a trespasser. In *Glasgow Corporation v. Taylor*[50] a child of seven who had died after eating poisonous berries growing in a public park was held not to have become a trespasser through its acts. The allurement exception is confined to preventing an act from changing the status of a child who has been permitted to enter land from that of a lawful visitor to that of a trespasser. It does not provide children who have entered land without permission with a method of establishing that they are lawful visitors. Any protection available for such children must be found in the provisions of the O.L.A. 1984.

At one time it was believed that a young child[51] who entered property might only do so on condition that it was accompanied by a responsible adult; if it was unaccompanied it would be classed as a trespasser.[52] The reason for adopting this approach was that it was felt that unaccompanied young children are at such risk that their presence on property might place the occupier under exceptionally burdensome duties. However, as a result of Devlin J.'s judgment in *Phipps v. Rochester Corporation*,[53] it is generally agreed that this approach is too unfavourable to children and that any

---

[48] [1921] 3 K.B. 578.
[49] [1923] A.C. 253.
[50] [1922] 1 A.C. 44.
[51] There are very few reported cases on this issue and the possible legal distinctions between children, young children and very young children have not been explored.
[52] *Bates v. Stone Parish Council* [1954] 1 W.L.R. 1249.
[53] [1955] 1 Q.B. 450.

problem created by the presence of young children on property is better dealt with as an issue of standard of care. An occupier will therefore fulfil any duty which is owed to a young child visitor by providing a level of precautions sufficient to enable an accompanying adult to safeguard the child. On this approach the fact that such a child enters land unaccompanied does not render it a trespasser.

If a person's permission to be on premises is revoked,[54] a reasonable time to leave will be allowed before he becomes classified as a trespasser.[55]

Because necessity is a defence to trespass if the entry is made for the purpose of safeguarding human life,[56] a rescuer who enters property to render assistance to an injured person will be a lawful visitor even if the person to whom assistance is provided is a trespasser.

4. The common duty of care

The standard of care imposed by the 1957 Act is found in section 2(2) which provides that:

> "2(2) The common duty of care is a duty to take such care as in all the circumstances of the case is reasonable to see that the visitor will be reasonably safe in using the premises for the purposes for which he is invited or permitted by the occupier to be there."

This is a statutory enactment of a standard negligence duty, that of taking all reasonable care as is called for by the circumstances, tailored to the area of occupiers' liability. Some of the cases concerning the standard of reasonable care which were discussed in Chapter 3 were actually decided as applications of this provision. The common duty of care is directed to making the visitor safe and no obligation is placed on the occupier to make the premises safe other than for the purposes of the visitor. The duty is owed to "visitors" and may also operate as an implied term of a contract in favour of persons who are entitled by its terms to enter the occupier's property.[57]

The section provides additional guidance as to its working in the following provisions:

> "2(3) The circumstances relevant for the present purpose include the degree of care, and want of care, which would ordinarily be looked for in such a visitor, so that (for example) in proper cases –
>
> (a) an occupier must be prepared for children to be less careful than adults; and
> (b) an occupier may expect that a person, in the exercise of his calling, will appreciate and guard against any special risks ordinarily incident to it, so far as the occupier leaves him free to do so.
>
> (4) In determining whether the occupier of premises has discharged the common duty of care to a visitor, regard is to be had to all the circumstances, so that (for example) –

---

[54] See post, pp. 379–380 for a discussion of the revocability of permissions to enter land.
[55] Robson v. Hallett [1967] 2 Q.B. 939.
[56] Esso Petroleum Co. Ltd. v. Southport Corporation [1956] A.C. 218; Rigby v. Chief Constable of Northamptonshire [1985] 1 W.L.R. 1242. See the discussion in Chap. 5.
[57] s. 5(1).

(a) where damage is caused to a visitor by a danger of which he has been warned by the occupier, the warning is not to be treated without more as absolving the occupier from liability, unless in all the circumstances it was enough to enable the visitor to be reasonably safe; and

(b) where damage is caused to a visitor by a danger due to the faulty execution of any work of construction, maintenance or repair by an independent contractor employed by the occupier, the occupier is not to be treated without more as answerable for the danger if in all the circumstances he had acted reasonably in entrusting the work to an independent contractor and had taken such steps (if any) as he reasonably ought in order to satisfy himself that the contractor was competent and that the work had been properly done."

Section 2(4)(b) establishes the important rule that the duty placed upon an occupier by section 2 is a delegable one.

5. Defences

A number of standard defences are available to an occupier in a claim brought by a visitor. The 1957 Act contains no express provision which makes the common duty of care subject to a defence of contributory negligence. However, there can be no doubt that the defence does apply. A defence of consent, which is termed assumption of risk and expressly equated to the common law defence of *volenti* is made available to the occupier by subsection 2(5). In addition, it is well established that exclusion clauses and notices, whether they derive their validity from a contract or not,[58] are capable, subject to the provisions of the Unfair Contract Terms Act 1977[59] of providing an occupier with a defence to this liability. In the context of personal injury litigation this means that only non-businesses are able to "restrict or exclude liability."[60]

Occupiers' liability to trespassers and non-visitors

The 1957 Act made no provision concerning an occupier's liability to those who entered his property without consent. The traditional view was that an occupier owed no duty of care to such an entrant but was merely obliged not to deliberately or recklessly cause injury to such a person. The courts made several attempts to improve the position of trespassers on the basis that the result was too harsh, particularly in the case of innocent trespassers such as children. The final result achieved which recognised an obligation on an occupier to treat a trespasser with what became known as "common humanity" probably provided a workable compromise between the competing interests in this area in that it was a subjectively based duty which fell short of that of reasonable care.[61] However, the Law Commission[62] was of the opinion that sufficient uncertainties remained to justify a statute which clarified the law. The result was the O.L.A. 1984 which

---

[58] See *ante*, p. 115.
[59] See *ante*, pp. 117.
[60] Unfair Contract Terms Act 1977, s. 2(1).
[61] *Herrington v. British Railways Board* [1972] A.C. 877 provided the basis for this approach.
[62] Report No. 75.

imposes a statutory duty of care on an occupier[63] which is owed to persons "other than his visitors." This wording creates a duty owed by an occupier to three classes of person who fall outside the protection of the 1957 Act: trespassers; those entering property while using a private right of way and persons who enter property in the exercise of rights conferred by an access agreement or order, under the National Parks and Access to the Countryside Act 1949.[64]

Under the 1984 Act it is necessary to distinguish two issues: when does a duty arise? and what is the standard of any duty which does arise? It is an oversimplification to say that the Act simply imposes a duty on an occupier not to be negligent to a trespasser. It does this only in relation to a defined category of trespassers. Those who fall outside this category are left unprotected. Section 1(3) defines the circumstances in which the protection exists:

> "An occupier of premises owes a duty to another (not being his visitor) in respect of any such risk as is referred to in subsection (1)[65] above if –
>
> (a) he is aware of the danger or has reasonable grounds to believe that it exists;
>
> (b) he knows or has reasonable grounds to believe that the other is in the vicinity of danger concerned or may come into the vicinity of the danger . . . ; and
>
> (c) the risk is one against which, in all the circumstances of the case, he may reasonably be expected to offer some protection."

The aim of this strangely worded provision is to strike a factually based balance between those trespassers who merit protection and those who do not. The subsection should make it virtually impossible for an occupier to deny the existence of a duty when he knows that children habitually trespass in order to play on his property. However, the burglar is likely to be beyond the scope of the duty either because the likelihood of his appearing is so low that subparagraph (b) will not be satisfied or because it is unreasonable in terms of subparagraph (c) to offer him any protection. It has been suggested that one of the major differences between this statutory duty and a common law duty of care is that the tests contained in subparagraphs (a) and (b) depend on the subjective factor of the occupier's actual knowledge, rather than imposing an objective test according to what he ought reasonably to have known.[66] It is to be hoped that the courts will be able to avoid interpreting the provision in this way as it is difficult to accept that the protection offered by a measure of this kind should vary according to the particular subjective knowledge of the occupier.

The standard of liability which is laid down by subsection 1(4) is a straightforward statutory version of negligence. The standard of liability is an objective one "to take such care as is reasonable in all the circumstances of

---

[63] Defined by reference to the 1957 Act.

[64] Those using a public right of way are excluded from this protection by s. 1(7). Such a person may be protected by the law concerning the responsibilities of highway authorities (see *post*, p. 247), but the person using a public right of way which is maintained by a private individual has no statutory rights and would need to rely on the common law which only imposes liability for misfeasance.

[65] *i.e.* the risk of persons other than his visitors suffering injury by reason of any danger due to the state of the premises or to things done or omitted to be done on them.

[66] Jones, (1984) 47 M.L.R. 713.

the case to see that he (the entrant) does not suffer injury on the premises by reason of the danger concerned." Factual issues such as the adequacy of fencing and whether a site should be kept permanently manned will be determined under this provision if a duty is established under section 1(3). Subsection 1(5) expands on the terms of section 1(4) by providing that the duty may be discharged in an appropriate case "by taking such steps as are reasonable in all the circumstances of the case to give warning of the danger concerned or to discourage persons from incurring the risk." This almost certainly makes it easier for an occupier to use a warning to discharge his duty as against a trespasser than against a visitor. The 1957 Act speaks of a warning not being "treated without more as absolving the occupier from liability, unless in all the circumstances it was enough to enable the visitor to be reasonably safe."[67] The reason for the 1957 Act requiring a higher standard to be met is presumably, that an occupier can be expected to tailor a warning to the specific risks which an identified visitor is likely to face on the property, whereas a warning directed at trespassers may have to be couched in very general terms and, when contained in a notice, may not be placed at the precise point at which the entry is made.

Subsection 1(6) of the 1984 Act expressly makes the statutory duty subject to the defence of consent (termed "assumption of risk"). It seems certain that the standard defences of contributory negligence and illegality will also be available. It is uncertain whether it is possible for an occupier to use an exclusion notice against someone who enters property without permission.[68] If such a clause is efficacious it escapes the controls on such notices created by the Unfair Contract Terms Act 1977[69] and it is unclear whether an occupier would owe no duty or whether the law would regard the judicially devised standard of "common humanity"[70] as a minimum standard which should be applied in any circumstances.

Those who fear that the 1984 Act will create intolerable burdens for occupiers may be able to take some comfort from the approach adopted by the House of Lords in the decision of *Titchener* v. *British Rail Board*.[71] This was a case fought under the different wording of the O.L. (Scotland) A. 1960. The House showed little sympathy for a trespasser in spite of the fact that a statutory duty of care was owed to her. The plaintiff who was aged 15 was hit by a train after she had gone onto the line through a gap in the fence of which the Board knew. The train had been driven with proper care and the case turned on the Board's failure to maintain the fence. The House of Lords held that given the circumstances of the case, including the age of the plaintiff and the fact that she was aware of the risks, the defendants had broken no duty to this particular plaintiff by their failure to maintain the fence adequately. In the alternative, had the defendants owed a duty, breach of it was not the cause of the injury as the plaintiff would not have been prevented from getting onto the property by a properly maintained fence and as the plaintiff was fully aware of risks which her conduct entailed, she was subject to the defence of *volenti*.

---

[67] s. 2(4)(a).
[68] The reasons for this difficulty are discussed at p. 116.
[69] The duty imposed by s. 1(4) does not count as negligence for the purposes of the 1977 Act.
[70] *i.e.* the common law duty established as being owed to trespassers by the decision of the House of Lords in *Herrington* v. *British Railways Board* [1972] A.C. 877.
[71] [1983] 3 All E.R. 770.

Defective premises

The obligations of vendors and lessors of property in relation to injuries caused by the state of a building constituted an immunity from the duty of care for many years. This was a result of the principle of "caveat emptor." The risks of defects in the building were placed on the purchaser or lessee of a building who was regarded as able to obtain protection by having it surveyed prior to the acquisition. With the expansion of the neighbour principle this immunity appeared increasingly anomalous and was accorded a restrictive interpretation by the courts. In particular, it was not extended by analogy to provide protection to building contractors and neither was it held to protect an owner or lessor in relation to dangers created by design or building work which he had undertaken personally.[72] The immunity was finally removed by judicial and statutory developments. In *Anns* v. *Merton L.B.C.*[73] the House of Lords held that the vendor of a building has no immunity in respect of injuries caused by defects resulting from negligence. Although the authority of *Anns* has now been overruled in relation to the cost of repairing negligently caused defects in a building,[74] it seems to be accepted that a duty of care is still owed by a building inspector and others connected with the provision of a building in relation to personal injuries or property damage caused by negligence. In *Department of the Environment* v. *Bates*[75] Lord Keith was of the view that it was the unanimous opinion of the members of the House of Lords which had overruled *Anns* that "the builder would be liable under the principle in *Donoghue* v. *Stevenson* in the event of the defect, before it had been discovered, causing physical injury to persons . . . "

The common law position in respect to leases is more complicated. In *Rimmer* v. *Liverpool City Council*[76] the Court of Appeal was of the view that the common law immunity of lessors which was enshrined in House of Lords authority[77] could only be reviewed by a decision of that House, although it was held on the facts of the case that the defendant council could not avail itself of the lessor's immunity as the injuries suffered by the plaintiff were the result of the defendant's negligent design work.[78] As a result it seems that it is still the position at common law that no duty of care is created by the simple act of letting a defective property, at least if the danger has not been created by work done to the premises by the lessor.

At the same time that these judicial developments were narrowing the immunity, Parliament achieved very much the same result, when it passed the Defective Premises Act of 1972. Section 3 of this Act provides that:

"3(1) Where work of construction, repair, maintenance or demolition or any other work is done on or in relation to premises any duty of care owed, because of the doing of the work, to persons who might reasonably be expected to be affected by the defects in the state of the premises created by the doing of the work shall not be abated by

---

[72] *Rimmer* v. *Liverpool City Council* [1984] 1 All E.R. 930; *Targett* v. *Torfaen B.C.* [1992] 3 All E.R. 27.
[73] [1978] A.C. 728.
[74] *Murphy* v. *Brentwood District Council* [1991] 1 A.C. 398.
[75] [1991] 1 A.C. 499.
[76] [1985] Q.B. 1.
[77] *Cavalier* v. *Pope* [1906] A.C. 428.
[78] See also *Targett* v. *Torfaen B.C.* [1992] 3 All E.R. 27.

the subsequent disposal of the premises by the person who owed the duty."

The statute applies to all "disposals" whether by means of sale or lease so long as the contract which gave rise to it was made on or after January 1, 1974. The drafting of the provision makes it fairly certain that the duty which it creates applies only in relation to positive work done by the owner to the premises prior to the disposal. Allowing a building to fall into a dangerous state through a failure to repair it will not suffice and the section therefore does not overturn the immunity of the lessor who has permitted the property which he lets, to fall into disrepair.

Section 4 of the Defective Premises Act places an additional duty of reasonable care on those landlords of premises who owe a contractual duty to the tenant to keep the property in repair.[79] This extensive statutory duty, which is not confined to dwellings, is owed to all persons; tenants, persons visiting the tenants, neighbours and passers by, whom the landlord might expect to be affected by the defects, so long as he knows, or ought in the circumstances to have known of the defect.[80] The duty is expressly extended to cases in which there is no duty on the landlord to effect repairs but he has retained a power to enter and do them at his discretion[81] and to cases of contractual licences to occupy property.[82] The duty created by this section overlaps with the common law torts of negligence, and public and private nuisance.

NERVOUS SHOCK

Introduction

The term "nervous" shock is used to denote a range of injuries which may be inflicted by accidents. The term is used by lawyers to denote a variety of forms of mental injury or psychiatric illness which are described under different names by the medical professions. The twentieth century has witnessed a steady liberalisation in the judicial attitude towards allowing recovery of damages for nervous shock. In this, the courts have followed developments in social attitudes. Psychiatric illness is now more readily recognised as a medical affliction; the variety of possible causes for it are more widely appreciated and, as a result, accident victims are more likely to seek compensation for this form of loss.

It is proposed to divide the discussion of nervous shock into three categories. They are: (a) mental illness consequential upon physical injuries; (b) shock caused by fear of injury to oneself; and (c) shock caused by the fact of or fear of injury to another (witness cases). Most of the discussion of nervous shock has been concentrated on the third of these categories, but a complete picture can only be provided by mentioning the others.

---

[79] A covenant to repair the structure and exterior of the premises is implied in a lease for a term of less than seven years of a dwelling by s. 11 of the Landlord and Tenant Act 1985. See *McAuley* v. *Bristol City Council* [1992] 1 All E.R. 749 for a case on the implication of an obligation to repair other parts of a property (in that case a step in the garden).

[80] This is not confined to cases in which the tenant has informed him of the defect.

[81] s. 4(4). *McAuley* v. *Bristol City Council* [1992] 1 All E.R. 749.

[82] s. 4(6).

There can be little doubt that the part played by nervous shock in the development of the tort of negligence has resulted in its receiving greater critical attention than would be justified by its practical importance. The history of the subject in relation to witness cases provides an excellent illustration of the evolution of negligence theory during the twentieth century. The isolated examples of such recovery which had occurred prior to the decision in *Donoghue* v. *Stevenson*[83] were swept up into the generalised theory which was thereby created. Nonetheless, problems remained. First, the relationship between issues of duty of care and remoteness of damage in this area was not totally clear. Secondly, the expansionary tendencies of the neighbour test[84] posed particular problems in relation to shock, in as much as a far wider range of views was possible as to when this form of loss was foreseeable than was the case in relation to damage caused by physical impact. Finally, the spectre of novel and indeterminate forms of liability was raised by the wide range of persons who might be foreseen as possible victims of shock. In modern cases it seems to be generally assumed that nervous shock raises an issue of duty of care. In the light of this, it was not surprising that Lord Wilberforce's two stage test for the existence of a duty of care[85] came to be used to control the ambit of liability for shock in the 1980s and it is notable that that test received its first significant challenge in this context.[86] Most recently, the decision of the House of Lords in *Alcock* v. *Chief Constable of the South Yorkshire Police*[87] (a case which concerned the disaster at the Hillsborough football ground) saw a more modern "proximity" approach to the determination of the existence of a duty of care being applied to a case of shock.

The range of recoverable losses which might be classified as damages for nervous shock represents a fairly haphazard picture. In the case of those who witness accidents to others it must be proved that a medically recognised condition has developed as a result of the shock.[88] On the other hand, a person who suffers actual physical injuries will recover compensation for distress and inconvenience as an element in any award of general damages for pain, suffering and loss of amenities which is made. If, in such a case, a person's grief or sorrow increases the amount of suffering incurred, the full loss is recoverable.[89] The statutory award of damages for bereavement,[90] which was introduced in 1982, is a partial remedy for emotional losses which is not confined to those who witness the death of another nor to those who can produce medical evidence of illness caused by the death. However, it is subject to its own limitations being available only to a restricted category of persons; being for a fixed sum and being available only upon the death of another and not, for instance, to the spouse of a person who suffers permanent and crippling injuries. In recent years the law of contract has become somewhat more liberal in the range of losses which it recognises as justifying compensation. Awards for such categories of loss as vexation, inconvenience and annoyance have become relatively commonplace on the

---

[83] [1932] A.C. 562.
[84] See *ante*, p. 30.
[85] See *ante*, p. 30.
[86] *McLoughlin* v. *O'Brian* [1983] 1 A.C. 410.
[87] [1992] 1 A.C. 310.
[88] See *post*, p. 206.
[89] *Kralj* v. *McGrath* [1986] 1 All E.R. 54.
[90] Fatal Accidents Act 1976, s. 1A. See *post*, p. 282.

breach of certain types of contract and there is some slight evidence of such awards occurring in tort in the professional negligence sphere in which contractual and tortious liabilities run in parallel.[91] In the light of these developments the restrictions placed by the law on the recovery of damages for shock in witness cases can only be regarded as one of the artificial rules evolved by the tort of negligence to avoid the risk of "indeterminate liability."

Mental illness consequential upon physical injuries

The subject of mental illness suffered by persons as a result of physical injuries which they have incurred in an accident has received little academic attention. It would, however, seem to represent a form of loss which is well recognised by the courts as a foreseeable result of a physical injury. No difficulties of principle seem to have been raised when a minor physical injury leads to substantial disability as a result of a psychiatric reaction to the injury. It is appropriate to apply the standard egg-shell skull rule to these situations because the problem is one of differing kinds of damage[92] and is therefore capable of being classified as one of remoteness of damage. The problems which have exercised the greatest judicial attention in such cases have been the practical ones of proving whether the neurosis was genuine, was in fact caused by the accident and whether and when the plaintiff was likely to recover.

Shock caused by fear of an injury to oneself

The possibility of damages being recoverable in such circumstances was established by the decision of *Dulieu* v. *White & Sons*[93] in which the plaintiff who was serving in a public house suffered shock as a result of fearing for her safety when the defendant's servant negligently drove his vehicle in such a way as to collide with the premises. This decision has gone unquestioned in subsequent years and is undoubtedly correct. A person who physically endangers another by his negligence can scarcely claim that it is unforeseeable that that person will be shocked by the danger if, by fortune, physical impact is avoided. The facts of *Dulieu* show that the authority may remain of use in traffic accident situations.

The fact that this area may remain of significance in view of the narrow range of circumstances in which witnesses of accidents to other persons are entitled to recover damages for shock was emphasised by the decision of Smith J. in *McFarlane* v. *E.E. Caledonia Ltd.*[94] to use *Dulieu* as the basis of recognising a duty of care in the case of a person who claimed to have suffered shock as a result of witnessing the Piper Alpha disaster in which an oil drilling platform was destroyed by fire and explosions with many deaths resulting. The plaintiff had not been involved personally in rescue attempts although the support vessel, on which he was working, had approached to within 50 yards of the burning platform in order to render assistance. It was

---

[91] See Dugdale & Stanton, *Professional Negligence* (2nd ed.), paras. 20.14–20.18.

[92] See Lord Ackner's speech in *Alcock* v. *Chief Constable of the South Yorkshire Police* [1992] 1 A.C. 310.

[93] [1901] 2 K.B. 669.

[94] [1993] P.I.Q.R. P241. Reversed (1993) 143 N.L.J. 1367 on the grounds that the defendant could not have reasonably foreseen shock to a person in the plaintiff's circumstances.

held that there was a plain and forseeable risk that a person of reasonable fortitude placed in the position in which the plaintiff found himself would have feared for his own safety.

Shock caused by the fact of or fear of injury to another

When dealing with cases concerning shock suffered by those who witness accidents it is important to distinguish between shock which constitutes a medically recognised illness suffered by the plaintiff and the emotions such as grief, horror, sorrow and annoyance which are very likely to be suffered in such circumstances. In witness cases this distinction represents the boundaries of liability, as a medically recognised illness is the only form of recoverable loss. The leading statement of this principle is to be found in the judgment of Lord Denning M.R. in *Hinz* v. *Berry*.[95] His Lordship was of the opinion that:

"In English law no damages are awarded for grief or sorrow caused by a person's death. No damages are given for the worry about the children, or for the financial strain or stress, or the difficulties of adjusting to a new life. Damages are, however, recoverable for nervous shock, or to put it in medical terms, for any recognised psychiatric illness caused by the breach of duty by the defendant."[96]

Cases concerning witnesses resemble those relating to rescuers[97] in as much as an independent duty is owed and broken towards the person who suffers the shock. That person's rights are not dependent on those of the person whose fate caused the shock to be suffered and are not affected by any defences which might be pleaded against him. In *Dooley* v. *Cammell Laird & Co. Ltd.*[98] the plaintiff recovered damages for shock although none of his workmates working in the ship's hold, for whose safety he feared, had in fact been injured. A point which has not yet needed to be decided is whether a person who has put his own safety at risk can be liable to another who suffers shock as a result of witnessing the occurrence. No objection was made in the House of Lords in *Bourhill* v. *Young*[99] on the basis that the plaintiff's shock was claimed to be the result of the fatal injuries which the deceased defendant had inflicted upon himself by his negligent driving.

In a number of cases[1] damages for nervous shock have been claimed by persons who had a history of nervous illness and who therefore might be thought to be peculiarly susceptible to the risk of suffering this type of damage. This situation should not cause difficulty in relation to shock suffered by witnesses as the decision on the logically anterior question whether a duty of care not to cause injury by shock exists resolves the question. If the answer is affirmative, a peculiar susceptibility merely goes to

[95] [1970] 2 Q.B. 40.
[96] [1970] 2 Q.B. 40 at 42.
[97] See *post*, p. 212.
[98] [1951] 1 Lloyd's Rep 271.
[99] [1943] A.C. 92. However, see Lord Robertson's views (1941 S.C. 395 at 399) of the case of the negligent window cleaner who falls and impales himself on railings, cited by Lord Ackner in *Alcock* v. *Chief Constable of South Yorkshire* [1992] 1 A.C. 310 at 401. These views are equally susceptible to the explanation that the witness of this accident had an insufficient relationship of love and affection with the window cleaner to recover for any shock incurred.
[1] *Chadwick* v. *British Railways Board* [1967] 1 W.L.R. 912; *Brice* v. *Brown* [1984] 1 All E.R. 997.

the extent of the loss; if not, the issue is an irrelevance. *Brice* v. *Brown*[2] is a good illustration of this. The plaintiff, who witnessed her daughter suffering an injury in an accident, had a history of mental illness but had been able to live a fairly normal life. She suffered a severe reaction to the accident which led to her attempting suicide and being admitted to a mental hospital. The defendant argued that no damages were recoverable as the plaintiff's reaction to the accident was unforeseeable. However, Stuart Smith J., having held that it was foreseeable that a person of normal susceptibility in the plaintiff's position would suffer some degree of shock, held it to be immaterial that the precise reaction could not have been foreseen. The only requirement was that the damage which had been suffered was of a kind which was foreseeable. The case was decided as an application of the standard distinction between the kind and extent of loss.[3] The speeches of Lords Wright and Porter in *Bourhill* v. *Young*,[4] a case which concerned a claim that shock had been suffered by a person who was close to the scene of an accident in which the defendant's negligence resulted in his death, seem to have proceeded on the assumption that the defendant could not have foreseen that the plaintiff would have suffered shock because the ordinary bystander can be expected to withstand the sight and sound of highway collisions without suffering an adverse reaction. These speeches are probably best regarded as dealing with the question of whether a road user owes a duty of care not to cause shock to a bystander who has no connection with the victim of the accident rather than as denying the possibility of the thin skull rule applying to cases in which a duty of care not to cause shock does exist.

The law on nervous shock suffered by witnesses of accidents is now to be found in the decisions of the House of Lords in *McLoughlin* v. *O'Brian*[5] and *Alcock* v. *Chief Constable of the South Yorkshire Police*.[6] Both decisions deal with the question of the appropriate test of the duty of care in this area. However, different approaches emerge from the speeches in the cases and the position after the later decision of *Alcock* is something of an uneasy compromise which leaves scope for considerable difficulties in the future. The basic problem is that the choice of a test of duty of care for this subject is fraught with difficulty. A simple application of the *Donoghue* v. *Stevenson*[7] "neighbour" test in this context raises the risk of extensive, uncontrolled liability. Indeed, the use of this test may be unworkable unless a degree of consensus can be reached as to the circumstances in which people are likely to be rendered ill by the sight of injury to others. Difficulties of this kind led to Lord Wilberforce commenting in *McLoughlin*[8] that "there remains . . . just because 'shock' in its nature is capable of affecting so wide a range of people, a real need to place some limitation on the extent of admissible claims." On the other hand, the adoption of rigid "control" factors in this area, in the sense of confining recovery to persons who are close relatives to those killed or injured in the accident and who are present at the scene of the accident or its immediate aftermath, may create difficult questions as to where to draw the line; for example, is a fiancé to count as a relative? Is it

---

[2] [1984] 1 All E.R. 997.
[3] See *ante*, p. 98.
[4] [1943] A.C. 92.
[5] [1983] 1 A.C. 410.
[6] [1992] 1 A.C. 310.
[7] [1932] A.C. 562.
[8] [1983] 1 A.C. 410 at 421.

really correct to disallow a claim by a person who witnesses the death, in an industrial accident, of a workmate with whom he has worked for years? The distinction between these positions need not be as stark as it may first appear. If the neighbour test is chosen to govern the law, any determination of what damage is reasonably foreseeable may well be influenced by the relationship and the physical proximity of the witness to the accident. However, there can be no doubt that the "neighbour" test, if adopted, will have its usual capacity to expand the coverage of the law; in the period after the decision in *McLoughlin*, when it was widely believed that the law was governed by a test of whether shock was reasonably foreseeable, courts allowed recovery in the cases of a person shocked by the sight of their house being destroyed[9] and by others who were called to the hospital to which their fatally injured relative had been taken[10] and who were asked to identify the body of their relatives in a mortuary.[11]

Alcock was the case brought against the police by a number of persons with respect to shock suffered as the result of the deaths of relatives in the Hillsborough football disaster. The majority of the plaintiffs were related in some degree to persons who were killed or injured in the crowd; some had been present in other parts of the stadium when the disaster occurred, but others had only seen broadcast television coverage of it. The House of Lords was faced by rival contentions: the plaintiffs argued that the law was based on an untrammelled reasonable foreseeability test whereas the defence took the view that compensation for shock could only be recovered by a class of plaintiffs limited to spouses and parents of victims who had been present at the scene of the accident or its immediate aftermath. The House refused to accept that either of these extreme views correctly stated the law. However, the members of the House differed to a degree in the methods which they used to achieve the result. Whereas[12] some used the test of reasonable foreseeability to determine the class of persons who are sufficiently related to the victim to recover damages for shock and only fell back on a test of proximity when considering the physical relationship of the witness to the accident, others[13] saw the whole issue as governed by the need to establish a requisite relationship of proximity (whatever that might be). In spite of this difference in the theoretical approach to the subject, three factors enumerated by Lord Wilberforce in *McLoughlin* v. *O'Brian*[14] were regarded as relevant to determining the result of the case.

1. The class of persons

The result of *Alcock* would seem to be that although close relatives of the victim are the category of person most likely to recover, the courts are not prepared to impose a rigid, fixed list of relationships as a requirement of law. What is required is evidence of the existence of a close relationship of love and affection between the victim and the witness. It may be possible to presume the existence of such ties in the case of spouses or parents and child,

---

[9] *Attia* v. *British Gas* [1987] 3 All E.R. 455.
[10] *Ravenscroft* v. *Rederiaktiebolaget Transatlantic* [1991] 3 All E.R. 73, reversed [1992] 2 All E.R. 470n.
[11] *Hevican* v. *Ruane* [1991] 3 All E.R. 65.
[12] Lord Keith is the clearest supporter of this approach, Lord Ackner and Jauncey would appear to have proceeded on similar lines.
[13] Particularly Lord Oliver.
[14] [1983] 1 A.C. 410 at 421–422.

but this should not exclude the possibility of the fact of such ties being proved in the case of other, possibly non-family, relationships, for example, unmarried couples may have lived together for many years in a relationship which displays the same elements of love and affection as would exist between a married couple. In spite of these hints that the courts might be prepared to adopt a relatively liberal approach, claims brought in *Alcock* in respect of the death of brothers and brothers-in-law failed on the facts of the case because no evidence of the necessary close ties had been adduced.

It is doubtful whether a bystander who suffers shock as a result of witnessing an accident involving persons with whom he has no connection is able to recover damages for shock. In *Bourhill* v. *Young*[15] the plaintiff claimed to have suffered a miscarriage as a result of hearing the sound of an accident in which the defendant, to whom she was unrelated, was killed. Her claim failed, both Lord Wright and Lord Porter taking the view that the ordinary bystander can be expected to withstand the sight and sound of road accidents. Although this is likely to represent the normal result, there is considerable support in the speeches in *Alcock* for the proposition that the infliction of shock on bystanders who are unrelated to an accident victim may not be wholly beyond the bounds of reasonable foreseeability in the case of a major catastrophe.

In *Chadwick* v. *British Railways Board*[16] the plaintiff suffered nervous shock as a result of his having assisted at the scene of the Lewisham rail disaster in which over 90 persons had died. His claim for damages was successful in spite of the fact that he was not related to any of the persons on the trains and had come to the scene after the accident had occurred. The case is commonly explained on the basis that the defendants should have foreseen that, if, by their negligence, they caused an accident, the presence of rescuers and the fact that they might be shocked by the harrowing sights. This result may now be best assimilated to the view expressed in *Alcock* that it may be foreseeable that persons unrelated to the victims of the accident may suffer shock as a result of a major catastrophe.[17] An alternative approach is to say that rescuers constitute, alongside close relatives, a class of persons which is likely to be especially favoured when issues of shock are raised.[18] The success of Mrs McLoughlin's claim has been explained on the grounds that by going to hospital to visit her family she was performing a function akin to that of a rescuer.[19]

2. Proximity to the accident

It is a well established rule that in order to recover damages for shock the plaintiff must have been present at the scene of the accident. The decision in *McLoughlin* v. *O'Brian*[20] extended this rule slightly when it permitted damages for shock to be recovered by a mother who was not present at the scene of a road accident involving her husband and children, but who suffered shock as a result of seeing them in hospital immediately afterwards;

[15] [1943] A.C. 92. See also *Mcfarlane* v. *E.E. Caledonia Ltd.* (1993) 143 N.L.J. 1367.
[16] [1967] 1 W.L.R. 912.
[17] See also the views of Lord Bridge *McLoughlin* v. *O'Brian* [1983] 1 A.C. 410. 442.
[18] Lord Wilberforce *McLoughlin* v. *O'Brian* [1983] 1 A.C. 410. 419.
[19] Lord Edmund-Davies *McLoughlin* v. *O'Brian* [1983] 1 A.C. 410. 424.
[20] [1983] 1 A.C. 410.

the requirement of presence at the accident was held to extend to persons who witnessed the immediate aftermath of the accident. This extension seems to be strictly limited by the use of the word "immediate," shock suffered as the result of having to identify the body of a loved one at a mortuary several hours after the accident would not seem to suffice.[21]

3. The means by which the shock is caused

The receipt of a report of the fact of an accident is insufficient to satisfy the proximity requirement. Central to this requirement is the assertion that the recovery of damages for shock depends on there having been a sudden and unexpected shock administered to the plaintiff's nervous system. Several categories of person are likely to be excluded from obtaining damages for shock as a result of this approach; for example, the person who suffers shock as a result of anxiety for the safety of close relatives who are known to be involved in a major disaster and a person who suffers a nervous breakdown as a result of the demands placed on them by having to live with and care for a disabled relative.

Alcock raised directly, the issue of whether a person who suffers shock as a result of watching a television broadcast or news item concerning a disaster in which a relative was injured or killed, can recover damages. In general, it would seem to be the result of *Alcock* that the necessary relationship of proximity cannot usually be made out in the case of broadcast pictures of a disaster, even if those pictures are broadcast live. The code of ethics under which television companies do not broadcast pictures showing the suffering of identifiable individuals will normally mean that even simultaneous broadcasts of disasters cannot be equated with a person being present at the scene of a disaster. However, the House seemed prepared for the possibility of exceptions, even on this point. For example, a live broadcast of an event at which a sudden unexpected tragedy occurred might defeat the attempts of broadcasters to shield the viewers from the reality of the disaster.

The future

A range of situations involving nervous shock remain for judicial investigation. The Hillsborough case, *Attia* v. *British Gas plc*[22] in which a plaintiff succeeded in establishing a duty of care as a result of shock caused by her witnessing the destruction of her house by fire and the decision in *S.* v. *Distillers Company (Biochemicals) Ltd.*[23] which allowed a mother to recover damages for shock suffered as a result of giving birth to a child disabled by the drug thalidomide, illustrate the wide variety of situations which may produce such damage.[24] Even after the decision in *Alcock* the boundaries of the duty of care in relation to shock remain far from easy to determine.

---

[21] *Alcock* v. *Chief Constable of South Yorkshire* [1992] 1 A.C. 310 at 403 per Lord Ackner. See also *Taylor* v. *Somerset Health Authority* [1993] P.I.Q.R. P262.

[22] [1987] 3 All E.R. 455.

[23] [1970] 1 W.L.R. 114.

[24] See also *Watson* v. *Willmott* [1991] 1 Q.B. 140 in which a child, both of whose parents had died as a result of the defendant's negligence, was held entitled to damages for the likely psychiatric damage suffered. The child was present at the scene of the accident, but the damage would seem to flow from its knowledge of the deaths.

SUICIDE

Cases in which damages are claimed on behalf either of the dependants of a suicide or by a failed suicide in respect of injuries suffered in the attempt, raise problems of policy as well as issues of causation, remoteness of damage and defences. In essence, these difficulties centre on the fact that an act of suicide was a criminal offence until 1961; that a suicide may be removed in time and circumstances from the initial accident and that a suicide might be attributed causally, by many people, to the actions of the deceased.

The policies at issue in this area have been debated in a number of cases. In *Hyde* v. *Tameside Area Health Authority*[25] the plaintiff had suffered severe injuries as a result of an unsuccessful suicide attempt whilst a hospital patient. Lord Denning M.R. based his rejection of the claim on notions of public policy, arguing that although suicide was no longer a crime it remained unlawful with the result that no person should be able to benefit from such an act and that the policy of the law should be to discourage such claims rather than to allow them to result in large awards of damages being made against public authorities. This approach cannot survive the decision of the Court of Appeal in *Kirkham* v. *The Chief Constable of the Greater Manchester Police*[26] in which it was alleged that the negligence of the police was the cause of the plaintiff's husband committing suicide while he was on remand in prison. The Court of Appeal rejected the approach contained in Lord Denning's dicta and held, furthermore, that *volenti* could not be pleaded against a person whose judgment was impaired by clinical depression. On the question of public policy, the court pointed out that the abolition of the crime of suicide was evidence that public attitudes had changed: in 1990 it would no longer constitute an affront to public conscience to allow such a claim to succeed.

For the purposes of analysis it would seem preferable to divide suicide cases into two categories. The first is that in which the plaintiff was an identified suicide risk and the defendant, who had responsibility for supervising him, neglected these duties with the result that the plaintiff was able to attempt suicide. *Selfe* v. *Ilford H.M.C.*[27] was such a case. Liability was there established on the grounds of a failure by a group of nurses to supervise properly a number of patients (including the plaintiff) who were identified suicide risks. In such a case the existence of a duty of care protects the plaintiff against a real and identified risk. *Kirkham* v. *The Chief Constable of the Greater Manchester Police*[28] extended this line of authority to the suicide of prisoners in police custody. In that case the plaintiff's husband had been remanded in custody on a charge of criminal damage. The police knew that the accused was a suicide risk and that he had attempted to take his life shortly before the arrest. However, they failed to follow the normal procedure of communicating this information to the prison to which he was remanded with the result that the prison failed to take precautions which, the judge held, would have prevented the suicide occurring. The husband took his life whilst in custody and his widow successfully sued the police under the

[25] (1981) 2 P.N. 26.
[26] [1990] 2 Q.B. 283.
[27] (1970) 119 Sol. Jo. 935.
[28] [1990] 2 Q.B. 283.

Fatal Accidents Act. The Court of Appeal held that the police had assumed certain responsibilities for the husband when they took him into custody, that they were therefore under a duty to take reasonable care to communicate proper information to the prison and that they were in breach of this duty.

The second situation is that in which an accident victim commits suicide as a consequence of a reaction to injuries caused by the defendant's negligence. These cases are factually similar to those of shock consequential on personal injuries. The leading decision is that of Pilcher J. in *Pigney v. Pointers Transport Services Ltd.*[29] The plaintiff in that case, which was brought under the Fatal Accidents Act, was the widow of a man who had suffered head injuries in an accident caused by the defendant's negligence. As a result of his injuries the husband developed an acute anxiety neurosis which led to him taking his own life some 18 months after the initial accident. The judge held the widow to be entitled to succeed. The fact that there was evidence that the husband had been inclined to worry prior to the accident was discounted on the basis that the defendant had to take his victim as he found him and the contention that the husband's own act had broken the chain of causation between the negligence and the death was answered by an application of the *Re Polemis*[30] rule of remoteness of damage. Death by suicide might not have been a kind of damage foreseeable as a result of an injury of this kind, but the death was directly traceable to the negligence. Although doubts have been expressed as to whether the authority of this decision can survive the rejection of *Re Polemis* by *The Wagon Mound (No.1)*,[31] the reasoning of Pilcher J. seems firmly based on egg-shell skull reasoning which has undoubtedly survived and there can be little doubt that had a claim been brought in time the husband would have been able to recover damages on account of his neurosis.[32] If this is correct the fact that the depression was so severe that it produced a suicide would surely be a difference of extent rather than of kind. The decision in *Pigney* can therefore be accommodated within the confines of accepted principle and it is suggested that it is correct. It has been argued that although a suicide may be a foreseeable consequence of an injury to the head, it will not be foreseeable if an injury to another part of the body is involved.[33] It is difficult to accept this argument which proceeds on a relatively artificial categorisation of injuries and explains the law in the light of the *Wagon Mound* principle, which is not the appropriate theory to apply to these facts. The wide range of injuries which has justified claims for subsequent mental illness[34] also points towards the argument being incorrect.

RESCUERS

The subject of injuries suffered by rescuers, those who intervene to protect another who is in a situation of danger, is commonly treated as part of the

[29] [1957] 2 All E.R. 807.
[30] [1921] 3 K.B. 560. See *ante*, p. 95.
[31] [1961] A.C. 388, see *ante*, p. 95.
[32] See *ante*, p. 205.
[33] Douglas, (1982) 126 Sol. Jo. 455.
[34] See *ante*, p. 205.

law of defences.[35] As the whole tenor of the case law on this subject in the last 50 years has been to deny that the defences of consent and contributory negligence can apply to such injuries, it is difficult to justify this approach. Indeed it is questionable whether the topic of injuries suffered by rescuers deserves special treatment as the usual rescue case would seem to be a straightforward application of standard principles of negligence.[36] The leading Canadian case of *Horsley* v. *McLaren: the Ogopogo*[37] which concerned the death of a person who was attempting to rescue another who had fallen overboard from a boat, is an example of the fact that if a person is endangered by an accident which has not involved any negligence, a person who is injured in attempting a rescue will have no basis on which to claim compensation. However, it will usually be foreseeable that if a person by his negligence places another in a situation of danger, a third party may incur risks by intervening to protect the endangered person, and it would be strange if the law were to discourage the selfless act of the rescuer by denying him recovery for his injuries. As Cardozo J. said in his often repeated statement in the American case of *Wagner* v. *International Railways Co.*[38]:

> "Danger invites rescue. The cry of distress is the summons to relief. The law does not ignore these reactions of the mind in tracing conduct to its consequences. It recognises them as normal. It places their effect within the range of the natural and probable. The wrong that imperils life is a wrong to the imperilled victim; it is also a wrong to his rescuer."

This simple truth took some time to establish itself as law in England. Certain authorities[39] gave rise to the belief that a rescuer's claim could be defeated on the basis that his act of intervening in a situation of danger either made him *volens* to the risk or broke the chain of causation from the negligence with the result that he would be deemed to be the effective cause of his injuries. This approach, which offered scant recompense for a person who had put his own safety at risk from humanitarian motives, was rejected by a line of authority founded on the decision of the Court of Appeal in *Haynes* v. *Harwood*.[40] In that case the plaintiff was a police officer who was injured whilst stopping a pair of horses which had negligently been allowed to run away along a busy street. The plaintiff's claim was successful, and although there are dicta in the judgements which might appear to base the result on the duty of a police officer to intervene to protect the lives and property of persons in the vicinity, such a restricted interpretation of the decision has not found favour. The case is authority for the right of any rescuer, if foreseeable, to recover for his injuries.

The right of a rescuer to seek recompense for injuries suffered in the course of a rescue is independent of that of the person being rescued. It is on this basis that a rescuer's claim may succeed in full even though the victim's claim

---

[35] Salmond and Heuston, *Law of Torts* (20th ed.), pp. 492–494; Winfield and Jolowicz on *Tort* (13th ed.), pp. 693–697.

[36] There is little authority on the position of the rescuer when the victim would have had an action on the basis of a tort other than negligence. One may, for instance, speculate that if an employer endangered an employee by a breach of statutory duty it might be that a rescuer could show that he too fell within the class of persons protected by the statute or that the employer owed a duty of care to him.

[37] (1972) 22 D.L.R. (3d) 545.

[38] (1921) 232 N.Y. Rep. 176.

[39] Particularly *Cutler* v. *United Dairies (London) Ltd.* [1933] 2 K.B. 297.

[40] [1935] 1 K.B. 146.

is denied on the basis of his being a trespasser[41]; is reduced on account of contributory negligence[42] or is removed completely by an exclusion clause.[43] This rule is particularly important in circumstances in which the rescuer suffers injury but succeeds in saving the person originally endangered from harm. If the rescuer's right to recovery was dependent on the victim's rights the fact that the victim in such a case has suffered no damage would produce the anomalous result that recovery would be denied to a rescuer on the grounds that his efforts had been successful.[44] These propositions derive from the decision of the Court of Appeal in *Videan* v. *British Transport Commission*[45] in which a Fatal Accidents Act claim was successfully brought on behalf of the dependants of a station master who was killed when attempting to rescue his two-year-old son from the path of a negligently driven motorised trolley. The child's claim for compensation for his injuries was denied on the basis that his presence on the line was unforeseeable and that only a foreseeable trespasser could succeed in a claim.[46] However, the logically attractive argument that if the victim was unforeseeable the need for a rescuer to intervene was equally unforeseeable, was denied. First, on the basis that the rescuer is owed an independent duty and that if the defendant fails to take reasonable care he should foresee the need for a rescue, even though the identity of the victim and the exact sequence of events which occurred may be unforeseeable. In effect, "negligence in the air" is sufficient to make the intervention of the rescuer foreseeable. Secondly, on the basis that the station master was someone whose presence on the railway line in the course of his normal duties was foreseeable. This second approach, which is tantamount to denying that *Videan* was a rescue case was favoured by the majority of the judges sitting in the Court of Appeal.[47] It therefore raises the possibility that if the rescuer had been a person not employed by British Railways (for example, a passenger waiting on the platform) recovery would not have been allowed. It is suggested that the courts would be reluctant to reach such a result and that they are, therefore, almost certain to adopt the wider "independent right" approach. Indeed, this was done at first instance in *Harrison* v. *British Railways Board*.[48]

It is now accepted that it makes no difference to a rescuer's rights whether he intervenes instinctively, on impulse or after a deliberate consideration of the risks involved. It would be unfair to discriminate between different rescuers on this basis.[49] Neither is there any restriction on recovery by a

[41] *Videan* v. *British Transport Commission* [1963] 2 Q.B. 650.

[42] *Videan* v. *British Transport Commission* [1963] 2 Q.B. 650 at 669, *per* Lord Denning M.R. In principle, the victim in such circumstances should be liable for a portion of the rescuer's damages.

[43] *Videan* v. *British Transport Commission* [1963] 2 Q.B. 650 at 669, *per* Lord Denning M.R. A possibility which is removed in relation of "business liability" by the Unfair Contract Terms Act 1977, ss. 1 & 2. See *ante*, p. 117.

[44] The contrary result was reached without discussion of the point in *Morgan* v. *Aleyn* [1942] 1 All E.R. 489.

[45] [1963] 2 Q.B. 650.

[46] This is no longer the appropriate test governing an occupier's liability to a trespasser. See *ante*, p. 199.

[47] Harman and Pearson L.JJ., although Harman L.J. gave passing approval to the rescuers independent right approach.

[48] [1981] 3 All E.R. 679.

[49] *Haynes* v. *Harwood* [1935] 1 K.B. 146, rejecting the contention that the rescuer could only recover if he had acted instinctively. This was based on certain dicta in *Brandon* v. *Osborne, Garret & Co. Ltd.* [1924] 1 K.B. 548.

professional rescuer. In *Ogwo* v. *Taylor*[50] the plaintiff was a fireman who was injured when tackling a fire which the defendant had started negligently. The defendant argued unsuccessfully that he could only be held liable for these injuries if the fire had created an exceptional risk over and above the ordinary risks faced by those employed to fight fires. The House of Lords held that there was no reason for applying such a disadvantageous rule to professional rescuers.

A point which remained unsettled by authority for many years was whether a rescuer could recover damages from a victim whose own negligence had created the situation of danger which created the need for a rescue. The logic of the "independent right" approach suggested that a rescuer should be able to recover from the negligent victim in spite of the fact that a person does not commit a tort by endangering himself. This result was confirmed by the decision of Boreham J. in *Harrison* v. *British Railways Board*[51] in which the plaintiff, a guard on a train, was injured when trying to assist the defendant who was attempting to board the train as it was accelerating out of the station. It must be correct that a person who by lack of reasonable care puts himself in a position of danger should not be treated more favourably than one who has by such conduct endangered a third party.

A vivid example of the application of rescue principles is to be found in the Canadian decision of *Urbanski* v. *Patel*.[52] In that case the defendant surgeon removed his patient's one and only kidney in the course of an operation under the mistaken impression that he was removing an ovarian cyst. The patient was forced to resort to dialysis until a suitable kidney donor could be found to enable a transplant operation to take place. The patient's father volunteered to donate one of his kidneys and a transplant was performed. The defendant conceded liability to the patient, but the case is significant for present purposes because the father succeeded in a separate claim in recovering his lost earnings and the expenses which he incurred during his hospitalisation. It was accepted that transplant surgery is nowadays a recognised technique for treating kidney failure and thus that it was foreseeable that a donor would come forward if the surgeon's negligence resulted in the patient losing her only kidney. The facts therefore fall within the rescue principle and show that it may apply, at times, even where the rescuer has consciously chosen to follow a course of action which was certain to produce these losses. If the losses claimed here were allowed it is difficult to see why a claim for the pain and suffering incurred as a result of the operation should not succeed. All of these losses would seem to have been reasonably incurred.

An injury suffered in an attempt to save property rather than persons was held to fall within the rescue principle in *Hyett* v. *Great Western Railway Co.*[53] It was there said to be natural to expect someone to intervene to put

---

[50] [1987] 3 All E.R. 961. This confirmed the earlier decision on similar facts of *Salmon* v. *Seafarer Restaurants Ltd.* [1983] 1 W.L.R. 1264 in which the defendant's argument seems to have been based on the idea enshrined in s.2 of the O.L.A. 1957 that skilled visitors can be expected to guard against ordinary risks inherent in their work. Woolf J. held that although the occupier could expect a fireman attending a fire at his premises to be skilled in protecting himself against the risks of fire, he could not be exempt from risks which would threaten a fireman who was exercising the normal skills of his profession.

[51] [1981] 3 All E.R. 679. See also *Chapman* v. *Hearse* (1961) 106 C.L.R. 112.

[52] (1978) 84 D.L.R. (3d) 650.

[53] [1948] 1 K.B. 345.

out a fire which had developed in a railway wagon loaded with paraffin. No firm distinction would appear to have been drawn in subsequent cases between interventions to save property and those intended to save life.[54] This is surely correct: negligence which endangers property may well constitute an indirect threat to persons in the vicinity and any attempt to draw a firm distinction between the cases might produce anomalies. Nonetheless, it is conceivable that the courts would be more prepared to find an intervention unreasonable and hence to break the chain of causation when only property is at risk.[55]

It does not follow from the fact that the courts will not automatically deem a rescuer's acts to break the chain of causation that principles of causation have no relevance in this area. It is, for instance, perfectly possible for an injury suffered by a rescuer to be deemed to have been caused independently of the danger. In *Crossley* v. *Rawlinson*[56] an AA patrolman was injured whilst running towards a lorry which was on fire when his foot went into a pothole. The risk which produced the injury in this case was not created or increased by the negligence which had caused the fire to start.[57] The decision in *Cutler* v. *United Dairies (London) Ltd.*[58] is possibly best justified, if at all, on similar principles. The plaintiff in that case intervened after the danger caused by a runaway horse had passed and in these circumstances it is possible to argue that his acts were not motivated by the original negligence.

In the great majority of rescue situations any contention that a rescuer has been contributorily negligent in the course of his acts would seem doomed to failure on the basis that a person acting in the "agony of the moment" should not be criticised for acts which might prove to have been unwise given the benefits of hindsight. This approach was adopted by the Court of Appeal in *Baker* v. *T.E. Hopkins & Son Ltd.*[59] when it allowed a claim brought in relation to the death of a doctor who had taken some precautions, which proved to be ineffective, to safeguard himself before going down a well which contained a lethal concentration of carbon monoxide, in an attempt to save two workmen who had been overcome by the gas. The court did, however, recognise that cases might occur in which a rescuer acted with such wanton disregard for his own safety that his injury should be attributed, presumably wholly or partly, to himself. This suggestion is almost certainly correct in theory, but, to date, no reported case has produced this result. It would seem likely that an extreme fact situation would be required before such a result will be achieved. A situation in which a rescuer is criticised for his conduct in the course of a rescue must be distinguished from one in which a person is injured whilst attempting to rescue another from a danger which his negligence has contributed to create. In the latter situation a finding of contributory negligence against the rescuer would seem unexceptional. A finding of

---

[54] The purpose of the intervention does not seem to have been raised in *Crossley* v. *Rawlinson* [1981] 3 All E.R. 674.

[55] Some authority for weighing the benefits against the risks is to be found in *Russell* v. *McCabe* [1962] N.Z.L.R. 392, although the plaintiff's actions in that case were undoubtedly reasonable.

[56] [1981] 3 All E.R. 674, criticised by Jones, "Remoteness and Rescuers" (1982) 45 M.L.R. 342.

[57] *Cf. Chapman* v. *Hearse* (1961) 106 C.L.R. 112, in which the death of a doctor who was struck and killed by a car whilst assisting at the scene of a road accident caused by the defendant's negligence was held to be the joint responsibility of the two drivers.

[58] [1933] 2 K.B. 297.

[59] [1959] 3 All E.R. 225. See also *Morgan* v. *Aleyn* [1942] 1 All E.R. 489.

this kind was made in *Harrison* v. *British Railways Board*[60] on the basis that the plaintiff guard's failure to apply the train's emergency brakes and his having given the driver a meaningless signal in a vain attempt to stop the train had contributed to create the dangerous situation in which he was injured whilst attempting to help the defendant to board the moving train.[61]

---

[60] [1981] 3 All E.R. 679.
[61] The question whether a rescuer whose acts increase the victim's injuries would be liable to the victim for these losses would undoubtedly turn on whether the rescuer's act could be deemed negligent, remembering that negligence in the agony of the moment may be difficult to prove.

Chapter Eleven

Strict Liability for Personal Injuries

INTRODUCTION

As was indicated at the beginning of the previous chapter,[1] this chapter will describe those areas in which strict tortious liability plays the leading or an important role as a remedy in the case of personal injuries or death. A more correct description of the subject matter of this chapter would be mixed liability. As will be shown, in almost all of the areas described, negligence operates as an alternative remedy to the strict liability.

Some of the areas described here, such as animals liability and liability for nuisance, are the modern equivalents of strict liability principles which have existed in English law for many years. However, the appearance in the Consumer Protection Act 1987 of strict liability for injuries caused by defective products, seems to herald the arrival of a new interest in strict liability instigated by the activities of the European Community. The product liability legislation has been followed by other proposals from the Community concerning liability for waste[2] and for the provision of services.[3] The dominance of fault liability for personal injuries in English law is therefore facing a real challenge from developments initiated in Europe.

DEFECTIVE PRODUCTS[4]

Liability for personal injuries and death caused by defective products can be founded on four distinct areas of law, three of which are part of the law of tort.

Contractual liability[5]

The doctrine of privity of contract, under which only the parties to a contract can sue or be sued upon it,[6] places the primary legal responsibility for injury caused by a defective product on the supplier of the goods. The Sale

---

[1] p. 189.
[2] See *post*, p. 248.
[3] See *ante*, p. 193.
[4] See generally Clark, *Product liability*.
[5] A detailed description of the law of sale of goods is beyond the scope of this book. See Atiyah, *The Sale of Goods* (8th ed., 1990).
[6] For a full description of the operation of the doctrine see Cheshire, Fifoot and Furmston's *Law of Contract* (12th ed., 1991), Chap. 14.

of Goods Act 1979 and the Supply of Goods and Services Act 1982 create implied conditions in contracts for the sale or supply of goods to the effect that the goods must be of merchantable quality and reasonably fit for the purpose for which they were supplied. In the case of such goods supplied to a consumer, it is impossible to use an exclusion clause to exclude or restrict this liability.[7] Although these provisions are commonly used to protect consumers against the problem of goods proving to be of poor quality they undoubtedly also provide a remedy for injuries caused by defective goods.

The contractual remedy has the advantage of giving an injured person who has purchased goods, rights against a retailer with whom he will have had dealings. However, it is strongly arguable that the liability should also be placed upon the manufacturer who benefits from the sale of the product, who may well instigate the sale through marketing and who has control over the quality of the product through the design and production process. It is the manufacturer who can best account for the risks created by the product in the price charged for it. Contractual liability may not shield the manufacturer from liability because a chain of contracts may have the effect of passing liability back to him from the supplier. However, this process may break down if one of the parties in the chain is insolvent or protected by an exemption clause and it is possibly a less efficient technique than that of allowing a direct remedy. Contractual liability is of no use at all to a person, such as the plaintiff in *Donoghue* v. *Stevenson*,[8] who is injured by defective goods, but who was not the purchaser of them.

Negligence

The decision of the House of Lords in *Donoghue* v. *Stevenson*[9] established that the general law of negligence applies to injuries caused by defective products. That case concerned the liability of a manufacturer to an injured person to whom the relevant goods had been passed by the purchaser. The fact that no contract existed between the parties to the proceedings was held not to be fatal to the plaintiff's claim in tort. As the development of negligence liability for defective products is derived from the authority of *Donoghue* v. *Stevenson*[10] it is scarcely surprising that the subject has become subsumed into the mainstream of negligence liability for personal injuries. Nowadays it can be said that general negligence principles apply to all persons concerned with the design, manufacture, repair, supply and distribution of goods and are owed to all who can reasonably be foreseen, as being affected by defects in them: purchasers, donees, employees of the purchaser, bystanders and others. The standard limitations placed on a negligence duty in terms of the available defences[11] and the recoverable forms of loss[12] apply. Although Lord Atkin's original formulation of the duty speaks of products intended to "reach the ultimate consumer in the form in which they left him, with no possibility of intermediate examination," it is accepted that the mere possibility of an inspection will not protect a manufacturer from liability[13]

---

[7] Unfair Contract Terms Act 1977, ss. 6(2), 7(2).
[8] [1932] A.C. 562.
[9] [1932] A.C. 562.
[10] [1932] A.C. 562.
[11] See *ante*, Chap. 5.
[12] See *post*, pp. 349–353.
[13] *Grant* v. *Australian Knitting Mills Ltd.* [1936] A.C. 85.

and it is probably correct to say that intermediate inspection is best regarded simply as a factor relevant to deciding whether damage to the plaintiff was a reasonably foreseeable consequence of the defendant's acts.[14]

The problem with a system of product liability based on negligence is that a person injured by a defective product faces a heavy burden in trying to prove that a manufacturer was negligent. The injured party is likely to lack information as to the cause of the defect and to have no expertise in relation to the design and production process. The remedy is preferable to the contractual one in disposing of the constraints of privity of contract, but, inferior to it because liability under this head does not depend on the plaintiff proving a particular result but on the much more difficult question of proving a particular cause of that result.[15]

The arrival, in the Consumer Protection Act 1987, of strict liability for injuries caused by defective products does not mean that negligence will fall into disuse: it will remain available to apply to the areas which are beyond the scope of the Act. For example, the statutory liability does not extend to the designer or to a supplier of goods unless that person falls within the definition of the producer. The tortious liability of such persons on matters such as design and defects caused by the storage of the goods and failures to supply them with appropriate warnings or instructions as to use will continue to be regulated by negligence. Negligence will also apply to those who place items of agricultural produce which fall outside of the statutory definition of products[16] on the market.

It is also possible that further development of negligence may produce remedies which apply in areas which are beyond the scope of the Act. A topical example is the question of the duties owed by manufacturers in relation to product recalls; the idea that a manufacturer of goods may owe a duty to monitor their safety after the time of sale and to warn consumers of dangers which are discovered. English law now seems to have embarked on a course of recognising the possibility of such duties. In *E. Hobbs (Farms) Ltd. v. The Baxenden Chemical Co. Ltd.*[17] a manufacturer of a product which was used to insulate buildings was held to have been negligent for failing to take reasonable care to warn its past customers and those, like the plaintiff, who had dealt with those customers, of the fact that the publicity material issued concerning the product, had been shown in the course of earlier litigation, to be wholly misleading as to the capacity of the product to resist fire.

The Consumer Protection Act 1987

The Consumer Protection Act 1987 introduced a regime of strict tortious liability for damage caused by defective products which is designed to overcome the problems inherent in the contract and negligence based law. The statutory remedy is in addition to those provided by the contract and by negligence, but seems likely to supplant the latter in the great majority of cases brought against manufacturers. Strict liability for defective products

---

[14] This was the view of Lloyd L.J. in *Aswan Engineering Establishment Co.* v. *Lupdine Ltd.* [1987] 1 All E.R. 135 at 153–4.

[15] The negligence remedy is also inferior in the forms of loss which are recoverable.

[16] See *post*, p. 222.

[17] [1992] 1 Lloyds Rep. 54.

combines the strictness of contract liability with tort's ability to give remedies beyond privity of contract. Irrespective of the contractual position, any injured consumer is given similar protection to a person who purchases goods directly. The Act is not confined to cases of personal injury and death.[18]

The idea of replacing negligence by a form of strict liability for injuries resulting from defective products, has its genesis in American jurisprudence.[19] However, it was the European Community's harmonisation programme which provided the impetus for its introduction. The new remedy was intended to provide benefits for both injured consumers and manufacturers of products. The injured consumer no longer has to face the burden of proving negligence in order to obtain compensation while the manufacturer is given a common set of trading conditions throughout the Community. Notions of consumer protection are central to this development. Losses caused by defective products should be channelled to the manufacturer who is best placed to exercise safety control in relation to modern products which, because of technological advances, are increasingly sophisticated. It is the manufacturer who is both the least cost avoider and the person who has the capacity to spread any loss incurred into society by means of pricing and insurance[20] whereas the injured consumer is seen as totally innocent and in need of greater protection than contract or negligence can provide.

Two general issues are raised by the Act's imposition of strict liability. The first is the general question of why this particular category of accident victims is given the protection of strict liability when others, such as the casualties of motoring, are left to depend on proving negligence? It is clear that this is answered, to some extent, by the move towards consumerism in the United States of America and Europe. Product litigation is viewed as a self-contained area in which strict liability shifts the losses caused by products from the consumer to those responsible for their production. The fact that the contractual remedy already imposes strict liability on the supplier of the product makes it easier to extend this level of responsibility to other persons involved in the production process.

The second, and more difficult, question is the extent to which the Act represents a real improvement over negligence. This may be impossible to answer until the courts have had the opportunity of interpreting some of the provisions in the statute which define the scope of the protection. However, many commentators are of the opinion that the Act fails to achieve its most basic aim, that of placing the risk of product failures unequivocally on manufacturers. In fact, the Act is likely to prove relatively effective in cases of defects which arise in the course of production. However, in the case of injuries caused by design decisions and stemming from any unforeseeable risks created by new products it may well have achieved no advance. The

---

[18] It also covers some areas of property damage. However, damage to the item itself or to another item of which it forms a component is excluded. In this case a contractual remedy has to be used. See pp. 349–353.

[19] See particularly the American Restatement of Torts (2d) s. 402A.

[20] American literature has tended to take the argument a stage further and to suggest that the creation of strict product liability by American courts should be seen as a response to the failure of the United States to develop a floor of welfare rights along the lines adopted in western Europe. Fleming, *The American Tort process*, Chap. 2; Bernstein, (1991) 20 Anglo-Am. L.R. 224.

ghosts of *Roe* v. *Minister of Health*[21] and *Bolam* v. *Friern H.M.C.*[22] continue to haunt this subject in spite of the statutory reform. The law has changed for the benefit of injured consumers, but it may not have changed substantially in relation to the most difficult cases.

1. Products

The statutory provisions apply to any goods which have been manufactured; to naturally occurring items, such as minerals, which have been "won or abstracted" and to any other products to which an industrial or other process which has contributed to their essential characteristics has been applied.[23] In spite of the title of the Act, its provisions are not confined to consumer goods: it extends to injuries caused by chemicals and major capital items such as aircraft. The strict liability imposed by the Act also applies to defects in components which are built into other items,[24] with the result that a component manufacturer will be liable for injuries caused by such defects, and to moveable goods which are incorporated into immoveables, for example, a central heating boiler which is attached to the structure of a house. It is unclear whether books and computer software, which may endanger persons if they contain inaccuracies, fall within the definition of "products."

Game and agricultural products are excluded from the statutory definition if they were supplied at a time before they underwent an industrial process.[25] It is therefore likely that raw foodstuffs will escape the Act, whereas tinned, frozen or processed food will fall within it. It is unclear whether activities such as the spraying of crops will count as an industrial process such as to bring the Act into operation; if they do not, liability for any damage caused by the spraying might be imposed on persons who process such items further up the chain of supply. However, some doubts as to the scope of the Act are created by its failure to define the terms "industrial or other process" and "essential characteristic." Would the spraying of food constitute such a process and is it correct to assume that tinned or frozen peas have essential characteristics different from raw peas? The degree of mechanisation and scientific knowledge applied to the practice of modern farming makes the exemption a difficult one to draw and an impossible one to justify. It is submitted, however, that many of the problems could be reduced and the aims behind the introduction of strict liability furthered, if the courts were to give a liberal interpretation to the notion of an industrial process.

2. The producer and other persons liable

The strict liability created by the Act is not imposed on every person involved in the design, production and marketing of goods, but is, nonetheless, liable to be applied to a wide class.[26] The primary responsibility rests with the "producer," defined as meaning[27] the manufacturer; the person who won or abstracted the item or the person who added essential characteristics to the item by processing it. Other persons who may be liable are a

---

[21] [1954] 2 Q.B. 66. See *ante*, p. 62.
[22] [1957] 1 W.L.R. 582. See *ante*, p. 72.
[23] This is the result of the statutory definition of a "producer" contained in subs. 1(2).
[24] s. 1(2)(c).
[25] s. 2(4). In such cases any tort remedy would have to be in negligence.
[26] If more than one person is liable the liability will be joint and several, s. 2(5).
[27] subs. 1(2).

person who holds himself out as the producer of a product,[28] as will be the case in relation to "own brand" products; a person who imported the product into the E.C.[29] and a supplier who fails to identify the producer when requested to do so.[30] The aim of these provisions is to attempt to ensure that the injured consumer has available within the E.C. a defendant who bears the responsibility for the safety of the item.

The main category of persons in the chain of supply who escape the Act's provisions are retailers, who simply remain liable to the first purchaser under contract unless they are caught by the "own brand" or "failure to identify supplier" categories. Designers, unless they are also the producer or a liable supplier, and suppliers of services such as installers and repairers (again unless caught as suppliers) are also excluded from the Act. All of the omitted categories of person may be held liable in negligence if it can be proved that a failure to take reasonable care on their part was the cause of the plaintiff's damage.

3. Defective

An item is defined as defective, for the purposes of the Act, if its safety "is not such as persons generally are entitled to expect."[31] This test is amplified by the provisions of subsection 3(2) to take account of:

"3(2) . . . all the circumstances . . . including –
   (a) the manner in which, and purposes for which, the product has been marketed, its get-up, the use of any mark in relation to the product and any instruction for, or warnings with respect to, doing or refraining from doing anything with or in relation to the product;
   (b) what might reasonably be expected to be done with or in relation to the product; and
   (c) the time when the product was supplied by its producer to another"

This provision creates what is known as a "consumer expectation test" of defectiveness. The test differs from that used in negligence in considering the performance of the product rather than the conduct of the manufacturer. It is possible that courts, when deciding whether a product was defective, will balance the risks created by it against its utility and thus operate a test which is not far removed from negligence.[32]

The statutory test of defectiveness makes allowance for the fact that many everyday products, for example razor blades and cleaning chemicals, are unsafe if abused; that some products, such as foodstuffs, may become unsafe fairly quickly because of normal deterioration and that the existence of a defect must take into account the marketing, packaging and any instructions or warnings issued with the item and the time at which it was supplied. The safety of the item is judged at the time when it is supplied by its producer to another.[33] As the criterion of liability is the expectation held by consumers in

---

[28] s. 1(2)(b).
[29] s. 1(2)(c). Not necessarily into the United Kingdom.
[30] subs. 1(3).
[31] s.3(1).
[32] Stoppa, (1992) 12 L.S. 210.
[33] This resurrects the "hindsight" problem found in negligence. The court trying a case has to put itself back into the position, in terms of knowledge, of the producer at the time when the item was first supplied. This is a difficult inquiry to undertake and one which is more difficult for the injured consumer than for the expert manufacturer.

general of the characteristics of a particular product it should follow that injury suffered, for example, as a result of any well recognised side effects of drugs falls outside the scope of the protection. The level of safety which consumers are entitled to expect from a particular product is likely to be a matter of debate in a significant number of cases. Although a consumer might be thought to be entitled to expect that no item emerging from a production process will give a lower level of safety than other items of the same type, it is also arguable that the standard imposed by the Act cannot be absolute because no consumer can realistically expect any production process to guarantee perfect safety. The test would appear to be an objective one which excludes from consideration the particular knowledge of specialists in the field. However, this may prove to be a difficult approach to maintain when a product is being marketed only to specialists or when the risks which it creates are known to specialists but not to consumers in general. For example, would a drug count as defective because it can have side effects which are known to the doctors who are prescribing it, but not to consumers in general: those to whom it is prescribed.

The "consumer expectation" test may afford consumers no additional protection than that which reasonable care does in relation to conscious design decisions as to the degree of safety to be built into a product as it is likely to permit a designer to weigh the advantages and disadvantages of different design solutions according to standards accepted in the industry. For example, the designer of a car is likely to have to reach a compromise between the degree of protection afforded in the event of an accident and the demands of fuel economy and performance. So long as his decision does not produce a design which fails to meet normal consumer expectations of safety, no liability will accrue for injuries resulting from the choice. This result has considerable similarity to the negligence test which grounds liability according to the standards adopted by reasonable designers. It is specifically stated in the Act that the fact that products marketed at a later date achieved a higher level of safety does not raise an inference that earlier examples were defective.[34]

4. Defences

The Act provides a number of defences to the liability which it creates. Liability here is strict rather than absolute[35] in the sense that, although it is no defence to show that all reasonable care was taken in putting the product onto the market, a number of defences are available. Once the plaintiff has shown that injury was the result of a defective product, the burden passes to the defendant to show that one of these defences applies. In practice, the most important defences are likely to be contributory negligence, which will be pleaded in cases in which the product has been misused, and the defence that the item was not defective when supplied.[36] Some categories of consumers, such as those injured by defective drugs, may face considerable difficulties in proving that their damage was caused by the product.

Considerable criticism has been levelled at the so-called "development risks" defence. Subparagraph 4(1)(e) creates a defence if the defendant can prove that:

[34] s. 3(2).
[35] See *ante*, pp. 58–61.
[36] s. 4(1)(d).

"the state of scientific and technical knowledge at the relevant time was not such that a producer of products of the same description as the product in question might be expected to have discovered the defect if it had existed in his products while they were under his control."

This defence is available to any of the persons who are subject to the regime of strict liability, irrespective of whether they were actually responsible for the design of the particular product. It was introduced on the basis that it was needed to ensure that the strict liability would not discourage innovation on the part of manufacturers. However, it has attracted strong criticism on the ground that it compromises the protective purpose of the statute by re-establishing something which is close to the standard of liability imposed by negligence for this category of risks.[37] The defence may lead to injured consumers, such as the thalidomide children, obtaining no advantage from the introduction of strict liability. The defence denies the protection of strict liability to the victims of unforeseeable or newly identified risks; those whom one might have expected to be the main beneficiaries of its introduction. It is also argued that the Act fails, at this point, to comply with the requirements of the E.C. Directive on which it was based.[38] The Directive allows Member States to use a narrower version of this defence only when the state of scientific and technical knowledge, as opposed to such knowledge possessed by producers of the kind of product in question, was not such as to enable the existence of the defect to be discovered.[39]

There are other defences of non-supply[40] and compliance with statutory requirements.[41] Component suppliers are allowed to argue in their defence that a defect in the component was due to the design of the product into which the component was incorporated or to compliance by its producer with instructions given by the producer of the subsequent product.[42] It is impossible to remove or limit the statutory liability by use of an exclusion clause[43] and the Act places no upper financial limit on the amount of damages recoverable.[44]

---

[37] It is arguable that the statutory defence might result in a producer owing a lower level of duty than negligence would impose. In *Vacwell* v. *B.D.H. Chemicals Ltd.* [1971] 1 Q.B. 88 a manufacturer who had chosen to market a chemical was held to have been negligent in failing to discover and warn of the risk that the chemical was highly explosive if brought into contact with water. The finding of negligence was based on a failure to conduct adequate research into the available scientific literature. If, which was not the case in *Vacwell*, the producers of products of the kind in question lack the scientific expertise to identify risks identified in research publications the "development risks" defence would be available to them although they might be negligent in failing to adopt an adequate programme of research into the characteristics of the product. The wording of the "development risks" defence allowed by Art. 7(e) of the E.C. Directive gives the *Vacwell* result.

[38] The E.C. Commission has accepted this view and started proceedings agaist the U.K. Government alleging failure to comply with the requirements of the directive. The Commission is, in any case, obliged to reconsider the acceptability of this defence in 1995.

[39] Art. 7(e).

[40] s. 4(1)(b) and (c). This would apply, for example, where the goods have been stolen from the manufacturer or can be shown to be fakes.

[41] s. 4(1)(a).

[42] s. 4(1)(f).

[43] s. 7.

[44] This is permitted by the Directive. Claims for property damage of less than £275 cannot be brought.

Consumer safety legislation

The Consumer Protection Act 1987 seeks to protect consumers by giving power to the Secretary of State to issue regulations governing the safety of products which are sold to the public. This provision creates a second area of strict tortious liability, albeit one confined to a restricted area. Breach of any obligation imposed by such safety regulations and which results in injuries is made actionable as an express form of breach of statutory duty by section 41 of the 1987 Act.

INJURY CAUSED BY ANIMALS[45]

Tort liability for personal injury caused by animals is an amalgam of strict liability and negligence principles. Strict liability has existed in this area for many years. The Animals Act 1971 effected significant alterations in the rules and removed many anomalies which had grown up over the years. However, the Act made no change to the basic structure of the law in relation to personal injuries claims and its drafting created a whole host of new difficulties which the courts are still attempting to resolve.

The assumption on which the law is based is that animals are, of their nature, unpredictable. It follows that if a person chooses to keep an animal which is likely to prove dangerous he does so at his peril. Conversely, if the animal belongs to a species which is commonly domesticated and regarded as harmless, there will be no liability if it does cause harm merely because the fact of the animal having a mind of its own might be said to create a foreseeable risk of injury. This second rule may be overturned on proof that the particular animal, although belonging to a species normally non-dangerous, had characteristics, known to its keeper, which made it dangerous. In such circumstances strict liability is again imposed.

Negligence has made incursions into this area of law and in 1953 the Goddard Committee[46] recommended the abolition of the common law rules of strict liability in favour of the simple imposition of negligence. In contrast, the Law Commission[47] was of the opinion that the unpredictability of animals coupled with the degree of risks created made this an area in which strict liability still had a useful role to play. It was this approach which found expression in the Animals Act 1971. As a result, negligence based on common law principles coexists with the statutory strict liability.

Strict liability
The keeper

Strict liability under the Animals Act may be imposed upon the person who is the "keeper" of the animal. The definition adopted can result in the liability being imposed on persons other than the owner of the animal. The Act defines the keeper in the following terms:

> 6(3) "Subject to subsection 4 of this section, a person is a keeper of an animal if –

---

[45] See generally North, *The Modern Law of Animals*.
[46] Cmnd. 8746 (1953).
[47] Law Commission Report No. 13.

(a) he owns the animal or has it in his possession; or

(b) he is the head of a household[48] of which a member under the age of sixteen owns the animal or has it in his possession;

and if at any time an animal ceases to be in the possession of a person, any person who immediately before that time was a keeper thereof by virtue of the preceding provisions of this subsection continues to be a keeper of the animal until another person becomes a keeper thereof by virtue of those provisions.

6(4) Where an animal is taken into and kept in possession for the purpose of preventing it from causing damage or of restoring it to its owner, a person is not a keeper of it by virtue only of that provision."

As a result of this definition it would seem to be the case that an animal may have more than one keeper, for example, where it is owned and possessed by different persons. In such a case there would be joint liability on the keepers.

Animals belonging to a dangerous species

The Law Commission was of the view that "It does not seem unreasonable that the keeper of a dangerous animal should bear the special risk which is created by keeping it; moreover, it is a risk against which he can more conveniently insure than can the potential victim."[49] This principle is adopted by subsection 2(1) of the Animals Act 1971 by the following words:

"Where any damage is caused by an animal which belongs to a dangerous species, any person who is a keeper of the animal is liable for the damage, except as otherwise provided by this Act."

The limited range of defences made available by sections 5 and 10 of the Act[50] means that this section is one of the primary statutory examples of strict liability in English law.

The strict liability which arises under subsection 2(1) attaches to any animal which belongs to a dangerous species. The fact that the particular animal is tame or has characteristics which render it harmless is of no importance. Furthermore, liability may extend to encompass forms of damage which fall outside of the characteristics which made the species fall within the category of dangerous animals. Both of these propositions are well illustrated by the pre-1971 case of *Behrens* v. *Bertram Mills Circus Ltd.*[51] in which the owner of a tame circus elephant which was said to be "no more dangerous than a cow" was held liable for injuries caused to bystanders when the animal charged a dog which had worried it.

The question of whether a particular species[52] counts as dangerous is decided as a matter of law according to the provisions of subsection 6(2). Under subsection 6(2):

"A dangerous species is a species –

---

[48] There is no authority on the meaning of this term. For a discussion see North, *The Modern Law of Animals*, p. 28.

[49] Law Commission Report No. 13, para. 14.

[50] See *post*, pp. 230–232.

[51] [1957] 2 Q.B. 1.

[52] For the problems raised by the definition of a species, see North, *The Modern Law of Animals*, p. 36 *et seq.*

> (a) which is not commonly domesticated in the British Islands; and
> (b) whose fully grown animals normally have such characteristics that
>   they are likely, unless restrained, to cause severe damage or that any
>   damage they may cause is likely to be severe."

This definition leaves a number of difficulties for the courts to resolve. The old common law learning which had classified many species and created a number of anomalies has been replaced by a new provision according to which all types of animals will have to be classified anew. Because the word "species" is defined by section 11 to include "subspecies and variety" it will be possible for courts to hold, as a matter of law, that particular varieties of an animal are "dangerous" whereas other varieties are not. For example, it was reported during the debate which preceded the passing of the Dangerous Dogs Act 1991 that a single example of a breed of Japanese fighting dog had been brought to this country. As the relevant classification under the Act relates to subspecies and varieties of dog rather than to dogs in general it would seem to be the case that such an animal would be subject to the regime of subsection 2(1) as it could not be argued that the "variety" was "commonly domesticated" in the British Isles. It is also a consequence of the wording of subsection 6(2) that, although the classification of animals as dangerous or non-dangerous is a matter of law, it is possible for the classification of a species to change if it becomes, or ceases to be, commonly domesticated.

This subsection is wide enough to encompass dangers created not only by a species of vicious propensities but also by characteristics such as bulk. The use of the adjective "severe" ought to serve as a restrictive factor.[53] The fact that an animal which is not commonly domesticated in the British Isles may well cause minor injuries such as scratching to those handling it would be unlikely to mean that it should be placed in the dangerous species category. To date, there have been no reported cases dealing with this issue.[54]

It would seem probable that in time, as occurred at common law, a body of authority will emerge on the question of whether a particular species is or is not dangerous within the terms of subsection 6(2). The provisions of the Dangerous Wild Animals Act 1976, which creates a system for licensing the keepers of dangerous wild animals may be of assistance in as much as a species within that statute's controls[55] is almost certain to be deemed a dangerous species for the purposes of the 1971 Act. The criterion for subjecting a species to the requirements of the 1976 Act are, however, such that exclusion from its ambit could not be deemed to render it automatically non-dangerous within the 1971 Act.

Animals belonging to a non-dangerous species

Strict liability for those animals which do not belong to a dangerous species is governed by subsection 2(2) of the Animals Act 1971 which provides:

---

[53] Note particularly, the different form of subparagraph 2(2)(a) in which a contrast appears to be drawn between likely damage and unlikely "severe" damage.

[54] If the short report of *Tutin* v. *Mary Chipperfield Promotions Ltd.* (1980) 130 N.L.J. 807 is accurate, the court would seem to have erroneously classified a camel as dangerous simply on the grounds that camels are not "commonly domesticated" in the British Isles.

[55] For the full list see the Schedule to the 1976 Act.

2(2) Where damage is caused by an animal which does not belong to a dangerous species, a keeper of the animal is liable for the damage, except as otherwise provided by this Act, if –

    (a) the damage is of a kind which the animal, unless restrained, was likely to cause or which, if caused by the animal, was likely to be severe; and

    (b) the likelihood of the damage or of its being severe was due to characteristics which are not normally found in animals of the same species or are not normally so found except at particular times or in particular circumstances; and

    (c) those circumstances were known to that keeper or were at any time known to a person who at that time had charge of the animal as that keeper's servant or where that keeper is the head of a household, were known to another keeper of the animal who is a member of that household and under the age of sixteen."

The drafting of this subsection is not easy. The first arm of paragraph (a) removes the requirement, which is part of the definition of a dangerous species, that any damage caused by the animal should be severe,[56] but continues to make liability turn on the word "likely." In *Smith* v. *Ainger*[57] Neill J. was of the opinion that the word "likely," in this context, could not establish a requirement that such damage should be shown to have been more than a 50 per cent. probability. He preferred to take the word to bear a meaning which comes close to setting a requirement that there is a foreseeable risk by using the phrases "such as might happen" or "where there is a material risk." It has also been suggested that the words "the likelihood of the damage or of its being severe was due to" in paragraph (b) would have been better rendered as "the damage was caused by."[58] In spite of these drafting difficulties, the effect of the subsection is relatively clear. Actual knowledge of the keeper of an animal of a non-dangerous species of characteristics which render it dangerous imposes strict liability. Actual knowledge is required. Actual knowledge of an employee or of a keeper under the age of 16 may be imputed to an employer or the head of the household respectively, but constructive knowledge, *i.e.* a situation in which the keeper did not know of, but ought reasonably to have appreciated, the risk, is not sufficient.[59] This is slightly surprising in view of the fact that the relevant characteristics need not be abnormal or unique to the particular animal in question; a perfectly normal characteristic will suffice if it is only present at particular times or in particular circumstances.[60]

    Common examples of the imposition of strict liability on the keeper of an animal of a non-dangerous species are the cases of the dog which has

---

[56] Thus knowledge of propensity to cause likely but not severe forms of damage, which would not render a species "dangerous" under subs. 6(2) may ground liability in relation to a non-dangerous species.

[57] (1990) *The Times*, June 6.

[58] *Curtis* v. *Betts* [1990] 1 W.L.R. 459 *per* Slade L.J.

[59] An action in negligence may be available in such circumstances. See *post*, p. 232. North, *The Modern Law of Animals*, p. 68, argues that the courts have been prepared to find actual knowledge on very slender evidence.

[60] The corollary is that if the characteristics are normal there is no liability under the Act.

previously attacked, or attempted to attack, a human[61]; an animal carrying a disease such as rabies, and (within the "particular times" criterion) the female animal which becomes spiteful when it is rearing young. In *Cummings* v. *Granger*[62] strict liability was imposed under the "particular circumstances" test in respect of the perfectly normal reaction of an untrained Alsatian guard dog to defend what it regarded as its territory by attacking a person who entered the yard in which it was left to run free at night.

Paragraph (b) imposes strict liability simply on the basis of a characteristic which is "not normally found in animals of the same species" and which, as a result of paragraph (a), must either be likely to cause damage, or, if not, mean that any damage which is caused is likely to be severe. There is no requirement that the animal should show vicious characteristics. The natural reading of the words is adopted. In *Wallace* v. *Newton*[63] liability was imposed upon the owner of a horse on the basis that the animal was "unpredictable and unreliable." The recognition of such characteristics as sufficient places the keeper of such an animal under potential liability for a wide range of undefined risks. The substance of the complaint in that case would seem to have been that the horse was unusually nervous and the decision may be better explained as restricted to such a characteristic.

Defences to strict liability

A number of defences to the statutory liability are provided by the Animals Act. For the most part these defences seem designed to ensure that the standard common law defences are available to claims arising under the Act.

Subsection 5(1) provides that:

> "5(1) A person is not liable under sections 2 to 4 of this Act for any damage which is due wholly to the fault of the person suffering it."

This merely confirms that the normal causation principles operate. Section 10 is of greater significance in making available the normal defence of contributory negligence.

Subsection 5(2) is in the following terms:

> "5(2) A person is not liable under section 2 of this Act for any damage suffered by a person who has voluntarily accepted the risk thereof."

This might be thought to amount to a simple application of the common law defence of *volenti*. However, this interpretation has been placed in question by the variety of views expressed by the members of the Court of Appeal in *Cummings* v. *Granger*[64] on whether the plaintiff was barred by this defence on the basis that she had entered the defendant's yard when she knew of the presence of the dog which she admitted to being scared of. The view taken by O'Connor J. at first instance[65] which was, in effect, that the plaintiff was *sciens* but not *volens*, is attractive and reconciles with much of the modern

---

[61] *Kite* v. *Napp* (1982) *The Times*, June 1. A similar result has been achieved in the case of a dog known to be likely to start fights with other dogs as it is likely that humans who become involved in the fight may be injured. *Smith* v. *Ainger* (1990) *The Times*, June 6.

[62] [1977] Q.B. 397. See also *Curtis* v. *Betts* [1990] 1 W.L.R. 459.

[63] [1977] Q.B. 397.

[64] [1977] Q.B. 397.

[65] [1977] Q.B. 397.

learning on the common law defence.[66] The Court of Appeal, in contrast, held the defence to have been established. Lord Denning M.R. seems to have founded his judgment to this effect on the proposition that the plaintiff's knowledge and actions could be construed as meaning that she had voluntarily consented to the risk. Ormrod L.J. reached the same result although he expressed his desire to read the statutory words in their ordinary meaning uncomplicated by the developed learning of the common law on *volenti*, especially as a species of strict liability was at issue. Bridge L.J. held that the evidence was all to the effect that the plaintiff appreciated the risk and chose to run it. It is suggested that this reasoning is unconvincing, based, as it is, on a failure to make the crucial distinction between a person incurring a factual risk and that person agreeing to exempt another from his legal responsibility for damage suffered. It is, of course, possible to argue that Parliament in enacting subsection 5(2), must be taken to have supposed that it would have some effect, but there is no suggestion in the statute that the defence was to be regarded as distinguishable from the common law defence. Indeed subsection 6(5) incorporates an element of common law thinking[67] into the subsection 5(2) defence by providing that:

"6(5) Where a person employed as a servant by a keeper of an animal incurs a risk incidental to his employment he shall not be treated as accepting it voluntarily."

This provision would seem to be effective to negative the defence even in situations in which the victim consciously assented to incur the risk, so long as it was a risk which was incidental to his employment.[68]

It should also be noted that subsection 5(2) may operate to justify the efficacy of exclusion notices used by those who keep dangerous animals in zoos and parks. The Unfair Contract Terms Act 1977[69] does not operate to place any restrictions on such notices, for although the premises would be classed as business premises, the form of liability being stricter than negligence would escape the statutory controls.[70]

A more specialised defence is provided by subsection 5(3):

"5(3) A person is not liable under section 2 of this Act for any damage caused by an animal kept on any premises or structure to a person trespassing there, if it is proved either –
 (a) that the animal was not kept there for the protection of persons or property; or
 (b) (if the animal was kept there for the protection of persons or property) that keeping it there for that purpose was not unreasonable."

Thus if a trespasser is injured by an animal not kept for protection, there is an absolute defence to any liability which may arise under the Act. As was the case with an occupier's liability to a trespasser, this rule, which treats all trespassers with equal disfavour, appears outmoded and may produce

---

[66] See *ante*, p. 109.
[67] Although it reverses the previous common law rule relating to criminals in *Rands* v. *McNeil* [1955] 1 Q.B. 253.
[68] For a discussion of the scope of subsection 6(5) see North, *The Modern Law of Animals*, pp. 73–76.
[69] *Ante*, pp. 117–120.
[70] Unfair Contract Terms Act 1977, s. 1(1).

undesirable results. For example, a child trespasser injured by a pet dog with known vicious propensities would be denied recovery.

If an animal is kept for the purpose of protecting persons or property and it is deemed unreasonable to keep this particular animal for this purpose the normal principles of strict liability apply, but, if it is reasonable to use the animal for this purpose the trespasser is again excluded from any liability which would otherwise arise. In *Cummings* v. *Granger*[71] it was regarded as reasonable, in 1971, for the proprietor of a scrap yard to allow an untrained Alsatian dog to run free in the yard at night in order to protect the property from theft. It was said that the use of a gentle dog for this purpose would have been fruitless. Nonetheless, it is commonly assumed that the criterion of reasonableness in this regard may have been altered by the subsequent enactment of the Guard Dogs Act 1975. This Act confers no civil law remedy[72] but creates a criminal offence of using a guard dog which is neither restrained nor under the control of a handler. The acts of the defendant in *Cummings* v. *Granger*, if now repeated, would constitute this offence and it can scarcely be supposed that a court asked to judge the issue under section 5(3)(b) would hold a criminal act to be reasonable.

There is support in the judgment of Bridge L.J. in *Cummings* v. *Granger*[73] for the suggestion made by North[74] that the criterion of reasonableness under section 5(3)(b) may involve consideration not only of the nature of the animal kept and of the property being protected, but also (and this involves adding a gloss to the statutory language) of the extent of any warnings given as to the animal's presence.

Negligence

Liability for personal injury caused by animals may also be founded on normal negligence principles. The leading House of Lords decision in *Fardon* v. *Harcourt-Rivington*[75] is authority for this proposition and shows that liability may possibly be founded on a person's negligent treatment of an animal which was not dangerous. In that case the defendant had left his dog in his parked car. After a time the dog became restless and whilst jumping around in the car broke a window with the result that a fragment of glass entered the eye of the plaintiff who was passing the car at that time. The House of Lords affirmed that the negligent handling of an animal of a non-dangerous species was a good cause of action, but held that the defendant had not in fact been negligent in failing to guard against what they regarded as a "fantastic possibility." In the leading "rescue" case of *Haynes* v. *Harwood*,[76] a further example of this species of liability, the defendants were held negligent for having left horses unattended in a busy road near to some schools. Damage resulted when the horses ran away after some schoolboys had thrown stones at them.

The decision in *Haynes* shows that the negligent handling of animals brought onto the highway is actionable on normal principles. Until 1971 there was, however, an immunity protecting a person who negligently permitted

---

[71] [1977] Q.B. 397.
[72] s. 5(2)(a).
[73] [1977] Q.B. 397 at 410.
[74] *The Modern Law of Animals*, p. 81.
[75] (1932) 48 T.L.R. 215.
[76] [1935] 1 K.B. 146.

an animal to escape onto a highway and cause an accident.[77] This immunity, which was based on rules relating to fencing obligations developed long before the advent of motor traffic, was reversed by section 8(1) of the Animals Act 1971, subject to an exception favouring persons having a right to place animals on unfenced common land; land in an area where fencing is not customary (for instance, moorland) or on a town or village green.[78] In spite of the enactment of section 8(1) negligence still needs to be proved to establish such liability. It would thus seem dubious whether a motorist injured whilst attempting to avoid a cat in the road would succeed in proving negligence against the owner of the animal, whose tendency to wander at will would seem liable to defeat all reasonable attempts to confine it.

It might be thought that negligence liability based on an animal's dangerous propensities would be unlikely to arise as a strict liability cause of action would be available. Indeed, the recognition of negligence liability in respect of animals has been coupled with assertions that, first, it cannot be established merely by proof that a defendant has failed to provide against the possibility that a tame animal of mild disposition will do something contrary to its ordinary nature, and, secondly, that even if a defendant's omission to control or secure his animal is negligent, an act on the part of the animal which is contrary to its ordinary nature cannot be regarded, in the absence of special circumstances, as being directly caused by that negligence.[79] This approach is obviously designed to ensure that negligence does not encroach on established principles of strict liability concerning non-dangerous animals. Nonetheless, two decisions of the Court of Appeal dealing with the pre-1971 species of strict liability have shown negligence to be capable of playing a not insignificant role in this area and, indeed, of introducing a degree of flexibility into the technical rules relating to strict liability.

The simple assertion that if there is no strict liability for damage caused by the propensities of a non-dangerous animal there can be no negligence liability, is certainly misconceived. In *Aldham* v. *United Dairies (London) Ltd.*[80] the defendant's servant left a pony attached to a milk cart unattended for half an hour whilst he made deliveries to a block of flats. The pony became restive and injured a passer-by. There was evidence that the animal was known to have become restive in such circumstances in the past and that some persons had been alarmed by its behaviour. On these facts the jury found that the defendants had no knowledge of any propensity on the part of the pony to attack humans, but nonetheless held them to have been negligent in leaving the pony unattended in view of its character. The judge gave judgment for the defendants, presumably holding that liability for negligence was precluded by the first finding. The Court of Appeal, however, allowed the appeal and held that liability could be founded on negligence. In *Draper* v. *Hodder*[81] a pack of Jack Russell terriers owned by the defendant ran into the next door garden and savaged the infant plaintiff who was playing there. A strict liability claim was unsuccessful as it proved impossible to identify the particular dog or dogs which had actually injured the child and also because the defendant lacked any knowledge of any propensity on the part of the

[77] *Searle* v. *Wallbank* [1947] A.C. 341.
[78] s.8(2). See *Davies* v. *Davies* [1974] 3 All E.R. 817.
[79] *Aldham* v. *United Dairies (London) Ltd.* [1940] 1 K.B. 507, *per* Du Parcq L.J., and *Searle* v. *Wallbank* [1947] A.C. 341, *per* Lord Du Parcq.
[80] [1940] 1 K.B. 507.
[81] [1972] 2 Q.B. 556.

dogs to carry out such an attack. Nonetheless, a negligence claim was allowed to succeed on the basis of expert evidence to the effect that a pack of such terriers was liable to attack any moving object and that the defendant, as an experienced breeder, ought to have been aware of this danger.

Of these two Court of Appeal decisions *Draper* is the more significant. *Aldham* seems to have turned on the terms of the particular question put to the jury. The limited nature of the question on the pony's propensity to attack humans did not cover all of the risks and negligence was used to fill the gap by grounding liability on the known restive characteristics. In modern law, in the light of *Wallace* v. *Newton*[82] it is relatively certain that such characteristics would serve to ground strict liability under subsection 2(2) of the Animals Act 1971. *Draper* in contrast, in grounding liability on imputed knowledge of dangerous characteristics, shows negligence to be capable of providing a significant supplement to strict liability. Proof of actual knowledge on the part of a defendant, as required by subparagraph 2(2)(c) of the Act, is likely to prove a difficult hurdle for a plaintiff to surmount and his chances of success will be significantly boosted if he has an alternative of relying on expert testimony as to what the reasonable keeper of such an animal ought to have known. The decision in *Draper* is therefore to be welcomed, even though it goes some way to undermining the logic of the statutory scheme of liability to be found in the Animals Act. It is, of course, good evidence of the encroachment of negligence into older established areas of tortious liability.

INDUSTRIAL INJURIES

The risks created by working conditions account for a significant percentage of accidents. *The Civil Justice Review* recorded that approximately 350,000 personal injuries were suffered at work every year in England and Wales.[83]

An employer will not incur tortious liability for injuries suffered by his employee merely because the employee was engaged, at the time of the injury, in work which involved an unavoidable risk to his health and safety. An employer is not strictly liable for injuries to his staff simply because he conducts business of a dangerous nature.[84] The risk in such cases is on the employee unless breach of a duty owed in tort can be established. To do this an employee must show either that the employer had failed to provide a safe system of work (in effect, that the employer has been negligent) or that the employer was in breach of a statutory safety duty. As breach of the latter kind of duty commonly entails strict liability, this is an area of mixed tortious liability. Negligence has a comprehensive application in the industrial context, whereas breach of statutory duty operates only in those particular areas which have been subject to statutory control. Breach of statutory duty may assist injured employees, in the areas in which it operates, by imposing a

---

[82] [1982] 1 W.L.R. 375.

[83] Civil Justice Review, *Consultation Paper: Personal Injuries Litigation*, para. 12. The Health and Safety Commission statistics record a lower level of accidents. The Commission's Annual report for 1990–91 reported provisional figures of 326 fatalities, 19,607 major injuries and 156,604 other injuries which caused more than three days loss of work. The Commission accepts that these figures, which are of accidents recorded under the Reporting of Injuries, Diseases and Dangerous Occurrences Regulations 1985 are affected by under-reporting.

[84] *Smith* v. *Baker & Sons* [1891] A.C. 325 at 356 *per* Lord Watson.

strict standard of liability. Although the existence of statutory requirements may influence the measures which an employer must take to satisfy the obligation of reasonable care, negligence and breach of statutory duty are theoretically independent of each other. The best example of this independence is provided by *Bux* v. *Slough Metals Ltd.*[85] In that case an employer argued that once a statutory regulation had been satisfied, the particular regulation stipulated that certain safety equipment had to be "provided" for the use of employees, no further additional duties could be imposed on him. This argument was rejected. The employer's compliance with the statutory duty did not preclude the injured employee from arguing that the employer had been negligent in failing to do more than "provide" and to require or persuade the employees to use the equipment.

Although this area has the appearance of being simply an application of general principles of tortious liability, several features peculiar to it should be noted. First, the duties which are imposed on employers are of a non-delegable nature, whereas negligence based duties are more normally delegable. Secondly, as a consequence of the decision of the House of Lords in *Smith* v. *Baker & Sons*[86] it is virtually impossible for an employer to plead successfully the defence of *volenti* against an injured employee. Finally, certain specialised rules of causation have been developed to meet the situation in which the employer has been put in breach of a statutory duty by the acts of the injured employee.[87]

The truth is that this area of tort reveals considerable tensions between competing policies. The compensatory purpose of tort is supported by the existence of strict liability in relation to certain categories of industrial injuries. Persons injured whilst engaged on productive work can be regarded as peculiarly deserving of legal protection as the injury can be seen as the result of an activity intended to benefit the national economy. However, a policy of favouring injured employees through the imposition of strict liability on employers is not carried through consistently. The dominance of negligence based thinking can be seen in the fact that some of the strict statutory duties in this area have been interpreted in ways which qualify their protective purpose by leaving scope for employers to weigh the risks created by a process against the costs of providing protection. Furthermore, the courts have never really provided a satisfactory answer to important questions such as the scope of the principle that the negligence duties which an employer owes to his employees are non-delegable.[88]

Breach of statutory duty

Industrial safety legislation may well stipulate detailed requirements which are to be fulfilled by employers. These requirements are commonly enforced by a criminal penalty. Tort liability derived from such statutory requirements and founded on the tort of breach of statutory duty has been available as a remedy for industrial accidents since the Court of Appeal held,

---

[85] [1973] 1 W.L.R. 1359.
[86] [1891] A.C. 325.
[87] Discussed in Stanton, *Breach of Statutory Duty in Tort*, pp. 129–133.
[88] *Cf. McDermid* v. *Nash Dredging & Reclamation Co. Ltd.* [1987] A.C. 906 and *Square D. Ltd.* v. *Cook* [1992] I.R.L.R. 34. The Employers' Liability (Defective Equipment) Act 1969 resolves a particular issue in favour of the interests of employees by opting for the non-delegable approach.

in *Groves* v. *Lord Wimborne*[89] that a breach of the Factories & Workshops Act 1878 which caused injury to an employee was actionable. The current position is governed by section 47 of the Health and Safety at Work Act 1974. It is intended that this statute and regulations made under it will ultimately form a self-contained code governing industrial safety. However, for the moment a great deal of older legislation such as the Factories Act 1961, the Mines & Quarries Act 1954 and the Offices Shops and Railway Premises Act 1963 remains in force. Although the older legislation generally made express provision for only a criminal law penalty for breach, a civil law remedy was normally inferred on the basis of *Groves*. Section 47 now makes express provision for the whole area. Breach of the general safety duties contained in sections 2 to 8 of the Act is not actionable in tort, whereas a breach of a duty created by a regulation made under the Act will be so actionable unless the regulation specifies otherwise.[90] Any results established by authority concerning the older surviving provisions, such as the Factories Act 1961, are saved for as long as those provisions remain in force.[91]

Although it can be argued that an employer who has control over a working environment and who selects his staff and obtains the financial benefits of their labour should bear the risk of any injuries which employees suffer whilst performing their tasks, it is clear that the liability of employers based on breach of statutory duty by no means creates a comprehensive system of absolute liability. As has been said previously[92] the absolute nature of the standard of liability imposed in *John Summers & Son Ltd.* v. *Frost*[93] is exceptional. The degree of protection conferred by the statutory regime varies greatly according to the wording of the particular provision with the majority of industrial safety provisions imposing strict, as opposed to absolute, obligations. Precautions are required to be taken only if it is "practicable" or "reasonably practicable" to do so; obligations to protect against "dangers" have been held only to require protection against such risks as are foreseeably present.[94] Furthermore, the statutes in question do not provide a comprehensive answer to issues of industrial safety. They tend to deal with only part of the problem, the physical conditions under which work is performed, whereas many industrial accidents are caused by other factors such as employee carelessness. In addition, the judicial interpretation of industrial safety legislation has been criticised as inconsistent. It is not particularly surprising that this should be so because of the difficulty which this form of legislation presents to courts of marrying the policy of tort of ensuring that compensation is payable to injured employees with that of the criminal law of protecting a person from the risk of being convicted on an ambiguity. It is undoubtedly the case that the courts have reduced the effectiveness of some industrial safety legislation by regarding it as passed to secure employees against limited categories of risk. For example, the requirement established by section 14 of the Factories Act 1961 to fence the dangerous parts of a machine has been held to be intended to keep the operator's body from coming into contact with those parts rather than to

[89] [1898] 2 Q.B. 402.
[90] s. 47(2).
[91] s. 47(1)(b).
[92] Ante, pp. 58–61.
[93] [1955] A.C. 740.
[94] For a more detailed discussion see pp. 59–61, above.

restrain broken parts of the machine which might fly off and cause injury to the operator.[95]

In short, whilst breach of statutory duty may be capable of imposing stricter duties than negligence and can shift the burden of proof onto the employer, the liability which it generally creates is strict rather than absolute and fault based thinking is undoubtedly present in many cases, both because of the interpretation placed on the wording of the statutory provisions and because contributory negligence is a defence to the tort which compels a court to assess an injured employee's fault against that of the employer.

Negligence

The strict obligations created in the industrial injury context by the tort of breach of statutory duty are supplemented by the more general requirement derived from the general law of negligence that an employer should take reasonable care of the safety of his employees. An employer's obligation to take such reasonable care is imposed both as an implied term of the contract of employment and by the general law of tort. It requires the employer to provide a safe system of work. This is traditionally stated to cover matters such as the provision of competent and properly trained staff; a safe place of work; proper materials, equipment and systems of work. However, it is essentially simply an application of the standard principles of negligence. It follows that an employer's obligation to provide for the safety of employees will be dependent upon considerations such as the ease and expense of providing the precautions balanced against the level of risk[96] and on the accepted practice in the particular industry. It was on such grounds that Mustill J. held in *Thompson* v. *Smiths Shiprepairers (North Shields) Ltd.*[97] that an employer could have owed no duty to employees to protect them against the recognised risk of damage to their hearing from exposure to excessive noise at work during a period in which there was general apathy to this risk in industry. It was only from the time that a reasonable employer would have taken precautions against this risk that the employer could be held to have broken the duty which was owed to the employees.

The obligation to provide competent and properly trained staff imposes a primary duty upon an employer which may on occasions need to be distinguished from the vicarious liability which derives from the employee's work. For example, an employer might be held liable on this basis for failing to stop horseplay amongst the employees even though these acts would not count as being in the course of the employees' employment.

The limits of an employer's obligation to provide a safe place of work and the effect of the fact that this duty is of a non-delegable character, were explored by the Court of Appeal in *Square D. Ltd* v. *Cook*,[98] a case which concerned an injury suffered by an employee who had been sent by his employer to work in Saudi Arabia on computer control systems installed in premises occupied by a third party. The injury was caused by the fact that a tile, which formed part of the floor of those premises, had been left out of

---

[95] *Carroll* v. *Andrew Barclay & Sons Ltd.* [1948] A.C. 477; *Close* v. *Steel Company of Wales Ltd.* [1962] A.C. 367.
[96] *Latimer* v. *A.E.C. Ltd.* [1953] A.C. 643.
[97] [1984] 1 Q.B. 405.
[98] [1992] I.R.L.R. 34.

position. The point at issue in the case was whether the fact that the employer's duty was of a non-delegable character meant that any negligence on the part of the occupier was automatically attributed to the employer. If this was the law the employer was effectively an insurer of the employee in respect of risks created by the occupier's negligence. The Court of Appeal favoured a more lenient approach and argued that it was absurd to suggest that an employer's duty to take reasonable care in relation to the provision of premises could create liability for dangers present on any site to which the employee was sent. This was particularly the case where an employee was sent overseas to work for an apparently responsible and reliable client. In result the employer's primary obligation of reasonable care was greatly circumscribed by the circumstances in which the employee performed his work. The employer was not vicariously responsible for all negligence on the part of the client to whom the employee was seconded and the fact that the duty was a non-delegable one did not increase the level of duty owed.

The employer's obligation to provide proper equipment is, however, more stringent than a standard negligence obligation because section 1 of the Employers' Liability (Defective Equipment) Act 1969 does create an example of vicarious liability. The section makes an employer liable for personal injuries suffered by employees in the course of their employment which are caused by defects in equipment provided to employees for the purposes of the employer's business resulting from a third party's fault. In effect, the fault of a manufacturer or supplier is regarded as the negligence of the employer, even if the defect in the item supplied was latent and could not be discerned by an employer using all reasonable care. The remedy benefits the employee because it means that the employer cannot argue that he discharged any duty of care owed to the employee by purchasing the equipment from an reputable supplier and because it creates a remedy against a person with whom the employee has daily dealings; he is not left to pursue a claim against a supplier who may be situated on the other side of the world or who may be impossible to identify. The compensatory purpose of the law is to the fore in this situation. Indeed, the provision was passed to reverse a decision[99] which was based on the same reasoning which reappeared in *Square D. Ltd* v. *Cook*.[1]

Several features of the liability created by the 1969 Act should be noted. First, it is owed only to employees and only in relation to personal injuries.[2] Secondly, it depends on the supplier of the equipment being shown to have been at fault: the employer is not made absolutely liable for injury caused by any defects in equipment supplied. "Fault," however, is given a wide meaning for the purposes[3] of this provision; it means "negligence, breach of statutory duty or any other act or omission which would give rise to liability in tort." In modern law this might result in the employer being held to be negligent on the basis of another's negligence or breach of the strict duty imposed by the Consumer Protection Act 1987, but not for breach of a contractual duty to ensure the quality of goods. Finally, the term "equipment" is defined by the statute to include, "any plant and machinery, vehicle, aircraft and clothing."[4] The House of Lords has consistently refused to

---

[99] *Davie* v. *New Merton Board Mills Ltd.* [1959] A.C. 604.
[1] [1992] I.R.L.R. 34.
[2] s. 1(1)(a) and 1(3).
[3] s. 1(3).
[4] s. 1(3).

narrow the scope of the protection by placing a limited meaning on the word. In *Coltman* v. *Bibby Tankers Ltd.*[5] it was held wide enough to include a ship which was alleged to have sunk as a result of defective construction and design, it was not to be confined to items which form part of a large whole. In *Knowles* v. *Liverpool City Council*[6] it was held to cover the case of a defective flagstone which broke whilst being handled. There was said to be no reason why Parliament should have chosen to enact a partial remedy confined to plant or machinery as opposed to items being processed or the materials used to produce them. As a result the Act applies to all articles provided by an employer for the purposes of his business.

The obligation to provide a safe working system is well illustrated by the facts of the *Bux*[7] Case. Employers may commonly owe a duty of care to employees to encourage or require them to use safety equipment even if there is no statutory obligation to do so, particularly if the employees' appreciation of the danger involved in the work has been blunted by familiarity. Even though an employer is not under a strict duty merely because an employee is injured whilst working in a dangerous environment it does seem to be the case that the obligation to provide a safe system of work entails warning the employee of inherent and unavoidable dangers.[8]

ANTENATAL INJURIES

The Congenital Disabilities (Civil Liability) Act 1976 creates a species of mixed liability for personal injuries. The Act resolves the problem which existed at common law as to whether a child is able to bring an action in respect of injuries caused to it by antenatal events.[9] This area of liability is correctly viewed as a species of mixed liability because the Act permits the breach of any tortious duty to give a claim to an injured child.[10] The examples most likely to occur are negligent medical treatment, exposure to industrial hazards (which might be strict or negligence based) and strict product liability in relation to defective drugs. The Act was introduced into Parliament as a result of pressure to remove one of the legal difficulties which had faced the thalidomide children[11] and was originally seen as a limited measure of law reform which would serve as a stopgap remedy within the tort system until more radical reforms were introduced following the publication of the Pearson Commission's report. That report, when it appeared,

---

[5] [1988] A.C. 276.

[6] [1993] 4 All E.R. 321.

[7] *Bux* v. *Slough Metals Ltd.* [1973] 1 W.L.R. 1359.

[8] *Withers* v. *Perry Chain* [1961] 1 W.L.R. 1314; *White* v. *Holbrook Precision* [1985] I.R.L.R. 215.

[9] In *Burton* v. *Islington Health Authority* [1992] 3 All E.R. 833 the Court of Appeal held, in a case brought by someone born in 1967, that such an action was possible. The possibility of a victim of an accident being pregnant is foreseeable and the duty of care owed to the unborn child crystallises into a full cause of action when the child is born. S. 4(5) of the 1976 Act replaces any pre-existing law in respect of births occurring after, but not before, July 22, 1976.

[10] But not an act which is solely a breach of contract. A child will have to establish that there was tortious liability if a drug purchased by its parent caused the damage. This will obviously be easier to achieve after the introduction of strict liability for defective products.

[11] Note, however, that the Act applies only to children born after July 22, 1976. It was therefore of no benefit to the thalidomide children.

criticised the Act as being based on erroneous assumptions as to the ability of the medical profession to identify the causes of congenital disabilities in children.[12] However, as a result of the failure of the Commission to produce an acceptable reform of personal injury law, the Act has remained in force.

The Act gives a child born with disabilities a right to claim damages in tort if it can prove that the cause of those disabilities was a tortious act which "affected either parent of the child in his or her ability to have a normal, healthy child, or affected the mother during her pregnancy, or affected her or the child in the course of its birth so that the child was born with disabilities which would not otherwise have been present."[13] This wording excludes the possibility of a "wrongful life" claim[14] but allows for claims in relation to both pre-and post-conception events. The child's rights are derived from those of its parent. The derivative tort approach is subject to one obvious, but important, proviso which allows a breach of duty to the parent and damage suffered by the child to combine to constitute the tort.[15] A child's father may be liable to it under the terms of the Act, but its mother cannot be liable except in relation to injuries resulting from her negligent driving.[16] The reason for this exclusion of the mother's liability is that it is felt that actions brought on behalf of a child against its mother would be likely to be destructive of good family relationships, particularly as claims might well be mounted in relation to conduct such as smoking or drug taking during pregnancy.[17] On the other hand, it is felt that the existence of compulsory insurance in the case of motoring justifies exceptional treatment.[18]

A number of defences are recognised by the Act. If a disability was caused by a pre-conception injury to the parent, there will be no liability if, at the time of conception, either or both parents knew of the risk of a child which was conceived being born disabled. Secondly, if the affected parent shared responsibility for the disability, the court may reduce the child's damages to such extent as it considers just and equitable, having regard to the extent of the parent's responsibility. The derivative nature of the remedy therefore means that the contributory negligence of one generation is visited upon the next.[19] Thirdly, a defendant who was acting at the relevant time in a professional capacity is not answerable to the child for anything which he did or omitted to do in treating or advising the parent "if he took reasonable care having regard to then received professional opinion applicable to the particular class of case; but this does not mean that he is answerable only because he departed from received opinion."[20] This provision, which merely restates the

---

[12] Pearson, paras. 1441–1452.

[13] s. 1(2)(a)(b).

[14] See *ante*, p. 191.

[15] s. 1(3).

[16] s. 2.

[17] The Pearson Commission recommended (para. 1471), by a majority, that neither parent should be liable under the Act. At present it would appear to be the case that conduct of the mother can be alleged by another defendant, such as a drug company, as constituting contributory negligence and thus reduce the child's damages under subs. 1(7).

[18] The Pearson Commission, having recommended the abolition of the general right to bring such actions against the child's father, would have included the father under this exception (para. 1472).

[19] The Pearson Commission (para. 1477) recommended that this defence should cease to be available.

[20] s. 1(5).

existing common law, appears to have been included in the Act as the result of an abundance of caution.

CARRIAGE BY AIR

Tortious compensation for personal injuries and death suffered by passengers in the course of commercial air transport is governed by a form of strict liability. In this area the advantages of strict liability are counterbalanced by the fact that awards of damages are commonly capped. The genesis of this form of tortious liability lies in a number of international treaties which seek to create a uniform system of liability governing international commercial air transport. The aims underlying these treaties were to protect airlines from the costs of obtaining insurance against unlimited liability and to avoid costly disputes as to the jurisdiction which was to deal with cases of injuries suffered in the course of international flights. In modern practice both aims seem increasingly outmoded. Considerable effort is expended in order to invoke the exceptions to the statutory caps and as a result airlines may be faced by claims which are effectively unlimited. Dissatisfaction is also expressed at the different levels of capped compensation which may be payable according to the origin and destination of the flight and at the different treatment accorded to commercial air passengers, persons on the ground injured by aircraft[21] and those injured in the course of non-commercial aviation.[22]

The relevant international treaties are incorporated into English domestic law by the Carriage by Air Act 1961 and regulations made under it and the law so created has also been extended, by analogy, to domestic internal flights. The picture is complicated in practice by the fact that different countries are signatories to different international treaties; the most important being the Warsaw Convention of 1929 and the Hague Protocol of 1955 which amended the original Convention. The United Kingdom is a signatory to both treaties. The majority of countries are signatories to the Hague Protocol; however, a minority, including the United States of America, have continued to operate the unamended Warsaw Convention. As a result, three sets of rules may apply to flights originating in, or arriving in, the United Kingdom: the Warsaw Convention rules, the Hague Protocol rules or the domestic United Kingdom rules (which are modelled on the Hague Protocol).

Domestic flights

The law governing the liability of carriers on domestic flights is to be found in Schedule 1 of the Carriage by Air Act (Application of Provisions) Order 1967.[23] This order applies to all carriage of persons by air for reward and to gratuitous carriage performed by air transport undertakings. Non-commercial flights are outside this regime and are controlled by standard negligence principles.[24] The Order creates a strict liability tort[25] under which a carrier is

---

[21] See *post*, p. 244.

[22] Normal uncapped negligence liability operates. See *Morris* v. *Murray* [1990] 2 Q.B. 6.

[23] S.I. 1967 No. 480.

[24] See *Morris* v. *Murray* [1990] 2 Q.B. 6.

[25] *American Express Co.* v. *British Airways Board* [1983] 1 W.L.R. 701.

liable for personal injury or death sustained by a passenger as a result of an accident which occurred on board the aircraft or in the course of embarking or disembarking from it.

The precise meaning of the terms "accident" and "embarking and disembarking" is a matter of dispute. The only reported English authority on these issues is *Adatia* v. *Air Canada*[26] which concerned a passenger who was injured whilst using a "travelator" within an airport terminal prior to reaching immigration or customs controls. The Court of Appeal reviewed the various approaches adopted by American courts and accepted that "embarking" and "disembarking" might cover activities other than ascending into or descending from an aircraft.[27] However, the court concluded that, whichever of these approaches was correct, it could not be said that a passenger who had reached the terminal and had left the control of the carrier was still in the process of disembarking. If this is correct, it is unlikely that an airline will bear responsibility, other than under standard negligence principles, for injuries which occur in the departure, arrival and transit lounges of airports. The definition of "accident" is a matter of great significance in view of the problems created by international terrorism for air transport. It may seem harsh, in the absence of negligence, to hold an airline strictly liable for injuries inflicted by terrorists on its passengers, but tort claims against terrorists will rarely be of value. If passengers injured in terrorist outrages are to be given a remedy by the law the choice effectively rests between relying on criminal injuries compensation or making the airline liable either by finding it to have been negligent or to be strictly liable on the grounds that the facts counted as an accident.

The strict liability of the carrier is qualified by an important exception, the Article 20 defence, which is that the carrier will bear no liability if it proves that it, its servants or its agents either took all necessary measures to avoid the damage or that it was impossible to take such measures. This provision renders the liability strict rather than absolute in giving the carrier a considerable burden to satisfy if liability is to be escaped from.[28] Standard rules of causation and contributory negligence apply.

The damages which may be awarded under this provision are calculated according to standard English law principles but are capped in amount in respect of each passenger injured.[29] Any contractual provision which has the effect of restricting the liability established by the Schedule or of fixing a lower limitation is declared null and void. It is, on the other hand, open to the carrier to agree a higher limit to his liability with his passengers.[30] The limit on damages imposed by the Order does not apply if the passenger proves that his damage was the result of "an act or omission of the carrier, his servants or agents,[31] done with intent to cause damage or recklessly and with knowledge

---

[26] [1992] P.I.Q.R. P232.

[27] For example, travelling across an airport by bus to where an aircraft is parked.

[28] It is submitted that the decision of Atkinson J. in *Chisholm* v. *British European Airways* [1963] 1 Lloyds Rep. 626 that this provision means that the carrier bears the onus of proving that the accident could not have been avoided by the exercise of "reasonable care" cannot be correct in the light of the plain words of Art. 20.

[29] The limitation is expressed as 100,000 S.D.R.s. In 1990 this was in the region of £75,000.

[30] This has been done by British and American airlines under the different treaties.

[31] In order for the carrier to be liable acts done by the servant or agent must have been within the scope of that person's employment.

that damage would probably result."[32] In practice, allegations of recklessness are an important technique for opening the door to full compensation.
However, the leading English case on the subject, *Goldman* v. *Thai Airways
International Ltd.*[33] shows that the overall result of the provision may not be
that different from the "wilful misconduct" exception found in the original
Warsaw Convention because the words "and with knowledge that damage
would probably result" add significant additional requirements which go
beyond the need to prove recklessness. In that case the plaintiff passenger had
been thrown from his seat and injured when the plane on which he was
travelling encountered severe clear air turbulence. The pilot had been
supplied with a weather chart which forecast moderate clear air turbulence
and his operations manual required him to order the wearing of seat-belts
when flying when turbulence was expected. He had failed to illuminate the
sign. The Court of Appeal held that the conduct of deliberately ignoring
instructions which were known to be for the safety of passengers demon-
strated a willingness to accept the risk and could be regarded as recklessness.
However, the concluding words of the provision imposed additional requirements before the cap on liability was removed. They required the pilot to
have actual knowledge of the consequences. The knowledge could not be
inferred; the consequence had to be "probable," whereas it is possible to be
reckless in relation to a "possible" consequence and it is probable that the
damage suffered has to be of the same kind as that which was anticipated. On
the facts the additional requirements were not satisfied. There was no
evidence that the pilot, who had never encountered turbulence of this
severity before, knew that injury to passengers would probably result from
his omission.

International flights

The general principles of liability applied to international air transport are
similar. International carriage is defined by the Warsaw Convention as either
carriage in which the point of departure and destination are in different
states, both of which are parties to the convention, or cases in which
departure and destination are in the same state but there is an agreed
stopping place in a second state (this state need not be a contracting state).
The fact that an aircraft overflies the territory of another country does not
make the flight an international one. The second category obviously applies
to "round the world" flights and has, less obviously, been held to operate in
the case of return tickets.[34] This interpretation is important in relation to
flights to the small number of countries which are not parties to the
international conventions. The best known example is Thailand. Mr Goldman's claim would not have been governed by the Hague Protocol but for the
fact that his ticket from London to Bangkok was a return one.

Two sets of rules govern international carriage. The majority of countries
now adhere to the Hague Protocol which is the model for the rules governing
English internal flights. International travel from the United Kingdom to
these countries is therefore governed by the rules already described.

---

[32] S.I. 1967 No. 480, Sched. I, Art. 25.
[33] [1983] 1 W.L.R. 1186.
[34] *Grein* v. *Imperial Airways Ltd.* [1937] 1 Q.B. 50.

A minority of countries has refused to adhere to the Hague Protocol. Flights to these countries from the United Kingdom are therefore governed by the older Warsaw Convention. The strict basis of liability remains the same as before as does the Article 20 defence. However, the compensation payable is capped at a lower level and the escape from the cap is dependent on proof of "wilful misconduct" rather than "recklessness" on the part of the carrier. The United States of America is one of the countries which has not adopted the Hague rules. However, the treatment of passengers travelling to the U.S.A. is better than it may appear at first sight because American courts have tended to award damages well in excess of the Warsaw limits by placing a liberal interpretation on the words "wilful misconduct" and because carriers flying to that country are required by the licensing authorities to enter into special contracts with their passengers under which the Article 20 defence is waived and the cap is increased significantly.

Injuries on land

Section 76(2) of the Civil Aviation Act 1982 places strict liability on the owner of an aircraft for damage to persons or property on land caused by the aircraft or by items falling from it while it is in flight, taking off or landing. This liability is uncapped. As a result, if an airliner crashes into houses the occupants of those houses have an unlimited strict liability claim for compensation against the owner of the plane whereas the passengers have a capped one against the carrier unless they can invoke the "recklessness" or "wilful misconduct" exceptions.

Rylands v. *Fletcher*

Strict liability in the English law of tort is often identified with the principle derived from the case of *Rylands* v. *Fletcher*[35]; a case which creates strict liability for the escape of dangerous items brought onto land.[36] Nowadays this is somewhat surprising. As we have seen, English law recognises a number of bases of strict liability for personal injuries, albeit that they are confined to particular types of activity. Although *Rylands* may have had the capacity in the early twentieth century to provide the basis of a general principle of strict liability for damage caused by dangerous activities, it can no longer do this because its operation has become so hedged by conditions that it can rarely be relied on to provide a remedy. Instead of treating the case as creating a general principle of strict liability courts have accorded the judgments a narrow literal reading.

As part of this process, it has become doubtful whether the tort derived from *Rylands* can actually provide a remedy for personal injuries. Authority exists which supports the view that the tort can play such a role.[37] However, doubts were raised by the decision of the House of Lords in *Read* v. *J. Lyons & Co. Ltd.*[38] That case featured an attempt by a person who had been injured by the explosion of a shell in a munitions factory to recover damages

---

[35] (1868) L.R. 3 H.L. 330.
[36] See Chap. 22 for a discussion of this tort in the context of damage to land.
[37] *Schiffman* v. *Order of St. John* [1936] 1 K.B. 557.
[38] [1947] A.C. 150.

for her injuries on the basis of the *Rylands* principle. The House rejected the claim, the ratio of the decision being that, as the plaintiff's injuries had occurred in the factory in which the shell was being manufactured, the requirement that there should have been an escape from the defendant's land had not been satisfied. Although the majority of the members of the House felt it unnecessary to express an opinion on the use of the tort as a remedy for personal injuries, Lord MacMillan's speech raised severe doubts as to whether this was possible. He took the view that *Rylands* could not provide a remedy for personal injuries because, as a general principle, it is now generally essential for a plaintiff in a personal injury case to prove negligence in order to achieve success. Such a general principle obviously requires qualification, but it can be interpreted as insisting that English law recognises negligence rather than strict liability as the only general principle for the recovery of damages for personal injuries. In view of the restricted role now played by *Rylands* and the fact that any further introductions of strict liability for personal injuries are certain to be based on statute there is much to be said for using Lord MacMillan's views as authority for expelling the tort from the personal injury field.

NUISANCE

Those who have a sufficient interest in land[39] which is affected by a private nuisance[40] are able to seek compensation for personal injuries resulting from the nuisance. It is rather strange that the law should allow a tort which deals primarily with injury to the amenity of land to give a personal injury remedy, particularly as it makes the capacity to bring a claim depend on the plaintiff having an interest in the land affected by the nuisance; a rule which makes sense if the protection of the use and enjoyment of land is the purpose of the tort, but which imposes an arbitrary nonsensical barrier to recovery if the tort is to act as a remedy for the losses caused by personal injuries. An additional problem is created by the fact that, as nuisance is in some respects a form of strict liability, its availability as a personal injury remedy means that there is some possibility of it giving a remedy when negligence cannot do so. The modern history of the tort suggests, however, that this advantage is merely theoretical. Nuisance has increasingly been influenced by negligence and cases of nuisances creating physical damage are the prime example of such influence. It has, therefore, become increasingly unlikely that the courts will accept a personal injury claim based on nuisance unless negligence can also be proved on the facts.

Dangers on or obstructions of the highway

Tort claims for dangers on or obstructions of the highway which constitute public nuisances have also come to be dominated by negligence thinking. The requirement that special damage must have been suffered by a plaintiff before a public nuisance will be actionable in tort is commonly satisfied by proof of personal injury. Familiar examples of this form of nuisance are items

[39] See *post*, p. 397.
[40] For a detailed discussion of the law on private nuisance see Chap. 20.

which fall into the road[41]; defective cellar flaps which endanger pedestrians[42] and obstructions which impede the flow of traffic. For the most part this area now seems to be completely assimilated to negligence. If a diseased tree creates a public nuisance by falling into the road the question is whether the defect was latent or could have been appreciated by a reasonable person in the position of the owner. Thus in *Caminer* v. *Northern & London Investment Trust Ltd.*[43] a landowner escaped liability when a tree on his property which was suffering from a disease of the roots which was not discoverable by reasonable examination, fell into the road injuring the plaintiff. Lord Parker C.J.'s judgment in *British Road Services* v. *Slater*[44] went even further and, taking the view that nuisance and negligence were becoming increasingly assimilated, discharged a landowner from liability for damage caused by a tree which was growing out over the highway on the basis that he had reasonably failed to appreciate that the tree could constitute a nuisance. However, in spite of these relatively modern cases, some isolated examples of the older strict liability thinking may still be recognised by the law. The best known example being the fall of an artificial projection into a highway.[45]

Even though the decision ultimately turned on causation, the decision in *Dymond* v. *Pearce*[46] creates the possibility of public nuisance allowing a small area of strict liability to exist in respect of non-dangerous obstructions of the highway. Any act which permanently or temporarily removes the whole or part of the highway from the public use of passing freely constitutes an obstruction. The defendant in *Dymond* had parked a lorry overnight on a dual carriageway road. He had left the vehicle parked under a street light and with its lights on. The plaintiff, who was a pillion passenger on a motor cycle, was injured when the cycle ran into the back of the lorry. The Court of Appeal held, in an action brought against the defendant, that the sole cause of the accident had been the inattention of the motor cycle rider. However, the majority of the court was of the view that the defendant's acts had created a public nuisance, that such a nuisance could be founded on an obstruction of the highway which did not create a danger and that it might be possible in rare cases for a claim to succeed in nuisance on such facts but to fail in negligence. In part this is said to follow from the fact that if a prima facie nuisance is proved, the burden of proof passes to the person creating it to justify it. Perfectly normal activities such as parking under street lights are potentially caught by this principle. The person who leaves a car or rubbish skip obstructing part of the road may be liable for special damage caused thereby even though no danger was foreseeable. The causation point reduces this possibility but does not remove it. If a plaintiff can prove that the obstruction was a partial cause of his injury he will be able to recover damages, subject to the defence of contributory negligence. It may well be that the decision of the majority can be discounted on the basis that it is simply wrong. Edmund Davies L.J. in his dissenting judgment adopted the more modern approach that it is essential to prove fault in order to establish liability for personal injuries suffered on the highway. On this reasoning an obstruction has to amount to a danger before it can be actionable in tort.

---

[41] *Wilchick* v. *Marks* [1934] 2 K.B. 56.
[42] *Heap* v. *Ind Coope & Allsopp Ltd.* [1940] 2 K.B. 476.
[43] [1951] A.C. 88.
[44] [1964] 1 W.L.R. 498.
[45] *Tarry* v. *Ashton* (1876) 1 Q.B.D. 314; *Wringe* v. *Cohen* [1940] 1 K.B. 229.
[46] [1972] 1 Q.B. 496.

Subsequent decisions have generally assumed that negligence must be proved in this kind of case, but the decision of the majority has yet to be overruled.

The liability of highway authorities

Special rules govern the liability of those who have the responsibility for maintaining and repairing the highway. Cases in this area have concerned failures to remove dangerous items such as ice and compacted snow from roads[47] and allowing roads and pavements to fall into disrepair with the result that motorists[48] or pedestrians[49] are injured. In origin, these rules have the characteristics of absolute liability as they are based on public nuisance.[50] However, they have come to be heavily influenced by negligence, in part because courts have felt that the reasonable road user should be capable of protecting himself against the minor dangers to his safety created by items such as uneven paving slabs.

At common law a person who has responsibility for the maintenance of a highway is liable for negligent misfeasance but has an immunity from liability in respect of non-feasance. As a result damages cannot be recovered for injuries caused by the fact that such a person allowed a highway to fall into disrepair. However, highway authorities, but not private individuals with such responsibility, are now under a statutory duty in relation to injuries caused by both types of negligence.[51] The preferable view is that this duty is a species of public nuisance which becomes actionable when a danger has arisen as a result of misfeasance or non-repair.[52] However, the negligence standard is imported into the area by the fact that the courts have only been prepared to accept that a danger has arisen on the basis of foresight of harm being suffered[53] and because the authority is given a defence in cases of failures to maintain if it can prove that it took reasonable care in the circumstances to ensure that the highway was not dangerous.[54]

OTHER EXAMPLES

Strict liability for personal injuries is also imposed by statute in the case of a number of other specific activities. The Nuclear Installations Act 1965 places strict liability for personal injuries and property damage caused by a nuclear incident upon the person licensed to operate the plant in question. Similarly the Gas Act 1964 stipulates strict liability for any damage which results from the underground storage of gas and it is the result of section 88 of the Control of Pollution Act 1974[55] that there is strict liability for injuries caused by the deposit of poisonous, noxious or polluting waste on an unlicensed site or in

---

[47] *Haydon* v. *Kent C.C.* [1978] Q.B. 343.
[48] *Rider* v. *Rider* [1975] Q.B. 505.
[49] *Griffiths* v. *Liverpool Corporation* [1967] 1 Q.B. 374; *Meggs* v. *Liverpool Corporation* [1968] 1 W.L.R. 689.
[50] Diplock L.J. *Griffiths* v. *Liverpool Corporation* [1967] 1 Q.B. 374.
[51] Highways Act 1980, s. 41.
[52] Diplock L.J., *Griffiths* v. *Liverpool Corporation* [1967] 1 Q.B. 374.
[53] *Littler* v. *Liverpool Corporation* [1968] 2 All E.R. 343n.
[54] Highways Act 1980, s. 58. The duty remains stricter than ordinary negligence because the defendant bears the burden of proving the defence and because the duty is only delegable if strictly defined requirements are satisfied (see s. 58(2)).
[55] This provision is to be replaced by s. 73(6) of the Environmental Protection Act 1990.

contravention of the terms of a licence. The European Community has produced a draft Directive,[56] modelled on the Directive on product liability, which would impose a harmonised regime of strict tortious liability on the producer[57] of waste throughout the Community.

[56] The text of the draft directive is reproduced at [1989] 3 C.M.L.R. 594.
[57] Under the terms of the draft, "producer" would be defined widely to include an authorised disposer of waste, a person who imported the waste into the Community and a person who is transporting it through the Community. The holder of waste would be treated as the producer on failing to identify the true producer.

Chapter Twelve

The Calculation of Tort Damages for Personal Injuries and Death

GENERAL PRINCIPLES

This chapter will describe the methods which the law of tort uses to calculate the sum of money to be awarded to a successful claimant in a personal injury or death case. The principles outlined in this chapter apply to all successful personal injury claims in tort, whether the basis of liability is an intentional tort, negligence or strict liability. In practice, the social security system shoulders most of the burden of providing immediate help to persons injured, and this is done irrespective of the degree of their suffering and of the cause of the injury. Its aim is to provide a basic level of protection against the hazards of life, rather than to provide full compensation for all damage suffered. A tort remedy, on the other hand, when, and if, it is available may accomplish a drastic transformation in the victim's financial circumstances. A high wage earner, or someone who suffers a serious or catastrophic injury which requires regular nursing attention, will have a lot to gain by bringing a successful tort claim because tort adopts the principle of providing a full and fair replacement of all sums lost by the victim. The tort remedy is subject to no financial ceiling and permits the recovery, so far as money can, of non-financial losses. The fact that tort is, to a large extent, administered by private insurance companies rather than the State means that little pressure exists to place upper limits on the compensation which it provides and that courts have been free to raise the level of damages to keep it in line with the declining value of money when they have deemed this to be necessary. A second important advantage of the tort system is provided by the fact that damages are calculated according to the needs of the individual plaintiff. As a result real, rather than notional, earnings loss can be compensated; partial earnings losses can be recognised and the particular expenses created by an injury, which will rarely be of a standard kind, can be met. These advantages exist in the realm of theory. In practice, the fact that the majority of tort claims are settled by a negotiation process which is bedeviled by uncertainties means that the promised precision is often unattainable. The rules described in the rest of this chapter represent the law which is applied in the small number of cases which reach the courts and which should serve as the basis on which settlements of claims are reached. However, research has suggested that the settlement process, under which over 95 per cent. of tort claims are determined, is dominated by uncertainties which tend to lead to the plaintiff receiving a far lower sum than would be awarded by a court.[1]

The actual sums awarded in the great majority of cases show how academic concentration on issues such as the adequacy of the multiplier technique to protect the long term disabled[2] is of no relevance to the great majority of accident victims. The research conducted by the Oxford Centre for Socio-Legal Research[3] showed that half of the settlements covered by the study (most of which were arrived at between 1973 and 1977) were for less than £500, nearly three-quarters were for less than £1,000 and that only one in nine exceeded £2,000. The average sum paid to victims who recovered anything was £1,135. Although the figures recorded in the 1990s would certainly be larger because of inflation, it is likely that certain conclusions based on this data would still be correct. First, the tort system tends to produce relatively low figures of damages and it is likely that the figure achieved is influenced greatly by the unequal bargaining relationship which exists between the victim and the defendant's insurance company. These practical pressures are liable to frustrate the aim of precise and full compensation in many cases. Secondly, future earnings loss is likely to be at issue in hardly any cases which settle in the normal range[4] and, as a result, the concentration of lawyers on achieving full compensation for the most seriously injured, is questionable.[5] Settlements in respect of financial losses deal mainly with pre-settlement losses. However, delays in achieving a settlement (the average settlement time recorded by the Oxford research was 19 months) means that tort cannot in practice provide instant protection for the short term living expenses for which the compensation is actually being awarded. In these circumstances it is not surprising to find that although 70 per cent. of the settlements recorded by the Oxford research included sums calculated to replace lost earnings, only 27 per cent. of victims used their compensation either for living expenses or to pay off loans incurred while they had been ill. In practice, sick pay and social security benefits provide instant protection for a victim's living standards and the damages awarded are used in the same way as "any unexpected lump sum windfall, such as a win on the pools."[6]

The calculation of common law damages has become a process of increased sophistication as a result of the virtual disappearance of jury trials in personal injury cases and the need to itemise the elements of an award in order to apply the rules concerning the payment of interest. Reasoned and detailed awards made by judges are more open to review by appellate courts and a considerable body of detailed law has emerged from the appeal courts in recent years.

The basic approach adopted by English law is that full compensation is to be provided for all financial losses incurred by the victim. An award of damages seeks to replace every £1 lost and to keep the victim in the state to which he had become accustomed (or conceivably in the state to which he aspired). Tort is a form of compensation which insists that the means of a

---

[1] Harris, *Compensation and Support for Illness and Injury*, p. 97 et seq.
[2] See *post*, pp. 256–264.
[3] See Harris *op. cit.*
[4] Harris reported that it was taken into account in only one case out of 51 in which detailed information was received from solicitors.
[5] Particularly given the low number of victims who obtain anything from tort.
[6] Harris *op. cit.* p. 122.

victim who has been injured are not to be reduced by the hand of fate whereas most other compensation systems set limits to the level of protection which they provide. Tort also attempts to expand the scope of protection further by awarding compensation for non-financial losses such as pain and suffering; few other systems do this.

The calculation of personal injury damages is dominated by the compensatory purpose of tort. Exemplary damages may on rare occasions be available in cases of intentionally inflicted personal injuries.[7] However, negligence cases cannot as a matter of law give rise to a claim for exemplary damages. The medical negligence case of *Kralj* v. *McGrath*[8] went further and rejected an argument that the nature of a defendant's conduct could justify an award of aggravated damages in a personal injury case. However, the court in that case did accept that if the plaintiff has a valid claim for mental distress or nervous shock, it might be possible to prove that the nature of the defendant's conduct increased the damage and justified a higher compensatory award.

Awards of damages are generally made as a single lump sum which cannot be varied in the light of subsequent changes in the victim's circumstances. However, two pieces of procedure remove some of the difficulties which may be caused by the lump sum approach.

First, a plaintiff may apply to the court for an interim payment,[9] that is, an award of money which will help to meet losses incurred before the final calculation of the damages is made. This is particularly useful as many accident victims will incur most of the additional expenses produced by the accident and will have the most difficulty in tailoring their commitments to a reduced level of income in the period immediately after the accident or at the time when the payment of their wages ceases. The final award of damages may still be some way in the future at this date even if liability is not in dispute. A court may award an interim payment so long as it is satisfied that the defendant is liable to the plaintiff for a substantial sum and that the defendant is insured, a public authority, or is a person whose financial means are such as to enable him to make an interim payment. The amount awarded as an interim payment will not exceed a reasonable proportion of the damages which the court believes are likely to be ultimately awarded to the plaintiff. If the defendant is not prepared to agree voluntarily to make such a payment the plaintiff may seek one by applying to the court.[10]

Secondly, the lump sum may create a particular problem for a victim whose injuries create the possibility of serious deterioration in his condition in the future. For example, a head injury may create the risk that the victim will develop epilepsy in later life. If a court merely calculates the appropriate award for such a condition and then discounts that figure on the basis of an estimate of the chances that the condition will occur, it will undercompensate the victim who develops the condition and overcompensate the one who is lucky enough to avoid it. This problem is dealt with, in part, by the

---

[7] Assault by police officers and by other persons in the course of a wrongful eviction would seem to be the most likely circumstances in which the requirements of *Rookes* v. *Barnard* will be satisfied. See *ante*, p. 148.

[8] [1986] 1 All E.R. 54.

[9] Under R.S.C., Ord 29, r.11.

[10] The Law Commission has noted that concern exists that such awards are not always sought in cases in which they might be appropriate. See Law Commission, Consultation Paper No. 125, Pt. IV.

Administration of Justice Act 1982[11] which allows a court to award "provisional damages." This amounts to a power to split the lump sum award in two[12] rather than the introduction of a form of periodic payment of damages. If it is established that there is a chance that at some time in the future the plaintiff will, as a result of a tort, develop some serious disease or suffer some serious deterioration in his physical or mental condition, it is open to the court to assess damages on the assumption that the contingency will not occur, but to declare the plaintiff entitled to return to court at a future date to obtain a further award if it does. The wording of the jurisdiction, and in particular its dependence on the word "serious" means that the procedure is only of use in a small number of cases. In *Willson* v. *Ministry of Defence*[13] it was held not to apply to the case of a person whose condition following from an ankle injury was likely to degenerate with the risk of osteoarthritis occurring. The jurisdiction was held to require a clear and severable risk as opposed to a progressive and common place deterioration of an existing condition. The procedure obviously does not apply to non-medical contingencies such as the risk that an accident victim will be disadvantaged in the labour market in the future because of his injuries. However, in spite of these limitations, an award of provisional damages is capable of producing a far more accurate result in those situations in which it does operate.[14]

Non-pecuniary Losses

The law of tort awards compensation for what are described as non-pecuniary losses or "general" damages: pain, suffering and loss of amenity. These are heads of loss which have no exact equivalent in financial terms. From one standpoint it might be possible to argue that any attempt to compensate for non-pecuniary losses is misconceived. The technique of compensation used in this area is bound to be imprecise and can do nothing to alleviate the actuality of the injury. However, the better view is almost certainly that the losses suffered are real and that tort, by providing compensation in respect of them, is correctly recognising that the consequences of a personal injury are not purely financial. The Pearson Commission suggested that three reasons might be given for the award of such damages[15]: they might serve as a palliative for those injured, particularly if no financial losses resulted from the injury; they might enable the victim to purchase alternative pleasures to those which have been lost and they might provide compensation for any unquantifiable or unforeseen financial losses which might be suffered. In effect, this last reason amounts to regarding damages of this kind as having the role of boosting the value of the overall award of damages. From the standpoint of deterrence theory it can also be argued that the true cost of an accident is more likely to be transferred to a

---

[11] S. 6 added a new s. 32A to the Supreme Court Act 1981.

[12] The plaintiff is only permitted to return to court on one occasion under this jurisdiction.

[13] [1991] 1 All E.R. 638.

[14] A.P.I.L. has argued, in its preliminary submission to the Law Commission, that this jurisdiction should be extended beyond the "one off" event and that power should exist to permit a plaintiff to return to court on more than one occasion. See Law Commission, *Consultation Paper* No. 125, Pt. V.

[15] para. 360.

tortfeasor if some attempt to quantify the pain and suffering is included in the damages payable.

The principle governing awards of damages for such losses can be described as being that awards should be of "fair" rather than "full" compensation. The notion of "fairness" has two particular implications. First, it reflects the fact that, as there can be no exact financial compensation for such losses, sympathy for the victims of accidents must not be allowed to produce massive awards of damages against the defendant. Secondly, it recognises that it is important to achieve consistency between the awards made to people who suffer similar injuries. It does not follow from this specialised and limited use of the word "fair" that it is open to a successful plaintiff who is disappointed by the level of damages awarded to appeal on the basis that it is unfair as not representing a sum which others might regard as appropriate recompense for such an injury.

Awards of damages for non-pecuniary losses comprise a significant proportion of many awards of tort damages and can add greatly to the overall value of the award, particularly in relation to minor injuries. Research conducted by the Pearson Commission revealed that two thirds of the money paid by insurers in respect of tort claims was for non-pecuniary losses and that it was the predominant element in small claims.[16] It is thought to be the case that whilst seriously and permanently injured victims are unable to obtain tort's promise of full compensation for financial losses because of the inadequacies of the multiplier technique,[17] the availability of damages for non-pecuniary losses means that those who suffer minor injuries tend to receive far more than their financial losses. This is in part because it is uneconomic for insurance companies to do anything other than seek to settle such claims.[18] If this is correct, the law is failing to concentrate the available resources on those victims who are most in need of help.

In order to overcome the problems of calculating awards for intangible losses of this kind a tariff of conventional awards for particular injuries has been evolved. In this way some predictability is introduced into the system. The tariff is a flexible one based on judicial knowledge of previous awards made by other courts.[19] Limitations exist to this approach; previous decisions are not binding precedents but are a general guide to the bracket of figures currently deemed to be an appropriate award for a particular injury.[20] Every case has to be decided on its own facts and a judge has considerable latitude in selecting a figure within the bracket. The conventional sums awarded for particular injuries are meant to take into account

---

[16] Vol II, paras. 519–521.

[17] See *post*, p. 258.

[18] Pearson *op cit.* para. 383.

[19] A number of publications exist to keep practitioners informed of the current levels of awards being made by the courts. See particularly Kemp & Kemp, *The Quantum of Damages*, and Munkman, *Damages for Personal Injuries and Death*. In 1992 the Judicial Studies Board issued a publication *Guidelines for the Assessment of General Damages in Personal Injury Cases* which is intended to give judges up to date information on the appropriate award for particular injuries. A number of computer information systems, such as LEXIS and LAW-TEL, also provide such information. In essence, these provide a practitioner with examples of previous awards classified according to the nature of the injury. The tariff used by the social security system in relation to the disablement benefit payable under the industrial injuries scheme represents a far more formalised version of this technique.

[20] The previous decsion may have been influenced by subjective factors relating to the plaintiff and be out of date as a result of the effects of inflation.

the normal level of disruption to a victim's life caused by such an injury. However, if the victim can show that an unusual level of disruption has been caused by the particular injury, for example if a keen amateur footballer suffers leg injuries, an upvaluation will be appropriate.[21] The conventional figures have been periodically upvalued to take account of the declining value of money in periods of inflation[22] and as a result care needs to be exercised when using sums awarded in older cases, as examples.

The three elements which form an award of damages for non-pecuniary losses, pain, suffering and loss of amenity, are usually compensated in the form of a single undifferentiated sum, which is commonly known as general damages. However, exceptional cases do occur in which it is necessary to distinguish between them. The award of damages for pain is made on a purely subjective basis: the greater the pain suffered by the plaintiff, whether as a result of the injury or of the consequential treatment, the higher the award. Conversely, if the pain is controlled by the use of drugs or if the victim has periods of unconsciousness the award will be reduced or eliminated.[23] The subjective element of suffering can be important even if the victim experiences no pain. In its widest sense suffering covers the whole disruption of the victim's life caused by the injury. Included in it are elements such as loss of marriage prospects and the opportunity of having children,[24] distress at the physical indignities suffered by a disabled person,[25] or by someone who receives a disfiguring scar and also the appreciation that one's expectation of life has been shortened.[26] However, a person's fear that they are about to suffer an injury or death does not justify an award of damages.[27] As a result of the decision of the House of Lords in *Hicks* v. *Chief Constable of South Yorkshire*[28] it seems likely that no award of damages for pain and suffering may be made in respect of the pain and suffering endured in the course of a person's death. The plaintiffs in that case, who were the personal representatives of two of the victims of the Hillsborough stadium disaster, failed to obtain damages as they were unable, on the facts of the case,[29] to produce evidence that the victims had suffered physical injuries prior to the crushing which killed them.

Awards for loss of amenity (sometimes referred to as loss of faculty) represent the simple fact of physical injury and consequential impairment of bodily function. An award of this kind is assessed on an objective basis and thus does not depend on the victim's appreciation of his fate. This has led, in

---

[21] Examples of this have included loss of enjoyment of a favourite hobby *Moelicker* v. *Reyrolle & Co. Ltd.* [1976] I.C.R. 253; the loss of a holiday *Ichard* v. *Frangoulis* [1977] 2 All E.R. 461; lost job satisfaction as a result of discharge from congenial employment; *Champion* v. *London Fire & Civil Defence Authority* (1990) *The Times*, July 5 and imprisonment as a result of sexual assaults and rape committed following personality changes caused by serious head injuries; *Meah* v. *McCreamer* [1985] 1 All E.R. 367.

[22] *Walker* v. *Maclean* [1979] 1 W.L.R. 760.

[23] *Skelton* v. *Collins* (1966) 39 A.L.J.R. 480; *Mills* v. *Stanway Coaches Ltd.* [1940] 2 K.B. 334.

[24] *Thomas* v. *British Railways Board* [1976] Q.B. 912; *Moriarty* v. *McCarthy* [1978] 1 W.L.R. 155.

[25] *Connolly* v. *Camden & Islington Area Health Authority* [1981] 3 All E.R. 250.

[26] *Davies* v. *Tenby Corporation* [1974] 2 Lloyd's Rep. 469; Administration of Justice Act 1982, s. 1.

[27] *Hicks* v. *Chief Constable of South Yorkshire* [1992] 2 All E.R. 65.

[28] [1992] 2 All E.R. 65.

[29] It would remain open to attempt to prove that such a loss had been suffered in the course of a slower death than that suffered by the victims in this case.

a series of cases,[30] to a person who had suffered catastrophic injuries and who was surviving in a coma, with little, if any, appreciation of the injuries suffered receiving a large award of damages for this element of loss. There can be no justification for this result other than the natural sympathy for someone who has been reduced to such a sorry state. The money can serve no useful function in alleviating the victim's suffering and is, in any case, awarded in addition to the sums payable for the victim's loss of earnings and the costs of care. No award is made for loss of amenity to the estate of a person who is killed; however, these living plaintiffs who are in a condition close to death are given awards at the very top of the conventional range of damages for injuries. Ultimately this money is likely to become a windfall for the beneficiaries of the estate of the victim. The Pearson Commission was of the opinion that no award of damages for non-pecuniary loss should be made to a person in a state of permanent unconsciousness.[31]

Different proposals for the reform of this area of law have been made. A majority of the members of the Pearson Commission favoured the elimination of small awards of general damages and proposed that none should be made for such losses suffered during the first three months after the accident.[32] The effect of this, particularly when coupled with the Commission's proposal of a full offset of social security benefits from damages, would have been to remove the incentive to bring a tort claim in many cases of less serious injuries. However, the proposal attracted a great deal of criticism, chiefly on the basis that it amounted to the removal of a well recognised and vested right, and there is little prospect of it being revived. More recently, it has been argued that the figures currently being awarded have failed to keep pace with inflation[33] and are unacceptably low. A number of methods have been proposed for overcoming this. In 1988 the Citizen Action Compensation Campaign proposed that a panel of experts should be set up with the task of producing official guidance as to the appropriate sums for particular injuries which it would be the courts' duty to follow.[34] A proposal to introduce this system made no headway in Parliament in 1989.[35] In 1992 the Association of Personal Injury Lawyers, in a submission to the Law Commission[36] proposed a two pronged approach of compelling courts to use the Retail Prices Index as a method of calculating the decline in the value of money from the time of previous awards and the use of jury assessment of compensation in a sample of cases in order to obtain an indication of the appropriate level of damages to be used by judges as guidance in other cases.

---

[30] *Wise* v. *Kaye* [1962] 1 Q.B. 638; *H. West & Son Ltd.* v. *Shephard* [1964] A.C. 326; *Lim Poh Choo* v. *Camden & Islington Area Health Authority* [1980] A.C. 174.

[31] para. 398.

[32] para. 388.

[33] In particular it is alleged that the decision of the Court of Appeal in *Housecroft* v. *Burnett* [1986] 1 All E.R. 332 that £75,000 was the appropriate award to be made in April 1985 in a typical case of tetraplegia has "capped" the whole range of awards at a level which is significantly lower, in real terms, than the figures which were being awarded in the 1960s.

[34] Berlins, Cahill & Winfield, *News from CITCOM* (1988), p. 2.

[35] It was contained in the Citizens' Compensation Bill 1989.

[36] Association of Personal Injury Lawyers, *Law Commission, 5th Programme of Law Reform: Personal Injury Damages Examination, preliminary submission* (1992).

FINANCIAL LOSSES

Two kinds of financial losses may afflict an accident victim. Earnings may be lost and increased expenditure may be incurred. In both cases it is necessary to distinguish between losses incurred prior to the date on which the award is assessed and those which may continue, possibly indefinitely, into the future. If, as will commonly be the case, the victim has returned to work before the assessment is made and suffers no residual effects from the injury, only past losses will be at issue and these will be capable of assessment with a fair degree of precision, although estimates may need to be made on such questions as whether the victim would have achieved promotion at work during the period at issue. Only about 8 per cent. of tort cases concern future financial losses, although about 20 per cent. of all tort compensation is paid out under this head.[37] It is these losses, those which continue beyond the date of the calculation, which involve the difficult task of estimating the future and which attract the greatest critical attention.

The multiplier

Cases in which the loss is to continue into the future create difficulties because the finality of an award of damages made in the form of a lump sum means that the court must speculate as to the plaintiff's post accident prospects and as to what might have happened had the accident not occurred. The technique generally adopted in cases of future financial losses is to calculate the net annual loss incurred by the plaintiff as the result of the accident (the multiplicand) and to multiply it by a figure (the multiplier), which represents the period over which the loss will be suffered, to produce the final figure of damages. Because the sum awarded as damages will not be taxed or subject to social security contributions, the multiplicand will be calculated on the basis of the victim's "take home" earnings after deduction of income tax and social security contributions.[38] It is for the plaintiff to prove the existence of factors such as promotion prospects which may increase the sum awarded. Conversely, it is for the defence to prove the existence of unusual factors which would decrease the multiplicand.

The multiplier which is chosen will be a figure lower than the number of years over which the loss is estimated to be likely to run.[39] There are two reasons for choosing a lower figure. First, it is assumed that the money awarded will be invested and produce income. The conventional range of multipliers used by the courts, which in extreme cases might reach a maximum of 18, assumes a rate of return of approximately 4½ per cent. on the capital. The plaintiff's needs are expected to be met from both capital and the interest earned on the capital and it is intended that the fund should be exhausted at the end of the period over which the loss is expected to be

---

[37] Pearson *op. cit.* para. 557.

[38] *B.T.C.* v. *Gourley* [1956] A.C. 185. *Dews* v. *National Coal Board* [1988] A.C. 1 applies the same approach to pension contributions.

[39] The multiplier in personal injury cases is calculated from the date of trial, rather than from the date of the injury. *Pritchard* v. *Cobden* [1987] 1 All E.R. 300. *Cf.* claims brought under the Fatal Accidents Act in which the method is to calculating the multiplier from the date of the accident.

suffered. A successful plaintiff will receive capital to replace earnings which would have been made in the future and, as some of the losses would have been incurred long after the award is paid, there is an element of acceleration for which the plaintiff must give credit. Secondly, it cannot be assumed that the plaintiff would, in the absence of the accident, have continued to earn at the rate established in the multiplicand. There must therefore be a discount to take account of contingencies such as unemployment or natural illness which might have reduced the earning capacity in any case. As Brett L.J. said in the leading case of *Phillips* v. *London & South Western Railway Co.*[40]

" . . . if no accident had happened, nevertheless many circumstances might have happened to prevent the plaintiff from earning his previous income; he may be disabled by illness, he is subject to the normal accidents and vicissitudes of life, and if all these circumstances of which no evidence can be given are looked at, it will be impossible to exactly estimate them; yet if the jury wholly pass them over they will go wrong, because these accidents and vicissitudes ought to be taken into account."

The traditional range of multipliers is regarded as taking account of these factors. Special cases may call for some adjustment to the multiplier.

1. Children

The most familiar special case is that of an award of lost future earnings made to a child. In such cases the very large element of acceleration and the great uncertainties will require a heavy discount to be made. In *Croke* v. *Wiseman*[41] the Court of Appeal held that a judge had failed to take account of such factors when fixing a multiplier of nine in relation to a child of seven (who had a life expectation of 33 years) and reduced the multiplier to five.

2. Young women

Differences of judicial opinion have been recorded as to whether it is appropriate to reduce the multiplier in a case of a young woman on account of the possibility that she would have broken her career and thus reduced her earnings in order to raise a family. First instance decisions have attempted to avoid this result which is regarded as discriminatory. In *Moriarty* v. *MacCarthy*[42] O'Connor J. chose to reduce the multiplier, but put the woman in an identical position overall to a man of the same age by awarding an additional sum of general damages to make up for the fact of her having lost the joy of raising a family. This solution is inelegant as it presupposes that a man who suffered similarly would not merit such an award of general damages. In *Hughes* v. *McKeown*[43] Leonard J. adopted a different approach and refused to reduce the multiplier on the basis that, even if the woman's career was broken in order to raise a family, she could be presumed to be supported by her husband during that period. Thus her injury deprived her of support in that period which was to be regarded as a species of economic loss. This approach would seem to take an unrealistic view of the state of a family's finances when a woman leaves employment to raise a family. It is

---

[40] (1879) 5 C.P.D. 280.
[41] [1982] 1 W.L.R. 71.
[42] [1978] 1 W.L.R. 155.
[43] [1985] 1 W.L.R. 963.

suggested that it would be more satisfactory if the courts were to admit openly that they regard it as unacceptable to vary the multiplier on grounds of sex and that they are therefore taking a policy decision to exclude this factor from consideration.

Criticisms of the multiplier

Severe criticism has been directed at the multiplier technique on the grounds that it leaves seriously injured accident victims undercompensated, because it does not take proper account of the affects of inflation and taxation on the real value of the award. In essence, these criticisms have amounted to arguing that lump sum payment of damages should be replaced, in cases of long term financial losses, by compensation in the form of periodic payments or, if this is impossible to achieve, that the current levels of multipliers should be recognised as inadequate and increased.

1. Actuarial evidence

It has been contended that the multiplier technique is almost wholly dependent upon judicial instinct and that a more scientific result could be achieved by the use of the statistical techniques developed by actuaries on behalf of life assurance companies to assess both prospective life expectancy and the capital sums required to pay an annuity to the beneficiaries of insurance policies.[44] This approach was closely tied, in the 1970s, to the contention that the level of awards then being made was too low and took insufficient account of inflation. Actuaries argued that their techniques were simply a scientific method, by the use of life tables, of achieving the result that the judiciary, when choosing a multiplier, was attempting to attain by little more than intuition. The Law Commission has supported this approach and recommended the introduction of a statutory provision entitling the parties to rely on actuarial evidence.[45] The Commission was critical of the decisions in *Taylor* v. *O'Connor*[46] and *Mitchell* v. *Mulholland (No. 2)*[47] in which appellate courts faced by attempts to upvalue awards by the use of actuarial evidence had reasserted the primacy of the multiplier method and had restricted actuarial evidence to the subsidiary role of checking the results obtained by the traditional method. In 1984 the Government Actuary's Department published a booklet of tables for use in Personal Injury Cases. Nonetheless, the judicial reluctance to use actuarial evidence has persisted. In *Auty* v. *N.C.B.*[48] Oliver L.J. castigated it as "little more likely to be accurate (and almost certainly less entertaining) than (that) of an astrologer" and in *Spiers* v. *Halliday*[49] a judge refused to admit the Government Actuary's Tables as evidence arguing that they were merely the product of private research and had not been officially adopted. The standard explanation for

---

[44] For a detailed description of the sophistication of actuarial techniques see Street, *Principles of the Law of Damages*, Chap. 5.
[45] Report No. 56, (1973), para. 230. The Commission has reasserted this view in 1992 in Consultation Paper No. 125 (para. 2.21) pointing to the fact that the majority of European countries use such evidence when calculating future losses.
[46] [1971] A.C. 115.
[47] [1972] 1 Q.B. 65.
[48] [1985] 1 W.L.R. 784.
[49] (1984) *The Times*, June 30.

the reluctance to use actuarial techniques is that they assume that everyone is average, whereas the multiplier can be tailored to fit the circumstances of the individual plaintiff. This is scarcely unchallengeable, as actuarial techniques are capable of accounting for differences in known facts. The task of estimating the future is better done on a rational statistical basis than on an irrational instinctive one. Furthermore, the advent of structured settlements[50] has produced the anomaly that the lump sum which forms the basis of the settlement is assessed on a multiplier basis whereas the annuity which that sum can buy is calculated by actuarial techniques. It has been argued strongly that even if actuarial evidence is confined to acting as a cross check on the conventional method, it shows that young, seriously injured victims are undercompensated in terms of the full compensation principle by the conventional level of multipliers used in personal injury cases.[51]

2. The multiplier and inflation

The question of the use of actuarial techniques is part of a wider debate concerning the ability of the multiplier to achieve the aim of full compensation for the seriously injured victim in a period of high inflation. This issue has been much debated over the years, but no acceptable method has emerged of adapting the traditional methods of calculating damages to cope with the fact that inflation is certain to devalue a capital sum which is intended to provide protection to an accident victim over a number of years. The judiciary have continued to assert that inflation cannot be taken into account when calculating awards. The reasons given for excluding inflation from consideration when an award is calculated, are not convincing. In practice, it is unrealistic to ignore the effects of inflation on large awards of capital,[52] but no consensus exists on how an allowance for inflation should be made. The disappointing thing is that the effort which has been expended has not been directed to overcoming the problems of making an allowance for inflation, but in explaining why it should be ignored. It has been said that to attempt to build into lump sum compensation "a protection against future inflation is seeking after a perfection which is beyond the inherent limitations of the system."[53] If this amounts to saying that long term inflation rates are so unpredictable that they cannot be used as the basis for a calculation, it is an argument which ignores the fact that courts are commonly required to estimate similar imponderables and which prefers simplicity at the cost of inaccuracy. A different argument, to the effect that a plaintiff can protect the value of capital by careful investment,[54] was effectively disproved by the practical evidence that it was impossible to protect large sums of capital in this way during the periods of high inflation experienced in the 1970s. An argument that to inflation proof awards of damages would give accident victims protection from inflation which is denied to the rest of society[55] cannot meet the criticism that other forms of income are, in practice,

---

[50] See *post*, p. 263.

[51] See the tables in Kemp & Kemp, *The Assessment of Damages*, para. 8–029.

[52] Lord Reid in *Taylor* v. *O'Connor* [1971] A.C. 115.

[53] Lord Scarman in *Lim Poh Choo* v. *Camden & Islington Area Health Authority* [1980] A.C. 174. See also Sir Gordon Willmer in *Mitchell* v. *Mulholland (No. 2)* [1972] 1 Q.B. 65.

[54] Lord Diplock in *Mallett* v. *McMonagle* [1970] A.C. 168; Lord Pearson in *Taylor* v. *O'Connor* [1971] A.C. 115.

[55] Megaw L.J. in *Young* v. *Percival* [1975] 1 W.L.R. 17.

protected against inflation.[56] Average earnings have stayed ahead of inflation and social security benefits are revised annually in line with changes in
the value of money.[57]

The most sophisticated, if not necessarily plausible, explanation yet
provided for judicial refusal to take account of inflation is to be found in the
speeches of the House of Lords in *Cookson* v. *Knowles*.[58] It was there said
that the range of multipliers conventionally used by the courts assumes an
income on the capital invested which is far lower than that which is likely to
be available from fixed interest securities in periods of high inflation;
investment of the damages in this way therefore gives some degree of
protection "in a rough and ready way" against inflation. This argument
assumes that there is an automatic link between interest rates and inflation.
In practice, Government manipulation of market interest rates as a technique
for managing the economy has shown this assumption to be over simplistic.
Even if the *Cookson* approach is accepted, the courts have not updated it in
the light of the introduction of inflation linked securities. In *Robertson* v.
Lestrange[59] Webster J. refused to depart from the traditional assumptions as
to the rate of return on capital as he did not accept that the court should
assume that an award of damages would nowadays be invested wholly in
index linked securities. This view has attracted forceful criticism,[60] but is
probably correct in the light of the availability in the market of non-index
linked securities which give a much higher rate of return.

Periodic payments and modified multipliers

The Pearson Commission agreed with the criticisms of the multiplier on
the basis that the range used assumes a rate of return from investment of
capital of approximately 4½ per cent. It regarded this assumption as
unrealistic because it did not take sufficient account of the high rates of
taxation which might be applied to the income earned on the capital awarded
as damages in the case of a seriously injured high wage earner[61] and because
the award of large capital sums was particularly vulnerable to inflation. The
Commission developed two proposals for overcoming these difficulties.

The approach preferred by the majority of members of the Commission
was the introduction of a system of paying damages for long term financial
losses in the form of periodic payments.[62] It was argued that it was only by
the adoption of such a technique that the aim of full compensation, of
replacing like with like, could be achieved for those whose injuries create a
need for substantial long term financial support. This form of award was
envisaged as becoming the norm for court awards[63] and was to be encouraged for settlements made out of court. The Commission feared that if

---

[56] Lord Scarman in *Lim Poh Choo* v. *Camden & Islington Area Health Authority* [1980] A.C.
   174 was clearly of the view that accident victims should not be in a better position than other
   persons who rely on capital, as opposed to income, to support themselves.
[57] See *post*, p. 286.
[58] [1979] A.C. 556.
[59] [1985] 1 All E.R. 950.
[60] Kemp, (1985) 101 L.Q.R. 556.
[61] As a result of which a significant percentage of the income produced by the capital might not
   reach the victim. At the time that Pearson reported the rate of tax applied to unearned income
   could reach 98 per cent.
[62] Pearson *op. cit.* Chap. 14.
[63] Plaintiffs could make a special case for receipt of a lump sum.

periodic payments were to be introduced merely as an option, insurance companies might pressure plaintiffs into accepting a lump sum in order to close their files on a case. The proposal was not free from difficulty. Two members of the Commission dissented from the recommendation and evidence conflicted as to whether the parties involved in the tort system would favour it.[64]

One of the advantages claimed for such a system is that the payments made to the victim are able to be adjusted to reflect changes in the value of money and other alterations in the victim's circumstances. The Commission believed that the periodic payments being paid to a victim should be uprated annually in line with increases in average earnings. However, this proposal immediately raised the question of whether insurance companies are able to guarantee paying inflation linked benefits without the Government underwriting the scheme. Periodic reviews of the level of damages in the light of changes in the circumstances of the individual victim are likely to create significant costs and it was not surprising that the Commission's recommendation in this regard was confined to varying the payments in the light of changes in the victim's medical condition and did not extend to changes of employment and levels of earnings, which might raise insoluble problems of causation. The theoretical attractions of periodic payment of damages for long term financial losses are undeniable if the goal of fully compensating victims is to be pursued at all costs. However, the difficulties involved in creating a system of periodic payments are very real. The Commission's recommendations have not been enacted.

As a fall back position, the Pearson Commission produced a scheme for "modified multipliers" which it envisaged would operate generally if the proposal for periodic payments proved unacceptable and also if a plaintiff opted to receive damages in the form of a lump sum rather than periodic payments. This proposal was worked out in great detail and incorporated into the calculation an estimate of the long term inflation rate and of the post accident tax rate which would be applied to the income produced by the damages. It would, on the assumptions made for the purposes of illustration[65] (which were based on much higher rates of taxation on investment income than those currently in force) have changed drastically the multipliers to be used in the most severe cases.[66] Again, these proposals are open to the charge that they represent a sophisticated pursuit after the unattainable goal

---

[64] The Law Commission had reported in 1973 (*Report No. 56*, para. 27) that a suggestion of a move to periodic payments had met "vehement opposition from almost every person or organisation concerned with personal injury litigation." Pearson (para. 572) reported that its wider consultation had produced "a somewhat different balance of opinion." Just over half of those consulted favoured a change along these lines. Harris *op. cit.* pp. 90–91, reported that 73 per cent. of successful claimants surveyed would not favour periodic inflation linked payments of damages, but that this was not surprising given the small sums recovered by these victims. A majority of those who had recovered in excess of £2,000 favoured the change.

[65] The long term inflation rate in relation to earnings was taken as 8 per cent. The tax rates used were those applicable in 1976/77 tax year.

[66] See Pearson *op. cit.* p. 147, Table 11. On the assumptions made the highest multiplier, awarded to cover a 40 year period would have increased from 18 to 62. Note that this assumes that there may be some categories of victim who obtain a negative return on their capital because the income is taxed so heavily that it cannot counter the decline in the value of the award attributable to inflation.

of perfect compensation. They would certainly be liable to produce a large increase in the sums awarded as damages in the most serious cases.

The Pearson Commission's acceptance of much of the criticism levelled at the traditional approach has not produced legislative reform and has had little influence on judicial decisions. In *Cookson v. Knowles*[67] Lord Fraser hinted that the courts might be prepared to amend their approach when he said that an upward revision of a multiplier might be appropriate in a case in which the victim's liability to tax after the award made it very difficult to protect the value of the award against the effects of inflation.[68] However, attempts to justify increased multipliers in this way have been rejected. In *Hodgson v. Trapp*[69] the House of Lords asserted that it is incorrect to make a specific addition to a previously determined multiplier for this purpose,[70] although it might be a relevant factor in favour of choosing a higher multiplier in a case in which a range of possible correct figures exists. The House regarded the extent of higher rate taxation to be levied on an award as one of the imponderables which faces a court and said that no justification exists for singling out this particular imponderable for special treatment. Several factors were said to require this decision. First, the whole exercise of assessing future political, economic and fiscal policies is inherently unscientific; the court was reluctant to see trials encumbered with expert evidence given by actuaries and economists aimed at presenting imponderables as scientific fact. Secondly, the problem of protecting the value of the award does not arise in relation to that portion of the damages which relates to pain and suffering. Such sums are not intended to replace financial losses and it cannot be assumed that they will be invested and produce income which might place the plaintiff in a higher tax bracket. Only a portion of the award, that relating to financial losses, raises the problem and the smaller the sum which does so the less likely it is that higher rate tax will be payable. Finally, it should not be assumed that the plaintiff will treat his damages as capital to be retained and invested. He may choose to purchase an annuity and, if this is done, repayments of capital will be tax free. Although the balance of the payments will be taxable it will require a very large annuity to be payable before a higher tax bracket will be reached. This decision has not escaped criticism.[71] Given the non-scientific nature of the process of defining an appropriate multiplier, the difference between making a specific addition to the figure and choosing a higher figure from a range of appropriate ones may not amount to a great deal in practice. More fundamentally, the decision is said to ignore the facts that the courts have not been worried about the possibility that future rates of taxation may vary when applying the rules [72] that damages be awarded net of tax and that the conventional range of multipliers assumes that tax will be paid on the income on the award at

---

[67] [1978] A.C. 556.
[68] However, the House of Lords threw doubt on this when they did not make such an adjustment in *Lim Poh Choo* v. *Camden AHA* [1980] A.C. 174. In *Hodgson* v. *Trapp* [1989] A.C. 807 the House of Lords regarded the decision in *Lim* as precluding the making of a special adjustment in the multiplier on account of inflation.
[69] [1989] A.C. 807.
[70] In doing this the House rejected the decision of the Court of Appeal in *Thomas* v. *Wignall* [1987] Q.B. 1098 in which such an addition had been made.
[71] Anderson (1989) 52 M.L.R. 550; Burrows, (1989) 105 L.Q.R. 366.
[72] See *ante*, p. 256.

standard rate. To the extent that the decision is linked to that to take no account of prospective inflation when assessing awards for financial loss, it ignores the fact that inflation is, according to the explanation given in *Cookson* v. *Knowles*, taken into account automatically by the operation of conventional discount rates. As a result, the decision can be regarded as another example of a failure by the courts to attempt to achieve the aim of full compensation.

Structured settlements

One method of overcoming the disadvantages of the lump sum, which has played an increasingly important role in the most serious cases since it first received the approval of the Inland Revenue in 1987, is the "structured settlement." Under this technique the defendant's insurance company uses some or all of the capital which would have been awarded to the plaintiff, to purchase an annuity under which regular payments are made to the victim (and possibly his dependants).[73] The advantages from the claimant's point of view are that the capital produced by the award will be subject to professional management; the removal of the risk that the capital sum will become exhausted while the needs created by the accident continue[74]; damages will be paid in the form of periodic payments which may be tailored to fit the victim's needs[75]; payments of income from the annuity are free of tax[76] and that it is possible for the payments to be index-linked.[77] At present the courts have no power to impose a structured award of damages on the parties and one can only be achieved by an out of court settlement. In addition, the technique is only suitable for cases of serious injury in which the injury is expected to continue into the future and is probably only merited if the damages are in excess of £50,000.[78] However, as experience of such settlements has grown they have been increasingly favoured as practical means of mitigating the problems created by the lump sum payment for the small number of seriously injured people who have a valuable tort claim. It is an option which is at present only available to those who want it and who can convince the defendant's insurance company that it is the appropriate form of award. However, arguments are now being made to the effect that courts should be given power to require structuring if the plaintiff wishes to receive compensation in such a form and for judges to suggest a structuring after a lump sum has been awarded.[79] Press reports of such settlements reached in the most serious cases suggest that they are capable of giving

---

[73] A lump sum element remains possible and is almost certain to be awarded for pre-settlement losses.

[74] This is particularly important when the victim's post-accident life expectation is unclear.

[75] It is commonly the case that only part of the overall award is structured as lump sums may be needed to meet particular needs. Provision may also be made within the structure for lump sum payments to be made at fixed points in the future.

[76] This would not be the case if he managed his own investments. In fact the liability insurer may also be able to take some advantage from the tax saving.

[77] Benefits such as index linking and increases at fixed points will have to be paid for in the form of a reduced level of benefit at some point.

[78] See Frenkel, (1992) 136 Sol. Jo. 30 who reported that, at the time of writing, the smallest settlement to have been structured was worth £65,000.

[79] A.P.I.L. Preliminary Submission to the Law Commission. See Law Commission Consultation Paper No. 125 for a detailed discussion of proposals to improve the present arrangements.

victims a very high level of financial protection and much more security than a lump sum award could offer.[80]

Loss of earnings

Claims for damages for loss of earnings raise a number of particular problems other than the general ones outlined above.

1. The lost years

Damages for lost earnings are awarded in full up to the expected date of the victim's death or retirement, whichever comes first. However, there are circumstances in which the award needs to run beyond the expected date of death. This is so when the life expectation of an earner who has others dependent on him is reduced by an accident. Earnings in the lost years, those which would have been lived but for the accident, cannot be recovered by the dependants under the Fatal Accidents Act if, at the time of assessment, the victim is still alive. The House of Lords decision in *Pickett* v. *British Rail Engineering Ltd.*[81] allows the victim to recover these losses as part of a personal injuries claim. The amount awarded under this head is restricted to the portion of the earnings in the lost years which would have been spent in the support of persons other than the victim. In this way money is obtained to support the dependants during those years.[82]

The calculation of awards of this kind has become a matter of complexity. The primary justification for making such an award, that of protecting the victim's dependants, seems to have been lost sight of.[83] The award is calculated according to the likely "surplus" in the plaintiff's income in the lost years. The surplus is the difference between the plaintiff's earnings and his personal expenditure. The judicially created notion of surplus lacks the capacity to mark out with precision the part of the victim's earnings in which others have a legitimate interest. The contrast with the precise limits which the Fatal Accidents Act places on the categories of relatives who may make dependency claims[84] is marked. In the case of a married person with dependants, earnings used to support the family obviously form the major part of the surplus.[85] However, somewhat surprisingly, awards made to married plaintiffs with dependants are not calculated in the same way as an award made under the Fatal Accidents Act to the dependants. The Court of Appeal decision in *Harris* v. *Empress Motors Ltd.*[86] requires that the part of the plaintiff's earnings which were spent on the family unit as a whole, on items such as housing costs, be apportioned between the individual members

---

[80] Press coverage of such settlements has tended to emphasise the maximum sum liable to be paid from the structure as opposed to the sum which will be paid in the most likely event. The Law Commission (Consultation Paper No. 125, p. 24 note 3) give the example of a case in which the sum of £1,042,413 was structured and in which press coverage spoke of the victim receiving £100 million.

[81] [1980] A.C. 136.

[82] Since 1982 this cause of action has not survived the victim's death. If the victim dies before trial the dependant's support is achieved by means of an action brought under the Fatal Accidents Act.

[83] Evans & Stanton, (1984) 134 N.L.J. 515 & 553.

[84] See *post*, p. 276.

[85] The logic of this is clear, although it is linguistically somewhat strange to have to regard earnings used to support dependants as part of a "surplus."

[86] [1984] 3 All E.R. 561.

of the family including the plaintiff. Under the Fatal Accidents Act the dependants are entitled to the whole sum.[87] As a result the dependants will receive a larger, and more appropriate, award if they are able to delay bringing proceedings until after the death has occurred. Dependants will continue to live in the whole house after the victim's death, not just in a portion of it.

Claims for damages for loss of earnings in the lost years brought on behalf of seriously injured young children have generally been denied on the basis of the high degree of speculation involved in determining what responsibilities the child, if uninjured, would have had in these years.[88] The better view is that there is no absolute bar to the success of a claim of this kind but that one will only be possible if the plaintiff produces convincing evidence of loss being suffered. As the child is unlikely to have dependants at the date of injury and may be unlikely to acquire any after the injury, any award made is almost certain to be a windfall.

The most difficult cases of lost years claims are those concerning young single people. In such cases the courts have assumed that a surplus would have existed in the lost years and have awarded a percentage of the pre-accident earnings even though the victim had no dependants at the date of the injury and is unlikely (as a result of the injuries) to acquire any who would require the protection of a lost years award. In *White* v. *London Transport Executive*[89] the victim's surplus was estimated as being 33 ⅓ per cent. of his earnings for five years and 25 per cent. thereafter (on the basis that the plaintiff would have had a higher level of personal expenditure when he left his parent's home). An even more remarkable decision was reached in *Wilson* v. *Stag*[90] when the Court of Appeal refused to allow a defendant to lead evidence of the plaintiff's extravagant lifestyle in order to prove that no surplus had existed or was likely to exist. It is difficult to understand why, in the absence of evidence to the contrary, the courts do not assume that young single people live to their means and have no surplus. Victims of this kind lack the dependants in whose interest the lost years award was created and should not be able to claim it.[91]

2. Loss of earning capacity

The principle of full compensation allows an award of damages to be made for lost earning capacity. Two situations are covered by the notion of lost earning capacity: first, cases in which the plaintiff had no earnings to lose at the date of the accident but is likely to have had some in the future but for the injuries[92] and, secondly, cases in which the accident had no immediate effect

---

[87] See *post*, p. 278.
[88] *Connolly* v. *Camden & Islington Area Health Authority* [1981] 3 All E.R. 250; *Croke* v. *Wiseman* [1982] 1 W.L.R. 71.
[89] [1982] Q.B. 489.
[90] *The Times*, November 27, 1985.
[91] There remains the possibility that such a victim will acquire dependants after the award. It is submitted that the correct approach if this prospect is raised is to make an estimate of this contingency and to discount the appropriate award accordingly. In fact, the authority on this issue derives from the period before the Administration of Justice Act 1982 prevented such claims from surviving for the benefit of a deceased person's estate. Awards in relation to the lost years were being made to protect the families which the deceased was likely to have acquired but for the death! It was impossible to justify this.
[92] Examples include the child, the student, and the non-employed housewife. *S.* v. *Distillers Co. (Biochemicals) Ltd.* [1970] 1 W.L.R. 114.

on the victim's earnings, but left him injured so that he is likely to lose his job[93] or be disadvantaged in regaining employment if he should subsequently find himself out of work.[94]

Calculating damages in a case in which the plaintiff was not earning at the time of the accident can be very difficult. In such circumstances estimation becomes guesswork. If the victim was temporarily unemployed at the time of the accident a fair estimation is possible of the level of earnings which would have been likely to have been obtained had work been found and of the chances of this happening. Other situations are much more difficult. The victim may have been a married woman who was contemplating a return to work when her youngest child reached school age or a child who was too young at the date of the accident to have any settled prospects. In such cases the courts have insisted that the plaintiff has lost something of value. To deny a remedy on the basis of uncertainty is to opt for the certainty of an incorrect result to avoid the uncertainties created by the situation. In cases concerning young children courts have based their calculation on any available information; at times they have calculated the multiplicand according to the national average wage[95] and, at others, by reference to the parents' earnings pattern.[96] Large awards based on little evidence of substantial loss have been reduced on appeal.[97] The older the child the clearer the prospects are likely to be.

In cases of loss of earning capacity the elements of acceleration and uncertainty may be so great as to make a detailed calculation in terms of multiplicand and multiplier, inappropriate. It is perfectly acceptable for the court to choose to award a single lump sum in such a case as an estimation of the loss.[98]

Expenses

A claim for damages for increased expenditure caused by an injury, which will commonly cover items such as nursing and attendance, travel, special clothing and special equipment, will be assessed in basically the same way as a claim for loss of earnings. Wrongful birth claims arising from failed sterilisations[99] have given rise to damages calculated according to the costs involved in raising a child. The precise basis on which allowable expenses are calculated will depend on applying the principle of mitigation to the facts of the case in order to determine whether the expenditure was reasonable. For example, no invariable result has emerged to govern a claim for attendance: loss of earnings may be appropriate if a relative has given up work to provide the services, or, alternatively, the commercial costs of providing the care may be reasonable. If the loss of earnings measure results in a very high figure it is possible that the lower cost of providing professional nursing services may be adopted.[1]

---

[93] *Foster* v. *Tyne & Wear C.C.* [1986] 1 All E.R. 567.
[94] *Moelicker* v. *Reyrolle & Co. Ltd.* [1976] I.C.R. 253.
[95] *Croke* v. *Wiseman* [1982] 1 W.L.R. 71.
[96] *Connolly* v. *Camden & Islington Area Health Authority* [1981] 3 All E.R. 250.
[97] *Cronin* v. *Redbridge L.B.C. The Times*, May 20, 1987.
[98] *Joyce* v. *Yeomans* [1981] 1 W.L.R. 549.
[99] See p. 191.
[1] *Housecroft* v. *Burnett* [1986] 1 All E.R. 332.

1. Housing costs

If the victim's injuries necessitate the provision of specially adapted accommodation or transport, the measure of damages should be confined to the conversion costs.[2] An award of the capital cost of purchasing the unconverted item would normally involve overcompensation. It is to be assumed that, but for the accident, the victim would have provided for his accommodation and transportation needs out of his earnings and if he has ceased to earn as a result of his injuries the normal costs of purchasing and maintaining the unconverted item will be covered in the award for loss of earnings.

However, this result is not an invariable one because the injury may make it necessary for the plaintiff to acquire more expensive accommodation than he would otherwise have done. The method of calculating damages in such a case was discussed in *Roberts* v. *Johnstone*.[3] In that case the most important point at issue related to the costs of housing the plaintiff. Her parents had purchased a bungalow for £86,500 to replace their previous house, which had been sold for £18,000. There was no dispute that the previous house was wholly unsuitable accommodation for a person suffering from the plaintiff's severe disabilities. In making the award the Court of Appeal asserted that the additional capital cost involved in buying the new bungalow was not the correct measure of damages because this would overcompensate the plaintiff by providing a valuable additional capital asset. Two alternative methods were suggested both of which were based on the additional annual cost of providing the housing over the plaintiff's lifetime. The first method was based on the loss of income on existing capital which had to be spent in acquiring the new property. The second on the interest payable on a mortgage needed to raise the necessary capital.[4] The difficulty with these approaches is that the attempt to avoid the problem of leaving the plaintiff with a capital asset which will pass ultimately as a windfall to her estate may mean that the plaintiff's immediate needs for accommodation are met from damages which were intended to cover other items of loss and, ultimately, in the damages proving inadequate to cover the total costs incurred.[5]

2. Medical care

Section 2(4) of the Law Reform (Personal Injuries) Act 1948 permits a victim to charge a tortfeasor with the costs of private medical care: it is not open to the latter to claim that this constitutes a failure to mitigate losses because the expense could have been avoided by obtaining treatment free of charge from the National Health Service. It is commonly thought that, although this provision may have had some logic in 1948 when the Health Service was in its infancy, it is now outmoded. The Pearson Commission recommended that the rule should be reversed so that the costs of private medical care would only be recoverable if the plaintiff could show it was

---

[2] *Moriarty* v. *McCarthy* [1978] 1 W.L.R. 155.
[3] [1989] Q.B. 878, discussed Stanton, (1989) 5 P.N. 56.
[4] However, the market interest rate for such mortgages was not used because the mortgage was likely to result in the plaintiff acquiring an appreciating asset. Instead a notional rate of 2 per cent. was used.
[5] In the event, the plaintiff in *Roberts* was awarded £21,920 in relation to housing costs when the annual interest costs of funding a mortgage of £68,500 would have been £6,233. It seems unlikely that the plaintiff was overcompensated by this award.

reasonable to incur them.[6] Some commentators, however, take the view that the provision should be retained because it avoids any dispute arising over the use of private medical services when Health Service treatment would be difficult, but not wholly impossible, to obtain. In particular, it may encourage accident victims to pay for treatment such as physiotherapy which may accelerate the rate of their recovery.[7] In practice, no award will be made if the victim is in receipt of NHS care as it will be impossible to establish any loss. However, the section has the potential of producing overcompensation in circumstances in which the expenses claimed by the plaintiff are calculated according to the cost of private care but free care is subsequently obtained under the NHS.[8]

3. Expenses incurred by others

An important question of principle is whether an accident victim can include in a claim for damages, expenditure which may have already been incurred on his behalf by another. Members of families provide a great deal of support in terms of services and the purchase of items to meet the needs of accident victims. In *Donnelly* v. *Joyce*[9] the infant plaintiff suffered injuries which required special clothing and nursing services. The clothing was supplied to him free of charge by his parents and the plaintiff's mother gave up work in order to provide the nursing. The Court of Appeal held that, although the parents could have no direct claim for their losses,[10] the value of the child's claim was unaffected by the parents' actions.[11] A similar result was reached in *Schneider* v. *Eisovitch*,[12] a case in which the plaintiff's need to arrange the repatriation of the body of her husband who had been killed in an accident in France was met by a relative flying to France at his own expense to make the arrangements. These authorities calculate the value of the damages which are to be awarded according to an objective assessment of the needs created by the accident. The result is that an accident victim is provided with a sum of money which can be used to meet the expenditure incurred by the family unit as a result of the injury. It has been argued that such an award should only be made on condition that the victim undertakes to pay it over to the person who incurred the expense, but no consensus has emerged as to how such an undertaking might be enforced and it seems likely that the notion will be rejected as it is not desirable to encumber situations of family generosity with quasi-contractual claims.[13] The Pearson Commission argued that the damages should be the absolute property of the victim to dispose of as he wished and that a duty to account would be extremely difficult to enforce.[14] It may be that the best approach to this issue is to treat the third party's generosity as a non-deductible collateral benefit akin to those examples of public benevolence which have always been regarded as

---

[6] para. 342.
[7] Association of Personal Injury Lawyers (A.P.I.L.): preliminary submission to the Law Commission.
[8] A.P.I.L. has argued that there is no evidence of this happening.
[9] [1974] Q.B. 454.
[10] They would be irrecoverable as a form of "pure" economic loss.
[11] The mother's loss of earnings was used to measure the cost of providing the necessary nursing. This is almost certainly an application of the principles of mitigation of damages.
[12] [1960] 2 Q.B. 430.
[13] *Hunt* v. *Severs* [1993] 4 All E.R. 180.
[14] para. 351.

insufficient to merit a reduction in any award of damages made to an accident victim.

PARTICULAR ISSUES

Overlap

Care needs to be taken when itemising damages under separate heads to ensure that two awards are not made in respect of the same loss. A variety of arguments have been heard in this context. On occasion, a perceived overlap has almost certainly arisen from a feeling that the overall level of an award was too high.

A good example of this difficulty is provided by the judgments in *Croke* v. *Wiseman*[15] which concerned the relationship of an award for loss of earnings made to a child plaintiff, to that of one made for the cost of future care. Lord Denning argued that if a child was incapacitated and had to be cared for, for the rest of its life, it was inappropriate to make an additional award for lost earnings. The erroneous nature of this contention, based as it is, on the linguistic ambiguity of the term "future care" was fully exposed by the judgement of Griffiths L.J. An overlap exists only if the care award is calculated on the basis of providing the accident victim with accommodation in a residential home.[16] If the award merely provides nursing services the victim continues to need accommodation and the normal requirements of life such as food and heating and these fall to be met from the award for loss of earnings.

Other examples of overlap have been suggested but it seems dubious whether they should be accepted. In *Fletcher* v. *Autocar and Transporters Ltd.*[17] the Court of Appeal was of the opinion that a considerable overlap might occur between an award for loss of earnings and one of general damages for pain and suffering and loss of amenity. The court argued that if the victim would have spent a part of his earnings on the pleasures of living, the result of the accident would be a considerable saving in his living expenses. The basis for this may be questioned; it would seem to proceed on the doubtful assumption that an award for pain, suffering and loss of amenities is intended to provide alternative pleasures for the victim. The preferable view is that the greater part of such an award is an objective conventional sum based solely on the degree of physical deprivation suffered. It is perfectly open to the victim to utilise his damages in the provision of alternative, and possibly expensive, pastimes to replace those which he cannot pursue as a consequence of the accident. The dissenting judgment of Salmon L.J. seems to be correct in arguing that courts should not look at the pattern of the victim's expenditure before and after the accident and that the victim's economic and social condition should be irrelevant to the calculation of a conventional award. Salmon L.J. took the view that it was only when a court makes an upward adjustment of a conventional figure on account of the plaintiff's having suffered a loss peculiar to his case that an adjustment in the overall award is appropriate. Lord Denning M.R.'s

---

[15] [1982] 1 W.L.R. 71.

[16] In such a case all of the needs normally met from a person's earnings will be covered by the charge for staying in the home.

[17] [1968] 2 Q.B. 322.

judgment in *Smith* v. *Central Asbestos Co Ltd.*[18] contains the even more dubious suggestion that the effect of a large award of damages for loss of earnings goes some way to increasing the plaintiff's satisfactions and thus should reduce the award to be made for loss of amenities.

The Law Commission[19] rejected the argument that awards of damages should be reduced because of overlap, especially insofar as such arguments were being used to justify placing a limitation on the global sum awarded. They believed that the correct approach is that courts should simply add together the different items of loss and that a firm distinction should be retained between awards for pecuniary and non-pecuniary losses. This is what is done in practice.

Compensating benefits

As the aim of an award of damages is to compensate the accident victim for the losses resulting from the tort it is necessary to consider whether any advantages have accrued to the victim which should be offset from the losses when the damages are calculated. The overall effect of the tort on the victim forms the basis of the calculation and the tortfeasor is entitled to take advantage of any circumstances resulting from the tort which reduce the victim's overall loss. For example, in *Meah* v. *McCreamer*[20] it was accepted that the financial benefit derived from being boarded free in prison outweighed any claim for loss of earnings which might have been brought by a plaintiff who had no well established earnings and who had been imprisoned as a result of crimes which were found to have been committed as a consequence of head injuries inflicted on him by the defendant. On a similar basis the Court of Appeal has held that a claim for the basic costs[21] of caring for a child which would not have been born had the doctors treating the mother taken reasonable care to diagnose and warn of the possibility of disabilities resulting from rubella, must have offset from it the savings in such costs derived from the fact that the parents decided to abandon their plans to have more children when faced by the difficulties of raising a child with severe disabilities.[22]

An accident victim may receive a wide variety of payments and services other than tort damages which are designed to alleviate the effects of the injury. If tort damages fall to be assessed after such payments have been made it is necessary to decide whether the value of such benefits should be deducted from the damages. If a deduction is made, the benefit will reduce the tortfeasor's liability; whereas, if it is not, the victim, in effect, receives double compensation for his losses. If the damages and the benefit are correctly regarded as different techniques adopted by society for the protection of accident victims there is a strong case for avoiding double compensation as society should not waste resources in compensating accident victims twice for the same loss. The Pearson Commission took this view in relation to social security benefits paid to an accident victim.[23] The Commission believed that as such benefits and tort damages were ultimately derived from

[18] [1972] 1 Q.B. 244.
[19] Report No. 56, paras. 193–201.
[20] [1985] 1 All E.R. 367.
[21] Excluding the additional costs created by the disability.
[22] *Salih* v. *Enfield Health Authority* [1991] 3 All E.R. 400.
[23] Chap. 13.

society there should be co-ordination by means of offsetting social security benefits in full from awards of tort damages. As will be seen, this result has been achieved to a great extent, although not in the form proposed by the Commission.[24] On the other hand, if it is accepted that the general level of damages awarded by courts provides inadequate protection for accident victims[25] it is possible to contend that double compensation in fact helps to achieve an acceptable overall level of protection and that moves to eliminate it should be resisted.

Many of the most important questions of deductions are governed by statute. However, where this is not the case the issue has fallen to the courts to decide. The courts have toyed with a number of techniques designed to produce a general solution to the problem. It has been asked whether the payment was "too collateral to"[26] or "too remote from"[27] the loss to be taken into account. Attention has been paid to the sources of the money paid to the victim and to whether the intention lying behind the payment was to replace the kind of loss suffered. None of these approaches offers much constructive help and recently courts have openly acknowledged the degree of discretion vested in them by adopting the approach that such issues should be decided according to the criteria of "justice, reasonableness and policy." In recent years the courts seem to have been in favour of deducting Welfare State benefits from damages unless there are overwhelming arguments against doing so.

The results obtained under the existing law are described in the following paragraphs.

1. First party insurance

It was established as long ago as 1874 in *Bradburn* v. *Great Western Railway*[28] that payments made to a victim from insurance policies effected to protect against the risk which occurred are not to be deducted from an award of damages made in respect of that risk. Such payments derive not from the accident but from the victim's wisdom in contracting the insurance. The logic of this causation based approach may be obscure, but the result is correct. It is undesirable to create a disincentive to insurance by giving the benefits of any payments made to the tortfeasor (or his insurers). A policy of deduction would make the victim who was wise enough to insure himself a net loser as he would have spent the premiums on the policy for no return. Double recovery is an acceptable price to pay to avoid this anomaly.

2. Charitable payments, disaster funds and benevolence

Payments from such sources are non-deductible on similar reasoning to that used in relation to insurance benefits. It cannot be supposed that those giving to the fund intended their generosity to benefit the tortfeasor by reducing his liabilities.[29]

---

[24] See *post*, p. 274.
[25] This is the view of the Association of Personal Injury Lawyers. See A.P.I.L.'s preliminary submission to the Law Commission.
[26] Asquith L.J. in *Shearman* v. *Folland* [1950] 2 K.B. 43 regarded this test as easier to formulate than to apply.
[27] See Lord Pearson's dissenting speech in *Parry* v. *Cleaver* [1970] A.C. 1.
[28] (1874) L.R. 10 Ex. 1.
[29] *Redpath* v. *Belfast Railway* [1947] N.I. 167.

3. Payments by employer

An injured employee may receive payments derived from his employment in a number of forms. The problem in such cases has been to decide whether to classify such payments as a form of insurance benefit or as a continuation of pay. It is well recognised that if pay continues to be received, in whole or in part after an injury, the amount paid reduces the loss which is incurred and lessens the tortfeasor's liability to pay damages.[30]

An employee who suffers permanent disablement may receive an ill health or disability pension from the pension funds which were intended to provide for his retirement. The House of Lords in *Parry* v. *Cleaver*[31] held that such payments are not deductible from damages as they are derived from a form of insurance. This result applies even if the scheme is non-contributory on the part of the employee: the employer will be contributing and the premiums are sums which the employer is willing to find in order to obtain the employee's services. In a sense the payments are a species of deferred remuneration.[32] More recent decisions have discussed the application of *Parry* to equivalent forms of benefit derived from the employment relationship. In *Hussain* v. *New Taplow Paper Mills Ltd.*[33] the House of Lords held that payments of long term sickness benefit made under the terms of a contract of employment were deductible because they amounted to a continuation of salary. This was the case even though the employer had, at his own cost, insured his liability to make such payments by taking out a permanent health insurance policy. In *McCamley* v. *Cammell Laird Shipbuilders Ltd.*[34] the employer had adopted the slightly different approach of taking out a personal accident group policy for the benefit of the employees. The plaintiff employee who suffered an injury at work and who was unaware of the existence of the policy and had made no contributions to it, received £45,630 from the employer after that sum had been paid out under the policy. The Court of Appeal took the view that the case was not within the "insurance money" area of non-deduction as the employee had in no way contributed to the premiums, but that the payment should be regarded as an act of benevolence and be disregarded when assessing the employee's damages. This was the result even though the benefit was effected through the medium of an insurance policy. In contrast to *Hussain* the insurance policy was not a technique used to secure the payment of sick pay. There is a very fine distinction between the cases which depends on the precise method chosen by the employer to provide employees with protection against long term illness and disability.

Other forms of payment derived from employment have also received attention. A redundancy payment which is made to an employee who is selected for redundancy as a result of disabilities caused by an accident will be deducted from an award of damages for loss of earnings made in relation

---

[30] Unless the payments are made as a loan on condition that they are to be refunded from any payment of damages which is ultimately obtained. Payments of statutory sick pay are treated as a form of social security benefit.

[31] [1970] A.C. 1. See also *Smoker* v. *London Fire & Civil Defence*, *Wood* v. *National Coal Board* [1991] 2 All E.R. 449.

[32] Such payments are only to be deducted when loss of pension rights is assessed. If the effect of an accident and a premature retirement is to reduce the employee's ultimate pension, any payments in fact received will be deducted on the principle of deducting like from like.

[33] [1988] A.C. 514.

[34] [1990] 1 W.L.R. 963.

to the injuries, unless it can be shown that the employee would have been made redundant even if he had not been injured.[35]

4. Voluntarily rendered services

As we have already seen[36] the value of gratuitous services rendered to an accident victim is not deducted from an award of damages. In practice this means that a victim who has suffered no loss because the acts of others have protected him against it will be able to recover the expense of meeting the loss. It may well be that the best explanation for these results is that they are analogous to the examples of public benevolence outlined previously.

The position is more difficult if it is the tortfeasor who makes *ex gratia* payments to, or confers other benefits upon, the victim. In industrial injury cases, in which the defendant is the plaintiff's employer, it is only logical to regard such payments as being on account of damages and to reduce any award of damages ultimately made, by the value of such sums.[37] However, a different result was reached in *Hunt* v. *Severs*.[38] In that case the plaintiff had been injured in a road accident caused by the negligence of the defendant who subsequently married the plaintiff and provided her with some of the care which her injuries necessitated. The defendant's argument that he should not be held liable to pay damages in respect of the cost of those services as this would mean that he was meeting those costs twice was rejected. Voluntary services rendered to the plaintiff from motives of affection were to be regarded as adventitious benefits which were, for policy reasons, not to be regarded as diminishing the plaintiff's loss. The reasoning of the court seems to have been based on a desire to avoid creating an incentive for a plaintiff to purchase the necessary services in the market or to enter into a formal contract for them as opposed to accepting support on a voluntary basis.

5. Income tax

Although the decision in *British Transport Commission* v. *Gourley*[39] excludes consideration of the question of income tax from most calculations of damages, the working of the Pay As You Earn (PAYE) system of income tax may produce savings in the tax levied on the victim's surviving income which should be deducted from damages awarded to replace lost income. Thus the value of a tax rebate received by an employee who is off work as a result of an accident[40] or a tax holiday enjoyed on his return to work[41] are to be deducted.

6. Deducting state benefits

In practice, the primary source of payments for the accident victim is the social security system. The Pearson Commission[42] recommended that the full value of State benefits should be offset against equivalent awards of damages. By transferring some of the financial consequences of a tort from

[35] *Colledge* v. *Bass, Mitchells & Butlers Ltd.* [1988] 1 All E.R. 536.
[36] *Ante*, p. 268.
[37] *Jenner* v. *Allen West* [1959] 1 W.L.R. 554.
[38] [1993] 4 All E.R. 180.
[39] [1956] A.C. 185. See *ante*, p. 256.
[40] *Hartley* v. *Sandholme Iron* [1974] 3 W.L.R. 445.
[41] *Brayson* v. *Wilmott-Breeden* [1976] C.L.Y. 682.
[42] Chap. 13.

the tortfeasor to the state this would be liable to reduce the deterrent value of a tort claim. However, when offsetting was finally introduced by the Social Security Act 1989 the approach adopted in the case of substantial claims was the radically different one of allowing the D.S.S. to recoup the value of benefits paid from the tortfeasor. In effect, the tortfeasor pays the full cost of the accident and indemnifies the D.S.S. for any expenditure it has incurred. Two sets of rules, which depend on the overall value of the money payable[43] to the victim, now govern the relationship of social security benefits to any award of tort damages for personal injuries.[44]

If the award of damages is for a sum of more than £2,500, section 22 of the Social Security Act 1989 requires the person who pays the compensation, be it the tortfeasor or his insurance company, to repay to the Department of Social Security the value of any "relevant benefits"[45] which have been paid to the victim. Before damages are paid a certificate must be obtained from the D.S.S. detailing the amount of benefit which has been paid to the victim. This obligation applies to all court awards and out of court settlements.[46] The total amount of damages payable is calculated without reference to the benefits. However, on receipt of the certificate there is an obligation to deduct the amount of "relevant benefits" paid or payable from the sum to be paid to the victim and to pay the deducted sum to the D.S.S.

These recoupment provisions apply to all payments of "relevant" social security benefits[47] which are made within the "relevant period." The definition of the "relevant period"[48] limits the recoupment to benefits paid in the five years from the day on which the accident or injury occurred.[49] However, the "relevant period" will be terminated before the end of the five year period by the tortfeasor making payment in final discharge of his liability. Any relevant benefits paid or likely to be paid, after the end of the relevant period are not deducted from the damages.[50] In this respect, the statute accepts the possibility of an award of damages in respect of future loss being payable in addition to benefits and a plaintiff who is to suffer a continuing loss is given an incentive to obtain a final settlement of his claim quickly in order to shorten the relevant period applied to his case.

The full value of the benefits certified as having been paid is deducted from the money payable by the tortfeasor, irrespective of whether the sum payable represents a head of damages equivalent to the form of benefit paid. This means, for example, that payments of invalidity benefit can be deducted from an award of damages for pain and suffering. In addition, a full, not a proportionate, deduction of all benefits paid is made even if the damages have been reduced on account of contributory negligence. These rules may

---

[43] Any sums payable as costs are excluded from the calculation as a result of an amendment introduced by the Social Security Act 1990, Sched. 1, para. 1.

[44] Different rules apply to cases under the Fatal Accidents Act 1976.

[45] See note 47.

[46] Including interim payments.

[47] "Relevant benefits" are defined by Reg. 2 of the Social Security (Recoupment) Regulations 1990 S.I. 1990 No. 322. All of the main social security benefits which are likely to be paid to those who suffer personal injuries, including Statutory Sick Pay which is not administered by the D.S.S., are covered. Invalid Care Allowance, which is payable to a carer rather than to the person receiving care is not included.

[48] s. 22(3).

[49] In the case of a disease, the five year period runs from the date of the first claim of a relevant benefit in consequence of the disease.

[50] s. 22(6).

seem anomalous but bring a degree of simplicity to the operation of the system. For example, the fact that the plaintiff's contributory negligence has no effect on the amount deducted removes a source of potential dispute by allowing the parties to reach a settlement to agree the sum which is to be paid in settlement of a claim but not the percentage deduction on account of contributory negligence which has been made in arriving at that sum.

These rules have attracted considerable criticism from those organisations which have been arguing that the current level of damages awards is too low.[51] The rules are condemned for introducing anomalies, for making it difficult to achieve a settlement and are regarded generally as benefitting the Exchequer at the expense of victims by removing the prospect of some degree of double compensation for the same loss. On the other hand, the Pearson Commission's view that both social security benefits and tort damages are ultimately derived from society at large and that it is unsatisfactory for society to be called on to pay twice for the same loss is unanswerable, unless it is felt that the levels of benefit provided under each head are unacceptably low and that an adequate level of compensation can only be achieved by accepting a degree of double counting. If double counting is unsatisfactory the exclusion of awards of damages of £2,500 or less, payments made under the Fatal Accidents Act and payments of "relevant benefits" paid after the "relevant period" has finished fails to remove the problem totally. The policy adopted by the judiciary before the enactment of section 22 of applying a full deduction from damages of all benefits which were not subject to express statutory provision is more attractive, but achieves no saving in public expenditure. At the time that section 22 was enacted it was estimated that recoupment of benefits would save the D.S.S. approximately £55 million every year.

In the case of awards of £2,500 or less, section 2(1) of the Law Reform (Personal Injuries) Act 1948 applies. This provides that damages[52] are to be reduced by the value of half of the "relevant benefits"[53] received by the victim in the first five years from the date of the accident. In such a case there is a degree of over compensation of the victim, the tortfeasor's liability receives a subsidy from the benefits paid and the D.S.S. is unable to obtain any recoupment of its expenditure from the tortfeasor. This provision creates a considerable incentive for the parties to settle their claim at £2,500 even if this is less than its full value and is a further example of the law favouring a person who suffers a minor injury. Section 2(1) is exhaustive as to the deduction of these benefits. In the unlikely event that any benefits are paid in such a case after the expiry of the five year period no deduction will be made.[54]

Savings made as a result of the victim receiving free care in a hospital or other institution maintained at public expense are regulated by section 5 of the Administration of Justice Act 1982. Such savings are deducted from an award for loss of earnings. The effects of this vary. The victim who has a home and family to support is unlikely to achieve savings beyond the cost of his own food and other personal needs. Savings on such items as the cost of

[51] See A.P.I.L.'s preliminary submission to the Law Commission.
[52] The operation of this provision is no longer confined to damages for loss of earnings.
[53] The same benefits as are subject to the recoupment provisions if the award exceeds £2,500.
[54] *Jackman* v. *Corbett* [1988] Q.B. 154 a case decided at a time when s. 2(1) applied to all awards not just to those of less than £2,500.

transport to work will not be included as they are not attributable to the victim's maintenance at public expense. More significant deductions may be made if the victim has saved the costs of lodgings or rented accommodation. Awards to children who receive long term residential care at the public expense are drastically curtailed.

Survival of injury awards

With one exception, all heads of personal injury damages survive the death of the plaintiff to benefit his estate. The exception is a claim for damages for lost earnings in the lost years.[55] This exception was introduced in 1982 to remove problems which had arisen as a result of this head of damage covering the same area of loss as an award made under the Fatal Accidents Act.

FATAL ACCIDENTS

If a tort causes a death two heads of claim may be available under the Fatal Accidents Act 1976: a dependency claim for financial losses and a bereavement claim for non-financial losses. Such claims are personal to the claimants and are distinct from any claim for personal injury damages which survives the victim's death to benefit his estate. The dependency claim is, in effect, a statutory exception to the rule which bars recovery of damages for pure economic losses.[56] However, as claims under the Fatal Accidents Act are only available if the victim had an action available to him at the moment of his death and as they are subject to any defences which would have been available against the deceased, they assume, to some extent, the appearance of a derivative action.

Dependency claims

1. Categories of dependant

The categories of person who may claim for loss of dependency under the Act are defined by section 1(3). Inclusion in the list does not automatically entitle an individual to recover and the fact that the person was actually dependent upon the deceased must also be established. On the other hand, the fact of dependency will not allow recovery by a person who does not fall within one of the statutory categories. A person, such as the manager of a pop singer or sports star, may be dependent on the other's earnings because of a relationship based on contract. However, such a relationship will not suffice; the Act confines recovery of financial losses to family relations of the deceased, but does include a wide range of such relations. The persons who may count as dependants are: the wife or husband or former wife or husband of the deceased (the class of former spouses extends to marriages which have been annulled, declared void or dissolved); any person who was living with the deceased in the same household immediately before the date of the death and had been so living for at least two years before that date and was living during that time as the husband or wife of the deceased; any parent or other

---

[55] Law Reform (Miscellaneous Provisions) Act 1934, s. 2(a) as amended.
[56] See Chap. 16.

ascendant of the deceased; any person who was treated by the deceased as his parent; any child or other descendant of the deceased (this includes stepchildren and illegitimate children); any person (not being a child of the deceased) who, in the case of any marriage to which the deceased was at any time a party, was treated by the deceased as a child of the family in relation to that marriage and any person who is, or is the issue of, a brother, sister, uncle or aunt of the deceased.

An award for loss of dependency under the Fatal Accidents Act is confined to consequences which result from the relationship recognised by the Act. Usually the application of this rule is obvious, but care is needed in cases in which relatives have engaged together in a joint business enterprise as the losses caused by the family relationship will have to be distinguished from those stemming from the business. The leading decision is *Burgess* v. *Florence Nightingale Hospital for Gentlewomen*.[57] In that case the deceased wife and the plaintiff husband had worked together as professional dancing partners. The wife's death resulted in a considerable drop in the husband's earnings as well as the cessation of the wife's earnings. The former sum was held irrecoverable as it represented losses based on the business rather than the personal relationship: it would have afflicted the plaintiff had his deceased partner not been his wife. However, the position was different in relation to the wife's own earnings. The husband was dependent upon these to the extent that they were used for the purposes of general family expenditure and he could recover this loss in a dependency claim. A business relationship may, on the other hand, be a device to transfer money to the spouse in a tax efficient manner. If this is the case, the reality is that what at first sight seem to be earnings are, in fact, derived from the marital relationship. In *Malyon* v. *Plumer*[58] the wife had been paid a salary by her husband's business for which she worked on a part-time basis. The salary exceeded the value of the services which she provided to the business and the excess could only be explained as being derived from the couple's marital relationship. When the income ceased on the husband's death the excess over the value of the work done formed part of the wife's dependency.

2. Assessing the dependency

A dependency claim is confined to the financial consequences of a death. These cover earnings spent on the dependants, savings made for their future use and the value of services rendered to them. The full compensation principle requires that non-essential items, such as holidays, are included in the calculation of the dependency.[59] This gives rise to the criticism that the Act allows the dependants of wealthy persons to be maintained at the standard of living to which they had become accustomed.[60] Losses other than a deceased person's earnings can be included in the calculation if they are capable of being translated into financial terms. The death of a non-earning spouse justifies an award under the Act, as any unpaid services from which that person's family benefitted need to be replaced and are capable of

---

[57] [1955] 1 Q.B. 349.
[58] [1964] 1 Q.B. 330.
[59] *K.* v. *J.M.P. Ltd.* [1976] Q.B. 85.
[60] The treatment of young widows by the social security system is much less favourable to them (see p. 288). Widowers, who can receive considerable protection on account of a dependency on their wife's earnings or services receive no equivalent protection from the social security system unless they become eligible for income support on their wife's death.

valuation: the cost of employing a housekeeper to provide these services is likely to be significant. The case of *Hay* v. *Hughes*,[61] which concerned the deaths of an employed husband and his non-employed wife, is a good illustration of this insofar as the multiplicands chosen to reflect the value of the services lost to the dependants resulting from the wife's death was only £100 a year less than that used in relation to the loss of the husband's earnings. The decision in *Regan* v. *Williamson*[62] took this process a step further. The judge declined to limit an award for the death of a non-employed wife and mother to the cost of providing for a housekeeper's services. He argued that the fact that the mother would have been available to her children for a greater number of hours per day than a housekeeper and was likely from motives of love and affection to have provided a greater level of services was an element which was capable of estimation in financial terms and which justified a significant increase in the award. Small awards have been made to the parents of a deceased child for the loss of the chance of a dependency in their old age.

Dependency claims under the Fatal Accidents Act are calculated according to the general principles relating to financial losses in personal injury cases. Different multipliers may be appropriate to account for the different periods over which the dependencies of wife and children are expected to run. A significant difference between dependency and personal injury claims is that the multiplier is calculated from the date of the death rather than the trial because the uncertainties as to what would have happened to the deceased run from the date of the death.[63]

A family's expenditure has to be apportioned between sums spent exclusively on its individual members and those which support the family unit as a whole by the provision, for instance, of housing, transport and heating. In the case of a family which consisted before the husband's death of a husband, wife, and two children, it is incorrect to divide the husband's income into four portions and to allocate one of these to each of the survivors. The survivors do not live in a quarter of the house; they live in the whole house. The correct approach is to assess the proportion of the earnings that was spent exclusively on each member of the family unit and the sum which supported general family expenditure. The only element of the deceased's earnings which is excluded from the award under the Fatal Accidents Act is the money which was spent exclusively on the deceased or to benefit persons outside the family unit (for instance, if regular contributions were made to charity). Support exists in recent cases for the use of conventional percentages to reflect the division of a family's income.[64] However, it is submitted that this approach runs the risk of losing sight of the different patterns of expenditure which may occur in different families. The dependency should vary according to factors such as whether both partners were working, the

---

[61] [1975] 2 Q.B. 790.

[62] [1976] 2 All E.R. 241.

[63] *Graham* v. *Dodds* [1983] 1 W.L.R. 808. However, in practice the uncertainties which are relevant to the calculation relate to both the victim and the dependant. If there has been a long delay in bringing the case to trial the latter uncertainties will have been reduced and it seems to be the case that this factor will merit an increased multiplier. *Corbett* v. *Barking, Havering & Brentwood Health Authority* [1991] 2 Q.B. 408.

[64] Webster J. in *Robertson* v. *Lestrange* [1985] 1 Q.B. 950 spoke of the conventional apportionment in a normal case as being 75 per cent. while the children were dependent and 66.6 per cent. thereafter.

amounts of their respective incomes and the resulting free income. The existence of children will obviously tend to increase the proportion of income which is included in the dependency. However, a couple's intention at the date of the husband's death to start a family will not increase a wife's dependency.[65] The court will apportion the global sum between the various dependants. The sums representing joint family expenditure will be allocated to any surviving parent, who will bear the responsibility for making the payments. If, however, as occurred in *Hay* v. *Hughes*,[66] the children are left with no surviving parents, it will be correct to allocate the sums to their claim.

It is impossible to state a universal rule for the correct method of calculating the value of lost services. As with the calculation of expenses in personal injury cases, everything will ultimately depend on whether the plaintiff can establish that the particular method adopted to meet the loss was reasonable in terms of mitigation. Commonly, the employment of a housekeeper or nanny at commercial rates will be deemed to be reasonable, but at other times a parent's or other relative's loss of earnings may constitute the appropriate measure.[67] If the cost of employing a nanny is adopted as the appropriate measure of damage in a claim for loss of a parent's services, the award must reflect the fact that the child's need for the mother's (or nanny's) services will decrease as it gets older.[68]

The value of a dependency is assessed according to the facts of the particular case. The appropriate award to make in respect of the services received by a child from its deceased mother will therefore be reduced if the mother's services were restricted by the fact that she worked.[69] If a married couple had separated at the date of the death or if there is evidence of instability in the relationship which might affect the level of support which was likely to be provided, a reduced[70] or no[71] award may be appropriate. If a claim is made[72] by a man or woman who was not married to the deceased, section 3(3A) directs the court to take into account, along with all other relevant factors, the fact that the dependant would have had no enforceable claim to financial support from the deceased as a result of the relationship.

3. Compensating benefits

The treatment of compensating benefits arising from a death is relatively simple because section 4 of the Fatal Accidents Act adopts a general policy of non-deduction:

> "In assessing damages in respect of a person's death in an action under this Act, benefits which have accrued or will or may accrue to any person from his estate or otherwise as a result of his death shall be disregarded."

The word "benefit" clearly excludes from deduction all social security benefits such as the various forms of widow's benefits, which become payable on death. This reflects a policy which is at variance to that favoured

---

[65] *Malone* v. *Rowan* [1984] 3 All E.R. 402.
[66] [1975] 2 Q.B. 790.
[67] *Mehmet* v. *Perry* [1977] 2 All E.R. 529.
[68] *Spittle* v. *Bunney* [1988] 1 W.L.R. 844.
[69] *Creswell* v. *Eaton* [1991] 1 W.L.R. 1113, the mother's earnings may well counterbalance this reduction.
[70] *Gray* v. *Barr* [1971] 2 Q.B. 554; *Stanley* v. *Saddique* [1992] 1 Q.B. 330.
[71] *Davies* v. *Taylor* [1974] A.C. 207.
[72] Under subs. 1(3)(aa).

in the case of personal injury claims. Somewhat surprisingly section 4 has survived the introduction of recoupment by the D.S.S. from tortfeasors of the value of social security benefits paid to personal injury victims.[73]

Section 4 also makes non-deductible a wide range of other payments which may be made on a death such as insurance moneys, sums paid to a widow from her deceased husband's former pension fund[74] and benefits accruing to dependants from their having inherited the deceased's estate. The result in the case of inherited assets is logical in most cases as possessions and capital owned by the deceased prior to death would have been likely to have been available to support the dependants before the death had the need arisen and there is little financial value in the transfer of title to the dependants. However, the result is more questionable when the estate includes sums owed to the deceased as damages in a personal injuries claim and surviving under the Law Reform (Miscellaneous Provisions) Act 1934. This problem is limited by the fact that awards of damages for bereavement[75] and for loss of earnings in the lost years, do not survive the victim's death. As a result, if an award of damages for loss of earnings survives to benefit the estate it will relate solely to the period of the victim's life before his death and there will be no overlap with any award for loss of dependency made under the Fatal Accident Act.[76] However, a surprising result of the present wording of section 4 is that an award made for pain, suffering and loss of amenity is not deducted from a Fatal Accidents Act award.[77] It is difficult to justify the receipt by the dependants of a sum assessed according to the degree of physical injury sustained by a victim who is now, *ex hypothesi*, dead. In the case of a catastrophic injury, as exemplified by the *West* v. *Shephard* line of authority,[78] the result further accentuates an already unacceptable result.

Changes in a dependant's family status following a death present the law with considerable difficulties. Such changes clearly do not constitute a benefit resulting from the death and are unaffected by section 4. The prospect of a widow remarrying, and indeed, the actual fact that she has remarried, is specifically excluded by section 3(3) of the Act from being considered when her dependency on her deceased husband is assessed. This provision allows a court to avoid the task of assessing a widow's remarriage prospects; but it can produce substantial overcompensation. The anomaly is accentuated by the fact that a widower's remarriage prospects remain relevant when assessing his dependency upon his deceased wife and a widow's remarriage prospects may be in issue when the value of her childrens' dependency upon her deceased husband is being assessed.[79] It is difficult to see how a totally satisfactory solution to the conflicting issues underlying this problem can be achieved.

A child's claim under the Fatal Accidents Act in relation to the costs of care is unlikely to be affected by the fact that others have undertaken responsibility on a voluntary basis for the provision of the services which the

---

[73] See *ante*, p. 274.
[74] *Pidduck* v. *Eastern Scottish Omnibuses Ltd.* [1990] 1 W.L.R. 993.
[75] See *post*, p. 282.
[76] *Murray* v. *Shuter* [1976] Q.B. 972.
[77] Such sums were deducted in full prior to the amendments to s. 4 introduced by the Administration of Justice Act 1982 and it may well be that the change was an unintended effect of the modifications introduced by that Act.
[78] See *ante*, p. 255.
[79] *Thompson* v. *Price* [1973] Q.B. 838.

deceased parent would have provided. The cases decided on this point are not, however, entirely consistent in their approach. It was established in *Hay* v. *Hughes*[80] that no deduction is to be made if the child merely receives care and support from relatives as an act of gratuitous generosity. A policy of making an objective assessment of the loss and of not deducting the value of voluntarily rendered services applies in such cases. In that case the plaintiff children, whose parents had been killed in an accident, were allowed to recover the costs of their future care, although they had been cared for since the accident by a grandmother who stated that she intended to continue to care for them whatever the outcome of their tort claim. The grandmother's services were held to derive, not from the death of the parents, but from her personal generosity; they did not constitute a benefit resulting from the death. In *Stanley* v. *Saddique*[81] the Court of Appeal achieved the same result in a different way by holding that a "benefit" had been obtained by the child from its being absorbed into a new family unit consisting of its father and stepmother and that this benefit was non-deductible as a result of section 4. Most recently, in *Hayden* v. *Hayden*[82] the Court of Appeal had the opportunity to review these authorities in the context of a case in which the defendant, who was the husband of the deceased, had given up work after the road accident in which she had died to look after the plaintiff child. The court followed the approach adopted in *Hay* and held that the services provided by the father were not a result of the death. Section 4 was therefore not regarded as relevant. McCowan L.J. stated that:

> "there is to be no reduction in the amount of damages which would otherwise be awarded to take account of care voluntarily provided in substitution for the deceased's motherly services. That principle cannot . . . be affected by whether or not the person providing the care was the tortfeasor."

A different result applies when the care provided to the child is matter of legal obligation, as opposed to generosity. In *Watson* v. *Willmott*[83] the care and financial support provided by adoptive parents was set off against the value of the child's dependency on its deceased parent. The result of this case is that a child's financial position will be greatly improved if adoption does not take place, at least until after the Fatal Accidents Act award has been calculated.

It would seem to be incorrect to take account of a surviving wife's earning capacity when assessing her dependency upon her deceased husband. She possessed that capacity before her husband's death. It follows that if she decides to return to work after the death her earnings should be left out of account. This approach was adopted in *Howitt* v. *Heads*.[84] However, the decision of the Court of Appeal in *Cookson* v. *Knowles*[85] seems to require the opposite result if the widow was working before the death and increased her earnings after it. It is suggested that the statements made in that case need to be confined to the particular facts; that is, to a situation in which the husband and wife were in effect indulging in joint employment. In such a case the combined earnings do not represent the value of the dependency and any

[80] [1975] 2 Q.B. 790.
[81] [1992] 1 Q.B. 330.
[82] [1992] 1 W.L.R. 986.
[83] [1991] 1 Q.B. 140.
[84] [1973] Q.B. 64.
[85] [1977] Q.B. 913.

losses in the wife's earnings do not flow from the personal relationship, but from the business one. *Cookson* should not be read as authority for reducing a wife's dependency as a result of her transferring to full-time from part-time work following her husband's death.[86]

Funeral expenses

Damages in respect of funeral expenses incurred by dependants of the deceased are recoverable under section 3(5) of the Fatal Accidents Act.

Bereavement

Section 1A of the Fatal Accidents Act allows an award of damages for bereavement. This is recognition of the non-pecuniary losses which result from a death.[87] The award is only available to two categories of person[88] damaged by a tortiously caused death: the husband or wife of the deceased and the parents of a deceased unmarried minor.[89] A Pearson Commission recommendation that it should also be available to children in respect of the death of either parent was rejected for several reasons: first, because the fixed sum might have to be divided between a parent and several children and could thus become a very small figure and secondly, because any sum awarded to such a claimant would be likely to be swamped by a much larger award for financial losses. Neither argument seems wholly convincing and the second one would justify denying the award to almost all spouses. The historical explanation for the restricted form of the award is undoubtedly that it was introduced by a Lord Chancellor who had no sympathy with the philosophy which lay behind it. He felt that no sum of money could provide compensation for bereavement and he therefore chose to adopt the narrower of the two sets of recommendations which had been made.[90] This attitude is by no means accepted by all commentators.[91] In practice, the bereavement award will be the only damages which are payable in the case of the death of a young person and there is a vocal body of opinion which holds that the level of the award represents an insulting recompense for the death of a close relation and that the cut off at the eighteenth birthday can produce unacceptable anomalies. To a great extent these arguments seems to be based on the "vindication" approach to tort liability[92] and one wonders whether any sum of money could be awarded which would not be criticised as inadequate.

The bereavement award is a fixed sum of £7,500.[93] When both parents are claimants the award is divided equally between them. The award does not survive for the benefit of the plaintiff's estate. As a result, if husband and wife

---

[86] However, *Cookson* was interpreted in this way in *Dodds* v. *Dodds* [1978] Q.B. 543.

[87] In practice, the award replaced the old award of damages for loss of expectation of life which, when it survived for the benefit of the victim's estate, achieved much the same purpose indirectly.

[88] F.A.A 1976, s. 1A(2).

[89] If the child was illegitimate the award is made to the mother.

[90] Law Commission Report No. 56 rather than Pearson.

[91] A.P.I.L.'s preliminary submission to the Law Commission contains a number of proposals for increasing the value of bereavement awards and for making them more widely available.

[92] *Ante*, p. 17.

[93] It was originally fixed in 1982 at £3,500. Power is given to the Lord Chancellor to increase it. A.P.I.L., in its preliminary submission to the Law Commission, has contended that it should be increased to £25,000 and inflation linked.

are both involved in a road accident and both die from their injuries, the fact that one outlives the other for a short period of time will not confer the value of a bereavement award on the estate of the person who is the last to die.

DAMAGES FOR INJURY AND DEATH: AN ASSESSMENT

It can be argued that too much attention has been devoted to assessing the ability of tort damages to meet the stated aims of the tort system, such as achieving full compensation of the financial losses suffered by personal injury victims and that too little attention has been paid to debating whether those aims should be pursued.[94] For example, a great deal of attention has been devoted to debating the adequacy of lump sum awards and complex alternative techniques designed to achieve full compensation for accident victims who suffer long term disability, in spite of the fact that it has been estimated[95] that the Pearson Commission's proposal to introduce periodic payments of damages would only have been the appropriate form of award in approximately 600 cases a year.

There can be no doubt that the fact that tort has remained committed to the goal of full compensation has allowed it to deal with forms of loss which other compensation systems, such as social security benefits, cannot reach. Non-pecuniary losses such as pain and suffering; partial earnings losses; the costs of care; protection of widowers and compensation for bereavement receive far more generous treatment from tort than from social security. The system's commitment to full earnings relation means that the pre-accident financial commitments of victims should be protected. But, on the other hand, tort can be criticised for devoting inordinate attention to the small number of the disabled who are fortunate to be able to pursue a tort claim to success and that the commitment to full compensation produces unacceptable results such as the full financial protection accorded to the dependants (and particularly the widow) of the millionaire. Tort claims for small amounts of non-pecuniary losses amount to little more than pleasant windfalls to the successful claimants who will generally be fully recovered by the time the damages are paid. If tort is to be regarded as one of the responses made by society to the problem presented by accidents and the disabled, there are strong arguments for saying that society's resources can be better directed; that tort should cease to be the only compensation system which does not cap the compensation awarded[96]; that measures should be taken to eliminate small claims and that those with high incomes should be encouraged to protect themselves by first party insurance.[97]

---

[94] Atiyah's *Accidents, Compensation and the Law* is a notable exception to this criticism.

[95] Atiyah *op. cit.* p. 120.

[96] In fact it does do this in the area of transport accidents. See p. 241 for a discussion of the capped strict liability tort remedy in the case of persons injured in the course of civil aviation.

[97] It would, in any case, be illogical for such a person not to protect himself and his family in this way in view of the variety of non-tortious circumstances which might damage his income.

Chapter Thirteen

Non-tortious Protection for the Accident Victim

This chapter will consider the variety of ways in which accident victims can obtain compensation for, or protection against, their losses without having to pursue a tort claim.

PAYMENTS DERIVED FROM EMPLOYERS

Benefits payable under the terms of the contract of employment play a significant role in the provision of financial benefits for accident victims. It is estimated that approximately 90 per cent. of employees are protected by some form of non-contributory occupational sick pay scheme and that approximately 1 million accident victims receive such payments each year.[1] The Pearson Commission statistics[2] showed that £125 million was paid to accident victims annually under the terms of occupational sick pay schemes. This sum, which would be significantly higher today, represented approximately five-eighths of the money paid by the tort system to such victims.

In general, occupational sick pay is most significant in protecting employees against short term income loss. The great majority of persons in full-time employment are protected by occupational sick pay schemes and although the details of such schemes vary it is common to find that they maintain employees on full salary for a period, less any statutory sick pay which is payable,[3] and then provide for a lower level of benefit[4] for a further period. The qualification conditions and the periods for which such payments are made vary significantly between different schemes. It is well recognised that white-collar employees tend to be provided with better protection than their blue collar colleagues and the available evidence suggests that men are better protected in this regard than women.[5]

Although occupational sick pay is the most significant benefit provided by employers which may assist the accident victim, it is not the only one. The

---

[1] Report of the Review Body on Civil Justice, Cm. 394 (1988), para. 391.
[2] para. 141.
[3] The arrival of statutory sick pay as the basic protection for short term absence from work caused by illness produced a greater degree of integration between State and employer provided benefits.
[4] Commonly half pay, which is likely to be topped up by State benefits.
[5] Pearson, para. 138.

role of occupational pension schemes is also important in providing coverage for long term disability and sickness. The majority of modern pension schemes make some provision for a disability pension for those who are forced to retire early for such reasons and invariably provide for a widow's pension in the case of death. Some employers also make permanent health insurance or insurance against the costs of taking private medical treatment available to their employers at favourable rates.[6]

INSURANCE PAYMENTS

First party insurance under which the potential victim of an accident buys insurance protection provides a significant degree of protection to accident victims. It has been estimated that approximately 250,000 accident victims benefit from private insurance payments each year.[7] In theory, first party insurance should be preferable to a liability system of compensation underpinned by third party insurance as a method of providing financial protection for accident victims. Many of the overheads involved in a third party system are avoided and the victim is the person best placed to assess the value of the insurance which needs to be bought. In addition, payments made under such a policy are less likely to be reduced on account of minor acts of misconduct on the part of the injured person. However, first party insurance is not a comprehensive answer in practice as it is purchased on a voluntary basis whereas third party insurance is compulsory in the case of the creators of certain risks. In addition, it seems certain that the amount of such cover as is purchased is often insufficient to provide the level of protection which is provided by tort and social security benefits. It is a rather strange feature of the present accident compensation system that people tend to buy first party insurance to protect their property, such as their cars and houses, but not their incomes. It is unclear whether the role of social security, sick pay and tort in providing such protection is the reason for or the consequence of this failure.

There are four types of first party insurance policy which may provide protection against the financial consequences of an injury or death. Life assurance is a familiar form of policy which provides protection in the form of lump sum payments and annuities to the dependants of a deceased. It is a form of policy which is widely purchased, in part, because it is used as a savings medium. Personal accident insurance may pay either lump sums or a pension in the event of the insured suffering a particular injury, this is commonly confined to serious specified injuries. Insurance of this kind is often marketed as a component of motor or holiday insurance. Private health insurance will enable a person to pay for medical care received outside of the National Health Service. Permanent health insurance which protects a person's income in the event of inability to work as a result of illness or injury, has not proved to be very successful because of its cost.

It is not entirely clear how extensive a role is played by first party insurance in the protection of accident victims. The Pearson Commission's estimate that in 1977 personal accident policies alone were paying approximately £50

[6] Group schemes are likely to be available at cheaper rates than an individual could obtain.
[7] Report of the Review Body on Civil Justice, Cm. 394 (1988), para. 391.

million a year to accident victims suggests that the role is substantial.[8] However, the Commission also found[9] that only 7 per cent. of accident victims had received benefits from first party insurance and that the amounts paid to these policy holders were small.

Social Security Benefits for the Accident Victim

The protection of accident victims is only one of the roles of the social security benefits provided by the Welfare State.[10] Benefits also exist to protect those who are vulnerable financially as a result of illness, unemployment or retirement. However, such benefits do play a significant role in providing protection to accident victims. Indeed, they have a strong claim to be regarded as the primary form of personal injury accident compensation.[11] It is estimated that approximately 1,800,000 accident victims are new claimants of social security benefits every year.[12] In terms of the amount of money paid to victims, social security benefits outperform tort damages; they pay more money to victims[13] and, in doing this, consume fewer resources in overheads. They adopt a technique which pays money automatically to those accident victims who qualify for them irrespective of the cause of their disability. Applications for benefit are determined as a matter of entitlement by the Department of Social Security with the possibility of appeals being made to tribunals and then to the Social Security Commissioners. As a result accident victims are freed from the hazards and expenses of litigation. The social security system can also offer successful claimants who suffer long-term disablement regularly paid pensions which are uprated annually in line with inflation.[14] The Pearson Commission commented[15] that advocates of the introduction of a no-fault system of accident compensation commonly failed to appreciate that the social security system already plays an extensive role of this kind and that even well informed commentators tended to underestimate the capitalised value of the inflation protected periodic payments available from the system.[16] What social security benefits do not do is attempt to pursue the ideal of full compensation; they provide a basic floor of financial protection rather than seeking to give a total indemnity against all

---

[8] The figure was approximately 25 per cent. of the sums paid by the tort system to all tort victims. However, by definition it excludes payments in respect of deaths which would be included in the figure for tort. It is also likely that certain forms of permanent health policies, in particular mortgage protection policies, have become more popular in the intervening years.

[9] para. 154.

[10] The Pearson Commission estimated that only 6 per cent. of social security expenditure was directed to accident victims.

[11] The Pearson Commission took this view. See para. 275 they are "quick, certain and inexpensive to administer, and . . . already cover a majority of the injured."

[12] Report of the Review Body on Civil Justice, Cm. 394 (1988), para. 391. Approximately 340,000 tort claims are lodged each year by accident victims.

[13] The Pearson Commission (para. 44) estimated that in 1977/8 social security expenditure on accident victims was double that of tort and was payable to seven times the number of beneficiaries.

[14] See Social Security Act 1986, s. 63 and Ogus & Barendt, *The Law of Social Security* (3rd ed.), pp. 379–381.

[15] para. 176.

[16] para. 182.

losses. Only those benefits which play a significant role in the provision of support for accident victims will be described in this section.[17]

There are three forms of benefit which may be relevant to accident victims. The standard forms of benefit which cover short- and long-term earnings losses, death benefits and expenses are derived from national insurance ideas and, for the most part, still make eligibility depend on the claimant[18] having insured himself by making an appropriate number of National Insurance contributions. The second form of benefit is confined to the victims of industrial accidents. This is a specialised area which at one time offered higher levels of benefit to such victims. Although many of the advantages given to the industrially injured have been removed in recent years, one major area, disablement benefit, survives. The third area of benefit is the means tested safety net provided by income support, family credit and housing benefits; this is designed to ensure that nobody falls below the poverty line.

Statutory sick pay

Statutory Sick Pay (S.S.P.), which was introduced by the Social Security and Housing Benefits Act 1982, has replaced sickness benefit[19] as the main protection for employees against the financial consequences of short-term illness and injury. The administration of the benefit is the responsibility of the employer rather than of the D.S.S. The introduction of the benefit transferred administrative, not financial, responsibility to employers as they were entitled to deduct their expenditure on the benefit in full from their liability to pay national insurance contributions.[20]

In form S.S.P. appears more closely related to payments under an occupational sick pay scheme than to a social security benefit. It is administered and paid by the employer and is subject to the deduction of normal income tax and national insurance contributions. It is paid for up to 28 weeks at one of two rates according to the earnings level of the claimant. The rate payable does not vary according to the claimant's marital status and no additions are payable in respect of dependent children. The fact that the benefit is payable for all sickness arising after the commencement of work means that it is more readily available than the old sickness benefit[21] and the many occupational sick pay schemes which require a minimum period of service before benefits become payable.

Invalidity benefits

The standard invalidity pension is only available to those who have satisfied certain contribution conditions. Such a pension is a long-term benefit which becomes payable to a person incapacitated from work as a

---

[17] Retirement pensions, unemployment benefit and child benefit (including one-parent benefit) are the main benefits which are not described here.

[18] Or possibly their spouse.

[19] Sickness benefit is still payable to those persons who have the requisite contribution conditions, but who have exhausted their entitlement to S.S.P. The usual example of this is a person who has had successive illnesses in the course of a year.

[20] But see s. 1(1) of the Statutory Sick Pay Act 1991 which restricts the sum recouped by larger employers to 80 per cent. of the payments made.

[21] Which was subject to contribution conditions.

result of illness or disease from the time when S.S.P. ceases. It is payable on an indefinite basis until retirement age.[22] A flat rate of benefit is payable, with additional payments if the claimant has dependants. An additional component, called invalidity allowance, is paid as a flat rate addition to these sums; the rate of this addition varies according to the age of the claimant when first incapacitated.

The contribution conditions applicable to invalidity pensions mean that children and non-employed persons who become disabled before they have established the necessary contribution record are excluded from the benefit. A benefit called Severe Disablement Allowance exists to provide for such persons, who would otherwise be forced to rely on the means tested Income Support. It is payable to a person who has been incapable of work for not less than 196 consecutive days and suffering from a disablement assessed at 80 per cent. or more.[23] This non-contributory benefit performs a valuable role, but it is payable at a rate significantly lower than the contributory invalidity pension. It is a flat rate benefit to which additional payments are added on account of dependants. There is also an age-related additional supplement.[24]

Death benefits

There are four benefits which may be payable on a death. They are: a funeral payment; a widow's payment (these two benefits are designed to meet the short-term financial consequences of a death); the widowed mother's allowance and the widow's pension (which both provide long-term support for those classes of widows who are regarded as unlikely, because of family responsibilities or age, to be able to return to work after their husband's death). As will be apparent from the names of these benefits, the system is designed mainly to replace income lost as the result of a death and is largely directed to the situation of a death of a man who had been working and supporting a family. Widowers who were dependent on the earnings of their wives, other persons such as disabled or elderly relatives who were dependent on the deceased and the widows of the elderly will not receive significant death benefits from the State and may have to fall back on means tested protection. The assumptions made by the social security system in relation to the employment roles of husband and wife and in the treatment of remarriage and a widow's return to work on her husband's death, are very different from those adopted by the tort system under the Fatal Accidents Act.[25]

1. Social Fund funeral payment

State assistance towards meeting the "essential" costs of a funeral is available from the Social Fund,[26] but is only available to persons who were claiming income support, housing benefit or family credit at the time of making the claim. In order to qualify for this payment, the claimant, or one

---

[22] The Invalidity Allowance continues into retirement as an addition to the standard retirement pension.

[23] This second condition only applies to claimants who become incapable of work after their 20th birthday. For the ways in which this condition can be satisfied see Ogus & Barendt *op. cit.* p. 147.

[24] This was introduced by s. 2(1) of the Social Security Act 1990.

[25] See p. 277.

[26] See *post*, p. 293.

of his family, must have taken responsibility for the costs of the funeral which must have taken place in the United Kingdom.

2. Widow's payment

This is a single lump sum payment[27] which is designed to offset any immediate financial problems caused to a wife by the death of her husband. Any married woman may claim it if her husband had previously paid the appropriate number of contributions unless at the time of her husband's death she was aged 60 or over and he was aged 65 or over and in receipt of a State Retirement Pension.

3. Widowed mother's allowance

This allowance provides long-term support for a widow who has children dependent on her at the date of her husband's death. It is payable from the date of the husband's death, in addition to the widow's payment, for as long as the widow is supporting a child under the age of 16 (or 19 if the child is in full-time education) or until she remarries.[28] The benefit consists of a flat rate payment, additional payments for each dependent child and an earnings related addition calculated according to the husband's contribution record. Eligibility for the allowance depends on the husband's having made sufficient contributions and the allowance is taxable and payable regardless of any earnings made by the widow.

4. Widow's pension

This is a long-term pension which is payable to a widow who was 45 or over at either the date of her husband's death or at the date when, because of the age of her children, she ceased to be eligible for widowed mother's allowance. The pension is payable as a flat rate benefit with an earnings related addition according to the husband's contribution record. Eligibility depends on the husband having satisfied the same contribution conditions as apply to widowed mother's allowance and the pension ceases to be payable when the widow reaches the age of 65, retires after the age of 60 or remarries. No increases in the pension are payable in respect of adult or other dependants and the flat rate benefit is paid at a reduced rate to widows who were below the age of 55 when it first became payable to them. The basic rate is reduced by 7 per cent. for every year that she was below the age of 55 and the reduced rate remains payable throughout the period that the widow claims the pension. The pension is taxed and payable irrespective of earnings in the same way as widowed mother's allowance.

Disability living allowance

This allowance was introduced in 1992 as a replacement for the former attendance[29] and mobility allowances. The new benefit is available to a wider group of the disabled than its predecessors were. The aim is to provide a non-contributory and non-means tested benefit which will meet some of the costs imposed by a disability. There are two components to this benefit: the costs of care required by a person in terms of nursing and a mobility

---

[27] It is fixed at £1,000. It has not been uprated since its introduction.

[28] The allowance is suspended for as long as the widow lives with another man as his wife.

[29] Attendance Allowance is retained for those whose care needs arise after the age of 65.

component for those who are unable to travel without assistance. Either or both components may be payable to a claimant. The level of allowance payable depends on the degree of disability; the care element being payable at three levels and the mobility at two.

Invalid care allowance

The costs involved in the provision of nursing services for the severely handicapped accident victim may be met, in part, by the payment of Invalid Care Allowance to the person who is providing the care. This is a flat rate non-contributory benefit which is payable with additional allowances for dependants to persons who are unable to work[30] because they are providing substantial services[31] in caring for a person who is in receipt of a disability living allowance.[32] As will be apparent, these stringent conditions will not be satisfied by many people who have responsibility for providing care for their relatives and others. The benefit was introduced in order to provide non-means tested state support for such persons. Since 1986 it has been available to a woman who is living with and is supported by her husband. The allowance is taxable and very small amounts of earnings are disregarded.

Industrial injuries and diseases

Disablement benefits are the only significant part of the Industrial Injuries system which has survived the reforms of social security provision introduced in the 1980s and 1990s. The older industrial injury and death benefits which offered an industrially injured person a higher level of protection than was available under normal social security provision have been abolished along with some of the supplements to disablement benefit and the reduced earnings allowance, which had itself replaced the disablement gratuity. The historical reason for the separate treatment of industrial injuries at the inception of the modern system of social security benefits in 1948 was that it was the successor to the system of Workmen's Compensation which had been paying a much higher level of benefit than was to be available from the new National Insurance benefits. Over the course of time the financial advantages (the industrial preference) of the Industrial Injuries scheme were reduced and it was not surprising that most of them disappeared in face of a policy of targeting benefits at those most in need and of cash limits imposed as a consequence of the policy of limiting public expenditure followed in the 1980s.

1. Disablement benefit

The basic conditions governing entitlement to disablement benefit under the industrial injuries scheme is that the claimant must have been an employee[33] who suffered either a personal injury caused by an accident arising out of and in the course of his employment or have developed a "prescribed disease" while working in a specified occupation. The requirement that an injury should have arisen out of and in the course of employment imposes a test similar to that used by the law of tort in the area of

---

[30] A claimant must be over the age of 16 and below retirement age.
[31] At least 35 hours a week is required.
[32] Or a constant attendance allowance payable under the Industrial Injuries Scheme.
[33] The self-employed are not entitled to benefit.

vicarious liability.[34] However, the "course of employment" is slightly wider as the result of specific statutory provisions[35] and the requirement that the injury arises out of the employment is assisted by a presumption to the effect that all accidents which arise in the course of employment arise out of it unless the contrary is proved. The second category (that of the industrial disease) recognises the fact that long-term exposure to hazardous agents at work can damage health without having produced any single occurrence which could count as an accident. A fixed list exists of diseases recognised as hazards for those engaged in particular occupations[36] and it is presumed that an employee engaged in such an occupation who develops a disease which is prescribed in relation to it, has contracted it from his employment. No benefit is payable in respect of diseases which fall outside the list, even if it can be proved that the claimant's illness is attributable to his occupation. This system has been criticised on the grounds that the process of prescribing diseases for particular occupations has been too slow. The Pearson Commission recommended that the system could be improved by allowing an employee to claim benefits from the industrial injuries scheme if he could prove that the disease from which he was suffering had been caused by his occupation and that it was a particular risk of the occupation.[37]

Disablement benefit is exceptional in being a social security benefit payable for loss of faculty. The disablement does not need to be producing any loss of earnings and can be temporary; indeed, the majority of recipients of the benefit obtain it for a limited period. The amount of benefit which is payable depends on a medical assessment of the claimant's condition in the light of the injury or disease suffered,[38] which is expressed in the form of percentages of disablement. This process, which allows for less subjectivity than the tort technique of assessing damages for non-pecuniary losses, is simplified by the fact that certain injuries, assuming that there are no complicating factors, have a fixed percentage allocated to them in advance. For example, total blindness or deafness are assessed as a 100 per cent. disablement whereas amputation of a leg at the knee counts as 60 per cent. No benefit is payable unless the disablement is assessed at more than 14 per cent.[39] and the medical assessment of disablement of more than 14 per cent. is rounded to the nearest 10 per cent. in order to simplify the actual payment of the benefit. Two rates of disablement benefit are paid, the higher going to claimants who are over the age of 18 or who have adult or other dependants. The capitalised value of such a pension to a person who will receive it in an inflation linked form over a long period of time is almost certainly greater than that of the conventional figure which would be awarded by a court in a tort claim for the non-pecuniary losses resulting from such injuries.[40]

No contribution conditions apply to disablement benefit: an employee is protected from the time that he first commences work. Minor injuries are

---

[34] See p. 131.
[35] For example, a person travelling to work in transport provided by the employer falls within the course of employment for these purposes.
[36] Industrial Injuries (Prescribed Diseases) Regns. 1985. S.I. 1985 No. 967.
[37] para. 887.
[38] In comparison with the claimant's previous condition.
[39] Except in cases of pneumoconiosis, byssinosis and diffuse mesothelioma in which case a 1 per cent. disablement suffices.
[40] See Atiyah, *Accidents, Compensation and the Law* (5th ed.), p. 287 for a detailed comparison.

excluded from this benefit by the rule which stipulates that no benefit is payable for the first 15 weeks after the accident. Protection against the consequences of such losses is only provided by statutory sick pay. The benefit is tax free, can continue to be paid after retirement age has been reached and, because it is regarded as dealing with a different kind of loss, has no affect on the claimant's entitlement to receive other benefits such as statutory sick pay and invalidity benefit.

2. Constant Attendance Allowance

This supplement, which is payable to persons in receipt of 100 per cent. disablement benefit and who depend to a substantial extent on attendance by some other person in connection with the necessities of life, is payable at a higher rate than the standard disability allowance.[41] Four different rates are payable according to the level of needs of the claimant. Those who receive either of the two higher rates will also receive a flat rate additional allowance called Exceptionally Severe Disablement Allowance if their disablement is likely to be permanent.

3. Dust diseases[42]

Two special schemes, which can provide compensation for those who develop certain diseases as a result of exposure to dust at work, exist outside of the industrial injuries scheme. Under the Pneumoconiosis, etc., (Worker's Compensation) Act 1979 employees who are in receipt of industrial disablement benefit in relation to such a disease but who are unable to bring a tort claim against their employer because he is no longer in business, may receive lump sum payments in substitution. A special scheme is also operated by the National Coal Board in relation to its employees who develop pneumoconiosis. Payments under this scheme, which was instigated in order to avoid the Board and its former employees becoming involved in lengthy litigation, are made on condition that the employee waives any rights which he might have against the Board in tort.

Means tested benefits

Many accident victims who are unable to work as a result of their injuries will not need to have recourse to means tested benefits because statutory sick pay and invalidity benefit will be payable to them in addition to sick pay payable under their contract of employment. The making of a sizeable award of tort damages may actually disqualify a person from receiving income support by taking him over the capital limits. However, some classes of accident victim may need means tested support; for example, the person who is rendered unemployed but not incapable of work as a result of his injuries from the time that entitlement to unemployment benefit ceases and the widow who is not entitled to a widow's pension. In addition, a person who has no income payable to him other than State benefits may be entitled to income support as a supplement to bring his income up to the prescribed level. The advent of non-contributory benefits such as severe disablement

---

[41] Unification of the different kinds of attendance allowance was proposed as long ago as 1978 by the Pearson Commission.

[42] For the history of these special schemes see Pearson, para. 789 and Atiyah *op. cit.* p. 297.

allowance and invalid care allowance has reduced the amount of reliance placed by accident victims on means tested benefits. However, it has been calculated[43] that in 1991, income support was being paid to 296,000 sick and disabled persons.

1. Income support

Income support is the basic means tested benefit, the role of which is to prevent people from falling below the poverty line. It is a cash benefit which pays the difference between a person's net income and the net amount required to meet the needs which he is assessed as having. An accident victim may receive some advantage in this process because his needs may be regarded as increased if he is disabled. Similarly, those engaged in caring for the disabled are eligible to receive an additional premium. The benefit is subject to no contribution conditions and a person who owns capital in excess of a specified limit will be disqualified. A person claiming the benefit must usually be available for work and actively seeking it; full-time employment[44] disqualifies a person from receiving the benefit.

Family members are assessed together for the purposes of income support; in the case of couples only one is able to claim the benefit. As a result the needs, income and capital of couples will be aggregated when the level of benefit to be paid is calculated and the fact that one partner is working will disqualify the other from receiving the benefit.

In addition to Income Support payments, lump sum payments to meet particular "one off" needs which it is difficult to budget for may be received from the Social Fund. Such payments are generally loans rather than grants, the loan being recouped from future payments of income support. The majority of such payments are formally paid as a matter of discretion[45] and it had been alleged that they are liable to be refused to those most in need because it is unlikely that the loan could be repaid.

2. Family Credit

A person who is left with a reduced earning capacity as a result of an accident may be entitled to receive Family Credit. This is a benefit which does not require the claimant to be unable to engage in work. The benefit exists to provide means tested protection for low earners who are disqualified by the fact of their earnings from receipt of income support. It is only available to adults who are engaged in full-time work[46] and who are supporting one or more children of school age. Entitlement to receive the benefit, which is tax free and varies according to the number of members in the family unit, depends on the family's net weekly income and capital falling below prescribed limits.

3. Disability working allowance

This means tested benefit was introduced by the Disability Living Allowance & Disability Working Allowance Act 1991 with the aim of protecting the finances of partially incapacitated disabled persons who engage in low

---

[43] Atiyah *op. cit.* p. 299.
[44] Defined as working an average of 24 hours or more a week.
[45] As opposed to being governed by regulations. The distinction should not be overrated as the discretion is actually exercised according to guidance issued by the Secretary of State.
[46] 24 hours or more per week.

paid work. It plays much the same role for the disabled as Family Credit[47] does for families. It is payable to anyone of the age of 16 or more who is engaged in full-time work but who is suffering from a mental or physical disability which would disadvantage a person in obtaining work. Entitlement to the benefit is means tested and the benefit payable is calculated according to the difference between the claimant's needs and deemed requirements in the same way as Family Credit.

4. Housing benefit and council tax benefit

These are separate benefits from Income Support which are administered by local authorities rather than the D.S.S. They are not intended to meet all housing costs; income support plays a large role in providing for the payment of the mortgage interest of home owners. However, rent rebates and allowances are handled as housing benefit while council tax benefit is an independent income related benefit.

Other State Benefits[48]

The mechanisms of the Welfare State may provide a variety of other forms of assistance for accident victims. The National Health Service obviously has a substantial role to play in relation to the treatment of injuries and rehabilitation and local social services departments may provide a variety of practical assistance, such as home helps, meals on wheels and travel concessions, for those who suffer long-term disablement.[49] In practice, it is reasonably clear that a great deal of the everyday help received by the disabled is provided informally by members of that person's family.

The State also provides some financial support for the victims of accidents through the mechanisms of taxation. Short-term earnings losses may be alleviated to an extent by the fact that the Pay-as-You-Earn system of income tax is likely to produce a refund of tax previously paid in the course of the tax year on the assumption that a full year's earnings would be made. Special tax reliefs against income are also available to the blind and to persons who are maintaining a disabled person. Gifts made to charities, which may go to support the disabled, attract tax relief.

Compensation for Criminal Injuries

Injuries caused by criminal acts are covered by two special compensation schemes. A criminal court when convicting an offender has the power to order that compensation be paid to the victim and the Criminal Injuries Compensation Board (C.I.C.B.) provides State funded compensation for some victims of criminal acts. The first method enables the criminal court's process to substitute for tort. It goes considerably further than the Civil Evidence Act 1968 which merely allows the fact of a criminal conviction to be evidence in subsequent court proceedings. It has the capacity to replace

---

[47] Being in receipt of family credit disentitles a person from receiving this benefit.

[48] For more detailed consideration see Atiyah *op. cit.* pp. 305 *et seq.* and Harris and others, *Compensation and Support for Illness and Injury*, Chap. 9.

[49] The Oxford survey found that 8 per cent. of accident victims had received some help of this kind. See Harris and others *op. cit.* p. 244.

tort proceedings entirely in circumstances in which the damage is at a level which allows the convicted person to fund the compensation. It is a cheap and relatively fast method of providing compensation which avoids socially wasteful duplication of proceedings. The provision of a State funded mechanism for the compensation of the victims of crime requires more justification.[50] The best is that it can be assumed that many offenders are not worth suing in a civil court or being made subject to compensation orders and that the victims of certain crimes deserve support over and above that which would be provided by social security. Compensation claims for many criminal offences, in particular those relating to traffic accidents breaches of industrial safety legislation, fall outside of this reasoning and are left to be dealt with by the mainstream of tort liability because they are underpinned by compulsory insurance. Nonetheless, in spite of the existence of the C.I.C.B. it is not unknown for civil claims to be brought against persons convicted of serious criminal offences.[51] The civil claim by the dependants of the victims of Peter Sutcliffe[52] and the *Meah* Cases[53] are well known examples.

Criminal Injuries Compensation Scheme

The present status of the Criminal Injuries Compensation scheme requires some explanation. Part VII of the Criminal Justice Act 1988 contains provisions which would convert the C.I.C.B. into a statutory body. The C.I.C.B. was originally established as a non-statutory body and made what were, technically, *ex gratia* payments to applicants. The intention behind the new provisions was to ensure that victims of crimes of violence had a statutory right to receive compensation from the State. Unfortunately, the backlog of work which has afflicted the C.I.C.B. in recent years has meant that it has not had the resources to implement the new scheme. As a result, the relevant provisions have yet to be brought into force and the scheme has continued to operate on the non-statutory basis. However, from February 1990 the non-statutory scheme was amended to incorporate some of the most important changes which the 1988 Act introduced. It is the 1990 version of the scheme which will be described here.

Entitlement

In order to obtain compensation from the C.I.C.B. an applicant must satisfy the Board, on the balance of probabilities, that he has suffered a personal injury[54] which is directly attributable to a "crime of violence" including arson or poisoning or was a dependant of a person who died as a result of such an offence.[55] No definition is provided of the concept of a crime of violence[56] but it is generally understood to confine the ambit of the

---

[50] See Atiyah *op. cit.* pp. 252–257.

[51] See *ante*, pp. 181–182.

[52] *Hill* v. *Chief Constable of West Yorkshire* [1989] A.C. 53.

[53] Particularly *W.* v. *Meah* [1986] 1 All E.R. 935.

[54] The injury must have been sustained within Great Britain. See para. 4 of the Scheme for the definition for these purposes. There is no requirement that the applicant be resident or domiciled in Great Britain.

[55] para. 4a.

[56] s. 110 of the Criminal Justice Act 1988 would have replaced the definition with a list of specified offences.

scheme to offences which require proof of an intent to cause death or personal injury, or recklessness as to whether such damage is caused.[57] A large number of criminal offences which may result in personal injury, including most motoring offences[58] and breaches of the Health and Safety at Work Act 1974, are excluded from the ambit of the scheme by the restriction to a crime of violence. However, the scheme is specifically extended to cover injuries directly attributable to "the apprehension or attempted apprehension of an offender or a suspected offender or to the prevention or attempted prevention of an offence or to the giving of help to any constable who is engaged in any such activity" and to "an offence of trespass on the railway." The final case was added in 1990 to conclude a long debate as to whether the scheme could provide compensation to train drivers who had suffered shock after a person had committed suicide in front of the train they were driving. The applicant has to satisfy the Board that the offence has been committed.[59] There is no requirement that the offender must have been apprehended, charged or convicted of the offence. Indeed, the applicant has to satisfy a lower standard of proof than that placed on the prosecution to obtain the conviction of the offender.

The notion of a personal injury is also not defined by the terms of the scheme but has been interpreted to cover the same losses, including shock, as are recoverable in tort. If the offence in question was a rape or another sexual offence the scheme expressly provides for compensation to be paid in respect of pain, suffering, shock and loss of earnings due to a consequent pregnancy.[60] A further award of £5,000 is made in respect of any child born alive having been conceived as a result of rape.[61]

The persons entitled to claim compensation are the victim of the criminal injury or the dependants of a victim who has died. A claim brought by dependants is available whether or not the death was the result of the criminal injury. A number of significant exclusions of persons otherwise entitled exist. Possibly the most important is the "household" exception which removes a considerable number of domestic violence cases from the scheme in order to avoid an award of compensation benefitting the offender or creating disharmony in family relationships. A person aged 18 or more who was living in the same household as the offender when the injury was sustained is excluded, unless certain restrictive conditions are satisfied. Also excluded are cases in which a person accidentally sustains injury while apprehending an offender, preventing the commission of a crime or assisting the police in such activities unless the Board is satisfied that the risk taken was an exceptional one which was justified in the circumstances.

Level

The compensation awarded by the scheme is calculated in the same way as common law damages for injuries and death.[62] Awards are made in the form of a lump sum, although interim payments and provisional awards are

---

[57] See Miers, *Compensation for Criminal Injuries* (1990), pp. 100–114.
[58] para. 11 creates a limited exception.
[59] The fact that no conviction could have been obtained because of the age, insanity or diplomatic immunity of the perpetrator does not remove the right to compensation. Para. 4.
[60] para. 10.
[61] So long as the mother intends to keep the child.
[62] Property damage is usually excluded: para. 17.

possible. Both financial and non-pecuniary losses may be compensated.[63] However, in order to limit expenditure, claims in relation to loss of earnings are "capped" at 1½ times gross average industrial earnings and many small claims are excluded by the rule that no award will be payable if the compensation will not exceed a minimum figure. This figure was raised to £1,000 at the start of 1992 from the previous level of £750. The fact that 41 per cent. of awards made by the Board in the year 1990/91 were for less than £1,000 shows that this increase marked a significant restriction on the scope of the scheme. The Board awards compensation for non-pecuniary losses according to guidelines which it occasionally publishes. At times these guidelines have fallen well below the figures recognised as appropriate for such injuries by common law courts. In W. v. Meah[64] two victims of rape and sexual assault were awarded £6,750 and £10,250 damages in a tort claim for their non-pecuniary losses. They had previously received C.I.C.B. awards of £2,750 and £3,600 respectively.[65]

The C.I.C.B. is given discretion to refuse or to reduce an award in a number of circumstances. These include a failure by the claimant to take reasonable steps within a reasonable time to inform the police of the offence and to co-operate with their investigations, a failure to give reasonable assistance to the C.I.C.B. and a failure to prove that the offender will not benefit from the award. The *maxim ex turpi causa non oritur actio* receives its widest application under the scheme. An award of compensation may be disallowed or reduced on the ground of criminal convictions or conduct of the claimant, even if that conduct is unconnected with the offence which gave rise to the claim. The Board's Annual report for 1990/91 records the case of a rape victim whose award was reduced by 50 per cent. on account of her previous criminal convictions.[66] It is not surprising to find that there is a contributory negligence style disqualification and, in order to avoid claims being the source of friction within families it is provided that in the case of an applicant who was under 18 at the time of the offence and was living in the same household as the offender the Board must be satisfied that it is in the interests of the claimant that the award is made. All social security benefits paid to the claimant are deducted from the award as are any awards of damages or compensation orders which have already been received by the claimant.

Procedure

The procedure used by the C.I.C.B. is not adversarial in nature. In most cases the claim is determined without an oral hearing. In serious cases, particularly those which involve difficult issues of quantification, costs may present a problem. There is no entitlement to legal aid to support an application to the Board and a successful claimant will not have his costs reimbursed by the Board. At the end of 1989 it was reported in the press that a claimant who had been awarded £407,000 by the Board was faced with costs of over £20,000 for legal and experts' fees.

---

[63] Both in personal injury and death cases. Bereavement damages are available.
[64] [1986] 1 All E.R. 935.
[65] The C.I.C.B. awards would be larger nowadays.
[66] The history of this power is reviewed in Miers *op. cit.* pp. 75–97.

It might be thought that the distinctive characteristics of the C.I.C.B.'s procedure would mean that claims would be processed quickly. At one time this seemed to be the case. In 1984/5 the Board reported that it had received 34,890 applications and processed 32 per cent. of these within six months and 75 per cent. within a year. However, more recently, the Board became a victim of its own success. At the end of 1989 it reported that the number of applications in that year was expected to have increased by 10,000 to 53,000 and that it was faced by a backlog of 85,000 uncleared cases.[67] The award of £407,000 mentioned above had taken six years to process. Some improvement in the position was noted in the year 1990/91 when, for the first time in 10 years, the Board resolved more claims[68] than it received.[69] The position may well improve significantly over the next few years as a result of the elimination of many small claims from the scope of the scheme. In 1992 it was announced that the Government was planning to substitute a tariff for the common law basis for calculating a C.I.C.B. award in order to speed up the processing of payments.

Assessment

The C.I.C.B., which in 1990/91 paid £109 million to the victims of crime, is seen by many persons as a success and as being particularly generous when compared to equivalent schemes operated in other countries.[70] However, the removal of many small claims from the scope of the scheme as a result of increases in the minimum award show that attempts are being made to limit the State's generosity.

The success of the Board in terms of coverage is not entirely clear. The number of claims it deals with is less than one third of the number of crimes of violence reported to the police. However, given the household exclusion and the fact that many crimes of violence may result in insignificant injuries the take up rate may be regarded as relatively successful in comparison to tort.

Compensation orders[71]

Section 35 of the Powers of Criminal Courts Act 1973[72] gives courts wide powers to order a convicted person to pay compensation for personal injuries, loss or other damage resulting from the offence. This jurisdiction is a convenient and rapid means of providing compensation to those damaged by criminal acts and one which enables them to avoid the expenses of civil litigation.

---

[67] The backlog was described by the House of Commons Home Affairs Select Committee as "scandalous." Staff were said to be being diverted from casework to the investigation of delays. The average number of cases dealt with annually by each member of the C.I.C.B.'s staff fell from 170 to 125 between 1980 and 1989. The backlog had dropped to 81,282 cases on March 31, 1991.

[68] 53,384.

[69] 50,820.

[70] In 1988 the Federal Republic of Germany paid approximately £13 million under its scheme and France paid £11 million.

[71] See generally Bailey and Tucker, *Remedies for Victims of Crime*, Chap. 5.

[72] Amended by the Criminal Justice Act 1988, ss. 104–106.

An order of this kind may be made on the court's own initiative or as a result of the victim seeking it.[73] The court has a discretion whether or not to make such an order, and as to its amount.[74] However, if it chooses not to make an order, it has an obligation to give its reasons.[75] The order may be combined with any other sentence or may be made on its own. In practice, the courts tend only to make such orders when the legal position and the amount of the loss is clear. Criminal proceedings to which the damaged person is not a party are not the ideal forum for considering complex issues of quantum. Criminal courts tend therefore to leave the more difficult cases to be resolved by civil proceedings or the Criminal Injuries Compensation Board.

This has tended to limit the utility of such orders in relation to personal injury cases, although magistrates have been periodically issued with guide-lines as to the appropriate awards in simple injury cases in order to encourage the use of the jurisdiction.

A number of other principles apply to such compensation orders. The most important is that the court must have regard to the offender's ability to pay the order when deciding whether to make it and when fixing its amount. The full compensation principle has no place under this jurisdiction. As a result of this it is commonly thought unsuitable to combine a compensation order with a custodial sentence[76] or to allow payments by instalments to continue for more than two years. An order should also not be made at a level which might encourage the offender to commit further crimes in order to fund it. If the court is of the view that the offender merits the imposition of a fine and should pay a compensation order but feels that the offender's means are insufficient to cover both, it is directed[77] to give priority to the compensa-tion order. Motoring offences are excluded from this jurisdiction[78] as are claims by the dependants of a deceased person other than claims for funeral expenses and damages for bereavement.[79]

Special rules[80] apply if the victim brings successful civil proceedings after a compensation order in relation to the same loss has been made in his favour. A civil court which finds in the plaintiff's favour will assess the damages due without reference to the compensation order. However, only the sum by which the damages exceed the order and any amounts of the order which have not been paid[81] may be recovered. A civil court's decision to award damages lower than a compensation order previously made is a ground for

---

[73] In practice this will involve the prosecution leading evidence which relates to the loss. Failure to adduce evidence as to the extent of the injuries can invalidate an order *R.* v. *Chorley Justices, ex parte Jones,* The Times, March 24, 1990. It is not unknown for the offender to offer to pay compensation as a way of seeking to mitigate his liability.

[74] The jurisdiction of a magistrates' court is limited to a maximum of £2,000 per offence.

[75] s.35(1) as amended.

[76] *R.* v. *Crosbie The Times,* December 12, 1990.

[77] s.35(4)(a).

[78] Except damage resulting from offences under the Theft Act 1968 and uninsured damage not covered by the Motor Insurers' Bureau. These exceptions do not relate to personal injuries.

[79] s.35(1) as amended by the Criminal Justice Act 1988, s.104.

[80] Powers of Criminal Courts Act 1973, s.38, as amended by the Criminal Justice Act 1988, s.107.

[81] Recovery as damages of sums unpaid under a compensation order requires leave of the court: s.38(2).

seeking a review of that order if it remains unsatisfied[82] but creates no right to reclaim sums paid under an order which has been complied with fully.

The advantages of compensation orders as a technique are clear. The victims of a criminal offence may obtain compensation without having to spend money or seek Legal Aid. Such compensation is not subject to the minimum payments rule applied to C.I.C.B. payments and, with the exception of motoring offences, applies to all criminal offences, not just crimes of violence. On the other hand, criminal proceedings may not be the most appropriate forum for the calculation of awards of compensation. The procedure is best suited to simple cases, for example, when the cost of damage to property is easily assessed. The procedure is wholly dependent on the offender having the means to pay the order and sums ordered to be paid may be limited to less than the loss incurred on account of the offender's means.

VACCINE DAMAGE PAYMENTS

The Vaccine Damage Payments scheme is an example of State funded compensation which is available to a very limited category of disabled persons. The existence of this scheme is the product of political necessity. For many years it has been official policy to encourage the vaccination of children in order to control the spread of and ultimately to eliminate certain diseases. However, in the 1970s public confidence in this programme was severely damaged by press reports which linked whooping cough vaccine with cases of convulsions and resulting brain damage in children. The official reaction was that public concern was unjustified. The causal link between the vaccination and the convulsions had not been established; statistically a number of young children would have been likely to have suffered convulsions in the period immediately following the vaccination. In any case, it was argued that the risk of a child suffering damage from the disease was greater than that of damage being caused by the vaccination. In spite of these arguments the number of children being vaccinated against the whole range of childhood diseases dropped[83] and the Government, faced by the possible breakdown in a major public health scheme and a resulting increase in the incidence of certain diseases, was compelled to act. The Vaccine Damage Payments scheme, which is now governed by the Vaccine Damage Payments Act 1979 was the major response in terms of compensation.

Entitlement

The compensation payable under the Act, irrespective of the medical condition and personal circumstances of the applicant, is a fixed sum of £20,000. This level of compensation is regarded as "woefully inadequate" by some commentators[84] but does leave vaccine damaged children £20,000 better off than other severely handicapped children. An applicant who wishes to obtain this compensation must show that a severe disablement[85]

---

[82] s.37(a).
[83] Pearson, para. 1381.
[84] M. Brazier, *Medicine, Patients and the Law* (2nd ed.), p. 189.
[85] This is defined as constituting an 80 per cent. disablement in accordance with the provisions of s. 57 of the Social Security Act 1975.

has been suffered as a result of a vaccination carried out as part of a government recommended programme.[86] In practice, the requirement of government recommendation confines the benefits of the scheme, in most cases, to children below the age of 18.

Payments under the scheme are made extra-judicially by the Department of Health.[87] An applicant must satisfy the Department, on the balance of probabilities, that he is entitled to compensation under the terms of the scheme. It is possible to have the Department's decision on issues of entitlement, extent of disablement or causation reviewed by an independent tribunal.

Assessment

In terms of protecting the disabled, the Vaccine Damage Payments scheme is a classic example of a right to compensation which resulted from political pressures and which gives preferential treatment to a very small category of disabled persons.[88] The Pearson Commission did not avoid this danger. The Commission[89] having taken the view that all handicapped children deserved help from the State went on to make the somewhat inconsistent recommendation that special provision should be made for children handicapped as the result of vaccine damage. They were said to deserve special treatment because their handicap was the result of their parents following an official recommendation that they should be vaccinated. There is particular force in this argument in relation to whooping cough vaccine which is one which is administered to children when they are of an age when the risk of the disease causing them severe damage is greatly reduced. The vaccine is administered because it is in the interests of society to reduce the incidence of the disease and thus to provide protection to children younger than those who are being vaccinated.

As is the case in respect of all handicapped children, it is unlikely that tort can provide effective financial protection. It will be exceptionally difficult to prove that the Government was negligent in recommending a vaccination programme to the public and scarcely easier to establish tort liability on the part of medical staff who administered a vaccination or the manufacturer of the drug. Proving causation is bound to be a problem for tortious and other forms of compensation in this area.

In practice, causation has proved to be the downfall of the Vaccine Damage Payments scheme. The difficulty of establishing the true cause of

---

[86] The diseases at present covered by the Act are: diphtheria, tetanus, whooping cough, poliomyelitis, measles, rubella, tuberculosis and smallpox. Power exists to add others to this list.

[87] The Pearson Commission recommended an absolute liability tort remedy giving rise to compensation calculated according to normal principles. This remedy would have been obtained through judicial proceedings. The scheme enacted is in a very different form.

[88] The Pearson Commission estimated that there are approximately 100,000 severely handicapped children. Approximately 90,000 of these are the victims of congenital handicap and 8,000 of diseases suffered after birth. Only 1,000–2,000 were suffering from prolonged handicap as a result of post natal injury of all kinds (paras. 1514–1520). Only a small proportion of these children were the victims of vaccine damage. The Association of Parents of Vaccine Damaged Children informed the Commission (para. 1388) that it had 356 cases registered with it of serious damage resulting from vaccination. 240 of these cases related to whooping cough vaccine.

[89] para. 1406.

brain damage and other disabilities in children is well recognised and the operation of the scheme has been regularly criticised by applicants who have found causation to be an insurmountable hurdle to their obtaining a payment from it. Similar problems have confronted those who have sought common law damages in relation to vaccine damage. In *Loveday* v. *Renton*[90] Stuart-Smith L.J. held that on the evidence before him it had not been established on the balance of probabilities that whooping cough vaccine could cause permanent brain damage in young children. The Government treated this as a test case on the question of causation in relation to this vaccine and ceased to make payments under the statutory scheme in relation to it.

ROAD ACCIDENTS: A PROPOSAL

In 1991 the Lord Chancellor's Department issued a consultation paper[91] which proposed the introduction of a limited no-fault compensation scheme for road accident victims. The proposal is that road accident victims whose claims in respect of their injuries are worth between £250 and £2,500, calculated on the same basis as at common law, should be able to obtain compensation on a no-fault basis. Claims for property damage would be excluded from this scheme and the defence of contributory negligence would not be recognised. However, it is suggested that compensation should not be awarded in relation to intentionally self inflicted injuries and views are being sought as to whether drink driving or the commission of other motoring offences should bar a claim. Under some versions of the proposal, drivers injured in single vehicle accidents would be given access to a compensation scheme, other than social security, for the first time. The provisional suggestion is that the payment of such compensation should be administered by private insurance companies, with disputes being resolved either by the courts or by private arbitration. The scheme would be funded by an increase in the insurance premiums charged to motorists. A central tenet of the proposal is that it should not be a charge on public funds.

Compensation payable under this scheme would be assessed in the same way as common law damages and would therefore extend to non-pecuniary losses. Such compensation would have state benefits offset from it in the normal ways. In view of the limits on the level of compensation payable this would usually entail a 50 per cent. deduction of benefits. The compensation would itself be offset from any tort damages which were obtained through litigation. Tort claims would remain available, and would be the main method of protection for those who were seriously injured in road accidents, however such a plaintiff would be able to obtain no-fault benefits within the limits of the scheme. A successful plaintiff who was awarded damages of less than the maximum obtainable from the no-fault scheme would be penalised in respect of the costs of the litigation by the court.

---

[90] *The Times*, March 31, 1988.
[91] Lord Chancellor's Department, *Compensation for Road Accidents: a Consultation Paper* (1991).

It is envisaged that such a scheme would replace litigation in the case of the smaller claims in relation to which it is least cost effective. It would provide fairer, simpler, faster and more comprehensive protection for an important category of accident victims at the cost of an estimated 5 per cent. to 7 per cent. increase in the cost of motor insurance.

PART III

ECONOMIC INTERESTS

Chapter Fourteen

Economic Losses: An Introduction

Cane has defined "economic interests" as those interests "for the invasion of which a finite sum of money can provide complete recompense."[1] A great part of English law is devoted to the protection of existing wealth and other economic interests. Tort has a part to play in this process alongside other bodies of law, particularly property law (in all its guises), which tends to have the aim of protecting existing wealth, and the law of contract, which is mainly concerned with the protection of economic expectations. In practice, tort plays an ancillary, but not insignificant, role alongside these bodies of law[2] and the protection which is also provided by the administrative compensation schemes which exist.[3] The sheer width of the context within which this area of the law of tort operates makes it impossible, within the length of this book, to make any substantial attempt at providing a detailed picture of the whole subject.

Tort and economic interests

The English law of tort draws a clear distinction between physical damage to property and damage to other economic interests. In the hierarchy of values recognised by tort, property receives a similar degree of protection to that accorded to a person's physical integrity but other non-tangible economic interests receive a lesser degree of protection, particularly when the damage is inflicted by negligence. This is in spite of the fact that a person's main interest in physical property is likely to be an economic one in as much as damage to property will usually call for expenditure to repair or replace it.[4]

It is not the case, however, that the English law of tort has an inherent dislike for the recovery of all forms of economic loss. A number of tortious remedies are available to protect people against the intentional infliction of economic loss[5] and a limited number of strict liability remedies also exist.[6]

---

[1] Cane, *Tort Law and Economic Interests*, p. 5.

[2] Cane *op. cit.* Chap. 6.

[3] Statutory compensation funds are a familiar feature of modern regulatory legislation. For example, the Banking Act 1987 features a deposit guarantee scheme which is funded by a levy on banks. The limitations of this scheme, particularly the fact that the maximum protection is limited to £15,000, were well exposed by the failure of the Bank of Credit and Commerce International.

[4] The reasons for the refusal to provide a general remedy in relation to negligently inflicted "pure" economic loss are explored in greater detail in Chap. 16.

[5] See *post*, Chap. 15.

[6] See Chap. 17.

Furthermore, if physical damage to the plaintiff's person or property has been caused by negligence, economic loss consequential on that damage is likely to be recoverable. Indeed, it is important to appreciate that the familiar situation of a tort claim for loss of earnings resulting from a personal injury is a claim for negligently caused economic losses: losses which are based on the plaintiff's expectation of financial benefits to be derived from a contract with a third party (the employer).

On the other hand the non-recovery, in the great majority of situations, of negligently inflicted "pure" economic loss cannot be easily brushed aside.[7] It is a fundamental rule of English law and many familiar legal rules assume the existence of this barrier to recovery. A good example is provided by claims brought by dependants of a deceased under the Fatal Accidents Act 1976.[8] Such claims are for financial losses resulting from physical damage tortiously inflicted on another person. The Act assumes that such losses would be irrecoverable at common law and creates an exception which allows recovery.[9]

REMEDIES FOR ECONOMIC LOSSES

The remedies made available by tort in relation to damage to economic interests are the standard ones of damages and injunctions.

Injunctions

The standard rules[10] concerning the availability of injunctions operate in this area of tort.[11]

Damages

The basic principle of tort damages, that the plaintiff should be awarded a sum of money which will place him in the position he would have been in had the tort not been committed, is applicable in cases of economic loss.

Tortious remedies for economic loss differ from contractual ones in not being founded on a promise. If a person invests and loses £1,000 in reliance on a misstatement that the investment will produce a return of £2,000 the tortious measure of damage will seek to replace the loss (*i.e.* the capital and the return which one could have obtained on it).[12] If a contractual action was

---

[7] This is discussed in Chap. 16.

[8] See *ante*, pp. 276–283.

[9] The insurance doctrine of subrogation makes a similar assumption. An insurer who pays out under the terms of his contract for damage to an item which he has covered has no direct claim agaist the tortfeasor for this loss but must sue in the owner's name. *Simpson & Co.* v. *Thomson, Burrell* (1877) 3 App. Cas. 279; *Esso Petroleum Co. Ltd.* v. *Hall Russell & Co. Ltd., The Esso Bernica* [1989] 1 All E.R. 37.

[10] See *ante*, pp. 154–155.

[11] Except that the right of trade unions to take industrial action against an employer is safeguarded from the risk that legitimate union activity would be restricted too readily by the rules which favour the grant of an interlocutory injunction. The Trade Union and Labour Relations (Consolidation) Act 1992, s. 221(2) requires a court which is considering such an issue to take into account the possibility of the defendant being able to establish a defence under the Act.

[12] Subject to the possible addition of consequential losses.

appropriate, on the grounds that the defendant had promised that the profit would be achieved, the plaintiff's damages would be measured by the value of the promised "expectation" (*i.e.* the £2,000). In *Doyle* v. *Olby (Iron-mongers) Ltd.*[13] the Court of Appeal emphasised this distinction in the context of an action for deceit. The vendor of a business had represented to the plaintiff, who proceeded to purchase it in reliance on the representation, that all of the business shown in the accounts resulted from over-the-counter sales. In fact the turnover shown had been misrepresented and approximately half the annual turnover was the result of the employment of a part-time representative. The judge awarded damages calculated on the basis of giving the successful plaintiff the profits which would have been made had the representation been true. However, the Court of Appeal disagreed and established that the tortious measure of damages is aimed at restoring the plaintiff's losses as opposed to the contractual measure's aim of meeting the disappointed plaintiff's expectation of prospective gains. The plaintiff's losses, in the circumstances, included the capital invested in the business and consequential losses incurred in attempts to ensure its success.[14]

The fact that the obligations at issue in professional liability cases are generally ones to take reasonable care and skill provides a further explanation for the measure of damage adopted in relation to economic losses. A good example of this is provided by *Swingcastle Ltd.* v. *Alastair Gibson*[15] in which the defendant surveyors admitted that they had been negligent when they valued a house at £18,000 knowing that the brokers with whom they were dealing would use the valuation report in efforts to obtain a mortgage on the property on behalf of their clients. The plaintiff finance company made such a loan to the clients in reliance on the valuation. The terms of the loan required the borrowers to pay an annual rate of interest of 36.5 per cent., which would increase to 45.6 per cent. if they fell into arrears. The borrowers defaulted on the loan and the plaintiffs attempted to claim damages from the surveyors calculated on the basis of the sums which should have been paid to them under the terms of the loan agreement. The House of Lords refused to accept that this was the correct basis of the calculation. As the valuers' obligation was merely one to take reasonable care and skill when valuing with a view to a third party lending money on the property, it did not extend to warranting the borrowers' performance of their contractual obligations to the lender. The plaintiff company was entitled to recover as damages its capital losses and a sum representing the loss of use of that capital, but the rate of interest in relation to the loss of use was to be calculated by reference to the interest rates which were generally available in the market rather than the exceptional contractual terms at which the plaintiff actually lent money to "high risk" borrowers.

Swingcastle shows that an award of damages which is designed to put the plaintiff into the position he would have been in had the tort not occurred may include not only lost capital but also the returns which would have been produced by the capital if it had been invested elsewhere. This may be the standard rate of interest available on money in the relevant period or the profits which the plaintiff would have made from an alternative business.

---

[13] [1969] 2 Q.B. 158.
[14] The decision in *Doyle* established the survival of a "direct consequences" test of remoteness of damage in deceit, as opposed to one of reasonable foreseeability. See p. 100.
[15] [1991] 2 A.C. 223.

The deceit case of *East* v. *Maurer*[16] emphasised that the correct measure, if
the latter method is chosen, is the profits which the plaintiff would have
made from another, hypothetical, business and not those which the defendant would have made had he continued to run the business which he sold. A
person who is moving to a new area and attempting to establish a business is
unlikely to be able to achieve the same levels of profit as a person whose
business is well established.

It is a well established rule in cases brought in contract alleging that a
surveyor has been negligent when surveying property on behalf of a prospective purchaser that, as the purpose of the work is to advise the purchaser as to
the purchase price, any damages awarded should be calculated according to
the difference between the price paid for the property and the price which
would have been paid had the survey been conducted with reasonable care.
Damages in such a case are not to be measured by the cost of putting the
property into a sound state of repair.[17] This remains the result even in
cicumstances in which the purchaser would have withdrawn from the
proposed sale had the survey been conducted with reasonable care.[18] It
seems certain that the same measure of damage would be applied to tort
cases brought against surveyors on the authority of *Smith* v. *Eric S. Bush*.[19]
Damages for injury to non-pecuniary interests, for instance, for the disappointment, annoyance and vexation caused by tortious conduct which
damages economic interests, are, almost certainly, not available in tort.[20]
However, it does seem to be the case that awards of exemplary damages may
be possible in some limited areas of intentional infliction of economic loss.[21]

---

[16] [1991] 1 W.L.R. 461.
[17] *Philips* v. *Ward* [1956] 1 W.L.R. 471.
[18] *Watts* v. *Murrow* [1991] 1 W.L.R. 1421.
[19] [1990] 1 A.C. 831.
[20] In spite of the fact that they are now recognised in limited areas of contract.
[21] See *ante*, p. 150.

Chapter Fifteen

Intentional Infliction of Economic Loss

INTRODUCTION

The torts which control the deliberate infliction of financial losses, in other words, those which set the boundaries of legitimate trade competition, present a complex picture. A number of torts exist. Some of these provide a relatively general basis for liability; whereas others, such as deceit, are species of liability for misrepresentation.[1] The different species of interference with trade and conspiracy are commonly, if not particularly accurately, referred to as the "economic torts."

The root of the modern law on the economic torts is the decision in *Lumley* v. *Gye*[2] which held that a person who directly induces another to break a contract with a third person commits a tort against that third person. The third person may pursue alternative remedies against the contract breaker in contract and against the inducer in tort. The tort of conspiracy based on agreements to inflict damage grew up alongside the tort of directly inducing a breach of contract and found its modern form in *Crofter Hand Woven Harris Tweed* v. *Veitch*.[3] The modern law on the subject of intentionally inflicted economic loss is attributable to the development by the Court of Appeal in *D.C. Thomson & Co Ltd.* v. *Deakin*[4] of the extended tort of indirectly inducing or procuring a breach of contract and to the fact that in *Rookes* v. *Barnard*[5] in 1964 the House of Lords resurrected the dormant tort of intimidation to give a remedy to a person who was damaged by the threat of an unlawful act. These decisions provoked the growth of tort liability based on the notion that it may, in certain circumstances, be tortious to interfere intentionally with economic interests.

English law encounters little difficulty in justifying a tort remedy in respect of intentionally inflicted economic losses. But this is subject to the overriding consideration that our society values competition in its markets. The law in this area must accept that it is legitimate for businesses to aim to advance their interests at the expense of those of their competitors. The role of the law is to mark out the limits of acceptable competition and to provide adequate remedies for unacceptable behaviour. It is for this reason that the concept of unlawful means assumes such importance in large parts of this subject; it is

---

[1] Specialised torts such as passing-off and torts relating to the protection of copyright will not be discussed here.
[2] (1853) 2 E. & B. 216, see *post*, p. 326.
[3] [1942] A. C. 435.
[4] [1952] Ch. 646.
[5] [1964] A.C. 1129.

the factor which marks the boundary between legitimate and illegitimate competition.

There are a number of reasons why the law on intentionally inflicted economic loss poses difficulties.

Competing analyses

This area of law has evolved rapidly in recent years with the result that the boundaries between the different torts are not firmly settled and there are different ways of explaining the subject into which the authorities need to be fitted.

The traditional picture of the subject is of a group of separate co-existing nominate torts which have grown up independently of each other. These torts are; inducing or procuring a breach of contract, intimidation, conspiracy and a more nebulous tort of interference with contracts or other business interests by unlawful means.

A more radical analysis of the law treats the decision in *Rookes* v. *Barnard*[6] as having started a process of generalisation of the liabilities in this area. According to this approach the tort of inducing a breach of contract has been subsumed by interference with contracts; a tort which renders actionable acts which merely hinder the performance of contracts even if no breach occurs. Furthermore, it has been argued[7] that the development has gone even further and that this tort, intimidation and much of conspiracy should now be regarded as simply varieties of an even more general tort of interference with trade by use of unlawful means. On this analysis tort nowadays provides protection against interference with economic interests which are not founded on contractual relations. This analysis will be accepted for the purposes of this chapter for the simple reason that the majority of modern cases are expressed to be based on the tort of interference.

However, the contention that the law now recognises a general tort of interference with business by use of unlawful means is not free from difficulty. First, differences of opinion exist as to which torts are within the ambit of the generalised tort. If use of unlawful means is an essential component, as it would seem to be, the root tort of direct inducement of breach of contract and part of conspiracy, which do not impose this requirement, must survive independently of the general tort. The scope of the tort is also problematic. It is not certain which economic interests are protected and neither is it clear whether results obtained in litigation concerning the old nominate torts can be transferred automatically to the generalised doctrine.

The industrial relations context

A large part of this area of tort has developed in cases concerning strikes and other forms of industrial conflict. This has had an unfortunate effect on the law in as much as some of the cases have had political overtones and many have come before the courts as emergency interlocutory proceedings in which employers have sought injunctions to halt strike action. These factors

---

[6] [1964] A.C. 1129.
[7] Carty, (1988) 104 L.Q.R. 250. The author regards interference with contracts as a "half-way house" in the development of interference with trade.

have not been conducive to a careful consideration of the range of difficult legal issues raised by the cases. However, it is a common misconception that these torts are only of relevance to labour lawyers. A significant number of recent cases have considered the role of this area of tort in relation to other commercial activities.

Unlawful means

A further area of difficulty stems from the fact that the centrally important concept of "unlawful" means has never been properly defined and that the scope of a considerable part of the subject depends on this definition. A minor breach of a regulatory criminal law or a breach of a contractual undertaking which simply creates an obligation owed to an individual rather than to society as a whole, may be regarded as raising completely different considerations from the commission of a serious criminal law offence.

Overlapping torts

Finally, it must be appreciated that the torts which operate in this context are not mutually exclusive. A single act may be actionable in a number of ways as one of a number of torts. For example, a trade union which organises a picket line at a factory gate in support of a strike may be directly interfering with contracts in so far as the moral pressure not to attend work which the presence of the picketing workers imposes on other employees, constitutes a direct inducement to those employees to break their employment contracts by not attending work. A knock-on, and intended, effect of this may be that the employer, deprived of staff, is unable to fulfil orders which customers have placed with him; it is therefore an indirect consequence of the union's action that the employer breaks these contracts. The union's acts therefore also constitute an example of indirect procurement (*i.e.* prevention of the performance) of a breach of contract and is actionable as long as the requisite elements of intention, knowledge and unlawful means are present. The first tort is, in fact, central to the issue of the second tort's actionability as the existence of unlawful means will depend on whether the employees broke their employment contracts. This possibility of interpreting a single set of facts as raising different torts has been of great importance in the context of industrial disputes because such conduct is protected by statutory defences against tort liability. These statutory defences have been drafted in a form which provides defences to named torts if certain conditions are fulfilled and such drafting has created an incentive for plaintiffs to seek to reinterpret facts as disclosing other forms of non-protected torts. The history of the economic torts in the 1960s and 1970s was one of judicial attempts to circumvent the statutory protection in order to give employers weapons to invoke against strike action and of legislative responses to these moves based on the assumption that the resolution of industrial relations difficulties is achieved more effectively by processes other than litigation. The resurrection of the tort of intimidation in 1964 in the case of *Rookes* v. *Barnard*[8] and the consequential emergence of torts based on interference, form part of the judicial moves in this battle.

---

[8] [1964] A.C. 1129.

INTERFERENCE WITH TRADE BY UNLAWFUL MEANS

The following requirements must be established before the tort of interference with trade will operate.

1. **Intention:** the defendant must be shown to have intended to interfere with the trading relationship in question.

2. **Knowledge:** the defendant must be shown to have known of the existence of the relationship.

3. **Interference:** the defendant must be shown to have interfered with the relationship. If this was done indirectly (through the medium of a third person) the effect on the plaintiff's trade must be shown to have been a necessary consequence of the defendant's acts.

4. **Trade:** the interest interfered with must be one recognised by the courts as meriting protection.

5. **Unlawful means:** unlawful means must have been used in the course of the interference. Not every form of illegality constitutes unlawful means for this purpose. A direct inducement of a breach of contract is exempt from this requirement and it is not clear whether a direct interference is similarly exempt.

6. **Damage:** the plaintiff must prove that damage has been suffered as a result of the defendant's acts.[9]

Even if all of these requirements are satisfied, the common law defence of justification may excuse the defendant from liability on the basis of his motives. Persons or organisations taking industrial action, such as strikes, may be able to invoke specialised statutory defences.[10]

Intention and motive

Since interference with trade is a tort based on the intentional infliction of economic loss it might be thought that a defendant must be shown to have had the plaintiff in mind as a specific target of his acts before liability will be established. However, the courts have not imposed a stringent intention requirement. In *Lonrho plc. v. Fayed*[11] Woolf L.J. took the view that the intention requirement would be satisfied by the fact that the defendant deliberately embarked on a course of action when he appreciated the probable damaging consequence of this to the plaintiff.

The plaintiff need not have been identified to the defendant other than as a member of a class of persons who are intended to be affected by the acts. For example, a union taking industrial action against an employer may commonly be held to have committed torts against the employer's customers or

---

[9] *Greig* v. *Insole* [1977] 1 W.L.R. 302. If the action is for a quia timet injunction a likelihood of damage if the interference proves successful must be shown.

[10] Trade Union and Labour Relations (Consolidation) Act 1992, Pt. V.

[11] [1990] 2 Q.B. 479.

suppliers. This result is confirmed by the decision in *Falconer* v. *A.S.L.E.F.*[12] in which a rail passenger sought damages from a trade union for expenses incurred when British Rail broke its contract to carry him as a result of a strike. The union argued that the tort of interference could not be established unless it could be shown that the plaintiff was the identified object of the defendant's action. The judge rejected this saying that it was sufficient that the plaintiff was an unidentified member of a class of persons which the union intended to inconvenience so that they would put pressure on their main target, in this case British Rail. A suggestion that the effect on the plaintiff was a consequence rather than the intention of the union's acts was dismissed as "naive."

On the other hand, it is certain that the mere fact that the defendant ought to have reasonably foreseen that harm would follow from particular actions will not suffice. If it did, the tort would be likely to undermine the restrictive rules relating to the recovery of negligently inflicted "pure" economic losses.[13] The result would seem to be that the defendant must either have intended to do harm to the plaintiff (although this need not be the predominant aim) or must have intentionally embarked on an act reckless of the fact that the probable consequence would be such harm. This approach is in line with Diplock L.J.'s dictum in *Emerald Construction Co. Ltd.* v. *Lowthian*[14] to the effect that the element of intention to procure a breach of contract is sufficiently established by proof that the defendant intended the party procured to bring the contract to an end if there was no lawful method available to him of terminating it. In such a case it is likely that the defendant will be held liable on the basis that a person is taken to have intended the reasonable consequences of his acts.[15]

In *Lonrho plc* v. *Fayed*[16] the Court of Appeal refused to accept that the test derived from the tort of conspiracy, to the effect that the defendant had to have the predominant motive of injuring the plaintiff before he could be held liable, applied to the tort of interference. It is well established that the fact that trade union members may have the predominant purpose of benefitting their own interests at the expense of those of their employer will not allow them to escape liability under this tort.[17]

Knowledge

The requirement that the defendant must know of the existence of the contract or trading relationship in question is closely related to the requirement of intention. The courts have had to strike a balance between conflicting considerations at this point. On the one hand, a person cannot be said to have intended to interfere with something of which he has no knowledge. Furthermore, a stringent knowledge requirement serves to protect those normal market activities of traders which are designed to benefit the trader at the expense of their competitors. On the other hand, the courts have been wary of attempts by defendants to escape liability for their deliberate attacks

[12] [1986] I.R.L.R. 331.
[13] See *post*, Chap. 16.
[14] [1966] 1 W.L.R. 691.
[15] For an example of this principle being applied to a case of inducing a breach of contract, see *Greig* v. *Insole* [1978] 3 All E.R. 449 at 489.
[16] [1990] 2 Q.B. 479.
[17] It would suffice to negative liability in conspiracy to use lawful means. See *post*, p. 327.

on the trading relations of others by pleading that they lack precise knowledge of the terms on which the others trade. As commercial people rarely volunteer information as to the actual terms on which they conduct their business[18] the tort would be emasculated by a requirement that the defendant should possess precise knowledge before liability can be established.

The decision of the Court of Appeal in *Emerald Construction Co. Ltd.* v. *Lowthian*[19] established that a person can commit the tort even though he does not know the precise terms of the contract; a general knowledge of its existence is all that is required. In that case the defendant union officials knew of the fact that the plaintiff was working under contract, but did not know the terms of that contract. Cases decided in the industrial dispute area have held the knowledge requirement to be satisfied on the basis of a trade union's general knowledge of the kinds of contract used in the particular area of commerce in which it operates. In *Merkur Island Shipping Corporation* v. *Laughton*[20] Lord Diplock said that there could hardly be anyone better informed than the International Transport Workers' Federation (a union representing seamen) as to the terms of the kinds of contracts under which merchant ships trade.

Interference

The defendant must be shown to have interfered with the relationship. A causation point may arise here in as much as it must be shown that it was the defendant's acts, rather than those of the person with whom the plaintiff had the relationship, which constituted the cause of the damage to those interests of the plaintiff which derived from that relationship. The person induced might actually have been keen to, and intending to, renege on the relationship which he had with the plaintiff. A good example of this is provided by the facts of *British Motor Trade Association* v. *Salvadori*.[21] It was there pleaded, in response to an allegation that the defendant had induced a breach of contract between motor dealers and persons who had bought cars subject to a covenant that the vehicle would not be resold for 12 months, that it was not tortious to induce a breach of contract by a person who was willing to breach it. This defence failed. The better view is that all that needs to be shown to establish the defendant's liability is that his acts amounted either to aiding, encouraging, procuring or co-operating with the acts of the person with whom the plaintiff had the relationship.[22] Liability in tort is therefore established on the basis of any conduct which goes to facilitate the damage to the relationship other than that which is wholly attributable to the acts of the person who was in the particular relationship with the plaintiff. If the interference with the plaintiff's interests occurred indirectly (through the medium of a third person) the effect on the plaintiff's trade must be shown to have been a necessary consequence of the defendant's acts.

---

[18] However, it is said that employers when involved in industrial disputes with trade unions may volunteer such information to the union when seeking an injunction in order to preempt a defence of lack of knowledge. Wedderburn, *The Worker and the Law* (3rd ed., 1986), p. 588.

[19] [1966] 1 W.L.R. 691.

[20] [1983] 2 A.C. 570.

[21] [1949] Ch. 556.

[22] Stone, [1991] J.I.B.L. 310.

A variety of forms of interference have been recognised in the cases. The traditional forms of the tort cover interferences in the form of both inducing a breach of contract, that is, using persuasion to achieve the end, and procuring such a breach which involves creating a situation in which performance becomes an impossibility, for example by calling a workforce out on strike with the result that the employer is unable to fulfil existing contracts. For a successful allegation of an inducement to be made there must be some evidence of pressure being placed on one of the parties to the contract; it does not suffice to show that the defendant has done no more than express a desire that others will break their contracts.[23] On the other hand, there need be no evidence that the pressure is proving, or is likely to be, successful in damaging the relationship at which it is aimed. In *Greig* v. *Insole*[24] it was alleged that bodies representing the established cricketing authorities had committed the tort of inducing a breach of contract by imposing bans on players who had signed contracts to play in a rebel "unofficial" series of cricket matches. Slade J. refused to accept that the defendants could escape liability by arguing that the ban was likely to prove unsuccessful in achieving its ends because the players were adamant that they intended to fulfil their commitments to the unofficial series. He held that an injunction against prospective damage could be awarded if it was proved that the inducement "if successful" was likely to cause more than nominal damage.

An inducement does not need to amount to an offer of an immediate advantage to the person to whom it is directed in order to count as an actionable interference. In *Bents Brewery Co. Ltd.* v. *Hogan*[25] a trade union's intention of preparing a programme in support of a claim for improved wages and conditions for the managers of public houses was held to be a "clear inducement" to those managers to comply, in breach of their employment contracts, with its request to provide information to support the claim even though the outcome of such a campaign must have been highly speculative.

Authority exists to support the proposition that the mere communication of information to a person must be distinguished from the placing of pressure on that person in such a way as to constitute an inducement. This distinction proved decisive to the result in *D.C. Thomson & Co. Ltd.* v. *Deakin*.[26] In that case the defendant union organised a boycott of the plaintiff company which maintained a non-union policy. The defendants communicated this information to Bowaters, a company which supplied paper to the plaintiffs. Not wishing to become embroiled in a dispute with its workforce over work destined for the plaintiffs, Bowaters chose not to instruct their employees to undertake work destined for the plaintiffs and failed to fulfil its contract with them. The plaintiff's claim for an injunction to restrain the defendants from procuring a breach of the contract of supply between the plaintiff and Bowaters failed, in part, because the Court of Appeal held that the union's communication with Bowaters amounted merely to the giving of information as to the existence of the boycott rather than to placing pressure on them. To modern lawyers the application of the distinction to these facts

[23] *Camellia Tanker S.A.* v. *I.T.W.F.* [1976] I.C.R. 274.
[24] [1978] 3 All E.R. 449.
[25] [1945] 2 All E.R. 570.
[26] [1952] Ch. 646.

seems artificial. The industrial relations reality was that Bowaters were likely to be faced by industrial action if they sought to fulfil the contract and one would expect an implied threat of this nature to be sufficient to amount to an inducement. But it does not follow that the distinction should not be maintained. It is perfectly reasonable, and desirable, for information concerning a firm's industrial relations prospects to be communicated to it and the courts should not be too ready to regard such communications as intentional attacks on their business relations with their suppliers or customers.

It would seem to be the case that an interference can also be made out on the basis that a defendant has intentionally entered into a contract with a person knowing that the creation of the contract will put that person in breach of a contract with another person. This was one of the reasons for the defendants in *British Motor Trade Association* v. *Salvadori*[27] being held to have committed the tort. The plaintiff organisation supported a policy whereby cars were sold, shortly after the end of the Second World War, subject to a term that the purchaser would not resell within 12 months. The purpose was to ensure that purchasers could not exploit the shortages which existed by reselling at a profit. The defendants engaged in a concerted attempt to acquire vehicles in breach of these contracts and to resell at a profit. Roxburgh J. held that an actionable interference with the contracts could be established on the basis of any active step to facilitate the breach of the contract conducted with knowledge of it. It was only in the alternative that the judge held that the defendants, by offering the car owners a sum greater than they had paid for the vehicle, had "induced" a breach of the contracts.

The leading case of *Rookes* v. *Barnard*[28] established that an interference in the form of threatening another person with an unlawful act is actionable. At the time of *Rookes* such threats were held to amount to the tort of intimidation, but more recently this area has been assimilated into the general tort of interference with the threat of an unlawful act counting as an actionable form of interference. Interference of this type covers two separate situations. In the "three party" situation the unlawful threat is directed at a person who is induced thereby to inflict harm on a third party (the plaintiff). *Rookes* provides an example of this. The defendants threatened an employer that strike action would be taken in breach of contract unless a particular employee was dismissed. The employer chose to dismiss the employee lawfully, with appropriate notice, in order to avert the strike. The House of Lords held that the defendants had committed a tort against the employee on these facts holding; first, that the tort of intimidation based on threats of an unlawful act exists and, secondly, that a threat of a breach of contract could constitute an actionable form of unlawful means. The "privity of contract" objection, that the plaintiff, as a non-party to the contract between the person threatening and the person threatened, could not sue if the contract was broken and should therefore not be able to sue on the basis of a threat to break it, was dismissed. Lord Devlin argued that in a three party situation the person threatened would either inflict damage on the third party in order to avoid the threat (in which case the contract would not be broken) or the threat would be carried out and it would be the person threatened rather

---

[27] [1949] Ch. 556.
[28] [1964] A.C. 1129.

than the third party who would be damaged. The third party's tort claim was based on the threat rather than on the breach of contract and assumed that no breach had occurred. The second form of intimidation, the "two party" form, is intended to provide for losses caused to the person at whom the threat is directed. For example, an employer may lose money as a result of refraining from fulfilling work if his workforce threatened to strike if he went ahead with it. The two party situation, which is relatively uninvestigated, creates particular problems because it may possibly provide tort remedies in circumstances which are already governed by the rules relating to anticipatory breaches of contract.

There is a suggestion in the judgment of Russell L.J. in the case of *Morgan* v. *Fry*[29] that not all threats of unlawful action constitute an actionable form of interference. The argument is that the potency of the particular threat made by the defendant must be measured and if it is found to be less than that which could have been achieved by a threat of a lawful act it will not be an actionable form of interference. The potency of the threat is thought to be more important than the technical question of whether what is threatened is lawful or not. This reasoning has considerable significance in cases concerning strike action because both employers and employees will commonly prefer the option of strike action, which is unlawful as constituting a breach of contract, to the theoretically lawful act of the workforce giving proper notice to terminate its employment.[30] It is unlikely to be in the interests of either side for the employment relationship to be severed.

Direct-Indirect

In *Greig* v. *Insole*[31] Slade J. drew the distinction between direct and indirect interferences in the following words:

> "I take it . . . that the phrase 'direct interference' covers the case where the intervener, either by himself or his agents, speaks, writes or publishes words or does other acts which communicate pressure or persuasion to the mind or person of one of the contracting parties themselves, while 'indirect interference' refers to a case where, without actually doing any of these things, the intervener nevertheless procures or attempts to procure a situation which will result or may result in a breach of contract."

An example of this distinction can be drawn on the facts of *D.C. Thomson & Co. Ltd.* v. *Deakin*.[32] It would have been open to the union, in that case, to "directly" interfere with the contract of supply between the plaintiff company and Bowaters by threatening or otherwise attempting to persuade Bowaters not to fulfil it or to "indirectly" interfere with it by addressing the pressure to the employees on whom Bowaters depended for the services needed to complete the contract. In the decision in *Middlebrook Mushrooms Ltd.* v. *Transport & General Workers Union*[33] it was held that the defendant union's conduct of distributing leaflets, which informed potential customers

---

[29] [1968] 2 Q.B. 710.
[30] A concerted act of this kind might amount to an actionable conspiracy.
[31] [1978] 3 All E.R. 449 at 486.
[32] [1952] Ch. 646.
[33] [1993] I.R.L.R. 232.

of a shop of the fact that the union was in dispute with the plaintiffs who supplied produce to the shop, could not amount to a direct interference with the contracts between the plaintiffs and the shops. The distinction between direct and indirect interference was said to be essentially one of causation and the question was whether the interference with the contract was imposed by the defendant in person (in which case the interference was direct) or through the agency of a third person. On the facts it was clear that any decision by the supermarket to discontinue dealings with the plaintiff would be the result of potential customers' reaction to the defendant's campaign rather than to the defendant's conduct itself. The interference was therefore indirect.

Indirect interference may be actionable, two or more stages removed from the interest interfered with, so long as the other conditions are satisfied.[34] The further removed the interference is from the interest the less likely it is that the requirements of intention and knowledge will be satisfied.

In the case of an indirect interference there is an additional requirement that the defendant must be shown to have used unlawful means.[35] This requirement is established in relation to indirect inducements of breach of contract and interferences with contract by *D.C. Thomson & Co. Ltd.* v. *Deakin*[36] and *Torquay Hotel Co. Ltd.* v. *Cousins*[37] respectively. The explanation given for the requirement is that it is needed to protect free competition. A trader may knowingly and intentionally disrupt a rival's trading relationships by "cornering the market" in a commodity essential for the rival's business, but, so long as there is nothing unlawful in what is done, the conduct represents free competitive markets at work and is not tortious.

An attack on vested contractual rights in the form of a direct inducement of a breach of contract is actionable in the absence of unlawful means. It is not entirely clear whether the more modern version of this tort, a direct interference with contracts or business, is similarly exempt from the requirement.[38] However, the better view is that to permit such a vague form of liability to exist would question the legitimacy of much normal trade competition.[39] The case of *Brekkes* v. *Cattel*[40] revealed some of the dangers of such a development. It raised the question of whether a group of traders who chose not to continue to deal with the plaintiff had committed the tort of direct interference with the plaintiff's contracts or trade. Although there may be circumstances in which it should be tortious for a person to use unlawful means to interfere with an established course of dealings,[41] this surely cannot be extended to holding liable a person who has himself lawfully refused to continue with a relationship to which he was a party, when there was no contractual obligation on him to continue. In *Brekkes*, Pennycuick V.C. supported this result when he said that all forms of interference with trade[42]

---

[34] *Merkur Island Shipping Corporation* v. *Laughton* [1983] 2 A.C. 570.

[35] See *post*, p. 323 for the meaning of unlawful means in this context.

[36] [1952] Ch. 646.

[37] [1969] 2 Ch. 106.

[38] The suggestion that this is possible in relation to interferences with contracts derives from Lord Denning M.R.'s judgment in *Torquay Hotel Co. Ltd.* v. *Cousins* [1969] 2 Ch. 106.

[39] Clerk & Lindsell on *Torts* (16th ed., 1989), para. 15.05.

[40] [1972] Ch. 105.

[41] See *post*, p. 322.

[42] Other than a direct inducement or procurement of a breach of contract.

(*i.e.* both direct and indirect) require proof of unlawful means to be actionable.[43]

Trade (the protected interests)

The question of what interests qualify for protection under the general tort is one which fixes the scope of the tort. As the majority of modern cases have been pleaded as interference with "contracts" rather than "trade" the limits of the protected interests have not often been investigated. The cases support the propositions set out below.

An attack on existing contractual relationships in the form of a procuring or inducing of a breach of contract clearly suffices on the authority of well established case law.[44] Hindering the performance of a contract by making it more difficult or expensive to perform even if no breach occurs, is now also well established as a form of the tort. This development is generally regarded as the explanation for the existence of the tort when an interference fails to procure a breach because an exclusion clause in the contract, possibly one designed to deal with the case of the contract being affected by industrial action, provides one party to it with a defence to an action for breach.[45] This was the case on the facts of *Torquay Hotel Co. Ltd.* v. *Cousins*.[46] In that case the plaintiff sought an injunction to prevent a trade union from interfering with a contract under which Esso was obliged to supply fuel oil to the plaintiff's business. The contract contained a term which absolved Esso from liability for a failure to supply which resulted from, *inter alia*, industrial disputes. Although there is support in the case for the proposition that the clause did not change the character of the breach of contract but merely protected Esso from being held liable for the consequences of any breach that did occur and that the facts were therefore capable of being construed as a procurement of a breach of contract, the modern approach is to accept that the case establishes that it is tortious to act in a way which interferes with the performance of a contract but does not amount to procuring a breach of it.

Inducing a lawful termination of a contract would similarly seem to be recognised as meriting protection on the authority of the House of Lords decision in *Rookes* v. *Barnard*.[47] In that case the employee was protected when unlawful means were used to induce his employer to dismiss him. The act of dismissal on the part of the employer was a perfectly proper act as due notice was given. The result in *Rookes* marked a major development in this area of tort; it was now protecting legitimate expectations (the employee's hope that he would continue to be employed) as opposed to being confined to vested contractual rights (the employee's entitlement to the appropriate notice prior to dismissal).[48] The significance of this was not lost to the courts. On one of the issues which arose in *Torquay Hotel Co. Ltd.* v. *Cousins*[49] the Court of Appeal granted an injunction against union members to stop them

---

[43] On the facts, the actions of the defendants were held to have amounted to unlawful means as an infringement of the Restrictive Trade Practices Act 1956.

[44] *Lumley* v. *Gye* (1853) 2 E. & B. 216; *D.C. Thomson & Co. Ltd.* v. *Deakin* [1952] Ch. 646.

[45] *Torquay Hotel Co. Ltd.* v. *Cousins* [1969] 2 Ch. 106; *Merkur Island Shipping Corporation* v. *Laughton* [1983] 2 A.C. 570. In the latter case Lord Diplock was of the opinion that the tort covered all prevention of due performance of a primary obligation under a contract.

[46] [1969] 2 Ch. 106.

[47] [1964] A.C. 1129.

[48] The facts of the case predate the introduction in 1971 of the remedy of unfair dismissal.

[49] [1969] 2 Ch. 106.

interfering with the creation of contracts which were to be made by the plaintiff with a supplier who was prepared to break the union's boycott of the plaintiff[50] and in *Hadmor Productions Ltd.* v. *Hamilton*[51] the House of Lords applied the tort of interference to commercial expectations of business which were not based on a contractual relationship. In that case the plaintiff television production company had sold a programme to Thames Television who had the right, but were under no contractual obligation, to broadcast it.

The move beyond the protection of vested contractual duties has also resulted in the recognition of the fact that inducing the breach of, or hindering the performance of, a statutory duty, is a form of the tort.[52] This is a logical consequence of extending the protection of financial expectations beyond those derived from a contract. In a mixed economy a range of services are provided under statutory duties and it would be anomalous to exclude this area of financial expectations from the ambit of the tort.[53]

However, there do seem to be limits on the kinds of financial interests which are protected. In *Lonrho Ltd.* v. *Shell Petroleum Co. Ltd.*[54] the House of Lords rejected the existence of a tort based on the wide principle that an action for damages is available to "a person who suffers harm as the inevitable consequence of the unlawful, intentional and positive acts of another." The court's attention in that case was directed to the different meanings of "unlawful," rather than the nature of the loss suffered. The focus of attention changed in a later case featuring the same plaintiff. In the first instance decision in *Lonrho plc* v. *Fayed*[55] Pill J. held that the right or freedom to mount a take-over bid for a company is not a business asset or a form of legal right to which the law will grant protection. However, the point is not concluded because when the case went to appeal, the Court of Appeal left the point open and the House of Lords subsequently regarded the plaintiff's case as arguable without making specific reference to this point.

It has been contended[56] that the scope of the protected interests should include equitable obligations, such as a company director's fiduciary duty to the company or an agent's duties to a principal. Such obligations commonly have their origin in and overlap with contract, but extend to cover a wider range of duties. However, on the only occasion on which the point has been directly put to a court, when in *Metall und Rohstoff A.G.* v. *Donaldson, Lufkin & Jenrette Inc.*[57] the plaintiffs alleged that the defendants had procured or induced breaches of trust, the Court of Appeal took the view that conventional principles of trusts law were sufficient to deal with the problem of persons inciting a breach of trust or wrongfully meddling with

---

[50] It is possible that the result depends on the fact that the claim was for an injunction as it would be impossible to maintain the status quo in the plaintiff's favour without providing this protection.

[51] [1983] 1 A.C. 191.

[52] *Meade* v. *Haringey L.B.C.* [1979] I.C.R. 494; *Associated British Ports* v. *Transport & General Workers' Union* [1989] 1 W.L.R. 939.

[53] However, in order to avoid this development undermining the result of *Cutler* v. *Wandsworth Stadium Ltd.* [1949] A.C. 398 it is essential that the statutory duty in question is one which would give rise to a cause of action vested in the plaintiff *Lonrho Ltd.* v. *Shell Petroleum Co. Ltd.* [1982] A.C. 173; *Barretts & Baird (Wholesale) Ltd.* v. *I.P.C.S.* [1987] I.R.L.R. 3.

[54] [1982] A.C. 173.

[55] [1988] 3 All E.R. 464.

[56] Clerk & Lindsell *op. cit.* para. 15.20.

[57] [1990] 1 Q.B. 391.

trust assets. The court concluded that it knew of no authority supporting the existence of a tort on such facts and said that it could see no sufficient justification for its introduction.

Unlawful means

The requirement of unlawful means is the central element in the modern tort of interference with trade, but, unfortunately, there are great difficulties in determining what kinds of conduct satisfy the criterion. The word "unlawful" has a number of meanings and a variety of conduct infringes different laws and can loosely be termed "unlawful." The simple view that everything which is a tort, crime or breach of contract counts as unlawful means cannot be accepted, but the problem remains of deciding what can count. There can be no doubt that the courts have only recently begun to grapple with this difficulty and have yet to reach a satisfactory conclusion.

It is the clear result of the leading decision of the Court of Appeal in *D.C. Thomson & Co. Ltd.* v. *Deakin*[58] that the breach of a contractual obligation will constitute unlawful means. On the facts of that case the employees of Bowaters had not been instructed to handle work destined for the plaintiff company and had therefore not taken any industrial action in breach of their contracts of employment. It followed that no unlawful means had been proved such as would render the defendant's actions an actionable indirect procurement of a breach of contract. In contrast, all of the elements of the tort were established in *J.T. Stratford & Son Ltd.* v. *Lindley*,[59] a case in which it was alleged that officials of a union had committed a tort by interfering with the contracts under which the plaintiff company hired out barges by placing an embargo on their members working barges owned by the plaintiff. The unlawful means was based on the fact that employees of the hirers (who were members of the union) had broken their contracts of employment by refusing to work on barges which were to be returned to the plaintiff's possession at the end of their period of hire with the result that the hirers broke their contracts with the plaintiff. *Rookes* v. *Barnard*[60] establishes that a threat of acts in breach of contract is also capable of counting as unlawful means: although contracts are private agreements concluded between individuals the House of Lords took the view that a threat to break a contract should count as a form of unlawful means because it might well be much more coercive than the threat to commit a crime or a tort. It has been suggested that this should not be regarded as an invariable result and that the potency of the particular threat should be considered.[61]

Criminal offences create particular difficulties. It is an oversimplification to regard all crimes as unlawful in this context. The correct approach is to distinguish between criminal offences according to whether they are actionable in the sense of giving rise to rights to claim compensation in tort. It is a matter of basic principle that not every breach of a criminal law statute grounds tortious liability to those injured thereby. The breach of statutory duty principle[62] exemplified by *Cutler* v. *Wandsworth Stadium Ltd*,[63] insists

---

[58] [1952] Ch. 646.
[59] [1965] A.C. 269.
[60] [1964] A.C. 1129.
[61] See the discussion of Russell L.J.'s views in *Morgan* v. *Fry* [1968] 2 Q.B. 710 at p. 319.
[62] See *ante*, p. 43.
[63] [1949] A.C. 398.

that actionability in tort depends on the construction put on the particular statute by the courts. In *Cutler* the House of Lords decided that a bookmaker had no rights to sue in tort for breach of statutory duty if damaged by conduct which constituted a criminal offence under the Betting and Lotteries Act 1934. This result requires the courts to hold that the same conduct does not amount to unlawful means. Otherwise the bizarre result would be possible, at least in the case of intentionally inflicted damage, of a plaintiff circumventing the *Cutler* result by framing his claim as one alleging that the defendant intentionally interfered with his trade by use of unlawful means. The approach of making a decision on the existence of unlawful means dependent on the issue of whether the criminal offence is independently actionable in tort, is almost certainly supported by the speeches in the House of Lords in *Lonrho Ltd.* v. *Shell Petroleum Co. Ltd.*[64] and by a case at first instance.[65] However, the question cannot be regarded as finally settled because the Court of Appeal was of the view in *Associated British Ports* v. *T.G.W.U.*[66] that it was arguable that a breach of statutory duty could constitute unlawful means even though that breach was not actionable at the suit of the plaintiff.[67] In support of this view the members of the court argued that there was no precedent for a requirement that the unlawful means should be actionable by the plaintiff and that earlier decisions, which had held that breach of the provisions of the Restrictive Trade Practices Act[68] constituted unlawful means, did not recognise the requirement.

Even the area of tortious conduct is not free from difficulty. The apparently obvious rule that unlawful means will be established by conduct which constitutes a tort, but not otherwise, may well be incorrect. Support exists for the proposition that unlawful means may be established by conduct which is capable of constituting a tort even though no tort has been committed on the facts. For example, a fraud directed at a third party will apparently suffice although the third party would have no cause of action because he has suffered no damage and the plaintiff has no claim in deceit because the fraud was not directed at him.[69]

Other possible forms of unlawful means have been recognised in the cases. Acts which amounted to a contempt of court were held to count in *Acrow (Automation) Ltd.* v. *Rex Chainbelt Ltd.*[70] Interference with the freedom of the press as guaranteed by the European Convention on Human Rights was said to suffice in *Associated Newspapers Group* v. *Wade*.[71] On a number of occasions[72] acts, in the form of an organised boycott of another business, which were presumed to be unlawful under the terms of the Restrictive Trade

---

[64] [1982] A.C. 173.
[65] *Barretts & Baird (Wholesale) Ltd.* v. *I.P.C.S.* [1987] I.R.L.R. 3.
[66] [1989] I.R.L.R. 305.
[67] Even though it held that an inducement of breach of statutory duty was only actionable as a species of interference with trade if that duty was actionable at the suit of the plaintiff. The House of Lords ([1989] I.R.L.R. 399) did not deal with the point.
[68] *Daily Mirror Newspapers Ltd.* v. *Gardner* [1968] 2 Q.B. 762 and *Brekkes* v. *Cattel.* The best explanation is that these cases, which were decided 10 years before *Lonrho Ltd.* v. *Shell Petroleum (U.K.) Ltd.,* simply failed to deal with the point.
[69] *Lonrho plc* v. *Fayed* [1990] 2 Q.B. 479. The point was not raised in the House of Lords [1992] A.C. 448. However, the House did not strike out as unarguable a claim of this kind.
[70] [1971] 1 W.L.R. 1676.
[71] [1979] 1 W.L.R. 697.
[72] *Daily Mirror Newspapers Ltd.* v. *Gardner* [1968] 2 Q.B. 762; *Brekkes* v. *Cattel* [1972] Ch. 105.

Practices Act 1976[73] have been held to be capable of counting as unlawful means, in spite of the fact that that Act creates a specialised procedure and court for determining whether such acts are actually unlawful.

Justification

The defence of justification allows a defendant to escape liability on the basis of his motives or commercial interests even though all of the constituent elements of the tort have been established. The existence of such a defence is well supported by dicta,[74] but by a small number of decisions. In contrast to the position in the tort of conspiracy, pursuit of one's own interests, or those of third parties,[75] is usually insufficient to establish the defence. In the words of Slade J. in *Greig* v. *Insole*[76] if the other conditions for establishing the tort are proved "it is quite irrelevant that (the defendant) may have acted in good faith and without malice or under a mistaken understanding as to his legal rights."

As a result of the limited nature of the defence of justification, trade unions have been forced to rely on statutory defences rather than common law justification when seeking to avoid tortious liability for strike or other forms of industrial action. Under the Trade Union and Labour Relations (Consolidation) Act 1992 persons or organisations taking strike or other industrial action may be able to invoke specialised statutory defences.[77] It seems to be generally accepted that normal trade union activities are not protected by the common law defence of justification.[78]

It has been held to be justifiable to induce breach of contract in order to uphold public morality. In *Brimelow* v. *Casson*[79] the defendant union officials were held to be able to invoke the defence in order to justify action taken to induce the plaintiff to pay a living wage to the chorus girls whom he employed. The defendants had supported their case by evidence that showed that the wages paid were so low that some of the girls had been forced to resort to prostitution to supplement them. More recently the defence has been successfully used in a commercial context. *Edwin Hill & Partners* v. *First National Finance Corp. plc.*[80] shows that the courts may now be more prepared to allow the defence of justification to be used on a more general basis to render lawful acts done in order to protect a person's commercial interests. The plaintiff had been retained by a developer to provide architectural services. The defendant bank had loaned money to the developer which was secured by a charge over the property. The developer was unsuccessful in raising the additional funds which were needed to enable the work to proceed. The bank, having doubts as to whether the value of the undeveloped property would be sufficient, if sold, to cover its loan, decided not to enforce

---

[73] Both of the leading cases on this issue were actually decided under the earlier 1956 Act.
[74] For example, the judgment of Romer L.J. in *Glamorgan Coal Co. Ltd.* v. *South Wales Miners' Federation* [1903] 2 K.B. 545.
[75] For example, the employees represented by a trade union.
[76] [1978] 1 W.L.R. 302.
[77] Trade Union and Labour Relations (Consolidation) Act 1992, Pt. V.
[78] But in *Cory Lighterage Ltd.* v. *Transport and General Workers' Union* [1973] I.C.R. 339, Lord Denning M.R. was of the view that a trade union could plead the defence of justification against a worker who might be thought to have brought the problem on himself by his own eccentric conduct.
[79] [1924] 1 Ch. 302.
[80] [1989] 1 W.L.R. 225.

the security but to provide additional finance to enable the development to proceed. Although the bank had no criticism of the skill or work of the plaintiff it felt that the commercial prospects of the development would be enhanced if a more prestigious firm of architects were responsible for the work. It therefore made the provision of additional funding conditional upon the developer dispensing with the plaintiff's services. When the plaintiff claimed that this constituted an actionable interference with their contract the defendants argued that justification was available as a defence. The Court of Appeal accepted that justification could be used, holding that a mortgagee who had a legal charge over property had equal, or superior, rights to deal with it to the plaintiff. It was accepted that the bank could have pleaded justification successfully if it had used its powers under the mortgage to sell the property or to appoint a receiver with the result that the plaintiff's contract was terminated and it was held that it could not be in a poorer position if it chose to take the less drastic step of funding the project to completion.[81]

DIRECT INDUCEMENT OF A BREACH OF CONTRACT

As has already been mentioned, this tort, which is the root of a great part of the subject of intentional infliction of economic loss, survives as a tort distinct from interference with trade by unlawful means. A direct attack on vested contractual rights is tortious without any need for the use of unlawful means to be proved. The conditions governing the tort are identical to those for interference with trade but for the absence of the requirement of unlawful means and for the need to prove that an actual breach of contract was induced or procured.

The leading case on this tort is *Lumley* v. *Gye*[82] in which the defendant had induced a well known singer to break her contract to work exclusively for the plaintiff. The Court of Queen's Bench held that this conduct amounted to the defendant having committed a tort against the plaintiff irrespective of the fact that the plaintiff might have had a valuable action in breach of contract against the singer. The reasoning in the case was based on older authorities which established that it was tortious to entice a servant to leave a master's service. However, the case marked an extension of this principle in so far as the singer was arguably not a servant in the strict sense and, as a result, the case opened the way to a tort which applies to liability for the inducement or procurement of a breach of any kind of contract.

CONSPIRACY

Conspiracy consists of an agreement[83] by two or more persons to do an act which is intended to injure another person. The tort requires proof of the agreement, of acts in pursuance of it and of resulting damage.[83a] It is

---

[81] It is not at all clear whether the defence could have been pleaded successfully had the new funding been provided on similar conditions by a bank which had had no previous dealings with the project.

[82] (1853) 2 E. & B. 216.

[83] Husband and wife can conspire together *Midland Bank Trust Co. Ltd.* v. *Green (No. 3)* [1981] 2 W.L.R. 1.

[83a] For discussion of the forms of damage on which the tort can be based see *Lonhro plc* v. *Fayed (No. 5)* [1994] 1 All E.R. 188.

distinguishable in its requirements from the criminal offence of conspiracy which is founded on the simple fact of the agreement.[84] Tortious conspiracies have traditionally been placed in two classes according to whether lawful or unlawful means were used by the conspirators. Both forms of the tort may be actionable. The surprising feature of the tort is that a conspiracy which uses only lawful means may be actionable in certain circumstances.

Conspiracy is nowadays regarded as an anomalous tort, but one which is too well established by authority to be removed from the law. Restrictions which have been placed on it, such as the predominant purpose test, have tended to reduce its importance. It has a number of roles: first, a conspiracy may render tortious an act which would not be actionable if done by one person alone, this amounts to saying that a lawful act may, exceptionally, be tortious if done by two or more persons with the intention of injuring a third. The tort therefore infringes the basic principle that a malicious motive cannot render a lawful act tortious. The second role of conspiracy is to enable claims to be brought against persons who would otherwise escape liability. The tort may give the plaintiff additional defendants to pursue who may be better placed to pay damages. A person who conspired with others to commit a tort, but who did not commit it himself will be liable in tort in this way. At times this has been used to bring trade union officials in as defendants to tort claims when the actual tortious acts were committed by the members who they represented.[85] The tort can be similarly used to pursue persons who commit commercial frauds. If a company has been left insolvent or if assets have been deliberately removed from it to defeat the claims of creditors, conspiracy can provide a remedy against the directors or others who arranged the manoeuvre.[86] The fact that a separate cause of action exists against each conspirator means that the tort can permit new proceedings to be brought against other conspirators if a judgment obtained against one conspirator has not been fully satisfied.

Conspiracies using lawful means

A conspiracy of two or more persons which does not have the predominant purpose of protecting or advancing the legitimate interests of the conspirators is actionable even if no unlawful means are used. The justification which is given for the existence of this form of the tort is that a person may find it far more difficult to resist an attack on his affairs by two or more persons than a similar attack mounted by a single individual.[87] This is far too simplistic a view to be acceptable; as has been pointed out,[88] a single large corporation may wield sufficient economic power to destroy many businesses. Economic power in a particular sector of industry may be concentrated in one firm or in many. It is this species of the tort which is regarded as anomalous.

---

[84] *Lonrho Ltd.* v. *Shell Petroleum Co. Ltd.* [1982] A.C. 173.
[85] *Rookes* v. *Barnard* [1964] A.C. 1129.
[86] For claims based on allegations of this kind see *Allied Arab Bank* v. *Hajjar (No. 2)* [1988] 1 Q.B. 944 and *Metall und Rohstoff A.G.* v. *Donaldson, Lufkin & Jenrette Inc.* [1990] 1 Q.B. 391.
[87] Lord Bowen in *Mogul Steamship Co.* v. *McGregor, Gow & Co.* [1892] A.C. 25. Carty refers to the tort as "a crude (and arbitrary) method of attacking abuse of market power."
[88] Lord Diplock in *Lonrho Ltd.* v. *Shell Petroleum Co. Ltd.* [1982] A.C. 173 at 189.

The leading modern authority on this form of the tort is *Crofter Hand Woven Harris Tweed Co. Ltd.* v. *Veitch.*[89] The defendants in that case were officials of a trade union which represented dockers and mill operatives working on the island of Lewis and the owners of mills on the island. They had conspired together to induce the dockers not to handle yarn which the plaintiff was importing from the mainland which was destined to be made into cloth and any cloth which the plaintiff intended to export from the island. The reason for this was that the plaintiff's product was undercutting the price of the cloth which was wholly produced on the island. The dockers carried out this instruction without any breach of contract on their part. The House of Lords held that these facts did not give rise to an actionable conspiracy. As no unlawful means had been used, the question whether the conspiracy was actionable in tort turned on the predominant purpose of the conspirators; if it was to advance or to protect the legitimate interests of the conspirators as opposed to being to injure the plaintiff it was not actionable. The motive of the conspirators is therefore fundamental to the legality of the acts which they take. On the facts of the case the predominant purpose had been to protect the bona fide and legitimate trade interests of the conspirators from competition rather than to inflict injury on the plaintiff.

The alternative scenario of a bad motive turning a conspiracy to do acts lawful in themselves into a tort is well illustrated by the facts of *Gulf Oil (G.B.) Ltd.* v. *Page.*[90] In that case the defendants who ran a number of petrol filling stations had been involved in disputes with the plaintiff company over a contract under which the defendants were to acquire petrol from the plaintiffs. In proceedings between the parties the plaintiff company had been held to have been in breach of its contract to supply the defendants. Subsequently the defendants hired a light aircraft and arranged for it to be flown over a horse race meeting, at which the plaintiffs were entertaining customers, towing a banner which displayed the words "Gulf exposed in fundamental breach." These words were justifiable[91] in the law of defamation as the statement was true. Nonetheless, the Court of Appeal held that there was clear evidence of a conspiracy between the defendants and, that as they had no immediate interest of their own to protect, it was arguable that they were simply acting out of revenge. A prima facie case of conspiracy to injure by use of lawful means was therefore made out.

As a result of *Crofter Hand Woven Harris Tweed Co. Ltd.* v. *Veitch*[92] it is necessary to decide whether the predominant purpose of the conspirators was to inflict damage on another or to protect their own interests. In delivering the leading speech in the case, Viscount Simon L.C. made reference to the problems that may be involved in attempting to isolate the predominant motive in a situation of mixed motives. This issue is to be determined as a question of fact. In practice, the result in *Crofter* shows that the existence of a legitimate motive is likely to justify a conspiracy even though the conspirators know that their acts are certain to cause damage to the plaintiff whom they dislike. As the acts of the defendants are, by definition, lawful, any genuine element of self-interest should render the acts non-tortious. It is only

---

[89] [1942] A.C. 435. See also *Mogul Steamship Co.* v. *McGregor, Gow & Co.* [1892] A.C. 25 (Conspiracy by traders to improve their commercial position vis-à-vis rivals).

[90] [1987] Ch. 327. But, see now *Lonhro plc* v. *Fayed (No. 5)* [1994] 1 All E.R. 188. Damages for injury to reputation, as opposed to financial losses, are no longer available in conspiracy.

[91] See *post*, p. 444 for a discussion of the defence of justification in defamation.

[92] [1942] A.C. 435.

when the acts are done for no reason other than to inflict damage on the plaintiff that it is permissible to regard them as tortious.

The wording used by the courts in relation to the predominant purpose test seems to have undergone a subtle change in the years since *Crofter* was decided. In that case Viscount Simon spoke of the conspirators being protected if their purpose was the lawful protection of any lawful interest. However, the modern cases have followed the lead of Lord Diplock in *Lonrho Ltd.* v. *Shell Petroleum Co. Ltd.*[93] and have phrased the test as justifying a conspiracy designed to advance the defendant's self-interest and thus to have denied that the court has any discretion to test the legitimacy of the interest being protected; in his speech in *Lonrho plc* v. *Fayed*[94] Lord Bridge spoke of the predominant purpose test as being "to further or protect their own interests." This may not be a matter of great consequence now that it is clear that this test is not applied to conspiracies to use unlawful means; however, while it did apply to such conspiracies it allowed persons who had conspired to commit criminal offences to escape liability for conspiracy because their actions were motivated by self-interest.

Different motives may be held by the different parties to a conspiracy and, if this is the case, it is possible that some conspirators may be held to have committed the tort while others have not. In *Huntley* v. *Thornton*[95] a dispute between the plaintiff and officials of the local district of his trade union was held to have ceased to have concerned the genuine interests of the union and to have degenerated into a personal vendetta conducted against the plaintiff by the officials. As a result the successful attempts made by the officials of that branch of the union to prevent him from obtaining work in that area was an actionable conspiracy; the acts were not taken to further the genuine interests of the union. However, no actionable conspiracy was established in respect of action which was taken against the plaintiff by officials of another district of the union who knew nothing of the circumstances of the case and who acted out of traditional motives of solidarity between members of a trade union. A case such as *Huntley* shows that the defendant's acts may be justifiable even though the material financial interests of the conspirators are not at stake. Indeed, conspirators may be justified if the predominant purpose of their acts is to give support to the non-financial interests of third parties. This is well illustrated by the result in *Scala Ballroom (Wolverhampton) Ltd.* v. *Ratcliffe*[96] in which officials of the Musicians' Union were held to be justified in organising a boycott against the plaintiff company which operated a colour bar in its ballroom.

Unlawful means conspiracies

The conventional view is that the predominant purpose test is not relevant to conspiracies which involve the use of unlawful means. In such cases the additional element of conspiracy adds little to the unlawful character of the acts, but may provide the plaintiff with additional defendants to pursue. For a period, during the 1980s, certain dicta of Lord Diplock in *Lonrho Ltd.* v.

[93] [1982] A.C. 173.
[94] [1992] 1 A.C. 448.
[95] [1957] 1 W.L.R. 321.
[96] [1958] 1 W.L.R. 1057.

Shell Petroleum Co. Ltd.[97] were thought to have applied the predominant purpose test to this form of conspiracy. This produced some remarkable results, which included findings that a conspiracy to defraud creditors[98] and a conspiracy to commit a conversion of assets worth £43 million[99] could not be actionable as conspiracies because the conspirators were motivated by self-interest and did not have as their predominant motive the infliction of harm on the plaintiff. The conventional rule was restored by the decision of the House of Lords in *Lonrho plc v. Fayed.*[1] In that case Lord Bridge stated the law in the following terms:

" . . . when conspirators intentionally injure the plaintiff and use unlawful means to do so, it is no defence to show that their primary purpose was to further or protect their own interests; it is sufficient to make their action tortious that the means used were unlawful."

The problems concerning the definition of unlawful means for the purposes of this tort are the same as those which arise in the case of interference with trade. It is slightly disappointing that the House of Lords when deciding *Lonrho plc v. Fayed*[2] did not take the opportunity of emphasising that the facts of *Lonrho Ltd. v. Shell Petroleum Co. Ltd.,*[3] which concerned an allegation that the defendants had committed a criminal offence which was held not to be actionable under breach of statutory duty essentially raised a case of conspiracy to use lawful means. Had this been done future difficulties concerning whether to apply the predominant purpose test to conspiracies to commit criminal offences might have been avoided.

DECEIT

The tort of deceit, otherwise known as fraud, operates in cases of intentional infliction of economic losses by means of misstatements. The tort requires the plaintiff to prove that the defendant knowingly or recklessly made a false statement to the plaintiff with the intention that he, the plaintiff, should act on it and that the plaintiff has so acted to his detriment. A common example is that of a person making false claims as to the value of a business in order to induce the plaintiff to purchase it.[4] An active representation is required in the sense that a claim cannot be based on a person's silence, but the representation can be in oral or written form. The representation can relate to matters of fact, law or opinion and, indeed, there are circumstances in which the tort can be based on a promise as a result of the proposition that "the state of a man's mind is a fact." This result is, however, confined to promises which were not intended to be kept at the time that they were made. It is not open to a person who intended that another should rely on his fraudulent statement to argue that the plaintiff could, or should, have checked the accuracy of the

---

[97] [1982] A.C. 173.
[98] *Allied Arab Bank Ltd. v. Hajjar (No. 2)* [1988] Q.B. 944.
[99] *Metall und Rohstoff A.G. v. Donaldson Lufkin & Jenrette Inc.* [1990] 1 Q.B. 391.
[1] [1992] 1 A.C. 448.
[2] [1992] 1 A.C. 448.
[3] [1982] A.C. 173.
[4] *Doyle v. Olby (Ironmongers) Ltd.* [1969] 2 Q.B. 158; *East v. Maurer* [1991] 1 W.L.R. 461.

information before placing reliance on it. A person can only be liable in deceit to persons who were intended to rely on the statement in question.[5]

Deceit is distinguished from the area of negligent misstatement[6] by the requirement of dishonesty. The leading case is *Derry* v. *Peek*[7] in which the plaintiff subscribed for shares in a tramway company on the faith of statements in a prospectus issued by the directors to the effect that the company was empowered to operate steam powered (as opposed to horse drawn) trams. Although the directors honestly believed this statement to be true, the correct position was that this power depended on the Board of Trade giving its consent and such consent was not forthcoming. The company was ultimately wound up and the plaintiff's investment was lost. The plaintiff's action against the directors alleging deceit failed. The House of Lords held that a claim under this tort could only succeed if the plaintiff proved that the defendant made the statement either (a) knowing it to be false; (b) without an honest belief in its truth, or (c) recklessly, not caring whether it be true or false.[8] On this basis the tort cannot be made out by proof that the defendant should not reasonably have believed in the truth of the statement. Proof of dishonesty or recklessness, rather than negligence is required. The defendant's lack of honest belief in what he said is tested subjectively. This means that he must be shown to have lacked an honest belief in the truth of the statement in the sense in which he understood it. A plaintiff does not prove a lack of honest belief by showing that a reasonable person would not have held such a belief or would have understood the statement in some other sense.[9]

The arrival of liability for negligent misstatement[10] has meant that deceit is now of limited importance. There are a number of reasons for opting for the negligence remedy. It is likely to be easier to prove because courts tend to demand a high standard of evidence before they will find a deliberate fraud to have been established. Furthermore there may commonly be doubts as to whether insurance cover will exist to pay any damages which are awarded for fraud. Finally, negligence is not subject to section 6 of the Statute of Frauds Amendment Act 1828[11] which provides a defence to a claim of deceit in the case of representations as to the credit of a third party which are not made in writing. On the other hand, an allegation of fraud may be a potent weapon in negotiations aimed at compromising a claim and, if deceit is established, the plaintiff will obtain the benefit of favourable rules of remoteness of damage[12] and no disclaimer or exclusion clause is likely to afford any protection to the defendant.[13]

---

[5] *Peek* v. *Gurney* (1873) L.R. 6 H.L. 377.
[6] *Post*, p. 339.
[7] (1889) 14 App. Cas. 337.
[8] There is no substantial distinction between the second and third categories.
[9] *Akerhielm* v. *De Mare* [1959] A.C. 789.
[10] See *post*, p. 339.
[11] *W.B. Anderson & Sons Ltd.* v. *Rhodes (Liverpool) Ltd.* [1967] 2 All E.R. 850.
[12] See *ante*, p. 100.
[13] *S. Pearson & Sons Ltd.* v. *Dublin Corp.* [1907] A.C. 351.

Chapter Sixteen

Negligently Inflicted Economic Loss

INTRODUCTION

As a general rule, "pure" economic loss is irrecoverable in the tort of negligence. It is a form of loss in relation to which no duty of care exists. "Pure" economic loss can be defined as loss of money or potential profits which are not consequential on physical injury to the plaintiff's person or property. Thus, earnings losses consequential upon a personal injury to the plaintiff or physical damage to his property are not "pure" and are actionable in negligence. However, damage is classified as "pure" when financial losses result from injury to another person, another person's property or are unrelated to any physical damage at all. If, for example, the manager of a pop singer were to lose earnings because of a tortious injury inflicted on the singer[1] those losses will count as "pure" economic loss and be irrecoverable. The same result occurs if a person loses money because of damage to property in which he has no title: contractual rights over that property are insufficient.

The law on this topic has been dominated by the question of whether negligence should recognise more extensive recovery of "pure" economic losses and the debate on this issue has been conducted against the background of the even more fundamental question of the capacity of the *Donoghue* v. *Stevenson* "neighbour" test to continue its advance into new areas. Indeed, the debate concerning the duty of care has centred in recent years on the recovery of pure economic loss. Whereas personal injuries now generally fall within the authority of *Donoghue*, "pure" financial losses have presented the neighbour test with its greatest challenge, one which it has signally failed to meet. The cases which have occurred in this area since 1963 are probably the most remarkable modern example of a collective judicial decision first to expand the scope of tortious recovery and then to retrace their steps. The result of this process is that it must now be accepted that although the test of reasonable foreseeability provides a workable general criterion for the imposition of liability in personal injury cases, it cannot do the same in relation to economic losses. There are three linked reasons for this. First, the financial consequences of acts or advice may be widely felt, whereas there will usually be only a small, or a readily defined, group of persons likely to suffer personal injury or physical damage to their property

---

[1] *Burgess* v. *Florence Nightingale Hospital for Gentlewomen* [1955] 1 Q.B. 349.

as a result of negligent conduct.[2] Secondly, there is the so-called "ripple effect"; financial loss suffered by one person may have financial consequences for others a long way removed from the immediate damage. Finally, there is the fear of what is called "crushing liability"; the fear that individuals may be destroyed financially by a liability that could have been easily spread across society by a non-liability rule and the related fear that the imposition of such liability will be counterproductive in deterrent terms because those at risk will discount it as very remote, will fail to acquire adequate insurance against it or will arrange their affairs so as to be judgment proof. From a different perspective it can be argued that the values at issue in personal injury cases are such that they cannot be automatically applied by analogy to the protection of a person's finances. In the hierarchy of values personal hurt and physical damage to property are regarded by our society as more deserving of protection than financial losses. Some forms of financial loss are what economists term "pecuniary externalities"; these are losses which should be expected to occur as a result of normal fluctuations in trading conditions.[3] A person who suffers economic loss by means of the "ripple effect" of losses derived from a tortiously caused accident falls within this category.[4]

An issue which has been central to the debate on the wider recovery of "pure" economic losses in negligence has been whether all questions concerning negligently inflicted economic loss are, or should be, capable of resolution according to a single test. Whereas general theories of negligence liability derived from *Donoghue, Anns* and (to some extent) from the case of *Hedley Byrne & Co. Ltd.* v. *Heller & Partners Ltd.*,[5] which concerned negligent misstatements[6] have approached the different situations which may arise under the heading of economic loss as representing varieties of a single basic problem, the "incremental" approach to duty of care issues adopted by the House of Lords in *Murphy* v. *Brentwood District Council.*[7] may now be opening the way to a more precise evaluation of the policies which underlie the typical fact situations. Nonetheless, as we shall see,[8] there is growing evidence that *Murphy* has failed to expel general theories from this area of law.

There are two linked criticisms levelled at the existing law on negligently inflicted pure economic loss.[9] First, it is said that the existing "pockets" of liability, those areas within which a duty not to cause pure economic loss still exists, draw the boundaries of recovery on an arbitrary basis and according to the vagaries of previous case law, rather than according to the underlying policies created by the circumstances. Secondly, it is said that the boundaries which are drawn are imprecise, illogical and unworkable. For example, it is difficult to accept that the decision of the House of Lords in *Hedley Byrne &*

---

[2] Even if this is not the case, the group (for example, passengers on an aircraft) is likely to be easily identified.

[3] For a development of this argument see Harris & Veljanovski in *The Law of Tort* (Furmston ed.), Chap 3.

[4] Indeed, such a person may have virtually no means of knowing that his losses can be traced to another person's negligent conduct.

[5] [1964] A.C. 465.

[6] Discussed *post*, p. 339 *et seq.*

[7] [1991] 1 A.C. 398. For discussion of the incremental approach to the duty of care, see p. 34.

[8] *Post*, p. 336.

[9] See particularly Stapleton, (1991) 107 L.Q.R. 249.

Co. Ltd. v. *Heller & Partners Ltd.*[10] establishes that negligent words constitute a severable, and workable, category of "pure" economic loss in relation to which a duty of care exists.

The issue of the recovery of pure economic loss also raises fundamental questions concerning the relationship between contract and tort and, in particular, the forms of loss which are recoverable in the different kinds of action. The central question in this debate is whether the tort of negligence has the capacity to provide a remedy for defective quality in the case of buildings and chattels. The traditional view is that it cannot because defects affecting the quality of an item can only give rise to a negligence action in tort if persons have been injured or other property damaged thereby. Damages can only be claimed in the tort of negligence for losses inflicted on the person or other property and not for defects affecting the item itself. A claim in relation to the defective nature of an item is the exclusive preserve of the law of contract. This result can be rephrased by saying that, in terms of tort, a claim for defective quality is irrecoverable because it is one of pure economic loss: a plaintiff cannot obtain compensation in the tort of negligence for his disappointed expectation that an item was of the value that he had supposed. A related argument is that only contractual agreements have the capacity to fix a standard of performance; for example, the effective life of a product. It is meaningless to say that a product has been designed or manufactured negligently because it failed to achieve a particular level of performance. The recognition of tortious liability in a situation governed by a contract might also unsettle well established contractual devices designed to control liability. If an employer and contractor agree that the latter's liability should be limited and if a subcontractor, who is out of privity with the employer, has obligations to the main contractor which are similarly limited, is it acceptable that the employer, who claims to have been damaged by the subcontractor's negligence, should be able to sue directly in tort free from the contractual limitations?

Alongside the fear that expanding the recovery of pure economic losses will undermine established principles of contract is the belief that it might also open the floodgates to indeterminate, uncontrolled and overextensive liability. The fear is that financial damage to one person may have knock on effects on others who might also be able to mount a claim if the law of tort provided a generous area of recovery: financial losses suffered by an individual may well have consequences for those who deal with him. In the area of misstatements, a related fear is that overextensive liability might be created by the fact of information being passed from person to person. The denial of a duty of care in relation to "pure" economic losses may be regarded as a necessary, if possibly arbitrary, control factor designed to avoid these consequences. It creates an easily understood test which strikes a suitable balance between the competing interests in the great majority of situations.

When considering these issues it should be borne in mind that what is an immunity to one person is to another an unrecoverable loss caused by the first person's negligence. Negligently conducted work in the construction industry is a good example of this. For most people the purchase of a house is the major investment of their lives. However, the complexity of the contractual arrangements under which buildings are erected means that there will often be a lack of contractual nexus between the plaintiff and the person, the

---

[10] [1964] A.C. 465.

designer, builder or supervisor, who is responsible for defects in the house. To many people the whole point of *Donoghue* v. *Stevenson* is to protect the consumer interest by allowing the tort of negligence to impose liability on a negligent person free of the constraints of privity of contract. Cases such as *Dutton* v. *Bognor Regis U.D.C.*,[11] which allowed the second purchaser of a house to use negligence as a remedy for her financial losses against persons with whom she had no contract, seemed to confirm that the courts were not prepared to allow traditional immunities to stand in the way of consumer protection. Professional acts create a similar difficulty. The nature of the professional functions of persons such as solicitors and accountants is such that they are unlikely to cause physical damage to their clients or other foreseeable third parties if they perform their work negligently. Unless their work is so bad that it causes shock to the client the normal form of loss will be financial. If this means that no duty of care in tort is owed in relation to such acts the position is somewhat anomalous because a duty is owed to the client under contract and because the closely analogous advisory functions of such professionals may attract a tortious duty under the authority of *Hedley Byrne & Co. Ltd.* v. *Heller & Partners Ltd.*[12] In fact, the extension of the duty of care to negligently performed professional acts occurred by means of a somewhat forced application of *Hedley Byrne* to a case of professional failure to perform work in the case of *Midland Bank Trust Co. Ltd.* v. *Hett, Stubbs and Kemp.*[13]

Economic analysis

A variety of analyses of the present law based on economic theory have been offered. At the simplest level it has been argued that the law should not concern itself with the financial losses resulting from accidents because they do not represent a social cost[14]: the losses suffered by an individual are offset by a transfer of wealth to another. Either other manufacturers increase their profits by supplying goods in substitution for those lost or the victim can increase production at other times to offset the loss. This argument cannot be generally applicable because substitute production is not invariably available to replace that which is lost and because real costs may be incurred in increasing levels of production to meet demands created by accidental damage, particularly if the increased demand only exists for a limited period. A more generally accepted argument is that the barrier to recovery achieves the aim of avoiding "crushing" liability. The interconnection of financial interests which exists between different people may mean that a tortfeasor is indirectly causing loss to a large and indeterminate class. The range and quantity of such losses may be difficult to predict and to insure against. For example, a minor road accident which blocks a tunnel may have a wide range of consequences for other road users who are delayed. To avoid this a non-liability rule spreads the loss thinly through society and avoids the disproportionality which might result from channelling the whole loss to the tortfeasor. A variant of this approach is proffered in relation to advisory work.

---

[11] [1972] 1 Q.B. 373.
[12] [1964] A.C. 465. Discussed *post*, pp. 336 and 339.
[13] [1979] Ch. 384, see *post*, p. 347.
[14] Bishop, (1982) 2 Ox. J.L.S 1. Bishop has retreated from this standpoint in his later writing. See *The Law of Tort* (Furmston ed.), Chap. 4.

Information may be appropriated and used by persons other than those who paid for its production. There is therefore a real possibility that those who invest resources in its production will be unable to obtain a realistic price for it. In economic terms this is liable to lead to the amount of socially useful information produced being less than that required by society and a rule which sought to impose liability on people who have not been recompensed for their work can only accentuate the problem. The immunity from liability in relation to many forms of information which have not been paid for can therefore be regarded as a technique which is intended to encourage the production of socially useful information. Finally, it can be argued that, in contrast with personal injury law, there is less need for the tort of negligence to provide protection in respect of economic losses because the working of the market, through contractual mechanisms, does most of the task. Information and services are usually acquired under contract and warranties of quality are a specific contractual creation. However, this is not an invariable rule. The courts have perceived certain areas of market failure which they have felt justify the recognition of a remedy in negligence.

The economic analysis of this area of law has identified certain areas in which the existence of a duty of care might be thought to assist in achieving an efficient result. Some commentators have argued that a clear distinction must be drawn between voluntary and involuntary relationships and that the voluntary category includes some which are classified as tortious because of the technicalities of privity of contract.[15] If information or work has been purchased specifically to benefit the interests of a third party to a contract the imposition of a liability rule which benefits the third party should create proper deterrent incentives against poor quality work by the party performing it. The doctrine of privity of contract can, in certain circumstances, produce a market failure by defeating the intentions of the contracting parties to benefit the third party and the recognition of a tort duty may be needed to reassert correct incentives.

A General Theory?

A search for a general theory governing the recovery of pure economic loss under the tort of negligence might seem doomed to failure. As we will see, extremely limited areas of recovery of such losses are now recognised and the recent approach to the duty of care seems to favour abandoning any search for a general theory in favour of ad hoc development of the law in relation to the different situations which may arise. However, there are some signs in recent cases that the authority of the case of *Hedley Byrne & Co. Ltd.* v. *Heller and Partners Ltd.*[16] is being used to justify limited, but significant, recognition of a general basis for the recovery of such losses in tort.

The modern debate on the recovery of pure economic loss in negligence stems from the decision of the House of Lords in *Hedley Byrne*[17] which recognised that in certain circumstances a duty of care can be owed in the case of negligent misstatements. *Hedley Byrne* itself was a case of pure economic loss: the plaintiff had lost money as a result of entering into dealings, in

---

[15] Harris & Veljanovski in Furmston (ed.) *op. cit.* Chap. 3.
[16] [1964] A.C. 465.
[17] [1964] A.C. 465.

reliance on a reference given by the defendant, with a client who subsequently went out of business. It was not clear at the time whether the case created an exceptional area of recovery for financial losses confined to the limited category of misstatements cases or whether it had the wider significance of opening the way to the recovery of pure economic loss caused by both negligent statements and acts. The wider interpretation, that negligent acts which cause pure economic loss can give rise to a duty of care, was argued for without success in a number of cases concerning economic loss following damage to property belonging to a person other than the plaintiff.[18] However, in the late 1970s an interpretation of *Hedley Byrne* which based its ratio on the close relationship between the parties and on the existence of reliance between them rather than on the fact of the negligence being by way of misstatement led to the recognition of negligence liability in tort for professional misfeasance and failures to act.[19] At the same time Lord Wilberforce's two stage test for a duty of care[20] was fostering a rapid expansion in the scope of the tort of negligence.

In the early 1980s the law moved rapidly and by 1982 it was a possible interpretation of the decision of the House of Lords in *Junior Books Ltd.* v. *Veitchi Co. Ltd.*[21] that pure economic loss, whether caused by misstatement or negligent acts, was being assimilated into the mainstream of negligence liability and that, as a result, tortious liability was entering the preserve of the law of contract by providing a remedy for defects in quality of purchased items. If this was the correct interpretation of *Junior Books, Donoghue* v. *Stevenson* seemed to be in the process of winning its greatest victory. A more conservative reading of cases such as *Ross* v. *Caunters*[22] and *Junior Books Ltd.* v. *Veitchi Co. Ltd.*,[23] was that they allowed recovery of negligently inflicted pure economic loss in tort where there existed a relationship of very close proximity between the tortfeasor and the victim. Even this test had the capacity to provide the basis of a general theory governing the recovery of such losses. However, two decisions of the Court of Appeal went a long way to rejecting this suggestion. In *Simaan General Contracting Co.* v. *Pilkington Glass Ltd. (No. 2)*[24] a nominated supplier of glass for a building was excused from tort liability to the main contractor when the colour of glass which was supplied failed to meet the contractual specification with the result that the main contractor did not receive payment from the building owner. The relationship between a contractor and a nominated supplier of materials for the purposes of the contract is similar in terms of proximity to that between the owner and building subcontractor which existed in *Junior Books*. However, the court held that the tort of negligence could not penetrate the preserve of contract to the extent of providing a remedy against a person whose work failed to meet a contractual specification and that the plaintiff's remedy was to pursue his contractual claims. It noted that the recognition of duties in tort might create difficulties if the contract contained exclusion clauses. Dillon L.J. went as far as to say that he doubted whether future

---

[18] See particularly *Spartan Steel and Alloys Ltd.* v. *Martin & Co. (Contractors) Ltd.* [1973] Q.B. 27.
[19] See *post*, p. 347.
[20] *Ante*, p. 30.
[21] [1983] 1 A.C. 520.
[22] [1980] Ch. 297.
[23] [1983] 1 A.C. 520.
[24] [1988] 1 All E.R. 791.

citation from *Junior Books* could serve any useful purpose. The facts of *Greater Nottingham Co-operative Society* v. *Cementation Piling and Foundations Ltd.*[25] showed an even greater degree of proximity because a contractual relationship actually existed between the parties. The defendant piling subcontractors had entered into a specific contractual warranty with the building owner under which they undertook obligations in relation to matters of design and the materials used. However, the contract made no provision as to the method of doing the work. The defendants were alleged to have been negligent in relation to the methods used and it was claimed that this had caused the owner to suffer economic loss. The owner's claim for this loss in tort was rejected in spite of the close proximity between the parties: the specific omission of a term relating to the method of doing the work from the warranty was held to show that the subcontractor had not assumed responsibility for this matter. In effect, the terms of the contract created a policy reason which excluded the implication of a tort remedy which would have given a different result.

There are signs that the decline in the fortunes of *Junior Books* has been halted, if not reversed, and that an alternative route to a general theory of recovery may now be being provided by the authority of *Hedley Byrne & Co. Ltd.* v. *Heller and Partners Ltd.*[26] The basis of this proposition is a return to regarding the authority of that case as establishing a general principle of tortious liability for negligently inflicted pure economic losses based on a party having assumed responsibility for work or on reliance being placed on that party's work. This approach does not confine the authority of the case to misstatements and is of particular importance to professional liabilities as the presence of assumption of responsibility and reliance may be relatively easy to establish in cases of skilled professional persons performing their professional functions. Authority supporting this view is provided by dicta in *Murphy* v. *Brentwood District Council.*[27] Lord Keith in his speech in that case regarded both *Junior Books* and *Pirelli General Cable Works Ltd.* v. *Oscar Faber & Partners*[28] as having been correctly decided as applications of the *Hedley Byrne* principle, which was itself founded on the existence of reliance, and Lord Bridge suggested[29] that *Junior Books* might be explained on the basis of a "special relationship of proximity sufficiently akin to contract to introduce the element of reliance so that the scope of the duty of care . . . is wide enough to embrace purely economic loss." If these dicta are to be regarded as stating the law correctly they are authority for the recognition of a general theory of tortious recovery of negligently inflicted financial losses which might provide a basis for attacking decisions such as *Simaan*. In effect, this approach has the capacity to provide authority for the continued actionability in negligence of some cases of pure economic loss resulting from negligent acts and, as such, may serve as the basis for a significant exception to the general rule of immunity derived from *D. & F. Estates* and *Murphy*. Post-*Murphy* cases seem to be accepting this approach.

[25] [1988] 2 All E.R. 971.
[26] [1964] A.C. 465.
[27] [1991] 1 A.C. 398 at 466.
[28] [1983] 2 A.C. 1. A House of Lords authority which permitted the owner of a factory to bring a case in negligence in respect of defects in the lining of the chimney against the engineer who had been employed to design the chimney.
[29] [1991] 1 A.C. 398 at 481.

In *Lonrho plc* v. *Tebbit*,[30] Browne-Wilkinson V.C. used it as the basis for refusing to strike out an allegation that a government minister had acted negligently and caused losses to the plaintiff, saying that it was arguable that the relationship between the parties was sufficiently proximate to give rise to a duty to prevent economic loss. The view that the decision in *Junior Books* is an application of the *Hedley Byrne* principle also formed part of the reasoning in May J.'s decision in *Nitrigin Eireann Teoranta* v. *Inco Alloys Ltd.*[31] However, the judge held on the facts of the case that the relationship between the defendant, who was a supplier of specialist pipework, and the plaintiff purchaser did not reveal the factors necessary to bring the case within the authority of *Hedley Byrne* and supported the view that professional relationships are more likely to meet the necessary conditions than those of purchaser and supplier.

If *Junior Books* is to be subject to a limited rehabilitation in this way, the authority of the professional negligence case of *Ross* v. *Caunters*,[32] in which a solicitor's negligent acts were held to create a duty of care owed to a third party who was intended to benefit from the work, is almost certain to survive.[33] A theory of professional negligence liability in tort founded on a neo-contractual relationship or the assumption of risk would seem liable to support the authority of the case, even though it is an example of pure financial loss caused to a third party beneficiary of a contract by professional misfeasance. Architects and engineers may need to face the fact that *Hedley Byrne* may be capable of restoring, in some situations, the tort liability in negligence which *D. & F. Estates* and *Murphy* suggested had disappeared. It would seem unlikely that a general theory supporting the existence of professional liability in tort could be built of the basis of a requirement of reliance. The problem with doing this is that the word "reliance" bears a variety of meanings according to the context in which it is used[34] and it is by no means clear that any form of relevant reliance will always be present on facts analogous to *Ross*. The preferable view is that reliance forms a common, but not essential, element in professional liability cases and that its role should not be misunderstood with the result that it is regarded as a precondition to liability.

Until it is clear that these implications of the latest dicta are correct and that *Hedley Byrne* is to be interpreted as giving rise to a general principle governing the recovery of negligently caused "pure" economic losses it is necessary to continue to describe the law in terms of the existing "pockets" of liability in which the existence of a duty of care in relation to economic loss has been discussed. These "pockets" will now be discussed.

Negligent Misstatements

One area in which the recovery of negligently caused pure economic loss is clearly established is misstatements. It is difficult to see why this area should

---

[30] [1991] 4 All E.R. 973.
[31] [1992] 1 All E.R. 854.
[32] [1980] Ch. 297. See *post*, p. 347.
[33] The authority of *Ross* has been affirmed, on limited grounds, by the decision of *White* v. *Jones*, *post*, p. 349.
[34] Stapleton, (1991) 107 L.Q.R. 249; Stanton *The Law of Tort* (Furmston ed.), Chap. 1.

be accorded special treatment. One possible explanation is that most advisory work is, by its nature, likely to result in financial losses rather than physical damage. However, certain forms of professional misfeasance, such as the drafting of documents by solicitors, have the same feature but are less likely to give rise to the recovery of pure economic losses. It may also be argued that the misstatements cases are examples of attempts to surmount privity of contract problems and that successful plaintiffs are persons for whom advice has been bought by another but who are denied a direct contractual claim by lack of consideration. However, this does not explain the imposition of a duty of care in the straightforward example of the giving of gratuitous advice which nobody has paid for and, again, the recovery of pure economic losses caused by negligent acts could also be justified by this explanation. Attempts to equate the areas of acts and statements by expanding the recognition of duties in relation to economic losses caused by acts have failed and the recovery of pure economic losses resulting from negligent statements has been subject to increased restraints as part of the retreat from *Anns*. The proximity requirement applied in respect to statements is far more stringent than that which *Donoghue* v. *Stevenson* applies to acts which cause injury or property damage; however, it seems positively liberal alongside cases such as *Simaan* and *Greater Nottingham*[35] which suggested that the proximity requirement derived from *Junior Books Ltd.* v. *Veitchi Co. Ltd.* in respect of acts leading to pure economic loss was virtually unattainable.

The root of the line of authority in respect of statements is the decision of the House of Lords in *Hedley Byrne & Co. Ltd.* v. *Heller and Partners Ltd.*[36] The case concerned a reference given by a bank and received by the plaintiff who was contemplating doing business with a company on terms which would make them personally liable should the client default. The reference given by the defendant bank concerning that company was favourable, but proved to be over-optimistic as the company collapsed leaving the plaintiff bearing losses. When the plaintiff sued the bank arguing that it had suffered financial losses as a result of the negligently given reference the House of Lords held that a duty of care could, in certain circumstances, be owed in relation to negligent misstatements. On the facts of the case a disclaimer of responsibility attached to the reference negated the existence of any duty. Most professional advisory work has always involved an obligation to use care and skill because the professional person is in a contractual relationship with the person receiving the advice. *Hedley Byrne* went further. It opened the door to liability for negligently given gratuitous advice; for information given in the course of pre-contract negotiations; for information supplied to third parties dealing with the professional person's client and, more contentiously, for information passed to and damaging third parties foreseeably affected by the work.

The words used by the members of the House of Lords to express their decision have been subject to much analysis and it is arguable that they have, at times, been mistakenly regarded as providing precise formulae governing the actionability of misstatements in tort. A number of different formulae can be extracted from the speeches in the case, but none of these, on examination, provide a great deal of assistance to those who have to decide cases in this area. For example, it is said that the parties must be in a "special

---

[35] *Ante*, p. 337.
[36] [1964] A.C. 465.

relationship" before a duty of care will be recognised. This amounts to saying little more than that the standard *Donoghue* v. *Stevenson* foreseeability test cannot be used. The notion of the special relationship is of limited assistance in facilitating a decision as to whether or not a duty of care should be recognised on particular facts as it expresses a conclusion rather than providing the means of arriving at one. It was also said by Lord Devlin that before a duty of care could arise, the relationship between the parties must be one which is "equivalent to contract." This is arguably more helpful in implying that direct dealing between the parties is required and, possibly, that the advice given must be of a character which commonly leads to persons purchasing it. A further test to the effect that the advisor must have "voluntarily assumed the responsibility" of the advice proving inaccurate can be positively misleading.[37] Any duty of care in relation to a misstatement can only be imposed by the operation of law. It cannot be an optional duty and it has been established that it can exist when the advisor is under a statutory duty to give the information[38] and in circumstances in which he purports to disclaim responsibility when giving advice.[39] The fact that a duty of care for misstatements has been held to exist where there has been no express assumption of responsibility shows the voluntary assumption to be a fiction which should not be taken seriously. In *Smith* v. *Eric S. Bush*[40] Lord Griffiths said that he did not regard the voluntary assumption of responsibility as a helpful or realistic test.[41]

If any general test defining the scope of the duty of care which exists in relation to statements is to be found in the case it would seem to rest on the fact of a person acting reasonably and foreseeably in placing reliance upon the special skill of another. In the words of Lord Morris:

> " . . . if someone possessed of a special skill undertakes, quite irrespective of contract, to apply that skill for the assistance of another person who relies upon such skill, a duty of care will arise . . . Furthermore, if in a sphere in which a person is so placed that others could reasonably rely on his judgment or his skill or upon his ability to make careful inquiry, a person takes it upon himself to give information or advice to, or allows his information or advice to be passed on to, another person who, as he knows or should know, will place reliance upon it, then a duty of care will arise."

The central elements in this test would seem to be the fact that the plaintiff has relied upon the defendant, the fact that such reliance was reasonable and the defendant's knowledge, or imputed knowledge, of such reliance. The decision in *Hedley Byrne* can therefore be seen to have left considerable scope for further elucidation.

Instead of regarding the words used in *Hedley Byrne* as the equivalent of a statute governing the recovery of financial losses caused by negligent misstatements, the courts have, for the most part, proceeded to decide cases on the

---

[37] The best example of the problems which can be created was provided by the Court of Appeal's application of the Unfair Contract Terms Act 1977 to disclaimers of misstatements liability in *Harris* v. *Wyre Forest District Council* [1988] 1 All E.R. 691. This decision was reversed by the House of Lords [1990] 1 A.C. 831.

[38] *Ministry of Housing and Local Government* v. *Sharp* [1970] 2 Q.B. 223.

[39] *Smith* v. *Eric S. Bush, Harris* v. *Wyre Forest District Council* [1990] 1 A.C. 831.

[40] [1990] 1 A.C. 831.

[41] Both Lords Roskill and Oliver supported this approach in their speeches in *Caparo Industries plc* v. *Dickman* [1990] 2 A.C. 605. For earlier discussion see Stanton, (1985) 1 P.N. 132.

basis of the then current general approaches to duty of care issues. In the late 1970s the influence of the *Anns* principle meant that little more than foreseeability that a statement would be reasonably relied upon was required to establish a duty. The retreat from the width of *Anns* has not been as dramatic in misstatements cases as in the case of negligent acts causing pure economic loss. The authority of *Hedley Byrne* has blocked the total disappearance of the duty. For a time, the courts used the three stage test[42] to the effect that damage to the plaintiff must be foreseeable as a consequence of the defendant's words; that there must exist between the parties a sufficient relationship of proximity and that it must be just and reasonable to impose a duty of care on the advisor. The result of this was that a stringent proximity requirement was imposed in misstatements cases and only a narrow band of relationships was recognised as capable of giving rise to a duty. The fact that a person may foresee that his words may be relied upon by a large class of persons who are personally unknown to him will not create a duty of care owed to them. The author of a legal textbook owes no enforceable duty in tort to readers of the book.

The relationship of the parties

More recently, as courts have continued to restrict the scope of the duty of care in negligence even further, the formulation of the misstatements duty has come to require a very close relationship to exist between the parties. In *Al Saudi Banque* v. *Clarke Pixley*[43] Millett J. held that no duty of care was owed by auditors of a company to banks which had made loans to the company treating certain bills of exchange, which proved to be worthless, as security. The banks had contended that the auditors ought to have appreciated that the company's business was dependent on bank finance and ought to have foreseen that any bank which made loans to the company would do so in reliance on the company's audited accounts. The plaintiffs argued that the high probability that a number of banks would place reliance on the audit reports was sufficient to establish the necessary relationship of proximity even though the identity of the actual future lenders was unknown to the auditors at the time that they did the work. The judge held that the proximity requirement was separate from that of foreseeability and was not satisfied in the particular circumstances in which the auditors had had no direct dealings with the banks. The high probability that some of a limited number of likely lenders would place reliance on the accounts did not, of itself establish the necessary proximity.

In his speech in *Caparo Industries plc* v. *Dickman*[44] Lord Bridge identified three requirements to be established before sufficient proximity will be established in such a case in the following words:

> "The salient feature of all these cases is that the defendant giving advice or information was fully aware of the nature of the transaction which the plaintiff had in contemplation, knew that the advice or information would be communicated to him, directly or indirectly and knew that it was very likely that the plaintiff would rely on that advice or information in deciding whether or not to engage in the transaction in contemplation."

[42] *Ante*, p. 33.
[43] [1989] 3 All E.R. 361.
[44] [1990] 2 A.C. 605.

Lord Oliver adopted a similar approach in slightly different terms:

"What can be deduced from the *Hedley Byrne* case, therefore, is that the necessary relationship between the maker of a statement or giver of advice (the adviser) and the recipient who acts in reliance upon it (the advisee) may typically be held to exist where (1) the advice is required for a purpose, whether particularly specified or generally described, which is made known, either actually or inferentially, to the adviser at the time when the advice is given, (2) the adviser knows, either actually or inferentially, that his advice will be communicated to the advisee, either specifically or as a member of an ascertainable class, in order that it should be used by the advisee for that purpose, (3) it is known, either actually or inferentially, that the advice so communicated is likely to be acted on by the advisee for that purpose without independent inquiry and (4) it is so acted on by the advisee to his detriment."

If these rules come to be generally used,[45] very close dealings will usually be required before a duty of care is recognised. The requirement is that the defendant should have actual knowledge of the plaintiff and of the form of his likely reliance, not that he should merely have foreseen the possibility of such reliance.

On this basis it seems reasonable to conclude that the proximity requirement will be satisfied where the parties have indulged in face to face dealings, whether the situation concerns gratuitous advisory work, the giving of pre-contractual information[46] or concurrent tortious liability for advice given to a client under a contract.[47] Although a case at first instance has held that a solicitor answering inquiries before contract as his client's agent does not owe a duty of care to a person who enters into transactions with the client in reliance on the advice,[48] the weight of authority would support the existence of a general rule to the effect that a duty will be imposed when a professional person supplies information to a third party at the instigation of his client,[49] particularly if the professional person is involved in discussing the information with the third party. It is more doubtful whether a duty will exist where information prepared for a particular purpose is merely forwarded by the advisor to a third party at the client's request.

If information is supplied to the client with the knowledge that the client intends to forward it to a third party for a particular purpose a duty owed to the third party may well arise. The cases of *Yianni* v. *Edwin Evans*[50] and *Smith* v. *Eric S. Bush, Harris* v. *Wyre Forest District Council*[51] establish that a duty will commonly be owed on this basis by a surveyor who conducts a valuation of property on behalf of a lending institution knowing that a prospective borrower will have provided the money for the valuation and is likely to rely on it. In such cases it does not matter that the valuation report is not released to the borrower. The implication created by the offer of the loan

---

[45] The alternative would be the abandonment of any general test in favour of "incremental development" of discrete areas of liability. See *ante*, p. 34.

[46] *Esso Petroleum Co. Ltd.* v. *Mardon* [1976] Q.B. 801.

[47] *Pirelli General Cable Works Ltd.* v. *Oscar Faber & Partners* [1983] 2 A.C. 1.

[48] *Gran Gelato Ltd.* v. *Richcliff (Group) Ltd.* [1992] 1 All E.R. 865.

[49] *Candler* v. *Crane Christmas & Co.* [1951] 2 K.B. 164 the dissenting judgment of Denning L.J. in this case was approved in *Hedley Byrne*.

[50] [1982] Q.B. 438.

[51] [1990] 1 A.C. 831.

that the valuation must have been favourable has been held to suffice, at least in the case of residential property at the lower end of the housing market. In cases of this kind it is common knowledge that the great majority of borrowers do not commission a private survey but rely on the valuation. This result is not based on there being a high probability of reliance on the work but on there being a very close "neo-contractual" relationship, the borrower having supplied the funds on the basis of which the valuer conducted the work.[52]

When it is known that information will be passed on by the recipient to another person, a defendant may owe a duty of care in spite of the fact that the identity of the ultimate recipient is unknown. In *Hedley Byrne* the bank giving the reference did not know the identity of the person who received it, it merely passed the information to the plaintiff's bank.[53]

It now seems clear that relationships more remote than those already outlined will not exhibit the required degree of proximity and will not give rise to a duty of care. In particular, the leading decision of *Caparo Industries plc* v. *Dickman*[54] established that a company's auditors do not owe a duty of care to persons who invest in or mount a successful takeover bid for a company merely on the basis that they can foresee persons who undertake such transactions placing reliance on the audited figures. A similar result was obtained in *Al Saudi Banque* v. *Clark Pixley*[55] in relation to an auditor's duties to banks which were making loans to the company. The fact that the audited figures are a matter of public record and that an auditor has a statutory duty to report the information to shareholders does not create a duty. The purpose for which an auditor reports to a company's shareholders is not to assist in the making of investment decisions. More generally, it is now clearly established that a person who supplies information to a particular person will owe no duty of care to third parties to whom that information is passed without his knowledge.[56]

The nature of the advice

Although skilled persons who give professional advice are likely to comprise the majority of defendants the scope of the *Hedley Byrne* duty of care is not confined to them. In *Mutual Life and Citizens' Assurance Co. Ltd.* v. *Evatt*[57] the majority of members of the Privy Council regarded *Hedley Byrne* as confined to cases in which the defendant is in the business of giving advice of the kind in question or had held himself out as competent to give it. This was said to be the only basis by which it would be possible to fix a standard with which to judge the defendant's work. However, the minority judges in the case rejected this approach and regarded foresight of reasonable reliance being placed on the defendant's words as the critical test. Subsequent English decisions[58] have expressed overwhelming support for the minority view.

---

[52] Millett J. in *Al Saudi Banque* v. *Clarke Pixley* [1989] 3 All E.R. 361, 368.
[53] Problems may arise as to the size of the class *Swingcastle Ltd.* v. *Alistair Gibson* [1991] 2 All E.R. 353.
[54] [1990] 2 A.C. 605.
[55] [1989] 3 All E.R. 361.
[56] *Smith* v. *Eric S. Bush, Harris* v. *Wyre Forest District Council* [1990] 1 A.C. 831.
[57] [1971] A.C. 793.
[58] *Esso Petroleum Co. Ltd.* v. *Mardon* [1976] Q.B. 801; *Howard Marine and Dredging Co. Ltd.* v. *A. Ogden & Sons (Excavations) Ltd.* [1978] Q.B. 574; *Lawton* v. *B.O.C. Transhield Ltd.* [1987] I.C.R. 7.

The rejection of the majority approach in *Mutual Life* shows a degree of liberality in the courts' attitude to the scope of the misstatements duty of care. However, some kind of business context is almost certainly a requirement for the imposition of a duty. Statements made or advice given on a family, domestic or social occasion will not be subject to a duty of care. In Lord Reid's words in *Hedley Byrne*[59]:

> "Quite careful people often express definite opinions on social or informal occasions, even when they see that others are likely to be influenced by them; and they often do that without taking the care which they would take if asked for their opinion professionally, or in a business connection . . . there can be no duty of care on such occasions . . . "

There are bound to be difficulties in deciding what is a social occasion. While there will be no problem in denying the existence of a duty of care in relation to advice given casually as to the quality of restaurants or public entertainments, the facts will not always be so simple. The case of *Chaudhry* v. *Prabhakar*[60] provides an illustration of the potential difficulties. The defendant had agreed, as an act of friendship, to advise the plaintiff as to her proposed purchase of a car. The defendant was not a trained mechanic but had had some experience on his own behalf in the motor trade. The plaintiff stipulated that she did not wish to buy a vehicle which had been accident damaged. The defendant advised her to purchase for £4,500 a car which was unroadworthy as a result of extensive and poorly repaired accident damage. The defendant had failed to inquire of the vendor whether the vehicle had been involved in an accident (some signs of repairs were obvious) yet informed the plaintiff that it had not been so damaged. In negligence proceedings based both on *Hedley Byrne* and on the fact that the defendant was acting as a gratuitous agent[61] the existence of a duty was conceded. The majority of the Court of Appeal regarded this concession as properly made in view of the gratuitous agency and the plaintiff's considerable financial interest in the transaction. However, May L.J. stated that he doubted that the concession was correct because he did not regard as "entirely attractive" the imposition of a duty of care on a family friend giving gratuitous help as a personal favour.

Even if advice is given on a business occasion the form in which it is given may negative the existence of a duty of care. In *James McNaughton Papers Group Ltd.* v. *Hicks Anderson & Co.*[62] the Court of Appeal held that the fact that accounts supplied to a prospective purchaser of a company by its auditors were clearly marked "draft" was one of the reasons why the recipient should not have placed reasonable reliance upon them. Similarly in *Howard Marine and Dredging Co. Ltd.* v. *A. Ogden & Sons (Excavations) Ltd.*[63] it was held that "off the cuff" answers given over the telephone on behalf of a firm that was hiring out barges did not create a duty of care, even though the answers related to the commercially important issue of the capacity of the barges. The inquirer who wished to place reasonable reliance on such answers was told to obtain confirmation of them in writing. A

---

[59] [1964] A.C. 465 at 482.
[60] [1988] 3 All E.R. 718.
[61] An agency may create duties of care owed to the principal independently of any duties owed in tort.
[62] [1991] 1 All E.R. 134.
[63] [1978] Q.B. 574.

specialised rule which has been established is that no duty of care can arise in relation to statements made as part of character references.[64] The basis for this is that such statements would, in the absence of malice, be incapable of giving rise to an action for defamation because the situation would be one of qualified privilege. It is said that plaintiffs should not be allowed to bypass the rules of defamation by framing their actions in negligence.[65]

The purpose for giving the advice

The scope of the duty of care recognised in a number of modern misstatements cases has been held to be limited by a consideration of the purpose for which the advice was given. Lord Oliver's speech in *Caparo Industries plc* v. *Dickman*[66] provides a leading example of this process. His Lordship defined the purpose of the statutory requirement that a company's accounts are audited as being to enable its shareholders to make an informed decision as to the exercise of their voting rights in the company: it was not to give investment information to those trading in the company's shares on the stock exchange. Therefore no duty of care was owed by the defendant auditors to persons who bought shares in the company in reliance on information obtained from a statutory audit.[67] By subjecting the *Hedley Byrne* duty of care to a purpose test the courts are giving themselves a tool which can block the recognition of a duty of care in spite of the existence of close proximity between the parties and the fact that the plaintiff regarded it as perfectly reasonable to rely upon the information.[68]

The purpose approach has had substantial use in the post-*Caparo* world. In *Mariola Marine Corporation* v. *Lloyds Register of Shipping*[69] it was held that the primary purpose of the classification scheme applied by Lloyds Register was to enhance the safety of persons and property at sea and not the protection of the financial interests of persons contemplating the purchase of a vessel and in *Al Nakib Investments (Jersey) Ltd.* v. *Longcroft*[70] it was held that the purpose of a prospectus published by a company in connection with a rights issue of shares was to assist persons in relation to that specific issue and not in relation to subsequent purchases of the shares in the market. A good example of the freedom of manoeuvre given to the courts by the purpose approach is provided by the litigation in *Morgan Crucible Co. plc* v. *Hill Samuel & Co. Ltd.*[71] In that case the plaintiffs, who had mounted a successful contested takeover bid for another company alleged that they had been damaged by placing reliance upon negligently produced profit forecasts, financial statements and other documents which had been prepared as part of the defence against the bid. At first instance the judge struck out the allegation as disclosing no cause of action saying that the purpose of defence

---

[64] *Spring* v. *Guardian Assurance plc* [1993] 2 All E.R. 273.

[65] The fact that *Hedley Byrne* was itself a case of a reference was not alluded to in *Spring*.

[66] [1990] 2 A.C. 605.

[67] See also *Berg Sons & Co. Ltd.* v. *Adams* (1992) 8 P.N. 167, in which the *Caparo* approach to the purpose of an auditor's duty prevented a duty of care being owed to a company in a case in which it was alleged that an unqualified audit certificate had permitted the company to continue trading and thus to increase the losses suffered.

[68] Many investors would regard the statutory audit, which is a matter of public record, as a piece of information of great significance to an investment decision.

[69] [1990] 1 Lloyds Rep. 47.

[70] [1990] 3 All E.R. 321.

[71] [1990] 3 All E.R. 330, Hoffman J.; [1991] 1 All E.R. 148, C.A.

documents produced in the course of a contested takeover bid was to assist shareholders in deciding whether or not to accept the bid, rather than to induce the bidder to increase the offer. The Court of Appeal, however, reversed this decision and held it to be arguable that a duty of care was owed on the facts because it is possible that one of the purposes underlying the issue of defence documents in the course of a contested takeover is to persuade the bidder to make the best possible offer for the company.[72]

PROFESSIONAL ACTS

Negligent acts on the part of professional persons such as solicitors may be an area in which a duty of care not to cause pure economic loss survives. It would be anomalous if this were not the case: professional work is a classic example of an area in which it is difficult to disentangle elements of misstatement (which would be actionable under *Hedley Byrne*) and misfeasance and in many of these situations it is inherently unlikely that a form of loss other than pure financial loss will be suffered.

The earliest case to support the existence of a duty of care in this context was *Midland Bank Trust Co. Ltd.* v. *Hett, Stubbs and Kemp*.[73] In that case a solicitor's failure to register as a land charge an option to purchase land meant that the client's interest was defeated by a subsequent transaction involving the property. Oliver J., in finding in favour of the client's claim in tort opened the door to concurrent tortious liability in negligence when a contractual relationship existed between the parties and allowed *Hedley Byrne's* ability to permit the recovery of pure financial losses to operate in a case of a professional person's failure to act. These developments were contentious. However, the advance of the negligence duty into the area of professional work causing financial losses was supported by Megarry V.C.'s judgment in *Ross* v. *Caunters*.[74] This case involved a disappointed beneficiary under a will. A solicitor, either through negligent advice or work, had caused a gift under a will which would have benefitted the plaintiff to be invalid. On the facts the solicitor had failed to warn that the will should not be witnessed by the spouse of a beneficiary and had failed to appreciate that the returned will was defective for this reason. The central problem is obvious: the solicitor's negligence has caused pure economic loss to a third party beneficiary to the contract. If this were not difficult enough other problems are also lurking just below the surface. First, if the justification for recovery in such cases is an extension of the *Hedley Byrne* principle, following *Midland Bank*, the central requirement of reliance may be missing. Reliance is normally thought to involve acting positively; that is, changing one's conduct as a result of the advice, not merely doing nothing on the assumption that everything will be all right. This is the distinction between "active" and "passive" reliance. The difficulty on the facts of *Ross* is that the reliance may not even reach the level of being passive; a named beneficiary under a will may know nothing of the intended gift until the testator's death.

---

[72] As this case was decided as a preliminary issue it is difficult to assess its true importance, but it provides some support for the contention that the boundaries of *Hedley Byrne* liability may have been drawn too narrowly by the House of Lords in *Caparo*.

[73] [1979] Ch. 384.

[74] [1980] Ch. 297.

Secondly, a successful claim on behalf of the beneficiary will have the result of inflating the value of the testator's estate. The money which the beneficiary was intended to receive will have passed to others and the disappointed beneficiary will acquire an equivalent sum from the solicitor. Thirdly, there is a problem concerning the nature of the loss suffered. In most situations of tort the plaintiff's assets have been reduced by the defendant's conduct. In this case the disappointed beneficiary has merely failed to receive a benefit, his existing assets are in no way devalued unless they can be said to include the expectation of the gift under the will.

In spite of these difficulties Megarry V.C. found in favour of the disappointed beneficiary. His judgment is something of a period piece. Although he emphasised the existence of a close relationship of proximity between the solicitor and the beneficiary who was identified by name as the recipient of the work, the main thrust of his approach was to cut this line of development free from *Hedley Byrne* and to base it firmly on *Donoghue v. Stevenson* as interpreted by Lord Wilberforce's two stage test for a duty of care. It is a classic example of the decision in *Anns* pushing the boundaries of the recovery of pure economic loss forwards. The twin decisions of *Midland Bank* and *Ross* established that in some circumstances a duty of care might be owed in respect of professional acts causing financial losses.

Neither of these decisions has been directly affected by the limiting of the scope of the duty of care concerning the recovery of negligently caused pure economic loss, but this process inevitably raised doubts as to their authority. However, the current case law provides support for some limited survival of a tort remedy for financial loss caused by professional negligence. In *Clarke v. Bruce Lance & Co.*[75] the Court of Appeal refused to extend *Ross* to place a solicitor under a duty of care to protect a beneficiary of a will by advising his client that transactions which he was planning to make concerning his property would affect the value of a gift previously made to the beneficiary under the will. In view of the fact that a solicitor's primary duty is to give effect to his client's instructions and that the duty argued for might have faced the solicitor with a conflict as to which party's interests to protect, this result was not surprising. However, the court seemed to accept that *Ross* was a correct decision on its facts. Further support for the survival of the tort action was provided by Lord Keith when, in his speech in *Murphy v. Brentwood District Council*,[76] he stated that he regarded the earlier decision of the House of Lords in *Pirelli General Cable Works Ltd. v. Oscar Faber & Partners*[77] as correctly decided as an application of *Hedley Byrne* principle. *Pirelli* was an example of the use of a tort remedy in a situation of concurrent liability in contract and tort. It involved an allegation by a client that an engineer had been negligent in the design of the lining of a chimney. At the least[78] this would seem to provide continuing support for the existence of professional negligence liability in tort when a professional person has been in a contractual relationship with the plaintiff. However, as it is the authority of *Hedley Byrne* which is being invoked as the basis for the survival of *Pirelli*, professional negligence liability in tort may well extend to non-contractual relationships in which a high degree of proximity exists between the parties.

---

[75] [1988] 1 All E.R. 364.
[76] [1990] 2 All E.R. 908.
[77] [1983] 2 A.C. 1.
[78] For a wider interpretation see *ante*, p. 338.

Most recently, in *White* v. *Jones*,[79] the Court of Appeal has expressly affirmed the authority of *Ross* and applied it to a situation in which a solicitor had failed to prepare the will as opposed to advising incorrectly in the course of the transaction. The Court took pains to turn its decision on the particular circumstances of the disappointed beneficiary situation: the negligence remedy was required to meet the justice of a case in which the contracting party (the estate) had lost nothing and the loser was outside the protection of the contract. The remedy allowed the testator's instructions to be carried through. The existence of a general remedy was, however, left in doubt because it was said to be a general rule that a solicitor owes a duty of care to his client and no-one else.

In spite of the qualifications expressed by the court in *White*, it is suggested that the approach of basing liability for professional acts on *Hedley Byrne* principles should be accepted. The solicitor's work in a case such as *White* is designed to confer a financial benefit on a third party. The law should recognise this to be a situation calling for the imposition of a duty of care not to cause economic loss. Anomalies can be avoided by ensuring that professional acts which cause economic loss are governed by tests equivalent to those recognised in the area of misstatements. On such a basis the professional person would need to know that the work being performed was directed to protecting identifiable economic interests of the plaintiff.[80] The plaintiff might not need to be identified personally, but would need to belong to a clearly defined class which was intended to benefit from the work. In the light of the reasoning in *Ross* and *White*, it is suggested that reliance should not be a requirement of a duty of care in this area.

DEFECTS OF QUALITY IN BUILDINGS AND CHATTELS

Cases concerning defects in buildings decided in the 1970s such as *Dutton* and *Anns* presented a challenge to the traditional refusal of the law to allow the tort of negligence to be a remedy for defects of quality.[81] These cases allowed recovery for defects in the structure of buildings on the basis that the defect was an "imminent threat to health and safety" of persons using the property. It was said to be an "impossible distinction" to allow tort damages for personal injuries or damage to other property but to deny it in relation to remedial work undertaken to avert such damage, even though the result of doing this was indirectly, and to a limited extent, to give protection to the property owner's expectation that he had made a good bargain when purchasing it. At times the "health and safety" requirement seemed to be little more than a fiction justifying the recovery of damages in tort for quality defects. Indeed, the courts at times tried to sidestep the difficulties by denying that economic loss was at issue. The cases were said to involve physical damage because the buildings themselves were suffering physical damage. The distinction between an item which was damaged in being defective in

---

[79] [1993] 3 All E.R. 481.

[80] There is support in May J.'s decision in *Nitrigin Eireann Teoranta* v. *Inco Alloys Ltd.* [1992] 1 All E.R. 854 for distinguishing professional work from that of suppliers and manufacturers with regard to the recovery of economic losses.

[81] The issues here would seem to be equally relevant to defects in both chattels and buildings. However, the bulk of the authority has concerned buildings.

itself and requiring repair or replacement and one which caused damage to persons or other property was lost from sight.

The high point of the expansion came with the decision of the House of Lords in *Junior Books Ltd.* v. *Veitchi Co. Ltd.*[82] This was a claim by the owner of a factory against a specialist subcontractor who had negligently laid the floor in the factory. The plaintiff sought compensation in tort for the cost of relaying the floor and the costs of the consequential disruption of its business, but did not allege that the defects had created a risk of injury to persons or property in the factory. In spite of this, the majority in the House allowed their claim. To the more radical commentators the decision opened the door to the recovery of pure economic loss in the tort of negligence whenever such losses were foreseeable and allowed negligence a role as a remedy for quality defects in purchased goods. A less revolutionary inter-pretation of the case accepted these consequences but confined them to a neo-contractual relationship; the parties in *Junior Books* were not quite in a contractual relationship, but they were one stage short of being in one and the close proximity which existed justified allowing tort to overcome a problem created by the harsh rules of privity of contract.

Neither of these interpretations of *Junior Books* can now be regarded as correctly stating the law. The governing rules and the rejection of a wide recovery for economic loss favoured by decisions such as *Junior Books* are to be found in the modern leading decisions of *D. & F. Estates Ltd.* v. *The Church Commissioners*[83] and *Murphy* v. *Brentwood D.C.*[84] *D. & F.* was a tort claim by lessees of a building against the main contractor in respect of defective plasterwork. There was no privity of contract between the parties. The claim was for replacing the fallen plaster, the costs of replacing plaster which was defective but which had not yet fallen and for the costs of disturbance. The speeches in the case revived the traditional view of the boundary between contract and the tort of negligence. Tort deals with damage which is suffered by person or property other than the item purchased. Warranties of quality do not run with the title of a property to benefit future purchasers on the basis of a tort right. In *D. & F. Estates* the cost of replacing defective plasterwork was held irrecoverable. The only possibility that conceivably gave rise to a claim in tort was that falling plaster might have caused damage to other items of property such as the carpets. In *Murphy* the House of Lords overruled its own previous decision of *Anns* on the scope of a local authority's duty of care when exercising statutory functions in respect of building regulations. The authority of *Anns* had not been directly in issue in *D. & F. Estates* and it had been arguable that the case was authority for the existence of an exceptional area of tortious recovery under which defects which created an imminent threat to health and safety were still actionable in tort in spite of the reassertion of the traditional principle of the forms of recoverable loss. This result would have applied to the negligence liability of the local authorities and builders but not to architects and engineers who were outside the ratio of *Anns*. In *Murphy* the House of Lords rejected the "imminent threat to health and safety" approach as unworkable and assimilated the negligence liability of local authorities

---

[82] [1983] 1 A.C. 520.
[83] [1989] A.C. 177.
[84] [1991] 1 A.C. 398.

and builders to the traditional rules which had been revived by *D. & F. Estates*.

Several important results flowed from these decisions. The most important is that the balance has shifted decisively in favour of bringing actions relating to defects in items such as buildings in contract rather than tort. A large number of cases decided in tort between 1972 and 1988 no longer represent the law because they deal with a form of loss which is now only recoverable in contract. The great majority of defects in buildings are not a form of loss which will be recoverable in tort as such claims are usually for the costs of repairing defective property. Even the most seriously damaged property is as likely to lead to the need to replace it as to claims for personal injuries or damage to other property. Professional persons working in the construction industry, who are likely to be out of privity of contract with the person ultimately damaged, may well have regained much of the immunity which they thought they had lost. The scope of parallel liability (the option of switching a claim based on contract into tort) is reduced for the same reason.

Complex structures: a possible exception?

As should be apparent, the result of these authorities is that the law has drawn a firm distinction between property which deteriorates (damages itself) because of a defect and items which cause damage to other items of property. This distinction has compelled lawyers to ask basic questions concerning the identity of items. Sophisticated things, for instance buildings and cars, will usually consist of components manufactured by a number of different firms. Even relatively simple items such as foodstuffs may be supplied to consumers in packaging which is likely to have been manufactured by someone other than the producer of the food. If food is ruined by negligently manufactured packaging or if negligently designed structural steelwork calls for repairs to the walls of a building do we have an example of a single item of defective quality or can we subdivide the item and say that defects in one item are damaging another?

The retreat of tort as a remedy for defects of quality means that recognition of the possibility of subdividing items is one of the few ways in which tort could continue to play a role. A growing body of authority dealing with chattels and buildings has aired the possibilities but has done little to determine exactly where the relevant distinctions are to be drawn. The issue first came to prominence in *Aswan Engineering Establishment* Co. v. *Lupdine Ltd.*[85] in which it was alleged that negligently designed packaging had caused the product which it contained to be lost through leakage. The question whether the plaintiff had bought one item or two did not ultimately have to be decided as it was held that there had been no negligence in the design of the packaging. However, both Lloyd and Nicholls L.JJ. did seem prepared to accept the proposition that it is possible to distinguish between a product and the packaging in which it is contained and between different components built into a single item. This case therefore provides some slight support for the possibility that packaging will be held to be an item distinguishable from its contents. However, it should be noted that Nicholls L.J. was reluctant to accept the existence of a duty of care on the manufacturer of the package in relation to loss of the product. It is significant that

[85] [1987] 1 All E.R. 135.

provision was expressly made in the Consumer Protection Act 1987[86] to stop claims of this nature. Section 5(2) blocks a strict liability claim from being brought under that Act for damage caused to the defective product itself or to a product into which a defective component was incorporated.

The issue next surfaced in *D. & F. Estates* where the suggestion was made by Lord Bridge that defective parts of a building may cause damage to other parts. For example, defective foundations may cause damage to the walls of the building. Lord Bridge suggested that as buildings were "complex structures"[87] they might be capable of being subdivided into their component parts and such damage could be treated as an example of a defective item of property damaging different property.[88] If correct, this was a very important exception to the redrawn distinction between contract and tort. It could apply to all persons working in the construction industry and to many faults which their work produced with the result that a significant tort remedy in respect of, what are essentially, defects of quality would survive.

The same judges returned to the issue in *Murphy*. As *Anns* was overruled in that case it was no longer necessary to explain the case away and it is not surprising that the members of the House found that the subdivision approach did not fit easily with the general approach to the scope of tort liability in negligence which they were reaffirming. The speeches in *Murphy* are problematic on this issue. At one level they can be regarded as a rapid retreat, the judges who mooted the possibility in *D. & F. Estates* as a way of explaining *Anns* being now keen to bury it before it undermined their conservative revolution. Their speeches support the view that it is unrealistic to subdivide a building into its component parts and that the structural elements constitute a single indivisible whole. The problem is that the members of the House then mooted exceptions to this which seem capable of undermining the purity of the theory favoured. Their rejection seems based on the simple case in which the building is erected in its entirety by a single contractor. It remains far from clear whether a negligent subcontractor or a designer remote from the contract may not continue to fall foul of a form of the subdivision approach. Lord Keith regarded wiring done by an electrical subcontractor as constituting a distinguishable part of the work, Lord Bridge agreed with this and added the example of a defective central heating boiler which exploded and damaged the fabric of the building, and Lord Jauncey contemplated the possibility that a structural steel frame for a building erected by a separate contractor could be held to have caused physical damage to other parts of the building. It seems that the members of the House may have underestimated the amount of subcontracting which occurs in the construction industry and have left scope for the subdivision argument to continue to complicate the law.

Defining what counts as a single item of property is not an easy task. At present the courts favour a distinction between integral parts of the structure and ancillary parts. The difficulty is that items such as wiring and structural steelwork would seem to be an integral part of a building to many people. An

---

[86] Discussed in relation to personal injuries in Chap. 12, *ante*.

[87] This terminology, which has gained considerable currency, is inaccurate in so far as the fundamental issue is that of identifying an item in distinction from others. As the *Aswan* decision shows the complexity of the item(s) at issue is irrelevant to this more fundamental issue.

[88] Lord Oliver treated the complex structures approach as a possible explanation of the continuing, if exceptional, authority of *Anns*.

alternative approach might be to distinguish between items built into the original structure and others added at a later date although there is nothing in the cases to support this. The problem may prove to be of particular significance to the professional negligence liabilities of engineers who may well be asked to design identifiable components of the structure such as the steelwork or the foundations. Architects, being responsible for the whole building, may be in a much more favourable position.

Conclusion

The immunity in respect of quality defects might be justified by arguing that the degree of protection which is provided by other legal mechanisms is adequate. In the case of buildings, private purchasers obtain the protection of section 1 of the Defective Premises Act 1972 and the National House Builders Council warranty in the case of new buildings and purchasers of all properties can opt to obtain a survey report.[89] Those who acquire commercial property can obtain some protection from survey reports and any contractual protection which they can negotiate in the form of collateral warranties.[90] In the case of defective products the implied contractual conditions recognised by the Sale of Goods Act 1979, supplemented by the provisions of the Unfair Contract Terms Act 1977, provides an effective remedy in the majority of cases. Privity of contract causes fewer problems in relation to defective products than it does in relation to buildings.

Contractual Interests/No Title to Property

In *Leigh & Sillavan Ltd.* v. *Aliakmon Shipping Co. Ltd.*[91] Lord Brandon summarised this area of the pure economic loss rule in the following words:

" . . . there is a long line of authority for a principle of law that, in order to enable a person to claim in negligence for loss caused to him by reason of loss or damage to property, he must have had either the legal ownership of or possessory title to the property concerned at the time when the loss or damage occurred, and it is not enough for him to have only had contractual rights in relation to such property which have been adversely affected by the loss or damage to it"

---

[89] Even if they do not do this there is the possibility of their obtaining protection from the tort duty recognised in *Smith* v. *Eric S. Bush (a firm), Harris* v. *Wyre Forest District Council* [1990] 1 A.C. 831.

[90] Collateral warranties are specific contractual undertakings entered into by designers and contractors to provide protection to parties (such as prospective tenants of a building or funding institutions). If it were not for the warranty there would be no contractual relationship between these parties. The use of such warranty agreements has increased dramatically in the wake of the disappearance of tort rights. In one sense this might be regarded as a "market solution" to the problem which shows that the intervention of tort was unnecessary, however, there is a suspicion that the variety of forms of warranty which have been given owes more to bargaining power than to the logic of the situation and is almost certain to create major problems in due course; it is possible that many of the warranties which have been given may provide the recipient with no real remedy if the property proves to be defective. If this is the case, we may actually be witnessing a market failure which calls for some form of intervention such as the reappearance of tort rights, or the imposition of standard contractual terms by legislation or use of standard form contracts.

[91] [1986] A.C. 785.

This rule can be traced back to several nineteenth century cases. In *Simpson & Co.* v. *Thomson, Burrell*[92] an insurer of a ship brought an action against a person who had negligently damaged the ship on the basis that the negligence had caused financial loss to him. The claim was rejected because the insurer's interest in the damaged vessel was purely contractual; the lack of any property interest in it at the time of the damage barred the negligence claim in tort.[93] In *Cattle* v. *Stockton Waterworks Co.*[94] the plaintiff was engaged on a fixed price contract to construct a tunnel on another person's land. A defective water main owned by the defendants fractured and flooded the workings and caused completion of the work to be delayed. The plaintiff's claim that the damage to the owner's property had rendered his contract less valuable failed. The decision was heavily influenced by the fear that to allow the claim would be to open the door to claims by a variety of other persons, such as the plaintiff's workmen, who might claim that their financial interests had been damaged by the negligence.

A modern application of this rule is illustrated by the "power cut" cases exemplified by *Spartan Steel and Alloys Ltd.* v. *Martin & Co. (Contractors) Ltd.*[95] In these cases the typical fact situation is that the defendant, by negligence, has damaged equipment belonging to the electricity board with the result that a power cut causes lost production and profits in factories in the area. It is accepted law that the owners of these factories can recover their losses in a negligence action against the tortfeasor if, and only if, foreseeable damage has been caused to their property by the power cut. In *Spartan Steel* the cut resulted in damage to metal which was being processed in a furnace and to the furnace itself. Financial losses consequential on these items of damage were recoverable, whereas losses incurred because the failure to restore the power supply meant that the furnaces could not be restarted even when they had been repaired could not be recovered. On the basis of this result, business losses caused in this way may or may not be recoverable according to the arbitrary factor of the nature of the process which is being used in a particular factory. If Business A, which uses a process which simply switches itself off when the power is cut, loses money as a result of a power cut it will not recover; however, Business B, next door, which uses a process which damages itself when the power is cut, and which suffers an equivalent loss of profits is treated more favourably.

The principle barring recovery in tort on these grounds came under attack as a result of the *Anns* principle but has clearly survived. Two important cases reaffirmed the rule. In *Candlewood Navigation Corp. Ltd.* v. *Mitsui O.S.K. Lines Ltd.*[96] the plaintiff was the time charterer of a ship which was damaged by the defendant's negligence. The charter, which gave the plaintiff contractual rights to use the ship, but no property in it, was rendered less valuable because the ship could not be used while necessary repairs were effected and because hire charges remained payable during this period. However, the Privy Council regarded the plaintiff's contractual interest in

---

[92] (1877) 3 App. Cas. 279.

[93] To overcome this result insurers have developed the practice (known as subrogation) of pursuing claims against tortfeasors in the name of the insured.

[94] (1875) L.R. 10 Q.B. 453.

[95] [1973] Q.B. 27. See also *Electrochrome Ltd.* v. *Welsh Plastics Ltd.* [1968] 2 All E.R. 205; *British Celanese Ltd.* v. *A.H. Hunt (Capacitors) Ltd.* [1969] 1 W.L.R. 959; *S.C.M. (United Kingdom) Ltd.* v. *Whittall & Son* [1971] 1 Q.B. 337.

[96] [1986] A.C. 1.

the vessel as insufficient to bring them within the protection of a duty of care. The House of Lords reached a similar decision in *Leigh & Sillavan Ltd.* v. *Aliakmon Shipping Co. Ltd.*[97] In that case a cargo was damaged by negligence whilst being shipped. At the time that the damage occurred the plaintiff had contractual rights to the cargo which was at its risk but no title to it. The House of Lords held the plaintiff's interest to be insufficient to justify the recognition of a duty of care. A tort duty imposed on these facts would have the potential of unsettling the well established contractual rules concerning the transfer of risk and title in contracts for the carriage of goods by sea. It was incorrect to use the authority of *Anns* to attack settled and long established rules of law. The plaintiff's position could have been protected by recourse to the normal operation of the rules concerning bills of lading and it was no part of the role of the law of tort to obviate the need for individuals to take normal precautions.

In view of the direction taken by these authorities it is slightly surprising to find that Parliament created a limited exception to the general rule by section 3 of the Latent Damage Act 1986. This provision governs the situation of a sale of property which is suffering from negligently inflicted latent damage. Because the damage was latent; that is it could not have been discovered at the time of the purchase by the exercise of reasonable care, the sale will have taken place at the full market price. However, the normal rule will be that only the person who had title at the time that the damage occurred, the vendor rather than the purchaser, will have a right to an action in negligence. The vendor, by selling at the full market price, will have lost nothing as a result of the negligence, whereas the purchaser will have paid too much but will be denied a cause of action because of having no title at the time when the item was damaged. Section 3 answers this by allowing the purchaser of property which was suffering from latent damage at the date of the purchase to succeed to any negligence based cause of action in relation to that damage which is vested in the vendor. In effect, the section protects the purchaser's expectation that he made a good bargain. The section was undoubtedly aimed at the house purchase situation, although as it is worded to deal with all property it has been suggested that it has the capacity to reverse the result in the *Aliakmon* type of case. In practice, its utility has been significantly reduced by the decisions of the House of Lords in *D. & F. Estates Ltd.* v. *The Church Commissioners for England*[98] and *Murphy* v. *Brentwood D. C.*[99] It is unlikely that a vendor of property will have suffered damage which is of a type recognised by the law of tort but which is at the same time latent.

Cases such as the *Aliakmon* deal with financial losses suffered by a person who has contractual interests over property belonging to another. No such contractual interest existed in *Spartan Steel & Alloys Ltd.* v. *Martin & Co. (Contractors) Ltd.*[1] which applied a similar result to trading losses alleged to have resulted from damage to a third party's property. A person may simply suffer business losses because his business is shut down as a result of another's negligence. For example, a shop may lose a day's trading because the defendant has negligently caused a fire with the result that roads leading to the shop are blocked off. As we have seen, as a result of *Spartan Steel*, only

---

[97] [1986] A.C. 785.
[98] [1989] A.C. 177.
[99] [1991] 1 A.C. 398.
[1] [1973] Q.B. 27.

those financial losses which are consequential on physical damage to the plaintiff's property are recoverable in the tort of negligence. This result may be thought to create some anomalies, but the general view is that liability has to stop somewhere and that the *Spartan Steel* rule provides a convenient and easily understood stopping place.

These cases produce a very arbitrary result in terms of placing incentives on persons who cause damage to property. If a person's income is reduced by damage to his property that loss is recoverable. However, if a third party is utilising that property for business purposes the losses resulting from the damage are excluded from recovery. The result of this in economic terms is likely to be to reduce the incentives on persons to take care not to damage property. The rule could only be justified in terms of deterrence if it could be shown that the incentive achieved by the rule which makes the tortfeasor liable for negligently caused physical damage is adequate to achieve a cost-justified level of care and that the additional incentives derived from holding a person liable for third party losses[2] do not justify the expense which would be incurred in processing claims by third parties and in shifting the losses.[3]

Government Supervisory Bodies

One of the consequences of the view that *Junior Books* established that a duty of care existed in respect of any foreseeable negligently caused pure financial loss was that a number of cases were brought against official bodies which bore responsibility for supervising and regulating the operation of a particular area of commercial activity. Faced by the prospect of government funded regulatory bodies having to underwrite the losses caused to investors by a business collapse, the courts have pursued a consistent policy of denying the existence of a duty of care in such circumstances. The fact that this is an area of potentially enormous liabilities is emphasised by the fact that the government's ad hoc scheme to compensate investors who lost money in the collapse of the Barlow Clowes investment company had paid out almost £150 million by the middle of 1990.

The leading modern authority on this subject is *Yuen Kun-yeu* v. *A.G. for Hong Kong*.[4] In that case it was alleged that the Commissioner for Deposit Taking Companies in Hong Kong had been negligent in failing to withdraw a licence from a company which had subsequently gone into liquidation leaving the plaintiff and fellow investors with losses. It was contended that the Commission had had reason to suspect that the company was being run fraudulently and speculatively and that investors had relied on the fact of its continued registration as indicating that it was a fit and proper body in which investments could be safely made. The Privy Council used a number of familiar arguments when denying the existence of a duty of care. Although it was foreseeable in the widest sense that investors might lose money if an unsuitable company was allowed to continue to trade, foreseeability of loss on its own does not create a duty of care. The legislature had intended to

---

[2] These are likely to be small as the remote chance of such losses occurring is likely to mean that the risk is discounted heavily.

[3] See D. Harris & C. Veljanovski in M. Furmston (ed.) *op. cit.* Chap. 3.

[4] [1988] A.C. 175. See also *Minories Finance Ltd.* v. *Arthur Young* [1989] 2 All E.R. 105 and *Davies* v. *Radcliffe* [1990] 2 All E.R. 536.

create the licensing system in the interests of the public as a whole rather than to create a duty enforceable by individual depositors. Recognition of the duty of care argued for would involve the Commission in liability for the acts of independent third parties and would face it with an additional burden when exercising its delicate task of deciding whether or not to revoke a licence (a decision to revoke could well prove damaging to investors). As no detailed and stringent system of supervision of deposit taking companies was created by the Ordinance there existed no sufficient special relationship to create a duty of care between the defendant and either the investors or the company.

At one level this result can be regarded as a device for protecting the public purse. If Parliament wishes to provide a mechanism whereby public funds are to be used to protect investors or other categories of consumer who trade in particular markets it should do this consciously: it should introduce legislation the underlying policy of which can be openly debated. The issue should not go by default simply because the logic of the neighbour test leads inevitably to the existence of a remedy.[5] In terms of economic analysis this is a classic example of a situation which poses a risk of exceptionally extensive and indeterminate liability. It is also an example of "asymmetry"; the defendant, being a public body, is likely to be conferring substantial benefits, without charge, on persons trading in the market and the immunity may be seen as the price which is to be paid to avoid the deterrent affect of liability discouraging the production of socially useful services.[6]

Statutory Negligence Remedies

A number of tortious remedies for negligently caused economic loss are created by specific statutory provision. These remedies were enacted to reverse the immunity from negligence liability for misstatements which was thought to derive from the decision of the House of Lords in *Derry* v. *Peek*.[7]

Misrepresentation Act 1967, s. 2(1)

This remedy co-exists with that created by *Hedley Byrne & Co. Ltd.* v. *Heller & Partners Ltd.*[8] It was the Parliamentary response to the supposed lack of a general negligence remedy for misstatements which *Hedley Byrne* also sought to meet. The remedies are not identical. The statutory remedy is confined to the parties to the contract which was entered into on the faith of the misrepresentation and the potentially wide scope of the *Hedley Byrne* "special relationship" and the difficulties which it creates are not relevant under the statute. Under the statute if a misrepresentation which induces the plaintiff to enter into a contract with the representor is proved the defendant bears the burden of proving that he was not negligent whereas the normal rule that the plaintiff bears the burden of proof applies to the common law remedy and, finally, the drafting of the statutory remedy requires that the rule of remoteness of damage which is applied to it is the deceit rule of

---

[5] The critics of the incremental approach to duty of care issues might argue that tort protection should not be regarded as unavailable simply because of a lack of previous authority.
[6] D. Harris & C. Veljanovski in Furmston (ed.) *op. cit.* pp. 53–54.
[7] (1889) 14 App. Cas. 337.
[8] [1964] A.C. 465.

"natural and direct consequences" rather than the normal negligence rule of reasonable foreseeability.[9]

Financial Services Act 1986

This statute contains the modern version of compensation remedies which were originally enacted in the Directors' Liability Act 1890 to reverse the actual decision in *Derry* v. *Peek*.[10] It creates a compensation remedy for damage caused by misstatements or omissions in the listing particulars[11] or prospectus[12] issued by a company in relation to issues of shares, debentures or other securities.[13] The duty imposed by the Act rests on all persons responsible for the particulars, but, as is the case under section 2(1) of the Misrepresentation Act, defences may be available if negligence can be disproved. The remedy has a significant advantage over the common law one in being available to persons who suffer loss as a result of the purchase of securities in the market.[14]

---

[9] *Royscot Trust Ltd.* v. *Rogerson* [1991] 3 All E.R. 294.
[10] (1889) 14 App. Cas. 337.
[11] s. 150.
[12] s. 166.
[13] Non-listed companies will remain subject to s. 67 of the Companies Act 1985 until Pt. V of the Financial Services Act 1986 is brought into operation.
[14] *Cf. Al Nakib Investments (Jersey) Ltd.* v. *Longcroft* [1990] 3 All E.R. 321.

Chapter Seventeen

Strict Liability for Economic Losses

INTRODUCTION

Strict liability for financial losses is a subject which has received little attention from commentators. Those areas which exist are examples of the different kinds of statutory torts.[1] In view of the limited scope given to negligence as a remedy for such losses, it is not surprising to find that the common law has not, in general, recognised strict liability in this area. What is slightly surprising is that examples of statutory torts protecting people against such losses are continuing to appear in an era in which common law protection against such losses based on negligence has retreated. The best explanation is that Parliament has identified the protection of individuals as of such importance in particular areas that special provision overriding the common law immunity can be justified. The Defective Premises Act 1972 is to be seen as a considered, and limited, Parliamentary response to the consumer interest in the quality of newly built dwellings. Some of the other remedies described in this chapter operate to supplement the primary enforcement mechanisms given to public bodies by particular legislation. The tort right gives a compensation remedy to an individual who has been damaged by conduct which the statute has declared to be unlawful.

There are no general principles governing the law's approach to this topic. Several of the best known authorities concerning the question of whether the tort of breach of statutory duty should be inferred feature claims for damages for financial losses alleged to have been suffered as a result of acts in breach of a statutory duty. The refusal of the House of Lords to infer the existence of a tort remedy in cases such as *Cutler* v. *Wandsworth Stadium Ltd.*[2] and *Lonrho Ltd.* v. *Shell Petroleum Co. Ltd.*[3] might be thought to indicate that the law generally does not recognise the tort when financial losses are at issue. This interpretation may well be correct but is no part of the reasoning in the cases which were decided on the narrower ground, that the statutes in question were not intended to confer individually enforceable rights on the defined class of society of which the plaintiff was a member. This emphasis on the construction test has effectively killed discussion of the issue of whether the tort of breach of statutory duty has a role to play in relation to financial losses.[4] Indeed, little discussion of this policy question has occurred,

---

[1] For the distinction between the different kinds of statutory tort see Chap. 2.
[2] [1949] A.C. 398.
[3] [1982] A.C. 173.
[4] It is still producing this result. See *Wentworth* v. *Wiltshire C.C.* [1993] 2 All E.R. 256.

in spite of the fact that an inferred breach of statutory duty tort has been recognised as a remedy allowing the recovery of financial losses suffered in the important area of competition law.

In spite of the absence of any general principle, Parliament can be seen to have created a number of significant examples of statutory torts and expressly created breach of statutory duty remedies which protect financial interests in relation to defective premises; copyright; competition law; landlord and tenant law; financial services law and employment law. Strict tortious liability for financial losses is an area of growing importance.

DEFECTIVE PREMISES

Section 1 of the Defective Premises Act 1972 creates an important example of a statutory tort which imposes strict liability for financial losses. This provision, the effects of which are confined to residential property, enacts a statutory warranty that dwellings are to be built properly. This is a consumer protection remedy which has been closely connected, in the past, with the guarantee scheme for residential property operated by the National House-Building Council. Although the link between the two forms of protection has now been broken, with the result that the section 1 remedy is now more generally available, the provisions of the N H B C scheme will be outlined in this section as it is likely to continue to provide an attractive alternative to litigation in many cases.

Section 1 imposes a wide ranging form of strict liability which applies to all persons who are involved in the provision of a "dwelling." The section provides that:

> "1(1) A person taking on work for or in connection with the provision of a dwelling (whether the dwelling is provided by the erection or by the conversion or enlargement of a building) owes a duty –
>
> (a) if the dwelling is provided to the order of any person, to that person; and
>
> (b) without prejudice to paragraph (a) above, to every person who acquires an interest (whether legal or equitable) in the dwelling;
>
> to see that the work which he takes on is done in a workmanlike or, as the case may be, professional manner, with proper materials and so that as regards that work the dwelling will be fit for habitation when completed."

This is a classic example of a strict liability consumer protection remedy which draws on both tort and contract. The standard of liability imposed by it is based upon the contractual warranties found in the standard terms of a building contract. But the contractual characteristics of the duties to do work "in a workmanlike . . . " or "professional manner, with proper materials" so that "the dwelling will be fit for habitation when completed"[5] are in marked contrast to the width of application of these duties, which are owed by any "person taking on work for or in connection with the provision of a

---

[5] The "fit for habitation" requirement states the result to be derived from compliance with the earlier obligations and is not an independent obligation. *Alexander* v. *Mercouris* [1979] 3 All E.R. 305; *Thompson* v. *Clive Alexander* (1992) 28 Con. L.R. 49. This is not the case in relation to the common implied terms in a building contract.

dwelling" to "every person who acquires an interest" in it. This is a wide ranging tort style duty which does not even require foreseeability or proximity. It is likely to be owed by a large group of persons: the architect, engineer or surveyor who designs or supervises building work as well as builders and subcontractors. The duty expressly applies to developers and others who arrange for work to be done, but do not undertake it personally.[6]

The statutory tort created by section 1 gives the disappointed purchaser of a dwelling a remedy which is generally superior to the alternatives available in the tort of negligence or in contract. The strict duty places a heavier standard of liability on a defendant than negligence would and proximity issues do not have to be considered. The duty was held by the Court of Appeal in *Andrews* v. *Schooling*[7] to cover acts of non-feasance, such as the omission of a damp proof course, as well as misfeasance. The forms of loss recoverable almost certainly extend to pure economic losses in the form of defects of quality in dwellings. This is a major advantage as this form of loss has been removed from the scope of the tort of negligence by recent decisions.[8] Some commentators have doubted whether the remedy extends this far[9] and it must be admitted that the drafting of the section fails to make clear whether the tortious or contractual characteristics of the "hybrid" remedy govern the categories of losses which are recoverable. However, all the evidence suggests that pure economic losses are covered by the section. The Law Commission[10] when it proposed the introduction of the remedy clearly intended it to cover defects of quality and, as it did so at a time before *Dutton* v. *Bognor Regis U.D.C.*[11] had set negligence on the ill-fated road to granting recovery of pure economic losses in cases of buildings, it is difficult to see why the retreat of negligence should have implications for the statutory remedy. It would be strange if a duty to do work in a workmanlike manner with proper materials with the result that the dwelling was fit for habitation when completed could only ground liability if damage to persons or property other than the building resulted.

The most important advantages that the remedy has over a contractual one are that the constraints of privity of contract are abandoned both in respect of those who owe the duty and those who may invoke it and that there is a complete bar placed on clauses purporting to exclude or restrict the statutory liability.[12]

However, the section 1 duty has some drawbacks when compared to a tortious duty based on negligence or to a contractual one. In particular, the phrase "the provision of a dwelling" means that section 1 is a consumer protection remedy which has no role in relation to commercial property and does not apply to works of alteration or repair undertaken by builders and

---

[6] s. 1(4).
[7] [1991] 3 All E.R. 723.
[8] See pp. 349–353.
[9] Fridman on *Torts*, para. 12.57 "there would seem to be no justification for interpreting the 1972 statute so as to permit an action for pure economic loss caused by breach of the statutory duties set out in the Act." See also Spencer, "The Defective Premises Act 1972 – Defective Law and Defective Law Reform" (1974) 33 C.L.J. 307 at 319–320.
[10] Report No. 40. The report draws a firm distinction between defects of quality and dangerous defects.
[11] [1973] 1 Q.B. 373.
[12] s. 6(3).

others on existing dwellings. Furthermore,[13] the words "A person taking on work" may not cover as wide a range of persons as are subject to a common law duty of care[14]; and the class of persons who can claim the protection of the statutory duty is limited to those who obtain an "interest in the dwelling" whereas a negligence duty would be owed to anyone foreseeably affected by the negligence. Finally, although this duty is similar to that imposed by contract, the requirement that the defect must result in the building not being fit for habitation when completed means that some trivial defects, which might be actionable in contract, fall outside the statutory protection because their consequences are insufficiently serious.[15]

The section 1 duty does not operate if at the time of the first sale or letting of the dwelling an "approved" guarantee scheme gave rights in respect of defects in it.[16] Between 1972 and 1979 this provision prevented the section 1 duty from operating in the case of any dwelling sold with the benefit of a guarantee issued under the auspices of the National House-Building Council. The N H B C scheme applies to almost all new houses and purpose-built flats sold in this country and, as a result, the operation of section 1 during this period was confined to the area of converted properties and to the small number of developers who did not belong to the Council. The exclusion of the statutory duty was of particular significance for contractors and professional persons who would be subject to section 1 as persons "taking on work." It is the vendor of the dwelling who enters into a contract in the N H B C form and the fact of his having done so excludes the operation of section 1 duties against himself and all the other persons involved in the provision of the dwelling. No version of the N H B C scheme has received approval since 1979 and the approval given to the 1979 version of the scheme has now ceased to be effective.[17] As a result the section 1 remedy is now an alternative to invoking the N H B C guarantees. It is likely that the great majority of complaints concerning defects in new dwellings will continue to be dealt with under the guarantee, rather than by resort to litigation.

The National House-Building Council Scheme

The provisions of the N H B C scheme, the latest versions of which have been marketed under the title of "Buildmark," have developed over the years in which the scheme has operated. The rules which apply to a particular property are those in force when it was first sold. The scheme is a combination of contractual responsibilities undertaken by the developer and owed to the first purchaser and his successors in title and a warranty and insurance role assumed by the Council itself. The developer's main obligation is that he enters into a general contractual warranty that the house has been, or will be built in accordance with the N H B C's requirements in an efficient and workmanlike manner and of proper materials and so as to be fit for

---

[13] Note also that the limitation period stipulated by subs. 1(5) runs from "the time when the dwelling was completed" whereas in negligence the standard rule is that time runs from the date when the damage occurred.

[14] Doubts have been expressed as to whether a local authority building inspector would come under the s.1 duty. *Sparham-Souter* v. *Town and Country Developments (Essex) Ltd.* [1976] Q.B. 858 at 869–870 *per* Lord Denning M.R.

[15] *Thompson* v. *Clive Alexander & Partners* (1992) 28 Con. L.R. 49.

[16] s. 2.

[17] See the note to s. 2 in the Noter Up to Halsbury's Statutes.

habitation. The protection provided by the Council is additional and varies according to whether the defect at issue arises and is reported during "the initial guarantee period," which runs for two years from the issue of the Notice of Insurance cover on the particular property or the "structural guarantee period," which runs from the conclusion of the initial guarantee period for a further eight years. The developer's contractual obligations under the scheme are made for the benefit of the first purchaser and of his successors in title, whether or not the benefit of the contract has been assigned. The fact that the scheme is designed to protect subsequent purchasers of the property is a deliberate improvement on the normal contractual position. The theoretical efficacy of this device in the absence of any assignment of the contractual obligations is dubious,[18] but as the Council's rules forbid a member from raising privity of contract as a defence and as the Council will underwrite the vendor's main obligations if he becomes insolvent, the practical result is that a subsequent purchaser of the property is protected by the scheme in almost all cases.

The scheme offers several forms of protection. First, insurance cover is given to protect purchaser's deposits lost through a builder's insolvency or to correct defects in the building which are of such a nature as to prevent the Council from issuing a guarantee on the building. Secondly, in the initial guarantee period the developer undertakes to remedy any defect arising in the dwelling as a result of a breach of the Council's requirements as to building standards. The Council's role during the initial guarantee period is that of an underwriter of this obligation. During the structural guarantee period the Council itself assumes primary responsibility for reimbursing the cost of "major damage" which is defined as that which requires "complete or partial" rebuilding or extensive repair work. The Council covers such damage so long as the defect results from a failure to comply with its technical requirements and is not covered by another insurance policy in force at the time of the claim. The developer's liability during this period is based on its having undertaken in general contractual terms "that the Dwelling has been or will be built in an efficient or workmanlike manner and of proper materials and so as to be fit for habitation."[19] Finally, protection is given if the N H B C acted as building inspector in relation to the building.[20] The Council will pay the cost of remedial work if a building which it has inspected develops defects, which fall beyond the scope of other N H B C protection, as a result of a failure to comply with building regulations. This protection is confined to defects which present an imminent danger to the physical health or safety of occupants of the building. When introduced in 1988 it was a real advance over that provided by tort against local authority building inspectors as no proof of negligence on the part of the N H B C inspector was required. It is now of even more significance in the light of the

---

[18] Obligations arising under an N H B C agreement were held to run with the land under Law of Property Act 1925, s. 78 in *Marchant* v. *Caswell and Redgrave Ltd.* (1976) 240 Estates Gazette 127. However, this result was doubted in *Kiljowski* v. *New Capital Properties Ltd.* (1987) 15 Con. L.R. 1 which also dealt with the requirements of proving an effective assignment.

[19] A remedy based on this obligation is only available during the structural guarantee period if the Council has disclaimed liability because it is not "major damage" or is beyond the financial limits of the cover. This residual contractual liability of the vendor is not underwritten by the Council.

[20] It may do this under the provisions of the Building Act 1984.

virtual disappearance of local authority tortious liability for negligently conducted building inspections.

The extent of the N H B C guarantee is subject to financial limits. The most significant of these restricts the amount recoverable in relation to a particular dwelling to the purchase price of the house or three times the national average purchase price (whichever is the lower). The cover is inflation-proofed during the 10 years.

The N H B C scheme is a good example of a guarantee scheme designed to overcome the difficulties which confront the purchaser or owner of a defective dwelling. The primary obligations arising under it are limited, but the retention of the standard contractual warranty, freed (in most cases) from the operation of privity, leaves the purchaser in as good a position as he would be under the Defective Premises Act. The role of the N H B C in setting standards for construction work, in inspecting work and in imposing on the vendor an obligation to remedy defects are all of practical importance. It is, however, the Council's role as insurer of the developer's main obligations which gives the purchaser the greatest protection. A remedy backed by the Council's assets is likely to be of more value than the conventional common law claim against an insolvent developer.

The retreat of the tort of negligence in recent years has removed the possibility of contractors and professional persons owing negligence duties in respect of quality defects in buildings. In relation to defects in residential property, the operation of the 1972 Act and the N H B C guarantee are now the major consumer protection remedies. No equivalent protection exists for commercial property.

COMPETITION LAW

Competition law[21] is the area which has seen the most notable growth in the availability of strict liability tort remedies for breach of statutory duty. There now seems to be an emerging consensus at both European Community and United Kingdom Government level that individually enforceable remedies have an important role to play in supplementing the regulatory machinery which exists to outlaw anti-competitive practices. At present two bodies of competition law, one governing the United Kingdom, the other European Community trade, exist alongside each other. Both can give rise to individually enforceable tort rights.

The position in relation to United Kingdom domestic competition legislation is that section 26(1) of the Fair Trading Act 1973 contains an express denial of a civil remedy based on contravention of any order made by the Secretary of State under section 22 of the Act. However, a breach of sections 1, 2, 9 and 11 of the Resale Prices Act 1976 (i.e. an unlawful agreement between suppliers or distributors or arrangements[22] intended to maintain minimum prices) and a failure to register a restrictive agreement under the Restrictive Trade Practices Act 1976 are actionable as an express form of breach of statutory duty as a result of sections 25(3) and 35(2) of the respective Acts. These remedies open the door to individual enforcement of these legislative measures by tort claims, irrespective of whether the Office of

---

[21] For a general survey of this area see Whish, *Competition Law* (3rd ed., 1993).
[22] Contractual or otherwise.

Fair Trading decides to investigate the matter and take enforcement proceedings. The annual reports of the Director General of Fair Trading suggest that a significant number of agreements which should have been, but have not been registered under the Restrictive Trade Practices Act 1976 exist. These are often unwritten agreements which have emerged from consultation and discussion between firms.[23] No breach of statutory duty cases of this kind have reached the law reports. However, it has been reported[24] that the Post Office invoked section 35(2) of the Restrictive Trade Practices Act against manufacturers of telephone cables who had operated an unregistered price fixing agreement to its detriment, and that the out of court settlement reached in this case was for the payment of damages of £9 million to the Post Office.

The availability of a tort remedy in English courts for breach of European Community competition legislation derives from the decision of the House of Lords in *Garden Cottage Foods Ltd.* v. *Milk Marketing Board*.[25] This case concerned an allegation that the defendant Board had broken Article 86 of the E.C. Treaty by deciding to restrict its sales of bulk butter to four distributors. The plaintiff company, which was not one of the four, had previously purchased 90 per cent. of its requirement for such butter from the Board. Article 86, which prohibits the abuse of a dominant position in the Common Market or a substantial part of it, has been held by the European Court of Justice to create direct rights vested in individuals which national courts must safeguard.[26] In the light of this, the House of Lords held[27] that breach of Article 86 gave a person damaged thereby a right to claim damages in an English court. In effect, the inference of the tort of breach of statutory duty was made on the basis of a breach of the Treaty provision. Lord Diplock, who delivered a speech which was agreed to by three of his brethren, summarised the decision in the following terms:

---

[23] The Annual Report of the Director General of Fair Trading for 1989 reported that the Office of Fair Trading had issued 32 notices that year seeking details of unregistered agreements. In 1988, 97 such notices had been issued.

[24] Annual Report of the Director General of Fair Trading (1978), p. 9.

[25] [1984] A.C. 130.

[26] *Belgische Radio en Televisie & Societe belge des auteurs, compositeurs et editeurs* v. *S.V. SABAM and N.V. Fonior* [1974] E.C.R. 51.

[27] It may overstate the authority of the case to say that it establishes the remedy. The case was heard on a preliminary issue as to whether an injunction should be granted. The Court of Appeal granted the injunction on the basis that, as serious doubts existed as to whether damages could be claimed, the injunction was the only effective remedy. The ratio of the House of Lord's decision, which reversed this, was that a private law cause of action which gave rise to an injunction must necessarily also give rise to a claim for damages. Lord Diplock found difficulty in seeing how it could be successfully argued that Art. 86 did not give rise to a cause of action of the nature of breach of statutory duty, but did not regard the matter as wholly unarguable and felt it unnecessary to decide the point. Although this appears to leave the point open, it is difficult to see how an argument that the tort should not be inferred can stand with the main ratio. In terms of legal reasoning Lord Wilberforce's dissenting judgment has attractions. It does not automatically follow from the proposition that Art. 86 has direct effect, that a new damages remedy should be inferred. We should distinguish between national courts establishing procedures to enforce rights created by Community law and those courts extending those rights by attaching new remedies to them. The directly applicable nature of the Article 86 right seems to have helped to satisfy the normal construction tests. But, is the normal construction test appropriate in the case of the E.C. Treaty which contains machinery governing its interpretation? See the doubts expressed by Oliver L.J. in *Bourgoin S.A.* v. *Ministry of Agriculture, Fisheries & Food* [1986] Q.B. 716.

"A breach of duty imposed by Article 86 not to abuse a dominant position in the Common Market or in a substantial part of it can thus be categorised in English Law as a breach of statutory duty that is imposed not only for the purpose of promoting the general economic prosperity of the Common Market but also for the benefit of private individuals to whom loss or damage is caused by breach of that duty."

In result this decision provides individuals injured by breach of Article 86 with an effective right to seek compensation or an injunction by bringing proceedings in an English court. This is a true example of inferred breach of statutory duty as the Treaty itself merely specifies orders to desist and fines (which are not payable to an injured party) as remedies to support the prohibition. The new remedy establishes a major new role for breach of statutory duty. In the period since *Garden Cottage* the courts have had no difficulty in extending its reasoning to breaches of Article 85 of the E.C. Treaty which prohibits agreements and practices which may effect trade between Member States with the object or effect of preventing, restricting or distorting competition.[28]

In practice it is very likely that the main role of these remedies will be to give businesses damaged by anti-competitive practices access to interlocutory injunctions in domestic courts. All of the reported cases have actually concerned claims for injunctions. Peter Gibson J.'s decision in *Holleran* v. *Daniel Thwaites plc*[29] was particularly significant in this regard because the plaintiffs were granted an interlocutory injunction on the basis that they had an arguable case that the defendant's actions which threatened their livelihood infringed Article 85 even though the European Commission had shelved its investigation of the issue. The judge commented that it was notorious that the Commission was overburdened with work and took the view that its decision not to act was a factor, but not an important one, relevant to the exercise of his discretion on whether to grant the injunction.

A further move in favour of encouraging tort remedies in this context was provided by the Government's publication in 1989 of a White Paper on Restrictive Trade Practices.[30] It was there proposed to replace the Resale Prices Act 1976 and the Restrictive Trade Practices Act 1976 with new domestic legislation along the lines of the European model. The policy of individually enforceable tort rights would be carried over from the 1976 legislation as the Government "remains convinced" of the need for private enforcement. It hopes that use of these remedies will grow over time and thus enhance the deterrent effect of the legislation and it hoped that the measures that it was taking in other spheres in relation to group actions[31] and contingency fees[32] would make such actions easier to mount.

FINANCIAL SERVICES LAW

The Financial Services Act 1986 creates a wide ranging framework of law which regulates the activities of persons who offer investment and other

---

[28] *Cutforth* v. *Mansfield Inns Ltd.* [1986] 1 C.M.L.R. 1; *Holleran* v. *Daniel Thwaites plc* [1989] 3 C.M.L.R. 917.
[29] [1989] 3 C.M.L.R. 917.
[30] Opening Markets: New Policy on Restrictive Trade Practices, Cm. 727 (1989).
[31] See *ante*, p. 177.
[32] See *ante*, p. 176.

financial services to the public. The task of defining and implementing rules
within this framework is delegated by the Act to the Securities and Investment Board (SIB) and to a number of self-regulating organisations and
recognised professional bodies. Section 62 of the Financial Services Act
expressly creates a breach of statutory duty remedy which is available to any
private investor[33] who suffers loss as a result of the breach of rules or
regulations imposed by the Act's provisions or of equivalent rules laid down
by a self-regulating organisation or a recognised professional body. No
particular relationship between the plaintiff and the person who is in breach
of the rules is required, although causation must obviously be established.
This provision thus creates a strict liability tort duty in respect of financial
losses caused by any breach of the Conduct of Business Rules issued by the
SIB or the breach of equivalent rules of the self-regulating organisations or
recognised professional bodies.

As in the case of the proposed legislative developments concerning competition legislation, the policy underlying section 62 is to allow individually
enforceable private law rights to supplement the role given by the legislation
to regulatory bodies. In part, this can be seen as a reaction to the view that the
criminal law has proved itself an ineffective mechanism in the fight against
fraud and other economic crimes. A private individual whose interests are
damaged by improper trading practices is, therefore, given a direct tort claim
for injunctive relief or damages. Although the person concerned will have to
bear the cost of such proceedings,[34] the initiative is in his own hands; he will
not have to convince a regulatory body to take action. American experience[35] has suggested that such provisions can be an important technique for
controlling misconduct by persons offering investment advice and similar
services to the public.

EMPLOYMENT LAW[36]

Recent legislation in the field of employment law has also created rights to
sue for breach of statutory duty in order to allow persons affected by a
breach of a statutory prohibition to recover any losses which they have
suffered. Once again breach of statutory duty is being used by the legislators
as a technique, independent of contract, which opens the door to enforcement of the prohibition by a wide range of individuals who might be affected
by its breach. At the time of writing no claims under these provisions have
been reported.

Sections 144, 145, 186 and 187 of the Trade Union and Labour Relations
(Consolidation) Act 1992[37] make it unlawful for a business to adopt certain

[33] The remedy was restricted to private investors by s. 62A which was introduced by the
Companies Act 1989. "Private investor" is defined by the Financial Services Act 1986
(Restriction of Right of Action) Regulations 1991, S.I. 1991 No. 489. For a full discussion of
the thinking which produced these amendments to the s. 62 remedy see Pritchard, (1992) 13
Company Lawyer 171 & 210.
[34] The exclusion of business investors from making a claim under s. 62 means that this form of
enforcement is in the hands of those least likely to have the means to invoke it.
[35] See the brief comments by Doyle at (1992) 13 Business L.R. 87.
[36] For the role of breach of statutory duty in relation to individual employment law matters see
Stanton, *Breach of Statutory Duty in Tort*, pp. 72–73.
[37] The provisions first appeared as ss. 12 and 13 of the Employment Act 1982.

practices in order to ensure that other businesses which supply goods or
services to it recognise trade unions or impose union membership requirements on the persons who are to perform work under the contract. A
contract term which imposes any such requirement is void and a person will,
in addition, contravene the sections if, in order to achieve either of these
purposes, he terminates a contract; fails to include a person in his list of
approved suppliers; excludes a person from an invitation to tender; fails to
permit a tender to be made or otherwise determines not to enter a contract.
Contravention of these obligations is made expressly actionable as breach of
statutory duty by sections 145(5) and 187(5) of the Act. The tort created by
these sections is in all probability one of strict liability. A claim under these
provisions is available to certain stipulated classes of persons such as those
excluded from lists of approved suppliers; those not permitted to tender and
those whose contracts are terminated. The list of potential claimants is,
however, extended by the inclusion of "any other person who may be
adversely affected by (the) contravention." An obvious category of claimants
under this head would be employees and subcontractors of the supplier who
lost work as a result of such a prohibited practice. Proof of loss will obviously
be easiest when an existing contract has been terminated, rather than when
the supplier has been prevented from attempting to obtain the work.

Section 18 of the Telecommunications Act 1984 imposes civil liability for
breach of the statutory duty owed by a licensed telecommunications operator to comply with an order issued by the Director-General of Telecommunications. This statute replaced a criminal offence which had previously
existed under the Telegraphs Act 1863 with civil liability which can be
enforced, under section 18(6)(a), by "any person affected by the contravention"[38] or by the Director-General. Section 18(7) ensures that the standard
of liability is not absolute by providing that "it shall be a defence . . . to prove
that he (the defendant) took all reasonable steps and exercised all due
diligence to avoid contravening the order." This defence is possibly designed
to protect an employer whose contravention is caused by industrial action
taken by his employees. It is not certain whether such employees would
themselves be liable for breach of the duty,[39] although the fact that section
18(6)(b) creates a tort of inducing a breach of, or interfering with the
performance of, the duty to comply with the order suggests that any liability
on the part of the unions or their members is not to be found under section
18(6)(a).

LANDLORD AND TENANT

An express statutory duty remedy is created by section 4 of the Landlord and
Tenant Act 1988 to deal with a case in which a landlord has failed
unreasonably to give consent to the tenant assigning, underletting, charging
or parting with the possession of premises in circumstances in which the
relevant lease stipulates that such consent must not be withheld unreasonably. Such a refusal could lead to significant economic loss in rendering the
tenancy valueless.

---

[38] s. 18(5).
[39] Carty, (1984) 13 I.L.J. 165.

Copyright and Dramatic & Musical Performers' Protection

Copyright generally raises no problems in terms of breach of statutory duty. A remedy for damages for infringement of copyright is available under sections 96 and 97 of the Copyright, Designs and Patents Act 1988. Although this remedy is undoubtedly of a tortious character, the subject of copyright is now so specialised as to form a subject of its own.

Two examples of expressly created breach of statutory duty remedies are also established by the 1988 Act. The first, section 103(1), provides a remedy for the infringement of what are termed "moral rights." The moral rights are the right to be identified as the author of a work; the right to object to derogatory treatment of a work; the right not to have a work falsely attributed and the right to privacy in respect of certain photographs and films. The second remedy creates a damages right in favour of a performer or other person in respect of an infringement of recording rights which they hold in a performance. This provision resolves, in favour of the existence of a remedy, the much debated problem as to whether the older Performers' Protection Acts could give rise to the implication of such a breach of statutory duty remedy.[40]

Consumer Protection

In view of the availability of contractual remedies based on the Sale of Goods Act 1979, it is not surprising that there is no evidence of breach of statutory duty being used to protect a consumer's expectation that his purchases would be advantageous. In this area, unlike some of the others described previously, there does not seem to be any policy of encouraging the emergence of tortious remedies as an enforcement mechanism.

For example, there is no authority to support the existence of a breach of statutory duty remedy in respect of the offences created by the Trade Descriptions Act 1968. It is generally assumed,[41] however, that the tort will not be inferred in such a case and that a disappointed purchaser will be left to pursue any remedies he might have for breach of contract, misrepresentation or under the Powers of Criminal Courts Act 1973.[42]

Section 170(1) of the Consumer Credit Act 1974 goes further and expressly restricts liability for breach of any requirement made by or under the Act to enforcement by those remedies which are expressly provided by the Act.

Other Areas

A notable example of an attempt to establish a statutory species of strict liability for economic loss occurred in *Merlin* v. *British Nuclear Fuels plc.*[43] In that case the plaintiffs sought compensation following the discovery that

---

[40] Stanton *op. cit.* pp. 68–71.
[41] Lowe & Woodroffe, *Consumer Law and Practice*, Chap. 13.
[42] *Ante*, p. 298.
[43] [1991] 3 All E.R. 711.

their house had been contaminated by radionuclides emanating from the defendant's plant at Sellafield. The publicity surrounding the discovery was such that the house was ultimately sold for £35,500 two years after it had been first offered for sale at £65,000. The judge held that the mere presence of the contamination in the house did not constitute damage to property; that the claim was effectively one relating to economic loss and the risk that the occupants of the house might develop cancer and that the plaintiffs' claim for damages under section 12 of the Nuclear Installations Act 1965 failed as that provision was confined to cases of physical damage to persons or tangible property.

Chapter Eighteen

Torts Concerning Land: An Introduction

The torts which protect interests in land are best divided according to the old forms of the tort of trespass. One area of the subject deals with direct interferences with land. These torts, trespass to land[1] and more modern statutory equivalents,[2] have as their primary task the protection of a person's interest in land from unwanted incursions. The other torts which are of relevance to interests in land, nuisance,[3] negligence[4] and the varieties of strict liability tort derived from the case of *Rylands* v. *Fletcher*,[5] deal with indirectly inflicted damage to land.

There are three kinds of loss at issue in this area of tort. Unfortunately the different torts which operate here do not confine themselves to a single kind of loss. The first kind of loss is that suffered as a result of an appropriation of, or an incursion onto, another person's land, tort is here being used to test which party has the right to use and exploit the land. The second form of loss is the more familiar one of physical damage to the land or to immoveable items, such as buildings, which form part of it. Tort is here pursuing its familiar purpose of providing compensation to repair damage done to a valuable asset. The third form of loss is an interference with a landowner's ability to use and enjoy land as he would wish free from unreasonable interference. This is a further remedy designed to protect the value of a person's assets. However, a wider range of forms of damage than simple physical hurt is being recognised and, as a consequence, this area of tort has some role to play in relation to the protection of the environment from various forms of pollution.[6]

The tort of trespass to land deals primarily with the first form of loss and the various forms of the tort of nuisance deal with the third, but both of these torts, along with other torts such as negligence and the tort derived from the case of *Rylands* v. *Fletcher*,[7] also provide a remedy for physical damage to land.

---

[1] See *post*, Chap. 19.
[2] See *post*, pp. 384–385.
[3] See *post*, Chap. 20.
[4] Discussed in this context at p. 406.
[5] (1869) L.R. 3 H.L. 330. See *post*, pp. 407–414.
[6] This role of tort is explored further at pp. 387–388.
[7] (1869) L.R. 3 H.L. 330.

REMEDIES

Two features of this area of law have had important consequences for the remedies which are available.

First, many cases which arise deal with conduct, such as incursions or pollution, which may persist over a long period of time. "One-off" events, which one might term accidents, and which are likely to give rise to simple claims for damages are not irrelevant, but are of less significance. It is therefore not surprising that injunctions designed to prevent wrongful conduct from continuing into the future have an important role to play in this context.[8]

Secondly, much of this area of tort, particularly the tort of trespass to land, has come to be regarded as having the primary purpose of protecting rights. As a consequence, courts have been reluctant to allow a defendant to, effectively, buy out those rights by paying damages in lieu of an injunction.[9]

Injunctions

Most of the leading cases on injunctions and the discretion to award damages in lieu of an injunction deal with damage to interests in land. These cases have been discussed in Chapter 7.

Damages

The measure of damages applied to cases in this area is simply an application of the general principles governing the award of damages in tort. However, there are a number of particular points concerning the measure of damages in tort cases concerning land which should be noted. A general point which applies in this context is that a person such as a lessee or reversioner who has a limited interest in a piece of land is only able to obtain compensation for the damage done by the tort to his particular interest.

Whatever the basis on which the measure of damages is calculated it will remain possible for the plaintiff to receive those consequential losses which are not too remote a consequence of the main loss. In cases concerning damage to interests in land the most familiar forms of consequential loss are likely to be loss of production and the costs of temporary relocation.

Incursions

Unlawful incursions onto land may not result in any lasting damage to it. In such circumstances it may be appropriate to seek to measure the damages to be awarded by the cost imposed on the plaintiff of having to acquire temporary alternative property or by the market rental value of the property unlawfully entered. It is now well established that a person whose land is trespassed upon can measure the damages by the rental value without

---

[8] See *ante*, pp. 154–155 for a discussion of the power of courts to grant injunctions or to award damages in lieu of an injunction.

[9] Common law damages can only compensate for losses which have been suffered up to the date of the trial. Compensation for future losses is awarded in lieu of an award of an injunction. See further *ante*, p. 155.

needing to prove that the property would have been let to another person if the defendant had not been in possession.[10]

If, as may well be the case in relation to an unlawful eviction, the entry is made with a view to making a profit for the person evicting, it is open to the court to award exemplary damages.[11]

Devaluation or repair

In cases of physical damage the question of whether the plaintiff can charge the cost of restoring the property to its original condition or should accept damages in the form of diminution in value and seek to acquire alternative property is to be decided as an application of the doctrine of mitigation of damage. If the property has only been partially damaged it will usually be reasonable for the injured party to opt to undertake repairs and to charge the cost to the tortfeasor.

If a building has been completely destroyed there may still be good reasons which make it reasonable to rebuild rather than move permanently to alternative premises with the disruption to family or business relationships which such a move may entail.[12] However, if there is no realistic possibility of reinstatement occurring the measure of damages will reflect the diminution in the value of the property suffered as a result of the tort. A good illustration of this approach was provided by *Taylor (C.R.) (Wholesale) Ltd. v. Hepworths Ltd.*,[13] in which the plaintiff company owned a building which they intended to demolish to allow for redevelopment of the site. The building was destroyed by fire as a result of the defendant company's negligence and the plaintiff's attempt to measure the damages by the cost of reinstating it was unsuccessful as there was no prospect of such work being undertaken. The fire was held to have conferred a financial benefit on the plaintiff in so far as the saving in the demolition costs outweighed the cost of the safety works which had to be undertaken as a consequence of the fire.

The leading discussion of the principles governing the date by reference to which the courts should calculate the cost of conducting repairs has occurred in the area of damage to buildings. In the leading modern decision of *Dodd Properties (Kent) Ltd. v. Canterbury City Council*[14] the Court of Appeal held that the cost of repairs to a building which had been damaged by negligence might be assessed as at the date of trial if it was reasonable for the plaintiff to delay undertaking the repairs. In the circumstances the defendant's denial of liability combined with the plaintiff's impecuniosity made such a delay reasonable and opened the way to the damages being calculated according to the cost of conducting the repairs at the date of the trial. This result would seem to be a further application of the doctrine of mitigation of damage.

---

[10] *Penarth Dock Engineering Co. Ltd. v. Pounds* [1963] 1 Lloyd's Rep. 359; *Swordheath Properties Ltd. v. Tabet* [1979] 1 W.L.R. 285.

[11] See *ante*, pp. 150–151.

[12] *Harbutt's Plasticine Ltd. v. Wayne Tank and Pump Co. Ltd.* [1970] 1 Q.B. 447. Some allowance may need to be made for betterment if items in the new building have a longer useful life than those which were destroyed.

[13] [1977] 1 W.L.R. 159.

[14] [1980] 1 All E.R. 928.

Damage to amenity

It is logical that any damages which are awarded in respect of an interference with the amenity of land should be calculated according to any diminution which has occurred in the value of the property. Because of the nature of the interference there will be no basis for calculating damages according to the cost of restoring the property to its original condition, assuming that the nuisance has now ceased. However, the grant of an injunction may mean that no lasting damage has been done to the value of the property and in such circumstances it may be appropriate to make a small award to reflect the inconvenience which the interference has caused. This was the situation which occurred in *Bone* v. *Seale*,[15] a case which concerned offensive smells which emanated from a pig farm. In that case the Court of Appeal held that the sum to be awarded as damages for past interference could be calculated by analogy to the sum which would have been awarded in a personal injury case for the loss of the sense of smell.[16] A person who has incurred expenses for the purposes of abating a nuisance which affects his property is entitled to recover any expenses reasonably incurred in the course of this work.

---

[15] [1975] 1 All E.R. 787.

[16] The Court of Appeal reduced the judge's award under this head from £6,000 to £1,000 commenting that the successful plaintiff in *Halsey* v. *Esso Petroleum Co. Ltd.* [1961] 1 W.L.R. 683 had been awarded only £200 as damages for a gross interference with the comfort and enjoyment of his property which had extended over a period of five years. In view of the very different interests at issue, the temporary nature of a nuisance which is stopped by a injunction and the fact that forms of nuisance other than smells may be more difficult to equate to a form of personal injury, the approach adopted in *Bone* should be regarded as questionable or as merely having been designed to show how unreasonable the judge's award had been.

Chapter Nineteen

Incursions onto Land

Introduction

This chapter deals with two areas of tort which provide a remedy to protect a person's possession of land against others who seek to enter it or to directly damage it. The torts which operate in this area are the traditional tort of trespass to land and the modern statutory tort created by the Housing Act 1988 which deals with unlawful eviction of residential occupiers.

TRESPASS TO LAND

Trespass to land can be defined as a direct interference with the plaintiff's possession of land. In common with other examples of tortious liability based upon trespass, liability for trespass to land does not depend on damage having been caused to the plaintiff. Liability is strict so long as the defendant entered the property voluntarily: he will only be excused if he can prove that the entry was involuntary. In so far as trespass is a tort based on intentional acts, the required intention is that of being on the land, rather than that of infringing another person's rights. Trespass does not involve balancing the competing interests of neighbours in the way that nuisance does.[1] These rules derive from the fact that the tort is used to test title to a piece of land as well as to give compensation for damage done to it. A person does not cease to own a piece of land just because another enters it thinking that it is his.

The characteristic form of this tort involves a person entering property which is in the possession of another without permission or other lawful justification. A common example is an attempt to evict a tenant who is lawfully in possession of premises. The tort may, however, take many other forms for example, removing minerals, soil, plants, buildings or other items attached to the property; placing unwanted buildings or other items on property or directly damaging land. An entry onto property is not essential. For example, throwing stones at the windows of a building from the road would amount to a trespass. In *Rigby* v. *Chief Constable of Northamptonshire*[2] the action of a police force of firing a C.S. gas canister into a building was held to constitute a trespass to the property.

In practice, actions brought under the common law tort of trespass to land regularly coexist and overlap with contractually based remedies. A tenant's

---

[1] See *post*, p. 390.
[2] [1985] 2 All E.R. 985.

right to remain in possession of rented property is protected by the tort of trespass to land; contractual rights to claim breach of the covenants in the lease which guarantee the right to quiet enjoyment and by statutes which provide for security of tenure,[3] render unlawful eviction a criminal offence[4] and make damages available to persons who are unlawfully evicted.[5] Actions founded on the tort of trespass may feature both claims for damages and applications for injunctions to compel a person to give up possession or to stop infringing the plaintiff's rights.

Possession

The tort of trespass is founded on an infringement of a person's possession of land. Possession can be defined for these purposes as having physical control of the land. What constitutes possession for these purposes varies according to the facts of the case. For example, a lodger or an occupier of a hotel room is not regarded as being in possession of the rooms in question although such a person might, in one sense, be regarded as having control of the room.

A tenant of property is regarded as being in possession. It follows that an owner of land can commit trespass against a person to whom a tenancy has been granted. This rule is extremely important; it is both the basis of a sizeable body of law concerning the wrongful eviction of tenants[6] and also bars an owner out of possession from invoking trespass against persons other than the tenant[7] except as a remedy for damage done to the reversionary interest.[8]

A person who is in possession of land can use the tort of trespass to defend that possession against any person other than one who has a superior right to possess the property. A person who has taken possession of land by trespass cannot resist a claim brought by the dispossessed occupier. However, such a person, if himself dispossessed by means of trespass, cannot be met by a defence that the original dispossessed occupier had rights over the land which were superior to his own.[9]

Permission

The existence of a permission (commonly known as a licence) to enter the land given by the person in possession of it[10] will mean that no trespass has been committed. As we have already seen when discussing occupiers' liability

---

[3] The primary legislation for residential tenancies is the Housing Act 1988. See also the Landlord and Tenant Act 1954, Pt. II (for commercial tenancies) and the Agricultural Holdings Act 1986 (for agricultural tenancies).

[4] See the Protection from Eviction Act 1977.

[5] See post, p. 384.

[6] The owner may also, in such circumstances, be liable for a breach of covenant under the lease and for the statutory tort of wrongful eviction created by ss. 27 and 28 of the Housing Act 1988 (see post, p. 384).

[7] The primary responsibility for protecting the land during the course of the tenancy rests with the person in possession (the tenant).

[8] For example, for damage to minerals or other items forming part of the land.

[9] This is the rule that English law does not recognise the *jus tertii* (the superior rights of a third party) as a valid defence to trespass.

[10] Or by a person having apparent authority to do so. See *Robson* v. *Hallett* [1967] 2 Q.B. 939.

such permissions can be implied.[11] A permission to enter which is not based on a contract is revocable and it is therefore open to an occupier of property to withdraw such a permission to be on land at any time for any or no reason. If this is done the visitor will have a reasonable time in which to leave the property by an appropriate route and will only be classed as a trespasser when this period of time has expired.[12]

Whether or not a contractually granted permission may be revoked at will depends on the terms of the contract[13] and on any statutory controls on the particular kind of contract.[14] The nineteenth century case of *Wood* v. *Leadbitter*[15] appeared to establish that a landowner who had permitted another to enter land under the terms of a contract could revoke the permission at will, subject to liability for breach of contract, with the result that a person who attempted to stand on his contractual rights would be deemed to be a trespasser and would be liable to be ejected from the property. The only true exception to this rule appeared to be a case in which the permission had been coupled with a grant, for example, where a person was given permission to enter land to cut and remove wood. The twentieth century has seen a number of devices being used to reverse this result. Permissions to enter land for a limited time and for a specific purpose, such as contracts permitting an individual to attend sporting events or theatrical performances, have been held not to be instantly revocable either because the notion of a grant has been extended[16] or because they have been construed as including an implied term to the effect that the permission will not be revoked until the purpose of the contract has been completed.[17] The merging of law and equity following the Judicature Acts and the consequential availability of injunctions to restrain revocation has been said to justify reversing the result in *Wood* in appropriate circumstances.[18]

A person who enters property with permission will become a trespasser if the scope of the permission is exceeded, even if this occurs in all innocence. A person may exceed the scope of a permission either by going beyond its geographical limitations[19] or by using the premises for purposes which were alien to the invitation.[20] A doctrine known as trespass *ab initio* is to the effect that any person who enters premises under the authority of law, as opposed to the authority of the person in possession of the property, and who in the course of the entry, exceeds the permission, will be deemed a trespasser from the moment of the original entry (*ab initio*) and not just from the time that the permission was exceeded. The only effect that this rule can have is to boost the damages payable for the tort by extending the period over which a trespass has taken place. The rule of trespass *ab initio* is derived from early seventeenth century authority[21] and it is not at all clear what purpose it is intended to serve. In so far as it would apply to public servants entering

---

[11] See *ante*, p. 196.
[12] *Robson* v. *Hallett* [1967] 2 Q.B. 939.
[13] *Minister of Health* v. *Bellotti* [1944] K.B. 298.
[14] As in the case of the protections granted to residential occupiers.
[15] (1845) 13 M. & W. 838.
[16] *Hurst* v. *Picture Theatres Ltd.* [1915] 1 K.B. 1.
[17] *Hurst* v. *Picture Theatres Ltd.* [1915] 1 K.B. 1; *Winter Garden Theatre (London) Ltd.* v. *Millenium Productions Ltd.* [1948] A.C. 173.
[18] *Verrall* v. *Great Yarmouth B.C.* [1980] 1 All E.R. 839.
[19] *Mersey Docks & Harbour Board* v. *Proctor* [1923] A.C. 253.
[20] *Hillen & Pettigrew* v. *I.C.I. (Alkali) Ltd.* [1936] A.C. 65.
[21] *The Six Carpenters' Case* (1610) 8 Co. Rep. 146a.

another's property under statutory authority it might be thought to have a punitive purpose analogous to awards of exemplary damages.[22] Trespass *ab initio* has been interpreted restrictively and criticised in twentieth century cases. In *Elias* v. *Pasmore*[23] the rule was applied restrictively in circumstances in which police officers had lawfully entered premises and arrested a man but had acted in excess of their warrant by seizing documents which they found there. It was held that any liability for trespass *ab initio* was confined to the goods and did not render the officers liable for trespass to land.

Strong criticism was subsequently levelled at the rule by dicta of Lord Denning M.R. and Salmon L.J. in *Chic Fashions (West Wales) Ltd.* v. *Jones*.[24] There is therefore a real possibility that the rule of trespass *ab initio* would be rejected, if directly challenged, as infringing the basic principle that a lawful act (the original entry onto the land) should not be rendered unlawful by subsequent acts.

Trespass to subsoil

Unauthorised mining of a person's land is just as much a trespass as an unauthorised entry onto the land. This is because a person generally[25] owns the right to exploit the minerals and other items below the surface of his property. However, there remains the possibility that a person may have been granted the right to mine and to extract minerals or other items from below the surface of another person's property.

A highway is regarded as having been dedicated to the use of the public for the purpose of passing and repassing and other reasonable and ordinary uses incidental to these. Several old authorities such as *Hickman* v. *Maisey*[26] establish that a person may commit a trespass against the owner of the subsoil beneath the surface of the highway by acts which exceed ordinary and reasonable use of it. In *Hickman* the plaintiff, who trained race horses on land which was crossed by a public highway established that the defendant, a racing tipster, had committed trespass against his land by walking up and down the road and taking notes on the performance of the plaintiff's horses in training with a view to publishing the information. His acts had exceeded the uses of the highway for which permission had been given and he was therefore a trespasser.

Trespass to airspace

It is well established that the owner of land has rights in the airspace above his property which can be protected by a trespass action. The problem has been to define the extent of those rights. The result of the present law is not wholly satisfactory, but it can be said with confidence that a landowner does

---

[22] However, it is not confined to public servants and the availability of awards of exemplary damages in cases involving excess of authority by public servants (see *ante*, p. 149) renders the existence of the increase in damages achieved by trespass *ab initio* unnecessary.

[23] [1934] 2 K.B. 164.

[24] [1968] 2 Q.B. 299. But note that Lord Denning subsequently favoured the use of the rule in his judgment in *Cinnamond* v. *British Airports Authority* [1980] 1 W.L.R. 582.

[25] Gold, silver and petroleum are vested in the Crown. Coal deposits are vested in the National Coal Board.

[26] [1900] 1 Q.B. 752. See also *Harrison* v. *Duke of Rutland* [1893] 1 Q.B. 142.

not own all of the airspace above his land without limits. However, the fact that the plaintiff is making no use of, and is not intending to use, the airspace into which the defendant has entered does not prevent a successful claim for an injunction to stop the trespass.

Trespass to airspace can arise in a variety of ways; for example, the placing of telephone wires, overhead cables, scaffolding or advertising boards over another's land. In *Kelsen* v. *Imperial Tobacco Co. Ltd.*,[27] McNair J. held a landowner entitled to an injunction ordering the removal of an advertising sign which the defendant had mounted on his property and which projected a small distance into the airspace above the plaintiff's land. The judge held the sign to constitute a trespass even though it did not interfere with the plaintiff's use of his property and granted the injunction requiring the sign to be removed on the basis that any award of damages would be nominal and therefore inadequate.

A recurrent problem in recent years has concerned the tower cranes used on construction sites. For safety reasons such cranes must be left free to turn with the wind and, in view of the size of such cranes and the sites on which they are used, they may well overhang neighbouring property. A consistent line of authority has held that, in the absence of permission, this constitutes a trespass. The leading modern authority is *Anchor Brewhouse Developments Ltd.* v. *Berkeley House (Docklands Developments) Ltd.*[28] in which Scott J. took the view that it was important that adjoining owners were left in no doubt as to their rights in relation to cranes. He held that an owner of land is not confined to complaining about incursions into airspace which interfere with the use and enjoyment of his property and which would therefore constitute a private nuisance. A landowner is entitled to reduce the airspace above his property into his possession and he is therefore entitled to complain of trespass if another takes possession of it. The judge was of the opinion that cases concerning aircraft[29] should be kept wholly separate from those dealing with neighbouring landowners, their cranes, scaffolding and advertising signs. He summarised his decision to grant the plaintiffs an injunction to restrain the cranes operated by the defendants from trespassing as based on the simple principle that "if somebody erects on his own land a structure, part of which invades the airspace above the land of another, the invasion is trespass."

The reason for Scott J.'s reluctance to extend the ratio of his decision to cases concerning aircraft was that there are statements of Griffiths J. in *Bernstein* v. *Skyviews & General Ltd.*[30] which support the view that airspace is only owned to the extent that it is used. The plaintiff, in that case, failed in an attempt to establish that the defendant company had trespassed into the airspace above his land. The defendant's business consisted of taking aerial photographs of large country houses and offering them for sale to the owners. The plaintiff regarded this activity as an infringement of his privacy and sought to establish that the aircraft had trespassed on the basis that the owner of land has unlimited rights to the airspace above his property. Griffiths J. rejected this contention, but did so on the basis that the rights of an owner to airspace are restricted to such space as is necessary for the

[27] [1957] 2 Q.B. 334.
[28] (1987) 38 B.L.R. 82.
[29] See below.
[30] [1978] Q.B. 479.

ordinary use and enjoyment of the land and the structures upon it. The subsequently decided cases on cranes show that this judgment cannot be taken to express a universally applicable rule.

Section 76 of the Civil Aviation Act 1982 provides that:

"(1) No action shall lie in respect of trespass or in respect of nuisance, by reason only of the flight of an aircraft over any property at a height above the ground which, having regard to wind, weather and all the circumstances of the case is reasonable . . . "

In *Bernstein* Griffiths J. gave this provision its natural reading. He refused to accept an argument made by the plaintiff, on analogy to *Hickman* v. *Maisey*,[31] that the section merely permitted entry into airspace above another's land for the purposes of passing and repassing and that the defendant's use of the airspace had taken them beyond the scope of the protection.

Defences

1. Statutory or common law authority

A wide range of common law and statutory authorities permit entry onto another person's property in the absence of any permission having been obtained. Common law examples include entries on public rights of way and entries made in order to abate a nuisance on neighbouring land. The best known statutory powers are those given to the police by the Police and Criminal Evidence Act 1984.[32]

2. Adverse possession

A person's right to recover possession of an interest in land is lost as a result of 12 years adverse possession of that interest by another person.[33]

3. Necessity

The defence of necessity[34] is available in answer to a claim for trespass to land. However, the defence operates exceptionally and is probably only available when life or property is threatened. The example which is most commonly given is that it would not amount to trespass to pull down a person's property in order to create a fire break which would protect other properties. This defence does not protect squatters who enter another person's property on account of homelessness. If this were not the rule no house would be safe from incursions.[35]

Until 1992 an owner of property had no right to enter another's land, against that person's will, in order to effect repairs to his own property, even if the state of the property constituted a danger to the public.[36] This rule could mean that buildings adjoining another's property could be impossible

---

[31] [1900] 1 Q.B. 752, discussed *ante*, p. 380. See also *Harrison* v. *Duke of Rutland* [1893] 1 Q.B. 142.

[32] See *post*, p. 429. For a comprehensive survey see Feldman, *The Law Relating to Entry, Search and Seizure*.

[33] Limitation Act 1980, s.15.

[34] See the discussion in Chap. 5.

[35] *Southwark L.B.C.* v. *Williams* [1971] Ch. 734.

[36] *John Trenberth Ltd.* v. *National Westminster Bank Ltd.* (1979) 39 P. & C.R. 104. The defence of necessity does not appear to have been pleaded expressly in this case.

to maintain or repair because of the other's refusal to allow entry to contractors and items such as scaffolding. However, the Access to Neighbouring Land Act 1992 now provides a procedure whereby a person may apply to court for an access order which will override the neighbour's refusal of consent and allow access for the purpose of effecting repairs. As an access order can permit entry to "buildings or other structures" it may be possible to obtain entry to another person's house or flat under this provision. The court will only make an access order if satisfied that the works proposed are necessary for the preservation of the whole or part of the applicant's property and that they cannot be carried out, or would be substantially more difficult to carry out, if entry upon the neighbour's land was not permitted. The court cannot, however, make an access order if it determines that it would cause the neighbour or any other person interference with, or disturbance of, his use of the neighbouring land or such hardship as would make it unreasonable to make an access order. A court to which an application for an access order is made has wide powers as to the conditions which it can impose on any order which is granted, except that an order that the applicant should pay for the privilege of entry cannot be made in relation to work to residential property.[37] The rights of access granted by the 1992 Act are limited to enabling a person to maintain existing property in good repair. The Act does not allow a court to grant an access order in order to assist a person to develop or improve land.[38] It is therefore not available to assist a developer who wishes to use a tower crane which, in the course of the construction work, would overhang another's land.

TRESPASS BY ANIMALS

Under certain circumstances it is possible to establish liability for trespass by animals. However, the general impossibility of controlling domestic animals such as cats is recognised. Liability can therefore only be established if it can be proved that a person who had control of an animal intentionally permitted or negligently failed to prevent it from entering another's property. It was on this basis that the joint masters of a pack of staghounds were held liable in *League Against Cruel Sports Ltd.* v. *Scott*[39] for the fact that their hounds had entered property owned by the plaintiffs on Exmoor.

Section 4 of the Animals Act 1971 creates a strict liability remedy for damage done to property by straying farm animals. The primary purpose of this remedy is to provide compensation for crops which have been damaged or destroyed by livestock which have strayed onto another person's land. The definition of livestock[40] used for the purpose of this provision confines the remedy to straying farm animals. As well as giving a damages remedy to the landowner on whose property such trespass occurs, section 7 of the Act entitles such person, under certain conditions, to detain the animals and to sell them as well as to recover any expenses which have been incurred in maintaining them. Subsection 5(5) of the Act provides an important defence:

---

[37] Strangely this would appear to exclude a builder repairing residential property with a view to resale from any obligation to pay for access.

[38] Although under s. 1(5) it is permissible to make improvements which are incidental to effecting the necessary repairs.

[39] [1985] 2 All E.R. 489.

[40] s. 11.

there is no liability if the animal strayed onto the plaintiff's land from the highway and its presence on the highway was a lawful use of it. In such a case the assumption is that the landowner should have kept his property securely fenced in order to avoid such incursions.

UNLAWFUL EVICTION

The social importance of housing has resulted in a large body of legislation which aims to give security to occupiers of residential property. This legislation has implications for tort because a residential occupier who is suffering harassment from, or who has been unlawfully evicted by, a landlord may seek compensation for losses or an injunction to prevent further harassment or to require the landlord to allow reoccupation of the premises. Claims of this nature may be based, depending on the facts, on the torts of trespass to land, nuisance or on breach of the landlord's contractual covenant to give the tenant quiet enjoyment of the premises.[41] In addition, statutory remedies may be available.

The Protection from Eviction Act 1977 creates a number of criminal offences relating to the harassment of residential occupiers and their eviction in the absence of a court order. In view of the protective purposes underlying this legislation it might be thought to be likely to give rise to an inference of the tort of breach of statutory duty. However, modern authority is opposed to such an inference being made. In *McCall* v. *Abelesz*[42] the Court of Appeal determined that no action for breach of statutory duty was available in respect of an offence of harassment under section 30(2) of the Rent Act 1965[43] on the basis that adequate alternative remedies based on trespass to land and contract existed. It seems very likely that the same result will apply to the other provisions of the 1977 Act.[44]

A residential occupier[45] of premises who is unlawfully evicted is given a statutory right to claim damages in tort by sections 27 and 28 of the Housing Act 1988. In the majority of cases an unlawful eviction will be one which has occurred in the absence of a court order. The statutory remedy is additional to other rights which may be available on the facts for breaches of any covenants in the lease or for trespass to land,[46] but makes no provision for injunctive relief. For the purposes of this provision "unlawful eviction" is defined as covering both: attempting[47] to unlawfully deprive a residential occupier of the occupation of the whole or part of the premises (for example,

---

[41] Claims brought in trespass and nuisance for wrongful eviction have the additional attraction that an award of exemplary damages is possible if the landlord's conduct falls within the "profit earning" category of such damages recognised by *Rookes* v. *Barnard* (see *ante*, p. 150). Significant use seems to be being made of this possibility in circumstances in which a landlord has ignored advice that an eviction should not take place without a court order having been obtained. See *McCaffrey* v. *Ekango* (1992) *Legal Action* (March) 15 and *Ramdath* v. *Daley* (1992) *Legal Action* (June) 12.

[42] [1976] Q.B. 585.

[43] Now s. 1(3) of the Protection from Eviction Act 1977.

[44] But *cf. Warder* v. *Cooper* [1970] 1 Ch. 495.

[45] Defined by s. 1 of the Protection from Eviction Act 1977.

[46] However, damages cannot be obtained for the same loss under both s. 27 and the other remedies (s.27(5)).

[47] Note that the consequence required by s. 27(2) means that an unsuccessful attempt is not actionable under the statute.

physical eviction and exclusion by acts such as the changing of locks), or as doing acts likely to interfere with that persons' peace or comfort or withdrawing or withholding services (*i.e.* harassment) knowing that this was likely to cause the occupier to give up occupation or to refrain from pursuing any right or remedy in respect of the premises. In either case the tort will only be complete if the consequence of the act is that the residential occupier gives up occupation of the premises. The statutory remedy is therefore not available to a tenant who remains in occupation of residential property in spite of acts of harassment. Under this section a landlord is liable for his own acts and for those of persons acting on his behalf. The remedy is available irrespective of whether there has been a successful prosecution of the landlord under the Protection from Eviction Act 1977.[48]

The right of action created by section 27 is lost if an occupier who has been unlawfully evicted is reinstated in the property before the statutory claim is finally disposed of.[49] If reinstatement has occurred any claim for damages brought by the residential occupier would need to be framed as one of breach of contract or trespass to land. The Court of Appeal in *Tagro* v. *Cafane*[50] accepted that a residential occupier has an unfettered right to defeat this defence by refusing reinstatement. However, an unreasonable refusal of reinstatement can lead to a reduction in the damages awarded. Section 27(7) gives the court power to reduce the damages on account of the conduct of the occupier, or those living with him, prior to the eviction or if, before proceedings under section 27[51] were begun, the occupier had acted unreasonably in refusing an offer to reinstate. On the facts of the *Tagro* Case it was held that the offer of keys to premises which had been wrecked did not amount to an offer to reinstate.

Damages awarded under these sections are calculated according to the difference in the value of the landlord's interest in the property according to whether the residential occupier does or does not have the right to occupy. It thus pays to a displaced occupier any profit, in terms of the value of the property, made by the landlord from the wrongful act and this profit is calculated according to the landlord's whole interest in the building rather than the part occupied by the plaintiff. The remedy is therefore restitutionary in allowing the plaintiff to recoup the profit made as a result of the wrong done to him.[52]

---

[48] Such prosecutions are infrequent. Partington & Hill, *Housing Law: Cases, Materials and Commentary*, pp. 265–266.

[49] s. 27(6).

[50] [1991] 1 E.G.L.R. 279.

[51] Not any other proceedings in relation to the eviction. See *Tagro* v. *Cafane* [1991] 1 E.G.L.R. 279.

[52] S. 28 does not, on its face, permit a punitive award of exemplary damages in excess of the restitutionary award. However, actions for wrongful eviction pleaded as trespass to land have permitted exemplary awards in excess of the profits made from the eviction. See *MacMillan* v. *Singh* (1984) 17 H.L.R. 120.

Chapter Twenty

Nuisance

INTRODUCTION

The tort of nuisance provides a remedy for a wide range of indirect interferences with land. Interference with the enjoyment of property by smell, noise or vibration; physical damage to the land; the encroachment of tree roots and branches; the withdrawal of support from the land and the blocking of rights of light all fall within the scope of the tort. Public nuisance, which commonly involves interferences with the use of a highway by the creation of an obstruction or danger upon it, is also capable of providing a remedy in the case of damage to land. The tort of nuisance overlaps to a considerable degree with part of the tort of negligence and is closely related to the tort derived from the case of *Rylands* v. *Fletcher*.[1] It is not uncommon to see all three causes of action alleged on a single set of facts.

The law of nuisance is one of the most difficult areas of the English law of tort. There are a number of reasons for this. First, there are different forms of the tort. Although both torts may be alleged on a single set of facts, the distinction must be drawn between the private nuisance, one which affects an individual in the use and enjoyment of his property, and a public nuisance. A public nuisance is a widespread one which affects the comfort and convenience of a whole class of society. Public nuisance is a criminal offence and only gives rise to an action in tort in the event of someone having suffered "special damage" from it; that is, damage over and above the inconvenience suffered by the rest of society. Public nuisance has taken on roles far removed from the more common forms of private nuisance. As we saw in Chapter 11, public nuisance in the form of dangers on or adjoining the highway may have much more in common with negligence than with normal examples of private nuisance which seek to protect a person's enjoyment of land.

The second reason for difficulty is that, whilst nuisance is primarily a tort which protects a person's interest in the enjoyment of land, subsidiary functions, such as providing a remedy for personal injuries and physical damage to the land itself and to other property on it, have been grafted on. In some respects nuisance is very unsuited to these additional roles.

Nuisance is also a victim of its history. It is a strict liability tort in the sense that liability does not depend on proof of negligence. However, as negligence has come to dominate tort, nuisance has increasingly been influenced by it. Drawing the boundary between negligence and nuisance is now one of the most difficult problems in the law of tort. In some areas, such as public

---

[1] (1868) L.R. 3 H.L. 330.

nuisance on the highway, the torts fulfil identical functions and are virtually indistinguishable.[2] In others they deal with totally different topics in completely different ways.

Nuisance in context

The tort of nuisance may, on occasion, deal with major issues of pollution control. It may provide an individually enforceable means of stopping pollution as well as a mechanism for compensating people who have been damaged by it. The leading case of *Esso Petroleum Co. Ltd.* v. *Southport Corporation*,[3] although decided as long ago as 1956, clearly has a great deal of topicality dealing, as it does, with oil discharged from a tanker and polluting a river estuary. At a more mundane level the tort operates to regulate the relationship between neighbours, often by means of injunctive relief rather than damages. The unifying feature of the tort is the protection of amenity in the sense of the use and enjoyment of property. Given the complexity of a developed, heavily populated, modern industrialised society the tort inevitably faces a substantial task in balancing the conflicting interests over the use of land.

Just as it is misleading to regard the tort of negligence as representing the whole of accident compensation law, so it would be wrong to believe that the protection of the environment and the control of pollution are dealt with exclusively by tort remedies in nuisance.[4] However, whereas the role of tort has been placed in its accident compensation context by much modern writing, it is only recently, as environmental law has come to be regarded as a subject in its own right, that the role of nuisance in the context of environmental protection has attracted considerable attention.[5]

The limits placed on the ability of nuisance to become a substantial remedy for the protection of the environment are real. The tort of private nuisance is only available to those who have a proprietary interest in land affected by the conduct. The notion of protecting the environment as an entity is alien to the common law's traditional individualistic stance.[6] Further problems are derived from the familiar difficulties[7] involved in litigation of funding, delays and in running class actions.[8] The law of nuisance uses essentially vague mechanisms of control based on reasonableness in the context of a particular community whereas, in practice, effective environmental protection is only likely to be achieved by the enactment and enforcement of precise and well publicised emission standards. Civil litigation over pollution may well raise problems of causation as difficult as those which beset medical negligence cases.

---

[2] See *ante*, Chap. 12.

[3] [1956] A.C. 218.

[4] The protection of the environment concerns a wider range of interests than protection against pollution. For example, the protection of the landscape would fall under the former but not the latter.

[5] The leading works on environmental law are Ball and Bell, *Environmental Law* (1991) and Hughes *Environmental Law* (2nd ed., 1992). Both contain chapters which deal with the role of the law of tort in protecting the environment.

[6] Note, however, that the E.C.'s Draft Directive on Liability for Waste marks a move towards the recognition of environmental rights.

[7] See Chap. 8.

[8] See *ante*, p. 167.

In view of these difficulties it is not surprising to discover that an individual's private law claim in tort is only one of a battery of legal and administrative controls which are relevant to the protection of the environment and the amenity of property. A variety of other possibilities need to be considered. For example, planning controls, restrictive covenants and restrictive obligations imposed by the terms of leases may effectively limit the uses to which a particular piece of land may be put in order to protect the amenity of other persons who live in the neighbourhood. In practice, planning controls aim to avert the most serious problems by ensuring that potentially conflicting land uses do not occur. A person who feels that his enjoyment of property is being adversely affected by one of a number of activities which are either prejudicial to health or a nuisance may be able to avoid the costs of civil proceedings by invoking the law on "statutory nuisance."[9] Local authorities,[10] through their environmental health departments, have power to take enforcement proceedings, which are ultimately criminal in nature,[11] for statutory nuisance. Other environmental protection agencies, such as Her Majesty's Inspectorate of Pollution and the National Rivers Authority also have substantial powers to regulate the levels of emissions of harmful substances into the environment and to bring enforcement proceedings against those who breach limits. These techniques may pre-empt the occurrence of a problem; may be effective in eliminating a problem which has occurred and may, in some circumstances, actually remove the possibility of a successful nuisance claim being brought.

Against this background the tort of nuisance can be viewed as a reserve power. It can be used to obtain an injunction against localised interferences and it is not dependent on the willingness of official bodies to take action. It remains the only remedy for those who wish to obtain financial recompense for interferences and damage which have already been endured. The editor of *Winfield & Jolowicz on Tort* summarised the position succinctly as follows:

> "The common law of nuisance remains necessary where the plaintiff seeks damages or where for some reason the public body is unable or unwilling to act, but we are witnessing here, as in other areas of tort, the steady ousting of private law by public law."[12]

The economic approach

Because much of the law of nuisance deals with injunctions, remedies which protect against future damage, and because the parties to such proceedings may have some form of relationship both before and after the event which precipitated the proceedings, it is more suitable than many other areas of tort to be the subject of an analysis according to market based economic theory. From the perspective of economic analysis, the tort of

---

[9] The law concerning statutory nuisances is contained in Pt. III of the Environmental Protection Act 1990 and the Noise & Statutory Nuisance Act 1993.

[10] District Councils and London Borough Councils.

[11] If an abatement notice is not complied with.

[12] (13th ed., p. 376). The decision in *Gillingham Borough Council* v. *Medway (Chatham) Dock Co. Ltd.* [1992] 3 All E.R. 923 emphasises this by holding that the planning process has the capacity to alter the character of an area and thus to negate the possibility that an activity will constitute a nuisance.

nuisance can be regarded as a technique for ensuring that the true costs of production processes are borne by those processes: if factories pollute the surrounding area they impose a cost on persons who live and work in that area in terms of reduced levels of amenity and (possibly) production. Any interference of this kind is likely to result in depressed land values. If the costs of such pollution are not channelled back to the creator the possibility arises of an economically inefficient level of production resulting from the fact that the activity is not obliged to bear the true level of costs which it imposes on society whereas the activities which are subject to the pollution will bear a greater level of cost than is justified and have their production levels reduced below the level which efficiency would call for.

In practice, a variety of reasons mean that it is difficult to accept this as an accurate analysis of the role of nuisance. At the simplest level a system of individual enforcement of pollution control through the litigation process is likely to produce a haphazard amount of loss shifting particularly in cases of widespread pollution. In practice, many people will not enforce their rights. Furthermore, the analysis presupposes that the creator of the nuisance is invariably the least cost avoider, whereas, in economic terms it would be more correct to regard a situation of nuisance as one of conflicting land use in relation to which the question of which of the parties is actually best placed to bear and distribute or avoid the loss should be open to debate. It was on this basis that Coase developed his famous theorem to the effect that an economically efficient result should be obtained in circumstances of unin-cumbered bargaining whatever allocation of liability is achieved by the legal process: if the result achieved by the courts is economically inefficient the parties will have an incentive to bargain over that result to achieve the "efficient" result.[13] In practice, the conditions which would enable such transactions to take place may often not exist. In the words of two leading commentators:

"It cannot be assumed that individuals have sufficient time, energy or inclination successfully to pursue their own self interest. Secondly, they are seldom in a position, either financially or psychologically to bargain with large corporations. Finally, the suspicion is that the average English householder is unlikely to perceive environmental protection as a problem involving individual rights and therefore requiring the assistance of the legal profession."[14]

These writers also note that there is likely to be a marked asymmetry between polluters and those who are subject to pollution with regard to access to information as to the costs created.[15] It is not surprising that recent discussions of the use of economic mechanisms to create incentives to avoid pollution (the "polluter pays" principle) are best regarded as supporting the

---

[13] Coase, "The Problem of Social Cost" (1960) 3 J.L. & Econ. 1.

[14] Ogus & Richardson, (1977) 36 C.L.J. 284, 316.

[15] This assumes that polluters are invariably large industrial enterprises and that the victims are private individuals. This need not always be the case. See, for example, *Bridlington Relay Ltd.* v. *Yorkshire Electricity Board* [1965] Ch. 436 in which the development of the plaintiff's business required a high degree of freedom from electrical interference. The result of the case, if not the reasoning of Buckley J., is compatible with the idea that when the interests of commercial enterprises clash in this way they should be left to achieve the most suitable result by bargaining.

creation of additional market mechanisms in a situation of market failure rather than as leaving the issue of pollution control to free market forces.[16]

In practice, the law has adopted two techniques which mean that it does not consider the respective economic interests of both parties in the course of seeking to identify the least cost avoider. First, the law concerning injunctions seems to aim to protect against interference with rights rather than to determine, from the perspective of conflicting land use, which of the parties is best placed to deal with the consequences of pollution. It is likely that an injunction will be granted if a substantial interference with the plaintiff's interests has occurred; irrespective of whether the defendant is the person best placed to bear the cost of eliminating the interference. Secondly, because the existence of a nuisance is assessed according to normally accepted standards of environmental amenity, it is likely to be ineffective in providing a remedy against well established sources of pollution, irrespective of whether they are cost justified.

THE ELEMENTS OF NUISANCE

The typical form of nuisance, the private nuisance, is an interference by a person with another's use and enjoyment of land. The proposition that everyone has a right to use their own property as they wish cannot be accepted without qualification. The law of nuisance has to perform a delicate balancing act to reconcile the conflicting interests which are created by competing, and prima facie lawful, land uses. Several of the leading modern cases on nuisance[17] have dealt with the disturbance faced by private property owners as a result of sports facilities operating close to their houses. The best example is *Kennaway* v. *Thompson*,[18] the facts of which were that the plaintiff had had a house built on land which she owned next to a lake although she knew, at the time, that the lake was used by a club for power boat racing and water skiing. Within a few years of the house's completion the plaintiff sought an injunction against the club complaining that its activities constituted a nuisance against her. By that time the club had become an international centre for power boat racing and, as a result, the number of days on which the lake was used had increased and larger and noisier boats had appeared. In deciding such a case the individual's interest in enjoying property free from interference is being balanced against another's interest in exploiting his property to its full potential and the public's interest in having sports facilities made available to it. There is no simple right or wrong answer to such cases. It is not surprising that the law has chosen to use a reasonableness test to strike a balance between these interests. This reasonableness test is not identical to that used in negligence. It relates to a different kind of injury; injury to amenity rather than to physical injury and it considers the issue from the plaintiff's perspective. The question is what an ordinary person in the plaintiff's position could reasonably have expected, rather than what ought the reasonable person in the position of the defendant to have done? The tort is thus "expectation" rather than "conduct"

---

[16] See Ball & Bell *op. cit.* pp. 79–85.
[17] *Miller* v. *Jackson* [1977] Q.B. 966; *Kennaway* v. *Thompson* [1981] Q.B. 88; *Tetley* v. *Chitty* [1986] 1 All E.R. 663.
[18] [1981] Q.B. 88.

based. On the facts of *Kennaway* the judge held that the club's activities had gone beyond the interference which the plaintiff could reasonably have expected and were therefore a nuisance. The Court of Appeal had to decide whether the judge's decision to use his discretion to refuse the plaintiff an injunction was justified. The judge had taken into account the public interest in obtaining sports facilities as evidenced by the large numbers of people who attended events organised by the club at the lake. It held that as a substantial interference had been caused a refusal to grant an injunction was not a proper exercise of the judge's discretion.[19]

The result of this approach in the case of industrial defendants is that the law protects them from liability if their activities only produce commonly accepted forms of pollution. In effect the law of nuisance which developed in the nineteenth century protected the emerging industries which were bringing wealth to the country by fixing the status quo as the criterion of liability for damage to the environment so long as they did not produce physical damage. More sophisticated controls on pollution required legal mechanisms other than the tort of nuisance.

A number of factors may be relevant to determining whether an activity constitutes a nuisance.

Protected interests

Nuisance actions are available in relation to a wide range of interferences with land ranging from subjecting it to such items as smoke, fumes, noise and vibration to the withdrawal of support and interferences with rights to light and other easements. The most obvious form of loss which is excluded from the protection is the loss of a pleasant view.[20] Buckley J. in *Bridlington Relay Ltd.* v. *Yorkshire Electricity Board*[21] took, *obiter*, the rather surprising view that interferences with a purely recreational use of land, in that case the ability to obtain television reception free from electrical interference, could not give rise to a nuisance action. As a matter of general principle it is difficult to see why recreational uses of land, which will commonly be reflected in the value of the property, should be excluded from the protection of the tort. It is therefore suggested that the judge's views in that case should not be followed.

Once a right to sue for nuisance has been established on the basis of an unreasonable interference with the use and enjoyment of land there do not seem to be any difficulties concerning the actual nature of the damage suffered. Successful claims for compensation in respect of physical injuries to person and chattels on the land are recorded.[22] Business losses which result from the fact that a property has been affected by a nuisance are recoverable. In *Andreae* v. *Selfridge*[23] a hotel owner was able to quantify the losses caused by the nuisance which affected the property according to the loss of custom incurred. Claims of this nature would not seem to be a true example of pure economic loss as the financial losses are consequential on a form of loss recognised as recoverable by the law.

---

[19] See p. 155.
[20] *William Aldred's* Case (1610) 9 Co. Rep. 57b.
[21] [1965] Ch. 436.
[22] Subject to the restrictions concerning who has the right to sue for private nuisance.
[23] [1938] Ch. 1.

The character of the area

The character of the locality in which the interference occurred is considered to be relevant to whether a nuisance has occurred. In the classic words of Thesiger L.J. "What would be a nuisance in Belgrave Square would not necessarily be so in Bermondsey."[24] It is therefore the case that a person who chooses to live next door to a factory cannot complain if subjected to the normal noises and smells associated with such premises.[25] A good example of this process was provided by the decision in *Halsey* v. *Esso Petroleum Co. Ltd.*,[26] a case which concerned the defendant's activities at a storage depot in an area of Fulham which contained both industrial and residential buildings. Veale J. decided the issue after considering what was the normal position with regards to smell and noise in that area of London. The results of this approach is that an activity may be deemed to be reasonable in one area but wholly unacceptable in another.

This rule has not escaped criticism.[27] At the simplest level, the locality rule is too imprecise to place any detailed control on the levels of interference introduced into the environment. In practice, different areas have varying and mixed characteristics and the test can do little more than legitimate minor everyday interferences and ban the most significant and unusual. In addition, the rule results, at least in relation to cases of non-physical damage, in nuisance being unable to be used to achieve any improvement in the environmental conditions of an area. The tort enables the status quo to be protected but leaves improvements to be achieved by planning decisions[28] and by administrative and legislative controls. The role of the tort as a secondary enforcement mechanism is clear from this.

However, although interferences such as the noise and smells produced by a factory will be judged according to the standards of the area in which the plaintiff's property is situated, the characteristics of the area will not be treated as relevant if the interference causes physical damage to the plaintiff's person or property. Interference of such a nature is regarded as unreasonable in any area. In the leading case of *St. Helen's Smelting Co.* v. *Tipping*[29] it was held by the House of Lords that the industrialised character of the neighbourhood was not to be taken into account as a relevant factor when trees growing on the plaintiff's land had suffered damage as a result of vapours emitted from the defendant's works. The distinction made between physical and non-physical damage is difficult to justify. It may be difficult to make in practice and both forms of damage are likely to reduce the enjoyment and value of the plaintiff's land. The distinction reflects the fact that the law regards physical damage as more important than non-physical damage to the use and enjoyment of property. The result can be seen both as an attempt to exclude claims in relation to kinds of interferences which are regarded as trivial and as recognition of the fact that a process of balancing of the competing interests of neighbouring parties is fundamental in the case of interferences causing non-physical damage but not in physical damage cases.

---

[24] *Sturges* v. *Bridgman* (1879) 11 Ch. D. 852.
[25] *St Helen's Smelting Co.* v. *Tipping* (1865) 11 H.L.C. 642.
[26] [1961] 1 W.L.R. 683.
[27] Ogus and Richardson, (1977) 36 C.L.J. 284.
[28] Such decisions can also produce deteriorations in the conditions in a locality. See *Gillingham Borough Council* v. *Medway (Chatham) Dock Co. Ltd.* [1992] 3 All E.R. 923.
[29] (1865) 11 H.L.C. 642.

Continuity

It is often said that some degree of continuity is required and that a nuisance cannot be established on the basis of a single occurrence. An isolated act of slamming a car door at night or playing music loudly will not constitute a nuisance because reasonable people tolerate a degree of such interference with their comfort. However, constant repetition of these acts might well count as a nuisance. In *Lambton* v. *Mellish*[30] the occupier of a house sought injunctions against two neighbours who had merry-go-rounds on their properties and who provided musical accompaniments for these amusements by the playing of organs. Chitty J. in granting the injunctions commented that a passer-by would not have regarded the music as a nuisance,

> "but the case is very different when the noise has to be continuously endured: under such circumstances it is scarcely an exaggeration to term it 'maddening,' going on as it does, hour after hour, day after day and month after month."

Although the continuity rule cannot be doubted it must be remembered that a single instance of damage to land may be evidence of a state of affairs which constituted a continuing threat to the property and was therefore a nuisance before the damage occurred. This was the case in *Sedleigh-Denfield* v. *O'Callaghan*.[31] A defectively constructed culvert on the defendant's land resulted in damage to neighbouring land through flooding. Although flooding only happened on one occasion the culvert constituted, even before the flood, a state of affairs which continually threatened the plaintiff's land. It was therefore a nuisance against which an injunction could have been obtained; the state of affairs provided the required element of continuity.

The time at which the interference occurred

Several of the leading cases show that the level of interference which is to be expected during the day may be unacceptable if it occurs at night or in the early hours of the day. In *Andreae* v. *Selfridge*,[32] the plaintiff hotel owner established that the defendant's activities of demolition and construction constituted a nuisance against his hotel. The court accepted that it was impossible to conduct such activities without the creation of noise and dust, but held that the defendant had created excessive interference, partly as a result of the hours at which the work had been undertaken. Similarly, in *Halsey* v. *Esso Petroleum Co. Ltd.*,[33] one of the reasons given for the plaintiff's success in establishing that the defendant's activities were a nuisance was that the vibration and noise which his house was subjected to occurred during the night and made it impossible for him to sleep. The converse of these results is that it is likely that a shift worker who was prevented from sleeping during the day by the activities of another would be expected to endure a greater level of interference.

[30] [1894] 3 Ch. 163.
[31] [1940] A.C. 880.
[32] [1938] Ch. 1.
[33] [1961] 1 W.L.R. 683.

Abnormal sensitivity

As a finding of nuisance is based on an interference going beyond that which might reasonably be expected to be encountered it cannot be based on the simple fact that a plaintiff was particularly sensitive to the interference. Thus, in the leading case of *Robinson* v. *Kilvert*,[34] the plaintiff tenant failed in his complaint that his landlord's use of adjoining property was damaging brown paper which he was storing. The heat which was emanating from the defendant's premises was not such as would have damaged ordinary paper and there was no evidence that it was inconveniencing the plaintiff's work-force. This rule does not prevent an abnormally sensitive person from succeeding in an action in nuisance; the abnormally sensitive do not have fewer rights than a normally sensitive person, but an abnormal sensitivity cannot increase a neighbour's duties. In *Hollywood Silver Fox Farm Ltd.* v. *Emmett*,[35] the plaintiff company alleged that the defendant's acts of firing a shotgun along the boundary of their adjoining properties had caused the vixens which they were breeding on their fur farm to fail to mate or to kill their young. This must surely have constituted an abnormal sensitivity. However, the plaintiff's claim succeeded, presumably on the basis that the defendant's acts would have constituted a nuisance against any user of the plaintiff's land.

Unlawful means

There is no requirement that the defendant be proved to have committed an act independently unlawful before liability in nuisance[36] can be established: excessive exercise of a person's prima facie rights is sufficient.

Malice

The general principle that the existence of malice cannot make a lawful act tortious[37] causes some difficulties in the context of nuisance because several nuisance cases seem to have regarded the defendant's motive as relevant to the question of whether the plaintiff's enjoyment of his property has been unreasonably interfered with. In *Christie* v. *Davey*[38] the defendant, who was in dispute with his neighbours over their playing of musical instruments, retaliated by maliciously making noises and playing instruments with the intention of annoying the plaintiffs. He was held to have committed a nuisance as it was not legitimate for him to use his property for the purpose of vexing and annoying his neighbours. A similar result was reached in *Hollywood Silver Fox Farm Ltd.* v. *Emmett*.[39] A possible reconciliation of these cases with the general principle is to say that the conduct in *Christie* and *Hollywood* would have been unreasonable even if done without malice.

---

[34] (1889) 41 Ch. D. 88. See also *Bridlington Relay Ltd.* v. *Yorkshire Electricity Board* [1965] Ch. 436.
[35] [1936] 2 K.B. 468.
[36] This applies to both private and public nuisances. See *Gillingham Borough Council* v. *Medway (Chatham) Dock Co. Ltd.* [1992] 3 All E.R. 923.
[37] *Mayor of Bradford* v. *Pickles* [1895] A.C. 587.
[38] [1893] 1 Ch. 316.
[39] [1936] 2 K.B. 468.

Nuisance and negligence

The relationship between negligence and nuisance is one of the more intractable problems presented by the law of tort. A number of important modern cases such as *Bolton* v. *Stone*[40] and *Goldman* v. *Hargrave*[41] show the two torts operating in parallel; the nuisance claim in *Bolton* was rejected by the House of Lords on the grounds that the plaintiff had failed to prove negligence. There is also judicial support for the view that the two torts are becoming increasingly assimilated[42] and plenty of evidence in a number of cases for the view that an occupier is only liable for a failure to abate those nuisances on his property of which he ought reasonably to have been aware.[43] Lord Reid was of the view that there exists a close relationship between the two torts. In his speech in *The Wagon Mound (No. 2)*[44] he said:

"It is quite true that negligence is not an essential element in nuisance. Nuisance is a term used to cover a wide variety of tortious acts or omissions, and in many negligence in the narrow sense is not essential. An occupier may incur liability for the emission of noxious fumes or noise, although he has used the utmost care in building and using the premises. . . . And although negligence may not be necessary, fault of some kind is almost always necessary and fault generally involves foreseeability, e.g., in cases like *Sedleigh-Denfield* v. *O'Callaghan* the fault is in failing to abate a nuisance of the existence of which the defender is or ought to be aware as likely to cause damage to his neighbour."

Lord Reid used this approach as the basis of his holding that the test of remoteness of damage in nuisance is identical to that in negligence, it is a test of reasonable foreseeability of the kind of loss. However, the difficulty with these words is that they do nothing to elucidate the distinction between "negligence in the narrow sense" and "fault of some kind." In the final analysis Lord Reid's words are no more than word play designed to enable him to avoid answering the problem.

In spite of all this evidence of the assimilation of the two torts, they have fundamentally different roles in many situations; negligence deals primarily with physical damage to person or property whereas private nuisance aims to protect the use and enjoyment of land. As we have seen, although both torts make use of a test of reasonableness, the tests are different. The nuisance form of reasonableness relates to the plaintiff's "expectation" rather than to the defendant's "conduct."[45] It is probably not an exaggeration to say that many of the difficulties encountered by writers in this area have stemmed from a failure to appreciate the significance of this distinction. The fact that a person could not have foreseen any damage to flow from an activity and has taken all normal and reasonable precautions in conducting that activity will not necessarily excuse him from nuisance liability as it may be unreasonable to conduct an activity in a particular area whatever precautions are taken.

A number of approaches have been suggested by writers who have sought to explain the distinction between nuisance and negligence.

---

[40] [1951] A.C. 850, discussed *ante*, p. 63.
[41] [1967] 1 A.C. 645, discussed *ante*, p. 74.
[42] Lord Parker C.J. *British Road Services* v. *Slater* [1964] 1 W.L.R. 498.
[43] See *post*, p. 398.
[44] *Overseas Tankship (U.K.) Ltd.* v. *Miller Steamship Co. Pty. Ltd.* [1967] 1 A.C. 617.
[45] See *ante*, p. 390.

One suggestion which has been put forward[46] is that the issue turns on the nature of the remedy which is being sought. It is said that if the plaintiff is seeking an injunction to prevent future occurrence of an interference the very fact of his making the claim renders it impossible for the defendant to argue that the damage is unforeseeable: the plaintiff is spelling the fact of the risk out. On the other hand, it is contended that a claim limited to seeking damages for past interference should be capable of being met by such a defence. This view is impossible to accept as it proceeds on an erroneous assimilation of the tort of negligence with the issue of foreseeability. Negligence, as a tort, involves additional consideration of issues of reasonable care. It does not follow from the fact that damage is foreseeable that a defendant is precluded from contending that he took reasonable care to avoid it.

A second suggestion is that negligence is relevant when the nuisance stems from an unintentional act but is irrelevant when the defendant has knowingly brought the activity which creates an interference onto his land.[47] This approach is certainly compatible with the cases concerning the liability of occupiers for nuisances introduced onto their property by the forces of nature or the activities of trespassers but there is little, if any, express support for it in the cases.

Another approach explains the position in terms of the different roles played by the tort of nuisance over the years. It is argued[48] that a strict form of liability was appropriate in the nineteenth century when nuisance was performing a planning function; in that period its role was to preclude activities from being conducted in areas in which they were inappropriate. Fault has no part to play in resolving issues of this kind. However, now that the planning function has passed to local authorities, nuisance deals with more mundane kinds of interference in relation to which it is easier to impose a requirement of fault.

It is suggested that the key to understanding the distinction between the torts lies in their history[49] and in the fact that nuisance has come to play a number of different roles. Nuisance is the older tort and had grown from the root of private nuisance. Essentially, it is a tort which protects a person's use and enjoyment of land. It is just as much an actionable nuisance for a landowner to be discouraged or prevented from going onto his property by the defendant's interference with it as it is if the plaintiff goes onto the property and is injured. This basis of the tort explains the requirement for the plaintiff to show an interest in the land affected: it is a tort against property. However, in spite of these roots, the tort has taken on the subsidiary role of providing compensation for physical damage to persons and property and, in practice, this has become the normal kind of damage alleged in public nuisance cases brought in tort. The great majority of the cases in which negligence has appeared to be a requirement of liability in nuisance have actually been cases of public nuisance in which physical damage to person or property has been at issue. It is suggested that the position is that modern courts, influenced by the dominance of the tort of negligence in the field of

---

[46] See further Winfield & Jolowicz on *Tort* (13th ed.), pp. 380–381.

[47] Salmond & Heuston on the *Law of Torts* (20th ed.), p. 76. See Winfield & Jolowicz *op. cit.* pp. 383–384 for a variant of this approach.

[48] See Fridman on *Torts*, p. 189.

[49] Newark, (1949) 65 L.Q.R. 480.

personal injury litigation, have refused to allow nuisance to offer a stricter form of liability in situations in which both torts are available, particularly when personal injuries or physical damage to property are the basis of the claim. On the other hand, when injury to amenity of land is in issue, very little thinking derived from negligence is relevant to the decision whether a nuisance has occurred. It is not acceptable for a person who could not foresee any physical injuries resulting from his conduct to be held liable for any which are caused simply because his conduct subjected his neighbours to an unreasonable interference with the enjoyment of their land. The contrary result would be particularly anomalous as a result of its being confined to claims brought by those with a proprietary interest in the land affected. As early as 1933 Talbot J.[50] distinguished defects in property which interfered with the enjoyment of a neighbour's property, for which nuisance was the appropriate cause of action, and those which created dangers, in which case the claim should be phrased as negligence.

THE RIGHT TO SUE FOR NUISANCE

It is commonly said to be the case that a plaintiff must be able to prove that he had some kind of proprietary interest in the land[51] affected by the interference in order to qualify to bring a claim in private nuisance. However, the authorites in this area reveal a variety of approaches. Some, which have seemed to require the plaintiff to have either a freehold or leasehold interest, have excluded persons who are merely licensed to use the land from bringing such a claim.[52] Others have seemed willing to protect virtually any form of occupation or possession.[53] The leading authority of *Malone* v. *Lasky*[54] is to the effect that lawful occupation, of itself, is insufficient. In that case, the plaintiff and her husband were permitted to occupy a dwelling by the husband's employer. The property was affected by a nuisance in the form of vibration caused by a generator on the neighbouring premises of the defendant. This vibration caused a bracket which supported the water tank in the lavatory to come loose and to fall from the wall injuring the plaintiff. The court held that as she had no interest in the property affected by the nuisance she could not maintain an action. As we have argued previously, this restriction, which might seem somewhat strange at first sight, betrays the origins of private nuisance as a tort which deals with interferences with the use and enjoyment of real property: the role of the tort as a remedy for physical injury to persons or property is secondary. The rule, in the absence of proof of negligence, can be said to produce an "inefficient" result by failing to channel some of the damage caused by pollution to the person responsible for it. There is no equivalent requirement in public nuisance. Anyone who can fulfil the requirement of showing special damage can bring a claim in public nuisance.[55]

---

[50] *Cunard* v. *Antifyre Ltd.* [1933] 1 K.B. 551.
[51] This notion extends to servitudes such as easements. Thus unreasonable interference with a right of way is a nuisance. *Thorpe* v. *Brumfit* (1873) L.R. 8 Ch. App. 650.
[52] *Metropolitan Properties Ltd.* v. *Jones* [1939] 2 All E.R. 202.
[53] *Foster* v. *Warblington U.D.C.* [1906] 1 K.B. 648.
[54] [1907] 2 K.B. 141.
[55] See *post*, p. 402.

Modern authorities which have dealt with harassment by telephone calls seem to support a liberal approach to this issue. At one level these cases may merely amount to recognition that members of a family unit, other than the person in whom the title is legally vested, have proprietary interests in a family's home. In the Canadian case of *Motherwell* v. *Motherwell*[56] it was held that a wife's status and right to live in the matrimonial home was sufficient to give her a right to sue in private nuisance. The subsequent English case of *Khorasandjian* v. *Bush*[57] went further in extending the *Motherwell* approach to provide a remedy to all other members of the family unit. In the words of Dillon L.J. "If the wife of the owner is entitled to sue in respect of harassing telephone calls, then I do not see why that should also not apply to a child living at home with her parents."

It remains to be seen whether these decisions should be regarded as accepting the authority of *Malone* but extending the range of persons who are regarded as having a proprietary interest or as rejecting *Malone* on the basis that any lawful occupation can justify a claim.

LIABILITY FOR NUISANCE

Liability for nuisance may be placed by the law on a number of people.

Creator

The person who creates a nuisance bears the primary responsibility for it. There is no requirement that such a person must have an interest in the land from which the nuisance emanated. A trespasser, even though he has no right to return to the property to abate a nuisance which he created, remains liable. Conduct on the highway, such as a picket line, which interferes with the use of property which adjoins the highway,[58] may constitute a private nuisance against the owner of that property.

Occupier

The occupier of land on which a nuisance arises may also be liable. This is obviously the case if he is the creator (liability may arise vicariously), but liability may also be based on the fact that an occupier has "adopted or continued" a nuisance which is present on his property. This rule, which may make an occupier liable for nuisances brought onto his property by a previous occupier,[59] a trespasser or the forces of nature, comes close to creating liability for non-feasance. If a nuisance is present on property, and the occupier had, or ought to have had, knowledge of it, a duty to abate it arises. This duty seems to involve a subjective standard of care.

The leading English case on this form of liability is *Sedleigh Denfield* v. *O'Callaghan*.[60] In that case the nuisance had been created by employees of the local authority who had trespassed on the defendant's property and

---

[56] (1976) 73 D.L.R. (3d) 62.
[57] [1993] 3 All E.R. 669.
[58] *Hubbard* v. *Pitt* [1975] 3 All E.R. 1.
[59] *St. Anne's Well Brewery* v. *Roberts* (1928) 140 L.T. 1.
[60] [1940] A.C. 880.

constructed a culvert to drain water from a ditch. Measures taken to prevent the culvert from becoming blocked proved ineffective and flooding of the plaintiff's neighbouring land occurred. The occupier was held liable in nuisance on the basis that he had "continued the nuisance"; his employees, who had knowledge of its existence, had not taken reasonable steps to remove it. In the alternative, the defendant had "adopted" the nuisance by making use of the pipe to rid his land of water. The position would have been different if the occupier had had no knowledge, or means of knowledge, of the trespasser's acts. This approach was applied to nuisances created by a predecessor of title of the occupier in *St. Anne's Well Brewery Co.* v. *Roberts.*[61] In that case, the nuisance, excavations which had rendered a wall unstable, was latent in the sense that the occupier had no means of knowing of it. The occupier escaped liability. The *Sedleigh-Denfield* approach was extended to nuisances which are produced by the forces of nature by decisions of the Privy Council and Court of Appeal in *Goldman* v. *Hargrave*[62] and *Leakey* v. *National Trust.*[63] In the latter case the defendant owned a mound of land from which soil and tree roots were falling onto the plaintiff's land. The court accepted the proposition that an occupier of land is under a duty to abate a naturally occurring nuisance on his property once the risk has become patent, but held that the duty was of a subjective character; the occupier's duty was to do what was reasonable in the light of his personal capacity to deal with the nuisance.

Owner out of occupation

The landlord of tenanted property is, as a general rule, not liable for nuisances which arise in the course of a tenancy; there is no automatic liability placed on a landlord for any use of the property by a tenant which amounts to a nuisance. However, there are important exceptions to this rule which deal with the problems which may arise as a result of the landlord's knowledge of the particular use which is to be made of the property by the tenant and with nuisances caused by the property falling into disrepair.

1. The purpose of the letting

It is clearly established that a landlord will be liable if he has authorised the creation of a nuisance by letting property for a specific purpose which is ordinarily certain to constitute a nuisance. However, a number of first instance decisions have expressed slightly different approaches to the question whether a landlord will be liable for activities of a tenant which constitute a nuisance because he can foresee the tenant indulging in them.

The plaintiff in *Smith* v. *Scott*[64] lived in a road in which the defendant local authority was buying up properties in which to house homeless families. In 1971 the defendant moved the Scott family into the house next door to that owned by the plaintiff. The council knew from previous experience that the Scott family were far from being ideal tenants and the conditions of the lease with them prohibited them from creating a nuisance. In spite of this the

[61] (1928) 140 L.T. 1.
[62] [1967] 1 A.C. 645.
[63] [1980] 1 All E.R. 17.
[64] [1972] 3 W.L.R. 783.

family caused such damage to the plaintiff's property and so much disturbance that the plaintiff moved out of his house into other accommodation. He brought proceedings against the council alleging that its knowledge of the Scott's tendencies to create such interference rendered it liable for the nuisance which had been created. Pennycuick V.C. rejected this claim holding that although a landlord would be liable if he had authorised a tenant to commit a nuisance, this principle was confined to situations where the nuisance had been expressly authorised or to where a nuisance was certain to result from the purposes for which the property was let. The rule was based on express or implied authority having been given by the landlord to the tenant and was not wide enough to cover a situation in which a landlord had merely foreseen that a nuisance might result. However, in the later case of *Tetley* v. *Chitty*[65] McNeill J. favoured a rule which would place wider responsibility on landlords. A council, which had let property which it owned with the intention that it should be developed as a track for go-kart racing, was faced by a claim that it was liable for the nuisance created by the noise of the go-karts. The ratio of the decision that the council was liable was that the noise was an ordinary and necessary (*i.e.* certain) consequence of the purpose for which the land had been let to the club. However, the judge expressed his obiter view, that a landlord should be held to have authorised a nuisance in any case in which the nuisance is a foreseeable consequence of the letting.

2. Nuisances caused by disrepair of the let property

A landlord's responsibility for nuisances caused by the state of the property during the course of a tenancy depends on the degree of control which the landlord exercises over the property once it is tenanted. In practice, the provisions of the lease under which the tenant acquires the property are likely to define the responsibilities of the parties as to keeping the property in repair. Such agreements will be effective to define the mutual rights of the landlord and tenant. However, when claims by third parties affected by the defects in the property are raised, the courts have been prepared to look behind the terms of such agreements at the reality of the degree of control which the landlord has exercised over the property in order to decide whether a landlord should bear responsibility for nuisances created on the property. Many of the results obtained in the older cases are now incorporated into section 4 of the Defective Premises Act 1972. The result is an area of nuisance which is heavily influenced by thinking drawn from negligence. As a result, a landlord who has a sufficient degree of control over tenanted property to be under a duty to neighbouring owners with respect to nuisances created by a failure to maintain or to repair it will only be liable for those defects of which he ought reasonably to have been aware.[66]

One rule which is clearly established is that if a landlord knows, or ought to have known, of the existence of a nuisance on his property prior to letting it, he cannot remove his responsibility to third parties for it merely by letting the property subject to a covenant under which the tenant accepts the responsibility for keeping it in good repair. Any other result would run the risk of the owner of property in need of repair being able to escape liability to

---

[65] [1986] 1 All E.R. 663.
[66] Except, possibly in the case of artificial projection over the highway. *Wringe* v. *Cohen* [1940] 1 K.B. 229.

third parties by letting it to a penniless company. In *Brew Brothers Ltd.* v. *Snax (Ross) Ltd.*[67] a landlord was held liable in nuisance because he ought to have known that a wall on the property was in a dangerous state before he let the property to a tenant. His liability was said to be based on his control over the property at the time when the nuisance arose which was before the time at which the property was let.

If a nuisance arises after a tenancy has been created the landlord's responsibility depends on the degree of control which he has over the property at that time. The necessary degree of control may be established in a number of ways.

The existence of an express covenant making the landlord responsible for repairs has this effect as a result of section 4 of the Defective Premises Act 1972. Under this provision a landlord[68] who has an obligation to maintain or repair premises and who knows, or ought to have known, of a defect in them owes a duty to take such care as is reasonable in the circumstances to all persons who might reasonably be expected to be affected to see that they are reasonably safe from the risk of damage to themselves or their property. It is relatively clear that this provision is intended to protect the interests of those who occupy neighbouring property as well as those who are endangered by entering the property subject to the tenancy. In the case of short term tenancies of residential property it is normal for maintenance of the structure of the building to be the express responsibility of the landlord. Section 11 of the Landlord and Tenant Act 1985 removes the need for an express covenant in many cases by placing a landlord under an statutory obligation to keep in repair the structure and exterior of dwellings let for a term of less than seven years.[69] As a result section 4 of the Defective Premises Act applies to the great majority of tenancies of residential property.

However, the landlord's responsibility may be established in the absence of an express or statutory obligation having been placed on him to conduct repairs. Section 4(4) of the Defective Premises Act 1972 extends the obligation created by section 4(1) to cases in which the landlord has merely retained a right to enter the property to carry out maintenance and repairs, as opposed to being under a duty to do this. This provision can lead to a landlord bearing the responsibility for a nuisance even though, as between the landlord and the tenant, the primary responsibility for the repairs was with the tenant.[70]

Several older decisions, which foreshadowed the provisions of the Defective Premises Act, hint that the actual exercise of control over tenanted property may be sufficient to place a landlord under liability for nuisances which arise on it even though there is no obligation upon him to repair or maintain and no right to enter to do such work has been retained.[71]

---

[67] [1970] 1 Q.B. 612.

[68] Note that the provision applies to rights of occupation granted by contract: s. 4(6).

[69] This is incorporated into the Defective Premises Act's provisions by s. 4(5).

[70] *i.e.* the landlord's power of entry was merely a reserve power for use if the tenant defaulted in his obligations.

[71] In *Wilchick* v. *Marks* [1934] 2 K.B. 56 (a case in which the landlord had a right, but no duty, to enter and conduct repairs) it seems to have been significant that the tenant's rent had been increased on the basis that the landlord bore the responsibility for the repairs. In *Heap* v. *Ind Coope & Allsopp Ltd.* [1940] 2 K.B. 476 (in which again the landlord had a right to enter) the fact that he had done repairs in the past seems to have been relevant to establishing that he had sufficient control over the property to be responsible for the nuisance.

Public Nuisances

A public nuisance is a nuisance which affects a whole section of society. Public nuisance is essentially a criminal offence. In relation to such nuisances the law takes the view that it is unreasonable to expect any individual to bear the responsibility for initiating proceedings for an injunction which would benefit a class of society as a whole. The right to seek an injunction to stop a public nuisance is vested in the Attorney-General and local authorities.[72] A public nuisance only becomes actionable in tort by an individual on proof that that person has suffered special damage as a result of the nuisance; that is, damage over and above that suffered by the rest of the community. There are two forms of public nuisance: those which affect land and those created by dangers on or obstructions of the highway.[73]

In the leading case of *A.G. v. P.Y.A. Quarries Ltd.*,[74] which concerned a claim that the defendant's activities constituted a public nuisance because showers of stones and splinters had been ejected from their quarry into the neighbourhood in addition to the noise and vibration caused by the quarrying activities, the Court of Appeal held that it was a question of fact whether a sufficient class of persons had been affected by the interference to justify a finding of public nuisance.

Public nuisances which affect land are similar in character to private nuisances. What is required is a widespread and unreasonable interference with the use and enjoyment of property. Any special damage suffered by the plaintiff will suffice to ground a cause of action, there is no requirement that the plaintiff have an interest in land affected by the nuisance. A good illustration of this difference is provided by the decision of the House of Lords in *Tate & Lyle Industries Ltd. v. Greater London Council.*[75] In that case the construction of ferry terminals by the defendant in the river Thames resulted in siltation which rendered it impossible for the plaintiff company to use the jetties which it had been licensed to construct in the river to serve its premises without dredging the channels. The plaintiff claimed for damages on the basis that its status as the owner of property fronting onto the river entitled it to the maintenance of a certain depth of water adjacent to the land. The claim failed on the ground that the obstruction of a public right of navigation did not amount to an interference with riparian rights and because the jetties were regarded as chattels rather than as part of the land. However, this obstruction was held to amount to a public nuisance because the Thames was a navigable river and the plaintiff could show that it had suffered special damage from the obstruction in spite of the fact that its proprietary rights had not been infringed.

In practice, there may be a considerable overlap between public and private nuisances which affect land because the element of special damage required to render a public nuisance actionable by an individual may itself constitute a private nuisance against the plaintiff's property. It was on this basis that Veale J. held in *Halsey v. Esso Petroleum Co. Ltd.*[76] that the noise of tankers entering and leaving the defendant's depot at night was actionable

---

[72] Local Government Act 1977, s.222.
[73] These nuisances usually feature personal injury claims. They are discussed at p. 245.
[74] [1957] 2 Q.B. 169.
[75] [1983] 2 A.C. 509.
[76] [1961] 1 W.L.R. 683.

as either a public or private nuisance by residents who were prevented thereby from sleeping in their homes. Conversely, proof of the existence of a large number of private nuisances may establish that a public nuisance has occurred.

Defences

The standard defences of contributory negligence and consent (in the form of consent to the activity which created the nuisance) are available.

Statutory authority

Some of the most important discussions of the defence of statutory authority are found in a series of nineteenth century nuisance cases brought against persons who had been authorised to conduct activities by Act of Parliament. The issues involved are well illustrated by *Hammersmith & City Railway Co.* v. *Brand*,[77] in which compensation was sought for vibration suffered by the plaintiff's home near to a railway line from a company which had constructed and operated the railway. The House of Lords rejected this claim on the basis that the vibration was an inevitable consequence of operating the railway and that a successful claim in respect of it would defeat the intention of Parliament which had authorised the operation. The plaintiff's remedy was to be found in any compensation provisions contained in the statute.

The result in a case of this kind is that Parliament has acted to achieve a supposed public benefit, albeit that certain individuals may be disadvantaged. The fact that the authorisation may lead to the expropriation of private rights gives rise to the argument that its scope will be read strictly against the person who seeks to rely on it. However, this important general principle of interpretation may face the conflicting desire of the courts to carry through the perceived intention of the legislature. These conflicting influences were central to the leading modern authority of *Allen* v. *Gulf Oil Refining Ltd*.[78] In that case the defendant company pleaded the provisions of a private Act of Parliament in defence to a claim that the operation of an oil refinery at Milford Haven constituted a nuisance to persons living in the vicinity. The Act in question contained express power to acquire the land required for the purpose of "constructing" the refinery and the power to construct and use certain ancillary facilities such as railway lines. There was no express provision empowering the "use" of the refinery. The plaintiff's argument that this meant that the refinery could only be operated if all pre-existing legal rights were not infringed was rejected on the grounds that it would make nonsense of the obvious intention of the legislature. Lord Diplock commented that Parliament could hardly be supposed to have intended the refinery to be nothing more "than an adornment to the landscape."

A statutory authorisation to undertake certain activities does not automatically negate liability for nuisance. The immunity will only extend to those interferences which are the inevitable consequence of the activity permitted. It will remain possible for the plaintiff to allege that the interference which

---

[77] (1869) L.R. 4 H.L. 171.
[78] [1981] A.C. 1014.

was suffered became a nuisance when it transcended these limits. Certain activities authorised by statute may be capable of being performed without any affect on others and, if this is the case, all nuisances created by such acts will be actionable.[79] On a similar basis damage caused by the negligent exercise of such powers will be held to fall beyond the scope of the immunity.[80] In *Tate & Lyle Industries Ltd.* v. *Greater London Council*[81] it was held that a statutory authorisation to construct ferry terminals would have had the inevitable consequence of causing additional siltation of the river bed, but that the design chosen had increased the problem beyond that which was inevitable. As the defendants were held to have been negligent in making this choice they were liable for the difference between the inevitable interference and that which actually resulted from the design chosen.

The approach adopted in relation to statutory authorisation of an activity was extended to planning permissions by the decision in *Gillingham Borough Council* v. *Medway (Chatham) Dock Co. Ltd.*[82] In that case the plaintiff local authority had granted the defendant company planning permission to use part of a former naval dockyard as a commercial port. It was envisaged from the outset of the development that the port would operate on a 24-hour-a-day basis and that access to the site for heavy vehicles was only possible through a residential neighbourhood. The plaintiff council, although aware of the environmental consequences of the development, was prepared to sanction the scheme in order to bring new business to the area which would counteract the employment consequences of the closure of the naval facility. Some years later the council, which had come to regard the environmental considerations as of greater importance, sought to restrain the passage of heavy goods vehicles to and from the port between the hours of 7 p.m. and 7 a.m. by alleging that it constituted a public nuisance. The defendants successfully argued that the existence of a planning permission authorising their activities meant that the claim must fail. Buckley J. was of the opinion that the central purpose underlying the making of a planning decision is that of balancing the interests of the community against those of the individual and that the remedies for those whose interests are affected by proposals lie in the rights granted by planning legislation to object to the proposal, to appeal against a decision and to have the matter referred to an inquiry or to the Minister. The judge held that a nuisance action cannot be allowed to defeat a decision properly reached under the planning process. A planning decision has the capacity to alter the character of the area and to render innocent activities which might have previously constituted a nuisance. On the facts of the case the residents had to accept that they now lived in the neighbourhood of a commercial port which operated 24-hours-a-

---

[79] *Managers of the Metropolitan Asylum District* v. *Hill* (1881) 6 App. Cas. 193. Lord Wilberforce's judgment in *Allen* adopts the wider and erroneous reading of this decision that permissive powers must be exercised in strict conformity with private rights. There can be no basis for distinguishing the effect of powers which must be used from those which a body may use at its option. This interpretation of the case was rejected by the House of Lords in favour of the proposition stated in the test in *London, Brighton & South Coast Railway Co.* v. *Truman* (1885) 11 App. Cas. 45.

[80] *Geddis* v. *The proprietors of the Bann Reservoir* (1878) 3 App. Cas. 430; *Sadler* v. *The South Staffordshire & Birmingham District Steam Tramways Co.* (1889) 23 Q.B.D. 12; *City of Manchester* v. *Farnworth* [1930] A.C. 171. See also the discussion of negligence in the context of public authority powers and duties, *post*, Chap. 25.

[81] [1983] 2 A.C. 509.

[82] [1992] 3 All E.R. 923.

day.[83] The judge emphasised that nothing in his decision prevented liability being based on unreasonable conduct of activities covered by a planning permission. The decisions to hold the defendants liable in public nuisance on the facts of *A.G.* v. *P.Y.A. Quarries Ltd.*[84] and *Halsey* v. *Esso Petroleum Co. Ltd.*[85] must therefore now be regarded as examples of unreasonable use of planning permissions.

Prescription and coming to the nuisance

It is no defence to allege that the plaintiff "came to the nuisance"; that is, that it affected the property before he acquired it. The new owner is entitled to assert rights which his predecessor waived. In the leading decision of *Sturges* v. *Bridgman* the defendant had used noisy machinery on his premises for many years without complaint from those living in the neighbourhood. However, the plaintiff, a doctor who lived in adjoining premises built a consulting room close to the defendant's machinery and subsequently complained of the noise. The Court of Appeal held that the plaintiff could not be met by the argument that he had brought the problem on himself by building the consulting room in close proximity to the machinery.[86]

Act of God

It is a defence to show that the interference was the result of an "act of god," in the sense of wholly exceptional natural events.

---

[83] It would be possible for the planning authority to use the planning process to place conditions on the defendant's operations or to revoke the permission, but this would involve it in paying compensation. The plaintiff council admitted that its purpose in bringing proceedings in nuisance was to avoid the payment of compensation.

[84] [1957] 2 Q.B. 169.

[85] [1961] 1 W.L.R. 683.

[86] A defence of prescription by means of 20 years use did not apply as time would only run against the plaintiff from the date that the nuisance first ocurred and that would only be when the consulting room was erected.

Chapter Twenty-One

Physical Damage to Land

A number of tortious causes of action have as their main aim the provision of compensation in relation to physical damage to land or buildings attached to it. As has already been noted,[1] trespass to land and nuisance may also provide a remedy in relation to such losses, but they are confined, respectively, to directly inflicted damage and interferences which have satisfied the required test of continuity and neither tort has the provision of compensation for physical damage to land as its primary function. The attention in this chapter will be on those torts which do provide compensation for damage caused to land indirectly and by one-off events.

NEGLIGENCE

Negligently inflicted damage to land, or to the buildings attached to it, creates no difficulties of principle. Examples recorded in the cases include: structural damage resulting from negligently conducted pile driving operations on a site close to that occupied by the plaintiff[2]; damage caused by a negligently driven vehicle colliding with the building[3]; a negligently caused fire being allowed to spread and damage the plaintiff's property[4] and negligently failing to repair a building so that it became a target for vandals with the result that damage was caused to adjoining property.[5]

The rules requiring a plaintiff to have an interest in the property affected by the negligence in order to avoid being held to have suffered pure economic loss[6] effectively mean that the same level of proprietary interest must be shown in a negligence claim in relation to land as in one brought in private nuisance.[7]

---

[1] *Ante*, p. 373.
[2] *Dodd Properties (Kent)* v. *Canterbury City Council* [1980] 1 All E.R. 928.
[3] *Hole & Son (Sayers Common)* v. *Harrison of Thurnscoe* [1973] 1 Lloyds Rep. 345.
[4] *Taylor (C.R.) (Wholesale) Ltd.* v. *Hepworths Ltd.* [1977] 1 W.L.R. 159.
[5] *Ward* v. *Cannock Chase D.C.* [1986] Ch. 546. A case of this nature may well also be actionable in private nuisance.
[6] See *ante*, pp. 353–356.
[7] See *ante*, p. 397. However, a person may still claim in negligence for personal injuries or damage to chattels suffered whilst on another person's land.

Rylands v. *Fletcher* LIABILITY

The tort based on the authority of *Rylands* v. *Fletcher*[8] may be available to provide a separate cause of action to a person whose land[9] is damaged by the acts of another. The tort is related to nuisance and is commonly pleaded as an alternative to it. However, it differs from that tort in that its operation is confined to dangerous activities conducted by the defendant. The availability of the tort is limited, nowadays, by restrictive conditions. However, it has one clear advantage over nuisance in that it is available in respect of an isolated incident: no continuity of interference is required.

We have discussed elsewhere and rejected[10] the possibility that this tort can provide the basis for a general principle of tort which imposes strict liability for dangerous activities. A more limited role which might be suggested for the tort is that it can provide compensation and injunctions for persons whose property is injured by the escape of chemicals, gases and other forms of pollution. The tort may now have the capacity to assume the role of an "environmental" tort. For many years it seemed possible that restrictions created by the non-natural user requirement would prevent *Rylands* from performing as effective a role in protecting the environment as nuisance. However, *Cambridge Water Co. Ltd.* v. *Eastern Counties Leather plc*[11] has opened the way for the tort to have such a role. The case concerned the pollution of a borehole used by the plaintiff to extract water for domestic consumption. The pollution was traced to repeated spillages of solvents at the defendant's tanning works. A claim for compensation failed on the basis that the defendant could not have foreseen the type of damage suffered by the plaintiff as a result of these spillages. The House of Lords refused to impose strict tortious liability for "historic pollution": *i.e.* the cost of repairing damage to the environment which was not appreciated when done. However, Lord Goff's speech did open the way to a greater role for *Rylands*[12] as he stated that the storage of chemicals on industrial premises is a "classic case of non-natural use."

The case of *Rylands* v. *Fletcher*[13] concerned a landowner who employed an engineer and a contractor to construct a reservoir on his land. They failed to take the necessary precaution of blocking up old mine shafts on the property and when the reservoir was filled the water broke through into the plaintiff's mines and flooded them. The defendant was held liable on these facts. Blackburn J. stated the law in the following terms:

> "We think that the true rule of law is that the person who, for his own purposes, brings on his land and keeps there anything likely to do mischief if it escapes, must do so at his peril, and, if he does not do so, he is prima facie answerable for all damage which is the natural consequence of its escape."

This principle was subsequently affirmed by the decision of the House of Lords in the case, Lord Cairns adding the requirement that the item in question must have been introduced to the property in the course of some non-natural user.

---

[8] (1868) L.R. 3 H.L. 330.
[9] The role of the tort in relation to personal injuries has been discussed in Chap. 11.
[10] See p. 38.
[11] [1994] 1 All E.R. 53.
[12] It may still have few advantages over nuisance unless there is an isolated escape.
[13] (1868) L.R. 3 H.L. 330.

It may be thought strange that the conditions of liability under the *Rylands* principle are shrouded in difficulty well over a century after the case was decided. However, these difficulties are created by the fact that subsequent cases reflect conflicting views as to the role of the tort. Some, particularly cases decided in the early twentieth century, treat it as authority for a general principle of strict liability protecting a variety of interests; others have interpreted Blackburn J.'s statement virtually as a statute with the result that the tort survives at the end of the century as a hidebound historical anomaly which is effectively a specialised form of nuisance. The imposition of restrictive conditions on the tort's operation means that it can no longer claim to be a general principle of tort liability.

It is probably the case that *Rylands* v. *Fletcher* does not apply to intentional or voluntary, as opposed to inadvertent, releases of an item.[14] Such a release would be actionable under the tort of trespass. Negligence based thinking has not had a significant influence on the working of the *Rylands* v. *Fletcher* tort[15]; its possible rigours have been mitigated by the interpretation placed by the courts on concepts such as non-natural use rather than by the importation of ideas from the more dominant modern tort.

Escape

The decision of the House of Lords in *Read* v. *Lyons*[16] is the best example of the restrictive approach. The plaintiff had suffered personal injuries as the result of an explosion while she was working in the defendant's munitions factory. Her claim for damages was obviously based on the assumption that *Rylands* establishes that injuries caused by dangerous activities attract strict liability; her pleading contained a simple statement of the facts and made no allegation of negligence. The decision effectively, if indirectly, rejected this approach by stating that it is an essential condition of *Rylands* v. *Fletcher* liability that there has been an escape from the defendant's property. This excluded the plaintiff's injuries from the scope of the tort because they had been suffered within the confines of the defendant's factory. Why this requirement should exist has never been entirely clear; it obviously has the potential to produce anomalies according to whether the victim is just outside the boundary of the defendant's property or not. It also has the effect of making the tort unavailable in relation to a great deal of damage resulting from ultra-hazardous activities.[17] The Court of Appeal in *Cambridge Water Company* v. *Eastern Counties Leather plc*[18] drew the very dubious distinction between liability for an *escape*, which was held to ground *Rylands* v. *Fletcher* liability, and for *actions*, for which it was asserted that there could be no such liability.

The best explanation for the requirement of an escape depends on acceptance of the view that the tort is a species of private nuisance and is

---

[14] This view was supported by Taylor J. in *Rigby* v. *Chief Constable of Northamptonshire* [1985] 2 All E.R. 985.
[15] The new rule on remoteness of damage may herald a shift. See *ante*, p. 101.
[16] [1947] A.C. 150.
[17] For example, it must now be doubted whether the plaintiff in *Honeywill & Stein Ltd.* v. *Larkin Bros.* [1934] 1 K.B. 191, whose cinema was damaged by flash photography, which at that time involved the lighting of explosive flares, could now recover under the principle.
[18] (1993) 5 *Journal of Environmental Law* 173.

therefore founded on interference with the land of another person. If this is correct the claim in *Read* was wholly misconceived because personal injury claims should not be brought under it, other than by a person whose land was affected by the escape. However, much of the older authority on the tort is not reconcilable with this view. What is clear is that *Read* marked the end of any possibility of the tort being the basis of a general principle of strict liability.

The *Rylands* v. *Fletcher* object

The other conditions of liability are very unclear. For example, it is difficult to discern any logic governing which objects are covered by the principle.[19] Blackburn J.'s words "something likely to do mischief if it escapes" provide the starting point in suggesting that the need is for something which creates a peculiar risk. In short, the principle applies to dangerous things. However, many everyday items may prove dangerous if mishandled and the courts have held some commonplace items, such as petrol in the tank of a car[20] and the storage of water in bulk,[21] to be covered by the principle. The sheer variety of objects which may require classification undoubtedly justifies the assertion that the question is ultimately one of fact.

The burden of establishing that an object is harmless (*i.e.* is not likely to do mischief if it escapes) rests on the person who accumulated it on land. It must be shown that the escape of any quantity of the item will be harmless.[22] As will be seen, even if an item is classified as being a *Rylands* v. *Fletcher* object, it remains possible that the requirement that it was brought onto land in the course of a "non-natural use" will prevent liability from arising.

Non-natural use

The requirement that the escape must have been the result of a *Rylands* v. *Fletcher* object having been brought onto the land in the course of a "non-natural" use of it by the defendant creates a vague criterion of liability which has been subject to different interpretations over the years and now probably prevents the tort operating in many situations. At the minimum it must mean that the escape of a naturally occurring danger, such as earth falls from naturally occurring features such as cliff faces,[23] are not within the scope of *Rylands* v. *Fletcher* even though they might ground liability in nuisance. In 1868 the distinction which was being made was probably between risks of this kind and those introduced onto property by human intervention. Indeed, the leading speeches in *Rylands* v. *Fletcher* seem to confirm this. Blackburn J. spoke of the new tort as being closely related to cattle trespass[24] (*i.e.* to the responsibilities of those who pasture livestock) and Lord Cairns (whose judgment gave rise to the non-natural use requirement) contrasted the

---

[19] Examples of items which have been held to fall within the principle are listed in Clerk & Lindsell on *Tort*, (16th ed.), para. 24.03. See also Stallybrass, (1929) 3 C.L.J. 376.

[20] *Musgrove* v. *Pandelis* [1919] 2 K.B. 43.

[21] *Rylands* v. *Fletcher* itself.

[22] *Cambridge Water Company* v. *Eastern Counties Leather* (1991) 4 *Journal of Environmental Law* 81. This point was not discussed in the Court of Appeal or House of Lords.

[23] *Leakey* v. *National Trust* [1980] 1 All E.R. 17.

[24] This is the common law version of the tort of livestock trespass which is now to be found in the Animals Act 1971. See *ante*, p. 383.

artificial construction of a reservoir with the natural collection of water on land.

Subsequently views changed and the requirement of non-natural use has been taken to involve the creation of an abnormal risk: "some special use bringing with it increased danger to others." This is obviously a much more stringent test which clouds the distinction between this requirement of liability and the need for a *Rylands* v. *Fletcher* object to be "something likely to do mischief if it escapes" by making the notion of increased danger central to both. As early as 1912, in *Rickards* v. *Lothian*,[25] the overflow of water from a domestic plumbing installation was held to be a natural use of land and to fall outside of the *Rylands* principle because it did not amount to a special use of land bringing with it increased danger to others. On the basis of such authorities it is possible for commentators to suggest that "the concept of non-natural user is now understood by the courts as being similar to the idea of unreasonable risk in negligence."[26]

However, the modern interpretation which is placed on the non-natural use requirement may go even further and prevent the tort from providing a remedy in relation to many of the potentially dangerous uses made of land in a sophisticated modern society. In 1947, the House of Lords, when deciding *Read* v. *Lyons*, gave some consideration to the question of whether the manufacture of munitions in an industrial area during the war could constitute a non-natural use. The issue did not need to be resolved but one member of the court did comment that the concept of a natural use of land should not be equated to a primitive use. Subsequently a court held that the manufacture of electronic components in a factory on an industrial estate was not a non-natural use.[27] Such cases give rise to a theory that many, if not most, industrial activities would not constitute a non-natural use of land. However the tide may have turned with Lord Goff's speech in *Cambridge Water Co. Ltd.* v. *Eastern Counties Leather plc.*[28] His Lordship, having held that the plaintiff's case could not succeed under *Rylands* because the form of loss suffered was unforeseeable, took the view that the storage of substantial quantities of chemicals for industrial use was a "classic" case of non-natural use of land. The fact that the activity was liable to benefit the community, by the creation of employment, was not sufficient to make the use a natural one. Unfortunately, his Lordship did not attempt to redefine the concept of non-natural use.

Must the plaintiff have an interest in the land?

The cases which discuss whether a plaintiff must have an interest in the land onto which the escape occurs cannot be reconciled. The difficulty almost certainly stems from the fact that different perceptions of the role of the tort have been held by different courts over the years. Some authorities have viewed *Rylands* v. *Fletcher* as a species of nuisance governing the relations of neighbouring landowners. If this is correct one might expect, by analogy with private nuisance, that the plaintiff would be required to have an

---

[25] [1913] A.C. 263.
[26] Winfield & Jolowicz on *Tort* (13th ed., 1989), p. 429.
[27] *British Celanese Ltd.* v. *A.H. Hunt (Capacitors) Ltd.* [1969] 2 All E.R. 1252.
[28] *Cambridge Water Company* v. *Eastern Counties Leather* [1994] 1 All E.R. 53.

interest in the property onto which the escape occurs. Authority for confining the tort in this way can be found in *Cattle* v. *Stockton Waterworks Co.*,[30] a case which has been followed in at least one modern case.[31]

A much wider approach to the tort is favoured in the line of authority which derives from the decision of the Court of Appeal in *Charing Cross Electricity Supply Co.* v. *Hydraulic Power Co.*[32] That case, which was decided at a time when the tort appeared to be developing into a generally applicable principle of strict liability, held it to apply to the escape of a dangerous item from one chattel, a hydraulic main laid in a street, to another, an electricity cable laid alongside it. It was said that the tort is not to be confined to claims between adjacent landowners. This result has been followed in more modern cases in which the escaping object damaged the paintwork of the plaintiff's car, which had been parked on the public highway outside his property[33] and when an escape from the defendant's land damaged property which was on the land of a third party, rather than on that of the plaintiff.[34]

Does the escape need to be from the defendant's land?

Blackburn J.'s requirement that the defendant should have accumulated the item on his land would suggest that the tort is confined to escapes from the defendant's property. However, this would impose a restriction on the tort which was more stringent than that applied in nuisance[35] and it is not particularly surprising to find that this restriction was not applied in the period when the tort was expanding.

A number of cases take the wide view that the escape must be from the defendant's control but need not be from land which he owns or occupies. The *Charing Cross* Case is a good example of this, the defendant in that case having only a licence to place his hydraulic main in land which belonged to another. When the point was raised more recently in a case in which the police had fired a C.S. gas canister from the road into the plaintiff's building,[36] the court adopted the wider view that the owner or controller of the escaping thing could be liable although he was neither the owner nor the occupier of the property from which the escape occurred.

Defences

The defences available as an answer to a claim brought under the principle of *Rylands* v. *Fletcher* reduce the utility of the tort even further.

1. Act of a stranger

Rylands v. *Fletcher* imposes a non-delegable tortious duty under which a person may be responsible for escapes which result from the acts of his

---

[30] (1875) L.R. 10 Q.B. 453.
[31] *Weller & Co.* v. *Foot & Mouth Disease Research Institute* [1966] 1 Q.B. 569.
[32] [1914] 3 K.B. 772.
[33] *Halsey* v. *Esso Petroleum Co. Ltd.* [1961] 2 All E.R. 145.
[34] *British Celanese Ltd.* v. *A.H. Hunt (Capacitors) Ltd.* [1969] 2 All E.R. 1252.
[35] See *ante*, p. 398.
[36] *Rigby* v. *Chief Constable of Northamptonshire* [1985] 2 All E.R. 985.

independent contractor[37] and others. However, the defendant will not be
liable if the escape was caused by the act of a stranger. In the analogous area
of damage caused by fire[38] Lord Denning M.R., having asserted that an
occupier of land is liable for damage caused by the escape of a fire caused by
the acts of his employees, independent contractors, guests and anyone else on
the land with his leave or licence, defined a stranger as "anyone who . . . acts
contrary to anything which the occupier would anticipate that he would do."
Edmund Davies L.J. adopted a narrower, and, it is suggested, more realistic
test: the stranger is a person over whose acts the occupier has no control. The
difficulty with Lord Denning's test is that it might hold a person liable for the
malicious acts of third parties over whom he had no control merely because
such acts could be anticipated. Courts have been reluctant in recent years to
permit negligence to impose such duties and it is difficult to see why the
Rylands v. *Fletcher* principle should be subject to different rules. The leading
cases on the point are consistent with the narrower test. In *Rickards* v.
Lothian[39] the defendant pleaded act of a stranger successfully against a claim
by the plaintiff that his property had been damaged by water flowing from
the defendant's property. The jury held this to have been caused by acts of a
malicious third party who had turned taps on and plugged the waste pipe.
The defence was also made out in *Perry* v. *Kendricks Transport Ltd.*[40] in
which the plaintiff child had been injured by the acts of other children
putting a lighted match into the petrol tank of a disused coach which had
been parked on the defendant's land.[41]

2. Act of God

The courts have placed stringent limitations on the scope of this defence
with the result that wholly exceptional circumstances need to be proved
before it will apply. If it is to be established, it must be shown that the escape
was the result of a wholly unforeseeable natural event against which it was
impossible[42] to provide any precautions. A heavy fall of rain or snow will not
therefore, without more, raise this defence; something wholly exceptional is
needed.

3. The plaintiff's consent

A defendant will not be liable under the tort if he can show that the
plaintiff consented to the activity which produced the escape. It seems to be
possible to establish this on the basis of either an express consent or the fact
that both the plaintiff and defendant obtained a common benefit from the
activity. If, for example, water escapes from one part of a tenanted property
into another[43] the fact that the water had been brought onto the premises for

---

[37] In *E. Hobbs (Farms) Ltd.* v. *The Baxenden Chemical Co. Ltd.* [1992] 1 Lloyds Rep. 54 it was
held that the landowner's liability extended not only to escapes from his land caused by the
negligence of the independent contractor but also to those caused by the negligence of the
manufacturer whose materials the independent contractor uses.

[38] *H. & N. Emanuel Ltd.* v. *Greater London Council* [1971] 2 All E.R. 835.

[39] [1913] A.C. 263.

[40] [1956] 1 W.L.R. 85.

[41] C.F. Atkinson J.'s *obiter* suggestion in *Schiffman* v. *Order of St. John* [1936] 1 K.B. 557 that
anticipated interference with property by children would not count as the act of a stranger.

[42] It is not sufficient to show that it was not reasonably possible to guard against this risk. Clerk
& Lindsell *op. cit.* para. 24.13.

[43] *Sachdeva* v. *Sandhu* [1989] 2 E.G.L.R. 273.

the joint benefit of all of the tenants will prevent a claim from being brought under the *Rylands* principle.

4. Statutory authorisation

Standard principles of statutory authorisation[44] apply to liability under the *Rylands* v. *Fletcher* principle. A mandatory obligation imposed by statute to conduct an activity which would otherwise fall within the scope of the tort excuses the defendant from anything expressly required to be done by the statute or for anything reasonably incidental to that requirement.[45] Negligence in the course of the activity will, however, ground liability as it will not be assumed that Parliament intended to authorise negligence.[46]

If the governing statute merely permits the activity the result will vary according to whether it contains a provision which makes the undertaker liable for nuisance. If it does not do this it will be necessary to prove negligence in order to establish liability. However, if a clause does impose liability for nuisance there will be no such requirement.

5. Causation and contributory negligence

If the damage is caused by the default of the plaintiff himself there will be no liability under the *Rylands* v. *Fletcher* principle. The Law Reform (Contributory Negligence) Act 1945 applies to reduce the damages to be awarded to the plaintiff if his conduct is a partial cause of the damage suffered.

6. Necessity

Necessity is not a defence to this form of liability because the tort does not apply to intentional or voluntary releases.[47]

Conclusion

Nowadays *Rylands* v. *Fletcher* has no defined role. The tort is so hedged with restrictions that it can rarely be predicted with certainty when it will apply. The case law is confused, in dire need of authoritative review and makes distinctions which are simply irrelevant to the substance of the issue: the control of activities on land which are dangerous and likely to cause pollution or physical damage. A great deal of the role which could be performed by the tort is handled satisfactorily by public and private nuisance. Indeed, it can be said that the tort is only of use in cases of non-continuous escapes from land, resulting from a non-natural user, which damage the amenity of land and affect a small area of society. The result in the *Cambridge Water Company* Case suggests that it may now be possible, in limited circumstances, to use the tort as a remedy for environmental damage. However, the advantages to be gained from this are limited as it may well be

---

[44] See *ante*, p. 121.
[45] In practice, a mandatory obligation of this kind is likely to be imposed on a public body charged with conducting an activity for the benefit of the public. In such circumstances it is possible to contend that the defendant falls outside the basic requirements of *Rylands* v. *Fletcher* because the defendant did not bring the item onto his land "for his own purposes." See *Dunne* v. *North Western Gas Board* [1964] 2 Q.B. 806.
[46] *Dunne* v. *North Western Gas Board* [1964] 2 Q.B. 806.
[47] This seems unlikely. See *ante*, p. 408.

that nuisance can perform the same task free from the difficulties which encumber the *Rylands* v. *Fletcher* principle.

FIRE DAMAGE

The common law position was that a person was strictly liable for damage caused to others by fires started on his premises.[48] This position was modified by the Fires Prevention (Metropolis) Act of 1774. This Act, which is still in force, provides that:

> "No action shall be maintained against any person in whose house, chamber, stable, or barn or other building or on whose estate any fire shall accidentally begin."

The result of this is that the question of what counts as an "accidental" fire is critical to the question of a landowner's liability. The Act places the plaintiff under the burden of proving that the fire was other than accidental. There can be no doubt that intentionally caused fire damage is not protected by the Act. However, twentieth century authority has gone much further and assimilated this area to the mainstream of liability by holding that all that the plaintiff needs to do to show that the fire was not "accidental" is to prove either negligence or that the fire was started under conditions which would make *Rylands* v. *Fletcher* applicable.

Negligence

The leading modern authority holding a negligently caused fire to count as non-accidental under the 1774 Act is *Balfour* v. *Barty-King*.[49] In that case the defendant had asked some workmen to attempt to thaw out some frozen water pipes in the attic of her house. One of these workmen negligently started a fire which spread to damage the plaintiff's adjoining property by attempting to thaw the pipes which were lagged with combustible material by means of a blowlamp. The defendant was held liable to the plaintiff on these facts.

The earlier decision of *Musgrove* v. *Pandelis*[50] established an important further limitation on the operation of the Act when it held that it would not apply to a fire which started accidentally but was then negligently allowed to spread. In that case a petrol fire started accidentally when the defendant's chauffeur was attempting to start the car's engine. It was found as a fact that the fire might easily have been rendered harmless had the chauffeur turned off the supply of petrol; however, he failed to do this and the fire spread and damaged the plaintiff's property. In spite of the fact that the Act uses the words "any fire shall accidentally begin" the damage was held to have been caused by a non-accidental fire. In effect, the fire was divided into two parts and the defendant was held liable for the second part because it was attributable to negligence. A similar result was reached in *Goldman* v. *Hargrave*[51] in respect of a landowner's negligent failure to control a fire

---

[48] Theoretically this still applies to fires which fall outside the ambit of the 1774 Act.
[49] [1957] 1 Q.B. 496.
[50] [1919] 2 K.B. 43.
[51] [1967] 1 A.C. 645.

started on his land by a lightning strike. In effect, these decisions place a landowner under a duty to take reasonable care to abate fires which arise on his property either accidentally or from natural causes. The extent of the measures required to fulfil this duty, in relation to fires caused by natural events, may well vary according to the capacity of the particular landowner to deal with the problem.[52]

Rylands v. Fletcher

It might be thought that damage caused by a tort, such as that derived from *Rylands* v. *Fletcher*, which does not require negligence to be proved would count as accidental. However, the contrary result seems to be accepted. This was the alternative ground given by the Court of Appeal for the finding of liability in *Musgrove* v. *Pandelis*.[53] The petrol in the tank of the car was treated as a dangerous thing falling within the *Rylands* principle and the 1774 Act was held not to classify fires started under such conditions as "accidental." This authority was applied, with some reservations, by Mac-Kenna J. in *Mason* v. *Levy Auto Parts of England Ltd.*[54] This case concerned the not unfamiliar situation of an unexplained fire starting in inflammable materials which the defendants had stored on their property and is important because, by accepting that *Rylands* can apply to such a case, it effectively moves the law towards imposing strict liability in such circumstances. It is not, however, a particularly convincing authority for several reasons: first, the judge was bound to follow the authority of *Musgrove* in spite of his having reservations as to the correctness of that decision on the point; secondly, he was of the opinion that the *Rylands* principle needed to be adapted to the fire situation which it did not fit precisely, particularly because it was the fire rather than the dangerous item which escaped and finally, he had doubts as to whether the non-natural user requirement was satisfied on the facts of the case. MacKenna J.'s reformulation of *Rylands* sets three conditions for liability for fire damage under *Rylands*: first, that the defendant must have brought onto his land things likely to catch fire and kept them there in such conditions that, if they did ignite, the fire would be likely to spread to the plaintiff's land; secondly, that he must have done this in the course of some non-natural user of the property and, thirdly, that the things must have caught fire and the fire must have spread and damaged the plaintiff's property.

Defences

Liability for fire damage based on negligence or *Rylands* v. *Fletcher* is subject to the standard defences which apply to those torts.

The duties imposed in respect of damage caused by fire are of a non-delegable nature. The *Balfour* case involved the occupier of premises being held liable for the negligence of a non-employee who had been invited onto the property to undertake work. However, the defence of act of a stranger

---

[52] *Goldman* dealing, as it does, with a fire started by lightning on property situated in the Australian outback may not be a helpful authority in relation to fires which occur in Great Britain, where most occupiers, whatever their personal capacity to extinguish the fire, will have fairly immediate access to the services of the fire brigade.

[53] [1919] 2 K.B. 43.

[54] [1967] 2 Q.B. 530.

does provide a limited exception to this result. The leading modern authority is *H. & N. Emanuel Ltd.* v. *Greater London Council*[55] in which the defendant council wished to have removed two prefabricated bungalows which had been erected on its property. The task of removing these buildings was a statutory function of the Ministry of Housing, which contracted the actual performance of the work to a firm of contractors under terms which prohibited the use of bonfires to dispose of rubbish. Nonetheless, the contractors did follow the common practice of lighting bonfires and one of these was negligently allowed to go out of control and spread to damage the plaintiff's property. The Court of Appeal held that the occupiers were liable for this damage on the basis of the tests outlined previously[56]: the contractors' acts were foreseeable and could not be classified as the acts of a stranger. The occupiers were therefore held liable for the negligence of a third party who was neither their employee nor an independent contractor performing work on their behalf.

GAS

Gas is a dangerous substance which falls within the *Rylands* v. *Fletcher* principle. However, gas is generally supplied under statutory powers which reduce the liability of the suppliers for damage caused by both escapes of gas and failures to remedy escapes of which the suppliers are notified to the level of negligence.[57] A species of absolute statutory liability is, however, retained in the case of the underground storage of gas.[58]

NUCLEAR INSTALLATIONS

The Nuclear Installations Act 1965 places strict civil liability on persons licensed to handle radioactive materials for damage to property which results from such handling or from an escape of radioactive material.[59]

DISPOSAL OF WASTE

Section 73(6) of the Environmental Protection Act 1990[60] creates strict liability for damage caused by the deposit of waste on land in such a way as

---

[55] [1971] 2 All E.R. 835. See also *Hobbs, ante* note 37.

[56] See p. 411.

[57] Liability in nuisance is also possible, however, the fact that there is a mandatory statutory duty to supply gas means that negligence in the course of the supply needs to be established in order to make out a claim in nuisance. *Dunne* v. *North Western Gas Board* [1964] 2 Q.B. 806.

[58] Gas Act 1965, s. 14. Although stated to be absolute this liability is not strictly so as it is subject to the defence of contributory negligence (s. 14(3)).

[59] The mere presence of radioactive contamination which devalues, but does not otherwise damage, the property does not suffice. See *ante*, p. 369.

[60] This provision is designed to replace, in slightly modified form, provisions previously contained in s. 88 of the Control of Pollution Act 1974. At the time of writing the new provisions had not been brought into force.

to amount to an offence under section 33 of the Act.[61] The liability is placed on the person who deposited the waste and on any person who caused or knowingly permitted it to be deposited.

Under the European Community's draft Directive on Civil Liability for Waste[62] it is proposed that the producer[63] of waste should be strictly liable for damage which it causes. The novel feature of this liability would be that it would extend beyond personal injuries, death and damage to property to injury to the environment. Under the scheme of the Directive a plaintiff would be able to recover both damages and the cost of restoring the environment to the state that it was in prior to the event. The burden of proving causation, on a standard of overwhelming probability, would rest with the plaintiff.

OIL POLLUTION

A special statutory scheme is created by the Merchant Shipping (Oil Pollution) Act 1971 in relation to oil pollution caused by tankers.[64] Under this statute the owner of a tanker is strictly liable for any damage caused by the escape or discharge of oil from the vessel. Damage, in this context, includes the cost of preventative measures reasonably taken to limit the losses and trading losses, such as those which might be suffered at a holiday resort which was afflicted by oil pollution. The liability under this provision is strict, there being limited defences to the effect that the discharge was the result of acts of war; exceptional natural phenomena; the intentional acts of third parties, other than servants or agents of the owner or the negligence of a government or other authority in relation to lights or navigational aids. Liability under this provision is "capped" unless it can be proved that the pollution was the result of intentional or reckless acts.

---

[61] Unauthorised or harmful deposit, treatment or disposal of waste. Section 73(6) also applies to offences under the supplementary s. 63(2).

[62] COM (89) 282 final (September 15, 1989).

[63] This term receives an extended definition.

[64] This scheme, which is the result of international conventions, supersedes all common law liabilities in this regard.

PART V

OTHER INTERESTS

Chapter Twenty-Two

Introduction

This section of the book deals with miscellaneous tortious remedies which protect less tangible, but still important, interests and with the special rules which apply to the tort liabilities of public authorities.

The "civil liberties" torts,[1] the majority of which are varieties of trespass, provide a person with a weapon with which to test the legality of interferences with his person or property. They therefore protect an individual's right not to have his person or property interfered with other than as a result of an act authorised by law. As a subsidiary aim they also protect the individual's reputation. Although much of this area of law is directly concerned with the activities of the police it has wider relevance to the protection of liberties as was well illustrated by the "Pindown" regime of confining children which was operated in childrens' homes in Staffordshire. This is an area in which tort remedies have been championed as a result of perceived inadequacies in extra-judicial remedies.

The tort of defamation[2] protects a person's reputation against unwarranted attacks. It plays a major role in regulating the activities of the press and has attracted much attention in recent years as a result of a number of highly publicised cases in which large awards of damages have been awarded to media personalities and politicians.

One interest which has not, as yet, received direct protection from tort is that of privacy.[3] However, recent discussion of the role and conduct of the press has led to suggestions that some form of compensation right for the infringement of privacy should be introduced.

The final chapter[4] will be devoted to the special rules which regulate the tort liability of public bodies. Many of the modern cases in this area feature claims for economic loss. However, the principles which govern recovery have developed separately from the mainstream of liability. This area of law has been revolutionised by the advent of new compensation rights based on principles of European Community law.[5]

---

[1] Chap. 23.
[2] *Post*, Chap. 24.
[3] See *post*, pp. 461–462.
[4] Chap. 25.
[5] See *post*, p. 479.

Chapter Twenty-Three

The Protection of Civil Liberties

INTRODUCTION

Tort has a significant role to play in the protection of civil liberties. A great deal of this role is performed by the different forms of the tort of trespass: trespass to the person,[1] to land,[2] and to goods.[3] The fact that these torts are actionable without any damage needing to be proved enables them to be used as a technique for asserting a person's claim to be free from unlawful interference by the police, public authorities and others. Once a person oversteps the bounds of lawful interference with another's person or property tortious liability will have been incurred and a claim for nominal damages will exist, whether or not actual damage has been suffered. As with any case alleging trespass, once a prima facie trespass has been shown it is for the defendant to justify his actions. If the defendant is a public authority which has deliberately abused its powers a claim for exemplary damages may be possible.[4]

TRESPASS TO THE PERSON: ASSAULT AND BATTERY

As we saw in Chapter 10, these torts have the protection of a person's basic rights to be free of unwanted physical interference as one of their roles. Their main use in the protection of civil liberties is as a remedy with which to challenge the legality of police conduct[5] in relation to the searching of, fingerprinting of and taking samples from individuals and the force used to effect an arrest. A second area of relevance, which has been touched on already,[6] is that of medical treatment given without the consent of the patient.

The power to conduct personal searches, and in certain circumstances to stop persons for this purpose, is now contained in a number of provisions of the Police and Criminal Evidence Act (PACE) 1984[7] as are the powers to take

---

[1] See *Chap.* 9.
[2] See *Chap.* 19.
[3] For a discussion of the rules governing this tort see Winfield & Jolowicz on *Tort* (13th ed.), Chap. 17.
[4] *Ante*, p. 149.
[5] And others such as customs officers and private security services.
[6] See *ante*, pp. 180–181. For a more detailed survey see Jones, *Medical Negligence* (1991), Chap. 6.
[7] ss. 1, 32, 55, 62 & 63.

fingerprints and intimate and non-intimate samples. In order for a search to be lawful the person being searched must be informed of the reason, unless the circumstances are such as to make the requirement unnecessary or impracticable.[8] A police force risks being held to have acted tortiously if it adopts a general policy of searching every person who is taken into custody. The necessity of conducting a search on each person must be considered in the circumstances of the particular case.[9] The mere fact that a police officer has followed the standing instructions issued to members of his force will not give automatic protection.[10]

The use of force by the police and others will often form part of an arrest and be justified by the common law or statutory powers of arrest.[11] However, the use of force may be justifiable in limited circumstances even if no arrest is effected by the defendant. First, any person has the right at common law to use reasonable force in self-defence or to rescue another person from an attack. Such a degree of force may also be used to resist an unlawful arrest. Secondly, there is a statutory right to use such force as is reasonable in the circumstances of the case in the prevention of crime or in effecting or assisting in the lawful arrest of offenders, suspected offenders or persons unlawfully at large.[12]

Trespass to the Person: False Imprisonment

The tort of false imprisonment, which is sometimes referred to as "wrongful arrest" is constituted by "the unlawful imposition of constraint on another's freedom of movement from a particular place."[13] The tort is a species of trespass to the person and, as such, is actionable without proof of damage. It is used to vindicate a person's right to personal freedom and has, as its primary role, the provision of a damages remedy to persons who have been subjected to constraints by the police or other security services such as store detectives in excess of that justified by law. Claims of this kind brought against the police, at times in combination with actions for battery and trespass to land, have attracted sizeable awards of exemplary damages.[14]

Constraint

The tort may be committed even though the plaintiff has not been confined in anything resembling a prison. In the words of Blackstone[15]: "(E)very confinement of the person is an imprisonment, whether it be in a common prison, or in a private house, or in the stocks, or even by forcibly detaining one in a public street." Arrest, rather than imprisonment, meaning a restraint on the plaintiff's liberty, better describes what is required. The constraint must clearly be total. A boundary must be defined and the plaintiff prevented

---

[8] *Brazil v. Chief Constable of Surrey* [1983] 3 All E.R. 537.
[9] *Ibid.*
[10] *Middleweek v. Chief Constable of the Merseyside Police* (1985) [1990] 3 All E.R. 662.
[11] See *post*, p. 425.
[12] Criminal Law Act 1967, s.3.
[13] *Collins v. Wilcock* [1984] 3 All E.R. 374.
[14] The plaintiff retains a right to jury trial in a case which includes a claim of false imprisonment or malicious prosecution (Supreme Court Act 1981, s. 69(1)(b)). A claim for battery or trespass to land or goods does not involve such a right.
[15] *Commentaries*, Vol.3, p. 127.

from going beyond it. A denial of a previous freedom to go wherever he chooses, for example, the blocking of a right of way which leaves the person free to go in other directions does not amount to an imprisonment. It was on these grounds that the plaintiff, who had been prevented from using a particular section of a highway because it had been set aside for the purpose of allowing spectators to view a sporting event, failed in a claim of false imprisonment in *Bird* v. *Jones*.[16] No constraint had been placed on the plaintiff's ability to proceed in all but one direction.

The tort will not be established if the plaintiff has available some means of escape from an apparent constraint. It is submitted that, given the role of the tort in protecting civil liberties, a means of escape should only discharge the defendant if he can prove that it ought to have been reasonably apparent to the plaintiff and that it was reasonable for him to avail himself of it. Courts should be critical of attempts by persons who impose constraints on others to avoid liability by arguing that the other had the means to avoid the constraint.

Tort lawyers have traditionally debated whether the plaintiff must have knowledge that he is under constraint for the tort to be committed. It is difficult to see why a requirement of knowledge should exist. The tort which exists to control conduct which infringes individual liberty and conduct in breach of a person's rights is no less obnoxious because the victim is unconscious, asleep or in ignorance of what is happening. The classic statement of the correct approach is that of Atkin L.J. in *Meering* v. *Grahame-White Aviation Co. Ltd.*[17]:

> "I think a person can be imprisoned while he is asleep, while he is in a state of drunkenness, while he is unconscious, and while he is a lunatic. Those are cases where it seems to me that a person might properly complain if he were imprisoned, though the imprisonment began and ceased while he was in that state . . . So a man might in fact . . . be imprisoned by having the key of a door turned against him so that he is imprisoned in a room in fact although he does not know that the key has been turned. It might be that he is being detained in that room by persons who are anxious to make him believe that he is not in fact being imprisoned, and at the same time his captors outside that room may be boasting to persons that he is imprisoned . . . "

This approach, which is irreconcilable with some strange nineteenth century authority,[18] received the emphatic approval of the House of Lords in *Murray* v. *Ministry of Defence*.[19] Although the views expressed in *Murray* were *obiter*, they express the current approach to the issue and should be regarded as concluding the debate. In the words of Lord Griffiths: "the law attaches supreme importance to the liberty of the individual and if he suffers a wrongful interference with that liberty it should remain actionable even without proof of special damage."[20]

---

[16] (1845) 7 Q.B. 742.
[17] (1919) 122 L.T. 44 at 53–4.
[18] *Herring* v. *Boyle* (1834) 1 C.M. & R. 377.
[19] [1988] 2 All E.R. 521.
[20] This statement was part of his Lordship's refusal to adopt the compromise position in the Restatement of Torts that the tort is committed if the plaintiff "is conscious of the confinement or is harmed by it." The requirement that harm be proved would conflict with the rule that trespass to the person is actionable *per se*. His Lordship was correct to reject it.

Lawful authority

A variety of justifications may be found for placing constraints on another person's freedom.

1. Consent

If a person consents to being constrained no tort will be committed. As a result a person who agrees to accompany a police officer to a police station will not be able to claim that he has been arrested.

2. Powers of arrest

A detailed review of the powers of arrest vested in the police and private citizens is beyond the scope of this book. However, an outline of the most important powers of arrest will be given as they are central to the tort of false imprisonment because they define the conditions under which the overwhelming majority of arrests are effected. False imprisonment is the remedy in the case of an arrest in excess of these powers. It renders the person who conducts such an arrest strictly liable in tort. An arrest which is justified in law, but which is conducted with the use of undue force, does not give rise to the tort.[21]

The law on arrest is contained in the Police and Criminal Evidence Act 1984. The power to arrest and the conditions which must be fulfilled differ according to whether the arrest is effected by a private person, such as a store detective, or by a police officer. Any person may arrest without warrant another who is in the act of committing an "arrestable offence"[22] or whom he has reasonable grounds for suspecting to be committing such an offence.[23] If such an offence has been committed, any person may arrest without warrant any person who is guilty of it or whom he has reasonable grounds for suspecting to be guilty of it.[24] Police officers have additional powers. In relation to past events, they need not prove that an offence has actually been committed. A police officer who has reasonable grounds for suspecting that an arrestable offence has been committed can arrest without warrant any person whom he has reasonable grounds for suspecting to be guilty of that offence[25] and can also arrest anyone who is about to, or whom he reasonably suspects to be about to, commit an arrestable offence.[26] Only a police officer is empowered to arrest a person without warrant in relation to a non-arrestable offence. He may do this if he has reasonable grounds for suspecting that such as offence is being, or has been, committed or attempted and it appears to him that service of a summons is impracticable or inappropriate; for example, where the person refuses to give his name and address or is reasonably suspected to have given a false name.[27]

---

[21] *Simpson v. Chief Constable of South Yorkshire Police, The Times*, March 7, 1991. It may give rise to a claim for battery.

[22] Defined by s. 24(1) to cover offences for which the sentence is fixed in law and offences for which a previously unconvicted person over the age of 21 could be sentenced to a term of five years imprisonment or more. Ss. 24(2) and (3) include other specified offences within the definition.

[23] s. 24(4).

[24] s.24(5).

[25] s.24(6).

[26] s.24(7).

[27] s.25(1).

Additional powers permit any person to use reasonable force, including detention, to prevent crime and to effect, or assist in, the arrest of suspected offenders, offenders or persons unlawfully at large. A surviving common law power entitles every person in whose presence a breach of the peace is being, or appears to be about to be, committed to take such reasonable steps as are necessary to preserve the peace, including the detention of the person threatening to cause such breach.[28]

Once an arrest has been effected, certain procedures must be complied with. If they are not continued detention will be unlawful. An arrested person must be informed that he is under arrest and of the reason for the arrest.[29] Once the arrest has been effected, a private person must take the arrested person before a magistrate or to the police as soon as is reasonably possible. The police are entitled to detain the arrested person, without charging him, for up to 24 hours.[30]

The fact that a plaintiff has been convicted of the offence for which he was arrested, and indeed that he pleaded guilty to it, does not conclude a claim for wrongful arrest in favour of the defence, at least in cases in which the claim is based on a failure to comply with procedural safeguards in relation to arrests. In *Hill* v. *Chief Constable for South Yorkshire*[31] the Court of Appeal refused to strike out the plaintiff's allegation of wrongful arrest, based on an alleged failure by the defendant's officers to comply with certain procedural requirements[32] of PACE 1984 at the time of the plaintiff's arrest, in spite of the fact that the plaintiff had pleaded guilty to and been convicted of the offence charged. The result would almost certainly have been different if the allegation had been that the arresting person had lacked reasonable grounds for suspecting the plaintiff to have been guilty of the offence.

It seems that minor constraints imposed on the liberty of third parties by those who are effecting the lawful arrest of another may not be tortious. In *Murray* v. *Ministry of Defence*[33] members of the army conducting security operations in Northern Ireland assembled the occupants of a house in a single room while they searched the premises and arrested the plaintiff. The suggestion that those assembled in the room might be able to succeed in a claim for false imprisonment was greeted with scorn by Lord Griffiths. He said "that very short period of restraint . . . was a proper and necessary part of the procedure for effecting the peaceable arrest of the plaintiff. It was a temporary restraint of very short duration imposed not only for the benefit of those effecting the arrest but also for the protection of the occupants of the house and would be wholly insufficient to found an action for unlawful imprisonment."

3. Detention in prison

If a court of competent jurisdiction orders a person to be detained, the detention is lawful. Subsection 12(1) of the Prison Act 1952 provides:

---

[28] *Albert* v. *Lavin* [1981] 3 All E.R. 878.
[29] A police officer must give this information even if it was obvious from the circumstances of the arrest.
[30] Subject to certain safeguards, this period may be extended to a maximum of 96 hours.
[31] [1990] 1 W.L.R. 946.
[32] Those imposed by ss. 28 and 37.
[33] [1988] 2 All E.R. 521.

"A prisoner, whether sentenced to imprisonment or committed to prison on remand pending trial or otherwise, may be lawfully confined in any prison."

It is because of this provision that false imprisonment claims which challenge the lawfulness of an arrest generally concern the brief period of time between the initial arrest and the plaintiff being brought before the court.

It follows from subsection 12(1) that no claim for false imprisonment can be brought against prison authorities by a prisoner who has been remanded in custody or sentenced to imprisonment by a competent court. A number of claims have been recorded of attempts by prisoners to use the tort as a basis for challenging the conditions under which they have been detained.[34] The argument on which these claims have rested is that the law's desire to protect individual liberty means that it will recognise and protect some residual liberties which survive the imposition of a lawful sentence of imprisonment. Claims of this kind have invariably related to the conditions under which the plaintiff is detained in prison. In view of the fact that the tort can only be established on proof of the complete restriction of an individual's freedom of movement and that this freedom has been lawfully removed in the case of a person committed to prison, it is not surprising that these claims have failed. In the leading case of *Hague* v. *Deputy Governor of Parkhurst Prison*[35] the House of Lords rejected such arguments on the basis that the realities of prison life did not allow a prisoner to retain any residual liberties which could be enforced by an action of false imprisonment. A subsidiary argument, that confinement of a prisoner in conditions which constituted a threat to his health could amount to false imprisonment, was also rejected. As a result of the case, the main remedy for challenging the conditions under which a prisoner is held is that of judicial review. The tort remedies which may be available in exceptional cases are misfeasance,[36] if a breach in bad faith of the Prison Rules is alleged, or negligence if, for example, the conditions of the imprisonment have caused foreseeable injury to the prisoner's health.

4. Mental Health Act 1983[37]

A number of powers, which permit a person to be detained compulsorily in a hospital for the purposes of assessment or treatment, exist under the provisions of the Mental Health Act 1983.[38]

5. Contractual claims

As a matter of general principle a person who has a valid contractual claim against another cannot detain that person as a way of enforcing payment. A creditor has no lien over the debtor's person. In the leading case of *Sunbolf* v. *Alford*,[39] an innkeeper who had attempted to detain a customer on account of an unpaid bill was held to have committed trespass to the person. His

---

[34] *Williams* v. *Home Office (No. 2)* [1981] 1 All E.R. 1211; *Middleweek* v. *Chief Constable of the Merseyside Police* (1985) [1990] 3 All E.R. 662; *Hague* v. *Deputy Governor of Parkhurst Prison* [1991] 3 All E.R. 733.

[35] [1991] 3 All E.R. 733.

[36] See *post*, p. 469.

[37] For a full survey of this area, see Hoggett, *Mental Health Law* (3rd ed., 1990), pp. 13–24.

[38] The majority of patients who enter hospital for treatment for mental disorder do so as voluntary patients and are free to discharge themselves and to refuse treatment.

[39] (1838) 3 M. & W. 248.

defence was viewed as giving rise to the "startling proposition" that a creditor could impose what might become life imprisonment on his debtor for a trifling unpaid sum.[40]

However, the *Sunbolf* rule seems to be subject to the proviso that a person who willingly subjects himself to another's confinement, often by the terms of a contract, cannot use false imprisonment as a means of demanding his release from the confinement at any time and on the terms which he chooses. It is suggested that this is the only proposition supported by the authorities of *Robinson* v. *Balmain New Ferry Co. Ltd.*[41] and *Herd* v. *Weardale Steel, Coal & Coke Co. Ltd.*[42] These cases do not support the view that a reasonable constraint may be imposed on another because of his breach of contract. The initial subjection to the constraint is critical. *Robinson*, the more difficult of the two cases involved a plaintiff who had contracted with the defendants that he would enter their wharf and be taken from it on a ferry boat. He changed his mind and sought to leave the wharf. The defendants forcibly prevented him from doing so when he refused to pay the prescribed exit fee of one penny. The Privy Council held that the defendants' conduct did not constitute false imprisonment as they were entitled to impose a reasonable condition upon the plaintiff's exiting from a place to which he had gone of his own free will. The result is difficult to reconcile with that of *Sunbolf* as it fails to distinguish the capacity to exact a charge (which is not in doubt) from the ability to enforce payment of that charge by detaining a person. Possibly the case might be interpreted as an application of *Bird* v. *Jones*[43] in the sense that the plaintiff was not imprisoned because he was free to leave the wharf by the ferry. However, Lord Loreburn's speech gives support to the far more questionable, and dangerous, proposition that one person is entitled to detain another until that other meets a reasonable condition.

In *Herd* the plaintiff was a miner employed by the defendant. Having descended the mine on a work shift which was due to run from 9.30 a.m. to 4 p.m. he became involved in a dispute over certain work which he regarded as dangerous. He refused to do the work and at 11 a.m. requested to return to the surface. The lift only became available for his use at 1.10 p.m. and he was not allowed to use it until 1.30 p.m. He claimed that the defendants had falsely imprisoned him for the 20 minutes during which the lift was available but he was not permitted to use it. The House of Lords rejected the claim. The reason for this seems to be that the plaintiff had consented to his freedom being constrained by choosing to go down the mine; he had contractual rights to be brought back to the surface, but he could not, in the circumstances, invoke false imprisonment in order to demand release at any time which suited him. In Lord Haldane's words:

"If a man gets into an express train and the doors are locked pending its arrival at its destination, he is not entitled, merely because the train has been stopped by signal, to call for the doors to be opened to let him out. He has entered the train on the terms that he is to be conveyed to a certain

---

[40] In that case the debt was 11/3d (54p). Note that attempting to leave premises, such as a shop, without paying for goods or services may amount to the commission of an offence which justifies an arrest.

[41] [1910] A.C. 295.

[42] [1915] A.C. 67.

[43] (1845) 7 Q.B. 742.

station without the opportunity of getting out before that, and he must abide by the terms on which he entered the train. So when a man goes down a mine, from which access to the surface does not exist in the absence of special facilities given on the part of the owner of the mine, he is only entitled to the use of these facilities . . . on the terms on which he entered."[44]

In essence, this is to say that trespass to the person does not impose liability for nonfeasance; *i.e.* the plaintiff cannot use the tort to force the defendant to assist him to go in any direction that he wishes. It is possible to regard the decision in *Robinson* as less convincing support for the same proposition.

6. Parental and other forms of discipline

Parents, as an incident of their general authority over their children, have the right to impose reasonable restraints upon their movements in order to safeguard their welfare or as a form of punishment.

Masters of ships and pilots of aircraft have statutory powers to forcibly restrain a person in order to protect the passengers or crew of the vessel or aircraft.[45]

TRESPASS TO LAND

The rules governing this tort have been described in Chapter 19. A wide variety of powers to enter land which is in the possession of another are granted by statute.[46] From the perspective of civil liberties the most important powers are those granted to the police to enter and search land.[47]

TRESPASS TO AND INTERFERENCE WITH GOODS

Challenges to attempts by the police, and other bodies,[48] to seize goods in the possession of another person may be mounted by use of tort remedies, such as trespass to and wrongful interference with goods.[49] Again, a wide variety of statutory justifications may provide a defence for such conduct.[50]

RELATED TORTS

Certain other torts which are not derived from trespass may be used to protect an individual's liberties. By far the most important of these is the tort of malicious prosecution.

---

[44] [1915] A.C. 67.71.
[45] Merchant Shipping Act 1970, s. 79; Tokyo Convention Act 1967, s. 3.
[46] A full description of these powers is beyond the scope of this book.
[47] For a full survey see Clayton & Tomlinson, *Civil Actions against the Police* (2nd ed.), Chap. 7.
[48] Such as the Customs and Excise.
[49] For the law on these torts see Clerk & Lindsell on *Torts* (16th ed., 1989), Chap. 23.
[50] Again, a full description of powers of seizure is beyond the scope of this book. For a survey of the powers of the police in this regard see Clayton & Tomlinson *op. cit.* Chap. 7.

Malicious prosecution[51]

This tort protects a person against the risk of his being deprived of his liberty by baseless malicious allegations that he has been guilty of criminal conduct. The tort, which is a species of the wider tort of malicious abuse of the judicial process,[52] protects a person's liberty and also his reputation against the damage which would be caused to them by an erroneous conviction. It is available against police officers and any other person who has initiated criminal proceedings against the plaintiff. It can be distinguished from the tort of false imprisonment in that it is capable of providing a remedy for the losses incurred by a person who has been remanded to prison by a competent court and to a person who is subjected to criminal process without having been arrested.[53] The public policy requirement of ensuring that persons are not discouraged from initiating genuine prosecutions means that the availability of the tort is subject to a number of restrictive conditions and that a plaintiff who alleges that the tort has been committed against him has to meet a heavy burden of proving four separate requirements.

The damages which may be recovered in such proceedings will cover damage to a person's reputation; damage flowing from the fact of detention and any consequential financial losses. The fact that a plaintiff in a case of this kind retains the right to require a jury trial[54] means that there may be considerable difficulty in predicting the sum likely to be awarded as damages. Exemplary damages may be awarded when a claim for malicious prosecution is brought against police officers or other public servants,[55] but the conduct of the plaintiff has been held to be capable of reducing any such award which is made in spite of the fact that the defendant has been held to have acted maliciously and with a lack of reasonable and probable cause.[56]

1. Fact of prosecution

To be liable under this tort a defendant must be shown to have initiated the proceedings which were taken against the plaintiff. This condition does not require the defendant to have conducted the prosecution personally. The mere reporting of facts to the police will not amount to the initiation of proceedings, whereas the laying of information before a magistrate will. Police officers remain liable for actions on their part which instigate a prosecution even though the conduct of that prosecution is in the hands of the Crown Prosecution Service.

2. Prosecution terminating in the plaintiff's favour

Although the proceedings brought against the plaintiff must have terminated in his favour before a malicious prosecution claim can be successful, it does not matter how this result is achieved. An acquittal on the merits of the case is not required and the plaintiff is not required to prove his innocence of

---

[51] See generally Clayton & Tomlinson op. cit. Chap. 8.

[52] Other actions may be available for the malicious instigation of bankruptcy or insolvency proceedings. However, malicious instigation of civil proceedings will usually not be tortious as the forms of loss recognised are strictly limited and do not extend to the costs incurred in defending such proceedings.

[53] It is an action on the case and is therefore not actionable per se.

[54] Supreme Court Act 1981, s. 69(1)(b).

[55] See ante, p. 149.

[56] Bishop v. Commissioner of Police of the Metropolis The Times, December 5, 1989.

the charge. An acquittal, a refusal by magistrates to commit for trial at committal proceedings, a failure to offer evidence or a successful appeal against conviction will all count as a favourable termination. Furthermore, a case will be held to have terminated in the plaintiff's favour if he is acquitted of the offence charged but convicted of a lesser offence or if he is acquitted on some, but not all, of the offences charged. It is just as much a wrong to inflate maliciously the charges against a person and to put him at risk of a greater level of punishment than is deserved as it is to bring baseless charges against a person who is wholly innocent. If the conviction stands, the tort claim fails even if the plaintiff is able to prove that the conviction was erroneous. If this were not the rule malicious prosecution would allow the civil courts to be used to obtain damages based on a conviction in criminal proceedings which had not been overturned.

3. Lack of reasonable and probable cause

The requirement that the defendant must have lacked reasonable and probable cause for instigating the proceedings against the plaintiff means that he must have lacked, at the time that he instigated the proceedings, an honest belief that the plaintiff was guilty of the offence charged. This requirement of proving a negative is a very difficult condition to satisfy unless the plaintiff has hard evidence that the prosecuting officers lacked an honest belief in the charges which were being brought. It is for the judge, rather than the jury,[57] to determine whether there was a lack of reasonable and probable cause.[58] The defendant is entitled to be judged at this point on the basis of those facts which he honestly and reasonably, albeit erroneously, believed to be true at the time that he initiated the prosecution. A police officer will therefore be able to rebut an allegation that he committed the tort by showing that he instigated a prosecution on the basis of allegations made against the plaintiff by persons who appeared to be reliable. The question for the court is whether the defendant thought that these facts gave rise to a case against the plaintiff which was fit to be tried. Before instigating the proceedings the defendant need not have investigated the strength of any defences which the plaintiff might have pleaded in answer to the charge. To expect the investigation of such matters as a matter of course before making a charge would impede the reporting of crime and might well give suspected persons the opportunity to destroy evidence.[59]

The reasonable and probable cause requirement must be kept separate from that of malice.[60] Although the existence of malice may be inferred from the lack of reasonable and probable cause on the defendant's part, a finding of malice does not prove that there was a lack of reasonable and probable cause for instigating the proceedings.[61]

4. Malice

The malice requirement means that the plaintiff must prove that the defendant had a wrongful and improper motive in initiating the proceedings

---

[57] This rule is said to have derived from the fact that juries were too ready to award damages in the event of unsuccessful prosecutions.

[58] Although the jury may be required to determine disputed issues of fact relevant to the decision.

[59] *Herniman* v. *Smith* [1938] A.C. 305.

[60] See *post*.

[61] *Glinski* v. *McIver* [1962] A.C. 726.

and that the predominant purpose of the defendant in bringing the proceedings must have been to harm the plaintiff rather than to uphold the law by bringing him to justice.[62] The mere fact that the defendant initiated the proceedings when he was angry or seeking revenge for the fact that the offence had been committed against him is insufficient to establish malice.

Misfeasance in public office[63]

Support exists for the view that misfeasance is available as a remedy for asserting rights in relation to areas such as deliberate breach of Prison Rules to the disadvantage of prisoners.[64]

Breach of statutory duty

Breach of statutory duty has had little role to play in this area. Its only appearance has been in a number of cases[65] in which it has been held to be impossible to bring an action for compensation founded on a breach of the Prison Rules.

NON-LITIGIOUS REMEDIES

Tort remedies are not the only method which a person may use to assert civil liberties. However, litigation has been pursued actively because of dissatisfaction with the non-litigious alternatives available. Tort remedies, if they are available, are seen by many commentators as the preferable choice because they can offer an independent and public adjudication of a grievance. Tort is seen as the only way of ensuring that the police are made truly "accountable" for their conduct. However, litigation has familiar disadvantages in being slow,[66] costly and possibly ineffective in achieving any improvement in the conduct of the persons charged with tortious conduct.

Complaints against the police[67]

The function of the Police Complaints Authority (PCA) which was set up under PACE 1984 is mainly supervisory. The actual investigation of complaints made against the police is conducted by the police as a matter of internal discipline. The purpose of the investigation into complaints made against police officers is to determine whether a breach of the criminal law or of the police Codes of Discipline has occurred and thus whether criminal

---

[62] *Glinski* v. *McIver* [1962] A.C. 726.
[63] Discussed *post*, p. 469.
[64] *Hague* v. *Deputy Governor of Parkhurst Prison* [1991] 3 All E.R. 733.
[65] *Arbon* v. *Anderson* [1943] 1 K.B. 252; *Becker* v. *Home Office* [1972] 1 Q.B. 407; *Williams* v. *Home Office (No. 2)* [1981] 1 All E.R. 1211; *Hague* v. *Deputy Governor or Parkhurst Prison* [1991] 3 All E.R. 733.
[66] The leading case of *White* v. *Metropolitan Police Commissioner The Times*, April 24, 1982 was resolved more than five years after the incident on which the claim was founded. Clayton & Tomlinson *op. cit.* p. 16 state that the average time taken to resolve such proceedings in a sample of representative cases was found to be three and a half years.
[67] See generally Clayton & Tomlinson *op. cit.* Chap 2 and Maguire & Corbett, *A Study of the Police Complaints System* (H.M.S.O., 1991).

proceedings or internal disciplinary action should be instigated. The provision of compensation to persons aggrieved by the conduct of the police is not one of the aims of the complaints procedure.

The procedure is initiated by the making of a complaint to the Chief Officer of the police force in question. There is nothing to stop a complaint being made in parallel with the bringing of civil proceedings in relation to the same incident. Indeed, it is common practice for police forces to regard the receipt of a solicitor's letter before action as a complaint which justifies starting the complaints procedure. The majority of complaints made against the police are either dropped or not proceeded with. However, if the complainant does decide to proceed there are two forms of procedure which may be used.

1. Informal resolution

The 1984 Act introduced a procedure whereby an informal resolution of minor complaints by such means as apologies may be reached. This procedure is only available if the complainant consents to it and the Chief Officer of Police in charge of handling the complaint is satisfied that the conduct alleged will not, if proved, amount to a criminal offence or a breach of the Code of Discipline. If an attempted informal resolution proves to be impossible a formal investigation into the complaint has to be made.

2. Formal investigation

If the nature of the complaint means that it falls outside the informal resolution procedure, or if an informal resolution has been attempted without success, the Chief Officer is obliged to ensure that a formal investigation of the complaint is conducted by a senior officer with a view to the taking of disciplinary or criminal proceedings against the officer concerned if the complaint is made out.

In a case in which the allegation is that a serious offence has been committed it must be referred to the PCA which has the right to order that the investigation be conducted by a member of another force and to impose conditions on the conduct of the investigation. The PCA is thus given a supervisory, as opposed to an investigatory role, in relation to complaints of this kind. The PCA is given a further supervisory role in that, even in a case in which it has not supervised the complaints process, it is entitled to receive a report from the Chief Constable explaining why he has decided not to send the papers on the case to the Director of Public Prosecutions with a view to prosecution.

Any disciplinary proceedings which are taken following the findings at the investigatory stage are the responsibility of the Chief Officer. The complainant will be entitled to attend certain stages of the disciplinary hearing. One significant factor which may tilt the balance in favour of a complainant bringing a tort action rather than relying on the complaints procedure is that the standard of proof imposed in police disciplinary proceedings is the criminal law one of "beyond reasonable doubt."

3. An assessment

This procedure has attracted considerable criticism on a number of grounds. One writer has summarised the criticisms as being "that complaints are not always investigated thoroughly and impartially; that serious wrongdoing by police officers goes unpunished; that the process is shrouded in secrecy and never adequately explained to complainants; that it grinds on for an unreasonably long time; and that it fails to satisfy people with genuine grievances."[68] The central criticism which continues to be made is that there is an urgent need for the introduction of an independent investigatory body. Both the Police Federation and the PCA have criticised the existing procedure as inadequate.[69] In the light of this it is easy to understand how the vagaries of the litigation system can look attractive to those with a grievance against the police. Litigation concerning allegations of police misconduct has increased substantially in recent years[70] and it has been asserted that it has a much higher rate of success in terms of proving misconduct than does the police complaints procedure.[71] Lawyers specialising in this area have taken the view that the pursuit of tort remedies against the police can be hampered by the initiation of a complaints investigation.[72] However, the complaints procedure is the only technique which can lead to a police officer who has misconducted himself being punished or disciplined.

Compensation for miscarriages of justice

Section 133 of the Criminal Justice Act 1988 allows for the Home Secretary to pay compensation to a person who has been convicted of a criminal offence but is then pardoned or has the conviction reversed[73] on the basis of new or newly discovered facts which show beyond reasonable doubt that the conviction constituted a miscarriage of justice. The Home Secretary determines whether the facts are such as to give a right to receive this form of compensation. The amount payable is then determined by an assessor.

---

[68] L. Lustgarten, *The Governance of Police*, pp. 146–147.
[69] For a summary see *Legal Action* (June, 1991), p. 9.
[70] See the table reproduced in Clayton & Tomlinson *op. cit.* p. 20.
[71] Clayton & Tomlinson *op. cit.* p. 13 state that in 1985 civil actions brought against the Metropolitan Police had a 49 per cent. success rate, whereas only 3 per cent. of complaints established misconduct.
[72] For a full discussion, see Clayton & Tomlinson *op. cit.* pp. 56–63.
[73] Defined as the conviction being quashed on an appeal out of time or on a reference by the Home Secretary to the Court of Appeal under s. 17 of the Criminal Appeal Act 1968.

Chapter Twenty-Four

Injuries to Reputation and the Protection of Privacy

This chapter deals with a number of topics which are linked, in many cases, by the fact that they deal with the conduct of the press and the other media. The tort of defamation is a complex area of law which provides protection for damage done by publications to a person's reputation. A related topic is the extent to which English law does, and should, provide any protection for acts which infringe a person's privacy. Finally, the chapter will consider a number of non-judicial mechanisms which may provide protection in relation to such matters.

DEFAMATION

Introduction

Defamation, the generic name for the torts of slander and libel, is an area of tort which has two aims. The first is to provide a remedy with which a person can protect his reputation from attack. This role of the tort aims to safeguard a person's reputation rather than his privacy; the tort provides a remedy against the publication of untruths as opposed to unfair revelations of long-forgotten truths or intrusions into a person's private life. It creates a significant incentive for newspapers to strive for accuracy. The other aim is to protect the right of freedom of speech and thus the ability of the press to investigate, and to bring to the public's attention, malpractice. There can be no doubt that these aims of the law can conflict and that the attempt to maintain a proper balance between them is one of the explanations for the complexity of this area of tort law.

Two related issues make the law of defamation topical. First, the survival of jury trial in the majority of cases[1] and the fact that it is the jury which assesses the damages awarded has led to the charge that outcome of cases is a "lottery" which commonly says more about the jury's attitude to press tactics than about the merit of the case and that the level of damages awarded can be excessive, unpredictable and encourages 'gold digging' claims. Secondly, awards of aggravated and exemplary damages may be available for defamation in spite of the fact that it is an area of law in which injury to reputation will commonly be presumed from the fact of the defamatory

---

[1] Supreme Court Act 1981, s. 69.

statement having been made. Defamation cases have produced well publicised awards of damages at levels which seem astronomical when contrasted with those made to persons who suffer serious personal injuries.[2]

The structure of the law of defamation has developed as a detailed set of rules and exceptions and difficult questions can arise in relation to the variety of meanings which a particular statement can bear[3] and the role of judge and jury in such cases. The outcome of cases can be virtually impossible to predict with certainty because important questions of fact and meaning will need to be resolved by the jury. In addition, some of the defences are difficult to state with precision because different terminology has been used in different cases. Others involve no more than lists of protected activities. A committee (The Faulks Committee), which reported in 1975 on the law, practice and procedure relating to defamation was of the opinion that some aspects of the law were unduly complex and technical, but that, to an extent, these difficulties were the inevitable consequence of the need to maintain a balance between the conflicting aims underlying the law. Unfortunately, the proposals which the committee made which were intended to simplify the law have not been enacted. A more limited set of proposals made in 1991 by a Working Party chaired by Neill L.J.[4] seems likely to produce some reforms.[5]

The law of defamation can only be understood properly as consisting of a conjunction of two issues. The first, whether the statement is defamatory, may well receive an affirmative answer. However, the stringency of this result is alleviated by the width of the defences which are available. The final result in a defamation case will be provided by the combined consideration of these two issues. In this area of law the available defences are of central importance.

What amounts to a defamatory statement?

For words to count as defamatory a number of requirements must be satisfied. The words must be defamatory in the sense of lowering the plaintiff's reputation; they must refer to the plaintiff; and they must have been published. In addition, different forms of damage may need to be proved according to the nature of the publication. The procedure in a defamation case requires the judge to decide whether, as a matter of law, the words are capable of constituting defamation and of referring to the plaintiff. In effect, the judge has an obligation not to allow the case to go to the jury if this is not established. If the judge allows the case to proceed, it falls to the jury to determine whether the words were actually defamatory of the plaintiff on the facts. The classic case on this issue is *Lewis* v. *The Daily Telegraph*.[6] The defendant newspaper had there published an article which stated that the police were investigating the affairs of a company of which the plaintiff was the chairman. The plaintiff brought a defamation claim which

---

[2] For a survey of the major awards made in 1991 and 1992 see (1992) 89/38 L.S.G. 29. The general approach of courts to has been discussed at p. 146.

[3] See particularly the case of *Bookbinder* v. *Tebbit* [1989] 1 All E.R. 1169 discussed at p. 445.

[4] Supreme Court Procedure Committee, *Working Group Report on Practice and Procedure in Defamation* (1991).

[5] It was reported in January 1993 that the Lord Chancellor had committed himself to acting on some of the proposals.

[6] [1964] A.C. 234. *Bookbinder* v. *Tebbit* is a further example of this in the different context of the defence of justification.

alleged, in part, that the words were understood to mean that he had been guilty of fraud or dishonesty. The judge's decision to allow the case to go to the jury on this allegation was held by the House of Lords to have been incorrect. It was decided that no reasonable person would infer guilt merely from the fact that an inquiry was taking place. As a result of this decision newspapers are left free to report that a person is "assisting the police with their inquiries."

Lowering the plaintiff's reputation

A simple inaccuracy in words published concerning the plaintiff will not render them defamatory because an inaccuracy will not always damage a reputation. A commonly accepted definition of defamatory matter is that which was given by Lord Atkin in *Sim* v. *Stretch*.[7] It is that it consists of "words which tend to lower the plaintiff in the estimation of right thinking members of society generally." It is clear, however, that no single watertight definition has gained universal acceptance. The Faulks Committee was of the opinion that a new statutory definition of defamation should be introduced to replace the common law in order to bring some simplification to the subject. Under its proposal, which was based on Lord Atkin's words, a statement would count as defamatory if "in all the circumstances" it "would be likely to affect a person adversely in the estimation of reasonable people generally."[8] This proposal has not been enacted. A number of points should be made about the surviving common law definition.

It is well established that words can be defamatory even though they contain nothing which is actually to the plaintiff's discredit. In the leading case of *Youssoupoff* v. *Metro-Goldwyn-Mayer*[9] an allegation that a Russian princess had been the victim of rape by Rasputin was held to be defamatory of her. The court said that it sufficed that the defendant had said something which might cause reasonable persons to shun or avoid the plaintiff. On a similar basis allegations of illness or insanity are potentially defamatory, even though they might be thought likely to invoke sympathy for the victim from those to whom they are published.

The identification of "right thinking members of society" can occasion particular difficulties as people's views on issues may differ. One group within society may regard the allegation as to the plaintiff's credit whereas others view it as reprehensible. Is it, for example, defamatory to allege of a doctor who has strong anti-abortion views that he has conducted abortions? The present law raises the possibility of a person suffering severe damage on the basis of his relations with a particular group of society yet being unable to invoke the protection of defamation because society "in general" rejects the views of this group.[10]

It is commonly said that spoken words of abuse cannot amount to defamation. It is more correct to say that in certain circumstances words

---

[7] (1936) 52 T.L.R. 669.
[8] para. 65.
[9] (1934) 50 T.L.R. 581.
[10] The Israeli Supreme Court in *Shaha* v. *Dandiryan* P.D. 39(4) (1985) 734 held that it was not defamatory to allege of a Jordanian citizen living within the Arab community in East Jerusalem that he had collaborated with the Israeli Government and supported its policy on the occupied territories. In effect, a statement which might have put the plaintiff's life at risk in the context of the community within which he lived was held not to be defamatory.

stated as a form of abuse may not be reasonably interpreted as bearing their literal meaning. The mere fact that words are spoken in the heat of the moment and with the intention of insulting or abusing the person about whom they are spoken does not render it impossible for them to constitute defamation.

Innuendo

It is perfectly possible for words which are not on their face critical of the plaintiff, and indeed for words which are prima facie complimentary, to constitute defamation. This is what is known as an innuendo. It is open to the plaintiff to offer the court an interpretation of the words, based on extrinsic evidence, which a particular class of reasonable persons might place on them which goes beyond their ordinary and natural meaning and which renders them defamatory of him. The best known example of this is the case of *Tolley* v. *J.S. Fry and Sons Ltd.*[11] The plaintiff was a well-known amateur golfer in the 1920s. He complained that the defendant chocolate manufacturers had issued an advertisement which depicted him playing golf. The drawing showed a bar of the defendant's chocolate in the plaintiff's pocket and a caddy who was likening the excellence of the plaintiff's golf to that of the defendant's product. Prima facie the advertisement was favourable to the plaintiff. However, he successfully alleged that the advertisement was capable of being defamatory of him because it would be understood to mean that he had agreed to his image being used for commercial purposes and thus that he had compromised his amateur status in the eyes of other amateur golfers. Words may therefore be defamatory on their ordinary and natural meaning and also in the light of facts and circumstances known to particular persons to whom they are published. Each innuendo constitutes a separate cause of action on which a plaintiff may found a claim and each must be separately justified. A person who publishes information critical of another must therefore be careful to ensure that his words do not carry any unjustifiable innuendo. The defendants in *Chapman* v. *Lord Ellesmere*[12] failed to achieve this. Following the discovery that a racehorse, which had won a race, had been doped, agents acting for the Jockey Club (the rule-making organisation for the sport) issued to the press and published on the Racing Calender a statement which recorded that stewards of the club had found the horse to have been doped and that the plaintiff, the horse's trainer, had been "warned off Newmarket Heath." This effectively amounted to the club withdrawing the plaintiff's licence to train horses for races run under its auspices. The words published were justifiable, in the natural and ordinary meaning, the plaintiff having been found to have offended not by administering the drug or by being a party to the administration but by having negligently allowed other persons to do this. However, the plaintiff was successful in proving an innuendo to the effect that the "warning off" meant that he had been party to the doping.

The type of innuendo described in the previous paragraph is traditionally known as the "true" innuendo. It must be distinguished from a "false" innuendo, which describes the process whereby the plaintiff, in order to assist his case, expressly pleads, without relying on extrinsic evidence, what

[11] [1931] A.C. 333.
[12] [1932] 2 K.B. 431.

is alleged to be the natural and ordinary meaning of the words. This is not truly an innuendo and does not create a separate cause of action. The "ordinary and natural" meaning of words cannot be divorced from the context in which they were used and, as a result, if the plaintiff chooses to restrict his complaint to a part of the publication the jury will be entitled to see, read and consider the whole of it.[13]

Reference to the plaintiff

The defamatory words must refer to the plaintiff. The question on this issue is whether an ordinary sensible person would understand the words to refer to the plaintiff. The strict nature of liability for defamation is shown by the rule that it is unnecessary for the defendant to have intended the words to have so referred, he need not have made an explicit reference to the plaintiff and he need not know of the plaintiff's existence or of the special facts which caused readers with particular knowledge to link the statement to the plaintiff. The only relevant issue is the understanding of the ordinary sensible person.

These principles are illustrated by a number of cases, the most important of which is *E. Hulton & Co.* v. *Jones*.[14] A newspaper published what appeared to be a humorous article about the behaviour of a fictitious person called Artemus Jones. Unknown to the author of the piece or the editor of the paper the plaintiff was known by that name. He brought an action for libel alleging that some of his friends had supposed the article to refer to him and that the words were actionable even though, as he admitted, the defendants had no intention of defaming him and did not know of him. The House of Lords, in upholding the claim, emphasised the strict nature of liability for defamation. The responsibility for defamation is based on what reasonable persons understand the defendant's words to mean rather than on what was intended. This approach was taken a stage further in *Newstead* v. *London Express Newspaper Ltd.*[15] a case in which the defendants, having published a true story about the trial for bigamy of a Camberwell man called Harold Newstead, were faced by a libel action brought by another man of the same name who lived in the same area. Again it was held that the recklessness or honesty of the author was not relevant. The protection for the publisher was said to lie in his giving a precise description of the person whose affairs he was describing. The risk of coincidence should not be borne by the innocent party who had no means of controlling the accuracy of the story.

The combination of the rules on innocent defamation with those on innuendo can make liability particularly strict at common law. However, the courts have not shrunk from the conclusion that the rules may operate together. In *Cassidy* v. *Daily Mirror Newspapers Ltd.*[16] the defendants published a photograph of a man, who was well-known in horse-racing circles, and a woman with a caption which recorded that the couple had announced their engagement to marry. The plaintiff, who was unknown to the defendants, was, and was known to be, already married to the man. She claimed damages for defamation on the basis that the publication libelled her

---

[13] *Thompson* v.*Bernard* (1807) 1 Camp. 48.
[14] [1910] A.C. 20.
[15] [1940] 1 K.B. 377.
[16] [1929] 2 K.B. 331.

by implying that she was an immoral woman who had cohabited with the man outside of wedlock. The Court of Appeal, in finding for the plaintiff, adopted the principle of *Hulton* that liability depends on the fact of defamation rather than the intention of the defendant. A newspaper's protection was said to lie in its making proper enquiry as to the truth of the material published. Although these rules are stringent, the Faulks Committee[17] was of the view that this is the correct balance between the interests of innocent parties and of publishers such as newspapers. Section 4 of the Defamation Act 1952[18] attempts to provide a procedure under which a person who has defamed another innocently can escape the full rigours of defamation liability by making an offer of an apology. However, the drafting of the section means that it has had little use.[19]

It is accepted that the ordinary sensible reader may read material such as newspaper articles in a fairly cursory fashion; such articles are intended to be so read and the defendant's words will be judged according to the interpretation that an ordinary sensible reader might give to them after such a reading. In *Morgan* v. *Odhams Press Ltd.*[20] the House of Lords held that the court should be realistic in its assessment of the way in which ordinary people read and draw information from such articles. The fact that such an article can be shown on careful analysis to contain discrepancies and inconsistencies is no bar to its constituting defamation as the ordinary sensible reader may very well be inclined to discount such inaccuracies, if indeed he notices them, on the grounds that newspapers commonly contain inaccuracies.

It is no defence for a defendant to show that the particular person to whom the defamation was published did not believe the truth of what was said.[21] The plaintiff may still suffer annoyance and hurt from the fact of such publication and fear that other reasonable persons will believe it. The plaintiff may therefore wish to attempt to restrain any further publication of such defamatory matter by means of an injunction.

It is commonly said that the requirement that the words must refer to the plaintiff means that it is impossible to defame a whole class of persons as the reference to any individual will not be explicit enough. The famous statement of Willes J.[22] that no lawyer could sue on the basis of a statement that "all lawyers are thieves" is often cited in this context. This should be approached with some care. Willes J.'s example is in fact little more than generalised abuse, and as we have seen, the reference to the plaintiff need not be express. The correct approach would seem to be to say that if a defamatory statement is directed at a whole class of persons an individual can only sue on it if he can show that reasonable persons would take him to be referred to. This approach is supported by the decision of the House of Lords in *Knupffer* v. *London Express Newspapers*[23] in which the defendants published an article concerning a Russian emigré group which operated in France and USA and described them as the "Quislings on whom Hitler flatters himself he can build a pro-German group in Russia." The plaintiff, who had been a leading

[17] para. 122.
[18] Discussed *post*, p. 449.
[19] See *post*, p. 449 for a discussion of this provision and of other proposals to introduce a procedure whereby an "innocent" defendant could make an "offer of amends."
[20] [1971] 1 W.L.R. 1239.
[21] *Morgan* v. *Odhams Press Ltd.* [1971] 1 W.L.R. 1239.
[22] *Eastwood* v. *Holmes* (1958) 1 F. & F. 347.
[23] [1944] A.C. 116.

member of the small English branch of this group claimed that the article defamed him. The House of Lords rejected this, not on the simple ground that the article was defamation of a class, but because there was insufficient material in the article to constitute a reference to him personally. The article said nothing about the views of particular members of the group and made no reference to the small number of members based in England.

Publication

Publication of defamatory matter is made when it is communicated to a person other than the plaintiff. The fact that defamation is defined as matter liable to lower the plaintiff's reputation in the eyes of others means that it is impossible to defame a person if the words are only published to him. If a true innuendo is alleged as the basis of the claim it must be shown that the words were published to a specific person or persons who would understand the innuendo. Words will not count as having been published if they come to the attention of third parties by the unauthorised and unforeseeable acts of others. On this basis no publication occurred when a letter directed to the plaintiff and alleged to be defamatory of her was opened and read by the plaintiff's inquisitive butler in an admitted breach of his duty.[24] It is, however, normal practice in modern business for secretarial staff to open and read correspondence addressed to persons for whom they work. If a letter is opened in this fashion a publication to a third party will have occurred.[25]

Every repetition of defamatory matter technically counts as a fresh publication giving rise to a new cause of action. It is on this basis that the author, publisher, printer and distributor of printed matter will all be independently liable for the tort. However, in the case of a widely publicised defamation, the practice is to bring a single action against those responsible and to regard the width and number of the publications as solely relevant to calculating damages.

The requirement of publication is commonly stated to be that the statement must have been published "maliciously." The use of "malice" is misleading in this context. As we have seen, a defendant may be held liable for defamation irrespective of his state of mind or intention when publishing; even if he is wholly innocent of an intention to damage the plaintiff.

Who can bring a claim?

Claims for defamation are not confined to individuals; it is well established that trading companies and other corporations have "trading reputations" which they can protect by defamation proceedings. Such bodies may find that their capacity to borrow money or attract staff has been damaged by defamatory statements and they are not required to show that a specific item

---

[24] *Huth* v. *Huth* [1915] 3 K.B. 32. It was held to make no difference that the letter was sent unsealed. Because of their nature, there is a presumption that the contents of postcards and telegrams has been published to the postal services.

[25] Marking the letter "confidential" or "private and confidential" would probably not be sufficient to stop publication occurring. The issue would turn on evidence of modern business practice and it is suggested that letters so marked are commonly opened by secretarial staff. Marking the letter "personal" should be sufficient to stop publication.

of loss has been suffered,[26] although any damages awarded must relate to financial losses and cannot extend to hurt and annoyance for the obvious reason that such bodies have no feelings which can be hurt.[27] One exception to this approach is that local authorities (and other government bodies) are not able to bring claims to protect their "governing reputations." In *Derbyshire County Council* v. *Times Newspapers Ltd.*[28] the House of Lords held that it would be contrary to the public interest for a local authority to be allowed to bring proceedings for defamation. It was said to be of the highest importance that the affairs of public bodies should be subject to scrutiny and observed that there is no bar on members or officers of an authority using the tort to protect their reputations against defamations concerning the exercise of their duties. The common law result was said to be consistent with that produced by the right to freedom of expression contained in the European Convention on Human Rights.

Defamation claims cannot be brought to defend the reputation of a person who is dead, no matter how much distress has been caused to relatives and acquaintances of the deceased. Furthermore the provisions of the Law Reform (Miscellaneous Provisions) Act 1934 do not apply to defamation proceedings with the result that the death of either party to a defamation action will cause it to lapse. It was reported that the death of the publisher Robert Maxwell resulted in a large number of defamation cases being discontinued. The reasons which are traditionally given for these rules are that defamation claims, in so far as they serve to protect a person against injury to feelings, are of a peculiarly personal nature and that it may be very difficult to achieve justice in such a case if one of the parties is unable to give evidence. Neither of these reasons would seem to be particularly compelling. It may be particularly unfortunate for a plaintiff to discover that a good claim has lapsed simply because of the death of the defendant; such a plaintiff may have already incurred substantial costs in pursuing the case. Other "personal" actions such as those brought for malicious prosecution, false imprisonment and pain and suffering do survive the death of either of the parties. The Faulks Committee was of the view that the decision to omit defamation from the 1934 Act was made merely because of the urgency of getting the legislation passed and proposed that a claim which had been started before the death (of either party) should be allowed to continue and that the estate of a deceased person should be entitled to start proceedings for an injunction or to recover pecuniary loss.[29] The majority of the Committee also recommended that a claim for a declaration with regard to the defamation of a deceased person should be available to close relatives of that person for five years after the death.[30] Nothing has been done to implement these proposals. In 1990 the Lord Chancellor's Department issued a consultation paper[31] on the question of whether a claim for defamation suffered during the lifetime of the person defamed should be allowed to survive the death of one of the parties. However, in 1991 the Department reported that the

---

[26] *South Hetton Coal Co. Ltd.* v. *North Eastern News Association Ltd.* [1894] 1 Q.B. 133. The Faulks Committee proposed to limit such claims to cases in which the plaintiff had suffered special damage or could prove that he was likely to do so (para. 342).

[27] Lord Reid in *Lewis* v. *Daily Telegraph* [1964] A.C. 234 at 262.

[28] [1993] 1 All E.R. 1011.

[29] para. 415.

[30] para. 421.

[31] *Defamation: Death of a party to defamation proceedings.*

divergence of views expressed during the consultation process had led it to
conclude that it was inappropriate to amend the law.

Who can be liable?

Every person who participates in the publication of defamatory matter is
liable for the defamation. It is on this basis that defamatory matter published
in a newspaper is likely to result in liability being imposed on the author, the
paper's publishers and editor, the printer and the distributor. A distributor
may be able to take advantage of a defence known as innocent
dissemination.[32]

The question of whether a person who publishes a libel is liable for damage
resulting from the fact that another person has republished it is decided
according to standard principles of remoteness of damage. A good example
of this problem occurred in *Slipper* v. *British Broadcasting Corporation*[33]
when a person who alleged that he had been defamed in a television
programme sought to be allowed to argue that press reviews of the programme which repeated the substance of the allegations were relevant to
assessing the loss which the defendant had caused to him. The Court of
Appeal refused to accept that this part of the claim disclosed no cause of
action and should be struck out.

What damage must be caused?

The kind of damage which must be proved for success in a defamation
action varies according to whether the defamation is classified as libel or as
slander. At the simplest level the distinction between libel and slander is that
between defamation which is published in a permanent form, such as writing
(libel) and that in transient form, such as spoken words or gestures (slander).
However, the distinction is not always clear cut[34] and modern technology
has created a number of problem cases. Legislation has tended to classify the
doubtful cases, stage plays,[35] television and radio broadcasts[36] as libel.

The distinction between libel and slander is only of relevance in relation to
the damage which must be proved in order to establish a cause of action. In
the case of libels, damage will be presumed to have resulted. Slanders on the
other hand, with certain exceptions, will not be actionable unless actual
damage, that is, the loss of some material benefit, is proved.

Four kinds of slander are, exceptionally, actionable without proof of
damage (actionable *per se*). They are: an imputation that the plaintiff has
committed a criminal offence punishable by imprisonment; an imputation
that the plaintiff is suffering from an infectious or contagious disease which is
likely to prevent others from associating with him; an imputation of adultery
or unchastity made against a woman or girl[37] and an imputation as to the
competence, honesty or fitness of a person in any office, profession, calling,

---

[32] See *post*, p. 450. The Faulks Committee (para. 309) proposed that this defence should be
extended to printers.

[33] [1991] 1 All E.R. 165.

[34] For example, Greer L.J. in *Osborn* v. *Thomas Boulter & Son* [1930] 2 K.B. 226 was inclined
to the view that dictation to a typist amounts to libel.

[35] Theatres Act 1968.

[36] Defamation Act 1952, s.1.

[37] Slander of Women Act 1891.

trade or business. This final form of slander can be actionable *per se* even though the conduct alleged did not take place in the course of the office, etc.[38]

The distinction between libel and slander attracts considerable criticism. It is difficult to accept that spoken words are invariably less damaging than written ones, particularly as the spread of slanders may be wholly uncontrollable whereas there may, on occasions, be some possibility of recalling defamatory matter which is in written form. A particular anomaly which can arise is that a person who records spoken defamatory words may bear a greater responsibility than their originator. The Faulks Committee[39] was of the view that the distinction between libel and slander was an historical accident and that the result was illogical, complex and unjust. The Committee discounted the objection that the distinction prevents the courts being faced by many trivial actions based on slanders and concluded that the distinction should be abolished and that the question of the damage which needed to be proven to establish a cause of action should be governed by the libel rules.

Defences

1. The defence of truth (justification)

Truth, known technically as the defence of justification,[40] is a complete defence to a charge of defamation. One of the many issues raised in the leading case of *Lewis* v. *The Daily Telegraph*[41] provides a good example of this. It is defamatory of a person to say that his affairs are being investigated by the fraud squad as this is likely to lower his reputation in the eyes of others. However, if the statement is true, as it was on the facts of the case, no tort has been committed.

The defendant bears the burden of proving the truth of his statement and the plaintiff is entitled to know what defence he has to meet. In recent years courts have tried to simplify proceedings by insisting that a defendant must state clearly in the pleadings the meanings which are intended to be justified.[42] If the defence of justification is established then the fact that the words were published maliciously or relate to conduct which has been long forgotten is irrelevant. This rule is justified on the basis that the publication of long forgotten facts about a person merely reduces his reputation to its correct level. It was suggested to the Faulks Committee that this defence should only be available in the case of statements of which publication was in the public interest. However, the Committee rejected this on the basis that the notion of public benefit would be virtually impossible to define, particularly in the case of private correspondence, and because it believed that damages for defamation should not be available in relation to statements of the truth, whatever the motive for publication.[43]

Justification creates particular difficulties as a result of the rule that the true meaning of words is for the jury to determine. It is therefore sensible

---

[38] Defamation Act 1952, s. 2.
[39] See Chap. 2.
[40] The Faulks Committee proposed that the defence should be renamed truth.
[41] [1964] A.C. 234.
[42] *Lucas – Box* v. *News Group Newspapers Ltd.* [1986] 1 All E.R. 177; *Morrell* v. *International Thomson Publishing Ltd.* [1989] 3 All E.R. 733.
[43] para. 138.

tactics for a plaintiff to plead the widest possible range of meanings that the words may be capable of bearing in order to attempt to increase the insult and the damages and to put the defence under the greatest pressure. A defendant who seeks to justify must face the possibility that a failure to convince a jury of the truth of the statements may result in the defence aggravating the hurt suffered by the plaintiff and hence increasing the damages payable.

The courts have evolved a complex set of rules to deal with this situation. If a statement is capable of bearing a number of meanings, for instance as a result of innuendoes, each meaning constitutes a separate potential defamation which must be justified. However, it is important to decide whether the statement has different meanings or whether it merely contains a number of different allegations addressed to the same charge. A number of difficult cases have concerned the scope of the charge which needs to be justified and have discussed whether it is open to the defence to raise other alleged acts of the plaintiff on the basis that the plaintiff has alleged that he has been charged with general rather than specific forms of wrongdoing. There is a delicate balance to be struck here. On the one hand the law should seek to stop the defendant extending the scope of the proceedings and increasing their cost by wide ranging allegations of general misdeeds on the plaintiff's part. On the other hand, the plaintiff should not be entitled to limit his complaint and hence the scope of the proceedings in such a way as to stop the defendant justifying the substance of the charge made. Given the infinite variety of circumstances in which this problem can arise it is not surprising that narrow factual distinctions have sometimes been made; however, it is suggested that the law has developed along the correct lines.

A good example of these difficulties is provided by *Bookbinder* v. *Tebbit*.[44] There it was alleged that the defendant, a leading politician, had, in the course of a speech given at an election meeting, defamed the plaintiff, who was the leader of a county council. The Council had adopted a policy of overprinting all stationery used in its schools with the words "Support Nuclear Free Zones." The defendant, in his speech, was alleged to have referred to the alleged cost of this policy and to have described it as a "damn fool idea." The plaintiff alleged that the words were defamatory of him because on their "ordinary and natural meaning" they bore the meaning that he had acted irresponsibly in causing a large scale squandering of public funds. The defendant argued that the words were incapable of bearing a defamatory meaning or, if they were, that he could rely on the defences of fair comment or justification. On the issue of justification he wished to adduce evidence not only in relation to the overprinting but also in relation to a wide range of other council activities which were alleged to constitute the squandering of public money. Faced with the prospect of the case causing a long and expensive review of the council's activities the plaintiff sought, and obtained, permission to amend his pleading to restrict the allegation that he had been defamed to the specific issue of the overprinting. The defendant, however, resisted the application to have the wider form of the justification defence struck out. The Court of Appeal allowed the plaintiff's application. It held that the words, in the context in which they were published, were not capable of raising a general charge of the squandering of public money and that a plaintiff ought to be free to prove the untruth of a specific charge

---

[44] [1989] 1 All E.R. 1169.

without having to face the burden of a trial directed to any number of preceding incidents.

However, the result in such a case is heavily dependent on the particular facts. It would be different if a specific allegation merely forms part of a general charge of misconduct made against the plaintiff. If this is the case, it is open to the defendant to plead in his defence any circumstances which may go to justify the general charge and the plaintiff will not be allowed to restrict matters raised by the defendant's pleading by limiting his claim to certain allegations. A good example of this is provided by *Williams* v. *Reason*[45] in which the plaintiff, a well known Rugby Union player, claimed damages on the basis that he had been libelled by an article which alleged that he had written a book for money in breach of his union's rules and while continuing to purport to be an amateur player. In the course of the proceedings the defendants sought leave to adduce evidence that the plaintiff had, whilst playing the sport, received payments from boot manufacturers in return for wearing their boots in matches. The Court of Appeal held that this evidence was admissible as justification for the publication on the basis that the articles complained of made a general allegation of "shamateurism," hypocrisy and deviousness on the plaintiff's part. The evidence relating to "boot money" was admissible in relation to the general sting of the libel.

It is therefore necessary to decide whether the evidence put forward as justification relates to separate and distinct charges from those complained of or goes to justify a "general sting" running through the publication. The distinction is a matter of fact and degree[46] and there is obviously room for considerable differences of opinion as to its application to particular cases. A good example of such differences is provided by a New Zealand case[47] in which the plaintiff, a parliamentary candidate, had been described as a man "who despised bureaucrats, politicians, women, jews and professionals." He brought defamation proceedings confined to the allegation that he despised Jews. The defence was unsuccessful in its attempt to lead evidence to justify the other charges; it being said that the publication consisted of distinct and severable allegations. A subsequent English decision[48] doubted this result on the basis that the words in the context in which they were used were capable of carrying the general sting that the plaintiff was an intolerant bigot who preached the politics of hatred for political advantage.

Where a publication contains two or more distinct allegations against the plaintiff and the defendant is only able to justify some of them he will be held liable at common law in respect of those which he is not able to justify. However, the evidence justifying some charges may, in practice, mitigate the damages awarded on the charges established. In Lord Denning's words the plaintiff ought not to "recover damages for a character which he does not possess or deserve."[49] Thus partial justification may mitigate damages on a successful charge of defamation. Section 5 of the Defamation Act 1952 takes this approach further and allows for a defence of partial justification to a defendant who makes a number of distinct allegations against a person and who cannot justify all of them. The defence is allowed to succeed in spite of

---

[45] [1988] 1 All E.R. 262.
[46] *Polly Peck (Holdings) plc* v. *Trelford* [1986] 2 All E.R. 84.
[47] *Templeton* v. *Jones* [1984] 1 N.Z.L.R. 448.
[48] *Polly Peck (Holdings) plc* v. *Trelford* [1986] 2 All E.R. 84 at 102.
[49] *Plato Films Ltd.* v. *Speidel* [1961] A.C. 1090.

the failure to prove the truth of all of the allegations if the untrue allegation would not materially harm the plaintiff's reputation, in view of the truth of the other allegations made. It therefore prevents a defamation claim being based on the untruth of allegations which are trivial in the context of the overall situation. It follows that a person who alleges that another has committed ten offences of theft but can only prove that eight were committed is likely to have a defence of justification available. The scope of this section is limited. It requires two or more distinct charges of defamation to have been made and it does not apply if the plaintiff only alleges that a single charge is defamatory of him nor if the defendant argues that there are no distinct charges but rather two or more allegations with a common sting.[50] It also seems unlikely that it protects a defendant who can only establish the truth of a lesser charge than that alleged. For example, if the defendant alleged that the plaintiff had been convicted of rape but could only establish a conviction for indecent assault.[51]

Criminal offences

Two special rules apply to statements which allege that a person has committed a criminal offence.

Section 13 of the Civil Evidence Act 1968 provides that proof that a person stands convicted of a criminal offence is conclusive evidence in defamation proceedings of the fact that that person actually committed that offence. This provision prevents defamation proceedings being used as a means of collateral attack on a criminal conviction and eases the task of persons who report or comment on the decisions of criminal courts.[52] No equivalent provision exists in relation to other lesser forms of disciplinary proceedings.

The defence of justification is subject to a special restriction when it is used in relation to those criminal offences which are covered by the Rehabilitation of Offenders Act 1974. This Act permits certain categories of convicted offenders to treat their conviction as "spent" and as not requiring disclosure after a set rehabilitation period. In spite of this policy, the defence of justification remains available to a person who reveals that another has been convicted of such an offence. However, the defence of justification can be defeated in such cases by proof of malice on the part of the person publishing the information.

2. Fair Comment: the protection of opinions and criticism

The defence of fair comment is commonly regarded as central to the law's protection of freedom of speech. The defence is designed to protect honest criticism from the law of defamation. The name of the defence is somewhat confusing as the defence may well protect extreme criticism which many persons would regard as unfair.[53] A number of requirements must be satisfied: the comment must relate to a matter of public interest; it must be an expression of opinion as opposed to an assertion of fact and the opinion must have been honestly held by the defendant: proof of malice will defeat the defence. The defendant must spell out the defence in the pleadings with

---

[50] *Polly Peck (Holdings) plc v. Trelford* [1986] 2 All E.R. 84.
[51] An example given in Duncan and Neill on *Defamation* (2nd ed.), p. 53.
[52] Previously they faced the task of having to prove the guilt of the convicted person.
[53] The Faulks Committee (para. 152) proposed that the defence should be renamed comment.

sufficient precision to enable the plaintiff to know the case that must be met.[54]

Proof that the statement relates to a matter of public interest is relatively easy to establish. Comments on any matter in which the public are legitimately interested are protected. As a result the defence covers comments on a wide range of matters ranging from the behaviour of public figures and institutions to the quality and fate of entertainments offered to the public.[55]

The distinction between expressions of opinion and statements of fact can be difficult to draw. If a defendant asserts facts the appropriate defence is justification.[56] The role of fair comment is to protect opinions rather than assertions of fact. A plea of fair comment will fail if it is impossible to disentangle the comment from statements of fact. It is a jury function to determine whether particular statements amount to assertions of fact or are comment and the decision of the House of Lords in *Telnikoff* v. *Matusevitch*[57] establishes that this decision turns, as a matter of construction, on the document in question and that reference cannot be made to the items on which the comment was based. Although critics[58] of this rule argue that it emasculates the defence, particularly in the context of a newspaper which wishes to publish a reader's response to another item, its supporters take the view that a publication should be judged on its own terms because this reflects the fact that those who read the publication may well not have access to the original work which provides the basis for the comment or assertions of fact in question. However, it is essential to establish the truth of the facts underlying the comment because a person is not allowed to invent facts and then to comment on them under the protection of free speech. This rule is subject to two exceptions. First, it is permissible to comment on untrue statements published under the protection of privilege so long as the report constitutes a fair and accurate report of the statements.[59] Secondly, section 6 of the Defamation Act 1952 enacts a rule equivalent to that concerning justification found in section 5. A defendant's plea of fair comment will not fail simply because some of the allegations of fact on which the comment was based prove to be unfounded so long as the expression of opinion was fair comment having regard to such of the facts as are proved to be true.

The facts upon which the statement of opinion is based need not be stated expressly in the publication. In *Kemsley* v. *Foot*[60] it was alleged that an article which was severely critical of the publications of the Beaverbrook press was defamatory of the plaintiff, another newspaper group, because it carried the headline "Lower than Kemsley." The plaintiffs argued that a fair comment defence could not succeed as nothing in the article supported criticism of the plaintiff. It was said to be necessary for facts to be provided so that a reader might be able to judge the criticism himself. The House of Lords held that the defence could be available on these facts as a sufficient substratum of fact supporting the criticism of the plaintiff could be drawn from the context of the publication.

---

[54] *Control Risks Ltd.* v. *New English Library Ltd.* [1989] 3 All E.R. 577.
[55] *London Artists Ltd.* v. *Littler* [1969] 2 Q.B. 375.
[56] *London Artists Ltd.* v. *Littler* [1969] 2 Q.B. 375.
[57] [1991] 4 All E.R. 817, discussed (1992) 55 M.L.R. 278.
[58] See the dissenting speech of Lord Ackner in *Telnikoff*.
[59] *Brent Walker Group plc* v. *Time Out Ltd.* [1991] 2 All E.R. 753.
[60] [1952] A.C. 345.

The title of the defence is potentially misleading. The criticism need not be "fair" in the sense that the jury should agree with it. Extreme, exaggerated or violent criticism may be protected. All that needs to be proved by the defendant is that the opinion was one which an honest, albeit prejudiced, person might legitimately have reached. There is no additional "subjective" requirement to the effect that the defendant must prove that the comment reflected his own, honestly held, opinion.[61] This rule means that a newspaper is often able to use the defence in relation to items written by others which it "publishes" whether or not the opinion expressed reflects the editorial views of the paper. It was on the basis that the defence has the capacity to protect unfair or extreme opinions that the Faulks Committee proposed to rename it "comment." It must be remembered, however, that the significance of the lack of a requirement of subjective belief in the definition of fair comment is qualified by the fact that the defence is lost if the plaintiff can prove that the defendant's comment was actuated by malice. If it can be shown that the defendant published with malice, either lacking an honest belief in the truth of the comment or, having such belief, published the comment from motives of spite, ill-will or for some other improper reason,[62] the defence will be lost even though other, albeit prejudiced, persons might have honestly held the opinion expressed.

3. Innocent defamation

As has been seen, the strict characteristics of liability for defamation mean that a defendant who acted in all innocence may be held liable. The provisions of section 4 of the Defamation Act 1952 offer a procedure whereby this liability may be avoided by the making of a proper apology. The section applies only to words which have been published "innocently." This is defined to cover circumstances either in which the publisher did not intend to publish them of and concerning the plaintiff and did not know of circumstances by virtue of which they might be understood to refer to him, or, where the words were not defamatory on their face and the publisher did not know of the circumstances by virtue of which they might be understood to be defamatory. In both cases, the publisher, in order to establish the defence, must prove that he exercised all reasonable care in relation to the publication. If these conditions are satisfied it is open to the publisher to make an offer of amends. This involves offering to publish or join in the publication of a suitable correction and apology and, where copies of a libel have been distributed by or with the knowledge of the person making the offer, to take such steps as are reasonably practicable for notifying persons to whom copies have been distributed that the words are alleged to be defamatory. If the offer of amends is accepted by the plaintiff and duly performed by the defendant no further proceedings between these parties in relation to this

---

[61] *Telnikoff* v. *Matusevitch* [1991] 4 All E.R. 817.

[62] The Faulks Committee recognised that the shifting of the burden of proof on these similar matters "poses a difficult task for the tribunal of fact" (para. 156) and proposed to redefine malice as a comment which "did not represent the defendant's genuine opinion" (para. 159). See Sutherland, (1992) 55 M.L.R. 278 for a discussion of the meaning of the word "malice" in the context of the defence of fair comment. Sutherland comments that the issue whether malice is proved by showing that the defendant intended to injure the plaintiff or by merely showing the existence of any motive other than that of expressing a genuine critical opinion is of particular importance to a person who publishes a defamatory statement of which he is not the original author.

matter are possible. It will not, however, protect other parties who were jointly responsible with the defendant for the publication. If the offer is not accepted, the person making it is given a defence in subsequent proceedings if he can show that the words were published "innocently" in relation to the plaintiff; that the offer was made as soon as practicable after the defendant received notice that the words were or might be defamatory of the plaintiff and that the offer has not been subsequently withdrawn. If the publisher was not the author of the words, it will also need to be proved that the words were written by the author without malice.[63]

The underlying purpose of section 4 is to ensure that cases of innocent defamation can be settled by the parties without recourse to litigation. However, the Faulks Committee,[64] whilst accepting that this was a valuable aim, condemned the section as containing "defects which render it difficult to operate if not unworkable"[65] and, in particular, criticised two features of the procedure which it suggested had resulted in little use being made of the section. The first was the requirement that any offer of amends must be accompanied by an affidavit specifying the facts relied upon as proving the publisher's innocence. This procedure was regarded as laborious, time-consuming and expensive. The affidavit requirement also places the publisher in a difficult tactical position because, if the offer of amends is refused, he cannot use evidence omitted from the affidavit in any subsequent proceedings to support a claim of innocence. The publisher therefore has a great incentive to ensure that all evidence relevant to the defence of innocence is collected and included in the affidavit which accompanies the offer of amends, but, he has to balance this need against the risk of his being unable to prove that the offer of amends was made as soon as practicable after the receipt of the complaint.[66] Secondly, there seems to be no reason in principle why a publisher who is not the author of the defamation should have a defence of innocence turn on whether he can prove that the original author wrote the words without malice.

The Neill Committee,[67] which reported in 1991, proposed that a defendant should be allowed to make an offer of amends, a published correction and apology, in relation to any libel which had not been published intentionally or recklessly. If such an offer was not accepted any issue of damages would be assessed by a judge rather than a jury. This proposal has been welcomed[68] but would still leave scope for a plaintiff to attempt to prove recklessness in the form of a failure to make such inquiries as could, and should, have been made.

4. Innocent dissemination

A defendant, such as a newsagent, bookseller or librarian, who is deemed to be the publisher of a libel because he distributed the document which contained it may be able to take advantage of a defence of innocent

---

[63] s. 4(6).
[64] Chap. 9.
[65] para. 281.
[66] In *Ross* v. *Hopkinson* [1956] C.L.Y. 5011 an offer of amends made six weeks after the complaint was received was held not to have been made as soon as practicable.
[67] Supreme Court Procedure Committee, *Working Group Report on Practice and Procedure in Defamation*.
[68] Robertson & Nicol, *Media Law* (1992), p. 95. It is reported, at the time of writing, that the Lord Chancellor is intending to introduce legislation which would establish this defence.

dissemination.[69] This defence allows a person to escape liability if he can prove: (a) that he distributed the publication without knowing that it contained a libel; (b) that there was nothing in the work or in the circumstances of its publication which ought to have led him to suppose that it contained a libel and (c) that he was not negligent in failing to appreciate that the publication contained a libel at the time that he distributed it. In *Vizetelly* v. *Mudie's Select Library Ltd.*[70] a decision taken by a library that it was too burdensome to check the contents of books to be issued and a failure to see recall notices placed in the appropriate trade press by the publishers was held to be sufficient prima facie evidence of negligence by the library for the issue to go to the decision of the jury.

The Faulks Committee[71] was of the view that this defence should be extended to protect printers and in 1991 the Lord Chancellor's Department committed itself to introducing legislation along these lines. Technological advances in the printing industry mean that printers may no longer need to read the material which they are typesetting and producing and it is therefore difficult to avoid the conclusion that they should be given the protection of this defence.

5. Consent

The consent of the person defamed is a complete defence. As a result a person who agrees to appear in a television programme to answer specific allegations concerning his conduct cannot bring a defamation claim in relation to those allegations.

The best known examples of this defence have concerned persons who, by agreeing to become subject to the disciplinary code of an association, have consented to the risk that the findings of disciplinary proceedings concerning them will be published. No complaint may be made in relation to true statements of the findings of disciplinary bodies published within the rules of the association. The leading cases, which both concerned horse racing, are *Chapman* v. *Lord Ellesmere*[72] and *Cookson* v. *Harewood*.[73] In the former case, the plaintiff, a trainer, had agreed to be subject to the rules of the Jockey Club. He alleged that he had been libelled by the publication, in the manner provided by the club's rules, of a finding by its stewards that a horse which he had trained had been found after a race to have been doped. This statement could be justified in its ordinary and natural meaning, but not on the innuendo that the plaintiff himself had been responsible for the doping. The plaintiff's assent to publication was held to provide a complete defence. He was held to have assented to the risk of being libelled by an innuendo when he agreed to be subject to the club's rules. In the words of Scrutton L.J. in *Cookson* " . . . these questions about innuendoes are quite beside the mark. If you get a true statement and an authority to publish the true statement, it does not matter in the least what people will understand it to mean."

---

[69] Support exists for regarding innocent dissemination as negativing the fact of publication as opposed to providing a defence, see the judgment of Romer L.J. in *Vizetelly* v. *Mudie's Select Library Ltd.* [1900] 2 K.B. 170. However, as the burden of proving innocent dissemination rests with the defendant it seems preferable to treat it as a defence.

[70] [1900] 2 K.B. 170.

[71] para. 309.

[72] [1932] 2 K.B. 431.

[73] [1932] 2 K.B. 478n.

This defence will usually be restricted to providing defences to innuendoes in circumstances in which the plaintiff had agreed to the publication of the truth. It is unlikely, but not impossible, that a court will find that a plaintiff consented to have untrue words spoken about himself. If this is the case the defence should still apply. To establish the defence the plaintiff must be shown to have authorised the publication. The mere fact that a person has jokingly told the libel about himself to a group of his friends does not amount to his assenting to others spreading the libel more widely.[74]

6. Privilege defences

These defences are based on the occasion on which a defamatory statement is published rather than on the content of the statement. In certain circumstances freedom of speech is regarded as of such importance that no defamation claim can be brought in relation to statements made on that occasion, even if the statement cannot be justified. There are two kinds of privilege defence to a defamation action: absolute privilege, which admits of no exceptions, and qualified privilege, which can be defeated by proof of malice on the part of the person publishing.

Privilege as a defence to a defamation action must be distinguished from several other kinds of privilege. Evidential privilege is a rule of evidence which enables a party to refuse to disclose documents to the other side of a dispute. The two forms of privilege are distinct even though they overlap; for example, documents passing between solicitor and client in relation to impending litigation are likely to be privileged in both senses. The important feature of defamation privilege is that no cause of action may be founded on a statement even though the document which contains it is before the court in evidence. Parliamentary privilege has similar effect to evidential privilege. This privilege is based on the principle that the Houses of Parliament are the exclusive judges of their own affairs and that their deliberations should be free from consideration by the courts.[75] This form of privilege excludes evidence relating to proceedings in Parliament from the courts. At times there is a complete overlap between the Parliamentary and defamation privilege because statements made by members of either House of Parliament in the course of proceedings are accorded absolute privilege in defamation proceedings. However, a defamation case may prove impossible to pursue because evidence is not admissible on account of Parliamentary privilege. This kind of privilege does not technically create a defence, it merely creates hurdles for the plaintiff who wishes to prove his case.[76]

Absolute privilege

In a limited number of situations freedom of speech is regarded as of such paramount importance that no claim for defamation is possible irrespective of malice on the part of the person who published a statement. Statements made on such occasions are said to attract absolute privilege. Absolute

---

[74] Cook v. Ward (1836) 6 Bing. 409.
[75] The basis of the privilege is Art. 9 of the Bill of Rights 1688.
[76] Parliamentary rather than defamation privilege is the explanation of the decisions in Church of Scientology v. Johnson-Smith [1972] 1 Q.B. 522 and Rost v. Edwards [1990] 2 All E.R. 641. In the Scientology Case the defendant pleaded the defence of fair comment, privilege was used to prevent the plaintiff from producing evidence of Parliamentary proceedings in an attempt to rebut that defence.

privilege attaches to three sets of circumstances: proceedings in Parliament; judicial proceedings and certain official communications.

Proceedings in Parliament

All statements made in the course of Parliamentary proceedings are absolutely privileged. This covers statements made by members of Parliament in debates and proceedings of committees and by other persons giving evidence to committees. Under section 1 of the Parliamentary Papers Act 1840 this privilege is extended to the publication by order of either House of its reports, papers, votes or proceedings. Statements made by M.P.s outside Parliament are not privileged. Press and other reports of Parliamentary proceedings and extracts from Parliamentary papers are only accorded qualified privilege.

Judicial proceedings

Statements made in the course of judicial proceedings[77] by judges, counsel, witnesses and the parties are absolutely privileged.

This species of privilege extends to professional communications between solicitor and client relating to judicial proceedings. It is doubtful whether communications between solicitor and client on other topics can attract more than qualified privilege. In *More* v. *Weaver*[78] the Court of Appeal held that all communications between solicitor and client relevant to a matter under discussion were absolutely privileged. However, in a subsequent decision[79] the House of Lords seemed to prefer the view that the privilege was of a qualified character but did not need to reach a final decision.

Fair and accurate contemporaneous reports of judicial proceedings heard publicly in the U.K. are also accorded absolute privilege.[80] This allows newspapers to publish accurate reports of the evidence given in judicial proceedings whether or not the court ultimately accepts the accuracy of that evidence. As judicial proceedings are open to the public and the evidence given therein is absolutely privileged it is logical to extend the privilege to reports of the proceedings. Non-contemporaneous reports are accorded qualified privilege.

Official communications

Statements made by one officer of state to another in the course of his official duty attract absolute privilege. In *Chatterton* v. *Secretary of State for India*[81] the Court of Appeal held that the plaintiff could not bring a libel action in respect of statements made by the Secretary of State for India to his Under Secretary in order to enable a Parliamentary question to be answered.

---

[77] Including proceedings of tribunals and inquiries exercising judicial functions.
[78] [1928] 2 K.B. 520.
[79] *Minter* v. *Priest* [1930] A.C. 558.
[80] S. 3 of the Law of Libel Amendment Act 1888. The section merely speaks of "privilege." It is generally assumed to create an absolute privilege.
[81] [1895] 2 Q.B. 189.

The absolute privilege was said to be necessary to safeguard the independence and freedom of action of state officials with regard to matters of state.

It is uncertain whether this form of privilege extends beyond statements made by government ministers and senior civil servants to protect the communications of other categories of public officials. In *Merricks* v. *Nott-Blower*[82] the Court of Appeal declined to strike out as unarguable a libel claim based on an official communication between a Commissioner and a Deputy Assistant Commissioner of Police.

Qualified privilege

Qualified privilege is an important defence which covers a wider range of publications but is less powerful than absolute privilege. This kind of privilege will be lost if the plaintiff can prove that the defendant's defamatory statement was published maliciously. The malice restriction is an important constraint on this defence as without it, the defence would offer significant opportunities to persons to publish unremediable libels. Malice, in this context, is defined as taking improper advantage of an occasion to make accusations which are known to be false or making a defamatory statement recklessly not caring whether it is true. Taking improper advantage of an occasion of privilege in the sense of intending to damage the plaintiff rather than to protect a legitimate interest or perform a duty also constitutes malice. However, malice is not to be established by proof that the defendant, although honest, was prejudiced or arrived at his opinion in an impulsive or irrational manner.[83]

Interests and duties

This is one of the more difficult areas of the law of defamation, but also one of the most important defences. It is difficult because the law is expressed in different ways by different writers, applies to a wide variety of situations and is dependent upon notions which are difficult to define such as moral and social duties. It is important because it offers the benefit of qualified privilege to communications made in a considerable number of everyday circumstances.

The form of the defence is best summarised in the speech of Lord Atkinson in *Adam* v. *Ward*.[84] An occasion is privileged if a statement is published on "an occasion where the person who makes the communication has an interest or a duty, legal, social or moral, to make it to the person to whom it is made, and the person to whom it is so made has a corresponding interest or duty to receive it. This reciprocity is essential." The defence recognises that

---

[82] [1965] 1 Q.B. 57.
[83] *Horrocks* v. *Lowe* [1975] A.C. 135.
[84] [1917] A.C. 309.

frankness is so important in certain forms of communication that defamation claims should not be possible unless the occasion is abused. The defence is best viewed as removing the need to prove justification, and as such, its scope should be carefully limited. It has the capacity to protect a wide range of communications but is particularly important in the case of character references and internal memoranda produced by companies and other organisations.

The central requirement of the defence is that both the publisher and the recipient have either a duty or an interest at stake in the communication. An interest or duty on one side only, for instance, the fact that the recipient has an interest in receiving the information which the other side has no interest or duty to give, will not be sufficient. Similarly, a publication may be privileged on the basis of a particular recipient's interest in it, but will not be protected if it is published to a third person who has no such interest. For the sake of ease of exposition it is proposed to discuss the meaning of duty and interest in this context separately. However, both factors can be relevant to the same case in as much as the defence can be claimed by a person who has a duty to communicate information to a recipient who has an interest in receiving it.

The meaning to be attributed to the notions of legal, social or moral duties on particular facts can cause difficulties. Courts have been left to decide these issues as best they can. In *Watt* v. *Longsdon*[85] Scrutton L.J. described the moral and social duties as those which were not enforceable by legal proceedings but which were recognised by English people of ordinary intelligence and moral principle. Greer L.J. in the same case asked whether the great mass of right-minded men in the position of the defendant would have considered it their duty, under the circumstances, to make the communication. On this basis, the Court of Appeal held that a director of a company had a duty and was therefore privileged when he passed on to the company's chairman uninvestigated and unfounded allegations as to immorality, drunkenness and dishonesty on the part of the plaintiff, who was the managing director of an overseas branch of the company. However, the court refused to regard as privileged, on the particular facts of the case, the communication of the same information to the plaintiff's wife. This decision strikes the correct balance. Persons in a position of authority must be entitled to pass accusations concerning the conduct of others to the appropriate authorities[86]; whereas to regard a person as under a general moral or social duty to pass uninvestigated allegations to the relatives of a person against whom charges are made would make qualified privilege a powerful tool for those who wish to blacken another's reputation. Similarly, it will only be in extreme circumstances that a journalist will be under a duty to inform the public of suspicions or speculations, even if they relate to a matter of legitimate public interest.[87]

---

[85] [1930] 1 K.B. 130.
[86] *Beach* v. *Freeson* [1972] 1 Q.B. 14.
[87] *Blackshaw* v. *Lord* [1983] 2 All E.R. 311.

Doubts, founded on the problem of defining a duty, exist as to the availability of qualified privilege to organisations such as credit rating bureaux which provide traders with information on prospective customers. In *Mackintosh* v. *Dun*[88] it was held that a bureau run for profit could not avail itself of the defence because its giving information with a view to profit excluded it from claiming that it was acting from a sense of duty or from legitimate self-interest.

However, in *London Association for Protection of Trade* v. *Greenlands Ltd.*[89] the House of Lords allowed the defence to be claimed by an unincorporated non-profit making body which made similar information available to its members. The distinction is difficult to justify and it is arguable that *Mackintosh* is wrongly decided in failing to accept that a profit making bureau has a social or moral duty to provide the information. It seems to be accepted that credit information provided by a paid agent is privileged.[90] An early version of what ultimately became the Consumer Credit Act 1974 would have accorded qualified privilege to all communications to or by credit bureaux and the Faulks Committee proposed allowing the defence to communications by, but no to, such bodies.[91] These recommendations have not been enacted and in view of the sensitivity surrounding credit information in the 1990s it may be argued that *Mackintosh*, by leaving such bureaux to seek protection, if at all, by the defence of justification, is the preferable decision. What is impossible to support is the application of different rules to different kinds of organisation.

Privilege based upon an interest is possibly easier to define. In order for interests to be at issue something tangible needs to be protected. Public interest in the sense in which it is used in relation to the defence of fair comment; *i.e.* the legitimate curiosity of the recipient of information, is not sufficient. This is not to say that the public at large may not have a sufficient interest in information, but that the information must relate to a tangible interest of the public at large before the defence will operate. Telling the public of an individual's suspected wrongdoing would not suffice in most cases (the accusation would need to be justified), but the situation would be very different if that individual was suspected of introducing poison into publicly available foodstuffs. This distinction is supported by the decision of the Court of Appeal in *Chapman* v. *Lord Ellesmere*.[92] Publication of the decision of the stewards in the Racing Calendar, a publication which was recognised as the proper medium for communicating such decisions to the racing fraternity, was held to attract qualified privilege; however, wider publication of the same facts through press agencies and the national

---

[88] [1908] A.C. 390.
[89] [1916] 2 A.C. 15.
[90] Lord Buckmaster *L.A.P.T.* v. *Greenlands Ltd.* [1916] 2 A.C. 15.
[91] para. 237.
[92] [1932] 2 K.B. 431. The case was mainly concerned with the defence of consent. See also *Blackshaw* v. *Lord* [1983] 2 All E.R. 311.

newspapers was not held to be privileged[93] as no legitimate interest existed in the wider class of readers.

Common interest on the part of publisher and recipient of a statement can be claimed in a situation in which these parties are in dispute with each other, and their interests are opposed.[94]

Reports

Even if absolute privilege is not available reports of the proceedings of many bodies attract qualified privilege.

Reports of Parliamentary proceedings[95] and published extracts from Parliamentary papers[96] are only accorded qualified privilege. Similarly, fair and accurate reports of judicial proceedings held in the U.K. which fail to qualify for absolute privilege (*i.e.* because they are non-contemporaneous reports) are accorded qualified privilege.

Section 7 of the Defamation Act 1952 extends qualified privilege to fair and accurate[97] newspaper or broadcast reports[98] of the proceedings of a wide range of bodies.[99] The defence is only available with respect to newspaper and broadcast reports[1] and therefore does not protect persons who make defamatory statements in the course of the proceedings of such bodies. This defence, although limited, extends the qualified privilege granted to the press to give information to the public beyond the narrow confines established by the common law in *Chapman* v. *Lord Ellesmere*. The defence is also subject to the condition that the matter at issue must be one of public concern and the publication must be for the public benefit.[2] The questions of whether the report is fair and accurate; whether the subject matter is of public concern and whether publication is for the public benefit are issues of fact which fall to the jury to decide.[3] Two forms of privilege are created by this section. The first category of cases[4] is governed by the normal

---

[93] The decision continues to represent the law on the matter of the interest required and would still govern any publication made by the disciplinary body itself. However, qualified privilege would now be available in these circumstances, if the publication was made by a newspaper, under the provisions of s. 7 of the Defamation Act 1952.

[94] *Osborn* v. *Thomas Boulter & Son* [1930] 2 K.B. 226.

[95] *Wason* v. *Walter* (1868) L.R. 4 Q.B. 73; *Cook* v. *Alexander* [1974] Q.B. 279.

[96] s. 3 of the Parliamentary Papers Act 1840.

[97] There is no requirement of contemporaneity.

[98] Broadcasting Act 1990, s. 166(3).

[99] The bodies covered are listed in the Schedule to the 1952 Act. The Faulks Committee recommended (para. 231) that list should be extended. This has not been done.

[1] The Faulks Committee (para. 229) recommended that it should be extended to books and other publications.

[2] s. 7(3).

[3] *Kingshott* v. *Associated Kent Newspapers Ltd.* [1991] 2 All E.R. 99.

[4] This covers fair and accurate reports of (1) proceedings of the legislature of any part of Her Majesty's dominions outside Great Britain; (2) any proceeding of an international organisation of which the U.K. is a member, or of any international conference to which the Government sends a representative; (3) proceedings in public of an international court; (4) any proceedings before a court in any part of Her Majesty's dominions outside the United Kingdom, or of any proceedings before a court-martial held outside the United Kingdom; (5) any proceedings in public of a body or person appointed to hold a public inquiry in any part of Her Majesty's dominions outside the United Kingdom; and also fair and accurate copies of or extracts from any register kept in pursuance of any Act of Parliament which is open to inspection by the public, or of any other document which is required by the law of any part of the U.K. to be open to inspection by the public; and a notice or advertisement published by or on the authority of any court within the U.K. or any judge or officer of such a court.

rules of qualified privilege. However, the second category[5] is unusual because the defence can be defeated by proof that the defendant has been requested by the plaintiff to publish a reasonable statement by way of explanation or contradiction, and has refused or neglected to do so, or did so in an inadequate or unreasonable manner.[6]

Ancillary privilege

If a business communication which contains defamatory matter is privileged, all incidental publications, for example, those made to employees such as typists, which reasonably occur in the course of its preparation will also be privileged.[7] The existence of ancillary privilege was attacked by Lord Denning M.R. in his judgment in *Bryanston Finance Ltd.* v. *De Vries*[8] on the basis that an original privilege existed in such circumstances: the employer and typist either had a common interest in the subject matter of the communications or the situation was one in which the person dictating had an interest in the matter dictated and the typist had a corresponding duty to

---

[5] This covers (1) fair and accurate reports of the findings or decisions of any of the following associations, their committees or governing bodies:

   (a) an association formed for the purpose of promoting or encouraging any art, science, religion or learning, and empowered by its constitution to exercise control over or adjudicate upon matters of interest or concern to the association, or the actions or conduct of any persons subject to its control or adjudication;

   (b) an association formed in the U.K. for the purpose of promoting or safeguarding the interests of any trade, business, industry or profession, or of the persons carrying on or engaged in any trade, business, industry or profession, and empowered by its constitution to exercise control over or adjudicate upon matters connected with the trade, business, industry or profession, or the actions or conduct of those persons;

   (c) an association formed in the U.K. for the purpose of promoting or safeguarding the interests of any game, sport or pastime to the playing or exercise of which members of the public are invited or admitted, and empowered by its constitution to exercise control over or adjudicate upon persons connected with or taking part in the game, sport or pastime, being a finding or decision relating to a person who is a member of or is subject by virtue of any contract to the control of the association;

(2) fair and accurate reports of the proceedings at any public meeting held in the U.K., *i.e.* a meeting held for a lawful purpose and for the furtherance or discussion of any matter of public concern, whether admission to the meeting is general or restricted;

(3) fair and accurate reports of the proceedings at any meeting or sitting in any part of the U.K. of:

   (a) any local authority or committee of a local authority or local authorities;

   (b) any justice or justices of the peace acting otherwise than as a court exercising judicial authority;

   (c) any commission, tribunal, committee or person appointed for the purposes of any inquiry by Act of Parliament, by Her Majesty or by a Minister of the Crown;

   (d) any person appointed by a local authority to hold a local inquiry in pursuance of any Act of Parliament;

   (e) any other tribunal, board, committee or body constituted by or under, and exercising functions under, an Act of Parliament, not being a meeting or sitting admission to which is denied to representatives of newspapers and other members of the public;

(4) fair and accurate reports of the proceedings at a general meeting of any company which is not a private company;

(5) a copy or fair and accurate report or summary of any notice or other matter issued for the information of the public by or on behalf of a government department, officer of state, local authority or chief officer of police (on this see *Blackshaw* v. *Lord* [1983] 2 All E.R. 311).

[6] s. 7(2).

[7] *Osborn* v. *Thomas Boulter & Son* [1930] 2 K.B. 226.

[8] [1975] 1 Q.B. 703.

take the information down. The majority of members of the Court of Appeal refused to accept that ancillary privilege did not exist; whilst it was accepted that Lord Denning's approach could work in some situations it was felt that it depended on a failure to distinguish the employer's motive in writing a letter from his having a legitimate interest to protect in the subject matter.

Remedies

1. Damages

The calculation of damages in cases of defamation is a subject beset by uncertainty and difficulty. Although the underlying principle remains that of giving pecuniary compensation for the loss suffered, a number of factors make it virtually impossible to forecast the exact sum likely to be awarded to a successful plaintiff. Central to this difficulty is the fact that the compensation is designed as redress for the inherently nebulous losses which flow from damage to a person's reputation. Embarrassment, hurt and loss of social esteem are not capable of translation into monetary terms with any degree of precision. The unpredictability of any calculation is accentuated by the fact that the majority of defamation cases have remained the preserve of juries with the inevitable result that it has been impossible for a tariff of awards to emerge.[9] Finally, a significant number of awards for defamation feature damages which have been "aggravated"[10] in some way by the conduct of the defendant and a smaller number may allow exemplary damages on the basis that the defendant has deliberately defamed the plaintiff calculating that the wrong is likely to produce a profit.[11]

There has been a great deal of criticism in recent years of the level of awards of damages for defamation made by juries to well known media personalities and politicians. The contrast with the level of awards made in the most serious personal injury cases suggests that plaintiffs who are successful in defamation cases are substantially overcompensated for what is essentially an intangible form of loss.

In theory a plaintiff's pre-existing reputation must be relevant to determining the level of losses which have resulted from a defamation. However, the law has encountered severe difficulties in devising a workable rule. The present law, which is derived from the leading authorities of *Scott* v. *Sampson*[12] and *Plato Films Ltd.* v. *Speidel*,[13] is that, although general evidence of the plaintiff's pre-existing reputation is admissible as evidence, it is not possible to admit evidence that the plaintiff's reputation had already suffered as a result of rumours to the effect that he had done that which the defendant also alleged against him in the words which give rise to the particular litigation.[14] Neither is it possible to adduce evidence of particular

---

[9] The Court of Appeal was given a greater power to interfere with awards of damages for defamation by s. 8 of the Courts and Legal Services Act 1990 (*ante*, p. 146). The Faulks Committee (para. 513) recommended that the function of the jury should be confined to indicating whether the final award should be contemptuous, nominal, moderate or substantial with the actual figure being chosen by the judge.

[10] See *ante*, p. 149.

[11] See *ante*, p. 150. The Faulks Committee recommended that awards of exemplary damages should no longer be available in defamation cases (para. 360).

[12] (1882) 8 Q.B.D. 491.

[13] [1961] A.C. 1090.

[14] Subject to the provisions of the Rehabilitation of Offenders Act 1974, it seems to be possible to bring evidence of previous convictions of the plaintiff as evidence of general reputation.

facts unconnected with the specific allegation which would tend to show that the plaintiff was, or should have been, of a bad character and had little reputation to defend. From one perspective both of these rules are justifiable: the first allows the plaintiff to attack defamatory words wherever they arise, the alternative would leave a person's reputation at the mercy of those who spread scurrilous rumours; the second avoids the risk of the proceedings being lengthened inordinately by evidence of misdeeds wholly unconnected with the subject matter of the alleged defamation. However, the result is that juries are presented with the task of drawing a virtually meaningless distinction: a general reputation (evidence of which is admissible) is inevitably based on rumours and specific instances of (mis)conduct (which are not admissible). Furthermore, the rule opens the door to highly artificial proceedings in which a plaintiff may be permitted to defend a level of reputation which he did not actually have as it is notoriously difficult to produce general evidence of a bad reputation unfounded on specific incidents.[15] The Faulks Committee accepted these criticisms and proposed that the rule should be changed to allow the defendant to give evidence of matters relevant to the aspect of the plaintiff's reputation with which the defamation was concerned.[16]

One problem which can arise as a result of the possibility of a number of people being liable in respect of the publication of similar defamatory matter is dealt with by section 12 of the Defamation Act 1952 which provides that in an action for defamation a defendant may give evidence in mitigation of damage that the plaintiff has recovered damages,[17] or has brought actions for damages for defamation in respect of the publication of words to the same effect as those on which this action is founded. In such a case the jury should be told that the plaintiff cannot recover twice for the same loss and should be directed to consider the extent to which the plaintiff's loss can be solely attributed to the libel which is before the court.

2. Injunctions

The availability of an interim injunction to prevent the publication or republication of defamatory matter is an issue on which a delicate balance has to be struck. Such injunctions can obviously serve a useful purpose in limiting the damage done by the defamation but should not be so readily available as to inhibit freedom of speech and criticism. The attitude adopted by the law is to make an interim injunction available only in the clearest cases.[18] A particularly important consequence of this is that the remedy is generally not available in any case in which the defendant intends to plead the defence of justification at trial. In the majority of cases it is therefore impossible to place a prior restraint on the publication of critical matter and

---

[15] Furthermore, cross-examination of the plaintiff as to other misdeeds is possible in order to question his credibility.

[16] para. 384(d). The Committee recommended that a person wishing to rely on evidence of this kind should be obliged to give notice of this intention in order to avoid the risk of the plaintiff being surprised by it. In 1991 the Supreme Court Procedure Committee's Working Group *Report on Practice and Procedure in Defamation* made a similar recommendation. It appears to be the case that the Government will introduce legislation on these lines in the near future.

[17] Including an agreed settlement.

[18] *William Coulson & Sons* v. *James Coulson & Co.* [1887] 3 T.L.R. 46.

investigative journalists therefore do not have to face the risk that their questions will be met by an injunction rather than answers.

PRIVACY AND RELATED MATTERS

English law recognises no specific right to privacy and does not make the infringement of a person's privacy a tort. This is not particularly surprising because the general idea that a person's privacy should be protected can cover a variety of interests including: protection from physical disturbance by such matters as trespass, harassment, eavesdropping, telephone tapping and photography; protection from having details of one's private life published and the appropriation of an individual's personality for commercial reasons.[19] In addition, the recognition of a general right to personal privacy is liable to impede the work of investigative journalists and thus to be criticised as undermining the freedom of the press. Recent widespread criticism of the conduct of certain sections of the press in the United Kingdom, which has led to calls for increased recognition of rights of privacy, has been answered by the comment that such protection would amount to a "rogues charter" and would work to the disadvantage of the general public.

The fact that infringement of a person's privacy is not itself a tort does not mean that a variety of tortious causes of action cannot be pressed into service in order to protect a person's privacy: trespass to land[20] and to the person; private nuisance[21]; defamation and malicious falsehood[22] may all be able to provide some assistance in particular circumstances. What it does mean is that there is no generalised principle which can be relied on to provide a remedy. The lack of such a principle means that there is always a risk that deserving cases fail because the facts do not precisely fit the requirements of a particular tort.

Proposed torts

These issues were addressed by the *Report of the Committee on Privacy and Related Matters* in 1990.[23] The Committee concluded that the problem of drafting a workable statutory tort of infringement of privacy could be surmounted but felt that a preferable solution lay in press self-regulation and the enactment of specific measures designed to protect individuals against particular forms of physical intrusion by the press. All of the proposals for legislation were therefore directed at rendering unlawful conduct which took place with a view to obtaining material for publication.[24] It was proposed to

---

[19] *Tolley* v. *J.S. Fry and Sons Ltd.* [1931] A.C. 333.

[20] See *Bernstein* v. *Skyviews & General Ltd.* [1978] Q.B. 479 for an unsuccessful attempt to use trespass to protect privacy.

[21] Dicta in *Bernstein* v. *Skyviews & General Ltd.* [1978] Q.B. 479 support this possibility. See also *Khorasandjian* v. *Bush* [1993] 3 All E.R. 669.

[22] See *Kaye* v. *Robertson* (1990) reproduced as Appendix I to the *Report of the Committee on Privacy and Related Matters* Cm. 1102 (1990).

[23] Cm. 1102 (1990).

[24] They would therefore cover conduct by journalists and by others who hoped to be able to sell the results to the press. Those publishing information so obtained would be outside the provision unless held to be conspirators or accessories.

render three kinds of conduct unlawful[25]: entering private property without the consent of the lawful occupant with the intention of obtaining personal information; placing a surveillance device on private property, without the consent of the lawful occupant, with the intention of obtaining personal information and taking a photograph, or recording the voice, of an individual who is on private property with the intention that the individual should be identifiable. It was further proposed[26] that it should be a defence to any such conduct that the act was done for the purpose of preventing, detecting or exposing the commission of any crime, or other seriously anti-social conduct or, for the protection of public health and safety or under any lawful authority. The Committee took the view that the primary method of controlling such conduct should be the criminal law as the criminal process could ensure a fast, effective and independent response when necessary. However, it also believed that conduct of this kind should be actionable in tort so that a person who was subjected to physical intrusions would have access to injunctive relief, damages and an account of profits.[27] When Sir David Calcutt Q.C. produced his report on the progress of press self-regulation in 1993[28] he repeated this recommendation with some minor amendments[29] and took the view that the issue of privacy was "sufficiently serious and worthy of detailed consideration" that the Government should take steps to consider the introduction of a general tort of infringement of privacy.[30]

The Government responded to this in a consultation paper[31] by recommending the creation of a new statutory tort remedy for those infringements of privacy which cause substantial distress, provided that such distress would have been suffered, in the circumstances, by a person of ordinary sensibilities. The proposed remedy would protect an individual, but not an institution, in relation to matters appertaining to health, personal communications and family and personal relationships. It would also extend to a right to be free from harassment and molestation. Defences of consent, lawful authority and absolute and qualified privilege would be available and, in addition, the public's "right to know" would be secured by a public interest defence which would allow invasions of privacy in relation to such matters as: crimes and seriously anti-social conduct; public health and safety; the discharge of public functions and the correction of misleading statements. It is suggested that: the standard remedies would be for injunctions and for damages for mental distress; that such cases should be tried by judge alone and that a recognised tariff of damages for mental distress limited to £10,000 should be used.

---

[25] para. 6.33.
[26] para. 6.35.
[27] para. 6.38.
[28] *Review of Press Self-regulation* Cm. 2135, (1993).
[29] See paras. 7.25–7.26 for the amended proposal. The main additions would render it unlawful to use a surveillance device other than on private property in relation to a person on private property and would introduce additional defences relating to (1) preventing the public from being misled by some public statement or action of the individual and (2) informing the public about matters directly affecting the discharge of any public function of the individual.
[30] para. 7.34.
[31] Lord Chancellor's Department, *Infringement of Privacy*, 1993.

Non-Judicial Complaints Mechanisms and the Media

As we have seen in the context of personal injury law considerable disincentives exist to the pursuit of litigation by private individuals.[32] These difficulties are accentuated in cases of press misconduct by the complexity of the law and the fact that legal aid is not available in relation to claims for defamation. The result is that extra-judicial mechanisms for obtaining redress, which may lead to a publisher being censured or publishing an apology or correction, assume an important role. The leading text on media law describes the Press Complaints Commission as "a poor person's libel court."[33] These extra-judicial remedies overlap with defamation in providing redress in cases of inaccurate reporting and go further that the law in attempting to protect privacy. However, they attract much criticism both on the ground that the redress which they provide for individuals is actually ineffectual and because they are seen to be hindering the abilities of the press to indulge in investigative journalism. It may well be that the task of controlling press malpractice cannot be left with a self-regulating body organised and funded by the industry which has championed the cause of press freedom.

Press complaints commission[34]

This body was set up in the wake of the Report of the Committee on Privacy[35] in 1990 to replace the Press Council. It is a non-statutory body funded by the newspaper industry. The Committee had taken the view that the newspaper industry should be given a limited period of time to show that self-regulation could provide an effective control over intrusive journalism and other unacceptable press practices and the Commission was the body given the task of providing this control. It is funded by the newspaper industry and a majority of its membership is drawn from persons with a press background.

The Press Complaints Commission has the role of enforcing a Code of Practice which was drawn up in the light of the recommendations of the Committee on Privacy. The present form of the Code differs in some significant ways from that which was proposed by the Committee on Privacy[36] and these differences were one of the reasons given for the conclusion that the press had failed in its last chance to impose effective self-regulation on itself.

The Code requires all members of the press to maintain the highest professional and ethical standards, having regard to the provisions of the Code and the need to safeguard the public's right to know. The Press Complaints Commission considers[37] and adjudicates upon claimed breaches of the Code. The fact that the Commission has no power to require the production of evidence which would enable it to investigate and make a determination on the accuracy of the contents of a publication means that it

---

[32] See *ante*, p. 163 *et seq.*

[33] Robertson & Nicol, *Media Law* (3rd ed., 1992), p. 40.

[34] For a more detailed discussion see Robertson & Nicol *op. cit* p. 526 *et seq.*

[35] *Report of the Committee on Privacy and Related Matters*, Cm. 1102 (1990).

[36] Both versions are reproduced in Appendix C of the *Review of Press Self-Regulation* Cm. 2135 (1993). Paras. 3.48–3.61 of the Review discuss the differences.

[37] The procedure is conducted on paper and does not involve a hearing or oral submissions.

may be an unsuitable vehicle for the resolution of factual disputes.[38] In the event that an adjudication criticises a publication the publisher is under an obligation[39] to print the adjudication in full and with due prominence. The Code itself covers a wide range of matters such as: the accuracy of reporting; the distinction between comment, conjecture and fact; privacy; access to hospitals; obtaining information by means of misrepresentation and subterfuge; harassment and the taking of photographs of person on private property; obtaining information by means of payment; intrusions into situations of personal grief and shock and the interviewing and photographing of children. A number of the provisions of the Code are subject to a "public interest" exception under which the provision of the Code does not apply if the journalist is engaged in: detecting or exposing crime or serious misdemeanour; in detecting or exposing anti-social conduct; in protecting public health or safety or in preventing the public being misled by some statement or action of an individual or organisation.[40] In this way the Code attempts to protect the public's "right to know" by creating a large and, at times, general, exception to the protection which it gives to individuals.

The bulk of the Press Complaints Commission's work seems to have overlapped with defamation[41] because the majority of claims which it has investigated have related to matters of accuracy in reporting.[42] The Commission's procedure is readily accessible, relatively quick and should not involve a complainant in the heavy expenditure likely in defamation litigation. However defamation actions are available against anyone who is to be regarded as the publisher of the words, whereas the Commission only has jurisdiction over newspapers and periodicals.[43] Furthermore, the Commission has no real capacity to investigate disputed facts and it has no power to act to prevent a publication. The only remedy which can be obtained from the Commission is the publication of an adjudication in the paper which carried the material complained about. A complainant who seeks compensation must therefore pursue the case at common law and one who seeks to block a publication has no chance of obtaining such relief from the Commission as opposed to the very poor prospects offered by an application to the courts.

A report produced by Sir David Calcutt Q.C. in January 1993[44] concluded that the Press Complaints Commission had not provided the effective mechanisms that the Committee on Privacy had sought and that the Government should, as a result, take measures to place the regulation of the press on a statutory basis. Sir David's conclusions as to the role and operation of the

---

[38] But the majority of cases referred to it relate to matters of accuracy. See note 42, below.

[39] Under the terms of the Code.

[40] The recognition of such exceptions is central to the criticism of the Code made by Sir David Calcutt Q.C. in the *Review of Press Self-Regulation*. The reality is that the exception is capable of permitting conduct which is tortious and which goes beyond the powers conferred on the police by PACE.

[41] The Commission does not formally require a complainant to waive any legal claim before it will process a case (as the Press Council did).

[42] In 1991 the Commission identified 1,118 complaints which raised a prima facie case of breach of the code. 740 of these related to matters of accuracy and only 80 to matters of privacy.

[43] Private citizens, the authors and publishers of books and distributors are therefore beyond the scope of the Commission's work. Radio and television broadcasts are dealt with by the Broadcasting Complaints Commission.

[44] *Review of Press Self-regulation*, Cm. 2135, (1993).

Press Complaints Commission following his previous report were summed up as:

> "The Press Complaints Commission is not, in my view, an effective regulator of the press. It has not been set up in a way, and is not operating a code of practice, which enables it to command not only press but also public confidence. It does not, in my view, hold the balance fairly between the press and the individual. It is not the truly independent body which it should be. As constituted, it is, in essence, a body set up by the industry, financed by the industry, and operating a code of practice devised by the industry and which is over favourable to the industry."[45]

The proposed Statutory Press Complaints Tribunal would have the task of enforcing a revised code of practice which would be less favourable to the press and would have three major new powers: it would be able to restrain publication of material obtained in breach of the code; it would be able to award compensation (up to a fixed limit) to persons damaged by a breach of the code and it would have the power to impose fines in the most serious cases.[46]

The initial reaction of the Government to these criticisms did not suggest that a great deal of enthusiasm existed for the creation of a specialised statutory tribunal administering both criminal penalties and tortious liability against the press. The press was generally hostile to the proposals on the basis that they would amount to an unwarranted infringement of the rights of a free press.

Broadcasting complaints[47]

The Broadcasting Complaints Commission is a statutory body the functions of which are governed by the Broadcasting Act 1990. It has the role of considering and adjudicating upon complaints of unjust and unfair treatment in broadcast programmes and unwarranted infringement of privacy in, or in connection with, the obtaining of material included in broadcast programmes.[48] As a statutory body it is given legal powers to view the offending programme and to see a copy of the transcript and of any relevant correspondence. Complaints will either be dealt with on the basis of written evidence or after a private hearing. The Commission has the power to direct the B B C or the Independent Television Commission to publish its findings in a specified manner. This will commonly involve broadcasting a summary of the findings at a time when the viewers of the original item would be likely to be watching the same channel.

The notion of "unfair or unjust" treatment covers matters of accuracy, including the difficult issue of the editing, selection and arrangement of material. The fact that intrusions into a person's privacy need to be "unwarranted" means that elements of the public interest are allowed to play a part.

---

[45] *Ibid.* Summary, para. 5.
[46] See *Review of Press Self-Regulation*, Chap. 6.
[47] For a more detailed discussion see Robertson & Nicol *op. cit.* pp. 545–559.
[48] Broadcasting Act 1990, s. 143(1).

Other controls

Many newspapers now appoint an "ombudsman" or "readers' representative" to consider and adjudicate on complaints brought by readers concerning the paper's conduct.

Both the Independent Television Commission and the Radio Authority have statutory duties with regard to such matters as: good taste and decency; matters offensive to public feelings; accuracy and impartiality. Equivalent, but non-statutory duties have been applied to the BBC. The BBC and ITC have promulgated codes of practice for those working on their behalf which cover a wide variety of matters including accuracy, impartiality, infringements of privacy and secret filming.

Two other bodies also have functions which may impinge on those of the bodies described previously. The Broadcasting Standards Council handles complaints from the public concerning matters of decency and the portrayal of violence, sex in advertising, video, radio and television programmes. The Advertising Standards Authority deals with complaints about misleading or unethical press or poster advertising and with failures of advertisers to meet their promises.

Chapter Twenty-Five

Public Authority Liability

INTRODUCTION

The torts discussed in this chapter cut across the general scheme of the book. What matters here is not the interest of the plaintiff which has been infringed, but the fact that the defendant is a public body or official. The majority of the important modern decisions on this topic concern economic losses. However, cases concerning personal injuries and individual liberties may also require special treatment if they fall into this area. Special considerations, and in the case of intentionally inflicted injuries, a special tort, apply and there is a very significant divergence growing between the approach of English and European Community law to these issues.

The central question to be addressed is whether tort actions are an appropriate means of redress for persons who have been damaged by the acts of public bodies. The traditional picture of administrative law in England and Wales is of a set of remedies for judicial review which an aggrieved person may use either to have acts or decisions of a public body invalidated or, in appropriate circumstances, to compel that body to act.

These remedies recognise that such bodies are accorded powers, by their enabling legislation, to develop policies as they think fit. A private person will only be able to obtain an administrative law remedy against a body which has exceeded the boundaries of the discretion conferred on it by the governing legislation (a body which acts in excess of its powers is said to have acted *ultra vires*) or which has failed to comply with essential procedural steps.

These remedies have traditionally been seen as the preserve of administrative law. The question of whether financial compensation can be obtained for damage suffered as a result of unlawful acts of public authorities is, however, of interest to tort lawyers, particularly because administrative law has not developed its own remedy. A body which is shown to have acted in excess of its powers will not automatically be liable to compensate those who are damaged thereby. In order for compensation to be obtained the injured person must prove a claim under traditional tort principles. The mere fact that a public body has acted unlawfully, that is, in excess of the powers granted to it, does not justify an award of damages to persons damaged. This would not present a serious difficulty if tort had developed adequate remedies, but it has not. The failure of both administrative law and tort to provide a satisfactory compensation remedy against public bodies has provoked serious criticism. The range of remedies available to an aggrieved individual may be thought to be incomplete. A person who is put out of business by an unlawful administrative act will have available to him remedies which will result in that act being declared a nullity and thus in his being allowed to recommence trade, but he may have difficulty in obtaining compensation for his losses.[1]

What special considerations have hindered the operation of tort law in this area? The most significant is that the policy making nature of the activities of public bodies makes them better suited to evaluation by the techniques of judicial review rather than to a challenge based on tort principles. Public bodies are given discretionary powers which they are free to exercise in developing what they consider to be appropriate policies. The courts cannot be permitted to substitute their own opinions of what is an appropriate course of action for those of such a body reached within the bounds of its discretion. This issue is particularly acute when a public authority has the task of balancing the demands of economy against the provision of adequate services for the public. For example, a health authority may decide to devote scarce financial resources to a particular area of its responsibility, such as geriatric care, when it knows that a consequence will be a deterioration in the services available to other categories of patients: fewer dialysis machines may be available to patients suffering from kidney failure. Can a patient who is denied treatment as a result of such a decision obtain damages in tort for any losses incurred? Tort principles are not well suited to test a decision of this kind which clearly creates a foreseeable risk of increased damage or a greater number of injuries to a category of patients. It may be impossible for a court deciding a private law claim of this kind for damages to give full consideration to the public interest in the matter. It is argued that the policy making functions of a public body are likely to be hampered by fear that a category of interested individuals which feels aggrieved by its policies will resort to a tort claim for damages. The business of government according to electoral mandate is not made easier by fear of judicial challenges.

There are a number of other subsidiary arguments as to why tort remedies should not be available against public bodies. In an era of strict controls on the spending of public authorities it may be felt to be inappropriate for such bodies to be forced to devote significant resources to defending cases and paying damages to individuals. Arguments familiar to tort lawyers are relevant here. An obvious one is the fear of opening the floodgates: the class of persons affected may be large and their losses great. As we will also see, a number of modern tort cases alleging negligence against public authorities have foundered on the traditional rocks of pure economic loss and liability for the acts of others.

Nonetheless, tort remedies may be available, in certain limited circumstances, to enable an individual to obtain financial redress for damage suffered as a result of administrative acts. The torts which are available can be divided into the traditional pattern of torts based on proof of intentional conduct (misfeasance), negligence and strict liability (breach of statutory duty). Misfeasance has shown steady growth in recent years; breach of statutory duty has occasionally offered a remedy and negligence has been through the familiar pattern of a phase of rapid advance followed by a steady retreat. In addition to these familiar forms of liability the decision of the

---

[1] The leading example of this is the case of *Bourgoin* v. *Ministry of Agriculture, Fisheries and Food* [1986] Q.B. 716.

European Court of Justice in *Francovich* v. *Italian Government*[2] opened up a whole new field of this kind of liability based on Community law but enforceable through national courts.

MISFEASANCE IN PUBLIC OFFICE

Misfeasance by a public official is a tort which is based on proof of malice. It is a specialised tort which is confined to the context of public authority liability. The policy behind the existence of the tort seems to be a punitive one designed to ensure that the highest standards of conduct are maintained by public officials. In his judgment in *Jones* v. *Swansea City Council*[3] Nourse L.J. explained the policy as follows:

"It ought to be unthinkable that the holder of an office of government in this country would exercise a power thus vested in him with the object of injuring a member of that public by whose trust alone the office is enjoyed. It is unthinkable that our law should not require the highest standards of a public servant in the execution of his office."

Misfeasance consists of intentionally abusing powers or breaking a duty. The act must be one done in bad faith or (possibly) without reasonable cause.[4] The general rule that an *ultra vires* act does not give a person injured thereby a right to claim damages is subject to an exception if it can be shown that the official in question acted intentionally. The decision of the Court of Appeal in *Bourgoin S.A.* v. *Ministry of Agriculture, Fisheries and Food*[5] confirmed that the tort is recognised by English law and that the necessary element of intention can be satisfied in two ways. The defendant must either have acted with the intention of injuring the plaintiff or must have knowingly committed an act in excess of his powers which could be foreseen as likely to injure the plaintiff. It is not necessary to show "targeted malice" in order to establish a claim for misfeasance: the defendant need not have had the infliction of injury on the plaintiff as the predominant motive of his acts. In *Bourgoin* this meant that the tort could be established if a deliberate breach of European Community legislation by the imposition of an import ban by the Ministry of Agriculture was proved. The fact that such a breach might be shown to have been intended primarily to benefit English producers provided no defence when it was shown that the act must necessarily have caused harm to rival French producers.

The necessary element of intention may not be easy to prove. This is particularly the case when the tort is alleged to have been committed by a body such as a council. The test in such a case is probably that, in order to succeed, the plaintiff must prove that the majority of councillors present, having voted for the resolution, did so with the object of damaging the plaintiff[6] or knowingly in excess of their powers. It seems possible that the malice of one councillor will taint the acts of others if, knowing of it, they

---

[2] [1992] I.R.L.R. 84.
[3] [1989] 3 All E.R. 162.
[4] *Calveley* v. *Chief Constable of the Merseyside Police* [1989] 1 All E.R. 1025.
[5] [1986] Q.B. 716.
[6] This was the view taken by Lord Lowry and agreed with by the other members of the House of Lords in *Jones* v. *Swansea City Council* [1990] 3 All E.R. 737.

acquiesce in decisions motivated by it, or if the one who has malice is in a position to direct the voting of the others by means of a party whip.[7]

As the tort is based on the malice or knowledge of the official rather than the nature of the act performed, misfeasance has significantly different features from those of the other torts available against public authorities. It is not subject to the "purpose of the statute" test[8] and it may apply to an abuse of a discretionary power. It has been held to apply to all abuses of power by public officials, whether or not the power being exercised is derived from statute. In *Jones v. Swansea City Council*[9] it was held applicable to a local authority's refusal to give consent to its tenant changing the use of premises, the refusal being in exercise of a power vested in the council by the lease applicable to the property. A similar act done by a private individual with the intention of injuring a lessee would not be actionable.

Misfeasance is a recently recognised tort which undoubtedly requires further elucidation. It has already been established that it is incapable of providing an alternative to an action for malicious prosecution brought against police officers as it might undermine some of the restrictions which are placed on the availability of that tort.[10]

NEGLIGENCE

In contrast to the special tort of misfeasance the operation of negligence in a situation of public authority liability is merely an application of standard tort principles, albeit one which may be subject to some special rules. The principles described here have been applied in cases concerning local authorities, health authorities, public corporations and even government ministers.[11] As in other areas of negligence liability, different approaches can be discerned in different eras. A period of expanding principle based on the authority of *Anns* has been followed by one which has introduced important constraints. The need for special "control factors" to apply in this area has been challenged[12] as duties of care have proved more difficult to establish, particularly in relation to omissions, control of the acts of third parties and financial losses.

The leading statements of the principles governing liability in this area derive from the speeches of Lord Wilberforce in *Anns v. Merton London Borough Council*[13] and of Lord Keith in *Governors of the Peabody Donation Fund v. Sir Lindsay Parkinson & Co. Ltd.*[14] In both cases the plaintiffs claimed to have been damaged by the defendant local authorities' negligent exercise of,

---

[7] This was the view of Roch J. in *Jones*. It did not form part of the ratio of the decision in view of the findings of facts on the evidence in the case.

[8] See *ante*, pp. 36 and 50–51.

[9] [1989] 3 All E.R. 162, C.A. the point was not discussed when the case went to the House of Lords, [1990] 3 All E.R. 737.

[10] *McDonagh v. Commissioner of Police for the Metropolis The Times*, December 28, 1989. Misfeasance might have circumvented the requirement that the plaintiff prove that the prosecution had been brought against him without reasonable and probable cause.

[11] *Rowling v. Takaro Properties Ltd.* [1988] A.C. 473; *Meates v. Att.-Gen.* [1979] 1 N.Z.L.R. 415; *Lonrho plc v. Tebbit* [1992] 4 All E.R. 280.

[12] For academic comment see Bailey and Bowman, (1988) 45 C.L.J. 430. The Privy Council favoured a similar approach in *Rowling v. Takaro Properties Ltd.* [1988] A.C. 473.

[13] [1978] A.C. 728.

[14] [1985] A.C. 210.

or failure to exercise, their function of approving construction work as satisfying building bye-laws. In *Anns* the House of Lords held that a local authority might owe a duty of care on such facts either if it conducted the inspection negligently or if it acted negligently and made an *ultra vires* decision not to exercise the powers at all. In *Peabody* this development was confirmed in relation to limited categories of plaintiff and loss.[15]

"Control factors": Operational acts and policy decisions

The approach which emerged on the basis of *Anns* accepted that negligence could be used as a damages remedy against a public body, but limited the impact of this by applying additional "control factors" to such cases. The "control factors" adopted by Lord Wilberforce distinguish negligence which occurs at the "operational" level from that which affects "policy" decisions. The distinction between these categories was said not to be absolute but to be one of degree and it was said to be possible for activities at the operational level to contain policy elements. The purpose underlying this distinction is to emphasise that the role of negligence is strictly curtailed when policy decisions are at issue. Public bodies are to be left free to develop their own policies and the primary responsibility for them rests in the political sphere. This distinction has fallen out of fashion in the courts but may still be of use in explaining the different functions which are involved.

The "operational" level denotes acts taken in the practical implementation of policies. The lack of, or reduction in, policy elements in operational activities means that negligence which occurs in such cases is actionable under normal principles. Many examples of this kind of conduct have undoubtedly survived the retreat of negligence as a public law remedy and still give a remedy. The law could not give immunity to a public body whose employee drove negligently in the course of his employment and caused a personal injury[16] or to a health authority whose employees administered treatment negligently. Although the building inspector who negligently approves the plans for, or the methods of constructing, property is no longer liable for the cost of repairing the property,[17] he probably still owes a duty of care to those who are injured by its dangerous nature.[18] Negligence liability for physical damage to property has been imposed upon a social worker whose failure to warn a community home of a child's propensities for arson resulted in damage to property close to the home[19] and on police who fired a CS canister into a building without ensuring that fire fighting equipment was present to deal with the consequences.[20] Examples of negligence liability based on the *Hedley Byrne* principle have arisen when a local authority employee conducts a valuation for mortgage purposes[21] and when a public body is charged with maintaining registers of information for the use and benefit of the public.[22] Advice given by officials on planning matters has

[15] See Chap. 16 for a discussion of the kinds of loss which are now recoverable in such a claim.
[16] *Marshall* v. *Osmond* [1982] 2 All E.R. 610. A claim for negligence against a police driver.
[17] Because of the change in the law concerning the recovery of "pure" economic loss in negligence. See *ante*, pp. 349–353.
[18] See *ante*, p. 202.
[19] *Vicar of Writtle* v. *Essex County Council* (1979) 77 L.G.R. 656.
[20] *Rigby* v. *Chief Constable of Northamptonshire* [1985] 2 All E.R. 985.
[21] *Smith* v. *Eric S. Bush (a firm)*, *Harris* v. *Wyre Forest District Council* [1990] 1 A.C. 831.
[22] There is no reported case precisely on this point, but see *Ministry of Housing and Local Government* v. *Sharp* [1970] 2 Q.B. 223.

provoked several pieces of litigation.[23] Successful claims for negligent mis-feasance resulting in pure economic loss have also been recorded,[24] but may now be of doubtful authority in the light of the nature of the loss.

The fact that a public body may have had the discretion to withhold a service will not protect it from responsibility for negligence which occurs when it chooses to provide the service. Lord Salmon was emphatic on this point in *Anns*: "I recognise that it may not be practical to inspect the foundations of every new building. This, however, is no excuse for negligent inspection of such foundations as are inspected."[25] Lord Wilberforce's speech in *Anns* would lead to the same result in the majority of cases, whilst allowing for the possibility of the council pleading in its defence that the damage resulted from a valid policy decision on its part to provide only limited inspections.

Anns established that negligence in the course of the formulation of policy can give rise to a private law claim for compensation. A private law duty can co-exist with the more familiar public law ones. The immunity from suit in respect of such activities was said to be great but not absolute and it even seemed to be possible to base a tort claim upon a public body's decision not to exercise discretionary powers. In *Anns* Lord Wilberforce said in relation to a local authority's function of inspecting foundations that "to say that councils are under no duty to inspect is not a sufficient statement of the position. They are under a duty to give proper consideration to the question whether they should inspect or not."[26] Lord Wilberforce's speech laid down two requirements to be satisfied before the tort claim can succeed. A person injured by the acts or failures to act of a public authority acting in the policy sphere must show (a) that the act, or failure to act, constituted a failure by that body to exercise its discretion properly, *i.e.* that it was acting *ultra vires*, and (b) that in doing so the body was failing to exercise reasonable care to protect a foreseeable plaintiff from harm. These requirements are not identical. The simple finding that an *ultra vires* decision has been made is not of itself proof of negligence. It cannot be assumed that the fact that an authority was mistaken as to the extent of its powers when making a decision automatically renders that decision negligent.[27] The result is that *Anns* did not allow negligence to be used to challenge policy decisions of a statutory authority arrived at within the boundaries of its discretion and that the individual who succeeds in establishing that injury was caused by an *ultra vires* act had to surmount the additional, and difficult, hurdle of establishing negligence before a claim for compensation could succeed.

The practical effect of this additional constraint on the recognition of a duty of care was to give extensive protection to an authority if it was established that the plaintiff's loss was caused by a "policy" decision. The most common examples of this sort of decision are cases in which a service is consciously withheld or restricted on financial grounds. A health authority faced by a limited budget may be unable to employ experienced staff or to purchase equipment which might save lives. A highway authority may decide

[23] *Coats Patons (Retail) Ltd.* v. *Birmingham Corpn.* (1971) 69 L.G.R. 356; *Davy* v. *Spelthorne B.C.* [1983] 3 All E.R. 278.

[24] *Ministry of Housing and Local Government* v. *Sharp* [1970] 2 Q.B. 223.

[25] [1978] A.C. 728 at 767.

[26] [1978] A.C. 728 at 755.

[27] *Rowling* v. *Takaro Properties Ltd.* [1988] A.C. 473; *Dunlop* v. *Woollahra Municipal Council* [1982] A.C. 158.

to remove street lighting in spite of the risk of greater numbers of accidents.[28] Policy considerations have also been considered to be relevant in cases in which policing tactics have been challenged. In *Rigby* v. *Chief Constable of Northamptonshire*[29] a police decision to use one form of CS gas delivery system rather than another was treated as a policy decision not reviewable by the court. Similar treatment has been accorded when the policies adopted in the treatment of offenders have resulted in increased risks to members of the public,[30] and where Government intervention in industry has been claimed to have proved damaging to individuals.[31] In such cases the normal method for a plaintiff to satisfy the requirement of negligence would probably be to show that the authority seriously misconstrued the relevant statutes under which it was purporting to act.[32] Defects in a service may be attributable either to simple negligence in operation or to a valid policy decision to restrict the service provided. As a result courts have found difficulty in making the distinction work and on occasions this produced a reluctance to allow the protection of "policy" to be invoked in the absence of clear evidence of a conscious decision to restrict or withhold a service for particular reasons.[33]

The abandonment of control factors

More recently the courts seem to have seen the difficulties involved in making the distinction between policy decisions and operational activities as a reason for abandoning the distinction altogether in favour of using the standard modern approach to determining duty of care issues.[34] At a general level it is now clear that one result of the increasingly restrictive and incremental approach to duty of care issues stemming from the *Peabody* and *Murphy* decisions is that the courts are no longer regarding cases featuring public authority defendants as requiring special principles for their resolution. Public bodies no longer require special protection from an expanding duty of care. The statutory context and the nature of the conduct in question remain relevant factors arguing against the recognition of a tort duty, but the cases are increasingly being decided according to standard principles.

A number of strands of reasoning can be identified in the cases. Possibly the most important is that of statutory purpose. Since the *Peabody* decision courts have taken the view that the statute under which the defendant authority acted must be considered in order to determine whether the purpose of Parliament in passing it was to protect persons in the plaintiff's

---

[28] *Sheppard* v. *Glossop Corpn* [1921] 3 K.B. 132.

[29] [1985] 2 All E.R. 985.

[30] *Home Office* v. *Dorset Yacht Co. Ltd.* [1970] A.C. 1004; *Vicar of Writtle* v. *Essex County Council* (1979) 77 L.G.R. 656. The later decision of *Hill* v. *Chief Constable of West Yorkshire* [1989] A.C. 53 produced a similar result but did not use the policy formula.

[31] *Rowling* v. *Takaro Properties Ltd.* [1988] A.C. 473; *Meates* v. *Att.-Gen.* [1979] 1 N.Z.L.R. 415. See also *Booth & Co. International Ltd.* v. *National Enterprise Board* [1978] 3 All E.R. 624 (a trial of a preliminary issue on allegations of breach of statutory duty).

[32] This is likely to be difficult. *Dunlop* v. *Woollahra Municipal Council* [1982] AC 158; *Rowling* v. *Takaro Properties Ltd.* [1988] A.C. 473.

[33] *Vicar of Writtle* v. *Essex County Council* (1979) 77 L.G.R. 656. A social worker's failure to pass information about a child to the home to which he was being sent was held to be "operational" negligence. There was no evidence that the officer was implementing a policy of withholding information about unsubstantiated allegations in the child's interests.

[34] *Rowling* v. *Takaro Properties Ltd.* [1988] A.C. 473.

position against the kind of loss which was suffered. The result is that negligence cases in this area, even those concerning operational activities, are subject to the construction test which is used to decide whether the tort of breach of statutory duty operates.[35] This is a very significant constraint on the recognition of negligence duties because of the line of authority[36] which has preferred to regard the functions of statutory bodies as being to protect the general public interest rather than to confer enforceable rights on individuals in relation to a specific form of damage. In *Peabody* the purpose of building bye-laws was said to be to protect the occupants of buildings against defects which created a threat to their health and safety. A claim for economic losses suffered by the developer of the site was therefore beyond the scope of the statutory protection. This lead has been followed in subsequent decisions. Government regulatory agencies licensing financial institutions to trade have been regarded as acting in the interests of the public as a whole rather than seeking to provide rights for individuals damaged by the activities of such bodies.[37] A grant giving body exercising a power to give or to withhold money has been held to be acting for the purpose of protecting the revenue rather than the recipient of the grant and his successors in title.[38] In *Hill* v. *Chief Constable of West Yorkshire*[39] it was accepted that the police owe a duty to the general public to enforce the law, but not that individual members of the public damaged by crimes were owed a duty.

Other arguments used in these cases are familiar features of modern negligence decisions. The reasoning supporting the plaintiff's claim in many of them seems to have had its roots in the assertion that, after *Junior Books*,[40] pure economic loss may be recovered in the tort of negligence on proof that it was reasonably foreseeable that it would be suffered. At the root of the authority of *Anns* was the belief that a public body owed a duty to supervise the acts of a third party in order to prevent that person's acts damaging others and that such authorities had the financial means to underwrite the failures of such third parties. None of these approaches is likely to find favour in the 1990s. Instead the courts have rejected the imposition of duties stating that the recognition of negligence claims in public authority cases would open the door to actions by large, possibly unlimited, classes of people and that the fear of tort liability might prejudice the efficient operation of public bodies.[41] Slightly surprisingly, the cases have not placed a great deal of emphasis on the financial constraints which have been placed on public authorities in recent years.

In the light of these developments the distinction between policy decisions and operational activities is probably disappearing from the law. The distinction has been stated to be unhelpful in the most recent cases and commentators are now taking the view that it is likely to distract attention from the central policy issue: the fact that the functions of public bodies such

---

[35] See Chap. 2, and Stanton, *Breach of Statutory Duty in Tort*, (1986) Chap. 3.

[36] *Atkinson* v. *The Newcastle and Gateshead Waterworks Company* (1877) 2 Ex. D. 441.

[37] *Yuen Kun-yeu* v. *Att.-Gen. of Hong Kong* [1988] A.C. 175; *Davis* v. *Radcliffe* [1990] 2 All E.R. 536.

[38] *Curran* v. *Northern Ireland Co-ownership Housing* [1987] A.C. 718.

[39] [1989] A.C. 53.

[40] *Junior Books Ltd.* v. *Veitchi Co. Ltd.* [1983] 1 A.C. 520. See pp. 337–339 for a discussion of this case.

[41] Lord Reid's rejection of this approach in *Dorset Yacht* [1970] A.C. 1004 in the words "Her Majesty's servants are made of sterner stuff" does not seem to have won the day.

as the police and those regulating financial markets involve weighing delicate issues of judgment and discretion as to the appropriate allocation of resources and that the nature of the task is therefore not readily amenable to evaluation by the tort of negligence. In *Rowling* v. *Takaro Properties Ltd.*[42] it was claimed that the defendant, the New Zealand Minister of Finance, had been negligent and owed a duty of care when refusing his consent to an arrangement which involved the issue of shares to a Japanese company as part of an agreement to provide finance for a project in New Zealand which had been undertaken by the plaintiff, a United States citizen. The Privy Council there emphasised that the distinction between policy decisions and operational activities cannot be conclusive as to the existence of a duty of care. Earlier proceedings had established that the minister had acted *ultra vires* in taking account of an irrelevant consideration, that the land in question should revert to New Zealand ownership, and the court was prepared to accept that the decision was capable of being described as one of a policy character. Nonetheless, it did not regard the question as being of a kind which was wholly unsuitable for judicial decision and the court considered a number of other factors as relevant to the imposition of a duty of care. It inclined to the view that no duty of care should be imposed but did not have to decide the issue as no breach of duty was established. In the later English decision of *Lonrho plc* v. *Tebbit*[43] the Court of Appeal cited *Takaro* as authority for the difficulties involved in distinguishing "policy decisions" from "operational activities." The court held that a government minister's decision to extract an undertaking from a company that it would not proceed with a planned takeover bid whilst the Monopolies and Mergers Commission was investigating the bid was a matter of public law but that it remained arguable that the minister owed a private law duty to the bidder to take reasonable care to release the undertaking as soon as it was no longer needed.

As with other developments in the duty of care stemming from *Peabody*[44] the effect has been to place a stringent limitation on the expansion of the duty of care principle which *Anns* had encouraged. The role of negligence as a remedy against public authorities is now limited.

Breach of Statutory Duty

It is not surprising that claims brought against public bodies for breach of statutory duty have been recorded. A wide range of functions are performed by public bodies acting in the performance of their statutory duties. If the tort could provide damages for anyone injured by a failure of a public body to fulfil its statutory duties, it would be an important strict liability remedy for a great number of *ultra vires* acts.

Some commentators take the view that breach of statutory duty is readily available as a remedy against public authorities.[45] However, there is little evidence in decided cases to support this and the authorities cited for the proposition are nineteenth century cases based on the discredited decision of

---

[42] [1988] A.C. 473.
[43] [1992] 4 All E.R. 280.
[44] See *ante*, pp. 33–34.
[45] Wade, *Administrative Law* (6th ed.), p. 772 *et seq.*

Couch v. *Steel*.[46] The modern approach,[47] which requires a statutory duty to be subject to the "statutory purpose" test, has the effect of excluding the great majority of statutory duties imposed on public authorities from the ambit of the tort. They are treated as intended to protect the interests of the public as a whole, rather than to confer rights upon a defined class of the public. Furthermore, the existence of specialised enforcement procedures, such as remedies of complaint to ministers, may raise a presumption against the inference of the tort.

The leading authority is *Atkinson* v. *The Newcastle and Gateshead Waterworks Company*[48] which concerned an action for damages brought by the owner of premises which had been destroyed by fire. The claim was based on an allegation that the defendant company had breached a statutory duty under the Waterworks Clauses Act 1847 to keep the pipes to fire plugs charged with water at a certain pressure. Under the terms of the statute breach of this duty made the company liable to a £100 fine. The Court of Appeal dismissed the claim that breach of the provision could also give rise to an action for damages. The duty was said to exist for the benefit of the public as a whole. When the defendants agreed to undertake the statutory duty, they did not intend to become gratuitous insurers of the whole area against the risk of fire. The duty could not be construed as having been passed with the intention of conferring a benefit upon a defined class of individuals.

It has been argued that this use of the "statutory purpose" approach serves the familiar underlying purposes of protecting discretionary decisions of public bodies from attack by a claim for damages[49] and of protecting public bodies, with limited resources against over-extensive liability. In *Re HIV Haemophiliac Litigation*[50] it was said that it was unlikely that Parliament when passing the National Health Service Act 1977 had intended to confer a civil remedy on all persons entitled to receive NHS benefits. Coupled with the difficulty of establishing a case in negligence against a public authority, the result is that decisions made by such an authority in the exercise of a discretion conferred by a statute as to the appropriate allocation of resources rarely give rise to claims for damages in private law proceedings. An authority's responsibility for decisions made within its discretion is a political one. The fact that breach of statutory duty would provide an unpredictable remedy, because it is not available when challenges are made in relation to statutory *powers*, as opposed to *duties*, is an additional reason for excluding the tort from this area.

The approach which *Atkinson* lays down has severely limited the capacity of breach of statutory duty to become a damages remedy against public authorities. Isolated examples of the inference of a strict liability species of the tort are recorded,[51] but they have been ad hoc decisions based on the construction of particular provisions and do not seem to reconcile easily with other authority. One case which might have provided a general authority for the ready inference of the tort against public authorities was *Dawson & Co.*

---

[46] (1854) 3 E. & B. 402, See Stanton *op. cit.* p. 34 for a discussion of the rejection of the approach supported in this case.
[47] See Chap. 2.
[48] (1877) 2 Ex. D. 441.
[49] Buckley "Liability in tort for breach of statutory duty" (1984) 100 L.Q.R. 204.
[50] (1990) 140 N.L.J. 1349.
[51] *Booth & Co. International Ltd.* v. *National Enterprise Board* [1978] 3 All E.R. 624; *Thornton* v. *Kirklees M.B.C.* [1979] Q.B. 626; *Meade* v. *Haringey L.B.C.* [1979] I.C.R. 494.

v. *Bingley U.D.C.*[52] The defendants, in breach of a statutory duty, fixed a plate which gave an inaccurate indication of the position of a fire plug with the result that the fire brigade was delayed considerably when it tackled a fire at the plaintiff's premises. The plaintiff successfully sued the authority for the additional damage caused by the delay, notwithstanding that the facts and the duty at issue were similar to those in the *Atkinson* case. There are statements in the Court of Appeal which support the inference of a breach of statutory duty remedy on the basis of the presumption of actionability in the absence of a specific remedy given by the statute[53] and on the authority of *Couch* v. *Steel.*[54] However the main ground for the plaintiff's success seems to have been that the defendant's conduct constituted a misfeasance in the carrying out of a statutory duty as opposed to mere non-feasance (the omission to perform an act). It is suggested that *Dawson* cannot be taken to establish a general approach as it is *Atkinson* which has been generally followed in subsequent cases. In addition, there is little logic in distinguishing misfeasance from non-feasance when a statutory duty to act exists. In *Dawson* the conduct at issue was negligence. If a case on facts similar to *Dawson* were to occur today it is suggested that a claim for a strict liability remedy for breach of statutory duty should fail on the authority of *Atkinson,* whereas a negligence claim might succeed as the conduct occurred at the operational level.

It might be argued that a group of cases decided in the late 1970s, *Booth & Co. (International) Ltd.* v. *National Enterprise Board*[55]; *Thornton* v. *Kirklees M.B.C.*[56] and *Meade* v. *Haringey L.B.C.,*[57] show an increased willingness on the part of the courts to make the inference of breach of statutory duty in cases concerning public authorities. However, this would be to place too great a weight on these decisions. *Meade* was not a claim for damages and there are strong arguments for saying that both it and *Thornton* are in conflict with earlier authority and should be overruled.[58] *Booth* is scarcely strong authority, as Forbes J. expressed his personal view that it was difficult to accept that Parliament had intended the relevant provisions of the Industry Act 1975 to create tort rights which could be enforced by individuals. However, he did not regard the plaintiff's claim to the contrary as so totally misconceived as to justify his striking it out as disclosing no cause of action. A consideration of cases concerning public authority liability in which it has been sought to use breach of statutory duty as a damages remedy confirms the dominance of the *Atkinson* approach in the post *Peabody* period.[59]

The most important modern English[60] authority on the topic is *Bourgoin S.A.* v. *Ministry of Agriculture, Fisheries & Food.*[61] We have previously

---

[52] [1911] 1 K.B. 149.
[53] See *ante,* p. 48.
[54] (1854) 3 E. & B. 402.
[55] [1978] 3 All E.R. 624.
[56] [1979] Q.B. 626.
[57] [1979] I.C.R. 494.
[58] See Stanton *op. cit.* pp. 80 & 83.
[59] *Re HIV Haemophiliac Litigation* (1990) 140 N.L.J. 1349; *R.* v. *Knowsley B.C., ex parte Maguire* (1992) 142 N.L.J. 1375; *Wentworth* v. *Wiltshire C.C.* [1993] 2 All E.R. 256. See also Stanton *op. cit.* pp. 79–84 for discussion of the pre-*Peabody* authority concerning the provision of welfare rights, education and other services.
[60] See the discussion of *Francovich* v. *Italian Government* [1992] I.R.L.R. 84 at p. 479 for the European law dimension.
[61] [1986] Q.B. 716.

discussed the role of breach of statutory duty as a damages remedy available in the English courts for breach of Article 86 of the E.C. Treaty.[62] *Bourgoin* raised the question of whether a similar approach could be applied to the case of a government department which had been held by the European Court to have broken another directly effective Article of the E.C. Treaty. The plaintiff, a French company, had imported turkeys into the U.K. under a general import licence. It was stopped from doing so when the defendant Ministry revoked that licence and replaced it by one which allowed imports only from countries which controlled a particular disease by the slaughter of affected birds. French practice was to control the disease by vaccination. The French Government successfully challenged this change in the European Court of Justice on the basis that it was a quantitative restriction on imports between Member States which breached Article 30. The plaintiff company then brought a claim for damages in the English court arguing that as Article 30 had, like Article 86, been held to be a directly applicable provision of the Treaty which conferred rights on individuals,[63] it should be held, on the authority of *Garden Cottage Foods Ltd.* v. *Milk Marketing Board*,[64] to be a provision which gave rise to a damages remedy on the basis of breach of statutory duty. The defendants argued, to the contrary, that the only appropriate remedy was an application for judicial review. A majority of the Court of Appeal upheld the defendants' arguments and refused to grant damages. The court gave a variety of reasons to support its decision: first, there is nothing in Community law which specifically requires that the domestic courts of Member States award damages as a remedy for breach of a directly effective provision; secondly, the measure in question was of a legislative, or quasi-legislative, character[65] and the European Court of Justice has determined that the Council of the Community is not liable in damages for legislative acts which breach those Articles of the Treaty which confer individual rights[66]; thirdly, an invalid act of a similar character would merely give rise in domestic law to a right to seek judicial review as an *ultra vires* act, done in good faith, does not *per se* give rise to a claim for damages. The *Garden Cottage* Case was distinguished on the basis that Article 86 created directly effective private rights in private individuals which were to be enforced against other private individuals and that Lord Diplock, in *Garden Cottage* had expressly excluded cases raising public law issues, which this claim under Article 30 was taken to be, from the principle that if a right could be protected by injunction it must also give rise to claims for damages. In the words of Nourse L.J. in *Bourgoin* "It is impossible to exaggerate the importance of the . . . question."A decision in the plaintiff's favour would have opened the door to a damages remedy in any case in which a Minister in good faith broke a provision of the E.C. Treaty which confers directly effective rights on individuals.

---

[62] See *ante*, pp. 365.
[63] *Ianelli and Volpi Sp.A.* v. *Ditta Paolo Meroni* [1977] E.C.R. 557.
[64] [1984] A.C. 130.
[65] The Court of Appeal has held the ratio of the case to extend to administrative acts, as well as to those of a legislative or quasi-legislative character. *An bord Bainne Co-operative Ltd.* v. *Milk Marketing Board (No. 2)* [1988] 1 C.M.L.R. 605.
[66] *Bayerische H.N.L. Vermehrungsbetriebe GmbH & Co. K.G.* v. *E.C. Council & Commission* [1978] E.C.R. 1209; *Koninklijke Scholten Honig N.V.* v. *E.C. Council & Commission* [1979] E.C.R. 3583.

It seems likely that the result reached in *Bourgoin* cannot stand in the light of subsequent decisions of the European Court of Justice which approach the matter from the standpoint of Community law.[67] However, the Court of Appeal's refusal to recognise a remedy was consistent with the general reluctance of English domestic courts to allow breach of statutory duty to be used as a damages remedy against public authorities exercising legislative or administrative functions in good faith. *Bourgoin* was clearly seen as a test case by those who were arguing that damages should be more freely available as a remedy for persons injured by unlawful administrative action. The House of Lords decision in *Garden Cottage*, in holding that a right to an injunction vested in an individual necessarily entails a right to claim damages for losses previously suffered, gave strong support to that view. Oliver L.J.'s long, and thoughtful, dissenting judgment in *Bourgoin* was founded on this logical application of *Garden Cottage*.

European Law

In *Francovich* v. *Italian Government*[68] the European Court of Justice established that European law recognises a right to obtain damages in a national court from a State for loss arising from that State's breach of its obligations under Community law. It is preferable to regard this right as a tort in its own right rather than as a species of breach of statutory duty founded on breach of the Community treaties and subordinate legislation.[69] On the facts of the case, the Italian Government had been held, in separate proceedings, to have failed to implement a Directive intended to protect employees in the event of their employer's insolvency. It was then held that employees who had incurred losses as a result of the lack of the protection which the Directive sought to achieve had a right to claim compensation in national courts from the State which had broken its Community obligations.

Three conditions are required by the judgment in *Francovich* before such liability can arise: first, the Directive in question must have sought to confer rights for the benefit of individuals; secondly, the content of these rights has to be determined by reference to the provisions of the Directive and, finally, a causal link must exist between the State's breach of its obligations under Community law and the damage suffered by the person affected. Although there is no express reference to the question in the judgment, it seems likely that this species of State liability is "absolute" in the sense that no particular state of knowledge or intention is required and no defences are available: all that is required is proof of breach of the Community obligation.[70] The decision gives no guidance on the principles under which the compensation provided for is to be assessed.

A "Eurotort" of this nature obviously reflects a fundamentally different approach to Governmental liability to that which is traditionally adopted by

---

[67] See the discussion of the *Francovich* decision in the next section and the speech of Lord Goff in *Kirklees Metropolitan Borough Council* v. *Wickes Building Supplies Ltd.* [1992] 3 All E.R. 717.

[68] [1992] I.R.L.R. 84.

[69] Decisions such as *Garden Cottage* might also be moved into this separate category of "Eurotort."

[70] See Ross, (1993) 56 M.L.R. 55 for a detailed survey of the issues raised and the possible implications of the case.

English law. A potentially wide new field of governmental[71] tort liability has been brought into existence. Two likely consequences of *Francovich* are: first, the Court of Appeal's decision in *Bourgoin* is wrong as the British Government had, on the facts, broken its Community obligations[72] and, secondly, if a plaintiff could show that his claim for personal injuries will fail as a result of the wording of the "development risks" defence established by the Consumer Protection Act 1987, whereas it should have succeeded under the, arguably, narrower wording of that defence allowed under the Directive from which the Act was derived, he will have a claim for damages against the British Government.

It remains to be seen whether the appearance of this form of governmental liability for breach of Community law will encourage a shift in the attitude of English courts and hence a move towards favouring the development of damages remedies in English law for governmental action which is unlawful in terms of domestic legislation.

A New Remedy?

It may be thought that the existing domestic tortious remedies for public authority liability are inadequate and that a new compensation remedy should be made available to persons injured by public bodies which act unlawfully or which delay unreasonably in reaching a decision. Under the present rules, misfeasance is confined to intentional acts; negligence cannot be established simply on the basis of an unlawful act and has retreated from the area and breach of statutory duty has no application to statutory powers and only haphazard, and unpredictable, application to statutory duties. A major review of administrative law[73] concluded that the existing torts could not provide a suitable remedy as they do not generally provide a compensation remedy for pure economic losses caused by unlawful administrative action or unreasonable delays. For example, a person who is deprived, in breach of natural justice, of a licence to trade should be able to seek judicial review to quash the decision but is unlikely to have a remedy to recover lost earnings unless misfeasance can be proved. A new remedy is needed. Its recognition should not create insuperable technical problems. *Ex gratia* payments of compensation following a finding of maladministration by a Parliamentary or Local Government Ombudsman are a familiar feature of the English administrative system and damages are a well established remedy in other European systems and have recently entered English jurisprudence as a result of the decision of the European Court of Justice in *Francovich*.

This proposal has considerable merits. Given the retreat of the common law remedies available against public bodies there is little alternative to legislation if an effective remedy is to be introduced. The central questions are whether any government would be prepared to open the door to the public expenditure involved and whether society can justify spending scarce resources on damaged individuals rather than on the public as a whole. The

---

[71] The identity of the bodies which are to be subject to such liability is not completely clear.

[72] The House of Lords doubted whether *Bourgoin* could survive, in the light of *Francovich*, in the course of its decision in *Kirklees Metropolitan Borough Council* v. *Wickes Building Supplies Ltd.* [1992] 3 All E.R. 717.

[73] Justice, All Souls, *Administrative Justice – Some necessary reforms* (1988). Chap. 11 deals with compensation remedies.

review mentioned previously[74] argued that limited expenditure would be involved because the quantity of claims would be small and, further, that the existence of a remedy would produce benefits as its deterrent effect would lead to better quality administration. One suspects, however, that it may be years before such a remedy is introduced.

[74] Ibid.

Index

DAMAGE *cont.*
trade, interference with, 314
vaccine damage *see* VACCINE DAMAGE
PAYMENTS
waste disposal, caused by *see* WASTE
DISPOSAL
DAMAGES
absolute property of victim, as, 268
aggravated damages, 148–149, 435
defamation, for, 435, 459
assessment of, 146
bereavement, for *see* BEREAVEMENT
AWARD; PERSONAL INJURY AND
DEATH
calculation of
causation, and, 85–87
mitigation, and, 147–148
contemptuous, 148
contributory negligence, and, 106–107
defamation, for *see* DEFAMATION
economic loss, for, 308–310
European Community legislation, breach
of, 43, 478–480
exemplary, 148–154, 157, 181, 251, 435
arbitrary or unconstitutional action by
servants of Government, 149–150
conduct calculated to make a profit,
150–151, 157
objections to, 153–154
fatal accidents, for *see* FATAL ACCIDENTS
funeral expenses, in respect of, 282
general damages, 145–146, 254
general principles, 145–147
injunction, in lieu of, 155
land, tort cases concerning
damage to amenity, 376
devaluation, 375
generally, 374
incursions, 374–375
repair, 375
malicious prosecution, for, 430
mitigation of, 147–148
partial justification, 446
recovery of damages in another action,
460
nominal, 148
non-compensatory, 148–154
pain and suffering, for, 18
personal injury and death, 174
aggravated, 251
compensating benefits, deductions for
benevolence, 271
charitable payments, 271
disaster funds, 271
fatal accident claims, 279–282
first party insurance, 271
generally, 270–271
income tax, 273
payments by employer, 272–273
state benefits, 273–276
voluntarily rendered services, 273
exemplary, 251
fatal accidents *see* FATAL ACCIDENTS

DAMAGES *cont.*
personal injury and death *cont.*
financial losses
expenses
generally, 266
housing costs, 267
incurred by others, 268–269
medical care, 267–268
generally, 250, 256
loss of earnings
capacity, 265–266
lost years, 264–265
unemployed plaintiff, 266
multiplier
children, 257
criticism of
actuarial evidence, 258–259
generally, 253, 258
inflation, 259–260
Pearson Commission, 260–263
generally, 256–257
modified, 261–263
periodic payments, 260–263
young women, 257–258
structured settlements, 263–264
general principles, 249–252
interim payments, 251
loss of amenity, 252, 254–255
lump sum award, 251–252
mitigation, 147
non-pecuniary losses, 252–255
"fairness", and, 253
Pearson Commission and, 252, 253,
255
overlap of awards, 269–270
pain and suffering, 252, 254
periodic payment of, 252, 260–263
structured settlements, 263–264
survival of injury awards, 276
public bodies, acts of, 467–468, 476–479
punitive, 148–154
purpose of award, 144–145
social security benefits, and, 273–276
special damages, 145–146
structured settlements, 263–264
DEATH *see* PERSONAL INJURY AND DEATH
DECEIT
deliberate fraud, 100–101
economic loss, and, 310, 330–331
false statement, 330–331
intention of defendant, 74
negligent misstatement distinguished, 331
remoteness of damage, 100–101
DEFAMATION
abuse, 437–438
amends, offer of, 449–450
apology, 449
claims for, who can bring, 441–443
consent, 451–452
damage caused by, 443–444
damages for, 146–147, 459–460
aggravated, 435, 459
exemplary, 435